New Testament

SCM CORE TEXT

New Testament

Richard Cooke

scm press

Published in 2009 by SCM Press
Editorial office
108–114 Golden Lane
London EC1Y 0TG

Second impression 2016

SCM Press is an imprint of Hymns Ancient and Modern Ltd
(a registered charity)
13A Hellesdon Park Road, Norwich,
Norfolk, NR6 5DR
www.scmpress.co.uk

British Library Cataloguing in Publication data

A catalogue record for this book is available from the British Library

978 0 334 04060 6

Typeset by Regent Typesetting, London
Printed and bound by
CPI Group (UK) Ltd

Contents

Preface

A Way into the New Testament

This book is an introduction to the New Testament by means of historical study. It offers a simple framework but one that I hope is fresh and stimulating both for beginning students and also for those who want to reacquaint themselves with the study of the New Testament.

It is a teacher's book rather than an academic's, designed to help readers grasp the subject and find a way in to what can be a bewildering mass of material. As such, I sometimes take unfashionable positions and for reasons of space have not always been able to cover every theory or idea about a particular part of the New Testament. As a Core Text it is intended to provoke ideas and discussion and to be a starting point for further study.

A few technicalities are:

- Dates before the Christian era are given as BC. All other dates mentioned are AD.
- I have usually avoided using the word 'Palestine' unless it is included in a quotation. For much of the first century the land was broadly divided into Galilee and Judea, so that is how I have referred to it.
- I have generally preferred to give my own translation of the New Testament. This avoids some phrases that have become over-familiar, though following the Greek sometimes means that the translation reads a little awkwardly. It is important to have a copy of the New Testament to hand to compare the renderings.
- Endnotes have been kept to a minimum. Where I have quoted from the same book more than once in a single paragraph I have usually given the reference in a note linked to the last quotation. Quotations are designed to make it possible for you to follow up the reference if you want to go deeper with the matter in hand. Therefore the endnotes supplement the more general suggestions for Further Reading at the end of each chapter.
- As far as possible I have restricted the notes and Further Reading suggestions to books rather than articles.
- A selection of web addresses is also given at the end of each chapter. These are designed to help you to begin surfing for others. These were all accessed on 26 March 2009.

I am grateful to the many people who have watched this project grow, especially the trainee Readers of Coventry Diocese over the last 15 years, for whom the structure was developed. Some colleagues have been especially supportive at crucial moments: Tony Bradley, the late Graham Smith and Christine Haines; Paula Gooder, David Runcorn and Mark Pryce are just a few of them, but I want to offer you all my thanks. At SCM Press, Barbara Laing offered enthusiasm and encouragement at the beginning of the process and Natalie Watson has been incredibly patient at the end. Paul Mileham kindly read the book and checked the biblical references at the last minute, saving me from some crucial errors. The congregations of St James Fletchamstead and the Edgehill/Kineton churches have unwittingly sampled a good deal of the content and kept me focused on why I was writing the book! Inevitably it's friends and family who bear the brunt of writing: thank you to Phil (Oswin) and Anne; to Kate, Patrick, Luke and Ciara for continuing to ask how it was going; and to Joyce for asking why it wasn't finished yet. William and Dig have helped me to understand some of the geography in chapter 1 and the film and drama references in chapter 5. Thank you both.

Finally, there are two people without whom the book would not be as it finally is. First of all, my Dad, who has faithfully proofread the chapters as they were finished. As ever, your support and love is quiet, practical and always to be counted on. I wouldn't have got here without you. And second, Barbara, who helped to put me back together when I was like Paul on the road from Athens. Thank you for understanding. This book is dedicated to the two of you, with my love and thanks.

Warmington Rectory
March 2009

1

The World of the New Testament

Discovering the New Testament

Imagine that you are an archaeologist, digging in a second-century village buried long ago in the sands of a desert. As you dig, your trowel strikes something solid and hollow. Putting the trowel down, you search with your fingertips, brushing aside the sand until beneath your exploring fingers you feel the outline of an earthenware jar. Carefully you locate its lid, and as you open the jar you find inside it a mixture of papyrus scrolls.

One by one you lift them out, counting as you do so. There are 27 items. The papyrus is brittle, and the ink is faded. The writing is in solid blocks of ancient Greek capital letters, with no gaps between the words and no punctuation. One is headed ΚΑΤΑ ΜΑΡΚΟΝ. Beneath the heading is a line of letters like this:

ΑΡΧΗΤΟΥΕΥΑΓΓΕΛΙΟΥΙΗΣΟΧΡΙΣΤΟ.

It looks at first like a code to be cracked. But your practised eye quickly divides the letters up into words, translating literally as you go: 'According to Mark. The origin of the good news of Jesus Christ.' Another scroll says, 'To the Corinthians. Paul, called messenger of Jesus Christ ...' A third begins, 'The Revelation of Jesus Christ which God gave to his servants to reveal to them what is shortly to happen.'

It is clear that you have found an ancient book collection and that it belonged to a group that had something to do with Jesus Christ. Glancing through the other manuscripts, you find that almost all of the 27 refer to Jesus Christ in their first line. Who was he? And what did he do to inspire such a wealth of writing about him?

You know that you will be able to answer these questions, because such a trove of written material about just one person from the first or second century is unique. Even the biographies of the greatest figures from the ancient world have to be constructed from scraps and fragments. But here you have 27 books connected to a single person. As you read on, you find that not only does the collection contain four versions of the life of Jesus, but there is also a narrative of what happened to his followers after his death, and no less than 21 letters, some general and some personal. From the handwriting you can deduce that all these documents were written inside the second half of the first century. In terms of ancient history this is a find beyond your wildest dreams.

From the 27 books you have found you will be able to reconstruct the story of Jesus Christ and the life of the community that was named after him in quite remarkable detail. It's like having a tiny corner of the ancient world illuminated by a spotlight, while the rest remains in the shadows.

Finding the way

Before you reach for your Indiana Jones hat and set off to sift the sands for the original New Testament I have to tell you it's not waiting out there to be discovered somewhere beneath the desert. The books of the New Testament coalesced gradually into the collection which we now have. But because we encounter it packaged neatly and translated carefully into the best contemporary language, with its principles still quietly echoing through modern Western culture, the New Testament does not seem to us to be an alien document from a strange land as it would do if we had just discovered it beneath the sands of a desert.

The New Testament belongs to a very different culture from our own, with different values and conventions, and even quite different maps. If you visit a foreign country today, you will probably buy a guidebook in advance. It will give you information about the country and its culture, and tips on how to understand local attitudes and customs. To understand the New Testament in its own terms we have to learn to be attentive to the beliefs and attitudes of the people who wrote it. So it may help to think of this book as a kind of guide to the New Testament. It is intended to be a 'way in'. It won't offer you everything you need to know, and it won't be a substitute for the experience of reading the New Testament itself, just as reading a guidebook is pointless without actually visiting the country it's about. But it may help you to know which questions to ask; perhaps it will challenge some of your own attitudes and beliefs too.

Teaching different groups over a number of years I have found that most people know more than they think they do; what they usually need is a framework to help them organize and place the knowledge they already have, to see how it all fits together. To go back to the analogy of the guidebook for a moment, the best ones will first introduce the country as a whole before breaking it down into smaller areas. So let's look at the world of the New Testament.

The world of the New Testament

A view of Vesuvius

On 24 August 79, a 20-mile high column of cloud shot into the blue Mediterranean sky above the Bay of Naples. Watching the whole thing in fascination was a man named Gaius Plinius Secundus (better known to later generations as Pliny the Elder). Alongside a prominent public career he had dedicated every minute of his spare time to the scientific study of the natural wonders of the world through reading the accounts of others. Now he realized that right in front of him was the opportunity to investigate a major natural phenomenon himself. He had the means at his disposal to do so, for he was also admiral of the Roman fleet in the western Mediterranean. A ship was ready and waiting for his command.

In the city of Pompeii, across the bay, showers of pumice stone fell like rain. They filled the streets, buried houses and blotted out the sun. Remarkably, some people stayed put, hoping the catastrophe would pass. Next morning a cloud of hot gas poured through the city, followed by a wave of lava. The city was frozen in time, preserving the food left on tables and a barking watchdog tied to a post. Among the human victims were 13 adults and children, huddled together in an orchard as the dust, stone and ash suffocated them. Their bodies were not recovered for almost 1900 years.

Pliny too became a victim of the volcano. He landed close to Pompeii, but quickly saw that there was no real prospect of organizing an evacuation or of putting back to sea. He died in the volcano's poisonous fumes. But perhaps he died happy, for he had seen at first hand an eruption such as occurs only once every millennium, an explosion 100,000 times more powerful than the first atomic bomb. In the end it was Pliny's scientific curiosity about the natural world that had killed him.[1]

Pliny's world, Paul's world

The eruption of Vesuvius occurred right in the middle of the period during which the New Testament was written, but you won't find Pliny or Pompeii mentioned in the New Testament. But his world was also the world of the New Testament, as a comparison between his life and the life of Paul shows:

- Paul passed close to Pompeii in 61. He was on his way to Rome as a prisoner, landed a few miles north of Pliny's villa at Puteoli and stayed with the Christian community there for a week (Acts 28.13).
- Pliny was active as a lawyer in Rome during the early 60s, when Paul was awaiting trial in the same city (Acts 28.30).
- Paul was originally imprisoned by Felix, the Roman governor of Judea (Acts 24.24). Felix was married to Drusilla, a princess from the

Herod family. Their son Agrippa died, like Pliny, in the eruption of Vesuvius.

- Pliny's death is described in a letter from his nephew to the historian Tacitus. It is from Tacitus that we hear of Nero's punishment of Christians in 65, a purge during which Paul and Peter met their deaths.[2]

Paul and Pliny ate the same kinds of food, spoke the same languages and were ruled by the same emperors. And this is also true of the other writers of the New Testament. Pliny's world was Paul's world too.

Pliny's Natural History

Augustus was the first Roman emperor, and he decided to count and value all the lands under Roman rule. He entrusted the survey to his close friend Marcus Vipsanius Agrippa. One of its by-products was the creation of the first public map of the world, completed in 5 BC and displayed in the Roman forum. Copies were sent to all the major cities of the empire so it could be widely seen. Luke's Gospel sets Jesus' birth in the context of a census in Judea ordered by Augustus (Luke 2.1) and, even though there are problems with identifying the actual census Luke is referring to, the story neatly underscores Augustus's desire to count, list and tax anything that might be his.

Seventy years later Pliny completed a similar survey of the natural world. His *Natural History* was a kind of counterpart to Agrippa's map. By dedicating the work to the imperial family Pliny symbolically offered them the whole inhabited world. Knowledge itself was placed captive at the feet of the Emperor Vespasian and his son, Titus.

From Pliny's *Natural History* we can gain a strong image of how a powerful Roman saw the world. In a stylized form it looked something like Figure 1.

Pliny offered his readers an armchair tour of this world. He tells some tall tales, such as the race of people who lived on an island in the Baltic and who had ears which were so big that they covered their whole bodies, so they had no need of clothes! In general, however, Pliny was a sober reporter of facts, especially about economic resources. Britain and Germany, for example, warranted little space because they were unproductive except as a source of slaves. Gaul, by contrast, was full of gold, silver, iron, lead and tin, so it paid many times over for the legions stationed there. Pliny was primarily interested in profit, as Augustus had been.

Europe was the centre of Pliny's world. He devoted half of his geographical description to it, and Rome was very definitely the hub, 'the central point around which knowledge is organized'.[3] Pliny's was unquestionably a political perspective, designed to boost the imperial family by celebrating the fabulous wealth that was now at their disposal and with the subtext that they had more even than Augustus.

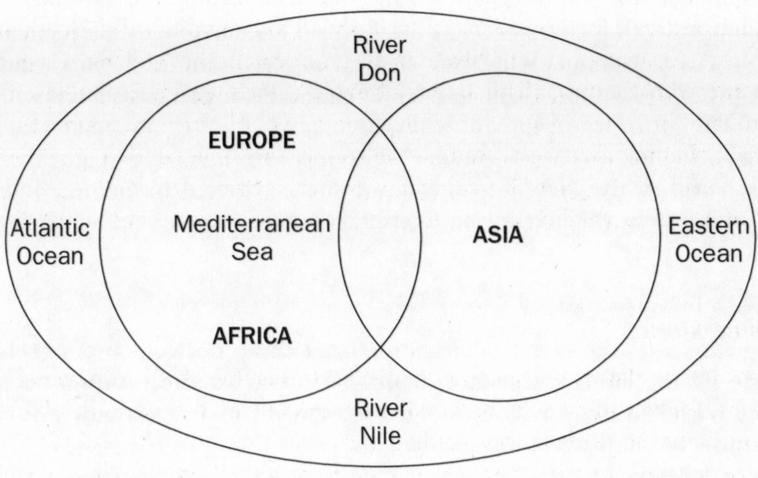

Figure 1 The world according to Pliny

The rest of the world also fascinated Pliny, however. He described West, North and East Africa, and mentioned the Chinese, who supplied a kind of semi-transparent muslin in which Roman matrons flaunted themselves, to Pliny's disapproval. Pliny described the island of Taprobane (Sri Lanka) in detail because the king had sent a delegation to Rome 30 years before, when Claudius was emperor.

India was a place of great rivers, many cities and powerful kings and an important component of the world trade system. Pliny estimated that Roman merchants paid around 50 million sesterces a year for goods from India, which they then sold on at a hundredfold profit. He estimated the value of eastern trade in total as being around 100 million sesterces a year, showing how important Roman trade links were with the Parthian empire, which stretched from northern Syria to India. (A *sestertius* was made up of four *denarii*, and one denarius was reckoned to be the daily wage of a labourer.)

Pliny described a big world. He had knowledge of the whole Eurasian land mass from the Atlantic to China, and while the extreme north was not of much interest to him (too cold for a warm-blooded Italian, perhaps) he was aware of the kingdoms of central and eastern Africa in the far south.

The size of the world described by Pliny is reflected in the New Testament. The body of Jesus was wrapped for burial in Jerusalem in a *sindon*

(Mark 15.46), fine linen cloth imported from Sind in north-west India (now Pakistan). The treasurer of the queen of Ethiopia apparently attended festivals in Jerusalem (Acts 8.27). Paul mentions the Scythians (Col. 3.11), a people who lived in the mountains beyond the Caspian Sea and whose cannibalistic habits Pliny described with horrified fascination. Paul dreamed of spreading the good news of Jesus into Spain (Rom. 15.24), the farthest west, though we're not sure that he ever got there. The world of the New Testament was not restricted to Galilee, Judea and the eastern Mediterranean. It stretched much further and wider than that.

Telling stories

Maps locate places and people in space. Stories locate them in time. By stories, I mean the way people make sense of their own existence within a complex web of memories of the past.

The Jews of the early first century told a story of how they had a right to freedom and independence under the lordship of their God. The Romans told a different story, about their right to rule the world and subdue any opposition in the name of peace. The Jewish revolt of 66–70, which led to Pliny's patron Vespasian becoming emperor, was a clash between two narratives which had become increasingly opposed to each other as Roman power became more and more naked and forceful during the 60s and Jews feared that it would crush them and their way of life.

The Jewish story was a noble and alluring one which outlived the destruction of the Temple in 70 and fed the dream of further revolt in 132. For some Jews, Roman victory in 70 led to a radical reworking of their story. So Josephus, a Jewish prince who at first fought the Romans and then became their tame prophet, concluded that God had abandoned his ancient people in favour of a new saviour, the Emperor Vespasian and his family. Josephus wrote up this adapted version of the story of Israel in several books, which give us a uniquely valuable historical background to the study of the New Testament.

Christians tended to find a way between these two stories. Critical of Rome, they had found a way of worshipping which valued but did not depend on the Jewish Temple, whose destruction they believed that Jesus of Nazareth had prophesied anyway. Thus they had begun to create their own narrative or narratives, and the writers of the books of the New Testament wove new stories around the life of Jesus to provide a framework by which Christians could understand the world.

Most of the rest of this book will look at the stories which the early Christians told and recorded in the books of the New Testament. Yet the Christian story was only one among a competing range which were being told in the first century. So what were those other stories like?

Alexander's story – the making of the Hellenistic world

Where does a story begin? Romans might begin their story with the founding of their city by Romulus and Remus, which they dated to 753 BC. Jews might look back to Moses or David in the distant past, or perhaps to the Maccabees who briefly freed the Temple from foreign rule in 164 BC. But many would have agreed that a new era had begun one spring day in 334 BC, when Alexander the Great, king of Macedon in northern Greece, set out to conquer the east.

The Persian Empire and the city-states of Greece had been at war sporadically for several centuries. Greek cities had progressively been established across Asia Minor and then extended eastwards into Syria and Egypt. A successful campaign by Alexander against the Persians would have safeguarded the trading rights and autonomy of these cities.

Alexander's father, the powerful but uncouth Philip of Macedon, had united Greece itself under his rule, but died before he could set out on this campaign. Alexander took on his father's mantle, but he was not just a Macedonian bully as Philip had been. He had been tutored by Aristotle, the finest mind in Greece, and he brought together the intellectual achievement of Greek culture and the raw power of the Macedonian army. It was a powerful and almost unstoppable combination.

Yet where moderation in all things had long been a Greek virtue, Alexander and the Macedonians valued excess. And there was nothing modest or moderate about Alexander's aim. He wanted to conquer the whole world, and he believed that he could do it.

It was a young man's dream. The astonishing fact was that, over the next 11 years, Alexander came closer than anyone else has ever done to make it come true. He did so as both Philip's son and Aristotle's pupil, undefeated in battle and restless in the pursuit of the knowledge of new lands.

By 327 BC, Alexander had reached the north of India, from which he believed that the ends of earth and the eastern ocean should be visible. When he didn't find them he sailed from the Indus River out across the Indian Ocean. When land was long out of sight Alexander believed that he must have reached the southern edge of the world. Then he turned back, preparing to go west and perhaps reach the Atlantic. But, still only 33 years old, he died in Babylon in 323 BC after a drinking contest. Alexander's was an extraordinary achievement, yet he died unfulfilled, having completed the conquest of only half the lands he had set out to dominate.

Others did not judge him by his own standards. Alexander captured imaginations for centuries to come. He showed what could be achieved by a human being. When Pompeii was excavated the largest and most striking mosaic discovered was of the youthful Alexander defeating the Persians. Three centuries after his death he remained an inspiration.

Alexander literally put the world on the map. His conquests defined the eastern world and gave it shape and content. The way to India was open, and by the mid second century BC trading links with China had been established, bringing silk to the west for the first time. Perhaps most significantly there was a legacy of Greek cities, initially populated by Alexander's soldiers who had tired of travelling, scattered across the east. This meant that 'After Alexander, the Greek language was the language of power all the way from Cyrene in north Africa to the Oxus and the Punjab in north-west India.'[4] Culturally the whole area which Alexander had conquered became 'Hellenistic' after the name the Greeks called themselves, *Hellenes*.

There was a measure of cultural unity, but political unity scarcely survived Alexander's death. In the relentless pursuit of new lands to conquer, Alexander had not established any infrastructure of government, and each kingdom he subdued had retained its existing political system. The empire was divided within a matter of years between Alexander's generals, whose descendants ruled the resulting states for the next two centuries.

Ptolemy, a childhood friend of Alexander, managed to claim Egypt for himself and was proclaimed king in 305 BC, for example. His descendant Cleopatra, queen of Egypt in the first century BC, was the last of his line. She was the lover of the Roman generals Julius Caesar and Mark Antony. The joint navy which she and Antony sent to fight Octavian, Antony's rival for power in Rome, was defeated at Actium off north-west Greece in 31 BC. Cleopatra and Antony committed suicide, and Octavian became the first man since Alexander to be able to claim to rule an empire. As Augustus he became emperor of Rome and brought the Hellenistic era to an end.

Or did he? Augustus certainly ushered in a new political order which transformed the economy of the Mediterranean under the protection of Rome. But culturally the lands once conquered by Alexander retained their Hellenistic character and their common language. However, the genius of Hellenistic culture as pioneered by Alexander was that beneath the veneer of Greek civilization traditional practices often remained undisturbed and retained their distinctiveness. The 'microecologies' of local and regional communities flourished, while Greek culture and language provided a means of 'connectivity' between them.[5] Martin Goodman comments that 'a surface Greek culture might disguise a variety of underlying local cultural patterns ... Greek culture provided opportunities for ... people not to abandon their native traditions but to express them in different ways.'[6] In this sense, Hellenistic culture was a subtle amalgam which was less a Greek takeover of local culture than a fusion and assimilation of that culture with Greek forms and styles, providing diverse communities with just enough common language and culture to enable them to communicate effectively with each other.

Hellenistic culture was more widespread than we might imagine. Rome would later take control of all the Hellenistic kingdoms ruled by Alexander's successors except for the Parthian Empire, which lay east of the Euphrates. The rise of the Roman Empire and the political boundaries which were eventually established between it and Parthia should not obscure the fact that, throughout the period when the New Testament was being written, Greek was the common language across the east, and the volume of trade ensured that there was widespread contact between the different empires.

The legacy of Alexander was the cultural and commercial unity of the east. There are signs of this unity in the New Testament: Matthew tells a story of 'wise men from the east', that is Parthia (Matt. 2.1–12); Paul became a Christian in Damascus at a time when the city was ruled by the king of Nabatea; he then spent three years in 'Arabia' (Gal. 1.17), another name for Nabatea. Nabatea was also where a woman named Babatha, hiding from the Romans in 135, left an archive of legal documents written in Greek, Aramaic and Nabatean which demonstrates the continued mingling of cultures beyond the eastern edge of the Roman Empire.

The Hellenistic world endured as a cultural phenomenon in the east long after the rise of the Roman Empire. The fact that the largest number of Jews outside Jerusalem was in Babylon meant that Parthia was an integral part of the Jewish world. Jews lived within the legacy of Alexander, but the Romans would claim that legacy as their own.

Augustus's story – the making of the Roman world

First-century Romans began their story with a saviour: Augustus. Augustus was a title rather than a name, meaning something like 'holy majesty', combining dignity, power and reverence. The Roman senate conferred it on Octavian in 27 BC, recognizing him as the most powerful man in the world.

Rome was certainly ready for a saviour. The city had been a latecomer to the power-plays of the ancient world. By the time the city's republic was formed, around 500 BC, Athens was already on the verge of its most creative century and Babylon was the richest city in the world. The sea-power of Carthage in North Africa dominated trade in the western Mediterranean.

The Romans quickly made up for lost time. In the mid third century BC they embarked on a series of wars against Carthage for control of the Mediterranean. In 146 BC, the Macedonians and Greeks picked the wrong moment to side with Carthage. Roman legions marched east for the first time. Macedon was conquered and the city of Corinth destroyed. Greece became Rome's captive. Isolated Carthage itself was savagely and brutally eradicated in the same year. For 17 days, the city burned until not a scrap of it was left. All its citizens were sold into slavery, and it was said that the fields were sown with salt, so that no crops could ever grow there again.

Carthage was a bleak example of the concentrated ferocity which struck anyone who dared to challenge the dominance of Rome. With good reason the Romans now called the Mediterranean simply *Mare Nostrum*: 'our Sea'.

In the face of this threat, the fabulously rich kingdoms of Asia Minor capitulated, one by one, to Rome. Their revenues poured into the city's treasury and into the coffers of those who managed to acquire administrative posts in the east. Yet all was not well in Rome. The republican system, which had served the city for centuries, was not adequate to rule such a vast empire. A few ancient aristocratic families had become immensely wealthy through the growth of empire, but it was the formidable Roman military machine on which success had been built. The working classes who were the foot soldiers of Rome began to use their dormant political powers to demand a bigger cut of the east's fabulous wealth for themselves, stirred up by populist politicians.

Decades of civil war followed until Julius Caesar became ruler for life in 48 BC. The Roman republic was effectively dead, though some of its defenders successfully plotted to murder Caesar in 44 BC, bringing about a further wearying decade of civil war. Caesar's nephew Octavian emerged as sole victor and the ruler of Rome and its territories in 31 BC.

Octavian, soon to be Augustus, rescued Rome from tearing itself apart under the strain of imperial ambition. Augustus was not only a consummate politician but also one of the greatest masters of spin the world has ever known. He pioneered a programme of cultural renewal in Rome, boasting that he found the city made of brick and left it clothed in marble, as befitted the centre of the world. Statues of Augustus, the bringer of peace, appeared everywhere and were disseminated across the Empire, promoting an image of the benevolent and all-seeing emperor who brought peace and prosperity. Where Hellenistic culture had tended to tolerate and even promote local expressions of art, imperial Rome standardized images in a uniform way. Local systems of government might be accepted for the time being, but Roman troops were quickly sent in if there were any awkward signs of independence.

Augustus also recognized that the years of expansion were over. After the humiliating defeat of Varus in northern Germany in the year 9, the boundaries of the empire were largely settled. In the east, across the Syrian deserts, the Parthian armies had also inflicted defeats on the Romans, which ensured that the Empire would be essentially Mediterranean in character. The Parthian frontier had to be secure to protect Rome's assets, and so Syria and Judea became strategically significant for the first time in the late first century BC, the eastern outposts of empire.

The Latin word for empire, *imperium,* literally means 'the power to give orders and to exact obedience to them.'[7] So the 'empire' was where the power of Rome was recognized, which did not necessarily mean direct government by Roman officials. In fact, it was a good deal cheaper to ensure that someone else did the hard work of administration. Formal concepts of nationhood and sovereignty did not mean much in the first century, and this can make it a fruitless task to decide whether particular places were part of the Empire or not. There was no Roman flag to be planted, and different emperors seem to have had different policies about direct and indirect rule. As James Dunn puts it, 'So long as taxes were paid and there was no undue unrest, the ruling hand of Rome was fairly light.'[8] The key to the Roman Empire was not glory, as it had been for Alexander, or national prestige, as was the case with nineteenth-century European imperialism, but the acquisition of hard cash and trade privileges.

Galilee in Jesus' time was not formally part of the Empire. But its rulers, Herod the Great and then his son Herod Antipas, could not have held power without the might of Rome behind them. A high proportion of the wealth generated in Galilee was paid to Rome in the form of tribute. The Roman Empire of the first century has perhaps its closest parallel in the British Empire of the early nineteenth century, which sat light to sovereignty and has been described as an 'empire of informal sway'.

Augustus claimed that the world was subject to his rule and in terms of the informal influence he had he was probably right. Yet he was wisely scrupulous about submitting to constitutional forms. He and his successors merely took the old title of *princeps senatus*, senior senator, and the legions continued to march under the letters *SPQR*, standing for the 'Senate and People of Rome'. But the reality of power was not in doubt. Greek speakers in the eastern half of the Empire had no illusions. They had no other word to describe Augustus but *basileus*: king.

Living in the first-century world

The stories of Alexander and Augustus offer some idea of how the world of the first century had grown and developed. But what was it like to live in?

Ruling the Roman world

At his death in 14, Augustus claimed that he had 'subjected the world to the rule of the Roman people'.[9] Though the claim was more rhetoric than reality in a sense Augustus's boast was true. For just as the emperor's power was often informal, so too was the Roman Empire.

Galilee and Judea are good examples. Herod the Great ruled these lands from 37 BC until his death in 4 BC, but he could not have done so unless his power had been guaranteed by the Roman governor of Syria. After his death his lands were split, on Roman orders, probably to ensure that his successors were not able to mount any kind of challenge to the power of Rome. Judea's dependence on Rome was shown by the way in which Herod's eldest son Archelaus was removed as ruler after the nobles of Judea and Samaria denounced him to Augustus, who dismissed him and brought the province under direct Roman rule in 6, though even then the high priest in Jerusalem seems to have retained control over the everyday government of the city and possibly beyond it.

In Galilee, Archelaus's brother Herod Antipas successfully ruled his portion of their father's kingdom. As well as Galilee in the north, Antipas ruled Perea, east of the Jordan, from 4 BC until 39 with comparatively little interference. Antipas's rule coincided with the whole of the life of Jesus of Nazareth. During that time Roman soldiers would rarely if ever have been seen in Galilee, which was policed by Antipas's own troops. In effect, Galilee was franchised to Antipas. In return he paid a handsome tribute to Rome and made a very good living for himself too.

Above all, Augustus's claim to world rule was true in economic terms. The ebb and flow of Roman rule in Judea and Galilee depended on commercial decisions about which rulers would exploit these lands most effectively. In the end, it was the balance sheet which mattered. Roman legions were awesome military machines, but they were very expensive to maintain and deploy. Provinces were only worth having if they had significant resources to exploit, and Pliny's *Natural History* is partly a catalogue of where they are to be found.

When Hadrian became emperor in 117, his first act was to withdraw troops from what is now Iraq, where they were part of a ruinously expensive war with Parthia instigated by his predecessor Trajan. Of all the emperors, Trajan was probably the one most keen to emulate Alexander. Hadrian, by contrast, was content like Augustus with a financially sensible empire, and set up boundaries around it for the first time, with walls and earthworks in Germany, Britain and North Africa. His decision showed clearly that the legacy of Augustus was a profitable bottom line.

The Mediterranean – an imperial lake

Romans were reluctant sailors. Carthaginians and Greeks were far more at home on the sea. But, rather as those who hate flying today regard it as a necessary evil, so sea-power underpinned communication in the Roman Empire. In earlier times, piracy had been rife across the Mediterranean, but in a single campaign in 67 BC the Roman fleet had swept the Sea clear of pirates. Trade boomed and the volume of sea traffic in the first two centuries of the Roman Empire was not replicated until the sixteenth century.

There were still natural hazards. Shipwreck was a constant threat, as the apostle Paul was painfully aware (Acts 27.14–24; 2 Cor. 11.25). Reasonable safety could be achieved by observing the sailing season, from late March to mid September. During this time, the Roman satirist Juvenal wrote, 'men at sea outnumber those on shore'.[10] In the closed season, some still attempted to sail: the risk was outweighed by the potential for greater profit (see Acts 27.9–12), for by the late first century it was cheaper to carry a cargo of wheat by ship from one end of the Mediterranean to the other than to take it 75 miles overland.

In his *Natural History*, Pliny describes how it was possible to travel by ship from Puteoli on the east Italian coast to Alexandria inside nine days, and from Cadiz to Rome in seven. These were exceptional times in light, fast-sailing craft, but cargo ships still routinely made the 'grain run' bringing Egyptian corn from Alexandria to Rome in six to ten weeks. The return trip was much quicker, since the prevailing wind was in the captain's favour.

Rome sat like an immense spider at the centre of the world economic web, swelled with the spoils of conquest and trade. It was a consumer city so vast that, according to Pliny, 'it must be admitted that no city in the entire world can be compared to it in size'.[11] He did not exaggerate. By the mid first century, Rome and its satellite towns had a population of over a million people, more than twice the size of Alexandria in Egypt, its closest rival, and greater than the eight next-largest cities of the world put together.

The book of Revelation lists cargoes destined for Rome, and their origins underline the worldwide reach of Roman trade: gold from North Africa; precious stones and pearls from India; fine linen and silk from China and India; cinnamon, spices, perfumes, ointments and frankincense from China and Arabia; marble, wine, oil, flour and wheat from Egypt and Syria; and cattle and sheep and carriages from Gaul; and 'the bodies and souls of slaves' from the limits of empire, in Germany and Scythia beyond the Danube (Rev. 18.12–13). The scale of Rome's consuming hunger is revealed by Monte Testaccio, the remarkable artificial hill still to be seen in the city, made entirely of broken pottery jars which carried olive oil. The number of pots suggests that, during the first three centuries of the Empire, at least 7 million litres of oil a year reached Rome.

Rome was unique among ancient cities in not being able to feed itself from its immediate hinterland. The other great population centres were situated at the heart of regional economies for staple foodstuffs, but the development of a market for consumer goods like silk, gems, spices, glassware and fine pottery spread trade empire-wide. Kevin Butcher concludes that archaeological evidence makes it 'quite clear that there was widespread movement of goods all over the Mediterranean and beyond, and on a considerable scale ... The amount of trade, its complexity and its nature mark the Roman imperial economy as something quite different from preceding and succeeding periods.'[12] The scale of trade in the first century was massive.

Culture and communication

Socrates famously described those who lived beside the Mediterranean as being 'like frogs round a pond'.[13] Like frogs, ships' captains hopped across the sea from one bit of land to another, seldom straying far from the coast, picking up and setting down passengers as they went. Paul's journey from Philippi to Caesarea is a good example of this kind of journey (Acts 20.6,13–15; 21.1–8). Although there was an imperial postal system, it was reserved for official use, so particular individuals, often slaves, acted as messengers and personally delivered letters. These letter-carriers were some of the best travelled people in the first century, an immense resource of knowledge about cities, peoples and cultures. They were an especially significant group within early Christianity, delivering the letters of Paul and other apostles to churches all around the Mediterranean.

Although most people can rarely have travelled further than their local market town, the spread of goods, merchants and messengers brought the wider world much closer to ordinary people than we might imagine. Wayne Meeks comments that 'the people of the Roman Empire travelled more extensively and more easily than anyone before them did or would again until the nineteenth century'.[14] The implications of this can be seen in the life of Jesus himself. He came from Nazareth, a small hill-village in lower Galilee of little significance. Only five miles away, however, was the town of Sepphoris, the administrative capital of the area, which had been rebuilt in the Hellenistic style by Herod Antipas. Excavations there have brought to light imported examples of Italian pottery and glassware, and also a theatre. There is no direct evidence that Jesus visited Sepphoris, but a few details in the Gospels suggest that even if he had not, he was familiar with some Greek customs. He mentions the 'place of honour' at a feast in one of his parables, and the Gospels portray him reclining at dinner in the Hellenistic fashion, for example (Mark 14.3; 12.39). The mention of *hypocrites,* a Greek word meaning an actor, which had no equivalent in Jesus' mother tongue of Aramaic, suggests that Jesus was able to speak some Greek and that he knew about the theatre in Sepphoris (Matt. 7.5; 22.18).

There is a vigorous debate on how Hellenized Galilee was in Jesus' time, and how widely Greek was spoken. But this debate should not detract from the overall picture which shows that someone who never travelled more than a few days' walk from the small village in which he grew up was familiar with these features of Hellenistic culture. As Dominic Crossan says, 'Nazareth, while certainly off the beaten track, was not very far off a fairly well-beaten track.'[15] In Jesus' time, Galilee was not directly ruled by Rome and was still nominally independent, but it participated in the same cultural world that Pliny later described.

Towns like Sepphoris played a crucial role by being places where there was a trade in ideas and stories as well as goods. Travelling philosophers went from town to town, debating as they went. Paul set up as a philosopher in Ephesus, holding discussions for a two year period in the 'Hall of Tyrannus' and as a result, according to Acts, everyone in the province of Asia heard his message (Acts 19.9–10). Stories also spread widely: 'no half-educated person in this [Mediterranean] world could be unaware of the stories in Homer's *Iliad* and *Odyssey*'[16] even if they had not read these classics for themselves. A copy of the *Aeneid*, Virgil's great Latin epic of the founding of Rome has been found at Masada in southern Judea, while a Greek prose translation of the work was widely known throughout the East.

The traffic in ideas and stories stretched out beyond the towns and cities. There was a delicate balance to be maintained between local and Hellenistic cultures. At the end of his time in Ephesus, Paul was accused of undermining the cult of the local goddess Artemis by the local silversmiths. The silversmiths relied on the sale of replica idols of the goddess for their livelihood and defended their local traditions fiercely against this man who had infected almost the whole province (Acts 19.23–41). Fears of a similar sort surface in Pliny's *Natural History* in his frequent complaint that luxuries from foreign lands have undermined the proud and austere traditions of Rome. The historian Tacitus saw little to celebrate in the way in which Rome had become, in his eyes, the place where 'all degraded and shameful practices collect and flourish'[17] from the whole empire. Captive Greece, with its Hellenistic culture, had taken the conqueror Rome captive, wrote the poet Horace.

As far as religion was concerned, the Roman view was that you couldn't have too many gods. These gods were identified as the 'spirits of place'; their local character was emphasized and in general the Romans were careful to respect local traditions. It was, after all, a good idea to have the local gods on your side. One of the most important Roman values was toleration of all gods. It was widely accepted that there were 12 Olympian gods, of whom Jupiter (Zeus to the Greeks) was the highest. Some local deities were co-opted into this group. Artemis of Ephesus, for example, had been worshipped for centuries there as Cybele, the mother goddess, before she was identified as a manifestation of one of the Olympians. Only two expressions of religion were ever actively suppressed under the Roman Empire in the first century: druidism in Britain and Judaism in Judea. In both cases it may have been because of the strongly nationalistic and intolerant nature of these beliefs.

Theories and presuppositions

Going back to the analogy of a guidebook, we have now completed a preliminary orientation and it is time to find a way of breaking down the mass of material about the New Testament in order to make it more easily understandable.

Most introductions to the New Testament divide up the different kinds of writing it contains: Gospels, letters and the book of Revelation, reflecting the order in which it is printed in our Bibles. It is also how the Old Testament is divided up and studied (into Law, history, writings and prophets). When the Old and New Testaments are seen as a single book, it makes sense to study the New in the same way as the Old. When I started teaching the New Testament this is the way I did it.

But I found that this approach was not very accessible to the people I was teaching, because it tends to focus on the writings themselves, rather than the context and process that produced them. This approach offers a lot of information but not much of a framework by which to understand the dynamic relationship between the different writings. By looking again at the process by which the New Testament was formed I came up with an alternative framework which embeds the writings of the New Testament much more clearly within their historical context. This framework is what underpins the book as a whole and offers a simple way in to the New Testament.

To some degree the frameworks which we use to study anything will determine what we see and what we overlook. All of us bring a network of presuppositions to the New Testament, and it's important at this stage to spend a few moments checking what they are. Presuppositions have aptly been called the 'spectacles behind the eyes'[18] because they affect everything that we see but we are not usually conscious of them until we stand back and try to become aware of them. As with spectacles, different lenses offer different perspectives. One set of lenses might be our own life experience; another might be our religious commitments, whatever they are; a third might be theories about the development of the early Church.

Theories of conspiracy, conflict and community

Particular theories of the development of the early Church can have deep, lasting and often unconscious effects on scholars. Three of the most influential theories which have been developed since critical historical study of the New Testament really began towards the end of the eighteenth century may be labelled as the theories, in turn, of conspiracy, conflict of traditions and isolated communities.

An early attempt to explain the rise of Christianity came from H. S. Reimarus in the mid eighteenth century. He argued that Jesus was a misguided Jewish teacher who tried in vain to lead a popular revolt, and whose memory was fraudulently manipulated by his followers for the sake of power and wealth. This conspiracy theory periodically resurfaces, especially when new documents from the period of the early Church are found, such as the Dead Sea Scrolls.

The theory relies heavily on the presupposition that the New Testament documents were meant to suppress the truth and mislead. This was a widely held view among intellectuals in the later eighteenth century, who were suspicious of the Church and all that it stood for, sometimes with good reason. Systematic scepticism of this sort, sometimes known as the 'hermeneutic of suspicion', is alive and well in contemporary journalism. But there are good grounds for considering that the Gospel writers and others did want to pass on the truth about Jesus, though we need to be aware that their standards of historical truth belonged to the first, not the twenty-first, century and that therefore their work must be approached critically.

The second, conflict of traditions, theory was formulated by F. C. Baur in the early nineteenth century. Baur found evidence of conflict between Paul and the other apostles, especially Peter, in some of the letters of Paul (see, for example, 1 Cor. 1.10–12; Phil. 3.1–12; Gal. 2.11). He then proposed that there had been two major parties in the early Church: Jewish Christianity of which James, Jesus' brother, was the figurehead; and gentile Christianity which was led by Paul.

At this point, like some kind of Frankenstein's monster, the theory began to take over. Baur proceeded to argue that any of Paul's writings that did not show strong evidence of the conflict must have been written by someone else in his name. In other words, he began to alter the evidence to fit the theory until he came to regard only the letters to the Romans, the Corinthians and the Galatians as actually written by Paul. Baur finally proposed that later attempts at mediation between the two parties led to the establishment of what he called 'early Catholicism', when the two major expressions of Christian faith were reconciled in the face of the external threat of heresy. Baur believed that this process must have taken almost 200 years, and as a consequence dated John's Gospel, which he thought to be the last book of the New Testament to be written, as late as 170, almost a century and a half after Jesus' crucifixion.

Baur's theory of the development of the early Church borrowed the contemporary philosopher Hegel's conviction that conflict is the basis of all development in human thought and history. Hegel's highly complex philosophy was based on the process of an original idea (the thesis) being distinguished from itself by its opposite (the antithesis), and the two then producing a higher, richer and fuller concept (the synthesis). Baur's theory of the development of the early Church clearly followed this pattern, but in the process it lost touch with the evidence. The presupposition behind Baur's theory was Hegel's view that conflict was the basis of all development.

Baur identified something very important when he noticed the evidence of conflict in the early Church. The problem was that, from the observation of some conflict, Baur elevated it to become the driving force of the whole process of development. Conflict was transformed from part of the analysis to its guiding principle. The discovery in 1934 of a manuscript of John's Gospel dating from around 125 was widely held to have disproved Baur's theory.

Yet, Baur's theory has neat simplicity about it. There were different understandings of Christian faith at an early stage and they sometimes led to conflict. The model has been extremely helpful as a means of studying what happened in the early Church, but it doesn't really seem to take all the evidence into account. For that reason most scholars today would not accept it. The identification of different traditions in the early Church is important, but we need not assume that they inevitably led to conflict.

The third theory relies on the idea of isolated communities. This model seems to have mushroomed without the case for it ever being fully argued. Put most simply, it assumes that each of the Gospels was written for a single local church, which developed in isolation from others. These churches have then been analysed to produce, as Richard Burridge puts it, 'reconstructions of communities each apparently unrelated to the rest of the Christian movement, each apparently treating itself self-sufficiently as *the* Christian social world'. A great deal of illuminating scholarship has grown out of this model, but the presupposition on which it rests is that communication in the first century was extremely difficult and that contacts between Christian communities were fleeting and rare. Evidence of trade networks suggests that this presupposition is wrong, and that, as Burridge continues, 'The early Christian movement was not a scattering of isolated, self-sufficient communities with little or no communication between them but quite the opposite: a network of communities with constant, close communication among themselves.'[19] The implication of this latter view is that the Gospels should be seen as dynamically related to, rather than insulated from, each other.

Checking our own presuppositions

These examples may offer some insight into the way in which presuppositions can both hinder and help us as we look at the New Testament. Perhaps this is the moment for me to be clear with you about what some of my own presuppositions are. Then you will be aware of some of the biases on display in the rest of the book, and perhaps be able to make allowances for them.

My academic training was first of all in the study of history, and only secondarily in theology. This means that I tend to value evidence and common sense more highly than theory, and try to ask practical questions (my social-scientist friends tell me that I am too suspicious of theory). I prefer to look for evidence rather than speculation. There are a lot of intriguing and exciting ideas in the study of the New Testament, but they have to be evaluated against the evidence that is available. Historians sometimes use a rule of thumb called 'Occam's Razor', which states that, in cases of difficulty, the simplest explanation is the one which is to be preferred. The value of evidence and the simplicity of explanations are therefore important criteria for me in trying to determine the truth.

My historical training also decisively affects what you will find in this book. My approach to the New Testament is historical rather than literary, for example, and I am sympathetic to James Crossley's view that New Testament studies have sometimes been 'focused too heavily on history of ideas rather than trying to find a range of down-to-earth social and economic *causal factors* that led to the spread of earliest Christianity'.[20] This book is intended as a 'way in' to the New Testament, and there are lots of exciting alternative ways of interpreting the New Testament; but I believe that the historical approach is the easiest preliminary approach for most people and that a grasp of the historical basis of the New Testament offers a foundation on which you can build if you want to take your studies further.

Finally, although this book looks at the New Testament historically, that does not mean that I think theology is unimportant. Every historian brings some kind of theology or ideological commitment to their studies, even if they do not call it that. Theology is basically a set of beliefs or convictions about the fundamental questions of existence, whether God exists and what the nature of reality is like. These kinds of issues have to be presupposed, but they decisively affect what you see when you study the New Testament. Is it possible that Jesus was able to heal people? Can there be any truth in the claim that he rose from the dead? Your theological or ideological pre-commitments will largely determine how you approach such questions. Theological commitments are not irrational, but they are properly the subject matter of other fields of study which are beyond the scope of this book. There's a kind of parallel with Gödel's theorem in mathematics, which proposes that 'systems of sufficient complexity to include whole numbers always contain propositions which are stateable but not decidable within that system.'[21] The existence (or non-existence) of God is similarly stateable but not decidable within a historical analysis.

My own theological commitment is as a Christian. I see the New Testament as more than just a collection of historical books. That doesn't stop me from appreciating the work of scholars who are not Christians, or make me assume that scholars who are have a hotline to the truth. But having a broadly orthodox Christian faith, including, for example, the readiness to believe that miracles are possible, does affect the way I study the New Testament. I might be wrong, of course; that possibility is deeply woven into the whole concept of faith. Yet, I have had enough personal experience that I identify with God to lead me to believe that purely human factors are not enough to account for the life and impact of Jesus of Nazareth.

These presuppositions lead me to a position where I have trust in the general historical reliability of the documents of the New Testament; where I recognize the importance of different traditions in the early Church; and where I see good communications and strong relationships between different Christian communities as a vital part of the development of the New Testament.

Before you go further you may wish to pause for a few minutes and note down your own presuppositions. How far are they the same, and how far do they differ from mine? If you are able to do this, it will make the rest of the book feel more like a dialogue and make it clearer why you disagree with me at times (and, I hope, sometimes agree too!).

Being aware of our own background beliefs and which theories they may dispose us to accept is vital because it enables us to look more objectively at the material in front of us. Theories are crucially important, but problems arise when they become so ingrained that they cease to be recognized as such, which was what happened with the theories of conspiracy, conflict and community. The process of moving from a simple explanatory framework or hypothesis through more and more complex qualifications to the abandonment of the first hypothesis in favour of a further more comprehensive one is how the process of intellectual discovery works.

By the end of this book, you may be happy with the rather simple (to some, simplistic) framework I shall use, but I hope you may have begun to develop your own more complex one. The important point is that you will be aware that any framework is an imaginative construction used to help us to understand the New Testament; it has to be, to some extent, imposed on the material. If a framework is properly constructed then it will be based on the material, even though it will have to go beyond it. As the historian John Lewis Gaddis puts it, 'coupl[ing] imagination with logic to derive past processes from present structures ... historians ... start with surviving structures, whether they be archives, artefacts, or even memories. They then deduce the processes that produced them.'[22] This book offers a framework for understanding the New Testament. It's what scientists call a 'heuristic model', that is, a speculative hypothesis developed to make the material studied intelligible. A heuristic model doesn't carry with it any assumption that it is true or false; the criterion for judgement is how useful it is.

The framework I shall use in the rest of the book is an imaginative but logical construction along the lines which Gaddis suggests all historians use. The 'surviving structures' available are primarily the books of the New Testament, alongside other documents (some Christian and some not) and some archaeological discoveries. Using these, I shall offer you a story of the development of the Church in the first century which seeks to account for the writing of what we now call the New Testament. The framework will form the basis of the structure of the book. I'm not making any big claims for it: it's really just a way of organizing the material so that you can understand it better. If it gives you a 'way in' to the New Testament and spurs you to go further and deeper in your studies then it will have done its job.[23]

How was the New Testament put together?

There was a process behind the collection of books which make up the New Testament. Why were some books included in the collection, and others left out?

The New Testament according to the Da Vinci Code

Dan Brown's phenomenally best-selling novel, *The Da Vinci Code* is a cracking read, as several million readers can testify. It includes an explanation by the character Leigh Teabing of how the New Testament was put together, which has proved surprisingly convincing and influential, even though Dan Brown did not intend his thriller to be a serious contribution to the study of the New Testament!

Teabing claims that the New Testament was invented by the Emperor Constantine in the fourth century, and that he selected just four gospels from some 80 or so which had claims to be included. These four gospels, says Teabing, were chosen for political reasons since they emphasized Jesus' divinity at the expense of his humanity, and boosted Constantine's claim to the imperial throne. The alternative Gospels, which offered the true story of Jesus, were suppressed and burned, he asserts. But some were preserved and rediscovered among the Dead Sea Scrolls and the texts found at Nag Hammadi in Egypt.

This simple account of the formation of the New Testament is wrong in most of its facts. Nevertheless it has a ring of truth for many readers because it makes use of a framework or narrative that frequently features in newspapers, magazines and television documentaries. This framework holds that the truth has been covered up by those whose vested interests would be threatened by it; a favourite target (as in *The Da Vinci Code*) is the Vatican. Only now, at the beginning of the twenty-first century, runs the story, can the truth be revealed.

Teabing's claim that new discoveries have suddenly revolutionized the study of the New Testament in the last 25 years is wrong. As Philip Jenkins writes, 'Particularly between about 1880 and 1920, a cascade of new discoveries transformed attitudes to early Christianity'. The texts found at Nag Hammadi and the Dead Sea, in 1945 and 1947 respectively, filled out a picture which had already emerged in clear outline, of Jewish and Christian beliefs in the first and second centuries which were far more diverse than scholars had previously imagined. (The Dead Sea Scrolls contain no Christian writings, despite Teabing's assertion; their full publication was not complete until 1991, but this seems to have been the result of incompetence rather than conspiracy.) Jenkins asks why, in this case, there has been an undeniable upsurge of interest in recent years. He concludes that there has been a 'fundamental change of attitude among scholars' related especially to postmodern scepticism about authority which sees 'orthodoxy and the institutional church ... as authoritarian, patriarchal, and narrow'.[24] Significantly, it's not what is there that has really changed, but the way it is seen. That is to say, the framework used to explain the early Church has changed to conform to the scepticism of contemporary Western society about those in authority. Cover-up stories are not hard to find in the media, and many of them do reveal important facts that have been hidden from the public gaze. But the formation of the New Testament does not appear to be one of them. How can we tell? By looking at how the New Testament was really put together.

Early collections of Christian books

Around 135, a successful businessman and evangelist called Marcion turned up in Rome with a large donation for the church there. Among other things, Marcion argued that it would be much simpler to make converts if the Church could agree on a single version of Jesus' life, based on the Gospel of Luke, instead of the several which were in existence.

Marcion had a pretty good case. Essentially, his point was that the Church's message could be packaged a good deal better (presumably it was his marketing skills that had made him a success in business). The differences between the Gospels were sometimes an embarrassment: the philosopher Celsus, Marcion's pagan contemporary, apparently said that Christians were like drunkards who couldn't get their story straight.[25]

On the other hand there were more than the four Gospels of Matthew, Mark, Luke and John in existence, including those attributed to Thomas, Peter and Philip. So if Marcion's plea for just one Gospel was not accepted, how many should there be? Was there anything magic about the number four?

What followed was not so much a competition for which books should be included in the canon (a word derived from the Greek *kanon*, a measuring stick or ruler) as a recognition of which books were already being widely used in worship and teaching and which had a good provenance. From their very early years, different Christian communities seem to have collected writings which documented the life of Jesus and the teachings of his early followers.

It is a sign of the importance which Christians attached to such writings that, when persecutions came, books were usually the first things to be confiscated by the Roman authorities. Facing a Roman proconsul in 180, the first African martyrs told him that they had a basket of 'books and letters of a man named Paul'.[26] This suggests two distinct collections, and it is likely that they had the New Testament as it now exists in embryonic form: the Gospels ('books') and Paul's letters.

Some of Paul's letters were collected by at least the late first century (see 2 Peter 3.16). The martyrs Ignatius and Polycarp in the early second century knew several letters by Paul, and Marcion knew all of Paul's letters now included in the New Testament, except for the letters to Timothy and Titus (often known collectively as the 'Pastoral Epistles').

By 180, there is evidence that the four Gospels of Matthew, Mark, Luke and John were becoming a standard collection and had begun to circulate as a single volume, and around this time, Irenaeus of Lyons passionately defended these four Gospels as the authoritative ones. Irenaeus' problem was this: if he were not to accept Marcion's argument for a single Gospel, why not have an infinite number of gospels? From his response it seems clear that he had not invented the idea of a fourfold Gospel, but that it must have already been current earlier in the second century. On the one hand, Irenaeus believed that one Gospel was not enough, but on the other hand that more than four was too many.

Irenaeus' argument for the authority of the four Gospels of Matthew, Mark, Luke and John was based on three grounds: first, that these four Gospels each had a strong connection to an apostle and had therefore been written early in the Church's life; second, that the consistency of these four had been widely recognized by the Church; third, that since the earth has four corners but is one, and the Old Testament has four covenants within it but is also one, and the divine throne is surrounded by four creatures witnessing to the one God (Ezek. 1.5–10, see also Rev. 4.6–7), so the gospel is 'in four forms, but united with one spirit'.[27] Irenaeus' third argument could, of course, have applied to pretty well any number. Seven would have been a better candidate, as it was generally reckoned to represent perfection. The fact that Irenaeus used the argument that something could appear in several forms and yet be one, and applied it to the number four, makes it clear that Irenaeus had not chosen the number himself but was passing on something which he himself had received.

Other gospels continued to be used in different churches for the stories they provided about Jesus. A *Gospel of Peter*, for example, was prized by the Christians of Rhosus in Syria around 200. Their local bishop, Serapion, at first encouraged them to continue reading it on the basis that it had apparently been written in the first person by the apostle Peter. When he received a copy himself he realized that, while much of it was helpful, there were 'some things added' which suggested that Jesus had not truly been human. This, he believed, could not have been Peter's teaching and so he said 'we reject with understanding the writings falsely ascribed' to the apostles and wrote in detail to the Rhosians about what was wrong with the *Gospel of Peter*.[28] The striking thing about this little episode is how charitable Serapion was about the *Gospel of Peter*. He does not appear to have banned the Rhosians from reading it, and fragments of a copy dating from somewhere between 500 and 900 found in Egypt in 1886–7 show that it was still very much in circulation more than three centuries later. It seems to have been an imaginative retelling of the story of Jesus, of a kind which is not uncommon still in sermons today. This seems to have been legitimate as far as Serapion was concerned, though it might expose the Rhosians to errors of understanding. What was not legitimate was linking this book with the apostles and taking it as Peter's direct teaching. By the end of the second century it seems that the four Gospels of Matthew, Mark, Luke and John had reached a recognized status as the authentic teaching of the apostles which would later be called canonical.

By the early third century the broad outline of the New Testament was emerging. The four Gospels were supplemented by the Acts of the Apostles, making a convenient five book collection which inevitably echoed the opening five books of Moses in the Old Testament. Ten letters of Paul made up a second section. But there were also other books which were read as authoritative in some places, such as the letter to the Hebrews (which was eventually included in the canon) and the *Revelation of Peter* (which was not). It was around this third group that there was dispute.

Forming the New Testament canon

In 303, the Emperor Diocletian inaugurated almost a decade of fierce persecution which nearly wiped out the Church. In an amazing reversal, which Christians did not hesitate to identify as a miracle, Constantine became emperor in 312. He genuinely believed that the victory was given to him by the Christian God and not only brought persecution to an end by proclaiming religious toleration, but used Christianity as a kind of glue to bind together his rather ramshackle empire.

The Church continued to reel from the ferocity and bitterness of the attacks it had suffered. It needed repairing and tidying up if it was to be fit for the purpose which Constantine had in mind. Under Constantine's influence issues such as whether Jesus should be understood as God or man or both were hammered out at the Council of Nicea in 325. Similarly, Constantine was eager to make sure that the untidiness at the edges of the New Testament canon was put right. His chaplain, the historian Eusebius, produced the first list of 27 books, which is identical with the one you will find on the contents page of a New Testament today. Eusebius' list is important because he was recording which books were recognized as canonical rather than arguing for a particular view. There was no real doubt over the collection of the Gospels by this time, nor over Paul's letters (though the letter to the Hebrews was sometimes regarded as written by him). Eusebius notes that some had doubts about the letters of James, 2 Peter, 2 and 3 John or Jude, and shows some nervousness about the Revelation of John (it would not have made comfortable reading for Constantine).

How might doubts about certain books be resolved? Eusebius describes the criteria which he believed had been used, echoing the principles of Irenaeus a century and a half before:

- First, was a book genuinely linked to an apostle? Mark was thought to have been Peter's assistant and Luke Paul's, so although they were not themselves apostles they were close to those who were.
- Second, was a book universally known? The *Gospel of Peter* and the *Gospel of Thomas* were excluded on this basis. The church in Rome was very fond of the *Revelation of Peter*; but no other church used this book in its worship so it too was excluded.
- Third, did a book agree with the 'apostolic usage', that is, the general sense of the apostolic writings?[29]

The importance of Eusebius' description is that it shows that the early Church had a critical process with which to assess the reliability of the books of the New Testament.

By the later fifth century, as the Church became more organized and became once more a missionary movement, there was widespread agreement on the 27 books of the New Testament. In part, this was a matter of practicality: which books should be translated into other languages in order to spread the gospel message? It also reflected an agreement which had emerged rather than been imposed.

There was agreement about which individual *books* were authoritative, rather than which *collection* of books was. So if there was later disagreement about the canon of the New Testament, it centred on whether individual books were trustworthy, not whether the whole canon should be dismissed. (The sixteenth-century Reformer Martin Luther, for example, wanted to exclude the letter of James on the grounds that he felt it did not reflect the 'apostolic usage', that is, it did not conform to his view of what was orthodox. Luther's views were not adopted by others.)

Very few Christian communities would have had a collection of all 27 books. The claim by Leigh Teabing in *The Da Vinci Code* that Constantine produced an 'official' version of the Bible probably reflects the emperor's order to Eusebius to procure 50 fine copies of 'the Sacred Scriptures' to present to the 50 new churches he had founded in his new capital of Constantinople. The point was that only the most important churches could expect to have a full set.

The formation of the New Testament was a critical process of sifting which books the Church genuinely believed to reflect the testimony and teaching of those who had been recognized in the earliest Church as apostles, that is, those commissioned and sent out by Jesus himself.

Four apostles

When we look at how the books of the New Testament reflect the testimony and teaching of the apostles an interesting trend emerges. Rather than finding books which are connected with twelve apostles (or thirteen if we include Paul who came late to the party but was most insistent that he, too, had been called by the risen Jesus) we can discern that there are four distinct groups:

- The first is of writings associated with Paul: his letters, the Gospel of Luke and the Acts of the Apostles (the second half of which is effectively a biography of Paul).
- The second is linked with the apostle John: the Gospel which bears his name, three letters and Revelation.
- Third, Mark's Gospel was widely held to be based on the reminiscences of Peter, who was also held to have written the two letters which bear his name.
- The fourth group seems to be a miscellaneous bundle of Matthew's Gospel, the letter to the Hebrews and the letters of James and Jude. Yet these books also have a kind of family resemblance because they are the books which most strongly reflect the Jewish origins of the Church.

Thus, when we look beneath the criterion of apostolic origin we find not a haphazard collection of 27 books but four coherent groups of writings. Each of the four groups contains a Gospel, and three are clearly identified with a particular apostle: Peter, Paul and John.

These three apostolic names are brought together in the New Testament itself, together with James, the brother of Jesus. Paul refers to Peter, John and James, as 'those reckoned to be pillars' who had given him 'the right hand of fellowship' (Peter is referred to by his Aramaic name Cephas, Gal. 2.9).

The four 'pillars' have been identified as the founding figures of four 'apostolic missions',[30] but I do not wish to make such sweeping claims, simply to use the four family groups of writings as a way in to understanding the collection of ancient books we call the New Testament. It seems reasonable to conclude that here we have the core group of apostles whose names were used to give authority to the writings of the New Testament. For this reason the miscellaneous group of writings which have a strongly Jewish flavour may be identified with the apostle James, the brother of Jesus, who had a central role in the earliest church in Jerusalem.

If we put the four groups into a table, they look like Figure 2.

James	Peter	Paul	John
Matthew's Gospel	Mark's Gospel	Luke's Gospel & Acts	John's Gospel
Hebrews	1 Peter	Romans	1 John
James	2 Peter	1&2 Corinthians	2 John
Jude		Galatians	3 John
		Ephesians	Revelation
		Philippians	
		Colossians	
		1&2 Thessalonians	
		1 &2 Timothy	
		Titus	
		Philemon	

Figure 2 Apostolic connections of New Testament books

The reality of how the New Testament was put together is of course more complex than this simple model suggests. The aim of this book is to use these four groups of writings as a device to help you to discover the New Testament more easily and to organize the knowledge you already have and the knowledge I hope you will gain as you read through it.

The pillar apostles and their books

The most important criterion for including a book in the New Testament was that it had a strong link with a particular apostle. But in what sense were the books listed above under each of the 'pillar' apostles connected to them?

At first sight you would think that Paul's would be the easiest connection to demonstrate. After all, surely his letters came from his pen? In fact scholars differ over how many of Paul's letters they think were genuinely written by him: Romans, 1 and 2 Corinthians, Galatians, Philippians, 1 Thessalonians and Philemon are agreed to be genuinely Pauline, but doubt has been cast on Paul's authorship of the other six on grounds of literary style and the theology contained in them. Luke's Gospel and Acts, connected with Paul in the early years of the Church by virtue of an associate of his named Luke (Col. 4.14), arguably differ from the theological views Paul presents in his letters. They also do not say that they were written by Luke, although the anonymous author of Acts identifies himself as a companion of Paul's (Acts 16.10–17).

At this point the suspicion of forgery arises, because it has been argued for a long time that many of the books which claim to be by apostles (like 2 Peter) were in fact attempts by later writers to borrow the authority of the original apostles for their own opinions. This phenomenon is usually known as pseudonymity.

Some scholars argue that it was a widespread and unexceptional practice in the ancient world to produce writings under the name of a dead mentor. There is some truth in this view, but the examples we know are almost all of writings published centuries after the supposed author's death. In such cases there was no attempt at passing off the documents as genuine. Pseudonymity, the argument runs, was simply a literary device. The New Testament books which may be pseudonymous were written within a few decades of the deaths of their supposed writers, so they were clearly intended to be read as if they were genuine. However, it is clear that during the second century there was a good deal of careful judgement to weed out books like the *Gospel of Peter*, which seemed to be apostolic but were in fact not so. Pseudonymity thus does not seem to have been a widely accepted phenomenon in the early Church.

A more detailed examination of these issues must wait until later chapters. At this stage, however, it is important to grasp that a connection between an apostle and a book did not imply that the book was written personally by the apostle in question. The ascription of a book to an apostle is more a statement of origins than authorship. Very few authors in the first century physically wrote the words on the page: they had scribes to do it for them. Paul drew attention to the unformed and amateurish style of his 'large letters' (Gal. 6.11). Handwriting was something he usually left to a scribe and Tertius, who actually wrote Paul's letter to the Romans, added his own greetings to Paul's (Rom. 16.22).

Writing in the first century was usually a collaborative exercise. Most of Paul's letters were sent from the apostle and one or more associates (Sosthenes, Timothy and Silas). How closely Paul supervised the letters that went out under his name is unclear. Scribes may have written to dictation in longhand, but perhaps more likely used a form of shorthand to transfer spoken word into written prose. They often gave advice on phrasing and style, and perhaps on structure too. It is possible that after Paul's death others wrote up his views in the same sort of way, continuing to convey his thought and perhaps using notes which he had left. Thus the letters of Paul which may have been written by others were like 'an afterwave or tail of the comet ... which is still able to tell us something about what went before'[31] and which had a genuine connection with apostle himself.

Each of the four groups shares its own 'family characteristics'. The first group, which I have linked with James, is strongly Jewish in its outlook. These books help us to see the roots of Christianity in Jewish faith. The second group, associated with Peter, reflects the expansion of this Jewish sect into the Greco-Roman world. The third group, linked with Paul, is much the largest and details the growth of the Church among gentiles. The fourth group, the writings associated with John, has a mystical tinge to it and reflects the development of the Church in the last decades of the first century.

In the rest of the book we shall look at these four apostles and the group of writings associated with each one in turn. Thus the chapters are paired: James with Matthew's Gospel, Peter with Mark's and so on. The first chapter in each pair will also look briefly at the letters linked with the apostle under discussion, while the second will take a comparative look at a particular theme in a 'spotlight' section at the end.

Each of the four groups of writings might be described as a stream of tradition. But all four streams flow from one source: Jesus of Nazareth himself. So in the final chapter we shall look at his life, death and what came after, the events which gave rise to this collection of 27 books which we call the New Testament.

Draw your own conclusions

- What are the presuppositions which you bring to your study of the New Testament? Where have they come from? How do they affect what you see when you read the New Testament?
- What is the value of reading gospels which are not in the New Testament such as *Thomas*?
- Do you think that the formation of the New Testament canon was a genuinely critical process?
- Do you agree that the link between certain apostles and the books of the New Testament is more about origin than authorship?
- Does it make any difference to how you read the New Testament if you believe that certain books were written pseudonymously?

Further reading

Reference books

It is important to have a modern translation of the New Testament: the *New Revised Standard Version* is probably the best currently available for study purposes. Learning New Testament Greek is obviously desirable if you want to wrestle with the text of the New Testament, but an interlinear Greek New Testament will provide some of the excitement of grasping the original meaning by offering a literal translation below the Greek text. R. K. Brown and P. W. Comfort (trs) (1990), *The New Greek-English Interlinear New Testament*, Carol Stream, IL: Tyndale House, also prints the NRSV alongside the text. A synopsis of the Gospels, which places the passages that are paralleled in Matthew, Mark and Luke side-by-side, is helpful. B. H. Throckmorton (1992), *Gospel Parallels*, Nashville: Thomas Nelson, is one of the best of these. Also useful is an atlas: J. Pritchard (1987), *The Times Atlas of the Bible*, London: Times Books, is one of the many available.

G. Vermes (2005), *Who's Who in the Age of Jesus*, London: Penguin, offers brief biographies of key people relevant to the New Testament. The series of four books comprising J. B. Green, S. McKnight and I. H. Marshall (1992), *Dictionary of Jesus and the Gospels;* G. F. Hawthorne, R. P. Martin and D. G. Reid (1993), *Dictionary of Paul and his Letters*; R. P. Martin and P. H. Davids (1997), *Dictionary of the Later New Testament and its Developments*; C. A. Evans and S. E. Porter (2000), *Dictionary of New Testament Background*, Downers Grove: IVP; all offer a wealth of information, from a moderately conservative perspective. It is to be hoped that they will be updated to take account of recent developments in scholarship. More broadly, J. Barton and J. Muddiman (eds.) (2001), *The Oxford Bible Commentary*, Oxford: Oxford University Press, is a one-volume commentary on the whole Bible by a variety of contributors. B. M. Metzger and M. D. Coogan (1993), *The Oxford Companion to the Bible*, New York: Oxford University Press, provides articles on both Old and New Testaments. A. Hastings, A. Mason and H. Pyper (2000), *The Oxford Companion to Christian Thought*, Oxford: Oxford University Press, ranges widely over Christian theology and has useful introductory articles on the New Testament and on Paul. F. L.Cross and E. A. Livingstone (1997), *The Oxford Dictionary of the Christian Church*, 3rd ed., Oxford: Oxford University Press, offers short entries on any imaginable subject including short summaries of all the books of the New Testament and brief histories of their interpretation.

Historical context

The best general survey is R. Lane Fox (2006), *The Classical World: an epic history of Greece and Rome*, 2nd ed., London: Penguin, which manages to be informative, entertaining and authoritative. Others include J.Boardman et. al. (eds) (1986), *The Oxford History of the Classical World*, Oxford: Oxford University Press, and C. Freeman (1996), *Egypt, Greece and Rome: civilizations of the ancient Mediterranean*, Oxford: Oxford University Press. S. Hornblower and A. Spawforth eds. (1998), *The Oxford Companion to Classical Civilization*, Oxford: Oxford University Press, offers a wide ranging feast of short articles on almost every aspect of the ancient world. Two more detailed works worth looking at are T. Holland (2003), *Rubicon: the triumph and tragedy of the Roman Republic*, London: Little, Brown, a narrative of the crisis which led to the end of the Roman republic and the beginning of the Empire; and P. Zanker (1988), *The Power of Images in the Age of Augustus*, Ann Arbor: Michigan University Press, which takes a detailed look at the way Augustus used architecture and statues as propaganda to spread the power of Rome.

Most general surveys tend to focus on Greece, Rome and the Western Empire. Some that do not are M. Goodman (2007), *Rome and Jerusalem: the clash of ancient civilizations*, London: Penguin, which sets the rise of the Roman Empire in the context of the later clash between Jews and Romans; and F. Millar (1993), *The Roman Near East 31BC–AD337*

Cambridge, MA: Harvard University Press. K. Butcher (2003), *Roman Syria and the Near East*, London: British Museum Press, covers the seven centuries of Roman rule in the east thematically.

The ruins of Pompeii offer a unique perspective on daily life in a Roman town during the Empire. A. Butterworth and R. Laurence (2005), *Pompeii: the living city*, London: Weidenfeld & Nicolson, provides a vivid portrait of the city and its people in the first century; M. Beard, (2008) *Pompeii: the life of a Roman town*, London: Profile, examines what the remains of the city can tell us about matters such as the home life, occupations, food, sex and religion of the inhabitants.

On travel and trade, L. Casson (1994), *Travel in the Ancient World*, 2nd ed., Baltimore: Johns Hopkins University Press, remains the best introduction. Two massive books offer more detail and range further than the first century: W. Schiedel, I. Morris and R. Saller (eds) (2007), *The Cambridge Economic History of the Greco-Roman World*, Cambridge: Cambridge University Press, offers several useful chapters; P. Hordern and N. Purcell (2000), *The Corrupting Sea: a study of Mediterranean history*, Oxford: Blackwell, is a ground-breaking survey of 3,000 years of history through the detailed examination of individual communities and regions.

A large amount of literature survives from the ancient world and is available in translation. It's worth trying to get to know some of this, because it offers an invaluable backdrop to the writings of the New Testament. It is easier to understand the Gospels, for example, if you have read a few of the *Lives* of eminent Greeks and Romans written by Plutarch in the later first century. Tacitus' *The Annals of Imperial Rome* offers a narrative of imperial politics from 14 to 66 and includes the story of the Fire of Rome in book 15. Suetonius' *Lives of the Twelve Caesars* is a gossipy and probably unreliable account of Rome's rulers from Julius Caesar to Domitian. Pliny the Elder's *Natural History* is too vast to read in full. A useful selection is available in J. F. Healy (ed.) (2004), *Pliny the Elder – Natural History: a selection*, 2nd ed., London: Penguin, and offers a good flavour of both Pliny's wide knowledge and some of the tall tales he collected. Pliny's death is described by his nephew in Pliny the Younger, *Letters* 6.16, 20. Josephus' *The Jewish War* is a gripping first-hand account of the Jewish rebellion against Rome and the destruction of the Jerusalem Temple in 70. Josephus's later and more measured work, *The Antiquities of the Jews*, is worth reading for his account of what led to the rebellion in books 15–20. These texts are all available in translation on the Internet.

Introductions to the New Testament

Of many general surveys of the New Testament, B. D. Ehrman (2008), *A Brief Introduction to the New Testament*, 4th ed., New York: Oxford University Press, does not privilege the canonical texts, but considers them with other contemporary Christian writings. While Ehrman is generally radical and sceptical in his views, J. Drane (1999), *Introducing the New Testament*, 2nd ed., Oxford: Lion, is fairly conservative. L. T. Johnson (2003), *The Writings of the New Testament: An Interpretation*, London: SCM Press, revised and updated edition, is a sane guide from a Roman Catholic perspective. I. Boxall (2007), *SCM Studyguide: The Books of the New Testament*, London: SCM Press, is accessible and clear.

On the history of the early Church, C. Rowland (2002), *Christian Origins: An Account of the Setting and Character of the most Important Messianic Sect of Judaism*, 2nd ed., London: SPCK, sets the story within the context of Jewish apocalyptic expectation. B. Witherington (2001) *New Testament History: A Narrative Account*, Grand Rapids: Baker Academic, is a useful introduction to what happened, when. The development of the early Church and the variety of theologies within it are explored in J. D. G. Dunn (2006), *Unity and Diversity in the New Testament: an inquiry into the character of earliest Christianity*, 3rd ed., London: SCM Press. A study with greater implications than merely the study of the Gospels is R. J. Bauckham (ed.) (1998), *The Gospels for All Christians*, Edinburgh, T.&T. Clark, a stimulating challenge to received opinions. On different approaches to interpreting the New Testament, see I. Boxall (2007), *SCM Studyguide: New Testament Interpretation*, London: SCM Press, and the excellent and comprehensive P. R. Gooder (2008), *Searching for Meaning: An Introduction to Interpreting the New Testament*, London: SPCK, which applies different methods of interpretation to individual New Testament passages and includes brief introductions from the leading exponents of each approach.

For the development of the canon of the New Testament, see H. Y. Gamble (2002), *The New Testament Canon: Its Making and Its Meaning*, 2nd ed., Eugene, Oregon: Wipf & Stock, for a good short introduction. Part III of M. Bockmuehl and D. Hagner (eds) (2005), *The Written Gospel*, provides a good survey of how the 'four gospel canon' developed. Definitive and weighty is B. M. Metzger (1997) *The Canon of the New Testament: its origin, development, and significance*, New York: Oxford University Press. B. D. Ehrman (2005), *Lost Christianities: the battles for Scripture and the faiths we never knew*, New York: Oxford University Press, considers the many books which did not enter the New Testament and why, and B. D. Ehrman (2004), *Truth and Fiction in the Da Vinci Code*, New York: Oxford University Press, is a more popular book which covers similar themes.

Websites

General

- Mark Goodacre's 'New Testament Gateway' at www.ntgateway.com is a more than excellent resource which offers well-organized links to a wide variety of web resources. It is far and away the best maintained site on the New Testament and definitely the place to start searching the web from.

- Comprehensive links to material on each of the books of the New Testament designed to be a resource for preachers but useful for all students can be found at 'The Text this Week', www.textweek.com.
- The *From Jesus to Christ* website at www.pbs.org/wgbh/pages/frontline/shows/religion covers the growth of the Church. It accompanies a 1998 PBS series, and also allows you to view the original television programmes which contain a large number of useful short interviews with leading American scholars.

The Roman Empire

- The website for another PBS series, 'The Roman Empire in the First Century', is at www.pbs.org/empires/romans. The clickable 'Map of the Roman Empire' enables you to access historical sources about individual provinces at www.intranet.dalton.org/groups/Rome/RMap.html. 'Google Earth Ancient Rome' allows you to visit first-century Rome itself in three dimensions at the fascinating www.earth.google.com/rome. A reconstruction of the map that Agrippa produced for Augustus can be seen at Agrippa map www.henry-davis.com/MAPS/AncientWebPages/118.html.
- The destruction of Pompeii and the life of the city before the eruption of Vesuvius is covered by the BBC history site at www.bbc.co.uk/history/ancient/romans/pompeii_portents_01.shtml

Texts

- The Perseus Digital Library offers the most comprehensive collection of classical texts in translation at www.perseus.tufts.edu/hopper/.
- Texts of books which were not included in the New Testament can be found at wesley.nnu.edu/biblical_studies/noncanon/; the *Gospel of Thomas* and other gospels can be found at www.gospels.net/.
- The amazing collection of documents left by Babatha in the Judean desert has a website at 'The Babatha Archive', www.pbs.org/wgbh/nova/scrolls/.

Notes

1 Pliny the Younger, *Letters* 6.16, 20.

2 Tacitus *Annals* 15.44

3 T. Murphy (2004), *Pliny the Elder's Natural History*, Oxford: Oxford University Press, pp. 19–20.

4 R. Lane Fox (2006), *The Classical World: an epic history of Greece and Rome*, 2nd ed., London: Penguin, p. 272.

5 The terms are from P. Hordern and N. Purcell (2000), *The Corrupting Sea: a study of Mediterranean history*, Oxford: Blackwell.

6 M. Goodman (2007), *Rome and Jerusalem: the clash of ancient civilizations*, London: Penguin, pp. 107–108.

7 P. S. Derow, 'imperium' in S. Hornblower and A. Spawforth (eds) (1998), *The Oxford Companion to Classical Civilization*, Oxford: Oxford University Press, p. 367.

8 J. D. G. Dunn (2003), *Jesus Remembered*, Grand Rapids: Eerdmans, p. 308.

9 Augustus, *Res Gestae* 1.

10 Juvenal, *Satires* 14.275.

11 Pliny, *Natural History* 3.67.

12 K. Butcher (2003), *Roman Syria and the Near East*, London: British Museum, p. 181.

13 Plato, *Phaedo* 109b.

14 W. Meeks (1983), *The First Urban Christians*, New Haven: Yale University Press, p. 17.

15 J. D. Crossan (1991), *The Historical Jesus: the life of a Mediterranean peasant*, San Francisco: HarperCollins, p. 18.

16 M. Goodman, *Rome and Jerusalem*, p. 107.

17 Tacitus, *Annals* 15.44 (tr. Grant).

18 The phrase, coined by N. R. Hanson, is discussed in J. Polkinghorne (1986), *One World: the interaction of science and theology*, London: SPCK, p. 9.

19 R. A. Burridge (1998), 'For Whom Were the Gospels Written?' in R. J. Bauckham (ed.), *The Gospels for All Christians*, Edinburgh: T.&T. Clark, pp. 21–22; 30.

20 J. G. Crossley (2006), *Why Christianity Happened: a sociohistorical account of Christian origins (26–50 CE)*, Louisville: Westminster John Knox Press, p. xiv (emphasis original).

21 Polkinghorne, *One World*, p. 106.

22 J. L. Gaddis (2002), *The Landscape of History: how historians map the past*, New York: Oxford University Press, pp. 40–41.

23 N. T. Wright (1992), *The New Testament and the People of God*, London: SPCK, especially Part II, offers a sustained and trenchant reflection on these matters.

24 P. Jenkins (2001), *Hidden Gospels*, New York: Oxford University Press, pp. 14, 15, 16–17.

25 Origen, *Contra Celsum* 2.27.

26 M. Hengel (2000), *The Four Gospels and the One Gospel of Jesus Christ*, London: SCM Press, p. 283, n.496.

27 Irenaeus, *Against Heresies* 3.11.8.

28 Eusebius, *Church History* 6.12.

29 Eusebius, *History of the Church* 3.25.

30 E. Earle Ellis (1999), *The Making of the New Testament Documents*, Leiden: Brill.

31 J. D. G. Dunn (1997), *The Theology of Paul the Apostle*, Edinburgh: T.&T. Clark, p. 13.

2

James – the Brother of Jesus

The bones of James?

The Jews of the first century buried their dead twice. After death, the body was prepared for burial, anointed with spices, wrapped tightly in a shroud and placed in a tomb carved out of rock. A year later, when the flesh and soft tissue had decomposed, the skull and remaining bones were gathered up and carefully washed before being replaced in the tomb, this time in an ossuary, a stone box which might already contain the bones of a close relative. This was the second burial. The name of the dead person was usually carved on the outside of the box, which was left in the tomb, usually with the ossuaries of other family members. Hundreds have been excavated from tombs around Jerusalem.

In the autumn of 2002, an ossuary bearing the Hebrew inscription '*Ya'akov bar Yosef achui d Yeshua*' was presented to the world at a press conference. The inscription means 'James, son of Joseph, brother of Jesus'. It was a highly unusual inscription, since most ossuaries simply record the name of the deceased and their father. Adding a brother's name suggested that he must be famous. James, Joseph and Jesus were all common names in first century Jerusalem, but their combination in this way immediately suggested that this was the James of the New Testament, 'the brother of the Lord' (Gal. 1.19).

There is a thriving black market in stolen archaeological artefacts in Israel. The 'James Ossuary' was one of these, and its finder was subsequently arrested by the Israeli authorities for adding the phrase 'the brother of Jesus' to an otherwise genuine inscription. Reactions remain polarized between those who continue to believe that the ossuary and the bones it contains are a genuine direct link to Jesus' family and those who believe it to be a forgery. The supporters have pointed out that if the bones genuinely belong to the brother of Jesus, then scientific tests could yield the DNA of the messiah. However, the bones are currently in the hands of the Israel Antiquities Authority, which is sceptical of their authenticity and will not authorize the tests.

Whether the bones are genuine or not, they are a powerful reminder that Christianity began among a real family and a real community which we can investigate as we would investigate any family or community of the past. We can find traces of James in Jerusalem in the mid 50s of the first century and he provides a direct link to Jesus and his family.

The 'brother of the Lord'

James is not very well known in the story of early Christianity, but he was a key figure. Two references in the Acts of the Apostles show this. First, in Acts 12.17 he is mentioned without any further identification, simply by name. Peter, miraculously released from prison, instructs those he meets to 'tell these things to James and the brothers'. Second, in Acts 15.13–21, James has the undisputed authority to act as chair and judge over the dispute about whether gentiles can become full members of the Church. Clearly, he was a major figure whom Luke did not need to introduce. He also crops up several times in Paul's letters as a significant figure. He is mentioned as 'the brother of the Lord' (Gal. 1.19) and the first of the 'pillar' apostles (Gal. 2.9). Paul records him as a privileged witness to the risen Jesus who takes precedence even over the apostles (1 Cor. 15.7). In Paul's story, it is to James that he reports on his final visit to Jerusalem (Acts 21.18).

James's importance is confirmed by the Jewish historian Josephus, who narrates the death by stoning of 'the brother of Jesus who was called Christ, James by name',[1] in Jerusalem in 62, making him the only New Testament figure apart from John the Baptist and Jesus himself to have his existence corroborated by an external source.

Yet the New Testament is largely silent about James. Apart from a passing comment in the Gospels, James is conspicuous by his absence from the story of his brother Jesus. One letter apparently written by him survives in the New Testament, but its later history is a chequered one. It refers to Jesus only twice and does not quote any of his words. James and the family of Jesus also became something of an embarrassment to the later Church, which wanted to claim that Mary remained perpetually a virgin, so there was little interest in James and his brothers and sisters. But what are we to make of this man and the faint traces of his life that are left to us? How do we make sense of someone who was clearly of major importance in the early Church, and yet whose life left apparently so little mark?

In the rest of this chapter we shall look first at James's background and family, finding that we can piece together a surprising amount of information about them. Then we shall follow his life as a, perhaps not always uncritical, follower of his brother, through to his later life as a patriarchal figure in the Jesus movement in its earliest years.

James the true interpreter of Jesus?

Many claims have been made in recent years for James as the authentic interpreter of Jesus in contrast to Paul, who came on the scene later and did not know Jesus personally. In this version of the story of the early Church, James was bequeathed the leadership of the movement which his brother started, but his role and importance in the early Church has, allegedly, been lost to history. Because of the propaganda of Paul, James was relegated to the shadows and information about him was suppressed. He did not make the grand claims, it is argued, that Jesus was the Son of God, which Paul and others later developed. Instead, James remained an orthodox Jew in Jerusalem at loggerheads with the philosophically sophisticated Paul who travelled the world.

The family of Jesus

The Gospel of Mark records that when Jesus returned to Nazareth from Capernaum the villagers asked 'Isn't this Mary's son, the brother of James, Joseph, Judas and Simon? Aren't his sisters here with us?' (Mark 6.3). Later tradition calls the unnamed sisters Salome and Mary, and though these names are not certain the tradition seems reliable. Matthew's Gospel repeats the story, and it is clear that the early Church recognized that Jesus was part of a family of at least seven children.

Dogmas about the perpetual virginity of Mary, which began to be formulated in the later second century, have led to elaborate theories accounting for this verse. The two chief ones are that Joseph was previously married and so these are step-brothers and -sisters to Jesus; or that the 'brothers' were actually cousins since family relationships were defined more widely in first-century Palestine, as they are today in Africa, for example. The question of the paternity of Jesus is not one which the texts directly enter into. The most obvious reading of Mark 6.3 is that it means what it says: these were Jesus' siblings, born of the same mother and brought up in the same environment.

What do we know about this family? There are three areas in which we are able to piece together some clues: their names; their link with the house of David; and their home village of Nazareth.

Being given a child to name is an awesome responsibility. In all cultures, names communicate in some way the ethnic identity and values of the parents. In Jesus' family the names mostly relate to important figures in the story of Israel, both distant and recent.

Jesus in Hebrew is Joshua, the one who led the people into the Promised Land. James's Hebrew name is Jacob, the founder of 'Israel' (Gen. 32.28). The next brother, Joseph, was named for Jacob's son and the hero of the later part of Genesis. Judas is Judah in Hebrew, another son of Joseph and originator of the tribe of David to which the family belonged; Judas was also the name of one of the Maccabean heroes who had briefly brought independence to Judah back in the mid second century BC. The third brother, Simon, also had the name of one of the Maccabees. Mary in Hebrew is Miriam, sister of Moses. Salome is a particularly interesting choice. It is a distinctively Palestinian name, rarely used by Jewish families who lived in the Diaspora. It is not biblical but relates to Alexandra Salome, a queen of the Hasmonean dynasty descended from the Maccabees, who ruled from 76 to 67 BC after her husband's death and who was noted for her piety and fairness. She was also the last monarch before the kingdom of Judah became a Roman province. The two girls' names evoke memories of strong, powerful and independent women. From these names we gain the picture of a pious family, steeped in the stories of the past, holding on to the dream of a free, independent and fiercely proud nation.

Some of the names link the family with the house of David, and so do a number of other references in the New Testament. There is no obvious importance in this link; yet Paul, for example, writing to the Romans in the 50s speaks of Jesus as a 'descendant of David' (Rom. 1.3–4) in a throwaway remark which adds nothing to his argument. The writer to Hebrews also recognizes Jesus' membership of the royal tribe of Judah even though it might have helped the argument about Jesus as the great high priest if he had come from the tribe of Levi instead. The Gospels of Matthew and Luke provide genealogies for Jesus and therefore the rest of his family, though these may not be quite what they seem. At other points in the New Testament there is anxiety about those who argue over genealogies (1 Tim. 1.4; Tit. 3.9) and neither Matthew nor Luke seem to be offering straightforward family trees. These are symbolic lists which differ from each other, notably by Luke providing 76 male names to Matthew's 40. Rather than pressing them for a literal basis it is more important to recognize in them a clear desire to demonstrate that Jesus' family was descended from the house of David. In an oral culture where births and deaths were not recorded on paper, family lists were important simply in order to establish descent from a famous ancestor.

Although David had received a promise that his family would occupy the throne of Judah for ever (2 Sam. 7.16), the line of kings had ended when Jerusalem was invaded by the Babylonians. Jehoiachin, the last king of the house of David, was taken into exile in 597 BC (2 Kings 24.12–15) and the prophet Jeremiah cursed him and his descendants (Jer. 22.30). This might not have been a problem for the house of David, as Jehoiachin was succeeded by his uncle Zedekiah, but when he and his children were killed it seemed that Jeremiah's prophecy had spelled the end for the direct line of David. Zerubbabel, Jehoiachin's grandson, was governor of Judah in the late fourth century BC and briefly raised hopes for a restoration (Zech. 1–8), but they came to nothing. The later Hasmonean royal house, which continued through Herod the Great's sons (their mother was the sister of the last Hasmonean king) had no connection at all with David's line. The Herodian kings were clearly puppets of Rome.

It was against this background that during the first century BC the idea of a messiah who was descended from David began to gain currency, something of which we have extensive evidence from the Dead Sea Scrolls preserved at Qumran. For Jeremiah's devastating curse against the royal house of David had been balanced by another prophecy, which promised that God would raise up, from that house, a 'righteous branch', a new shepherd (Jer. 23.5). Using this prophecy and Isaiah's similar words (Isa. 11.1), some began to look for a messiah from a sub-branch rather than the direct line of David. This is not so surprising if we recall that blood mattered more than seniority in the family in such matters. David himself was a relatively obscure member of Jesse's family (1 Sam. 16.1–13), and it was not unusual for kingship to pass over an older son to a more obviously gifted younger one. Suddenly any family that traced its ancestry back to David might become aware of a new destiny beckoning.

Growing up in Galilee

The family of Joseph and Mary grew up in the village of Nazareth, in Galilee. Galilee was part of the ancient northern kingdom of Israel, and had been depopulated after Israel was conquered and sent into exile by the Assyrians in 722 BC. Under the Hasmonean kings in the early first century BC the region was settled by groups of Jews from Judea. The archaeology of Nazareth suggests that it was occupied already when the southern settlers came, but existing inhabitants seem to have been forced to become Jews or move on. By the time Jesus and James were growing up there it was very definitely a Jewish village, and the names Judas, Simon and Salome recalling Maccabean and Hasmonean figures within the family suggest that the family had been part of the settler movement. Galileans would have had relatives scattered across Judea, with common grandparents and great-grandparents. This makes sense of the connection of Joseph with Bethlehem, the 'city of David', the story of Mary visiting her cousin in 'the hills of Judea' (Luke 1.39), as well as the ease with which James later seems to have taken up residence in Jerusalem. Paula Fredriksen comments that 'spiritually ... the chief city of Galilee was Jerusalem';[2] the cultures were the same, and Galileans would not have felt that they were strangers in the big city when they headed south to celebrate festivals in the Temple. Ties of faith and family were strong.

There was a strategy behind the settlement of Galilee, which was similar to the twentieth-century *kibbutz* programme. Nazareth may have been an example of this. The name has never been satisfactorily explained, but one suggestion is that it derives from the Hebrew *nezer*, meaning shoot or branch. Obviously this would recall the prophecies of Isaiah and Jeremiah, raising the temperature of messianic expectation. This would certainly make sense of the puzzling comment in Matthew's Gospel that the family settled in the village 'so that what was spoken through the prophets should be fulfilled: he shall be called a Nazarene' (Matt. 2.23). Nazareth does not appear in the Old Testament so Matthew's meaning must be more subtle. What prophecies (he is clear that they are plural) can he mean? The pun on *nezer* doesn't work in the Greek which Matthew wrote, but he seems undeterred. He may be referring to the Nazirite vows which dedicated a child to God from birth, but the likelihood is that, as elsewhere, Matthew is weaving a subtle and many-textured meaning. Nazareth, 'branch-town', would be a good place for a messiah of the line of David to come from.

All these strands lie in the background and were as much part of the early life of James and the other siblings as they were of Jesus himself. We see a family proud of its heritage, fervent in its faith, and perhaps aware that they might have some special part to play in the return of God's Kingdom through a messiah of the line of David.

Family faith

If we can use the clues offered by the names that Mary and Joseph gave to their children, it seems that the family was a pious one which cherished hopes that Israel might one day be free once more. The Hebrew tradition emphasized the responsibilities of both parents in teaching the young about the faith (see Prov. 6.20, for example) and the early chapters of Luke's Gospel provide a picture of Mary as a devout young woman who would have influenced her children greatly. But, given the dynamics of first-century society, Joseph would have set the spiritual tone for the family. What was his faith like?

One small clue in Matthew's Gospel helps us to begin to place Joseph: when he found that Mary was pregnant, and knew that it was not by him, 'being just and not wanting to make an example of her, he decided to divorce her without any fuss' (Matt. 1.19). In other words, Joseph decided to break his betrothal to Mary and divorce her in accordance with the commandment to 'purge the evil from among you' (Deut. 22.21). But he did not interpret the Law literally (which would have entailed returning Mary to her father's doorstep where she would have been stoned). Instead he resolved to take the merciful route of ending the marriage quietly. (The story ends differently because Joseph has a dream which persuades him not to divorce Mary.)

The implication of this verse is that Joseph decided to act this way because he was 'just' or 'righteous' (*dikaios*). Although it is a very small clue to use as the basis for describing the family in which Jesus and James grew up, read together with other clues scattered around the Gospels we can grasp something of the atmosphere in which their faith was formed. James himself later acquired the nickname 'the just'.[3] It suggests a person noted for, but not extreme in, their piety. Joseph's intended treatment of Mary shows this. Instead of applying the Law literally and unsparingly, he used 'an intelligent combination of principle and compassion'[4] and reflected the character of God by being merciful.

Another clue lies in Luke's stories of Jesus in the Temple as a baby and then at the age of 12. A sacrifice was made after Jesus' birth in Jerusalem (Luke 2.22–4), and his parents went 'year by year to Jerusalem for the feast of Passover' (Luke 2.41). This seems to have been a family which followed the traditional devotion to the Temple as a place of pilgrimage and worship. Where do these clues place Joseph in the spectrum of Jewish belief in the first century?

The writer Josephus, our best source for Jewish faith and practice in the first century, divided Jews into three 'philosophies' or schools of thought: Pharisees, Sadducees and Essenes. But it would be misleading to assume that each of these formed a single homogeneous party. Today we might say that English politics is divided into three main parties, but it would be foolish to think that all Labour Party members hold the same views as one another and the same is true for Conservatives and Liberal Democrats. Each party is in fact a coalition of broadly similar views and some significant disputes. The same was true of Jews in the first century.

The Essenes attracted more attention than the other two groups. Pliny knew that they lived on the western shore of the Dead Sea and were 'a people unique in the whole world, remarkable above all others' who had nothing to do with women, renounced sex and money and 'kept company only with palm trees'.[5] There was, of course, more to being an Essene than that, and Josephus says that in fact there was a 'second order' who did marry and that the Essenes were not confined to the Dead Sea region but also lived in cities and towns across Palestine. Essenes underwent a two-year initiation period and followed a strict rule of life. Purity was a particular concern, and they washed frequently and were fastidious with regard to food. In general they were opposed to the Temple in its existing form, believing that it had been compromised by the Hasmoneans and Herods, but despite their ambivalent feelings many of them continued to use the Temple. The Qumran Community, which appears to have been Essene in its beliefs and may have been what Pliny knew about, differed from other groups in rejecting the Temple and its priesthood totally, forming a complete alternative and waiting for God's apocalyptic action to restore them to power. The community's writings, preserved in the Dead Sea Scrolls, are a powerful mixture of deep faith, bitter hatred of God's enemies, passionate love of God and bloodthirsty curses. Overall the Essenes were probably the most extreme kind of Jews in the first century, the zeal of some spilling over into fanaticism. It seems unlikely that Joseph and his family were much influenced by the Essenes. Regular attendance at the Temple does not suggest the ambivalence of Essenes, and apart from anything else, the emphasis on celibacy which even married Essenes shared (having sex reluctantly and purely for procreation) is hard to square with a family of several children!

The Sadducees seem to have been almost entirely an aristocratic group, based in Jerusalem. Josephus describes them as generally rude, haughty and proud, uninterested in other people. They claimed to follow the Law as it was written in the Torah, rejecting any later traditions, though as can be seen today, the Bible is far from self-explanatory and they had their own (frequently unacknowledged) forms of interpretation. Among other things, this led them to reject the idea of a future life or a resurrection of the dead. It is probably right to say that the effect of this, in contrast to the Essenes of Qumran, was to remove any real hope of apocalyptic intervention by God. The Sadducees were hard-line in their views of punishment. Though they held their own nationalist ideals, in practice they were politically conservative and prepared to accommodate to Roman rule so long as their own elite position was safeguarded. A pregnant bride-to-be would attract the full penalty of Moses' Law as far as the Sadducees were concerned. Joseph was neither aristocratic nor hard-line enough to be part of this group.

Finally, the Pharisees. This group came to prominence under Queen Alexandra Salome in the mid first century BC, and Josephus portrays them as having significant power among the people. They were distinguished from the Sadducees by supplementing the Law with the 'traditions of the elders', that is, a body of cases and judgements built up over centuries, which required intensive study and deep knowledge. The Pharisees' awareness of the complexity of biblical interpretation led them to be much more lenient in judgements than the Sadducees. Sometimes, however, these traditions went way beyond the requirements of the Torah, such as the practices of *corban* and hand washing which were criticized by Jesus (Mark 7.1–13). The Pharisees did have a strong future hope of the resurrection and vindication of the righteous. Josephus refers to a 'fourth philosophy', sometimes thought to be the 'Zealot' party. There is little evidence that this was a serious alternative, and Josephus emphasizes that this group was really a subset of the Pharisees. They were those who were prepared to die for their beliefs. In practice the Essenes tended to withdraw from society and remain uninvolved as they waited for God's intervention, while the Sadducees upheld the political status quo. Therefore the Pharisees were likely to be those who produced people prepared to die for the sake of Israel and the Law, and who might come into conflict with the Romans or their puppets, the Herodian kings. This doesn't mean that all Pharisees took such a radical stance, only that those who did almost certainly came from this background and were prepared to take risks, as they saw it, for the glory of God. Joseph might conceivably have had sympathies with the Pharisees. His intended treatment of Mary is just the blend of law-observance and mercy which the best Pharisees showed in their judgements. Obedience to the Law by attending the festivals and offering sacrifices in Jerusalem also fits with Pharisaism. How widespread the Pharisaic party was in Galilee in the early first century is hard to say. It would probably have been difficult for a carpenter in Nazareth to maintain the level of purity and devotion expected of Pharisees, but not impossible; the family's names also suggest a characteristic Pharisaic blend of pride in the patriarchs and evocation of more recent nationalistic achievements.

Josephus estimated the strength of the three groups at the beginning of the first century. There were few Sadducees, though their influence was substantial, 4,000 Essenes and 6,000 Pharisees. Josephus tends to exaggeration when he counts, but even taken at face value these are small figures. He also estimated the crowd in Jerusalem for Passover 65 as around 3 million. Therefore the proportion of the population which actively belonged to the Essenes or Pharisees was very limited. Returning to the analogy of modern political parties for a moment, while most people have a settled idea of which one they normally vote for, very few are signed up as party members. The rules of life which the Essenes and Pharisees encouraged did not come with membership cards. Most people fell outside these rules. Yet, in modern British political life there is a general agreement on some issues; the value of a National Health Service and state-funded schools, for example. Not only do all three parties support these things, so do those who have never belonged to a political party and even those who switch their allegiance at different elections. There is both diversity and deep agreement here, and the same is true of Jewish faith in the first century. Joseph might have been a Pharisee; but it is more likely that he was simply a pious Jew who believed what most people believed and took the practice of his faith seriously.

The underlying agreement on practice and belief among Jews in the first century has been called 'common Judaism' by E. P. Sanders and its overall approach summed up by the phrase 'covenantal nomism'.[6] By this Sanders means they believed that the God of Israel had made the world and freely chosen them by grace to be his people, making a covenant with them; as his people he asked them to reflect his nature gratefully and joyfully and to do so by being obedient to the Law (*nomos*) which God had given them. All three parties and those who belonged to none agreed on this. How, then, did an ordinary family like Joseph's, which probably belonged to none of the three parties but may have seen some virtue in the Pharisees' approach, put their faith into practice?

Practising the faith

Judaism in the early first century had not become the 'religion of the book' which it was later to be. For one thing, books as we now know them were only just beginning to be produced in the first century and were used for writing notes, not recording the Scriptures; for this, scrolls were used. Although there seems to have been general agreement on which scrolls counted as the sacred writings of the Law, the prophets and the writings by the first century, few people had easy access to them. Outside Jerusalem or special centres like Qumran hardly any were able to see the whole corpus. Scrolls were expensive and not easy to obtain. We hear of there being a scroll of the prophet Isaiah in Nazareth (Luke 4.17–20) but we do not know how many other books of the Hebrew Bible such a village might have had. Almost certainly not the whole set.

This is why the Law assumed such an important place. The Sadducees of course accepted the Law only and not the other writings, but in practice others did virtually the same. In the caves at Qumran 86 copies of the books of the Law, either Genesis, Exodus, Leviticus, Numbers or Deuteronomy, have been found; the latter is often seen to be a summing up of the Law and accounts for 30 of the 86. Of the other books of the Hebrew Bible there are 119 copies, of which 36 are of the Psalms and 21 Isaiah.[7] We should be wary of seeing the Qumran community as in any way a guide to how ordinary people behaved, but in this at least it may give us an indication of which books circulated in greater numbers than others. Clearly the five 'books of Moses' were the best-selling scrolls of the day. But while the Pharisees would have found ways of actually reading the texts, ordinary people would generally have had to be content with hearing them (we shall consider how widespread literacy was later). In Matthew's Gospel, Jesus seems to make a distinction between talking to those who have 'heard that it was said' (e.g. Matt. 5.21) and the Pharisees and priests, to whom he says 'have you not read?' (e.g. Matt. 12.3, 19.4, 21.16, 22.31).

For ordinary people observance of the Law probably amounted to four things. These were:

- reciting the summary of the Law (Deut. 6.4–5, 'Hear O Israel ...' – the first word, *shema*, was used as a shorthand for this) and the ten commandments as well as praying twice a day;
- observing the Sabbath as a day of rest, which included studying the Law by attending the synagogue;
- keeping purity laws by both avoiding certain foods and also undergoing ceremonial washing regularly (ranging from once a year to once a month);
- visiting the Temple for Passover (spring) and possibly the other major festivals of Pentecost (early summer) and Tabernacles (autumn) as well as supporting the Temple financially through a tax.

We can imagine Joseph's family waking to hear him reciting the *shema* and praying; joining him at the synagogue on the Sabbath; keeping strictly to the prescribed foods and participating in ceremonial washing; and being part of an annual pilgrimage to Jerusalem (see Luke 2.41). Depending on how strict Joseph was in his faith, the children may also have seen him binding a miniature copy of the Law contained in a small leather pouch called a phylactery around his forehead as he dressed for the day.

Journeys to Jerusalem may have punctuated the year, though since attending a festival would have taken up about two weeks when the travelling time from Galilee is included it is likely that Passover was the only festival the family regularly attended. They would have put aside during the year a 'second tithe' which was intended to cover their expenses for the journey and the cost of buying animals in Jerusalem for sacrificial offerings (see Deut. 14.26). Once in Jerusalem and having found lodgings or set up camp with other families who had accompanied them from Galilee they would go to one of the large immersion pools near the Temple to wash. The next day the children would go to the Temple with their parents and witness the slaughter of the lamb which the family offered, and the rituals that surrounded it. Later they would join in the feast back at their lodgings, eating the meat that had been sacrificed. Jerusalem would be crowded, perhaps filled with as many as half a million people, making an extraordinary atmosphere. E. P. Sanders comments that it must have seemed 'like Christmas: a blend of piety, good cheer, hearty eating, making music, chatting with friends, drinking and dancing'.[8] For children an awareness of the Temple's central role in their faith would have been one of their earliest memories.

For boys, of course, a distinguishing mark of their faith was circumcision. Widely derided by sophisticated Greeks and Romans who saw the practice as unmanly and barbaric, it signified obedience to the Law. Its origin reminded the people of the covenant which God had made with them through Abraham (Gen. 17) and emphasized that they were chosen. Circumcision in particular and the Law in general were seen as God's gracious gift to them, rather than a hefty burden to be carried in order to win his favour. The almost ecstatic adulation of the Law (see Psalm 119, for example, an infectiously joyful celebration) conveys clearly that Jewish faith was not a dour religion which depended on good works to gain favour with God. Circumcision might have attracted derision, but that was countered for most Jews by the sure knowledge that God had chosen them and made them beloved. Theirs was a faith of joy and celebration in a world of hard work and suffering. This seems to have been what Joseph passed on to the children of his family.

Making a living in Nazareth

When Jesus was dedicated in the Temple as a baby, his family offered the sacrifice of the poor: two doves instead of a lamb and one dove (Lev. 12.8, Luke 2.24). But once they were settled in Nazareth it is likely that the family was better off. Joseph is traditionally known as a carpenter, though this rests on a single reference (Matt. 13.55). If he was, then his business was much more than simply being the village handyman. *Tekton*, the Greek word for carpenter, also applies to someone involved in the general building trade. Carpenters were in demand especially for making roofs, doors and door-frames as well as making furniture, tools and generally mending broken things. Herod Antipas's new town of Sepphoris lay within about an hour's walk from Nazareth. It is not hard to imagine Joseph being employed in Herod Antipas's grand attempt to emulate the building achievements of his father Herod the Great, or his sons accompanying him, though there is no direct evidence for it.

It was expected that all Jewish boys would learn a trade once they crossed the threshold into adulthood at the age of 12. Jesus is once referred to in the Gospels as a carpenter himself (Mark 6.3), and it seems likely that James and the other brothers also learned Joseph's trade. Jesus seems to have left Nazareth in his early twenties and on the basis that Joseph seems not have been present in the period covered by the Gospels (the late 20s and early 30s), probably because he had died, that would have left James as the breadwinner of the family having inherited his father's business. But before learning a trade there would have been education. What might that have involved in early first-century Galilee?

Education – reading, writing and languages

For James and his brothers and sisters as they grew up, their whole lives would have been suffused with a deep and practical spirituality which was based on the observance of the Law. The emphasis on the Law led to important practical consequences for the boys in terms of schooling.

Among Jewish adult males, because of the emphasis on the written Law, the literacy rate was probably significantly higher than the average for the ancient world, which has been estimated at a maximum of around 10%, with higher rates in the cities and lower ones in the remoter countryside.

Instruction in the Law began at an early age for boys, and schools had spread through Judea and Galilee during the first century BC, usually associated with synagogues. The Gospels mention a synagogue building in Nazareth in the early first century (Mark 6.2; Luke 4.16) and though there is no direct archaeological evidence there, one has been excavated at Gamla, also in Galilee. The 'attendant' who looked after the biblical scrolls (Luke 4.20) would also have been the person whose job it was to instruct the boys of the village. Though the context was different, the curriculum would have been the same as it was in the Jerusalem schools: the memorization of the Scriptures in the primary phase, followed by acquaintance with approved interpretations of the Law until the end of schooling at 12 or 13.

The language of education would have been Hebrew and its contemporary cousin Aramaic, and the texts studied were the Scriptures and commentaries on them. But there is also evidence that skills acquired by studying the Bible may have been more widely useful. Surviving documents from the ancient world are rare, being fragile and dispensable. But, in recent years, a number have come to light which show society in general and Palestine in particular as being much more reliant on reading, writing and official documents than we might assume. The documents reveal a world where quite ordinary people seem to have carried documents about important matters in their lives with them. Towns and even some villages had record offices where archives of important decisions were kept, such as decisions made by the local council, legal cases, land deeds and details of mortgages and loans. In Jerusalem records of priestly families were kept, to ensure that qualification to work in the Temple could be proved. All these things suggest that the world in which James grew up was a place where reading and writing, if not widespread, were at least highly important.

The society of Galilee and Judea in the first and early second centuries was multilingual. Hebrew was the language of the Scriptures, Aramaic the language of the street. Greek had spread across the whole of the east in the wake of Alexander the Great's army four centuries earlier. By the time of Herod the Great it had become well-known enough for it to be used in inscriptions in Jerusalem, including within the Temple precincts. Some estimate that as many as a fifth of the population of the city spoke Greek in the first century. But there was resistance to this Hellenistic cultural imperialism, rather in the way that in contemporary France there have been attempts to outlaw Americanized terms such as *le weekend* to preserve French culture. Establishing schools across Palestine was part of this anti-Hellenistic movement, associated with Maccabean nationalism. Even the cultured and well-educated Josephus, who was not prone to admitting weakness, confessed that he struggled to grasp Greek grammar and pronunciation as an adult, suggesting that his Greek was of the 'pidgin' kind, picked up piecemeal and for functional purposes. Anyone involved in a business such as building and woodworking would have needed some acquaintance with Greek to understand bills, for example. Masons' marks on buildings tended also to use Greek characters to show how the stones fitted together. Latin was also in use; but it seems unlikely that it was widely understood. The archaeological find of Herod the Great's cellars in his fortress of Masada suggests that a few people did have to know the language. Identical jars were labelled in Latin but some contained wine while others were filled with *garum*, the famously pungent Roman fish-sauce. Serving the latter to drink instead of the former would have led to rapid execution for the wine-steward! (One of Jesus' later followers was Joanna, wife of Herod Antipas's steward, Chuza, Luke 8.3.) We can be fairly certain, therefore, that James and his brothers had some knowledge of Greek as well as a command of Hebrew and Aramaic, but that it was the latter two which were the main means of communication in synagogue, school and home.

Whether they could write as well is another matter. Strange as it seems to us, for whom reading and writing blend into one, in the ancient world these were separate skills, with writing generally restricted to professional scribes. 'Scribes' are a feature of the Gospel accounts of Jesus' ministry and while this group was primarily named because they copied the Scriptures, it seems that a good many Pharisees may have earned their living by writing ordinary documents for those who needed them across the country. Most letters (even personal ones) were written from dictation by a scribe. Scribes were also necessary to make notes of legal cases and council debates which were comprehensively recorded in local registry archives. The scribes were a significant group and their existence draws attention to the fact that while reading may have been a more widespread skill than we might expect, and 'only the most isolated hamlets in Herodian Palestine may have lacked anyone who could read',[9] writing was a far more specialized and professionalized accomplishment.

It's likely that James and his brothers could read Hebrew and Aramaic and hold a basic conversation in Greek; but they would have needed to find a scribe to write for them when it came to communicating by letter or legal document.

Sibling rivalries? Jesus, his mother and his brothers

In his twenties, Jesus headed south and probably became a disciple for a time of John the Baptist. Abandoning one's family, especially if it was done after Joseph's death, was a potentially shameful thing to do, an avoidance of responsibilities. Given the closeness of blood ties and the economics of family life in first-century Palestine it would be surprising if such behaviour did not set up significant tensions between Jesus and his brothers, especially James, the next oldest. This may account for the ambivalence to be found in the few stories found in the Gospels of Mark and John about Jesus' family.

John states uncompromisingly that 'Even his brothers did not believe in him' (John 7.5). On the basis of this verse it has been assumed that James and Jesus' other brothers did not follow him during his ministry and were antagonistic towards him. But belief is a complex issue in John's Gospel. Only when Jesus has risen from the tomb does the beloved disciple see and believe and even then he does not understand (John 20.8–9). So the fact that Jesus' brothers did not believe at an earlier stage in the story does not necessarily put them outside the company of Jesus' followers. And when the passage is read a little more closely it emerges that the context is a discussion of strategy: the brothers tell Jesus that if he is serious about his mission, then Jerusalem at festival time is the place to gather support. He objects that they do not understand the dangers, and tells them to go without him on the grounds that the 'right time is not yet here' (John 7.6). Like belief, the 'right time' is another of John's themes. It also emerges in the other passage in John which illuminates relationships within the family, the story of the wedding at Cana (John 2.1–11). There are hints of an uneasy relationship here between Jesus and his mother, as he refuses to do what he is being advised to do. He addresses Mary as 'woman', which is not necessarily disrespectful but is certainly a rather formal and distant way of speaking to his mother. The basis for refusing the request in this story is also because 'my hour has not yet come' (John 2.4). Yet, and here is another similarity, in both stories Jesus does do what his family suggest, but secretly so as not to draw attention to himself. At Cana, he steps in and works a miracle; and he later follows his brothers to Jerusalem. There are, of course, issues here about how strongly we can press John's Gospel for detailed historical information about Jesus' family relationships. But, on the basis that a negative judgement of Jesus' family as his followers usually derives from John 7.5, it is important to pursue it. The two passages in John's Gospel which deal with this issue are not wholly negative at all. After all, Jesus seems to be open to his brothers' advice about heading to Jerusalem, implying that they have some involvement in the movement which has arisen around him. What John seems to portray is an edgy relationship, but not one of outright rejection on either side.

When read in the light of assumed antagonism between Jesus and his family based on John 7.5, Mark's contribution seems to show an outright rejection. But, read in the light of a more nuanced account of John's portrayal of family relationships, it provides a subtly different picture. The situation is that Jesus has returned to 'a house' (Mark 3.20, by which we assume Mark means his home in Capernaum) but is hemmed in by crowds seeking healing (as in Mark 1). His brothers set out to rescue him because 'they said, "He is beside himself"' (Mark 3.21). Mark characteristically diverts to a related saying to allow time for the family to arrive (Mark 3.22–30) and when they are outside they send him a message through the crowd. But Jesus famously looks around and asks rhetorically 'Who is my mother and my brothers? ... Whoever does the will of God is my brother, sister and mother' (Mark 3.33–4). If you have already decided that Jesus and his family are at loggerheads this saying is a pretty conclusive rejection. But if, on the other hand, the relationship was more complex this saying may simply function to widen Jesus' family without necessarily rejecting his blood relatives. To assume that this saying means Jesus wholly rejected his family underestimates the level of exaggeration that may be at work here in a way we tend not to do with other sayings (as James Dunn points out, 'If we treated such sayings as

Mark 10.15 ... in the same way, we could conclude that the kingdom consists only of little children'[10]). And, as is often the case with Mark, the Gospel then rushes on to narrate further stories without fully completing the episode. What happened to the family? Did they follow Jesus on the way? Or wander back, disgruntled, to Nazareth?

The next time we meet the family they are indeed back in Nazareth. In Mark 6.1–6, Jesus has returned to his 'native town'. The local people are scornful when he speaks in the synagogue: 'How does this man know these things? What is this wisdom he has been given? How do the works of power he does come from his hands? Isn't he the carpenter?' (Mark 6.2–3). Jesus, replying, says 'A prophet is not scorned except in his native town, among his family and in his own house' (Mark 6.4). The reply is specific in homing in on the immediate family. Nazareth's scorn seems to turn on the contrast between what is expected of a local carpenter and Jesus' apparent claim to be a wise man whose hands have turned from woodworking to healing. Perhaps this too was the basis of the family's fears about his sanity recorded in the earlier passage. Jesus' new lifestyle, forsaking the family business and setting up as a wandering prophet who had gathered a band of disciples around him, was simply not what they had expected for him. And they would not have been unaware of the dangers such a choice could lead to, not only for Jesus but for them too.

What does seem unusual is the close association of Jesus in all the passages considered (except John 7.3–10) with his disciples. They accompany him to Cana, surround him in Capernaum, and stand beside him at Nazareth as we might otherwise expect his family to do. The choice of the symbolic number of 12 (Mark 3.16) made an important claim to status: it was a clear signal that Jesus was seeking to create a new Israel. Within the group there was jostling for position (see Mark 10.35–41). In the first century you would expect his family to be involved in such a movement and to have significant places within it (there have been many ingenious attempts to identify Jesus' brothers with members of the Twelve especially since the names James, Judas and Simon are included in the lists, but since they require, for example, James to have a father called Alphaeus they do not convince). If his family was ambivalent about Jesus, their absence may be explained. But it does not answer the question why they were absent: was it Jesus' intention or their own? There is some evidence that the latter was the case, which may also explain why, later, they did come to play a significant part in the movement Jesus left behind.

The non-canonical *Gospel of Thomas* includes a passage in which the disciples ask Jesus who their leader should be when he is no longer with them himself. He replies 'go to James the just, for whose sake heaven and earth came into being.'[11] While the overall authenticity of *Thomas* in its present form is highly suspect, it does contain some sayings of Jesus which are probably genuine and not recorded elsewhere. This saying is significant because it bridges a gap in our understanding. How did James go from being sceptical about his brother's mission to later assuming leadership of it? The answer of *Thomas* is clear: because Jesus wanted him to. Given the apparently motiveless importance of the line of David in descriptions of Jesus' role (see above), James as another in David's line may have assumed a greater significance in the movement than he wished at first to bear.

None of the Gospels mention Jesus' brothers around the time of the crucifixion, leading to the apparently strange entrusting of Mary to the beloved disciple in John's Gospel (John 19.26–27). Jesus' burial too takes place without reference to his family. Many of Jesus' closest followers seem to have fled by this point and the absence of his brothers who were most likely to be the next targets for arrest may not be very significant.

To sum up, we have seen that there is evidence that James was probably not antagonistic to Jesus during his ministry, as is often supposed, but that he probably assumed the role of providing for the family in the absence of both Joseph and Jesus. He and the rest of the family may have had trouble understanding why Jesus acted as he did and have had legitimate concerns about what Jesus was getting involved in. But he did have some involvement in his brother's ministry, and Jesus may have asked him to assume leadership of the movement he was to leave behind.

After the crucifixion

Luke mentions the family of Jesus as being present in the upper room before the day of Pentecost (Acts 1.14). In his Gospel, Luke played down any misunderstanding between Jesus and his family. He also told an extended story of the risen Jesus' appearance to Cleopas and an unnamed companion (Luke 24.13–35). This Cleopas (or Clopas) was regarded in the early Church as being Joseph's brother, and thus uncle to his family. His wife (like Joseph's, named Mary) also features in the story (John 19.25). This puts Mary, Jesus' mother, and her sister- and brother-in-law close to Jesus during the last week of his life.

Paul includes James in his list of those to whom the risen Jesus appeared (1 Cor. 15.7), but there is no other reference to this event in the New Testament. The much later *Gospel to the Hebrews* embroidered a story of Jesus' appearance to James, but other than the bare fact that Paul says it happened we have no information. However, this puts James in the same situation as Peter, who is also recorded by Paul as having seen the risen Jesus, but without any other New Testament account giving details. This may partly be because the resurrection appearances are not explained at length: the accounts are impressionistic rather than detailed and exhaustive. Some have seen an encounter between James and the risen Jesus as being the cause of James's 'conversion' to being a follower of his brother. This view is based on the assumption of conflict between them at the time of Jesus' ministry and is clearly patterned on Paul's shift from persecutor to believer after having his vision of Jesus on the road to Damascus. This approach is unhelpful for two reasons: first, as we have seen, the relationship between Jesus and James was probably complex and ambiguous but not antagonistic; second, James is regarded by Paul as among the first witnesses to the resurrection and this puts his experience in a different category from Paul's, which occurred when the initial sequence of appearances was over (hence Paul notes the abnormality of what happened to him, 1 Cor. 15.8). The evidence suggests that, as for Peter, James's vision of the risen Jesus was confirming rather than converting.

In Luke's story, Cleopas and his companion return from Emmaus and report to 'the eleven *and those who were with them*' (Luke 24.33), and Jesus then appears to them all. 'Those who were with them' probably included James: Luke's account of the same period in Acts specifically mentions that Mary and 'his brothers' were with the disciples (Acts 1.14). James seems to have completed his journey from the edge of his brother's movement to the centre. He also seems to have completed a move from Nazareth to Jerusalem, which was to be his home until his death 30 years later.

After Pentecost – the Twelve and 'the brothers'

After Pentecost the movement of Jesus' followers began to take a new shape as an alternative sect within the spectrum of Jewish faith which we described above. What might have been a short-lived messianic movement that flourished around Jesus as its charismatic leader began to settle into a particular way of being Jewish.

Without Jesus to lead it, how would the fledgling sect gain direction? Though Jesus had appointed 'the Twelve' as his disciples, hereditary principles were strong. Jesus' redefinition of family boundaries (seen in Mark 3.30–5) did not exclude his blood family from his movement. Paul refers in passing to 'the brothers of the Lord' (1 Cor. 9.5), as travelling missionaries. He gave no further explanation but assumed that they were well enough known in Corinth for him not to need to do so. James's later significance as leader of the Jerusalem church, coupled with Paul's passing reference, suggests that the brothers formed a group similar to but distinct from the Twelve: 'the brothers of the Lord had the same authority as the apostles, but were not normally called apostles.'[12] Evidence from later centuries reveals a tradition within the eastern Church of leaders drawn from among Jesus' blood relatives. This has led some to suggest that the early Church was governed by a kind of 'Christian caliphate', though this is putting the case too strongly. The succession of leaders was not dynastic in the sense of a 'royal family'; but it does look likely that, especially in the church which developed to the east of Jerusalem among the Jews scattered across Mesopotamia, Jesus' brothers and their descendants played a significant role. Since our only major source for the early development of the Church is Acts, which focuses exclusively on the Church in the west, we cannot draw firm conclusions; but it seems likely that James had an important role in the Church from very early on, alongside the Twelve.

This conclusion begs the question why, if this were the case, James himself was not proclaimed as messianic leader, to continue where Jesus left off? As Tom Wright puts it, James turned out to be 'a great leader: devout, a fine teacher, well respected by other devout Jews ... *But nobody ever dreamed of saying that James was the Messiah.*'[13] Why not? The answer, of course, is that the early Christians did not believe that they needed a replacement messiah: Jesus would return to them, one day, and in the meantime 'apostles' or messengers were needed to spread the good news of his Kingdom. The role of leader of the movement in Jerusalem was like that of the servants in several of Jesus' own parables: to mind the master's estate while he was away. Who better to do this than his brother James?

As the story is told in Acts it is clear that by the time of the death of King Herod Agrippa in 44, 'James and the brothers' held a leading position in the Jerusalem church (Acts 12.17). Some argue that Luke is suggesting here a shift in power from Peter and the Twelve to James and the soon-to-be-centre-stage Paul. But there is no real evidence that Peter was ever the leader-figure for the Jerusalem church, and Acts never says that he was. In the early phase he is presented as spokesman but never sole leader. His role seems most importantly to have been as the chief eyewitness to the ministry of Jesus. When Paul first visited Jerusalem in 37, it was to Peter and James and no other apostles that he went (Gal. 1.18–19), suggesting that they shared the leadership of the Church well before Peter's departure to 'another place' (Acts 12.17), which left the leadership with James alone.

So in the first ten years or so of the life of the Church it seems that James moved from being on the edge of Jesus' followers to the centre. It is quite possible that this was the result of Jesus' own wishes. Until this point the Church seems to have developed as a Jewish sect, largely for Jews and continuing to observe all the Jewish laws and rituals which James would have known since childhood. But a new era of expansion was about to open up, spearheaded by the mission of Barnabas and Paul to the gentiles of Asia Minor. This would leave James in the hot seat of deciding what was a faithful reflection of his brother's teaching.

The community in Jerusalem

Jesus' movement had drawn its strength from Galilee. That was where his base and his support had been. But his last week was spent in Jerusalem, he died in the city and it was the place where his followers first claimed to have seen him after his resurrection. It is clear that the movement he left behind had its centre in Jerusalem, close to the Temple. Jerusalem was where his followers experienced what they took to be a sign of confirmation and vindication: the coming of the Holy Spirit at Pentecost (Acts 2.1–4).

Early years and growth

Jerusalem was by no means foreign territory to James and others from Galilee. They would have been familiar with the city from visits for the festivals and perhaps at other times too. The links between Jerusalem and Galilee were strong. For all Jews, Jerusalem was the centre of their symbolic world. Whether they lived nearby or not, they saw it as 'the joy of the whole earth' (Ps. 48.2) and it filled their imaginations. Pliny too considered that it had been 'for long the most celebrated city of the east, not just Judea'.[14] Population numbers are hard to calculate for Jerusalem. It swelled enormously for the three major festivals, but between them may have shrunk to under 100,000. This would still have made it one of the 20 largest cities in the world. It was also centrally placed between the two cultures that dominated the first-century world. Eastward it looked to the ancient civilizations of Mesopotamia with their long and deep traditions of learning and religion, under whose control the city had been for centuries. Westward lay the traditions of Greek philosophy and art, now overlaid by the burgeoning power of Rome. Jerusalem lay between these two cultures and participated in them both, while many Jews continued to yearn for their own distinctive culture and faith that set them apart from either east or west. The city was dominated physically and spiritually by the Temple, one of the most imposing structures of the ancient world, as it had been rebuilt by Herod.

Acts is basically the only source we have for the development of the church in Jerusalem, and many have questioned its reliability. This is a crucial issue for the life of Paul as well, where at least his letters provide additional information, and we shall consider it in more detail in later chapters. But it is important here to enter a note of caution. First, I am working on the assumption that Acts is a relatively late work, separated from the Church's early years in Jerusalem by as much as six decades. If this is the case, then by the time Luke wrote the Temple had long been destroyed by the Romans and the city was a shadow of its former self. Second, Luke has vigorously culled his sources to fit in only those stories which serve his greater purpose across his Gospel and Acts. The problem with this is not so much what is included as what is not. He is very schematic in his presentation of his material: the aim is to show how the good news goes from Jerusalem to 'Judea, Samaria and the ends of the earth' (the latter being defined as Rome, Acts 1.8). This leads to frustratingly imprecise information such as Peter's departure to 'another place' (Acts

12.17), after which he disappears from the story apart from a cameo appearance at the Jerusalem conference. It also leads Luke to smooth over what may have been sharp differences at the time but which with hindsight seemed less important; he has been accused, for example, of presenting a highly idealized portrait of the harmony of the early community in Jerusalem (e.g. Acts 2.44–5). In particular he wrote long after the arguments about the admission of gentiles to the Church had ended, and may therefore not have caught the real anguish that the decision to accommodate them involved. For these reasons we can only sketch the outline of the development of the church in Jerusalem very lightly. It is another case where the models and presuppositions which you bring to the material largely determine what you find. So for those who focus on conflict as the agent of change, disputes are magnified; for those who assume a more harmonious approach Acts can sometimes be too uncritically accepted at face value. What then is the portrait of the community in Jerusalem which Luke paints in the early chapters of Acts, and how far is it accurate?

Luke gives a summary statement of four features of the life of the early church in Jerusalem: the believers 'faithfully followed the teaching of the apostles, in sharing together, in the breaking of bread and in the prayers' (Acts 2.42). The succeeding verses expand a little on the headlines (Acts 2.43–7). We shall briefly look at each of the four features in turn.

First, Luke wishes to show an unbroken continuity between the ministry of Jesus and the mission of the Church. The early chapters of Acts clearly parallel the early chapters of his Gospel and are powerfully reminiscent of Jesus' early days in Galilee, characterized by healing and preaching. But where the Galilee preaching consisted of parables about the Kingdom of God, in Acts the message is about Jesus himself. Luke's avowed aim is to continue in this sequel the account of what Jesus '*began* to do and to teach' (Acts 1.1) in the Gospel. The expanding statement focuses on 'wonders and signs' (Acts 2.43) rather than what we would consider teaching, suggesting that the two were seen by Luke as different sides of the same coin. The issue of healing miracles is a complex one and on this ground alone many previous generations have rejected Luke's claim to provide historical information. But few would now deny that at least the perception of Jesus as a miracle-worker is crucial to understanding him in his first-century context. It is striking that the supercharged atmosphere of the early chapters of Acts changes markedly in the second half of the book; miracles become rare. It may be enough to conclude that the early church in Jerusalem understood itself as continuing the work of Jesus in as close a way to the master as possible. This was not a new movement but the continuation (in some sense perhaps, the completion) of the mission of Jesus.

Second, the believers shared possessions and income equally. This, as Richard Hays points out, is 'the fulfilment of two ancient ideals: the Greek ideal of true friendship and the Deuteronomic ideal of covenant community'.[15] Greek and Roman philosophers described ideal friendship in terms of sharing goods; the Hebrew Scriptures described the community of Israel in the promised land as one where 'there will be no one in need among you' (Deut. 15.4, cf. Acts 4.34). Because it so clearly relates to both Greek and Hebrew ideals, such radical sharing has often been discounted as Luke's invention. But it is a logical extension of Jesus' explanation of his mission in terms of the Jubilee, proclaiming good news to the poor in the 'year of the Lord's favour' (Luke 4.18–19) and the 'common purse' which Jesus and the 12 disciples operated (John 12.6); and, though it appears never to have been practised again on the same scale, it also lies behind Paul's great 'collection' for the poor of Jerusalem which dominated the latter part of his active ministry. Therefore it may well have a genuine historical basis and is paralleled in the practice of some Essene groups. Nor was it without problems, as is shown by the episode of Ananias and Sapphira (Acts 5.1–10) and the case of the Greek-speaking widows who complained that they were not receiving their fair share of the common meal (Acts 6.1–2).

The common meal (Acts 2.46), the third feature, was a single symbolic embodiment of the radical sharing which Luke draws attention to, and remained central to following Jesus. It was a development of Jesus' practice, brought to a climax in the Last Supper and continued in the early Church. This practice set those who obeyed Jesus' teaching apart from other Jews, and ultimately it was table-fellowship with non-Jews which would cause the split away from Jewish faith later in the first century. But making sure all had a fair share was a problem, later also to be encountered by Paul in the church at Corinth (1 Cor. 11.20–21). In Jerusalem the dispute brings the diversity of the early community into focus.

This diversity may at first sight be masked by the fourth feature, which is worship. Jesus had been ambivalent about the Temple in his teaching. The accusation against him at his trial was that he had sought to destroy it, and he had overturned the tables of the money-changers there (Mark 11.15–18). But there is little trace of this ambivalence in Acts. There the believers are portrayed after Pentecost as participating fully in the worship of the Temple (Acts 2.46, 3.1). In other words, they behaved as wholly orthodox Jews with regard to worship, but with a new message to tell about Jesus.

Yet even orthodox Jewish faith was far from monochrome. There were many different varieties. Luke presents the early community in Jerusalem as a wholly Jewish phenomenon (Acts 2.5) but we would be foolish to think that this implies unity. The widows who were going short at the common meal were Greek-speakers ('Hellenists', Acts 6.1). These people would have been Jews who had probably been born abroad and for whom Greek rather than Aramaic was their first language. Given the circumstances of the time, this was a highly political issue. The more nationalistic Jews sought to preserve Hebrew and Aramaic by rejecting the use of Greek, but plenty of others found no difficulty in embracing both cultures. However, it is likely that the Greek-speakers were better-off than their Aramaic-speaking cousins, in itself perhaps sufficient reason for the dispute at the meal. The issue was resolved, according to Acts, by the appointment of seven men who all had Greek names and of whom one, Nicolaus, was a proselyte who had become a Jew (Acts 6.5). Looking a little more closely at this episode suggests that underneath the harmonious surface of the Acts account there were real tensions.

The diversity of Jewish faith was itself reflected in the early Christian community. Yes, all the believers were Jews in the early years, but what kind of Jews? The answer is a variety, from extreme nationalists to those who wished to co-operate fully with the Romans, and from extreme Pharisaic law-keeping (see Acts 15.5) to the relatively lax observance of the Diaspora. But essentially there were two main groups, reflected in Luke's account: 'the Jerusalem church had two factions separated by language and culture ... [and] almost from the very beginning if not actually from Pentecost on, was culturally pluralistic.'[16] The task of leadership from the beginning would therefore have been trying to establish the kind of harmony which Luke portrays in the aftermath of Pentecost.

How big was this community? Luke is specific about this: after Pentecost 3,000 were added to the 120 who had stayed faithful to Jesus after the Passover events (Acts 2.41; 1.15). This number has often been discounted as fancifully inflated in the past but it has recently regained credence: it may correspond to about 1% of the expanded size of Jerusalem at Pentecost-time. Certainly if Jesus had 5,000 followers at one stage in Galilee (Mark 6.44) a number of these could have rejoined the movement in Jerusalem if they were there for Pentecost. When visitors from further afield (mentioned in Acts 2.9–11) are considered, the figure begins to appear plausible. Luke's later figure of 5,000 (Acts 4.4) may simply be a way of marking that significant growth had happened. Whether it was sustained we do not know, and the imprecise 'thousands' mentioned to Paul when he arrived in Jerusalem in 56 (Acts 21.20) do not add much to our knowledge. There also is no obvious symbolic value to the figures, another factor in favour of their substantial accuracy. Sometimes there is an objection that a community of this size would have had a more significant impact on Jerusalem. That probably depends whether you expect it to differentiate itself sharply from its Jewish roots. Since the community seems to have understood itself as a reform movement within the boundaries of orthodox faith there was no need for such differentiation. The 'persecution' of the infant Church in the early chapters of Acts is actually more like the attempted suppression of a new sect. The substance of the advice by the leading Pharisee Gamaliel perhaps reflects this mushroom-like growth: we have seen popular movements come and go before, he says, let's see what happens to this one. If it lasts, then we can believe it is from God (Acts 5.34–39). It is also likely that the effect of the growth of the church in Jerusalem was diluted by the mobility of the population. Probably many of those whom Luke counts went back to their homes, as in the story of Philip and the Ethiopian eunuch, a high official from eastern Africa (Acts 8.26–39).

Belief in Jerusalem

What did the community in Jerusalem believe? The basis of their beliefs was not very much different from other Jews, but like other parties such as the Essenes they had their own very distinctive additions. Luke gives four examples of sermons preached in the early days in Jerusalem (Acts 2.14–36; 3.12–26; 4.8–12; 5.29–32) and although it is unlikely that these are verbatim accounts of what was said 'We may with some confidence take these speeches to represent ... the *kerygma* [message] of the Church at Jerusalem at an early period'.[17] The common characteristics are: a reference to prophecies being fulfilled; the death of Jesus on a cross; his resurrection from the dead; a call to repentance which will be followed by restoration seen in terms of the 'new age' of the Holy Spirit. Significantly Jesus is not spoken of as God's son and his death is not linked with the forgiveness of sins; nor is there apparently much interest in his life either. The future focus of the message also seems to relate to the restoration of Israel primarily, and only secondarily to the world, following the pattern of later prophecy. The exaltation of Jesus to the right hand of God was regarded as a temporary measure until 'the time of the restoration of all things' – the coming of God's Kingdom in its fullness in the last days (Acts 3.21). It was the latter, imminently eschatological, belief that marked out this group most: 'They saw themselves simply as a fulfilled Judaism, the beginning of eschatological Israel ... a messianic renewal movement.'[18] In other words theirs was a message from Jews, for Jews and about Jews, centred on Jerusalem, waiting for the time of restoration to come. They may not have been alone in this: Luke records Simeon and Anna around the time of Jesus' birth, who waited in the Temple for the 'consolation of Israel' and the 'redemption of Jerusalem' (Luke 2.25, 36–38) and Josephus mentions various prophets in the city too. Hegesippus, a second-century Church historian, describes James as 'entering the Temple alone, begging forgiveness for the people so that his knees became hard like a camel's',[19] perhaps continuing the practice of the earliest believers in Jerusalem.

Eventually the hotter-headed among both followers and opponents of the Jesus movement in Jerusalem came to blows. Luke describes how Stephen, one of the seven Greek-speakers chosen to help in the administration of the common meal, fell into an argument with some Diaspora Jews 'from the synagogue of the Freedmen' (Acts 6.9). The fact that some of the members of this synagogue were from Cilicia has led to speculation that one of them was Paul, a native of that area who is introduced into the story soon afterwards (Acts 7.58). The accusation against Stephen was that he was threatening the Temple and the Law (Acts 6.13). Although Luke says this was not true, the content of Stephen's speech suggests that he certainly had developed a devastating critique of their confidence and complacency about the Temple and the Law (Acts 7.44–53). Stephen's stoning, clearly portrayed as mob violence rather than due process of law, set off a backlash against Jesus' followers in Jerusalem (Acts 7.58—8.1). The relatively peaceful early phase of the community's existence was over.

The effect of persecution was to spread the faith across Judea and Samaria. Now for their own safety many of the leaders of the Church had to leave Jerusalem. Almost certainly Luke has exercised his trademark simplification here: broadly speaking the Church was centred in Jerusalem at first and then expanded, but there are signs within Acts itself that the picture was more complex. How do we account for there being enough followers of Jesus in Damascus, beyond the normal jurisdiction of the high priest, for example, for Paul to know that they were a genuine threat (Acts 9.1–2), unless the Church had already been established there? But what Luke wants to signal is a shift in emphasis. From being a passive community waiting faithfully for the dynamic in-breaking of the Kingdom in Jerusalem, the church there was poised to become a hub from which many missions would eventually radiate.

Caesarea, Antioch and the arrival of the gentiles

During the previous two centuries Jewish settlers had colonized Galilee and Samaria (which lay between Galilee and Jerusalem) as well as Idumea (beyond the southern Judean desert). Luke suggests that after an initial few years based solely in Jerusalem (perhaps 30–4), the Church began to expand more widely along the same lines. The impression given is that this was a sudden and explosive growth, but in fact by reconstructing the chronology of Paul we can see that Acts 8—12 actually covers about 14 years (34–48). Luke gives representative details of the work of Philip, like Stephen one of the seven Hellenists chosen to help the apostles (Acts 6.5), in Samaria and in the cities of the coastal plain including the Roman administrative centre of Caesarea. The picture is of the gradual growth of the Church across the ancient land of Israel and beyond. After initial work there is a suggestion that there was some sort of 'apostolic inspection' (in the case of Samaria by Peter and John, Acts 8.14).

Many of the inhabitants of these areas had become Jews (in some cases because they were forced to convert). But many had not, and while Jerusalem was a largely Jewish enclave, outside it the population had a far more mixed ethnic identity. This made it likely that Jesus' followers as they spread the gospel more widely would encounter pagans who wished to join them. Luke picks out two cities as places where this happened.

They are Caesarea and Antioch, the two cities where we might guess such an encounter to be most likely.

Caesarea had a sizeable Jewish population but they were a minority in a model Greco-Roman city built by Herod the Great and dominated by a huge statue of the Emperor Augustus. The central temple was also dedicated to the cult of the emperor, from whom the city of course took its name: it was 'a monument to power and paganism'.[20] According to Josephus, tensions there were the flashpoint from which the Jewish revolt of 66 began. Luke brings the city into his story by having Peter summoned there as the result of a vision by a Roman centurion named Cornelius who has become a follower of Jesus (Acts 10.1–6). Peter seems to have been on an inspection tour of the communities that had sprung up in the Jewish cities by the coast (Lydda and Joppa, Acts 9.32, 36), but Philip had already branched out into the pagan cities (Azotus, once the Philistine stronghold of Ashdod, and Caesarea itself, Acts 8.40). It is clear in the way that Luke tells the story that he wishes his readers to understand that Peter's crossing of an important boundary was a divine not human initiative (see Acts 10.47–8). Yet Peter hears the message while staying with 'Simon, a tanner' (Acts 9.43), whose occupation would have been an unclean one according to some Pharisees. Although the boundaries between Jews and gentiles would have been quite easy to draw in Jerusalem, in a mixed city like Caesarea they would have been much harder to establish. Cornelius was not an outright pagan, but a 'God-worshipper', someone who was in sympathy with Jewish faith (Acts 10.2). Though sympathetic to Jewish faith Cornelius would not have been circumcised. According to Acts, Peter baptized Cornelius and, on returning to Jerusalem, had to answer for his actions (Acts 10.48—11.3). It seems quite likely that other gentiles had already been baptized. But this was a high-profile case (a centurion was an important figure and so was an apostle). If Peter's role was to inspect the new communities which were springing up, the accusation against him would have been that the gamekeeper had turned poacher.

Meanwhile, others from the Jerusalem church had scattered more widely. Some ended up in Antioch, 300 miles north of Jerusalem, the third or fourth greatest city in the world with a population of which perhaps 10% were Jews. It was the major crossroads of the world, lying at the apex of the 'fertile crescent' and commanding land and sea routes to all four points of the compass. It lay between east and west, but more accessibly so than Jerusalem, and was a real melting pot. The fourth-century teacher Libanios wrote that 'if a man had the idea of travelling all over the world ... Antioch ... would save him journeying.'[21] As at Caesarea, the lines between Jews and gentiles were perhaps not so easy to recognize in daily life.

'Some men of Cyprus and Cyrene, coming to Antioch, even spoke to the Greeks, proclaiming the Lord Jesus' (Acts 11.20, the term 'Greeks' here is problematic, as many manuscripts read 'Hellenists' and are followed, for example, by the NRSV; in the context, however, only 'Greeks' makes sense). In other words, Antioch was the home of the first church to include a substantial number of gentiles. Luke's grasp of chronology is often very imprecise by our standards, and this makes it likely that the developments in Antioch were not sudden but gradual. Again we see a pattern of inspection as a trusted envoy of the Jerusalem apostles is sent to see what has happened (Acts 11.22). And here in Antioch 'for the first time the disciples were called Christians' (Acts 11.26).

Thus, by the mid 40s the Jerusalem community had become the centre of a web of churches across Palestine and Syria. This was partly the effect of a calculated attempt at suppression, not only after Stephen's death but also, later, by Herod Agrippa (Acts 12.1), which probably had the effect of reducing the size of the church in Jerusalem. This latter persecution was harsher than before, and led to the death of the disciple James, the brother of John, by public execution (Acts 12.2). The church was also poor. The economy of Jerusalem was an unstable one, dependent largely on income from the many visitors for festivals. There was limited local employment. These factors pushed prices for basic items up and led to significant hardship and the need for support from the wider network of churches (Gal. 2.10), especially when added to a famine, one of which occurred in 46–7 (Acts 11.28).

The churches beyond Jerusalem were not only composed of Jews but included gentiles who had come from a variety of backgrounds, many of whom were God-worshippers, sympathetic to Jewish faith but not to the point of circumcision. Barnabas and Paul, leaders of the Antioch church, seem to have had an idea to take the gospel to the Greek cities of Asia Minor. Paul later claimed this had come to him as a revelation, by which he may have been referring to his foundational commission to take the gospel to the nations (Gal. 1.16). They sought the sanction of the leaders in Jerusalem and set off to proclaim the gospel to the gentiles (Gal. 2.1–10). Back in Jerusalem, some of those who had been with the movement from the beginning questioned this development. The basic issue that presented itself was very simple but of profound importance: did you have to be a Jew to be a Christian? James was to find himself in the position of being arbiter in the dispute.

Christians or Jews?

Paul's letter to the Galatians still burns on the page 2,000 years after it was written. Two people in particular attract Paul's wrath: Peter (always called *Cephas,* his Hebrew name, with heavy irony) and James.

Although the sequence of events is hard to determine and has been exhaustively reconstructed in many different ways the general outline seems clear. Once Barnabas and Paul set off on their missionary campaign to Asia Minor the familiar 'apostolic inspection' of the church in Antioch took place, probably led at first by Peter. A later wave of visitors from Jerusalem ('some people from James' hisses Paul, Gal. 2.12) tried to change the behaviour of the church and to enforce an orthodox Jewish separation of tables between Jews and gentiles to maintain purity. Peter acquiesced and so, for a time, may Barnabas have done also (Gal. 2.13).

Paul immediately saw the principle which was at stake: the common meal was the central and distinctive ritual of the Christian community and segregated tables meant that it would be lost. Common devotion to Jesus overrode any other distinctions: you did not need to be a Jew to be Christian. Others believed that the issue could easily be resolved: any gentile men who were Christians should simply submit to circumcision. If they refused to do so, they were just not prepared to meet the cost of commitment.

Members of the group opposing Paul are identified as being Pharisees who saw no contradiction between their faith in Jesus and their Pharisaism (Acts 15.5). They have often been called 'Judaizers' because of their demand that gentiles needed to be 'Judaized'. To us they seem an extreme group, but they would not have appeared so at the time. They shared a common background with Paul, who had been trained as a Pharisee, which probably gave an added edge to the conflict. Paul identifies them with James (Gal. 2.12) but it is not clear if James ever really thought like them. He may well have wavered. There was no right or wrong, orthodox or heretical view at the time. It was a new issue, which had to be resolved.

The strategy of Paul and Barnabas was, obedient to Paul's call, to take the gospel to the gentiles. The Jerusalem leaders, obedient to the practice of Jesus, were afraid of cutting off the roots that sustained them. Paul and Barnabas, accustomed to the cosmopolitan world, felt they could handle the tension which growth would bring. The Jerusalem apostles, accustomed to a largely Jewish context, were anxious that the Church would cease to be distinctively Jewish at all. Acts says that Paul and Barnabas were sent by the Antioch church down to Jerusalem to raise the question there (Acts 15.2–3). This may have been a significant change in the dynamic between the churches. In effect the church at Antioch was challenging the authority of the mother church in Jerusalem, largely at Paul's instigation. This was clearly a major flash point in the growth of the Church.

The conference at Jerusalem: what happened and what was at stake?

The meeting in Jerusalem was almost certainly more heated than Luke's judicious and gentle account in Acts 15 suggests (contrast the passion of Gal 2.1–10!). However, it is important to remember that Luke was probably writing 30 or 40 years later when the emotions had cooled right down.

Luke describes the crucial events as follows (Acts 15.4–21):

- A group within the Jerusalem church composed of Pharisees argued for the essential nature of circumcision for salvation.
- Peter began by saying that gentiles were accepted by grace, just as Jewish believers were.
- Paul and Barnabas gave evidence of the manifest work of the Spirit among the gentiles.
- James as leader of the Jerusalem church ruled that gentiles should be welcomed and entry should not be made difficult for them, on the grounds that the inclusion of the gentiles is prophesied in the scriptures.

Circumcision, it was agreed, was not required. However, James's main concern seems to have been to keep gentile converts away from pagan temples. Thus his four stipulations were: don't worship idols by eating in temples; don't offer blood sacrifices; don't offer strangulated sacrifices either; don't engage in sacred prostitution. It was a judicious judgement, steering between two extremes and disowning those who had caused trouble in Galatia and Antioch (Acts 15.24). James's speech clearly delineates a theological view that would enable the Church to include gentiles.

James's views do seem to be different from Paul's, however. For one thing, his argument is based on the appeal to the Hebrew Scriptures (primarily Amos 9.11–12, though allusions to other prophets are woven into the dense quotation of Acts 15.16–18), where Paul's was apparently derived from the manifest success of the mission to the gentiles (Acts 15.12). And where Paul would later argue in Romans for the redefinition of the people of God to include the gentiles, with a centrifugal dynamic, James sees the gentiles coming to Jerusalem as a sign of the restoration of the house of David, a centripetal dynamic. There was sufficient agreement to make progress possible, but it perhaps underlines once again the diversity of belief already present in the Christian community.

If the decision had gone against Paul and Barnabas, then the growth of the Church among the gentiles would have effectively been disowned by the leaders of the foundation community. If the conference had required circumcision, then Christianity would have remained a reform movement within Judaism. But in that case there might have been a real possibility that the unprecedented growth among the gentiles, which Paul and Barnabas clearly identified as the work of God, would result in a split between Jewish and gentile churches. Tension remained between Jewish and gentile expressions of faith for some time, and the parties at the conference were not to know that within a few years the issue would die because of the destruction of Jerusalem, and with it the influence of the Jerusalem church.

James – leader in Jerusalem and patriarch of the east?

James's position as chair of the conference brings him to a new prominence in the story. But once again we are aware of how much Luke has left out of the story: this is, after all, only the second direct mention of James in Acts, and it is clear that he now has considerable authority not only in the Jerusalem church but in the movement as a whole. It seems that from this point on (the conference probably took place in 49) James held an unassailable position of leadership.

As well as expansion westwards, as Acts records, there was probably also significant development of the Church towards the east. Many Jews had remained in Mesopotamia after the exile to Babylon in the sixth century BC: 'an immense multitude, not to be estimated by numbers'[22] according to Josephus. By the first century more Jews lived outside Judea and Galilee than within them. Many were scattered in a diaspora across the Roman Empire, but still more lived to the east of Jerusalem. Babylon had the largest Jewish community outside Jerusalem itself, and taxes were collected in Mesopotamian cities before being transferred to the Temple in caravans made up of thousands of pilgrims, ensuring frequent contact and a sense of participation in the daily sacrifices there. Aramaic remained the language of choice, supplemented by Greek, across the whole area. Visitors to Jerusalem from the east are placed first in the list which Acts provides for those who saw the events of Pentecost. Richard Bauckham points out that 'whereas Palestine's incorporation in the Roman Empire was a very recent development, Palestine's participation in a cultural world which stretched east to Mesopotamia and Persia was very old and influential in countless ways', and continues that 'Though scholars ... tend to think Christianity did not reach Mesopotamia in Paul's lifetime or even in the first century, it has to be said that the constant communication and travel between Jerusalem and the eastern diaspora makes it virtually incredible that it did not.'[23] Even if eastern Christianity flourished only half as much in the early years as its western counterpart did, it would still have been a very strong movement.

Later developments certainly suggest this. Eusebius preserves a tradition that when the Christian philosopher Pantaenus travelled to India around 180, he found a copy of Matthew's Gospel in Hebrew already there, perhaps left by Bartholomew, one of the original apostles. But frustratingly little is known of eastern Christianity.

One possible piece of evidence is the *Odes of Solomon*, a late first- or early second-century collection of psalms or hymns probably from Edessa in northern Mesopotamia, which became the first 'Christian' kingdom in the early third century. It is not clear whether the *Odes* are Jewish or Christian or perhaps Gnostic. Several of the *Odes* speak of a messiah who has come, and one speaks with startling imagery of the Trinity: 'The Son is the cup, the Father is he who was milked and the Holy Spirit she who milked him.'[24] Perhaps the most important thing we can deduce from the *Odes* is the fluid nature of the faith they express. James Charlesworth concludes that they seem 'to stand at a three-way junction: some will proceed ahead to Judaism, others will move on to full-blown Gnosticism, and others will progress to orthodox Christianity'.[25] They certainly testify to a vibrant but as-yet-unformed faith.

The eastern Diaspora occupied in a sense the hinterland of Jerusalem, bound more closely to it than the western Diaspora. The temple authorities communicated with Jews across the whole area by means of circular letters giving instructions and judgements on how festivals and other religious observances should be kept. The letter sent from Jerusalem to the new gentile Christians as a result of the conference seems to be written along the same lines (Acts 15.23–9). So, too, does the letter of James, which is addressed to 'the twelve tribes in the Diaspora' (James 1.1) and was known and accepted in the eastern Church before the western one. This may be taken tentatively to imply some sort of patriarchal role for James across all the churches of the eastern Diaspora. We simply cannot be sure, since the evidence is so slim, but the hypothesis is an intriguing one.

What happened to James and the Jerusalem church?

After the story of the conference in Jerusalem, the narrative of Acts heads firmly westwards and follows Paul's exploits across the Roman Empire. James and the Jerusalem church appear only once more, when Paul returns to Rome for Pentecost 56. There are suggestions of tensions between the two apostles (Acts 21.18–25) and Paul's subsequent use of his Roman citizenship to protect himself took him out of a Jewish milieu and into a Roman one which, as far as we know, he never left. Luke never mentions the Jerusalem church again.

But we are able to piece together some of the story. The main source here is Josephus. He records that, during the power vacuum which followed the unexpected death of the Roman governor Festus in 62, Ananus the high priest took the opportunity to have 'the brother of Jesus called the Christ, named James and some others'[26] arrested on the charge of opposing the Law. They were tried and stoned to death but the judgement so offended those in Jerusalem who were zealous for the Law (probably Pharisees) that the high priest was removed from office as a result.

From this story we can deduce that James was a critic of the high priest and that the accusations of laxity with regard to the Law which had led to the death of Stephen and the arrest of Paul (Acts 6.14; 21.28) were still current. Equally we can see from the way Josephus tells the story that the accusations were not, in James's case at any rate, true.

Six years passed between James's death and the Roman army's attack on Jerusalem in 68. It was to take the Romans two years to break down the defences and finally to kill thousands of Jews, burn the city and destroy the Temple. Pliny, writing a few years later, described it simply as 'a grave'.[27]

Where were the Jerusalem Christians when the Temple was destroyed? No doubt some were involved in the revolt, but Eusebius preserves a tradition that they had left the city in response to a prophecy about its impending destruction before the revolt broke out and settled in the town of Pella, across the Jordan (Pella was one of the 'ten towns' in the predominantly gentile region of Decapolis).[28] A later tradition suggests that they returned to the city after its destruction and retained a presence there, keeping the importance of sites such as the tomb of Jesus alive. But the city was no longer significant and it would have been hard to make a living there. Probably the majority of Jerusalem Christians scattered across the churches, and it may be that a good many of them eventually found their way to Antioch, which seems to have become the predominant church in the east. Overall, the destruction of the Temple as the central place of devotion for Jews also spelled the end of the Jerusalem church as the hub to which all the other churches related.

The faith of the Jerusalem church has sometimes been characterized as 'Jewish Christianity'. It is a term that those who were part of it would not have recognized. They were Jews who might possibly, later on, have thought of themselves as 'Christian Jews' as some might also have considered themselves as 'Pharisaic Jews.' We know of a group in the east during the second century known as the 'Ebionites' whose name means 'the poor ones'. They seem to have committed themselves to lives of poverty, exact observance of the Law including mandatory circumcision, and when they prayed they faced towards Jerusalem. They also saw Jesus as a perfect human being but stopped short of believing that he was God. The Ebionites appealed to the memory of Peter and James as support for their views and seem to have used an Aramaic version of Matthew's Gospel. Regarded later as heretical, to Bart Ehrman they 'sound very much like the ... opponents of Paul in Galatia'.[29] They drop out of historical view in the fourth century and none of their writings survive. But James Dunn suggests that 'The heretical Jewish Christianity of the second and third centuries apparently has no closer parallel than the earliest Christian community in Jerusalem ... [and] could quite properly claim to be more truly the heir of earliest Christianity than any other expression'. He continues, however, that it was a form of faith that had failed to change with time, fossilized like a fly caught in amber: 'simple Jewish messianism was no longer adequate'.[30] The Ebionites' devotion to Jerusalem is a moving but sad feature, as they prayed towards a Temple which was no longer there, remembering a Jewish saviour and excluding the gentile majority whose inclusion had changed the Church utterly.

Paul's passing comment about 'the brothers of the Lord' (1 Cor. 9.5) suggests that the rest of Jesus' brothers became, like James, followers and members of the early community in Jerusalem. It also suggests that they travelled, like Paul himself and Peter. More than that we cannot really say, though later traditions suggest that their influence was predominantly in the eastern churches (where their descendants Abris, Abraham and James became bishops in the second century). After James's death Symeon, son of Clopas and James's cousin, became leader of the Jerusalem church until he was martyred around 100. Symeon's death seems to have been because he was of the line of David and therefore a potential threat. In a similar way the grandsons of Jude, named Zoker (Zechariah) and James, were questioned by the Emperor Domitian in the late 80s. They successfully defended themselves on the grounds that their rough hands showed they were simple farmers from Nazareth, not pretenders to the throne of Israel. Thus we see that the family of Jesus continued to be remembered and to have positions of leadership in the Church well into the second century.

The letter of Jude

We know a little more about Judas or Jude, one of the other brothers of Jesus. His name appears as the author of the last letter in the New Testament, and he is identified as 'a servant of Jesus Christ and the brother of James' (Jude 1). It is unclear when the letter was written. There is nothing in it to suggest that it was not written by Jude, as it claims to be. Jude had intended to write a general letter to his audience, but finds that he must now write to tell them how to combat those who 'have crept in' (Jude 4) and are undermining their faith. He attacks these false teachers (Jude 8–19) and then gives brief advice on what to do: 'pray in the Holy Spirit, keep yourselves in the love of God, wait for the mercy of the Lord Jesus Christ in eternal life, and have mercy on those who are wavering' (Jude 19–21). The situation seems to be one which was widespread in the Church by the end of the first century, and the letter has some similarities with the letters of John.

The letter of James

The destruction of Jerusalem may have meant the end of the Christian community there as a central reference point for the Church, but Eusebius' story of the flight to Pella was intended to reassure his readers that contact with the traditions of the earliest church had not been lost. The sayings of Jesus and stories about him survived and so did some of the teaching of James himself. This teaching is contained in the letter of James.

The letter of James seems to speak a different language from the other letters found in the New Testament. At the most basic level, Jesus is mentioned only twice (James 1.1; 2.1), and if his name were removed from these verses nothing distinctively Christian would remain. Like most of the other writings of the New Testament, the date of the letter of James is uncertain. Some place it around the time of the Jerusalem conference, others as late as the second century on the grounds that it does not appear in the lists of New Testament books until after 180. The primary argument in favour of it being a late work (and therefore, of course, not written by James, since he died in 62) has been that its Greek is too polished to carry conviction as the composition of an author so identified with his Jewish roots. More recent research, which shows how widespread the use of Greek in first-century Palestine was, has made this line of approach untenable, though the Greek of the letter is very good and probably implies that a scribe polished it. On the grounds that the strongly Jewish tone of the letter reflects the character of the Jerusalem church it seems much more likely that it was written some time between 50 and 70 and was put into its final form by a literary collaborator either with James or soon after his death.

James's letter is unlike the other letters of the New Testament in that its primary purpose is to instruct in behaviour rather than belief. Paul's letters combine both approaches, but an emphasis on right belief is usually uppermost. Some have drawn a distinction between ortho*doxy* (right belief – *doxa* in Greek) and ortho*praxy* (right conduct – *praxis* in Greek), with James concerned for the latter. The kind of writing we find in James, therefore, has been called *parenesis* or ethical instruction. It follows that the closest writings to it are not to be found in the New but the Old Testament, and the Jewish writings of the last two or three centuries BC. The letter of James is a loosely formed set of sermons and sayings best grouped with other 'wisdom writings' ('like the Book of Proverbs but without as many one-liners'[31]).

The wisdom tradition embodied a critical, common-sense approach, which often looked at the world in a sideways fashion, deflating pomposity and questioning widely accepted views. A leading example was the teaching of Ben Sira who lived in the late third and early second centuries BC. His teachings were collected in the book of Sirach (also known as Ecclesiasticus), and they form a good model for interpreting the letter of James. Ben Sira's concern was to find a way of interpreting Jewish laws and traditions so that they remained fresh and viable in the face of Greek ideas and culture. In doing so he frequently alludes to the Hebrew Scriptures, but only rarely quotes from them.

Comparing the letter of James with Sirach to some extent explains the absence of any direct quotation of Jesus' sayings. Just as Ben Sira alluded to and reworked what he had inherited, so James seems to refashion the teaching of Jesus. Two examples show how this is done. James 1.5 seems to take the same thought about the generosity of God and the disciple's need to ask, expressed in Matthew 7.7, 11, and rephrases it. Similarly in James 1.6 the need to ask without doubting is linked with an image of the waves of the sea; Matthew 21.21–2 contains the same thought, and even mentions the sea too, but using a different image. There are at least 36 such subtle connections between James's letter and the teachings of Jesus. This leads Richard Bauckham to conclude that 'James is a sage who has made the wisdom of Jesus his own. He does not repeat it; he is inspired by it. He creates his own wise sayings ... guided by his special attentiveness to Jesus' wisdom as his major authoritative norm.'[32] In this sense James is acting very like Ben Sira, seeking to interpret traditional material for a new age in order for it to survive. This is why it seems likely that the letter is itself probably a creative reworking of James's own teaching, completed after his death.

Martin Luther wanted to reject the letter of James from his German New Testament of 1522 because he believed that it contradicted the teaching of Paul, who was for him the pre-eminent apostle and teacher of the Church. The focus of debate lies in James 2.14–26, which seems to contrast sharply with Paul's teaching, especially in Galatians and Romans, about the importance of salvation by faith and not by works. But James does not suggest that works, in the sense of right actions, are enough on their own for salvation: faith is always presupposed. This is an orthodox first-century Jewish faith, expressed through works of obedience to the Law. Paul, writing in a gentile context, approaches the matter very differently. He wants to free new converts from the potential burden of foreign demands being placed on them by those who want them to be circumcised. Yet he too is very concerned that they should also behave well.

The main themes of James's letter connect with what we have seen to be important issues for the life of the early community in Jerusalem. They are in a situation of suffering (James 1.2), they are poor (James 2.5) and they are waiting for the 'coming of the Lord' (James 5.7). Above all we see in the letter a Christian faith that is very close to its Jewish roots, concerned about acting righteously and obediently. Judaism is not superseded but fulfilled by faith in Jesus the messiah.

The letter to the Hebrews

The same concern about whether Judaism was superseded or fulfilled by Jesus dominates the letter to the Hebrews, which seems to belong to the miscellaneous group of writings that reflect strongly the Jewish roots of the New Testament. Hebrews is very much the 'odd one out' of the books of the New Testament. Its reception into the canon was slow, and it alone came to be regarded as anonymous. Many authors have been suggested, including Barnabas, Apollos and Clement of Rome.

In 1900, long before it was fashionable to do so, the great German scholar Adolf von Harnack suggested that Paul's female associate Priscilla was a good candidate, but argued that her identity as the author was subsequently suppressed because she was a woman. There are three main points in favour of Harnack's proposal. First, the letter's concluding greeting is from the 'saints in Italy' (Heb. 13.24) and the only other people from Italy mentioned in the rest of the New Testament are Priscilla and her husband Aquila (Acts 18.2). Second, Priscilla had a teaching role and instructed Apollos (Acts 18.26). Third, the letter includes women among the heroes of faith (Heb. 11.11, 31, 35). None of these pieces of evidence is very strong, however. The first point is probably not significant; the second applies equally well to Aquila; and the third would suggest that the author of Matthew's Gospel might have been a woman too, since he includes women in the genealogy of Jesus (Matt. 1.3, 5, 6, 16). The author of Hebrews refers to himself as male at one point (Heb. 11.32, the point is not clear in English), a small but telling indication. In fact Priscilla and Aquila seem to have been a team, never mentioned separately (Acts 18.2, 18, 19, Rom. 16.3, 1 Cor. 16.19, 2 Tim. 4.19). It is more likely that they were joint authors of Hebrews, but the case is far from proved. Origen, in the early third century, concluded that 'who wrote the letter, in truth, God knows'.[33] We are probably not likely to improve on this conclusion, though the tantalising possibility remains that this book might have been co-authored by a woman.

Who the 'Hebrews' who received the letter were is also hard to say. But the concluding greetings use a technical term for leaders (*hegoumenoi*, Heb. 13.7, 17, 24). This term was also used by Clement of Rome in the late first century, but it does not occur anywhere else, suggesting that the context is Rome. Clement himself uses Hebrews in his own first letter to the Corinthians, showing that it was known in Rome by the time Clement wrote in the very late first century.[34]

The emphasis of Hebrews on suffering and the possibility of danger ahead (Heb. 12.4; 13.3) suggests that it may have been written around the time of Nero's persecution in 65. But it is equally likely to have been written after the destruction of the Jerusalem Temple in 70, in response to Pharisaic attempts to tighten the boundaries of acceptable belief within the synagogues. (The apparent emphasis on the continuing process of sacrifice, Hebrews 9.25, is not decisive here: it was widely expected that the Temple would be rebuilt after 70.)

Nevertheless the concern of the Hebrews is clear: how should they regard Jesus? This, as we saw above, was a stumbling block to the Ebionites who were Christian but would not accept Jesus as God. Since there is evidence that the Hebrews were forsaking their commitment to follow

Jesus (see Heb. 10.32–4), much of the letter is devoted to proving his central importance, as the headline opening makes clear: 'In many and varied ways long ago God spoke to the forefathers by the prophets. But now he has spoken to us by the Son' (Heb. 1.1–2).

Is Hebrews really a letter? Its place in the New Testament after Paul's letters and before the letter of James suggests that it is, but it fits the pattern uneasily. It has none of the usual features of a letter, such as greetings or mention of the author's name and circumstances. It contains the 'longest sustained argument'[35] to be found in the New Testament and the author claims that it is a 'message of exhortation ... in a few words' (Heb.13.22). It seems better to categorize it as an extended sermon than a letter.

This is important because, though other letters in the New Testament contain sustained argument, they primarily address problems and issues that have arisen in the early Christian communities (Romans is to some extent an exception to this among Paul's letters). Hebrews, though it too is addressed to a pastoral situation, has a crisis of confidence rather than conduct in view. The writer encourages the recipients to continue in the faith, to persevere and, in doing so, to reflect the character of the God whom they worship (see Heb. 11—12).

The process of argument is careful and deeply rooted in rabbinic forms. The first seven chapters take the readers through the Hebrew Scriptures, offering a new interpretation which points to Jesus as the fulfilment of the promises to Israel. Chapters 8—10, the heart of the book, introduce the idea of a new covenant. A new covenant implies that the old one was a temporary measure which would one day be set aside: 'For the Law is a shadow of the good things to come, and not those things themselves' (Heb. 10.1). Jesus is portrayed as the mediator between God and humanity and also the sacrifice who restores the relationship between heaven and earth. He is thus both priest and victim. The author of Hebrews, deeply embedded in Jewish ways of life and thought though he (or she) may be, never doubts that Jesus has fulfilled the demands of the Law and superseded it. The Temple is no longer necessary (see Heb. 8.13). Whenever the letter was written, its application to the situation after the destruction of the Temple is obvious.

The picture of Jesus to be found in Hebrews is a fascinating one. He is often described in adoptionist language, that is as one who has become the Son of God after his resurrection and was not born that way (Heb. 1.4, 9; 2.10; 3.2; 5.5, 7; 7.16). Yet he is also described as the Son through whom the world was made (Heb. 1.2–3) in terms very similar to the opening of John's Gospel, implying that he was the pre-existing Son of God. There seem to be two strands here which have not been fully assimilated with each other. But the direction of developing thought about Jesus is clear, towards the highest possible understanding of him. It is significant that this development is found in such a strongly Jewish document. It points towards the eventual divergence of Christianity and Judaism.

The remaining chapters of Hebrews offer a catalogue of heroes of faith (Heb. 11—12), followed by a short list of instructions to believers about behaviour (Heb. 13). The list of heroes intriguingly parallels the one which concludes the book of Sirach, which we saw earlier was an influence on the letter of James. That list ends with the high priest Simon, son of Onias, who restored the Temple. Simon is the climax of the story of Israel's 'famous men' which Ben Sira told (Sirach 44—50), 'a great high priest, magnificently robed, splendid in his liturgical operations, coming out of the sanctuary after the worship to bless the people'. Tom Wright notes that in Hebrews 'Instead of the present high priest in the Temple being the high point towards which all Israel's history was tending, it is Jesus, the true High Priest ... [who] has brought Israel's story to its paradoxical climax.'[36] The same idea can be found in Matthew's Gospel, to which we shall turn next, which is equally firm in the conviction that in Jesus the true end of Israel's story is to be found.

James the Just

One of the major themes of James's letter is the need for compassion, for 'mercy wins out over judgement' (James 2.13, see also 5.19–20). Harshness has no place, and there is an inevitable link here with James's own story. In the later Church he was known as 'the Just' (or 'Righteous'), a description that we saw early in this chapter applied in Matthew's Gospel to Joseph, James's father (Matthew 1.19). In that case it was used to explain Joseph's gentle treatment of Mary, not requiring the full punishment of the Law on his new bride. James the brother of Jesus was similarly remembered as a man of piety and prayer, a Jew of a compassionate kind. His witness remains the closest to the Jewish roots of Christianity, yet he remains a shadowy figure of undoubted importance, glimpsed rather than seen fully. Probably that was how he would have wished it. If there ever had been any rivalry between James and Jesus there are no signs of it in James's later life. He was content to be described as the 'brother of Jesus', the way Josephus introduces him. His letter gives some idea of his beliefs, but there is another strand of evidence to the early phase of Christian Judaism which we must now go on to investigate. This is the Gospel of Matthew, which preserves within it many of the emphases which were distinctive in the early community in Jerusalem and the thought of James, the brother of Jesus.

Draw your own conclusions

- How would you describe the relationship between James and Paul?
- Do you think James was a follower of Jesus during his brother's lifetime?

- How would you describe the beliefs of the church in Jerusalem?
- What was really at stake in the Jerusalem conference?
- Is James best characterized as a wisdom teacher?
- Would James have described himself as a Christian?

Further reading

James and the family of Jesus

The best recent attempt at a survey of James's life is the second part of H. Shanks and B. Witherington (2003), *The Brother of Jesus*, New York: Continuum. On a more technical level, J. Painter (1999), *Just James: the Brother of Jesus in History and Tradition*, Minneapolis: Fortress, looks at the relevant biblical passages as well as later traditions. B. Chilton and J. Neusner (2001), *The Brother of Jesus*, Louisville: WJKP is a useful collection of essays. On the family of Jesus see R. J. Bauckham (1990), *Jude and the Relatives of Jesus in the Early Church*, Edinburgh: T.&T. Clark.

On the Letter of James, see R. J. Bauckham (1999), *James: Wisdom of James, the disciple of Jesus the sage*, London: Routledge; and P. J. Hartin (2003), *James*, Collegeville: Liturgical Press, a commentary in the Roman Catholic *Sacra Pagina* series.

Jewish background

On Jewish faith in the first century E. P. Sanders (1992), *Judaism: Practice and Belief 63BCE – 66CE*, London: SCM Press, is rightly regarded as indispensable. M. Goodman (2007), *Rome and Jerusalem*, London: Penguin is also a masterly survey, though in the context of the destruction of Jerusalem in 70. S. Goldhill (2005), *The Temple of Jerusalem*, London: Profile is a short 'biography' of the centre of first-century Jewish faith.

The Qumran community and its writings are richly illustrated and examined in P. R. Davies, G. J. Brooke and P. R. Callaway (2002), *The Complete World of the Dead Sea Scrolls*, London: Thames & Hudson, while A. Millard (2000), *Reading and Writing in the Time of Jesus*, Sheffield: Sheffield Academic Press, gives a judicious survey of this important aspect of the background to the New Testament.

Herod the Great's life and times are comprehensively examined in P. Richardson (1999), *Herod the Great: king of the Jews and friend of the Romans*, Edinburgh: T.&T. Clark, while T. Rajak (2002), *Josephus: the historian and his society*, 2nd ed., London: Duckworth, does the same for the writer from whom most of our information about Herod is derived. The links between Josephus's writings and those of the Christian communities are carefully surveyed in S. Mason (2003), *Josephus and the New Testament*, 2nd ed., Peabody: Hendrickson.

Websites

- Details and discussion about the forgery or authenticity of the James Ossuary can be found at the website of the *Biblical Archaeology* magazine: www.bib-arch.org.
- The 'Josephus Home Page' which offers backgrounds and texts, is at www.josephus.org/
- Resources for the study of the letter of James can be found at 'The Text this Week', www.textweek.com/epistlesrevelation/james.htm. On Hebrews, see www.textweek.com/epistlesrevelation/hebrews.htm.

Notes

1 Josephus, *Antiquities* 20.9.

2 P. Fredriksen (2000), *Jesus of Nazareth King of the Jews*, London: Macmillan, p. 183.

3 *Gospel of Thomas* 12.

4 R. E. Brown (1977), *The Birth of the Messiah*, New York: Doubleday, p. 127.

5 Pliny, *Natural History* 5.73.

6 E. P. Sanders (1992), *Judaism: Practice and Belief*, London: SCM Press, p. 262.

7 P. R. Davies, G. J. Brooke and P. R. Callaway (2002), *The Complete World of the Dead Sea Scrolls*, London: Thames & Hudson, p. 165.

8 Sanders, *Judaism*, p. 128.

9 A. Millard (2000), *Reading and Writing in the Time of Jesus*, Sheffield: Sheffield Academic Press, p. 168.

10 J. D. G. Dunn (2003), *Jesus Remembered*, Grand Rapids: Eerdmans, p. 596 n. 239.

11 *Gospel of Thomas* 12.

12 R. J. Bauckham (1990), *Jude and the Relatives of Jesus in the Early Church*, Edinburgh: T.&T. Clark, p. 59.

13 N. T. Wright (2003), *The Resurrection of the Son of God*, London: SPCK, p. 562 (emphasis original).

14 Pliny, *Natural History* 5.15.

15 R. B. Hays (1997), *The Moral Vision of the New Testament*, Edinburgh: T.&T. Clark, p. 123.

16 D. A. Fiensy (1995), 'The Composition of the Jerusalem Church' in R. J. Bauckham (ed.), *The Book of Acts in its Palestinian Setting*, Carlisle: Paternoster, p. 235.

17 C. H. Dodd (1936), *The Apostolic Preaching and Its Developments*, London: Hodder & Stoughton, p. 21.

18 J. D. G. Dunn (1990), *Unity and Diversity in the New Testament*, 2nd ed., London: SCM Press, p. 239.

19 Eusebius, *History of the Church* 2.23.6.

20 N. Faulkner (2002), *Apocalypse: the Great Jewish Revolt against Rome* AD *66–73*, Stroud: Tempus, p. 39.

21 Quoted in C. Kondoleon (ed.) (2000), *Antioch: the lost ancient city*, Princeton: Princeton University Press, p. 11.

22 Josephus, *Antiquities* 11.133.

23 R. Bauckham (2000), 'What if Paul had Travelled East rather than West?', *Biblical Interpretation* 8 (1/2), pp.173, 180.

24 *Odes of Solomon* 19.1–2.

25 J. H. Charlesworth, '*Odes of Solomon*' in C. A. Evans and S. E. Porter (eds) (2000), *Dictionary of New Testament Background*, Leicester: IVP, p. 751.

26 Josephus, *Antiquities* 20.9.

27 Pliny, *Natural History* 5.73.

28 Eusebius, *History of the Church* 3.5.3.

29 B. D. Ehrman (2003), *Lost Christianities*, New York: Oxford University Press, p. 100.

30 Dunn, *Unity and Diversity*, pp. 244–5 (emphases removed).

31 B. D. Ehrman (1997), *The New Testament: a Historical Introduction*, New York: Oxford University Press, p. 384.

32 R. J. Bauckham (2001), 'James and Jesus' in B. Chilton and J. Neusner (eds), *The Brother of Jesus*, Louisville: Westminster John Knox Press, pp. 115–16.

33 Eusebius, *History of the Church* 6.25.

34 *1 Clement* 36.

35 L. T. Johnson (1999), *The Writings of the New Testament: an interpretation*, London: SCM Press, p. 463.

36 N. T. Wright (1992), *The New Testament and the People of God*, London: SPCK, p. 410.

3

The Gospel of Matthew

Jerusalem, Summer 70

A Roman soldier leaned his spear in the corner of the room and took a last look around the house. Cups, plates, bowls and other signs of everyday life lay scattered and smashed across the courtyard. In this house, he and the other soldiers had released the tension that had built up through three months of bitter, bloody and desperate street-fighting. They had sustained many more casualties than they were used to, and in this house they had taken revenge.

In front of him lay the butchered bodies of the Kathros family. They were among the elite high priests and treasurers of the Temple, which is why they lived just a long stone's throw from the Temple itself. From the kitchen came groans. The hand of a young woman stretched out pleading for mercy. But the soldier hardly heard the sound amid the chaos of a city where almost every house was meeting the same fate.

He picked up one of the coins scattered across the floor. The writing on it was in Hebrew. It wouldn't be much use to him, and he had already looted more treasure than he could easily carry. He tossed it back on to the floor and set light to the pile of debris he had hastily gathered. In a moment or two the flames caught and he stumbled out of the door into the street, coughing from the smoke. Inside, the fire roared and blackened the plaster of the wall and the wooden ceiling collapsed with a crash. His centurion wouldn't be impressed when he reported without his spear, but then again, in the circumstances perhaps he wouldn't notice.

The 'Burnt House' on Tiferet Yisrael Street in Jerusalem remained hidden and ruined for 19 centuries until it was excavated. It offers silent but powerful testimony to the ferocity the Romans unleashed on Jerusalem in the summer of 70.

Those Jews who escaped from the ransacking of the city with their lives were utterly desolate. Their great city and the Temple itself lay ruined and shattered. Simon Goldhill comments that 'the destruction of the Temple by the Romans meant that the heart was ripped out of Jewish practice. The political, social and religious order which the Temple had provided was lost.'[1] The end of the Temple meant the end of the sacrificial system and the end of the festival pilgrimages, which had shaped the life and religious practice of Jews in Judea, Galilee and right across the Roman Empire and beyond. What did it now mean to be a Jew? Jewish identity would have to be redefined.

It was out of this situation that the Gospel of Matthew was written.

Matthew's Gospel

Matthew's Gospel breathes the same distinctively Jewish air as the early church in Jerusalem. For this reason the Church of the first few centuries regarded this Gospel as the closest to the original preaching of the apostles and placed it first in the New Testament.

Only a very few scholars would attempt to defend this view today. There is very good evidence that Mark's Gospel was the first to be written and that Matthew used the structure and much of the material provided by his predecessor. However, the strongly Jewish and eastern flavour of Matthew's Gospel means that many of the important themes which we have observed in the Jerusalem church in the last chapter are echoed here. In particular this Gospel is concerned to provide a body of teaching and to give guidelines for right conduct among believers, almost amounting to a 'new Law'. (Although the final form of the Gospel is very unlikely to have been written by Matthew the disciple, for simplicity's sake I shall refer to the author as 'Matthew' in the rest of this chapter; but since the quotation marks would probably become irritating, he will simply be called Matthew.)

Where was Matthew's Gospel written?

Most scholars place the Gospel's origins somewhere in the Roman province of Syria. A few clues scattered within the Gospel point to this:

- Jesus is called a 'Nazarene' (Matt. 2.23), a description given to the earliest Christian Jewish believers in Jerusalem (see also Acts 24.5);
- Jesus' fame spread 'throughout Syria' (Matt. 4.24) a detail which parallel passages do not include (Mark 1.39; Luke 4.44);
- The woman Jesus meets in Phoenicia is described as 'a Canaanite' (Matt. 15.22), probably a local term; the parallel passage simply describes her as 'gentile, Syro-Phoenician by birth' (Mark 7.26).

A few more clues lie outside the text in the writings of Ignatius, bishop of Antioch early in the second century. Ignatius uses phrases which occur in Matthew's Gospel but not in any of the others, suggesting that he knew it well. He also stresses Jesus' virgin birth and descent from David, both important motifs for Matthew's stories of Jesus' birth.

One tiny but revealing clue points to Antioch itself as the home of Matthew's Gospel. The curious story of the coin in the fish's mouth, which is unique to Matthew's Gospel, equates the rate for the Temple tax (two drachmas) with a *stater* (Matt. 17.24, 27). Only in Antioch did this exchange rate apply.

The evidence is painfully slim, so 'the great city of Antioch on the Orontes is only the most probable of many hypotheses.'[2] It does, however, fit the fact that this most Jewish of the Gospels has also embraced the mission to the gentiles (Matt. 28.19) and holds the synagogues at arm's-length. They are frequently referred to as 'your' or 'their' synagogues, and associated with hypocrisy and punishment (Matt. 4.23; 6.2, 5; 10.17; 23.34).

Antioch largely took the place of Jerusalem as the centre of Christian activity in the east after the destruction of the Temple. The church there was mixed, with strong Jewish and gentile congregations, the scene of early disputes about whether Jews and gentiles could belong to the Church on an equal basis (Gal. 2.11–21; see also Acts 11.19). The city was also a marketplace for goods and ideas, situated at the crossroads between east and west. The philosopher Libanios later wrote that 'if a man ... sits in our market-place, he will sample every city; there will be so many people from each place with whom he can talk',[3] a situation unchanged since the first century. It also had a long-standing and numerous Jewish population which suffered humiliation after 70, when the golden cherubim from the Holy of Holies in the Jerusalem Temple were displayed on the city gate and the synagogue deliberately destroyed to make way for a new amphitheatre. How could Jews live faithfully in the face of such attacks on their most cherished beliefs? So, though the case is not proved, Antioch is a good place to imagine Matthew's Gospel being composed, a city where the issue of how Judaism would cope with a radically altered world was of vital importance.

Being Jewish after 70

In 66, a young priest named Eleazar persuaded his colleagues not to offer sacrifices for the well-being of the Emperor Nero in the Temple at Jerusalem. Florus, the Roman governor, at first reacted too softly and then, too late, over-harshly. His troops indiscriminately massacred 3,500 men, women and children in Jerusalem, including Roman citizens. The city rose in revolt, and the token Roman cohort of 600 men stationed in Jerusalem was pinned down in its headquarters, the former royal palace of Herod the Great. They eventually realized that their situation was hopeless and ignominiously surrendered in order to escape with their lives.

A Roman force dispatched under Cestius Gallus to teach the rebel city a lesson unaccountably halted its advance at the Temple gates and then retreated back towards the coast. On the way, Jewish guerrilla troops made the most of their familiarity with the rocky terrain, descending from the hills to pick off the heavily armed legionaries as they slogged up to Caesarea Maritima. Around one in five of Gallus's 30,000-strong army were killed and the Romans hastily abandoned armour, weapons, supplies and even one of the legion's sacred eagle standards as they fled. Jerusalem became the centre of an independent Jewish state once again. For many it was a sign that God had re-established his Kingdom.

The might of Rome was in no mood to tolerate such humiliation. Nero dispatched the veteran general Flavius Vespasian to avenge the defeat. He began a patient but thorough campaign to secure the Empire's eastern frontier, moving through Galilee and gradually closing in on Jerusalem. But then Nero died suddenly and unlamented, in 68. His death created a power vacuum in Rome. Vespasian found himself in charge of the largest army in the Empire and unexpectedly in a position to become emperor. Leaving his troops under the command of his son, Titus, he set off to claim the imperial throne.

The conflict between the Jews and the Empire probably escalated far beyond what either party expected or intended through an unfortunate combination of circumstances. Even the catastrophic destruction by fire of the great Temple itself in 70 may have been an accident. But once it had happened and Jerusalem had been reduced to ruins, with only a portion of its ancient walls and towers left standing, it was too good a propaganda opportunity for Titus and Vespasian to miss. Total victory over the Jews meant that they could present themselves as the saviours of Rome against foreign danger and defiance. And the Temple treasury offered just what a family of undistinguished pedigree and little wealth needed to claim the throne: huge amounts of gold.

Titus followed his father back to Rome and the following spring they celebrated a Triumph. Jewish rebels were marched through Rome in chains. Simon of Giora, their last commander in Jerusalem, was executed at the end of the Triumph, a symbol of what happened to those who defied Rome. Unprecedented treasures were displayed for the populace to marvel at. Pride of place belonged to those from the Temple, including the sacred menorah, the seven-branched candlestick which had commemorated the victory of the Maccabees. But the climax of the spoils of war was a scroll of the Torah, the Jewish Law. 'There could not be a clearer demonstration that the conquest was being celebrated not just over Judaea but over Judaism.'[4] The Triumph was replicated in many eastern cities, and celebrated on Vespasian's coinage which proclaimed '*Judaea Capta*' (Judea conquered). All these things underlined the power of Rome, and of the new emperor.

Vespasian also instituted a tax, which was an annual reminder to his Jewish subjects of their defeat. The tax sent to Jerusalem for the upkeep of the Temple was the chief means by which Diaspora Jews demonstrated a link of piety to the homeland. Now, of course, it was no longer needed so Vespasian diverted it to rebuild the temple of Jupiter in Rome, a calculated insult to the monotheistic Jews. The tax was demanded from all Jews, male and female above the age of three years, across the Empire. Men who refused to pay were subjected to humiliating public examination to see whether they were circumcised or not. Vespasian's tax made it quite clear that it had become imperial policy to penalize all Jews, not just those who lived in Judea. They were a convenient target group. They had been manoeuvred into a position of becoming perpetual enemies of the state, and they remained so in Roman eyes long after Vespasian and his emperor-sons Titus and Domitian were dead.

Three monuments were built in Rome itself to mark the victory of the new Flavian imperial dynasty, all paid for from the looting of Jerusalem. The temple of Peace announced a new era of harmony and housed the vessels from the Jerusalem Temple. The great Colosseum was built with Jewish slave labour. And the Arch of Titus was decorated with scenes of Roman soldiers carrying the menorah through the city.

Back in Judea some might have thought the Triumph a little premature. Some Jewish rebels held out for three more years after the destruction of Jerusalem and tied up a large number of Roman troops in the process. The last stand was at Masada, Herod the Great's extraordinary fortified palace overlooking the Dead Sea and the bleak Judean desert. There in 73–4 just under 1,000 Jews held out against 15,000 Roman soldiers through the winter. By Passover it had become clear that the game was up. Eleazar, the Jewish commander, made a passionate speech to his men offering them a desperate plan. Rather than face the bleak alternatives of crucifixion or slavery at Roman hands they should draw lots and kill each other, he said. When dawn broke the legionaries advanced into an eerily silent fortress. They found no resistance, for the defenders and their families had preferred death to the loss of freedom.

At least, that was the Jewish historian Josephus's account. He was an apologist for Vespasian, to whose side he had defected during the revolt, which he had begun as a rebel commander in Galilee. Josephus had quickly spotted the writing on the wall for the rebels, and claimed to have prophesied Vespasian's rise to power in 67, long before anyone else had dreamed of it. A tame Jewish prophet was a useful addition to Vespasian's entourage and Josephus gratefully fulfilled the role. Part of that role was to rationalize the destruction of the Temple and the Flavian attack on Judaism. This he did by the simple expedient of claiming that God had willed it so. The fire that destroyed the Temple was a providential sign that God had switched his favour from Jerusalem to Rome. Josephus bought wholesale the Flavian propaganda version of, as the historian Suetonius later put it, the 'ancient superstition ... that out of Judaea at this time would come the rulers of the world. This prediction, as the event later proved, referred to a Roman Emperor'.[5] The story of the suicidal defenders of Masada forms the climax to Josephus's narrative of the Jewish rebellion. It perfectly dramatizes Josephus's argument that there was no future hope for an independent Judea and no remaining role for a Temple whose God had fled to Rome.

Others took a different view. Those who cherished nationalist views expected that the Temple would be rebuilt, just as it had been after its previous destruction 600 years earlier. When a temple was destroyed it was normal Roman practice to rebuild it, lest they offend the god of that place. But Jerusalem was an exception and in 132–5 there was a further revolt under Simeon Bar Kokhba which once again established an independent Jewish state and issued coins showing the image of the Temple on them.

The Emperor Hadrian suppressed the Bar Kokhba revolt with a savagery even more brutal than Titus had displayed. The names of Jerusalem and Judea were wiped from the map, as if they had never been. They became respectively a newly built pagan city inhabited solely by gentiles called Aelia Capitolina (after Hadrian's family name, Aelius), and Syria Palaestina (after the Philistines, the ancient tribe dispossessed by the Jews 1,000 years before). Yet still hope did not die. Detailed instructions for service in the Temple were freshly written in the third-century *Mishnah*, and as late as the mid fourth century there was a genuine attempt by the anti-Christian Emperor Julian to rebuild the Temple, though it ultimately came to nothing.

Most Jews, however, recognized after 70 that the Temple had gone for good. This might have meant, as the Roman emperors seemed to wish, the end of Jewish identity and culture altogether. But, just as the faith had proved resilient and flexible in the face of disaster centuries before, so now there were those who had resources at hand for a radical rethinking of what it meant to be a Jew.

Prominent among these were the Pharisees. Their stress on the Scriptures, alongside the growth during the first century of synagogues and schools within villages and towns, offered a way of practising Jewish faith that could survive the loss of the Temple. Their approach had always been a flexible one in contrast to the conservative Sadducees, who seem to have vanished after 70. The Sadducees' views were so inextricably linked with the priesthood and the ritual of the Temple that there was simply no role for them in a Temple-less future. The Pharisees later claimed that Vespasian himself had sanctioned the setting-up of a school at Yavneh (sometimes known as Jamnia) by Rabbi Yohanan ben Zakkai. To him was ascribed the saying that whereas the world had been held in being by the Temple, the Law and faithful works of love, now only the latter two were necessary. In fact a slow process of redefinition took place lasting, according to one estimate, 'five centuries ... of disaster and deterioration'.[6] It culminated in the development of rabbinic Judaism and the *Talmud*, in which 'prayer service and study replaced the ritual of the Temple',[7] though the form of the service was often an imaginative description of what had once taken place in Jerusalem.

In many ways post-Temple rabbinic Judaism was a new faith, markedly different from its parent though of course umbilically linked to it. It had a younger sibling too, also new yet vitally linked to Second Temple Judaism. This was Christianity, a fourth option to put next to Josephus's Roman one, the continuation of nationalist hopes and the Pharisees' radical rethinking. Matthew's Gospel is the best example we have of this fourth option.

Christian and Jewish?

In the early days of the church in Jerusalem all the followers of Jesus were Jews first and Christians second. They were simply another sect (though a small one) among the many which included Sadducees, Pharisees and Essenes.

The expansion of the Church among the gentiles, spearheaded by Paul, led to new questions about the role of the Law. The conference at Jerusalem in 49 made a landmark decision that gentiles who became Christians were not bound to keep the whole Law (see Acts 15.23–29). Christians who had been born Jews, however, like James the brother of Jesus, continued to observe the Law as they had always done and to worship in the Temple when they could, while also offering private devotions to Jesus. Yet they also remembered Jesus' predictions that the Temple would one day be destroyed and 'every stone laid upon another will be thrown down' (Mark 13.2; Matt. 24.2), a prediction which most probably led to his death (see Mark 14.55–63; Matt. 26.59–66).

The Christians were therefore perhaps not so surprised when Jerusalem was put to the torch. Like the Pharisees, they had theological resources to hand which would enable their faith to survive the destruction of the Temple, indeed to thrive as a result. Many may have expected that the Roman attack on Jerusalem would usher in the last days, when Jesus would return from the heavens. But when this did not happen they were able to incorporate the end of the Temple and the sacrificial system into their theology with little effort. The awaited return of Jesus would just take a little longer than anticipated. These beliefs alone would probably have been enough to lead to the voluntary or forced removal of Christians from the synagogues, reflected in Matthew's Gospel.

Into this setting, perhaps in the baggage of a traveller from Rome to Antioch, dropped a copy of the Gospel of Mark. Here was a document which told the story of Jesus concisely but with un-put-downable excitement. But it was written for a gentile audience and did not address the questions of those who wrestled with the destruction of the Temple. So someone – we do not know who it was, but it seems unlikely to have been the apostle Matthew, about whom we know nothing beyond fleeting glimpses in the Gospels – set out to write a 'new edition of the Gospel of Mark that answered the questions with which he was now confronted.'[8]

One obvious change to make was the alteration of 'Kingdom of God' to 'Kingdom of Heaven', since no devout Jew would easily read a book which used the sacred name of God so cavalierly.

As the author sharpened his pen he reflected on the main themes which he needed to draw out. Jesus must be shown to be greater than the greatest figures of Jewish faith, Moses and David, and worthy of worship as God's son. How could he take the skeleton of Mark's Gospel and put new flesh upon it?

The Gospels of Mark and Matthew – which came first?

Why do we think that the arrival of Mark's Gospel was the spur to the writing of Matthew's? Couldn't Matthew's Gospel have been written first?

The two Gospels share broadly the same structure and also have a great deal of material in common. For this reason they, and the Gospel of Luke which also shares much of the same material, are known as the 'synoptic Gospels'. About 80% of Mark's Gospel appears in Matthew's, forming 55% of the contents of the latter. The similarity between the two is often word-for-word in the original Greek, so close as to be clear even in translation. Obviously, then, there is a strong relationship between them.

It is, of course, logically possible that Mark's Gospel was based on Matthew's, and was an abridged version. This view (often known as the 'Griesbach hypothesis') has probably been the majority view through the history of the Church. But very few scholars hold it today. 'Markan priority', that is that Mark's Gospel came first, is widely accepted for the following reasons:

- *Matthew often cuts down what Mark wrote* even though his Gospel is longer overall. The story of the feeding of the 5,000, for example, is much shorter in Matthew's Gospel (Matt. 14.14–21, Mark 6.34–44; for another example see Mark 2.1–12 and Matt. 9.1–8). It's normal for a later version to be tidier and shorter than an earlier one.
- *Matthew prefers smoother links between sentences and uses past tenses* where Mark has a rather breathless and rough style. Mark likes to begin sentences with 'And' and to write in the present tense (this is not always obvious in English translations which remove some of the roughness). So the sudden 'And a leper comes to him ...' in Mark is given a context in Matthew and put in the past: 'Coming down from the mountain, many crowds followed him and behold there was a leper coming towards him who knelt before him' (Mark 1.40; Matt. 8.2). Again, it is unlikely that the smoother version would have come first and been made more jerky and rough.

- *Matthew often amplifies difficult or enigmatic sayings of Jesus* where Mark leaves them unexplained: Matthew expands Jesus' prohibition on divorce, for example, by adding the crucial words 'except for unfaithfulness' (Mark 10.11; Matt. 19.9). It is unlikely that a later version would make a passage more confusing, therefore Mark's Gospel probably comes first.
- *Matthew removes potentially embarrassing details* about the human nature of Jesus. Three examples of absence are: in conflict with the Pharisees Jesus heals a man apparently because he is angry with his opponents (Mark 3.4–5; Matt.12.12–13); Jesus' family want to restrain Jesus because they fear that he is mad (Mark 3.7–22; Matt. 12.15–24); and when a woman reaches out to Jesus and is healed, Jesus asks who touched him (Mark 5.25–34; Matt. 9.20–2). It's highly unlikely that a later writer would have wanted to make Jesus out to be more emotional, mad or ignorant.
- *Matthew is sometimes inconsistent* in his revisions of Mark. This has been called 'editorial fatigue'[9] by Mark Goodacre. For instance, in the account of the death of John the Baptist, when Mark calls Herod Antipas 'king' Matthew revises this to the correct term of 'tetrarch' at the beginning of the story, but lapses into following Mark by calling Herod 'king' later in the same passage (Mark 6.14, 26; Matt. 14.1, 9). This would be unlikely to have happened if Matthew's Gospel came first and Mark's second.

All this internal evidence strongly suggests that Mark's much shorter Gospel came first and was a source for Matthew's.

Adding to Mark's Gospel

Matthew often cuts down Mark's descriptions of events for reasons of both economy and theology. But he also often expands his source in three different ways. First and most obviously he adds a lot of new material which is completely independent of Mark's Gospel, most of it in the form of teaching such as the Sermon on the Mount (Matt. 5—7), and also a lengthy family tree and details about Jesus' birth and early childhood (Matt. 1—2). Second, Matthew sometimes adds quotations from the Hebrew Scriptures to the passages that he has copied from Mark's Gospel to underline the point that, in Jesus, ancient prophecies have been fulfilled (see, for example, Matt. 4.12–17 and Mark 1.14–15; Matt. 8.16–17 and Mark 1.32–4). Third, Matthew makes some telling short additions to Mark's text. The most obvious example is when Peter first articulates his belief that Jesus is the messiah (Mark 8.29). According to Matthew, Peter also recognizes that Jesus is 'the son of the living God'. Then Matthew adds a new section where Jesus blesses Peter and gives him a new name and role (Matt. 16.16–19). Where did all this material which Matthew added to Mark's Gospel come from?

Although it seems pretty certain that Matthew used Mark's Gospel as his main source, it is intriguing that 'All the early Christian writers who expressed an opinion, from the late second century onwards, pronounced in favour of the priority of Matthew.'[10] Not only that, but they also suggested that Matthew was originally written in Hebrew. This is a real puzzle, since Mark's Gospel is in Greek and Matthew's often uses exactly the same words. It seems obvious that Matthew's Gospel as we know it cannot have been written in Hebrew.

One argument that explains why this opinion was held so strongly is that in the early Church a Gospel bearing the name of an apostle, as Matthew's does, would have greater prestige than one which did not. Hence, argues Mark Goodacre, 'Matthaean Priority was a reflex of the (for them) related fact that Matthew was directly apostolic, whereas Mark and Luke were only indirectly apostolic.'[11] But this view is undercut by the fact that John's Gospel was almost unanimously placed last on the grounds that it was written last. If the apostolic-prestige argument were correct, then John's Gospel would have come first or second (there are a few rare examples of John's Gospel being placed second in the order, but the earliest traditions did not do so).

Papias, the bishop of Hierapolis in Asia Minor who lived from around 60 to 130, said that 'Matthew wrote the sayings (*logia*) in the Hebrew language, and every one interpreted them as he was able'.[12] Some argue that he meant 'in a Hebrew (rhetorical) style' not 'in the Hebrew language',[13] implying that Matthew's book was not actually written in Hebrew, but rather in a Hebrew rabbinical teaching style. Compared with Mark's Gospel this is certainly true and in the context of Papias's whole discussion of the Gospels (not just Matthew) he is perhaps comparing the style rather than the language of Matthew with Mark. But this is not the obvious meaning of what Papias wrote.

There is in fact another example from the first century of a book which was apparently written first in Hebrew but in its existing Greek form shows no sign of its ancestry. Josephus begins his book *The Jewish War* by saying that he 'decided to translate into Greek the books I wrote a while ago in my own tongue and sent among the upper barbarians in the East.'[14] The *War* as it stands shows no signs of a Hebrew first edition. If Josephus had not volunteered the information no one would suspect that this was the case. He also notes that this version was for the 'upper barbarians', that is to say, the Parthians, Babylonians and the Jews of the eastern Diaspora, for whom Hebrew or Aramaic was the common language. This preliminary version of the *War* may have been very different from the final one. Tessa Rajak considers that it may have been 'in the nature of a plain report'[15] unlike the later polished Greek text.

This example from Josephus suggests that it is possible that the sayings which Papias mentions might not correspond to the Gospel as we now have it and could have been written in Hebrew or Aramaic. In the early second century the traditions about Jesus were still in a fluid state (see the suggestion that there were many more stories about Jesus still in circulation, John 20.30; 21.25). So much so that, though Papias knew at least the Gospels of Mark and Matthew and probably the now lost *Gospel of the Hebrews*, he also preserved five further books of Jesus' sayings because he preferred the 'living voice'[16] of eyewitnesses, a few of whom were still alive.

Papias said that others 'interpreted' or 'translated' Matthew's material, so maybe what he meant was that original sayings material from Matthew the apostle was taken up by other, later hands and worked into the shape of the Gospel as we know it, also incorporating Mark's Gospel along the way. Could it possibly be the case that the apostle Matthew stands behind this Gospel?

The apostle Matthew and the Gospel of Matthew – is there a connection?

This Gospel was linked with Matthew, one of the 12 disciples, also known as Levi and identified as a tax-collector (Mark 2.14; Matt. 9.9; 10.3), from very early on in the second century. We know nothing of Matthew outside the Gospels. But the Gospel could just have a connection with him.

First of all there seems no reason why it should have been linked with Matthew, rather than one of the more prominent disciples, unless it had some kind of link with him. Second, recent research suggests that, alongside the existence of a significant body of oral material about Jesus, it is quite likely that there were some simple early written records of his sayings too. Tax-collectors were among the relatively few who had to be able to write, and Alan Millard says that 'To imagine some of them opening note-books they carried for their day-to-day business ... and jotting down a few of the striking sayings they had heard ... is quite feasible'[17]. Third, since tax-collectors had to be able to order and keep track of complex accounts and records in a way that would have been beyond the previous experience of fishermen, for example, it may be that Matthew's role within the group of disciples was to keep some sort of record of Jesus' prophetic words just as Judas's task was to manage the common purse, which the group kept (John 12.6). A similar role had been performed for the prophet Jeremiah by Baruch, who wrote down his master's words (see Jer. 36.4).

These pieces of circumstantial evidence suggest that it is not beyond the bounds of possibility that some of the material in Matthew's Gospel could go back to the disciple after whom the Gospel is named. This is not to say that Matthew the tax-collector wrote the Gospel as we now have it, but simply to suggest that the sources behind it might go back to the apostolic circle, as the early Church believed. The early Church might therefore have considered Matthew's the oldest of the Gospels because some of the material in it was the most primitive – maybe stretching back to the band of disciples themselves.

Treasures new and old – what were Matthew's sources?

Matthew probably thought that Mark's Gospel was good as far as it went. Traditionally it was identified with Peter's memories of Jesus, and whether this is true or not it does read as if it is the testimony of one person. By contrast Matthew, based probably in Antioch and reasonably close to both the people and places which Jesus had known, was surrounded by lots of information. He seems to have had access not just to individual witnesses of the life of Jesus, but to a whole reservoir of communal memory about him. The trouble with Mark's Gospel, from Matthew's point of view, was that it didn't go far enough. There was so much more to say, and Matthew seems to have had the resources to hand to say it.

Four things stood out as gaps in Mark's Gospel, three specific and one general. It began abruptly, ended on a cliff-hanger and, though it portrayed Jesus as a great teacher, it actually related almost nothing of what he taught. And it did not really make much of Jesus' Jewish background or the Scriptures which the Church had been quick to believe that Jesus fulfilled. Matthew's job was to fill these gaps. We can sum up the task which Matthew set himself quite simply: to 'fix' his predecessor's Gospel by adding new material and to show his fellow Jews how Jesus Christ was good news for them in the new circumstances following the destruction of the Temple.

A substantial part of the material which Matthew added to Mark's Gospel consists of sayings of Jesus. Some of this material is shared with Luke's Gospel and scholars have reasoned that perhaps Luke and Matthew each had independent access to a collection of Jesus' sayings now lost to us. This collection has been called Q. (Q is referenced by using chapter and verse numbers from Luke, so 'Q.6.41–2' = Luke 6.41–2 and Matt. 7.3–5.)

Q is short for *Quelle*, the German word for source or wellspring. The idea was first proposed in the 1830s and given its name by Johannes Weiss in 1890. It is a theory which has come to be widely accepted. It makes sense to consider some of the questions which surround Q when we discuss Luke's Gospel, so we shall reserve the main discussion of it until then. But it is clear that Matthew did have access to sayings of Jesus which either Mark did not know or chose not to use. Indeed C. F. D. Moule suggests that perhaps what 'Papias meant by *logia* sayings ... is something like what critical scholarship has labelled "Q" – a collection, or a group of collections, of sayings of Jesus'.[18] How far back did this collection (or collections) go, and what might its origins have been?

When the *Gospel of Thomas* came to light in 1945 at Nag Hammadi in Egypt it gave the theory of Q a new lease of life. *Thomas* was a collection of Jesus' sayings in exactly the form (though differing in content) which scholars imagined Q to have had. It consists simply of 114 sayings without any sign of a narrative of Jesus' death and resurrection attached.

Some scholars have built on this example and reconstructed Q, its implied theology and the community which, it is believed, gave rise to it. It's important not to get too carried away with Q. It is a hypothetical document, no copies of it exist and it has to be reconstructed entirely from the Gospels of Matthew and Luke. Therefore it should have some pretty strong historical health warnings around it. Nevertheless some features of Q seem clear.

It appears to have come from among the villages of Galilee. Two features in particular point to this. The imagery of the Q sayings is predominantly rural and agricultural: trees, grain-baskets, grass and milling, for example, all feature (Q. 6.43–4; 11.33; 12.28; 17.2, 35; Matt. 7.17–18; 5.15; 6.30; 18.6; 24.41). There also seems to be a level of distrust about towns in general and Jerusalem in particular. The latter is mentioned only as a place of temptation where prophets meet their deaths (Q. 13.34–5; Matt. 23.37–9).

Q also seems to have been a collection that had grown without any deliberate structure. Although there are 'some patterns through catchword connections, thematic groupings, and elaborated themes, the whole reveals no sustained sequential coherence ... Put simply, Q lacks a literary design'.[19] Of course, this might be because we do not have it in its entirety; but it does seem likely that Q represents a mass of raw material. Some of the groups of sayings have a prophetic flavour to them (John the Baptist's eschatological teaching has an important role, see Q. 3.7–9, 16b–17; Matt. 3.7–12), others are much more clearly wisdom pronouncements (for example, Q. 12.22b–31; Matt. 6.25–33). A few sayings, such as the one about the need for labourers in the harvest (Q. 10.2; Matt.9.37) suggest, according to James Dunn, 'elements given an enduring shape already in the pre-Easter context of Jesus'[20] and point to an early origin.

Was Q a written source? The verbal agreements between the Gospels of Matthew and Luke have suggested this for a long time, but more recently this idea has come under attack. Dunn points out that the extent of that agreement is often limited, but that the variations are 'inconsequential', begging the question why 'the second author should have bothered to change the text of the first'.[21] He argues that the differences make more sense if the sayings were passed on orally and that they are 'just the sort of variations one would expect from story tellers painting a vivid picture for a spell-bound audience'.[22] Dunn may be overstating his case. In a first-century society of limited literacy in which papyrus, scrolls and books were a scarce resource, oral and written records co-existed and interacted with each other. Once material was written down it did not therefore cease to circulate orally and in societies which are not dependent on books memorization was an important skill. The Emperor Hadrian, for example, was able to 'recite from memory books that he had just read'.[23]

Matthew facilitated memorization by the way he arranged his material. He felt at liberty, for example, to rearrange the sequence of miracles in Mark's Gospel and to combine them with other miracle stories to form a block rather than being scattered through the story. These miracle stories are then told in groups of three:

- a leper, a centurion's servant, Peter's mother-in-law (Matt. 8.2–15);
- a storm, some demons, a paralysed man (Matt. 8.23—9.8);
- a daughter, two blind men, a dumb man (Matt. 9.18–34).

Between these triplets come sayings of Jesus which put the miracles into context. Throughout the rest of the Gospel we also find patterns of threes. For example:

- three temptations and three quotations (Matt. 4.1–11);
- three actions: almsgiving, prayer and fasting (Matt. 6.1–18);
- three symbolic actions: entry to Jerusalem, cleansing the temple, cursing the fig tree (Matt. 21.1–19);
- three prayers and three returns to the disciples (Matt. 26.36–46).

These easily remembered patterns were a means of passing on what he had received.

The scribe whose task it was to preserve the tradition in a written form had a vital role. But scribes were not solely required to transmit what they had received. At times they had an important creative role for, as Samuel Byrskog says, 'even the ancient scribes, who were among the most literate in their society, can be seen as performers, not merely copyists of written texts, being deeply influenced by the oral culture in which they lived'.[24] They were responsible for the safeguarding traditions but also for organizing the material into easily memorized sections and incorporating new elements within it. Within the constraints of the normal length of a scroll they had to make judicious decisions about what could be included and what could not.

Matthew's Gospel contains within it a portrait of just such a scribe who, 'having become a disciple of the Kingdom of heaven is like the master of a house who brings out of his treasure what is new and what is old' (Matt. 13.52). It is important to catch the sense here that the scribe was, as Matthew has been described, 'more tradent than theologian, more exegete and commentator than innovator ... concerned above all to pass on the traditions ... he had received'.[25] Matthew seems to have been primarily a teacher, who had to decide how to structure the material he had before him in such a way that the traditions he received would remain alive in the memories of his pupils.

Matthew's Gospel also contains a fair amount of unique material. Some of this may be his development of a particular episode, but a good deal of it seems to have come from another source. The most obvious examples of this are the family tree and birth stories with which Matthew begins the Gospel, and which are quite different from Luke's versions. There are also ten parables, many sayings and a few details of the passion story as well as Jesus' farewell to his disciples at the end of the Gospel, which only Matthew includes. This material could have derived from Q as well, but we don't know whether it did, because Luke did not use it. But it looks likely that Matthew was able to supplement what he had received from Mark's Gospel and Q with other sources, perhaps both written and oral ones.

So as he began to write his own version of the story of Jesus, Matthew had in front of him a complex set of sources: a copy of Mark's Gospel; a written collection of sayings which might partly have had its origins with the disciples of Jesus; well-known sayings of Jesus which he had memorized; and several scrolls of the Jewish Scriptures, or at least a collection of quotations from them which he believed foretold events in Jesus' life. Perhaps there were other people around him, for writing was rarely an isolated occupation in the ancient world and, since there were no desks and scrolls were hard to keep open, the sheer physical difficulty of the task would have been too much for one person.

Perhaps if Matthew were writing his Gospel today, with twenty-first-century technology available to him, he might have been a web-page designer. Key words on a web page can be highlighted and hyperlinked to further pages of explanation and pictures which expand and explain more fully what you have just read or seen. Matthew's Gospel similarly is filled with references to things which are 'off-stage': he weaves complex patterns of numbers, leaves clues to other events and makes quotations from and allusions to the Hebrew Scriptures. This can make it a complicated book to read, and a web version would make it easier to understand. But Matthew did not have the wonders of the web at his command. Instead he had to combine the variety of material which he had into a single scroll and leave the readers to do the work. How did he do this?

The structure of Matthew's Gospel

Clearly Matthew thought the basic plot and order of Mark's Gospel were good things. He didn't really tamper with either of them. Instead he made frequent small corrections, tidying up Mark's notoriously colloquial Greek and removing odd things which he didn't think were appropriate (such as Jesus' angry response to the Pharisees, Matt.12.12–13; Mark 3.4–5).

He did spot that Mark's apparently unordered and fast-moving Gospel fell into five major narrative sections, and that the central episode occurs when Jesus' true identity is revealed. Jesus is recognized by Peter as the messiah and shortly afterwards is transfigured and seen with two of the great heroes of Judaism, Elijah and Moses (Mark 8.27—9.8; you can imagine Matthew shaking his head as he corrects Mark's order to Moses and Elijah, Matt. 16.13—17.8). Into this structure Matthew then added seven major sections of his own. The result looks like Figure 3, with Matthew's additions unshaded and in italics (N and D stand for Narrative and Discourse).

It's almost a cut-and-paste job.

As Davies and Allison point out, 'The primary structure of the Gospel is, then, narrative (N) + discourse (D) + narrative (N) + discourse (D) etc., and the plot is determined by the major theme of each narrative section and discourse.'[26] The additions generally supplement and draw out the meaning of the narrative blocks which Matthew has taken over from Mark's Gospel.

Five books

Back in 1918, B. W. Bacon noticed that if you discount the first and last of Matthew's additional sections you end up with five major teaching discourses, each of which ends with the formula phrase, 'And when Jesus had finished ...' (Matt. 7.28–9; 11.1; 13.53; 19.1; 26.1–2). The first of these discourses is given from a mountain top (Matt. 5.1). You don't have to be a genius to spot the parallel here. For Jews, the great teacher was Moses, who left behind five books and received the Law on Mount Sinai. Therefore, said Bacon, the structure of Matthew's Gospel presented Jesus as the new Moses, bringing a new Law. He went on to propose that each of Jesus' teaching discourses was designed to parallel the Pentateuch, from Genesis to Deuteronomy.

Bacon's thesis was certainly provocative, but it hasn't commanded conviction. It takes a good deal of special pleading to see any connection between the themes of the five discourses and the five books of Moses. And why is five so special anyway? After all, Mark's Gospel can be divided into five sections, as in Figure 3, and no one thinks that it therefore is echoing the first five books of the Bible.

Nevertheless, Bacon was on to something important. His legacy has been to help us to see that 'By giving such prominence to the five discourses, the evangelist stresses the continuing importance of the teaching of Jesus for his own day.'[27] They are at the heart of the portrait of Jesus which Matthew had received from his own sources independently of

Mark's Gospel. But Bacon has rightly been criticized for failing to take account of the two other sections which Matthew added to Mark's structure, the genealogy and birth stories of Jesus, and his resurrection appearances. Since seven was a particularly significant number for Jews, representing wholeness and perfection, it may be that Matthew felt that the addition of seven sections made Mark's Gospel complete.

Gospel of Mark	Gospel of Matthew
	The Ancestry and Birth of Jesus (1—2)
The Prologue (1)	The Prologue (3—4) N
	Teaching about Discipleship (5—7) D
The Kingdom in Galilee (2—7)	The Kingdom in Galilee (8—9) N
	Teaching about Mission (10) D
	The Kingdom in Galilee continued (11—12) N
	Teaching about the Kingdom (13) D
	The Kingdom in Galilee continued (14—15) N
Turning Point—Jesus revealed (8—9)	Turning Point – Jesus revealed (16—17) N
The Kingdom in Jerusalem (10—15)	*Teaching about the Community (18) D*
	The Kingdom in Jerusalem (19—23) N
	Teaching about the End-times (24—25) D
	The Kingdom in Jerusalem continued (26—27) N
The Epilogue (16)	The Epilogue (28.1–8) N
	Resurrection appearances (28.9–20) N

Figure 3 The structure of Matthew's Gospel

The opening of the Gospel

Finding the right opening to any book is a hard task. A great deal hangs on it. It must capture attention and draw the reader in to the story. In the ancient world, the first few sentences of a book were doubly important since they functioned as the equivalent of the eye-catching cover and the publisher's 'blurb', as well as the introduction to what followed.

Matthew's opening is puzzling to us. He begins with Jesus' family tree, a catalogue of names. It's hardly the most scintillating way in.

But Matthew knows what he is up to. His opening section, which functions as a setting for Mark's narrative which he will join up with presently, is like a diptych which offers two different views of the same thing. The genealogy will show how Jesus fulfils the hope of Israel. The story of the wise men will show how he does the same for gentiles.

Genealogy and ambiguity

Most contemporary readers skip the first 17 verses of Matthew's Gospel and cut to the chase, beginning with verse 18: 'Now the birth of Jesus was like this ...' But the family tree that Matthew gives us is full of the kind of clues which readers will later learn to pick up in the rest of the Gospel.

English has a very rich and wide vocabulary, which makes it a more precise language than most others. New Testament Greek had a much more limited range of words available to a writer, but this also offered a skilled writer greater opportunities for teasing ambiguity.

What this means in practice is that where, in English, you generally have to choose a word that expresses a single meaning, in Greek the equivalent word may have several meanings. Matthew was a master of ambiguity and exploited the fact that words cannot always be tied down. The opening of his Gospel is a case in point, and English versions do not serve us very well. Three regularly used versions of the opening words of the Gospel are as follows:

- A record of the genealogy of Jesus Christ (NIV);
- An account of the genealogy (or birth) of Jesus the messiah (NRSV);
- This is the list of the ancestors of Jesus Christ (Good News Bible).

There's nothing wrong with these translations, and they make sense in the light of what follows. The NRSV hints that there may be more at stake by noting that 'genealogy' could be rendered 'birth'. But none of them is able to capture the rich ambiguity of what Matthew wrote in four Greek words: *Biblos geneseos Jesou Christou*. Even if you don't know Greek at all, you can probably spot that the second word is very like 'genesis', meaning beginnings or origin. It is also, of course, the name given to the first book of the Hebrew Bible. Matthew's phrase could easily be translated: 'The book of Genesis of Jesus Christ'.

To a Jewish reader these four words would open a whole range of meanings. The same phrase is used in the Greek version of the book of Genesis, which was current in the first century. So when Matthew uses it, it conjures up associations with the creation of the world (Gen. 2.4) implying that Jesus' birth was like the creation of a new world. But it also reminds an attentive reader who knows Genesis of the family tree of Adam (Gen. 5.1).

In that case, and more generally in such genealogies, it was the first person who gave their name to the family tree. Here Matthew names the tree after Jesus, the last person in it. The effect of this surprising reversal is to make Jesus into the goal towards which all his ancestors were heading, the fulfilment of all the hopes of the Hebrew Scriptures.

Matthew seems intentionally to exploit the ambiguity available to him. The function of this ambiguity is not to confuse but to make the reader or hearer think. For the apparently dry section at the beginning of the Gospel is actually also a tightly woven pattern of clues and allusions to who Jesus is.

At the end of the genealogy Matthew sums up, drawing attention to three marker points in the story of Israel: Abraham, David and the exile in Babylon (Matt. 1.17). Each has significance. Beginning with Abraham signifies that this is a Jewish story, to be understood within the framework of God's dealings with the people of Israel. Yet it is also a reminder that the fundamental promise given to Abraham was that 'through your descendants all the nations of the world shall be blessed' (Gen. 22.18). Israel was chosen to bring salvation to the world.

The second marker, David, was the defining king of Israel, and a 'righteous branch' or *nezer* who might be a second David was looked for in first-century Palestine and this word may lie behind the name Nazarene for Syrian Christians. Seeing Jesus as the Davidic messiah was especially important within Christian Jewish circles but not so significant in the gentile churches of the west. Once again, the genealogy affirms links with Jewish tradition.

The third marker point is unexpected: the exile to Babylon. This cataclysmic event in 586 BC had been seen by the prophets as God's punishment on his people for their sins. It had been followed by a later return to Judea and the rebuilding of the Temple. Yet few of the promises of a restored Israel had become reality. Six hundred years on, the Temple lay once again in ruins and foreign rulers dominated the land. By choosing the exile as a marker here, Matthew implies that the whole sorry period between the exile and Jesus had been preparation for the arrival of the saviour, the providential work of God. And if that was the case, how should the present ruin of the Temple be seen? Clearly, yet mysteriously, as God's work too. Here was hope for Jews still reeling from the cataclysm of 70. Josephus was wrong: God had not transferred his favour to Rome. Instead he had provided a saviour, yet one whom, sadly, the heirs of Abraham had spurned. Matthew's Gospel would be an attempt to help them see where it had all gone wrong and that Jesus was truly the one who would 'save his people from their sins' (Matt. 1.21).

Matthew's summing up of the genealogy is not done yet, though. As well as the three markers he makes another point. He writes (I have attempted to keep some of Matthew's word order so we can see the effect he wants to achieve):

> so there were from Abraham to David generations fourteen;
> from David to the exile in Babylon generations fourteen;
> and from the exile in Babylon until the Christ generations fourteen (Matt. 1.17).

The refrain 'generations fourteen' is unmistakable. What is its significance?

First of all, it is noticeable that Matthew has his sums wrong! The first set of names contains 14 generations only if David is counted there as well as in the second set, and the third set of names contains only 13 generations. Why this is so is hard to say. But Matthew must be up to something because to make the scheme work he has actually cut out several kings (so Josiah was actually the *grand*father of Jechoniah, Matt. 1.11). Why does Matthew stress fourteen? Fourteen in itself was not a special number, but it was twice seven, the Jewish sacred Sabbath number. Three fourteens thus breaks down into six sevens, meaning (rather neatly) that Jesus is the beginning of the seventh set of seven. But Jesus is not the fourteenth of the third set. He is the thirteenth. The most compelling explanation of this is that Matthew was setting up the expectation of a further 'generation' of Jesus when he would usher in the end of the third set of generations and inaugurate the restoration of Israel, but Davies and Allison note that 'Discrepancies between stated totals and actual totals are not uncommon in biblical and extra-biblical literature'.[28] The significance rather than the accuracy of the number is what matters.

There is a further significance to the number fourteen, however. Hebrew was written without vowels, so David was spelt DVD. In ancient languages, the letters of the alphabet each had a numerical value so DVD = 4 + 6 + 4 = 14. Thus the stress on fourteen seems to be a further clue to the importance of Jesus as the descendant of David, but one which could only be understood in Hebrew rather than the Greek in which the Gospel was written, perhaps another hint that a Hebrew or Aramaic source lies behind Matthew's Gospel.

What about the women?

The genealogy of Jesus in Matthew's Gospel contains the names of five women: Tamar, Rahab, Ruth, Bathsheba, Mary (Matt. 1.3, 5, 6, 16). Matthew's is a pretty resolutely masculine Gospel in which women play little part: even in the stories of the birth of Jesus it is Joseph rather than Mary with whom God communicates. So why are these women here? Especially since there are plenty of other women in the story of Israel who might have been mentioned, like Sarah and Rebecca.

There are two clues. The first lies in the description of Bathsheba, mother of Solomon, who is referred to not by name but as 'the wife of Uriah' (Matt. 1.6). Uriah was a Hittite foreigner, and by marrying him Bathsheba disqualified herself from the people of Israel. The other women mentioned are also non-Israelites whom God used in unexpected ways. In other words Matthew draws attention to the way in which God is not bound by his own rules. Within the account of the origins of Jesus, gentiles are present. The second clue lies in the fact that the conceptions of the children born to these women were all, to some extent, scandalous. It is this point which makes a link with Mary, the fifth woman. The circumstances of the birth of her child will seem, outwardly, to be scandalous too. But, like the children of the other mothers in the genealogy, this child also will be the means by which God acts.

Matthew has set a puzzle for those who read or hear his book. Commentators often feel that they have to decide between the options, but it is likely that Matthew has more than one meaning in mind and is seeking to make his readers curious and to engage them in a dialogue. Something as apparently simple and formal as a family tree can hide within its branches many secrets, all of which point to the identity of Jesus. Like the good teacher that he is, Matthew does not serve the meaning up to his readers on a plate. He expects them to work it out for themselves.

Wise men from the east

After setting Jesus clearly in his Jewish context, Matthew tells the story of Jesus' birth (Matt. 1.18–25). But before he reaches the point at which Mark began his Gospel he embarks on a story about wise men from the east who come to visit the infant Jesus (Matt. 2.1–12).

Like the genealogy, this story reads strangely to contemporary western ears, not helped by its retelling in countless nativity plays. Why did Matthew include it, from the mass of material which we may assume was available to him? What purpose did its selection serve?

In Matthew's time many Jews lived to the east of Antioch. There, just as in Judea and Antioch, Jews would have been shocked by what had happened to the Temple. Five hundred years later the Babylonian Talmud would become the pinnacle of rabbinic scholarship, the basis for the medieval renaissance of Judaism and one of the greatest religious achievements in history. But back in the first century Jews of the eastern Diaspora must have been tempted to give up on their faith and adopt the religious practices which flourished around them, especially Zoroastrianism.

The east was home to the great wisdom traditions of the ancient world. The great philosophers of Greece, so admired by the Romans, were latecomers by Mesopotamian standards. There the wisdom tradition stretched back thousands of years, 'a timeless, abstract world' to the Greek and Roman authors who wrote about it 'of astronomical and astrological learning, of "Chaldeans" skilled in discerning the decrees of fate'.[29] Detailed observations of the skies had been kept since *c.*3800 BC. Understanding what was happening in the heavens might give early warning of divine intentions, and enable rulers to take steps to ward off possible evil. Since about 500 BC, sophisticated mathematical methods had been developed to predict the movements of stars and comets: 'Some of these functions are very elegant, and the process of their discovery and integration into consistent arithmetical "theories" represents the first true scientific revolution.'[30] Yet the spread of Hellenistic culture following the conquests of Alexander the Great in the fourth century BC had led by the first century to a decline in traditional wisdom practices. The last text of astronomical observations to survive is from *c.*75. Rome's eastward expansion, of which the destruction of Jerusalem was an important signal, would reach its peak with the Emperor Trajan's conquest of Babylon in 114. Though the Romans withdrew from what is now Iraq under Hadrian shortly afterwards, Trajan's eastern adventure spelled the end of the ancient eastern cultural world.

Matthew's story of wise men from the east makes sense against this background. They journey west because of a star they have observed. Ingenious attempts to identify the star as a supernova or conjunction of planets and thereby to date the year of Jesus' birth largely miss the point of Matthew's story. Heavenly portents were believed to accompany important events in Matthew's world, and at the end of the Gospel there will be darkness when Jesus is on the cross, as the sun itself hides its light (Matt. 27.45). In the star seen by the wise men, 'The testimony of the Scriptures ([Matt.] 2.5) is supported by the testimony of nature.'[31] The best minds of the east, skilled in reading the signs in the heavens, see the significance of Jesus in stark contrast to king Herod (Matt. 2.3–8). Their wisdom leads them to bow down and worship the child, offering him gifts fit for a king (Matt. 2.11).

The wise men are gentiles, the first to appear in Matthew's Gospel. Their gifts may signify the gathering of the gentiles to worship in Zion at the end of time (see Isa. 60.1–6), but more mundanely they represent the most valuable commodities of the east, the basis of its trading wealth. In other words, in this story the wisdom and wealth of the east are laid at Jesus' feet.

Jesus is thus shown to be the fulfilment of both Jewish and (eastern) gentile traditions by the genealogy and the story of the wise men. In an apparently dry recital of names Matthew introduces several themes of central importance to his Gospel. Jesus is presented as the goal towards which Israel has been heading, he is placed as the saviour promised since the exile, and his link with David is emphasized; and the idea that God works through gentiles has been introduced as well.

All of these themes addressed the situation which Jews faced after the destruction of the Temple. But they were all, almost certainly, themes which the church in Jerusalem and the east in general had been developing for several decades. Matthew's Gospel is not a polemic against 'gentile Christianity', but it is a corrective against a reading of Jesus' story that does not clearly locate him as the heir to the promises of Israel and the fulfilment of God's promises to the whole world through his chosen people.

Just as Matthew offered hope to Jews reeling from the events of 70, so he also offers hope to gentiles in the east, fearful of the disintegration of their ancient culture in the face of the onslaught of Rome. Facing the end of ancient certainties, Matthew's Gospel begins with a confident assertion that in Jesus a new king has come who is worthy of the worship of Jew and gentile alike.

A new Moses and a new Law?

Jesus' five discourses in Matthew's Gospel are probably meant to remind the audience of Moses and to draw a comparison between him and Jesus. Jesus is sometimes seen as the 'new Moses' according to Matthew. This is not quite correct.

Matthew named the genealogy with which his Gospel opens after Jesus, its last term, rather than Abraham, its first. In doing so he turned the normal conventions of family trees upside down. Matthew sees the relationship between Jesus and Moses in the same way. So it is not that Jesus follows Moses, as his readers might have expected, rather that Moses prepares the way for Jesus. This is a sign of just how deep Matthew's devotion to Jesus was, for such a view would be deeply offensive to Jews, which may be why it is never stated in so many words.

Some sort of comparison between Jesus and Moses seems to be set up in the first four chapters of the Gospel. As he did with the genealogy, Matthew here seems to leave a trail of clues for discerning readers to work out for themselves. As he tells the story of Jesus, some 'edited highlights' of the early chapters might look like this:

- systematic killing of male children (Matt. 2.16);
- Jesus in the desert, revelation of his role (Matt. 3.13, 16–17);
- Jesus baptized in the water of the Jordan (Matt. 3.13–16);
- Jesus tempted in the desert (Matt. 4.1–11, quoting Deut. 8.3; 6.16, 13);
- Jesus on a mountain, sits down to teach (Matt. 5.1).

Now admittedly these highlights are scattered, but they are rather like 'the pieces of a jigsaw puzzle; and, when they are all put together, a distinct image stares back at us'; yet the image is not 'the face of Moses but rather ... a picture of which he is only a part'.[32] If we look at the story of the book of Exodus, its 'edited highlights' might be rather similar to Matthew's story of Jesus:

- systematic killing of male children (Ex. 1.22);
- Moses in the desert, revelation of his role (Ex. 3.1—4.17);
- Moses and the people pass through the water of the Red Sea (Ex. 14.21–2).
- Moses, on a mountain, receives the Law (Ex. 19.20).
- The people are tempted in the desert (Ex. 32).

Interestingly, the sequence of parallels isn't quite right.

There is another way in which the story of Israel and Matthew's story of Jesus can be read in parallel. This time we can make the following links:

- Jesus goes to Egypt (Matt. 2.13–14): the people of Israel go to Egypt (Gen. 46.1–7).
- Jesus crosses the Jordan (Matt. 3.13): the people of Israel cross the Jordan to the promised land (Joshua 3).
- Jesus goes into the desert and is tempted for 40 days (Matt. 4.1–2); the people of Israel go into the desert and wander for 40 years (Ex. 15—Deut. 34).
- Jesus arrives on a mountain and sits down to teach (Matt. 5.1); Moses receives the Law at Mount Sinai (Ex. 20—3).

Once again the parallels are there, especially if you remember that Matthew began his Gospel with an allusion to Genesis (Matt. 1.1, 18); here Jesus' story is told as a parallel of the story of Israel. But once again they don't occur in quite the right chronological sequence.

This may be because chronological sequences were not as important in the ancient world as they are to us. But it may also be because the inexact parallel teases and intrigues. Matthew probably inherited several of these jigsaw-like puzzles. This kind of exercise, known as typology, sees the foreshadowing of present events in those of the past, and the fact that Paul used a similar technique when he wrote to the Corinthians, making the same equation between the Israelites passing through the Red Sea and baptism (1 Cor. 10.2), suggests that it was common in the early Church. The point is that Matthew manipulates his material in such a way that 'in Matthew's opening chapters we have to do not just with parallel personages (Jesus and Moses) but with parallel plots ... Matt. 1.1—5.2 contains a predictive structure which leads the reader to anticipate ... the revelation of another law'.[33] The inexactness of the parallels leads the reader to reflect on which is the real thing and which the shadow. Matthew's aim is to show, by several possible routes, that the stories of Moses, the Exodus and the people of Israel, all point to Jesus.

Matthew has arranged the discourses symmetrically. Richard Burridge has pointed out that when the length of these five sections is compared they form the pattern shown in Figure 4.[34]

The balance of the teaching sections points to another technique which Matthew likes. This is a kind of bracketing device which scholars call *inclusio*, where a particular phrase encloses sections of a text. The idea of Jesus as Immanuel, 'God with us', for example, occurs at the beginning of the Gospel, as Jesus' birth is announced (Matt. 1.23) and at the end as Jesus says 'I am with you always' as he sends his disciples out into the world (Matt. 28.20), enclosing the whole story and emphasizing its overall theme.

The first discourse – Matthew 5.1—7.29 (The Sermon on the Mount)

By the time we arrive at the first discourse, expectation is running high. This will be no simple restatement of the Law of Moses but will go beyond it (Matt. 5.17). It will be based on Jesus' own authority, signalled clearly by the formula 'You have heard that it was said ... but I say to you' (Matt. 5.21–2, 27–8, 31–2, 38–9, 43–4). The end of Moses' own teaching on a mountain is echoed at the end of Jesus' Sermon on the Mount (Deut. 32.45).

The theme of this first discourse is discipleship. It begins with a series of blessings, which address head-on the question why, if the Christian Church is the vehicle of God's purpose, it seems to be undergoing suffering rather than receiving the blessings that orthodox Jewish theology would have expected. The answer is that blessing is postponed until the end of the present evil age. Without drawing attention to the fact, these beatitudes also function to answer the same question about Jesus. Why, if he was the fulfilment of God's promises to Israel, did he suffer and die on a cross? Matthew's answer is the same: in order that he should be vindicated by God. The form of the blessings leaves 'little doubt that Jesus is remembered as one who spoke in this form',[35] though Matthew may have added four of them from another source (Matt. 5.3–12; Luke 6.20–3 omits Matt. 5.7–10).

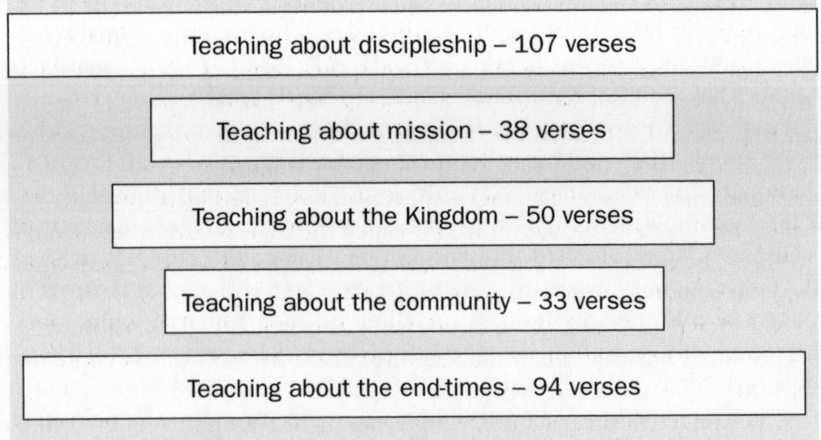

Figure 4 The five discourses of Matthew's Gospel

Jesus goes on to a reinterpretation of various key points of the Law: murder, adultery, divorce, oath-swearing, retaliation and love of enemies (Matt. 5.17–48). The Law is not set aside, but its underlying implications are brought out. The effect is to show that Jesus' ethic is far from being a relaxation of the demands of the Law but is actually more strenuous in many ways. The target is an outward show of religious scruples for the sake of attention. God knows the truth (Matt. 6.1–8).

A pattern prayer is given which again may have been expanded by Matthew (Matt. 6.9–15, see Luke 11.2–4) as well as instructions which assume the continuation of the Jewish practice of fasting (Matt. 6.16–18). These are especially interesting since Jesus was criticized for not fasting (Matt. 9.14), so this instruction may well indicate that the practice of the later Church has been added to Jesus' original teaching. Sayings on a variety of topics (Matt. 6.19—7.12) are followed by warnings about staying on the right track in order to enter the Kingdom of Heaven (Matt. 7.13–27).

The second discourse – Matthew 10.1—11.1

The theme of the second discourse is mission. It begins with Jesus commissioning the disciples, conferring his authority on them to do the same things that he was doing: casting out evil spirits and healing the sick (Matt. 10.1, see 9.35). Such activity clearly situates the mission of the Church in the eschatological context of a battle between good and evil at the end of time. The introductory section where Jesus speaks of the harvest (Matt. 9.37) uses an image that 'is typically a metaphor for the divine judgement' (see Matt. 3.12); therefore it is clear that, for Matthew,

'The mission of the twelve and of the post-Easter church belongs to the latter days.'[36] How then are the 12 disciples, who are now formally listed, to fulfil their role as heralds of God's rule (Matt. 10.2–4, even their number has eschatological significance, see Matt. 19.28)?

First they are to go to Israel alone and not to venture among either the 'nations' (that is, the gentiles) or even the Samaritans (Matt. 10.5–6). Although this was almost certainly Jesus' practice, it is plausible that a later gentile mission may have been in his mind. Here we see part of Matthew's 'spin' on Jesus, presenting him as one who observes most of the conventional Jewish attitudes of his day. So although the Gospels of Luke and John portray Jesus as travelling through Samaria, while Mark has an extensive section which takes place in the gentile area of Decapolis, Matthew carefully sidesteps these potentially tricky issues by not mentioning them at all. This is the only point in the entire Gospel where the Samaritans are mentioned. But Matthew clearly follows the view that God's promise was given to Abraham so that Israel might be the means of salvation for the whole world. As we have seen, however, Matthew seems to have had a strong liking for patterns and order, so he may here simply be reflecting the logical sequence of salvation: to Israel first, then Samaria and finally to the ends of the earth (see Acts 1.8).

By their presence, as they travel across Israel, the disciples are to bring the Kingdom of Heaven with them. They are to travel light, stopping where the Kingdom is welcome, ignoring the places where it is not. They have a dangerous task ahead of them. Just as they share Jesus' task, so they will share the suffering he suffers (Matt. 10.7–23). These trials are clearly seen to be part of the tribulations of the end-times (Matt. 10.22–3).

The good news is that, in the light of the future reign of God, they have nothing to fear. Ultimately God is working out his purpose of salvation and by aligning themselves with that purpose their reward will come, even if it is accompanied by division and present loss (Matt. 10.26—11.1).

In this discourse there seems to be a blurring of time. Jesus is ostensibly speaking to his disciples half a century before, but much of what he says directly addresses the situation for Matthew's own day. Being chased out of 'their synagogues' is not something that happened to his disciples in Jesus' own time, and the language and details of the passage seem designed to remind hearers of Jesus' own handing over and arraignment before governors and kings (Matt. 10.17–18). Ulrich Luz's comment on the Sermon on the Mount applies equally to all the discourses: it 'does not recount an episode from the historical past, like the speech of a grand statesman in a book of ancient history. Instead it is "spoken to the winds", directly addressing present-day readers'.[37] This is entirely appropriate for Matthew, since at the end of the Gospel he portrays Jesus promising his continuous presence with his disciples 'every day till the end of the age' (Matt. 28.20). How can this be, since Matthew and his readers obviously know that Jesus is not physically present any longer? The answer is, through the living voice of his teaching passed on by his faithful servants like Matthew.

The third discourse – Matthew 13.1–53

The third discourse is also the central one. Given Matthew's penchant for patterns, we expect that it will get to the heart of Jesus' message, and we're not disappointed. Its theme is the Kingdom of Heaven.

The two previous discourses have been private teaching delivered to the disciples, but this one is for the 'many crowds' who gathered around him. Unlike the previous discourses it is not filled with direct instructions, but comes in Jesus' characteristic form of parables (Matt. 13.2–3). Also unlike the previous discourses, this one is firmly based on material from Mark's Gospel and is effectively an expansion of the main teaching section of Mark's Gospel (Mark 4.1–33).

To Mark's parables of the Sower and the Mustard Seed, Matthew adds the parables of the Weeds, the Yeast, the Treasure, the Pearl and the Net. He also includes Mark's explanation of the Sower and adds an explanation of the parable of the weeds.

The parable of the Sower and its explanation is the keynote for Matthew as it had been for Mark. At its heart lies the question why, if Jesus was the messiah, he had not been recognized as such by the people of Israel and ushered in the last days. The onus for Jesus' rejection is placed back on those to whom his message came (which is why this parable is sometimes referred to as the parable of the soils). The parable of the weeds and its explanation sets this rejection within the context of eschatological conflict.

Though the parables in this discourse seem to be given publicly (Matt. 13.34–5), it is clear that the disciples are Jesus' authorized interpreters who have received the 'secrets of the Kingdom of Heaven' (Matt. 13.11). Jesus explains to them in private what the parables mean. They have received the revelation of God, and their task is to pass on what they have learned. Perhaps for this reason, Matthew removes a brief section on the theme of secrecy (Mark 4.21–9).

This discourse is significant because, alongside its content, Matthew is also able to portray Jesus as a teacher of wisdom. A little earlier in the Gospel, Jesus says 'Take up my yoke upon you and learn from me' (Matt. 11.29), a saying unique to Matthew's Gospel, which is virtually a quotation from Sirach (Sir. 6.19–31). But it is significantly different in one respect, for Sirach spoke of Wisdom and the Law. Jesus speaks of himself where the Wisdom of God and his Law might be expected. This is a huge self-claim to make, underlined by the further saying that 'one greater than Solomon is here' (Matt. 12.42).

The fourth discourse – Matthew 18.1—19.1

The fourth discourse takes place after the great turning point of the Gospel, when Jesus is recognized as the messiah by Peter and shortly afterwards is transfigured (Matt. 16.13—17.8). Matthew has taken this plot hinge from Mark, but adds an important extra dimension to Peter's role, emphasizing that it is on this rock (punning on the meaning of Peter, *Petros,* a rock) that he will build his Church (Matt. 16.17–19). Matthew's is the only Gospel to use the word 'church', though it is commonplace in the writings of Paul and throughout Acts. This suggests that it was not coined until after Jesus' time.

Matthew wants to make it clear that the Church was the intention of Jesus. Peter's change of name may well be a reminder of the change of Abram's name to Abraham, 'the father of many nations' (Gen. 17.5), the founding moment of the people of Israel itself. (Abraham himself is described as the 'rock from which you were hewn', Isa. 51.1–2.) The role of the Church is to be the spearhead of God's attack on the forces of evil (Matt. 16.18–19).

Prior to this episode Jesus has been rejected in his home town and John the Baptist, herald of God's judgement, has been put to death (Matt. 13.54—14.12). Pharisees and scribes from Jerusalem have come to question and test Jesus, and Jesus has characterized their teaching as yeast – something which easily spreads and infects whatever it touches (Matt. 15.1–20; 16.1–11).

This amounts to a sustained rejection of Jesus by the very people who should have welcomed him. The crowd, consisting of the ordinary people, does welcome him and 'they glorified the God of Israel' as a result (Matt. 15.31). The powerful in Israel by contrast do not live up to their vocation and so a vacancy occurs for a new people of God. The Church is created to fill this gap, and it is Peter's perception of Jesus' true identity which opens the way for its foundation (Matt. 16.16–19). On his faith a new community will be founded, as Israel was founded upon the faith of Abraham.

The fourth discourse therefore deals with the issue of life within the Christian community: 'How often should one forgive a brother? What is the procedure for excommunicating someone? These ecclesiastical questions are appropriate precisely at this point because Jesus has just established his church.'[38] In many ways this discourse develops ideas present in the first, showing what it might mean to apply the Law in a way that takes seriously the commandment to do good to those who oppose you and to love your neighbour as you love yourself (Matt. 5.44; 22.39). The emphasis of the whole discourse is on the kindness of God, exemplified by the place of children, who were a largely disposable commodity in the ancient world. Yet since God cares for the weak and humble, children have a special place in his new community (Matt. 18.1–10). A clear procedure for reconciliation is offered (Matt. 18.15–17). Even when forgiveness seems to make no sense at all, it is still to be practised (Matt. 18.23–35), in this new community which God has established.

The fifth discourse – Matthew 24.3—26.1

By the time Matthew's story is interrupted by the fifth discourse, Jesus has reached Jerusalem and the shadow of death has begun to loom over him. Mark offers the only discourse in his Gospel at this point (Mark 13), and its punctuation of the action may have been what gave Matthew the idea of introducing a similar device earlier in the story's flow. This is a long section, equivalent in size to the opening Sermon on the Mount.

The discourse opens in front of the Temple, with Jesus' prediction that it will one day be destroyed (Matt. 24.1–3). This will be a sign that the end of the age is near, but 'AD 70 does not exhaust the significance of ... eschatological events still to come.'[39] There is more in store, and the scheme underlying the wars, persecutions, sacrilege, tribulations and coming of the Son of Man (Matt. 24.6–31) is based on the prophet Daniel (Matt. 24.15, see Daniel 7—12).

So far, so similar to Mark's Gospel. Matthew adds a strong element of judgement by including a series of parables: the Thief in the Night, the Faithful and Unfaithful Slaves, the Bridesmaids, the Talents, the Sheep and the Goats (Matt. 24.42—25.46). The last of these gives a full-dress vision of the Son of Man in his glory sitting in judgement on the nations. Yet the basis of his judgement is simple action, such as feeding the hungry, welcoming strangers, clothing the destitute, caring for the sick and visiting those in prison. Amidst the cosmic apocalyptic battle going on all around, disciples of Jesus are, against all odds, to keep on showing their faith through everyday acts of kindness and love (Matt. 25.31–46).

Teaching is not enough

The material which Matthew used to extend Mark's Gospel may well, as we saw earlier, have been older than Mark's Gospel itself. Q and the other pre-Gospel sources are impossible for us to recover except from the snippets which were preserved in the Gospels as we now have them. Therefore we should be wary of drawing any firm conclusions about these sources. Nevertheless it has been obvious to scholars since the Q hypothesis was first proposed that none of the material which Matthew includes about the death of Jesus seems to have come from Q. Therefore, some have argued, perhaps the earliest form of a Gospel consisted solely of an account of Jesus' teaching. And in fact, when the *Gospel of Thomas* came to light it was exactly such an account.

A few scholars regard *Thomas* as equal in status to the four canonical Gospels, but most recognize that though it is 'a valuable collection of

114 sayings of Jesus, many of which may reflect the historical teachings of Jesus', these sayings 'appear to be framed within the context of later Gnostic reflections'. The message it contains is significantly different from the four canonical Gospels, for 'this was a Gospel ... concerned about salvation but that did not consider Jesus' death and resurrection to be significant for it, a Gospel that understood salvation to come through ... correctly interpreting the secret sayings of Jesus.'[40] Could Q have shared a similar theology? It might have done. But we have no evidence of any form of Christianity which ignored the death and resurrection of Jesus and saw his sayings as the means of salvation until the second-century Gnostics. So it seems unlikely that Matthew's source of sayings rejected the idea that Jesus' death was the basis for salvation. It may simply have been a source of sayings – and the story of Jesus' death and resurrection was independent from it.

Certainly it is clear that Matthew shared Mark's theological views on the matter. He added substantial teaching content to Mark's Gospel, but he did it in such a way as not to change substantially either the structure or the message of the story of Jesus which Mark had told.

The death of Jesus is crucially significant in Matthew's Gospel, but because Matthew added predominantly teaching material to Mark's Gospel, Jesus' passion does receive proportionally less space in his Gospel: a reduction from 40% of the Gospel to 25%. Matthew left out very little of Mark's crucifixion narrative, however, and added some elements to it. It is only because of the additions that he made earlier in the Gospel that it seems as if the death of Jesus is less important for Matthew. Matthew's Gospel includes a number of details in the passion narrative which underscore the cosmic significance of Jesus' death, especially the extraordinary eschatological resurrection scene that takes place in the middle of the passion (Matt. 27.51–3), which we shall examine in more detail at the end of chapter 5.

If Matthew did receive a set of Jesus' sayings without an account of his death and resurrection it does not look as if he would have considered them enough. His Gospel is a fusion of teaching material with the traditions about Jesus which affirmed the central significance of the cross and empty tomb as the basis of Christian belief. It seems to have been very clear in Matthew's mind that, in Jesus, God had not merely spoken but also acted.

Perhaps it is not surprising, then, that this Gospel also strongly emphasizes the importance of actions, not just words. In the parable of the Sheep and the Goats, it is on the evidence of actions not words that judgement is given, for example (Matt. 25.31–46, see also 7.21). The teaching of Jesus elucidates his actions, and informs the actions of his disciples. But on their own the sayings are not enough for salvation.

New and old

In an influential phrase Graham Stanton speaks of Matthew's Gospel as 'A Gospel for a New People'.[41] It is both an exposition of the Jewish roots of Christianity and also a manifesto for a new kind of Judaism altogether.

It is important to remember that in the aftermath of the Temple's destruction, several groups were jostling to be seen as the future of Jewish faith. Of these groups the synagogues, strongly influenced by the Pharisees, and the churches were to become the most significant. But in the decades after 70 they could both claim to be the legitimate heirs of Second Temple Judaism. James Burtchaell sums up the situation like this: 'The synagogue and the church were two innovative rivals who simultaneously and energetically framed their biblical canon and interpretation, moral code and liturgical usages, in attentive conflict with one another, in a definitive season of self-definition for both peoples.'[42] Matthew's Gospel is best read and understood within this setting.

The challenge for Matthew was thus to perform a delicate balancing act, reassuring devout Jews on the one hand that Jesus had not abandoned the Law, as some of the more extreme versions of gentile Christianity seem to have done, and yet on the other not watering down the confession of Jesus as Lord and Son of God, the focus of Christian worship from the beginning. It's an act he performed remarkably well, and it accounts for one curious feature of his Gospel: that it is simultaneously the most Jewish and the most anti-Jewish of the Gospels (though John's runs it close on the latter score).

Matthew reserves some of his strongest and most vitriolic language for the denunciation of the scribes and Pharisees (Matt. 23.15–36). The parables told just before that passage emphasize beyond doubt his view that the Jews had rejected Jesus (Matt. 21.33—22.14). And it is notoriously only Matthew who records the cry of the 'whole people' of Jerusalem in front of Pilate, baying for Jesus' death with the words 'His blood be upon us and upon our children' (Matt. 27.25). We shall look at whether the Gospels offer the basis for the shameful Christian record of anti-Semitism when we consider John's Gospel in a later chapter. But it should be clear that Matthew himself would not have condoned the violence and persecution that subsequently became such a stain on the history of the Church. Perhaps the passages against the Jews are best read as a form of prophetic oracle, like Amos, Jeremiah and the early parts of Isaiah: 'even though God's judgment is inexorable, these judgment oracles never mark the absolute end of the people, or of God's dealing with them. Always on the horizon is the word of promise and the hope of restoration.'[43] Matthew's own Jewish identity, strongly reflected in the Gospel, must have fuelled the intensity of his denunciations, and made him deeply concerned for the future of the people of Israel. He could not have conceived of a Christian faith cut loose from its Jewish moorings, a view which the Church in general a century later continued to uphold in the face of Marcion's attempt to consign the Old Testament to the rubbish bin of history.

More than any of the other Gospels, Matthew's attempts to give a handbook of instruction for the new people of God. It provides 'a set of authoritative traditions to be set alongside the law and the prophets', and though 'Matthew does not use the phrase "the law of Christ" ... he would not have been unhappy with this term.'[44] To gentiles Matthew urges that, since Jesus followed in Moses' footsteps, if they ignore Moses they ignore Jesus too. To Jews who wanted to know why Christians held the beliefs they did, Matthew tried to show that in Jesus one greater than Moses had come.

Spotlight on the beginnings of the Gospels

One of the most obvious features of Mark's Gospel that seemed to require 'fixing' by Matthew was the absence of any narrative of Jesus' birth. Krister Stendahl once suggested that the two questions about Jesus which Matthew was answering were: who was he and where was he from? Stendahl drew attention to the fact that the drastic differences between the approaches Luke and Matthew took in answering these questions 'should warn against treating Matt. 1—2 and Luke 1—2 as alternative birth narratives.'[45] Traditionally the two sets of birth stories have been harmonized to tell a single story. But it is often the differences between the Gospels which are the most illuminating feature of them. How do each of the four Gospels answer these questions?

Mark is in a hurry. It looks as if who Jesus was and where he came from are not questions in which he is much interested at this stage in his Gospel. He cuts quickly to John the Baptist by the Jordan (Mark 1.4), and before long Jesus begins his mission in Galilee (Mark 1.14). There are no preliminaries here such as we find in the other three Gospels.

Mark's whole Gospel will be a journey during which Jesus' identity is gradually unveiled, culminating in the final recognition that 'Truly, this man was the Son of God' (Mark 15.39) spoken, perhaps ironically, by a Roman centurion beneath the cross.

What Mark does give, through the Gospel, is clues to Jesus' identity. And the first couple of verses function rather like this. First Mark tells his audience that this is the beginning of 'the good news of Jesus Christ'. He may not have written 'the Son of God', which is missing from some of the earliest manuscripts of Mark's Gospel. It may have been effectively the title of the book, in which case 'the Son of God' fits well. After all, if this is the opening line then it rather gives the game away about who Jesus is! As Morna Hooker observes, 'reading the rest of the Gospel is rather like reading a detective story when someone has told you how it ends.' However, Jesus' identity is revealed several times in the early part of the Gospel (for example, Mark 1.11, 24). What Mark actually does in the introductory part of the Gospel (Mark 1.1–13) is to reveal 'the secret of Jesus' identity, so that in the pages that follow we may appreciate the significance of events which are misunderstood by almost all the characters in the drama'.[46] So perhaps Mark is answering the questions of who Jesus was and where he came from after all.

The second and third verses of the Gospel apparently quote from the prophet Isaiah; in fact Mark has combined three quotations here (see Ex. 23.20; Mal. 3.1; Isa. 40.3), but all of them point not to Jesus but to John the Baptist. It is the briefest of pointers to the Hebrew Scriptures, but places John as Jesus' forerunner with extraordinary economy before moving swiftly on. In a single sentence Mark establishes what John's Gospel will elaborate over a whole paragraph (John 1.6–15).

Overall Mark doesn't worry too much about information at this stage in his Gospel. His audience is invited to hear the clues, follow the journey and see whether, by the end, they too can echo the identification of Jesus as the Son of God.

For Matthew, Mark's opening was clearly not enough. He wanted a good deal more background on Jesus. We have already looked in some detail at the structure and content of the opening which Matthew added to Mark's Gospel, so we will not spend long on Matthew's account here. The first two chapters of the Gospel focus on the origins of Jesus in such a way as to anticipate questions that might have been raised about Jesus. If the early Christians said that Jesus was the messiah, the Son of God, as Mark suggested, then there were some obvious ripostes, interestingly summed up in John's Gospel: 'Some said, this man is the messiah, others said "But surely the messiah doesn't come from Galilee? Doesn't the scripture say that the messiah comes from the line of David and from Bethlehem, the town of David?"' (John 7.41–2). Stendahl pointed out that chapter 1 focuses on personal names and chapter 2 on geographical ones. Thus chapter 1 establishes that Jesus is indeed of the line of David and how he came by his name (Matt. 1.25), and chapter 2 explains how he came to be known as 'the Nazarene' (Matt. 2.23).[47]

Matthew's concern is to weave the story of Jesus into a longer and deeper story than Mark's quick-fire account allowed. By establishing how 'Jesus of Nazareth' could be the messiah, Matthew answers the obvious objections and can proceed with Mark's story of the baptism of Jesus (Matt. 3.1ff). But these objections would have been largely Jewish ones. In the wider world other questions remained to be answered.

There are differences between Matthew's and Luke's accounts of the birth of Jesus because they have different ways of answering the question, 'Who was Jesus and where was he from?' Where Matthew focuses on Jesus, Luke begins the story with the birth of John the Baptist. Why does he do this?

Mark too started with John: we saw above that Mark's brief compiled quotation from the Old Testament was about John the Baptist rather than Jesus. So Luke simply follows Mark's lead, but at much greater length in this approach.

Where Matthew likes to spell out the ways in which the story of Jesus fulfils the ancient Scriptures (see for example Matt.1.22–3; 2.15), Luke takes a more allusive approach. So Mary's song of praise at the news that she will bear a child strongly echoes Hannah's prayer when she hears that she is to give birth to Samuel (Luke 1.46–55; 1 Sam. 2.1–10) but the connection is not made explicit by Luke. This is characteristic of Luke's Gospel, which does not presuppose knowledge of the Jewish background to the story of Jesus as Matthew's does. For those who wish to follow up the clues left by Luke it is possible to do so; but if the audience is unaware of the details it does not hamper the telling of the story. Instead Luke has a different answer in mind to the questions 'Who and where from?'

Alone among the four Gospel writers, Luke gives a setting for the story of Jesus in the history of the world. This is done for the story of Jesus' adult life and ministry (Luke 3.1), but Luke has already offered a similar marker for the birth of Jesus: 'And it happened in those days that a decree was sent out from Caesar Augustus that all the world should be registered ...' (Luke 2.1). The question of whether Luke was confused about this decree will be examined in chapter 7; too much of a focus on it has tended to obscure what Luke was trying to say here, and the contrast he appears to draw between Jesus and Augustus.

Augustus was hailed by the Roman poet Virgil as the saviour of the Roman world, who brought peace and prosperity. Inscriptions set up in public places across the Roman world proclaimed the 'good news' of Augustus's rule. It is against this background that Luke too tells a story of good news of a saviour who brings peace (Luke 2.10–14). This is who Jesus is for Luke: the true saviour who brings genuine peace.

Yet this message is revealed not to the good and the great but to the poor and humble; Mary, a young woman from Galilee and some shepherds from the fields around Bethlehem. The saviour of the world himself is laid in a manger, the feeding trough for animals, among the simple people of his nation. In the story that follows, Luke more than any of the other Gospel writers will stress the impact of Jesus on the poor and humble who are close to the heart of God.

But why would a saviour of the world come from a Jewish background? Luke carefully locates the opening scene of the Gospel in the Jerusalem Temple (Luke 1.5ff), but the genealogy of Jesus is traced right back to Adam (Luke 3.23–38), offering a universal frame to the story. The implication is that God had intended the salvation of the world to come from the Jews, but that it should reach out to the whole world, as in fact Luke will show. The final scene of the Gospel and Acts is set in Rome itself with Paul preaching to the gentiles (Acts 28.17–31); the whole two-volume work might have been subtitled 'How we brought the Good News from Jerusalem to Rome'.

The prologue to John's Gospel widens the scope even further in answering the questions 'Who and where from?' John starts with 'the Word' (*logos*), a multilayered idea, which is hard to pin down, referring at least to Jewish Wisdom, a personified agent of God, and also the Stoic philosophical school's concept of the divine principle of natural order in creation. Certainly John's opening phrase, 'In the beginning ...' sends the reader back to the opening of the book of Genesis. The whole of creation is in view here.

And the Word is the underlying principle of the creation. Who was Jesus? In fact from this passage it is clear that, for John, he is nothing less than God himself even if the precise relationship eludes definitive explanation (John 1.1). Once again John the Baptist figures significantly (John 1.6–8, 15), but his role is more clearly subordinate when seen in the elongated perspective which John offers.

John answers the questions about Jesus quite simply: Who is he? God. Where does he come from? God. As Andrew Lincoln notes, 'it might well be claimed that most of the Christological affirmations of an ecumenical confession, such as the Nicene Creed, are already implicit in the prologue read within the Gospel as a whole.'[48] The rest of the Gospel shows the working out behind John's identification of Jesus.

Draw your own conclusions

- Describe the situation for which you think Matthew's Gospel was written. How effectively do you think Matthew addresses the concerns of the post-Temple period?
- What is the relationship between the Gospels of Matthew and Mark? Could Matthew's be the older, and if so in what sense?
- What do you think Matthew believed was the right way to understand the relationship between Moses and Jesus? How would an orthodox Jew of the late first century have answered the same question?
- Did Matthew intend there to be a 'new people' of the Christians?
- Why are the beginnings of the Gospels so different?

Further reading

Commentaries

W. D. Davies and D. C. Allison (2004), *Matthew: a shorter commentary*, London: T.&T. Clark, is a thorough survey. R. T. France (1985), *Matthew*, Grand Rapids: Eerdmans, and D. Harrington (1991), *The Gospel of Matthew*, Collegeville: Liturgical Press, are both excellent popular commentaries.

Other books

U. Luz (1995), *The Theology of the Gospel of Matthew*, Cambridge: Cambridge University Press, is a stimulating read, full of insights based on Luz's magisterial three-volume commentary. W. Carter (2004), *Matthew: storyteller, interpreter, evangelist*, 2nd ed., Peabody: Hendrickson, deftly weaves together historical and literary approaches, building on W. Carter (2000), *Matthew and the Margins: a religious and socio-political reading*, Maryknoll: Orbis.

Two more specialized studies which have proved influential are J. D. Kingsbury (1988), *Matthew as Story*, 2nd ed., Minneapolis: Fortress and G. N. Stanton (1992), *A Gospel for a New People*, Edinburgh: T.&T. Clark. The latter is a profound study focusing especially on the Jewish–Christian tensions in the Gospel.

On the openings to the Gospels, see M. D. Hooker (1997), *Beginnings: keys that unlock the Gospels*, London: SCM Press, a brilliant short reading of the prologues to all four Gospels. E. D. Freed (2001), *The Stories of Jesus' Birth: a critical introduction*, Sheffield: Sheffield Academic Press, and R. E. Brown (1993), *The Birth of the Messiah*, 2nd ed., New York: Doubleday, both concentrate on the Gospels of Matthew and Luke. R. E. Brown (1988), *A Coming Christ at Advent* and (1978), *An Adult Christ at Christmas*, Collegeville: Liturgical Press are each very short commentaries on the first two chapters of the Gospels of Matthew and Luke.

Websites

- The 'Matthean Studies Home Page' is at www.class.uidaho.edu/jcanders/Matthew/gospel_of_matthew.htm, and the 'Text this Week' links for Matthew's Gospel can be found at www.textweek.com/mtlk/matthew.htm.
- The 'International Q Project' has the reconstructed text of Q at www.chass.utoronto.ca/~kloppen/iqpqet.htm. General resources on Q can be found at www.ntgateway.com/synoptic-problem-and-q/q-web-materials/.

Notes

1 S. Goldhill (2006), *The Temple of Jerusalem*, London: Profile, p. 80.

2 U. Luz (1995), *The Theology of the Gospel of Matthew*, tr. J. Bradford Robinson, Cambridge: Cambridge University Press, p. 18.

3 Quoted in C. Kondoleon (2000), *Antioch, the Lost Ancient City*, Princeton: Princeton University Press, p. 11.

4 M. Goodman (2007), *Rome and Jerusalem*, London: Penguin, p. 453.

5 Suetonius *Vespasian* 3 (tr. Graves).

6 N. Cantor (1996), *The Sacred Chain: a history of the Jews*, London: HarperCollins, p. 79.

7 Goldhill, *The Temple of Jerusalem*, p. 95.

8 Luz, *Theology of the Gospel of Matthew*, p. 19.

9 M. Goodacre (2001), *The Synoptic Problem: a way through the maze*, London: Sheffield Academic Press, p. 71.

10 Goodacre, *The Synoptic Problem*, p. 76.

11 Goodacre, *The Synoptic Problem*, p. 80.

12 Eusebius, *History of the Church* 3.39.

13 R. H. Gundry (1994), *Matthew: a commentary on his handbook for a mixed church under persecution*, 2nd ed., Grand Rapids: Eerdmans, pp. 619–20.

14 Josephus, *Jewish War* 1.3.

15 T. Rajak (2002), *Josephus: the historian and his society*, 2nd ed., London: Duckworth, p. 176.

16 Eusebius, *History of the Church* 3.39.

17 A. Millard (2000), *Reading and Writing in the Time of Jesus*, Sheffield: Sheffield Academic Press, p. 223.

18 C. F. D. Moule (1981), *The Birth of the New Testament*, 3rd ed., London: A.&C. Black, p. 105.

19 J. Reed (2000), *Archaeology and the Galilean Jesus*, Harrisburg: TPI, p.180.

20 J. D. G. Dunn (2005), 'Q1 as oral tradition' in M. Bockmuehl and D. A. Hagner (eds), *The Written Gospel*, Cambridge: Cambridge University Press, p. 56.

21 Dunn, 'Q1 as oral tradition', p.49.

22 Dunn, 'Q1 as oral tradition', p.52.

23 D. Danziger & N. Purcell (2005), *Hadrian's Empire*, London: Hodder, p.15.

24 S. Byrskog (2000), *Story as History, History as Story: the gospel tradition in the context of ancient oral history*, Tübingen: Mohr Siebeck, p.140.

25 W. D. Davies and D. C. Allison (2004), *Matthew: a shorter commentary*, London: T.&T. Clark, p. xxv.

26 Davies and Allison, *Matthew: a shorter commentary*, p. xxiv.

27 G. N. Stanton (1989), *The Gospels and Jesus*, Oxford, Oxford University Press, p. 60.

28 Davies and Allison, *Matthew: a shorter commentary*, p. 10.

29 F. Millar (1993), *The Roman Near East 31BC – AD337*, Cambridge, MA: Harvard University Press, p. 495.

30 J. Britton and C. Walker (1996), 'Astronomy and Astrology in Mesopotamia' in C. Walker (ed.), *Astronomy before the Telescope*, London: British Museum, p. 52.

31 Davies and Allison, *Matthew: a shorter commentary*, p. 22.

32 D. C. Allison (1993), *The New Moses: a Matthean Typology*, Edinburgh: T.&T. Clark, p. 195.

33 Allison, *The New Moses*, pp. 195–6.

34 R. A. Burridge (1994), *Four Gospels, One Jesus?*, London: SPCK, p. 78.

35 J. D. G. Dunn (2003), *Jesus Remembered*, Grand Rapids: Eerdmans, p. 412.

36 Davies and Allison, *Matthew: a shorter commentary*, p. 146.

37 Luz, *Theology of the Gospel of Matthew*, p. 44.

38 Davies and Allison, *Matthew: a shorter commentary*, p. xxiv.

39 Davies and Allison, *Matthew: a shorter commentary*, p. 417.

40 B. D. Ehrman (2003), *Lost Christianities*, New York: Oxford University Press, pp. 64, 58.

41 G. N. Stanton (1992), *A Gospel for a New People: studies in Matthew*, Edinburgh: T.&T. Clark.

42 J. T. Burtchaell (1992), *From Church to Synagogue*, Cambridge: Cambridge University Press, p.280.

43 R. Hays (1997), *The Moral Vision of the New Testament*, Edinburgh: T.&T. Clark, pp. 433–4.

44 G. N. Stanton (2003), 'The Law of Christ: a neglected theological gem?' in D. F. Ford and G. N. Stanton (eds), *Reading Texts, Seeking Wisdom*, London: SCM Press, p. 175.

45 K. Stendahl (1960), '*Quis et Unde?* An Analysis of Matthew 1–2' in G. Stanton (ed.) (1983), *The Interpretation of Matthew*, London: SPCK, p. 57.

46 M. D. Hooker (1983), *The Message of Mark*, London: Epworth, pp. 6, 5.

47 Stendahl, '*Quis et Unde*?', p. 60.

48 A. T. Lincoln (2005), *The Gospel According to St John*, London: Continuum, p. 98.

4

Peter – from Galilee to Rome

Rome, summer 64

In the heated late July of 64, a great fire broke out in Rome. For a week and a half it raged through the streets. When at last it died down and the smoke which had hung over the city began to disperse, the Emperor Nero and his advisers saw that three districts were totally destroyed and seven more badly affected. Only four had escaped damage. It was well known that Nero had wanted to rebuild Rome on a fittingly imperial scale, and now he took the opportunity to place an enormous Golden House as his palace in the centre of the city, set within pleasure gardens through which roamed wild animals. The Golden House was dominated by a bronze statue of Nero that was 120 feet high.

The ashes were scarcely cold before gossip began to suggest that the fire had been started on Nero's orders. He looked for scapegoats to blame and found a group called Christians, who mostly lived in the districts which the fire had not touched. They were rounded up and many were burned alive to provide torches to illuminate the gladiatorial games which Nero put on to ingratiate himself with the people of Rome.

Peter was one of the victims, according to the early traditions of the Church. And deep beneath the Vatican lies a tomb which, from at least the third century, was identified as Peter's. Prayers were scribbled on the walls from early on, and the tomb was considered to be a link with the very earliest followers of Jesus. If the traditions connected with James and Matthew which we have looked at in the last two chapters provide a window on to the strongly Jewish basis of early Christianity, the stories which cluster around Peter take us to Rome in the 60s from Galilee in the 20s and 30s.

Peter's life

Peter's death must have sent a shock wave through the early Church and it is worth spending a few moments thinking how his obituary might have been put together when the Church across the Mediterranean heard the news. His death marked the beginning of the end of an era when the stories of what Jesus did and said were told by those who had been with him at the time.

Peter was born at Bethsaida on the north-eastern shore of lake Galilee, but he later had a house and fishing business in Capernaum, three miles or so to the west. He was attracted by the renewal movement of John the Baptist in Judea, and it was probably there that he met Jesus, whose disciple he later became. Jesus gave him the nickname Peter, the Greek form of the Aramaic *Cephas,* both of which mean 'rock'. It was by this name that Peter became known, so much so that his real name, Simon, virtually faded from view.

He travelled with Jesus, became part of his closest circle and entered Jerusalem with him. But, despite his bravado, Peter denied that he was Jesus' follower. After Jesus' death Peter claimed to be one of the first witnesses of the resurrection. After Pentecost he became spokesman for the movement in Jerusalem and later seems to have had a roving commission among the Christian communities which had sprung up across Judea and Galilee and to have had some role in the church in Antioch. Although he may have been the first among the apostles to accept gentiles as equal members of the Church, Peter later appears to have wavered over the question of whether it was necessary for converts to embrace Judaism.

After the conference of apostles in Jerusalem in 49, which seems to have agreed that gentiles did not have to be circumcised in order to belong to the Church, Peter's ministry is much harder to follow. The later chapters of Acts follow Paul, while we know almost nothing of Peter. He may have continued to be active in the church in Antioch, and Paul mentions a party identified with Peter in the Corinthian church, which suggests that Peter was in Corinth at some point. A letter apparently from Peter is addressed to those in Pontus, Galatia, Cappadocia, Asia and Bithynia, the provinces of Asia Minor (1 Peter 1.1), but that is all the evidence there is of Peter's activity among the churches there. The letter also suggests that the writer is in 'Babylon', well-known early Christian code for Rome (1 Peter 5.13).

These seem to have been the facts. But how do we explain the extraordinary story of how a fisherman from Galilee ended up dying a martyr's death in Rome 40 years later?

Galilee, Greek and garum

The family of Jesus and James had names that reflected the nationalistic past of Israel. Peter and his brother Andrew had names that reflected a different background. Peter's birth name, Simon, was a common name derived from Simeon. Unlike the family of Jesus and James, who were probably first-generation settlers from Judea, it is likely that Peter's family had been in Galilee for a long time. Peter's father was called Jonah, after the local hero who was the only Hebrew prophet to come from the area. But Peter's brother had a Greek name, Andrew (*Andreas*). The disciple Philip also had a Greek name and was, like Peter and Andrew, a native of Bethsaida (John 1.44). It seems that both Philip and Andrew were Greek speakers (John 12.20–2). This makes it unlikely that they shared the pious nationalistic background of Jesus and James, where speaking Aramaic rather than Greek was a matter of fierce pride. All this suggests that Peter's family had deep roots in Galilee and were less concerned about nationalism and the integrity of Israel.

Peter's native Bethsaida and his later home, Capernaum, were only three or four miles apart on the north-west shore of Lake Galilee. They were separated by the River Jordan, and for most of Peter's life this meant that they were under different rulers.

The will of Herod the Great in 4 BC had divided his kingdom after his death between his sons, and this meant that Philip received lands on the north-eastern quarter of the Galilee lake shore, while Herod Antipas inherited all of the western shore. Philip's subjects were a mixture of Greeks, Syro-Phoenicians and Jews; Antipas's were entirely Jewish. The River Jordan formed the boundary between the territory of the two brothers. We do not know why Peter and his brother moved from Bethsaida to Capernaum, but a plausible suggestion is that by doing so they would be able to pursue all of their business under the one ruler, Antipas, and thus avoid paying extra tolls.

The division of northern Galilee had the effect of raising the status of Capernaum, which became an important customs post between the territories of Philip and Antipas. This may have been why a centurion lived there, though he was probably retired from military service and had become the enforcer of toll collection (Matt. 8.5; Luke 7.30). There was also a regular tax-collector, Levi (Mark 2.14; Luke 5.27). Capernaum's population in the first century was between 600 and 1500 people, making it one of the larger villages in the area, but it was still materially quite poor.[1] There is no evidence of mosaics or marble in Capernaum, sure signs of wealthy inhabitants.

Antipas had a clear strategy in his rule of Galilee: to make it as Roman as possible. The flagships of this enterprise were the two cities he built: at Sepphoris, close to Nazareth, which he named *Auctocratoris* in honour of Augustus; and at Tiberias, named after Augustus's successor Tiberius, overlooking the lake. Antipas himself was more Roman than Jewish. His role, and that of many other similar rulers, seems to have been as a 'tool of imperial policy, ruling "backward" areas, "civilizing" them (for instance, by encouraging the growth of cities and towns in the areas they ruled) and preparing them for full incorporation into the Empire'. When a territory finally became part of the Empire, therefore, this 'was a sign of its success rather than an indication that its ruler had been incompetent'.[2] The early imperial era was thus an exciting one for those who, like Antipas, had a high enough economic status to exploit the new opportunities it offered.

The development of the whole Mediterranean basin as a unified market made the development of trade from areas like Galilee possible for the first time. Antipas took full advantage of the new conditions. Galilee was naturally blessed with water virtually all year, making the hill-country fertile in grain which was exported throughout the region. But it was the lake, fed primarily by the Jordan but also by many tributaries running down from the hills, which was the jewel in Antipas's economic crown.

Capernaum, according to Josephus, was the site of a fertile spring which enabled perch especially to thrive there. This made the village an integral part of the Galilean fishing industry which was rapidly expanding in the first century. Apart from the Passover lamb, meat is never mentioned in the Gospels. It was fish that formed the protein in most people's diet (see Matt. 7.10; Mark 6.38; John 6.9). Fresh fish could command high prices and it was usually beyond the means of the poor; they ate cheaper dried and salted fish, usually broiled to make it taste better (see Luke 24.42). Lake Galilee was and still is a huge freshwater fish pond, and fish was big business in the first century.

Recent developments in fish-processing techniques had made it possible for fish to become a cash crop for the first time. Fresh fish don't stay fresh for long, so fish had not been a very useful commodity in previous centuries. In the first century BC pickling in salt had become an effective way of preserving fish for a long time: 'The process not only preserves the perishable fish: it uses the parts that would be unpalatable when the fish was fresh, and it makes transportation more efficient by eliminating the weight of water and concentrating the protein.'[3] The saying 'Salt is good' (Mark 9.50; Luke 14.34), was probably a popular phrase around the Galilean lake-shore, for salt had brought prosperity.

The centre of the industry was Tarichea, whose Greek name means simply 'preserving town'. In Aramaic it was called Magdala which means 'tower', a reference to the tall buildings where fish were dried and then salted for export. It was renowned for the smell and grime which hung over it. (Tarichea was the home town of Mary Magdalene.) Capernaum was one among a number of fishing villages which dotted the shores of the Lake.

In a rather bland diet, the ability of pickled fish to tickle the taste buds made it a highly prized asset. Romans had an almost obsessive appetite for a salsa-like relish called *garum* which was made like this:

> Use fatty fish, for example, sardines, and a well-sealed (pitched) container with a 26–35 quart/liter capacity. Add dried aromatic herbs possessing a strong flavor, such as dill, coriander, fennel, celery, mint, oregano, and others, making a layer on the bottom of the container; then put down a layer of fish (if small, leave them whole, if large use pieces); and over this add a layer of salt two fingers high. Repeat these

layers until the container is filled. Let it rest for seven days in the sun. Then mix the sauce daily for twenty days. After that it becomes a liquid (*garum*).[4]

(It tastes rather like Worcester sauce, with the consistency of Marmite!)

Pliny commented loftily on the link between fish and luxurious living: in his view 'shellfish are the prime cause of the decline of morals and the adoption of an extravagant life-style'.[5] Breeding and eating fish had become a craze in Rome and spread across the Empire as a means of adopting Roman identity. There was much money to be made from the insatiable demand for seafood.

In the Mediterranean itself stocks of fish are relatively low, and the closed season for sailing during the winter meant that fishing boats sat idle on the beach for several months each year. Lake Galilee's advantage was that fishing was possible in every season and so production did not have to stop when the winter came. There was a local market to satisfy (kosher *garum* was a speciality), but some of the jars of *garum* and preserved fish produced in Galilee were for export, generally in Asia Minor or Greece, but in some cases as far away as Rome itself. Galilean *garum* was not top quality but it was always available. This was the fishing industry in which Peter was a key worker. Thanks to a historic low water level in 1986, it is possible to see the remains of the kind of fishing boat with which the surface of the lake teemed in Peter's time.

The 'Jesus Boat'

Held in a steel cradle, the dark timbers are still unmistakably a boat after all these years. Kept in darkness and carefully lit for visitors at the Yigal Allon Centre in Galilee the boat is 8 feet wide and 25 feet long consisting of a recycled keel of robust Lebanese cedar and ribs which are mostly of oak. It is big enough to have had a crew of five; four at the oars and one to steer, with room for about 12 passengers or an equivalent cargo.

When the water level of Lake Galilee fell in 1986 the remains of the boat began to protrude from the mud in which it had been buried for centuries. Its wooden construction allowed for pretty accurate carbon-14 dating. This placed the average date at which the timbers were cut at 40 BC, plus or minus 80 years. Archaeologists therefore conclude with some confidence that this was one of the fleet of small fishing boats that shuttled across Lake Galilee in the mid first century. It's exactly the kind of boat that Peter and Andrew, James and John would have used. The complexity of its patchwork carpentry suggests that someone skilled in working with wood was also pretty integral to their fishing enterprise. Perhaps inevitably it has become known as the 'Jesus Boat'.

Cooking pots and a lamp discovered with the boat conjure the image of long, cold nights out on the Lake, with the crew perhaps taking it in turns to snatch a little sleep in the stern on the 'pillow' (Mark 4.38), most likely a sandbag used for ballast.

Fishing on Lake Galilee was until recently done with seine nets. These have small mouths (about the size of a tall man) and then widen in the centre to three times that size. They can be up to 1300 feet long and are designed to catch complete shoals of fish, which is why patience is required even in such a fertile fishing ground as Galilee. It would not be uncommon to wait all night and catch nothing, only to find the early sun on the water bringing a shoal to the surface (see Luke 5.1–9; John 21.1–8). In general such nets were used from shore, the boat taking the mouth out to the deeper water where the fish swam, and waiting there at anchor until the catch was made. Then the shore team would pull in the full net (Matt. 13.47–8). Fishermen would also be highly skilled in interpreting the signs of the weather so that they didn't get caught in the middle of a storm (Matt.16.2–3).

To stand in front of the 'Jesus Boat' today is to feel the tangible presence of first-century Galilee and the bustle of the fishing industry which formed the background to Jesus' ministry, the livelihood of Peter and the prosperity of the region.

Class in Galilee

Fishing may have been a good business to be in during the first century and its exponents may have made a good deal of money. But they were not posh. The Roman orator Cicero, writing in the mid first century BC, considered that 'the least respectable trades are those which pander to the pleasures of the flesh, as Terence [the playwright] says: "Fishmongers, butchers, cooks, chicken-farmers – and fishermen"'.[6] Fishermen were regarded as representative of 'opportunism and poverty, proverbially wild, but [also] a familiar and parasitical accompaniment to all that was best about stylish living'.[7] Apart from anything else, fishermen tended to smell of their catch! Peter and his companions were stereotyped as 'unschooled, ordinary men' (Acts 4.13), but such a description probably just means that they had not had a formal training in the Law as, for example, Paul had.

There are some signs that Peter and Andrew were reasonably well off. They were in partnership with James and John who themselves had 'hired men' (Mark 1.20, Luke 5.7–11). When they went off with Jesus it seems that the business could carry on without them, and they could return to it when they wished. But to characterize Peter as 'middle class' and comfortable, as some do, is wide of the mark. The first-century economy did not work in the same way that the contemporary Western free market does. Society was not structured into upper, middle and working classes.

It was more complex than that and more closely resembled the kind of pattern found today in some African and Latin American countries.

At the bottom of the economic pile were the peasants, who scratched a living from the soil. Though their standard of living was low, nevertheless they owned land, which was inalienable according to Jewish law. Therefore they could expect to be poor but reasonably secure.

At the top of the pile sat the aristocratic landowners, led by the Herodian royal family. Herod the Great had been renowned for at least 68 building projects, which were 'stunning in their size, boldness and complexity'.[8] Herod Antipas continued his father's building mania, but such projects had to be paid for. One means of raising the cash was to increase taxes on those who were economically productive, the middle group between the peasants and the ruling elite.

Antipas raised taxes to pay for his own lifestyle and building projects, but there were additionally the poll tax and the Temple tithe, as well as tributes, tolls and customs duties. Staples like salt, grain, fruit and nuts could be taxed at between a third and a half of their value. Trying to calculate the tax burden of first-century Galilee is an extremely imprecise exercise, ranging from under 20% to over 40% of income. E. P. Sanders's careful reckoning suggests that for a Judean farmer perhaps 28–33% of income went in taxes of one kind or another. Though rightly sceptical of the wilder estimates of heavy taxation, Sanders concludes that 'the people were hard pressed ... The wealthy did not sit down each night and try to devise ways of making the peasantry more comfortable. The populace was a resource to be utilized.'[9] In Galilee we can assume that the burden was even heavier, since the tribute paid directly to Rome by the Judeans (12.5% according to Sanders) would be higher for Galileans in order to allow a substantial cut to go to Antipas. No ruler wanted to provoke his subjects to revolt so they finely balanced the equation between maximum productivity and minimum protest. Antipas seems to have been particularly successful in doing this and managed to maintain a fragile peace throughout his reign (4 BC–AD 39).

In such a system the last people to benefit were those whose hard work had produced the profits. There was no return benefit such as free schooling or healthcare, as there is in taxation systems today: money taken in tax was money lost to the taxpayer. Any economic surplus generated was creamed off by the ruling elite, and 'Architectural grandeur increased at one end of Galilean society by making poverty increase at the other.'[10] Simmering resentment at the way in which hard work gained no reward was a major cause of the rising in Galilee in 66, according to Josephus, showing how skilfully Antipas had kept the lid on any potential unrest during his time. Many people were caught in a debt trap as they attempted to pay all the taxes required of them and still remain afloat financially. (Jesus' parable of the unmerciful servant describes exactly this situation, Matt. 18.23–35.)

Antipas's policy was to enforce the collection of taxes more efficiently than had been done before. Occasionally the people of Galilee expressed a preference for direct rule from Rome, possibly because it would mean that their masters would be further away, their taxes would go direct to Rome, and they would no longer have to pay for the privilege of being ruled by the Herod family.

Peter and Andrew were among a group of people who were neither poor but secure peasants on the one hand, nor rich aristocrats on the other. Fishing was a precarious living with periods of both feast and famine. The tax burden on fishermen seems to have been particularly high because fishermen were at the centre of a very complex web of transactions, and the equipment required to do their job (boats) was expensive.

To keep their boats at sea fishermen needed a lot of skills and commodities which they did not have themselves: sailmakers and weavers were needed to provide sails; farmers to grow flax for making nets; stonemasons to make anchors; carpenters to make the boats themselves and keep them in repair. Each of these suppliers would pay tax on their work and passed the cost on, pushing up the price of what they did for the fishermen. Once the catch was landed, tolls and customs were demanded by the owners of the harbours (usually Antipas again, who had built most of those on the western shore as an investment). Then the catch needed processing and prices for the raw fish were kept low to increase the processors' margins. Beyond them there was the cost of carrying and shipping the fish for export. It is possible that the trip Jesus took with his disciples to Tyre and Sidon, the major Mediterranean ports for the Galilean fishing industry, was to accompany a cargo of dried fish for export to save the cost of paying a carrier (Mark 7.24, 31).

Peter and Andrew and those like them were also liable to have their profits confiscated at the whim of a tax official. So the economic group to which the brothers belonged was not middle class in the conventional sense, but rather caught in the middle of the economic system: landless, carrying a heavy tax burden, and with very little security.

Why does this background matter? The social and economic status of Peter is important for understanding what it might have been that attracted him to become a follower of Jesus. Seeing Peter as 'middle class', comfortably off and living a pleasant and settled life, leaves the impression that he may have sought something intangible and 'spiritual', or that it was Jesus' personal magnetism, or simply the unattractiveness of the hard work of fishing which led him to leave his nets to go and fish for people (Mark 1.17–18). But if Peter was a fisherman insecurely struggling under the burden of Antipas's taxes, who had already left Bethsaida in an attempt to escape the customs net, maybe Jesus' message of the Kingdom of God appealed on a more immediately practical and political level.

So what might the call to become part of the Kingdom of God have sounded like to Peter?

Opposing kingdoms

In the mid 20s a new prophet burst on to the scene in Judea. He emerged from the southern wilderness threatening the imminent judgement of God on Jerusalem. He prophesied the coming of 'the powerful one' (Mark 1.7), a figure who would enact the judgement of which he was the messenger. He called on all who heard him, rich or poor, clean or unclean, to accept a baptism which identified the baptized with turning away from sin towards the righteous rule of God. His message is summed up by Matthew as being 'Repent, for the Kingdom of heaven is near' (Matt. 3.2).

Crowds flocked to John. Among them were Peter's brother Andrew, and Jesus (John 1.35–41). John's Gospel suggests that it was in this setting that Peter first met Jesus and there is not necessarily a conflict between this encounter and the story of Jesus calling his disciples to follow him in a new mission back in Capernaum (Mark 1.16–18). What matters is that John the Baptist's announcement of a Kingdom attracted some Galilean followers and that they later took the message back to their northern home with them.

What would the notion of the Kingdom of God have meant to those who heard it proclaimed in Galilee in the early first century? The Hebrew Scriptures contained a powerful vision of a Kingdom of God, which would have been dynamite to economically struggling people like Peter. The Law prohibited the kind of exploitation which was rife in the Galilee of Jesus' day. In particular it was clear that the people of Israel were forbidden to make loans at interest to the poor (Lev. 25.35–7); that security on a loan should not include taking anything essential to livelihood (Deut. 24.6, 10–13); that debts and slavery bonds should be cancelled every seven years (Deut. 15.1–2, 12–14); and that land was to be restored to its original family owners every fiftieth (Jubilee) year (Lev. 25.10).

These provisions of the Law may have been utopian and never fully practised. However, they gave a clear indication of what God's Kingdom might look like – and it was obvious that it was not like the regime of Antipas, which was dedicated to maximizing profit for the elite, not safeguarding the needs of the most vulnerable. To speak of the Kingdom coming implied the arrival of God's rule of justice and righteousness in very practical economic terms. And this was what Jesus did (Mark 1.15). To someone in Peter's position a kingdom announced in terms of liberation and Jubilee (Luke 4.16–21) might have been enough to make him set off in search of a better world.

It was a dangerous path to take. For it was clear that by joining Jesus, Peter would be joining the opposition to the status quo of Antipas and the Roman power which lay behind his rule.

Peter among the disciples

When I read J. R. R.Tolkien's *Lord of the Rings* as a teenager, there was one character who stood out for me. Aragorn captured my imagination and it was through his eyes that I watched the story of Middle Earth unfold. In the strange hobbit- and elf-filled world Aragorn's humanity shone out and won my sympathy. I hoped that I saw a lot of myself in this sometimes troubled but always chivalrous man. Without him I would have found it very hard to grasp the story, but sympathizing with his character gave me a way to understand it.

The character of Peter in the Gospels is rather the same. He is the most frequently mentioned of Jesus' disciples. His nickname means 'the rock' and it's not hard to imagine him as a very solid, big fisherman. He means well but he often gets things wrong. Readers usually feel a strong affinity with him. He humanizes the story, and we see it unfold through his eyes.

But what is image and what is reality here? The Gospels are literary creations and Peter is a character within them. As Pheme Perkins says, 'His role is primarily functional. Peter provides a personality for the circle of disciples'.[11] Without him the strange story of Jesus would be difficult for us to grasp.

The picture of Peter varies from Gospel to Gospel but his role remains largely the same in all of them. Peter is not the first of the disciples to be called to follow Jesus but he is always mentioned first in lists of the disciples, suggesting that he was in some sense the foremost among them (the call is in Matt. 4.18–22; Mark 1.16–20; Luke 5.1–11; John 1.42; the lists are in Matt. 10.2; Mark 3.16; Luke 6.14). He seems to have been the spokesperson for the group and he has a crucial role in first identifying Jesus as the messiah (Matt. 16.16; Mark 8.29; Luke 9.20). But Peter fails Jesus at the crunch moment: the story of his threefold denial of Jesus is told in the first three Gospels and implied in John's (Matt. 26.69–75; Mark 14.66–72; Luke 22.56–62; John 21.15–17). Peter is also strongly connected with the resurrection appearances of Jesus, except, rather curiously, in Matthew's Gospel (Mark 16.7; Luke 24.34; John 20—1; also 1 Cor. 15.5).

In Mark's Gospel Peter and the other disciples are unable to grasp Jesus' significance and there is often real frustration on Jesus' part at their lack of understanding. Peter is the one who recognizes Jesus' true identity for the first time, yet he also fails to understand what Jesus then says about being a suffering messiah and earns a blistering rebuke (Mark 8.29–33; Matt.16.16–23). In one of his telling additions to Mark, Matthew softens the rebuke by including Jesus' words about Peter being the rock on whom the Church will be built (Matt. 16.17–19). Matthew thus seems to have remembered Peter as a central figure in the Church, stemming from his companionship with Jesus. For Luke, Peter's role among the disciples is less significant; yet he also seems to have become a more respected figure: Jesus' rebuke of him is omitted and his denial of Jesus is not portrayed as an outright one, for example. In Acts, Peter has an important role in the early chapters but his story fades out as Paul's takes centre stage. John implicitly compares him with the 'beloved disciple' who grasps the meaning of Jesus intuitively while Peter plods behind (for example, John 20.1–9). As we saw in chapter 1, Paul speaks of Peter as one of the 'pillars' of the Church, though he may well have been speaking ironically (Gal. 2.9).

The harmony of this portrait across all these different books suggests that, while Peter is drawn as a complex character and has an important function in the narratives as someone with whom readers can identify, underneath the characterization there is the basis of a real person who was close to Jesus. For whatever reason, Peter does not seem to have been a leader of the group of disciples after Jesus' lifetime to any marked degree. But many stories about Jesus which included him were current in the early Church and he was considered to have been the basis for them himself. This is something we shall consider in greater detail in the next chapter when we look the extent to which Mark's Gospel might reflect the reminiscences of Peter.

Witness to the resurrection?

Peter is twice mentioned first among those to whom the resurrected Jesus appeared, even before Jesus' appearance to the disciples as a group (Luke 24.34; 1 Cor 15.5). Yet there is no narrative of a private encounter between him and the risen Jesus in the New Testament. James Dunn wonders whether this 'reticence ... could possibly reflect Peter's own reticence on the subject' and surmises that the conversation between the risen Jesus and Peter at the end of John's Gospel may preserve a memory of it. Perhaps, he writes, 'throughout Peter's life the appearance to Peter was retained as personal testimony and never allowed to become church tradition as such'.[12] Others have claimed that the perhaps lost ending of Mark's Gospel contained the narrative of Peter's encounter with his risen master. In short, Peter's role in the resurrection appearances of Jesus is something of a puzzle, and one that seems beyond resolution. It is a useful reminder of how much we do not know about the world of the New Testament.

Peter and Cephas

Although Peter initially appears in Acts as the central figure in the Jerusalem church at and after Pentecost, the responsibility of leadership seems soon to have been taken on by James the brother of Jesus. This left Peter free to fulfil the command to go out with the good news 'in Jerusalem, and in all Judea and Samaria, and to the ends of the earth' (Acts 1.8). He seems to have had a travelling brief among the congregations throughout Judea (Acts 9.32) and this work may have developed into a more widespread ministry across the scattered population of Jews around the Mediterranean. More Jews lived outside Judea than inside, and the first expansion of Christianity was through the synagogues, perhaps aided by the return of those who had been present in Jerusalem at Pentecost (Acts 2.9–11). There would certainly have been more than enough work for Peter to do among the Diaspora Jews, telling the stories of Jesus.

At some point, perhaps after Barnabas and Paul had set out to take the gospel across Asia Minor, Peter spent some time in the church at Antioch. This is where he and Paul clashed. (The dispute is covered in more detail in chapters 2 and 6.) Peter aroused strong passions in Paul, who refers to him in his letters by the Aramaic name 'Cephas' (with the isolated exception of Galatians 2.7–8). Paul is at pains to establish his own apostolic credentials and to play down any sense of being Peter's 'junior partner'. He says that there was an agreement that Peter should go to the Jews, and Paul to the gentiles, though we have only Paul's word for this (Gal. 2.7–8). In effect such an agreement would have given Peter an apostolic role across the Mediterranean within the congregations of Christian Jews in the 40s and 50s, and certainly something like this itinerant ministry is hinted at by the mention of Peter's wife accompanying him on his travels (1 Cor. 9.5). At this point, with Christianity still a reform movement within Judaism, it might have been useful to Peter to call himself Cephas to emphasize his solidarity with his fellow Jews.

Some scholars continue to follow the pattern of F. C. Baur in seeing Peter and Paul as antagonists representing mutually exclusive versions of Christianity. Though they clearly clashed at Antioch and may have done so again in Corinth, where Peter, Apollos and Paul all had followers (1 Cor. 1.12; 3.22) there is no real evidence of long-term, entrenched animosity. Rather, Paul may have found his (probably older) colleague frustrating. As C. K. Barrett notes, the evidence suggests that Peter 'was easily frightened, and therefore easily influenced and used ... Paul ... could not simply repudiate Peter; yet Peter, in the hands of those who made use of him, was on the way to ruining Paul's work in Corinth'.[13] Paul recognized Peter's pre-eminent place as the first apostolic witness of the resurrection (1 Cor. 15.5) and went to Jerusalem 'to enquire of Cephas' early in his life as a Christian (Gal. 1.18): as C. H. Dodd drily remarked, 'we may presume they did not spend all the time talking about the weather'[14] but that Paul received his detailed knowledge of Jesus' life from this period. The evidence of Galatians shows that Paul recognized the value of Peter's testimony about Jesus, even while disagreeing with him over some crucial issues of interpretation.

Paul's references to Peter are rather guarded. Peter does not seem to have been a particularly deep thinker and was sometimes unaware of issues of principle which Paul, with his razor-sharp intellect, readily spotted. But Peter had been with Jesus and he was able to tell spellbound audiences the good news Jesus had proclaimed in words and actions. Paul lacked Peter's crucial gift of actually having been there with Jesus.

Peter in Rome

Peter's trail goes cold after Acts 12; but there was a very strong tradition from as early as the end of the first century that Peter died in Rome in the persecution that followed the great fire of 64. The church in Rome recognized Peter, if not as its founder, at least as its pre-eminent figure from an early stage. Rome was not disputed as the repository of the apostolic tradition of Peter, and no other church ever claimed to be his final resting place. So we can be pretty certain that the travelling apostle did end up in the chief city of the world.

Rome – the great city

Anyone who has seen the film *Gladiator* will have some idea of the impact of the first sight of Rome on a traveller, even though the film is set some 200 years later than Peter's time. The city was an extraordinary sight as you approached it. It stretched as far as the eye could see, sprawling across its famous seven hills. Once through the streets the newcomer would be dwarfed by great public buildings and blocks of flats called *insulae*, which rose to a dizzying six storeys. And there were people everywhere. In a world of small communities, Rome was a chaotic, crowded and noisy behemoth.

Rome's population had grown in number by perhaps as much as five times in the first century BC. Nothing like it had occurred before, and would not do so again until the Industrial Revolution over 18 centuries later. The strain of such rapid and unplanned expansion quickly began to show.

In the face of a city bursting at the seams, Augustus turned it into a building site. The poet Horace described a typical street scene: 'A builder rushes past, hot and sweating, with his mules and labourers. Stone and wood spin on a giant crane. Mourners vie for their place with hefty carts. Here there's a crazy dog and there a pig wallows in the mud.'[15] By the end of the first century AD around 650,000 people lived in the city itself, a figure which grew to over a million if you included the surrounding towns too. Pliny the elder celebrated the city in an orgy of measurement. There were 265 crossroads, he reported, and 37 gates within walls which were almost 21 miles long. There were over 60 miles of streets, and 'if the height of the buildings were also added then it would be a fair estimate to make that the magnitude of no city in the entire world could be compared to it.'[16] Rome might not be the most ancient city in the world, it might not have the cultural and intellectual *cachet* of Athens or house any of the wonders of the world, but it was undoubtedly the biggest, a fitting capital for the most powerful empire the world had ever seen.

Yet there were two Romes. One was a miracle of cleanliness, where water from distant mountain streams poured into the city through aqueducts and filled public fountains and the cisterns of well-to-do houses. The other Rome was awash in filth as inhabitants of the *insulae* emptied their chamber pots into the narrow and sunless streets below. Attempts were made to use this human waste to fertilize the gardens beyond the city walls but it was a losing battle. The richest of the city's 14 districts gleamed with new marble and their citizens conducted their business in the pleasant and sophisticated surroundings of the baths. Meanwhile the poorest districts resembled cesspits, the people living cheek-by-jowl in crowded slums under constant threat of fire and collapsing walls. These streets were littered with rough shelters built against walls or even in the graveyards. As many as a third of the city's inhabitants lived off official grain handouts, which were provided largely to keep them from rioting. Splendour and squalor co-existed within a stone's throw of each other.

Nero, who became emperor in 54, was 'pathologically vain and jealous', a man ruled by 'Egotism and cruel perversion'.[17] But he also had a deep interest in the arts (his final words as he committed suicide were allegedly, 'what an artist dies in me'). He hankered after completing the work, which Augustus had begun, of planning and building a new Rome. Other Roman cities across the Empire were admirably well planned, with rectangular street patterns and carefully designed public spaces. Rome's haphazard and down-at-heel appearance hardly reflected the great city's standing in the world. Nero's ambition to create a fittingly grand city was no secret. Nor was his increasingly ruthless pursuit of his own way: in 59 he had his mother killed and in 62 he compelled Seneca, his tutor and moral guide to retire, removing anyone who might moderate his excesses (Seneca was forced to commit suicide in 65). Nero embarked in his latter years on an arbitrary reign of terror beyond anything even Rome had seen before.

This was the setting for the fire of July 64. It was perhaps the most destructive disaster of its kind that has ever happened (the Great Fire of London in 1666, for example, burned only half as long and affected a much smaller area). As the majority of the population of Rome struggled with the loss of possessions and accommodation, not to mention the countless deaths of friends and relatives, Nero quickly unveiled his plans for rebuilding the city. Alongside sensible redesign of houses, streets and neighbourhoods he included a vast and opulent Golden Palace set in a landscape of parks, lakes and massive colonnades. The Palace created a vast rural idyll in the middle of the city, where thousands had lived before and was topped by a huge golden statue, 20 times life-size, of Nero himself. Understandably the people began to suspect that the fire, which had conveniently made these architectural dreams a reality, might have been begun on the orders of the emperor himself.

Few historians today believe that the rumour had a basis in fact, any more than the story that Nero serenaded on his fiddle while the city burned. What is significant, however, is that the historian Tacitus recorded 50 years later that the rumour still had its supporters: it fitted Nero's well-deserved reputation perfectly. The fire was an important moment in Nero's reign, for it tipped the balance of power and saw him begin an increasingly desperate struggle to retain political control.

To sidestep the accusation that he was prepared to destroy his own subjects and their city if they stood in the way of his artistic ambitions, Nero had to find some plausible culprits. In 65, his gaze fell on an obscure and previously insignificant group within the city who were 'hated for their shameful actions, and called by the common folk, Christians'.[18] Peter was among them.

Rome – the church

How and when the church was established in Rome is unclear. Luke records Jews from Rome being present on the day of Pentecost in Jerusalem (Acts 2.10); Paul's companions Priscilla and Aquila seem to have been Christians already when they arrived in Corinth from Rome in 49 (Acts 18.2); Paul's letter to the church in Rome, written in the mid 50s, included thanksgiving that their faith was 'known throughout the world' and sent detailed greetings to a substantial number of different people (Rom. 1.8; 16.1–16). Thus it seems that when Paul finally reached Rome himself in 60 and the Christians there came out to greet him (Acts 28.15), theirs was probably one of the longest-established, largest and best-known of the churches around the Mediterranean. Tacitus records that a 'huge crowd' of them were executed by Nero. Peter's first letter speaks of him as a 'fellow-elder' (1 Peter 5.1), suggesting that he was present in Rome, though not as the pre-eminent leader of the church there as later tradition asserted.

It seems likely that most of the Christians lived in the poorest, lowest-lying, roughest and most densely populated parts of Rome: primarily in Trastevere and the area surrounding the Appian Way. It is probably significant that these districts also comprised two of the busiest areas of Rome. Trastevere lay on the east bank of the River Tiber and was the harbour-quarter, where ships that had sailed up from Ostia on the coast unloaded their cargoes. The Appian Way was the main highway into Rome from the south. Both districts were flooded with new people, new goods and new ideas.

The Christians of Rome seem to have been predominantly poor. Among the list of 28 to whom Paul sent greetings it is possible to gain some idea of the social status of 13. Of these 'probably four persons are freeborn and at least nine are of slave origin',[19] though some Roman Christians were wealthy enough to pay customs revenue as well as taxes, implying that they were traders (Rom. 13.7).

The earliest Christians in Rome were, as everywhere else in the first two decades, Jews. Jews had lived in Rome for several centuries, and by the time of Nero there may have been around 50,000 of them resident in the city, approaching 10 per cent of the total population. The Roman writer Suetonius said that the Jews were expelled from Rome under the Emperor Claudius because they kept causing disturbances 'at the incitement of *Chrestus*'[20] in 49. (*Chrestus* is widely agreed to be a version of *Christus*, though the name was a relatively common one.) The size of Rome made the authority structure of the synagogues in the city looser than elsewhere, offering greater opportunity perhaps for Christian Jews to argue the case for their new message. It is significant that this first reference to Christians in Rome associates them with causing trouble.

But why did the Christians become Nero's scapegoats? Tacitus remarked, with reference to the Christians, that 'every degraded and shameful practice collects and blossoms in the city'.[21] He meant that Rome was host to all the variegated religious expressions which could be found across the Empire, a matter in which he was something of an expert since in 88 he became one of the priest-guardians of foreign cults in the city. Jews had been expelled from Rome in 139 BC and again in AD 19 apparently because of their reluctance to assimilate to Roman customs. This made them useful 'unRoman' targets whenever the rulers wanted to remind the city of their own patriotic credentials, 'a symbolic statement of the purification of the city'.[22] If this was true of orthodox Jews, how much more did it apply to Christians, especially if they had provoked the disputes which led to the expulsion of Jews in 49? Suetonius noted the punishment of Christians under Nero, but did not link it with the aftermath of the fire: rather they suffered for their 'new and mischievous religious belief',[23] he says. Tacitus considers that the Christians were convicted 'not so much for the crime of arson as for hatred of the human race'.[24] The chief reason for the scapegoating of the Church may have been that Christians were not tolerant of beliefs that were different to their own, and denounced them. An important feature of Roman religion was its diversity and inclusiveness. All beliefs were welcome so long as they did not claim to be exclusive. The districts in which the Christians lived were religiously very mixed and unchecked by the controls on the practice of new faiths which applied in the older parts of the city. Antagonism to other beliefs and vigorous preaching might have been enough to make Christians seem to be mischievous haters of the human race in Roman eyes, and a threat to the precarious peace of a volatile city. We can also guess that followers of a religion whose founder prophesied judgement, and which used fire as an image of that judgement, may well have fitted quite neatly into the category of potential arsonists.

And it seems that the two districts in which most of the Christians lived were among the four unscathed by the fire. Peter Lampe concludes that 'Those who had saved their own skins and had watched the fiery spectacle from the safety of the other shore [of the Tiber] became easy targets for suspicion ... For demagogic purposes this situation must have appeared ideal.'[25] As far as Roman police procedure of the first century was concerned, it was an open and shut case.

We know enough of the rough nature of justice under Nero to imagine the wave of terror which broke upon the Roman Christians once the emperor had settled on them as his targets. Soldiers breaking down doors, whole families arrested, routine torture of witnesses, the leaders singled out for degradation; this became the daily experience of those who were suspected of being Christians.

> Their deaths were a mockery. Dressed in the skins of wild beasts they were ripped to death by dogs, nailed to crosses or set alight as torches to illuminate the night when the day had passed. Nero opened his gardens for the spectacle and showed them in the Circus where he mixed with the crowd or stood in a chariot. Despite their deserved punishment the victims were pitied; they suffered not for the public good but the savage appetites of a single man.[26]

Tacitus's characteristically terse description opens a window on to the horrors which the Christians in Rome experienced.

Where was Peter in all this? We have no information beyond the bare tradition that he died in the persecution. There are legends, such as the story of how Peter fled the city only to be met by Christ walking the other way. 'Where are you going, Lord?' he asked. 'I am going to be crucified again' Jesus replied. So Peter returned to the perilous city and was crucified upside down because he felt himself unworthy to die as his master had done. There is no evidence behind this story, apart from the implication at the end of John's Gospel that Peter suffered crucifixion (John 21.15–19), but it encapsulates the importance of the persecution of the Roman church for later generations. As Rodney Stark notes, 'That Peter could gladly follow his Savior to the cross ... must have been a powerful reinforcement of faith for Christians not asked to pay such a price for belonging'.[27] Even the hard-hearted patrician Tacitus seems to have been moved to pity at the story of the suffering of the Christians under Nero. Peter became, at the last, a hero. Despite his earlier failures, Peter came good in the end and he would be an inspiration to future generations of Roman Christians.

Peter's letters

Two letters in the New Testament bear Peter's name as their author (1 Peter 1.1; 2 Peter 1.1). Scholars generally regard 1 Peter as coming from the apostle; they are far more doubtful about 2 Peter. As we saw with the discussion of authorship in chapter 1 the designation of an author may have more to do with the origin of a particular text than with who physically wrote it. The actual writer of 1 Peter appears to be Silvanus or Silas (1 Peter 5.12) who may have had a significant role in its composition. Silas was a respected member of the Jerusalem church who accompanied Paul and co-authored some of his letters (see Acts 15.22–40; 16.19–24; 17.4, 10; 18.1–5; 2 Cor.1.19; 1 Thess. 1.1; 2 Thess. 1.1).

An atmosphere of persecution hangs over Peter's first letter. The author warns his readers of the 'fiery trials' that some are suffering (1 Peter 4.12), and the image of fire is also used elsewhere (1 Peter 1.7). Some commentators have plausibly seen in these references connections with Nero's punishments. Yet the prevailing type of persecution which Peter seems to have in mind is social and verbal rather than physical (see 1 Peter 2.12, 23; 3.9,16; 4.14). Perhaps this may be accounted for by the fact that while the letter comes from 'Babylon', which is usually early Christian code for Rome (1 Peter 5.13), it is specifically addressed to the churches of Asia Minor (1 Peter 1.1). Peter's response is a peaceful one. He assumes that gentle words and a kind attitude will turn away antagonism (1 Peter 2.12; 3.15). Therefore this letter may well have been written before the persecution by Nero in which Peter lost his life. The atmosphere is one of gathering clouds rather than outright darkness.

However, if 1 Peter is closely identified with the onset of persecution by Nero, it becomes almost logically necessary that 2 Peter, which claims to be later (2 Peter 3.1), should have been written after Peter's death. It reflects a different set of issues, and it is argued that these would not have arisen until after 65. Most likely it is an example of a letter written in the name of an apostle to assume the mantle of his authority. It seems to be in fact a letter from the church in Rome to other churches, motivated by pastoral concern for them (2 Peter 3.1). The use of Peter's Aramaic personal name, Simeon (2 Peter 1.1) suggests that the writer knew Peter well, which may have given him the confidence to write on his behalf, passing on a version of what he had said (2 Peter 1.13–15). Adopting the apostle's persona may simply have been a way of speaking on behalf of the whole Roman church, and rather than being 'a fraudulent means of claiming apostolic authority' in fact 'embodies a claim to be a faithful mediator of the apostolic message'.[28] Clement of Rome wrote on his own behalf to the Corinthians in the late first century, so it is plausible that 2 Peter dates from earlier than that, perhaps around 80.

If 2 Peter was written around 80, then this would place it roughly in the same period as the composition of Matthew's Gospel. Like Matthew's

Gospel, this letter is a means of conveying apostolic teaching. Unlike 1 Peter, 2 Peter's concern is not withstanding suffering but the dangers of false belief. It claims to be written near to the end of the apostle's life (2 Peter 1.14), and represents his final words to his flock, rather as Deuteronomy sums up the teaching of Moses, and similar to a number of contemporary Jewish 'Testaments'. In many ways it is a very Jewish letter, quoting from the writings of contemporary Judaism and re-emphasizing the Hebrew roots of the gospel in the face of Hellenistic challenges. Second Peter also uses (perhaps re-uses) material found in the letter of Jude, and may be a pre-existing polemic both writers found useful.

The memory of Peter

Peter was remembered in the early Church as someone who bridged the gap between James and Paul. He is portrayed this way in Luke's account of the Jerusalem conference which was called to adjudicate on whether gentiles had to become Jews in order to participate in the Church (Acts 15.7–11).

There seems to be some truth in the portrait. Where James and the Jerusalem church represented the Jewish roots of the Christian movement, while Paul and the gentile churches represented the future, Peter straddled both expressions of faith. A close companion of Jesus (as neither James nor Paul had been), he was alert to new opportunities (see Acts 10), though he was always concerned to retain links with the past (see Gal. 2.11–13). Pheme Perkins comments that Peter is a fascinating figure because, among the 'Diversity in the early Christian communities ... no figure ... encompasses more of that diversity than Peter.' He continues that 'the complex diversity of Judaism and Jewish Christianity at Jerusalem and in Syrian Antioch created rough waters which were not always easy to negotiate.'[29] Peter did not always get the negotiating right. He seems not to have had the organizational or strategic grasp of James or Paul, nor the penetrating insights that came to be associated with John. What he did have, and offered as a gift to other followers of Jesus, was an unrivalled insight into Jesus himself, born out of their close companionship.

Peter's role was not to organize or strategize but to remember and to tell what he remembered. A striking confirmation of this crucial role is the two weeks which Paul spent with him, presumably learning everything he could from the man who knew more than anyone else about the human Jesus (Gal. 1.18). But what would happen after his death? How would the story remain alive?

After the Fire, and the persecution which followed it, the church in Rome must have been shattered. Joachim Jeremias once vividly described the scene like this:

> When the surviving members of the Church of Rome reassembled ... they found that many of their number were missing, the most important being the Apostle Peter ... They recalled those unforgettable occasions when St Peter had related his reminiscences of the earthly life of Jesus – of his call to discipleship, his confession at Caesarea Philippi, Gethsemane, and his denial of Jesus on Maundy Thursday evening. So it occurred to them to ask St Peter's fellow-worker, Johanan, surnamed Mark, of Jerusalem, who had escaped the persecution, to write down everything he could remember about the Apostle's teaching. Mark complied with their request.[30]

Jeremias based this reconstruction on Papias's comment, written about 130, that 'Mark, having become the interpreter of Peter, wrote down accurately but not in order, what he remembered of the things said or done by Christ.'[31] Papias's view was followed by other writers, who considered Mark's Gospel 'the reminiscences of Peter'.[32]

How accurate this view may have been we shall consider in the next chapter, but it shows that Peter was remembered in the early Church for his role as the 'memory man' among the apostles, the primary provider of testimony to the life of Jesus. He was the link between the first beginnings of Jesus' movement in Galilee in the late 20s and the Christian community in Rome in the 60s, which was significant enough to attract the attention of the emperor himself. He had come a very long way indeed.

Draw your own conclusions

- If you had to write an obituary of Peter, how would you sum up his life?
- What were the economic pressures on Galilean fishermen in the first century?
- Why do you think Peter followed Jesus?
- What was Peter's role among the disciples? Has it been exaggerated for literary effect in the Gospels?
- What were the similarities and what were the differences between Galilee and Rome in the first century?
- When do you think Peter's letters were written, and who do you think wrote them?

Further reading

Peter's life and reputation are examined in P. Perkins (2000), *Peter: Apostle for the Whole Church*, Edinburgh: T.&T. Clark. The evidence about Peter in the Gospels is carefully considered by J. P. Meier (2001), *A Marginal Jew III: companions and competitors*, London: Doubleday, pp. 221–45.

The Galilean background to Peter's life is outlined well in K. C. Hanson and D. E. Oakman (1998), *Palestine in the Time of Jesus: social structures and social conflicts*, Minneapolis: Fortress. J. L. Reed (2000), *Archaeology and the Galilean Jesus*, Harrisburg: TPI includes a particularly useful chapter on Capernaum. J. D. Crossan and J. L. Reed (2001), *Excavating Jesus: beneath the stones, behind the texts*, London: SPCK contrasts the kingdom of Herod and the Kingdom of God. The story of the excavation of the 'Jesus Boat' and its background is told in S. Wachsmann (2000), *The Sea of Galilee Boat: a 2000 year old discovery from the sea of legends*, Cambridge, MA: Perseus Books.

On the city of Rome, R. Lane Fox (2006), *The Classical World: an epic history of Greece and Rome*, 2nd ed., London: Penguin, Part 6 provides the general background. M. Goodman (2007), *Rome and Jerusalem: the clash of ancient civilizations*, London: Penguin, gives an outline of life in the city of Rome, pp. 38–52, and J. Carcopino (1941), *Daily Life in Ancient Rome*, Harmondsworth: Penguin remains a rich compilation of the literary evidence.

The church in Rome has been carefully and exhaustively studied in the remarkable P. Lampe (2003), *From Paul to Valentinus: Christians at Rome in the first two centuries*, London: Continuum. Suetonius's life of Nero in *The Lives of the Twelve Caesars* is worth reading, while Tacitus's narrative of the fire of Rome in *The Annals of Imperial Rome*, 15.37–44 should not be missed.

Websites

- K. C. Hanson's 'The Galilean Fishing Economy and the Jesus Tradition' is a technical but fascinating analysis of the economic and social background at www.kchanson.com/PTJ/fishing.html.
- 'Peter and Paul and the Christian Revolution', based on a PBS series, focuses more on Paul than Peter, but gives useful background on Rome, www.pbs.org/empires/peterandpaul/footsteps/index.html. If you haven't done already, try visiting first-century Rome in three dimensions at www.earth.google.com/rome.
- Resources on the letters of Peter are at www.textweek.com/epistlesrevelation/1peter.htm and www.textweek.com/epistlesrevelation/2peter.htm.

Notes

1 J. L. Reed (2000), *Archaeology and the Galilean Jesus*, Harrisburg: TPI, p. 152.

2 K. Butcher (2003), *Roman Syria and the Near East*, London: British Museum, p. 89.

3 P. Hordern and N. Purcell (2000), *The Corrupting Sea: a study of Mediterranean history*, Oxford: Blackwell, p. 196.

4 Gargilius Martialis, *De Medicina et de Virtute Herborum*, 62, quoted in I. G. Giacosa, A. Herklotz and M. T. Simeti (1994), *A Taste of Ancient Rome*, Chicago: University of Chicago Press, pp. 27–8.

5 Pliny, *Natural History* 9.104 (tr. Healy).

6 Cicero, *On Duties* 1.42.

7 N. Purcell (1998), 'Fishing' in S. Hornblower and A. Spawforth (eds.), *The Oxford Companion to Classical Civilization*, Oxford: Oxford University Press, p. 283.

8 P. Richardson (1999), *Herod the Great: King of the Jews and friend of the Romans*, Edinburgh: T.&T. Clark, p. 174.

9 E. P. Sanders (1992), *Judaism: practice and belief 63BCE–66CE*, London: SCM Press, p. 168.

10 J. D. Crossan and J. L. Reed (2001), *Excavating Jesus*, London: SPCK, p. 70.

11 P. Perkins (2000), *Peter: apostle for the whole church*, Edinburgh: T.&T. Clark, p. 21.

12 J. D. G. Dunn (2003), *Jesus Remembered*, Grand Rapids: Eerdmans, pp. 844, 846.

13 C. K. Barrett (1982), *Essays on Paul*, London: SPCK, pp. 37–8.

14 C. H. Dodd (1936), *The Apostolic Preaching and Its Developments*, London: Hodder & Stoughton, p.16.

15 Horace, *Epistles* 2.2.

16 Pliny, *Natural History* 3.67.

17 R. Lane Fox (2006), *The Classical World*, 2nd ed., London: Penguin, p. 505.

18 Tacitus, *Annals* 15.44.

19 P. Lampe (2003), *From Paul to Valentinus: Christians at Rome in the first two centuries*, London: Continuum, p. 183.

20 Suetonius, *Life of Claudius* 25.4

21 Tacitus, *Annals* 15.44.

22 M. Goodman (2007), *Rome and Jerusalem*, London: Penguin, p. 386.

23 Suetonius, *Nero* 16.2 (tr. Graves).

24 Tacitus, *Annals* 15.44.

25 Lampe, *From Paul to Valentinus*, p. 47.

26 Tacitus, *Annals* 15.44.

27 R. Stark (1996), *The Rise of Christianity*, San Francisco: Harper Collins, p. 187.

28 R. J. Bauckham (1983), *Jude, 2 Peter*, Waco: Word, pp. 161–2.

29 Perkins, *Peter: apostle to the whole church*, p. 184.

30 J. Jeremias (1957), *The Unknown Sayings of Jesus*, London: SPCK, p. 2.

31 Eusebius, *History of the Church* 3.39. See also 2.15.

32 Justin Martyr, *Dialogue with Trypho* 106.3.

5

The Gospel of Mark

What kind of animal?

If Mark's Gospel were an animal, what kind of animal would it be? And what are the qualities that would make it that animal?

There are many ways of approaching the Gospels, and imagination has an important role in interpretation. From the late second century people connected the four Gospels with four creatures seen in a vision by the prophet Ezekiel (Ezek. 1.4–28). The four creatures were a human being, a lion, an ox and an eagle. Matthew's and Luke's Gospels were always identified with the human and the ox, and before long John's was identified with the eagle. That left the lion for Mark's.

The symbols were widely used in medieval Christian art as a teaching aid, perhaps most famously in *The Book of Kells* (which was created around 800 and is now preserved in Trinity College, Dublin). Richard Burridge points out that the 'imagery was used for summaries of the gospel message, that Jesus was born as a man, sacrificed like an ox, rose again triumphant like a lion, and ascended like an eagle, extending his wings to protect his people.'[1] The symbols remind us that there are more ways to interpret the New Testament than simply through reason and words.

Approaching the Gospels indirectly in this sort of symbolic way is especially useful for Mark's Gospel, which seems to be designed to evoke an emotional rather than an intellectual response. Mark's Gospel, according to some of those who have pioneered the study of it as a narrative, 'presents us with a "story world", a world that engages and grips us, a world such as we experience when we get "lost" in reading a novel or watching a film'.[2] Mark does not appear to be very concerned with the objective outside world as he tells his story, unlike Luke who works hard to connect his narrative to outside events (see for example Luke 3.1–2). This doesn't mean that the events Mark describes were invented by him or that they are meant to be read as fiction. Rather, he presents a different reality in his story which can challenge the ordinary world his readers inhabit. In the rest of this chapter we shall find the parallel with storytelling in drama and films especially useful to understand the techniques which Mark uses in the story world of his Gospel.

Symbolic imagination

Why choose the lion to represent Mark's Gospel? This Gospel is a fast-moving, action-packed account of Jesus' life, unpredictable and bursting with energy, all qualities you might find in a lion. But there is also a latent danger about lions, a ferocity that inspires terror, and this quality too can be found in Mark's Gospel. Jesus inspires not faith but fear in his followers at times (see, for example, Mark 4.41; 16.8). The Jesus whom Mark portrays is, like a lion, at once both magnificent and frightening.

Michael Sadgrove, reflecting on the images in Graham Sutherland's modern interpretation of the traditional symbols in the tapestry of *Christ in Glory in the Tetramorph* in Coventry Cathedral (1962), writes that

> Like all symbols, the four creatures elude explanation. A symbol is not a sign, like a red traffic light, that means one thing and one thing only. A symbol opens up possibilities, draws me into its world, stretches my imagination, asks questions. I respond to a symbol at many different levels. Its perspectives are constantly shifting, even as I look at it. I can never say I have grasped its full meaning. That is its glory.[3]

Allowing your imagination to work on what kind of creature you would use to describe Mark's Gospel can produce some surprising intuitive insights. You don't need to be bound by the traditional lion imagery. Your own image, when you think about what qualities it represents, may also help you to express what you think are the main themes of the Gospel of Mark.

Who was Mark?

Mark's Gospel itself, like the other three, gives no clear answers to the question of the author's identity, nor to the time and place of writing. There is no strong scholarly consensus on by whom, when or where it was written. The Gospel could have been written at more or less any time between 40 and 75, and many settings have been proposed: Rome, Alexandria, Antioch, Syria and Galilee being the most convincing. No wonder Morna Hooker concludes that 'All we can say with certainty … is that the gospel was composed somewhere in the Roman Empire – a conclusion that scarcely narrows the field at all!'[4]

In many respects the setting and precise date of the Gospel is not so important: it is meant to tell the story of Jesus for a wide audience rather than a specific one. Nevertheless, some idea of where the Gospel came from does have a bearing on how we read it, because an understanding of a possible 'life-setting' (a phrase often used, from the German *Sitz im Leben*) helps us to make sense of why the story is told in a particular way and why certain themes predominate. To take one simple example, what is the significance of the young man who tries to accompany Jesus in the Garden of Gethsemane (Mark 14.51–52)? None of the other Gospel writers use the story, so did it have a special meaning for Mark's original audience? We shall never know.

There is little evidence in the Gospel itself regarding a date for its writing. A possible marker is Jesus' prophecy of the destruction of Jerusalem with the warning 'let those in Judea flee to the hills' (Mark 13.14). Since the same prophecy in Luke's Gospel has been amended to fit with what had actually happened in 70 (Luke 21.20–1) this suggests that Mark's Gospel was written before the Temple was destroyed. But this is not really strong enough evidence to be definitive. An alternative approach is to argue that Jesus is portrayed as a 'law-observant Jew' in Mark's Gospel and that therefore the book must have been written before 'the mid 40s ... when we start to get the first indication of notable nonobservance [of the Law] in earliest Christianity'.[5] This view deserves deeper investigation but it is not strong enough to convince.

A different approach comes from recognizing that one thing on which virtually all readers of Mark's Gospel agree is that suffering is a major theme within it. This makes it plausible that the Gospel was written to address a situation where suffering was an important question for the Christian community. Two obvious settings present themselves: Rome in the mid 60s in the aftermath of the Great Fire, or Galilee in the late 60s or early 70s around the time of the Jewish revolt against the Romans. Both of these settings have their champions.

Rome in the 60s was believed to be the setting during the first few centuries of the Church. Papias, in the same passage which we looked at in connection with the origins of Matthew's Gospel, identified the author of this Gospel as the Mark who is called Peter's 'son' (1 Peter 5.13). He also claimed that someone called 'the elder' had said this to him:

> Mark, having become the interpreter of Peter, wrote down accurately, but not in order, what he remembered of the things said or done by Christ. He had not heard the Lord or followed him but later ... followed Peter who adapted his teaching to his hearers' needs without aiming to give an ordered account of the Lord's sayings; so Mark made no mistake in writing things down as he remembered them. He was very careful not to leave out anything he had heard, and not to relate any of them wrongly.[6]

Since Papias's testimony apparently comes from someone older than himself, this description of the origins of Mark's Gospel reaches back well into the first century itself.

Papias intended to link the Gospel with John Mark, who was well-known in early Christian circles. The church in Jerusalem met in his mother's house (Acts 12.12) and he had accompanied his cousin Barnabas, and Paul, though he was not always in favour with the latter (Acts 12.25; 13.13; 15.37–9; Philemon 24; Col. 4:10; 2 Tim 4.11). Though he was an associate of the apostles, Mark was not himself a prominent leader in the Church and would have been an obscure choice to be linked with the Gospel if it had not been connected to him from the beginning. However, if you take away the reference in 1 Peter we have only the word of Papias's shadowy 'elder' for this view, which was repeated several times in the second and third centuries. Modern scholars have tended to see Papias's identification of Mark's Gospel with Peter as simply 'an early part of the process of claiming Peter's authority'[7] by the church in Rome.

That Mark wrote down what Justin Martyr in the second century called the 'reminiscences of Peter'[8] became the consensus for many centuries, though some agreed with Augustine that Mark was merely 'a kind of follower and abbreviator of Matthew'.[9] In the nineteenth century it was established that Mark's Gospel was the original, which Matthew copied and augmented. Because of this it was argued that as the earliest, Mark's Gospel was also the most historically reliable. The generally unquestioned association of Mark's Gospel with Peter further buttressed this consensus.

Three great German scholars of the early twentieth century, Karl Ludwig Schmidt, Martin Dibelius and Rudolf Bultmann overturned the consensus. Using 'form criticism' (in German *Formgeschichte*) they examined how Mark's and the other Gospels were composed of many independent and apparently unrelated oral units ('forms' or *pericopae*). Because Mark's was the earliest of the Gospels the form critics believed that his work was closest to the primitive traditions about Jesus; but they argued that Mark's role was to do little more than haphazardly thread together the precious stories about Jesus, which had been told among the Christian communities for several decades, 'like pearls on a string'. It followed that, as Dennis Nineham put it in an influential commentary, Mark's Gospel 'cannot ... be derived *directly* from St Peter or any other eyewitness ... [because] all of it, without exception, seems to bear the characteristic marks of community tradition'.[10] The Gospel writers became compilers rather than creative writers or theologians, the mouthpieces of community traditions, not the recorders of eyewitness testimony.

Papias's claim that Mark was the interpreter of Peter therefore came under attack from several angles:

- *Marcus was a very common name in the first century.* There must have been many of them in the early Church. There is no reason to assume that the author of the Gospel should be the same person as the one who was a companion of Paul and Peter even if they shared the same name.

- *Peter is no more prominent in this Gospel than the others.* We might expect Peter to have a higher profile in this Gospel if his eyewitness testimony lay behind it, but once the Q-sections have been taken into account his place in the story is pretty much the same. On the other hand, Mark's portrait of him is harsh compared to the other Gospels, leading some scholars to argue that Mark's Gospel is actually an attack on him and the other apostles, seeking to recall believers to the true teaching of Jesus and away from the leaders of the later Church. If this were the case, then clearly Mark's source could not be Peter himself!
- *Mark does not seem to be at home with the geography of Galilee and Judea.* While the background to the Gospel is 'remarkably true to the conditions of Palestine in Jesus' day', nevertheless the 'numerous vaguenesses and inaccuracies are most naturally explained if [Mark] was *not* directly acquainted with Palestine'.[11] Mark's account of the journeys of Jesus certainly requires rather hectic movement around Galilee. At one point he travels from Tyre and Sidon to Galilee through the Decapolis (Mark 7.31, 'as though a man should travel from Cornwall to London via Manchester'[12]). Mark describes the journey from the western shore of Lake Galilee to Bethsaida as going 'to the other side' (Mark 6.45), when it is only a few miles away and still just on the western shore itself. And Mark says that Jesus entered Jerusalem through 'Bethphage and Bethany' when the order would be the other way round for a traveller coming by the Jericho road (Mark 11.1).
- *Mark seems confused about the customs of Passover.* He says that 'the first day of unleavened bread' was the day on which the sacrificial lambs were slaughtered, when in fact it was the day after the ritual killings took place (Mark 14.12). Surely, the argument runs, no one brought up in Jerusalem would make such a mistake?
- *The vivid details often used to underpin the claim that this Gospel was based on eyewitness memories are rare exceptions.* The 'pillow' in the fishing boat and the 'green grass' at the feeding of the 5,000 (Mark 4.38; 6.39) contrast with the other stories in the narrative, where 'local colour and extraneous detail which eyewitnesses provide is missing'. Instead of 'lively personal touches ... we are given a story of stark simplicity, a story "worn smooth" by repetition'.[13]

In short, for all these reasons the tide turned decisively against accepting Papias's portrait of Mark's Gospel as the memories of Peter and in favour of the argument that it was composed of many community traditions.

If the church in Rome after the Fire and ensuing persecution did not seem such a good setting for the composition of Mark's Gospel, then Galilee or Syria in the late 60s or early 70s became a good alternative. Ched Myers's work is the most impressive and thoroughgoing application of this life-setting to Mark's Gospel; he says that it 'reflects the daily realities of disease, poverty, and disenfranchisement that characterized the social existence of first-century Palestine's "other 95%."' Myers situates the writing of the Gospel very precisely in 69, just before the destruction of the Temple, and argues that it is a plea for 'non-aligned radicalism' between Jewish nationalism and Roman imperialism. This non-violent approach is 'a heroism of the cross, not the sword ... [a] struggle to put an end to the spiral of violence and oppression that [God's] reign may truly dawn'[14] and the Gospel is an appeal to those caught in the spiral to come and join a middle way between the forces which are about to meet in a bloody and destructive holocaust. Yet the evidence for this view is entirely circumstantial, as several scholars have pointed out. It may simply be that there can be no answer to the question of who wrote the Gospel, where and when.

On the other hand, Papias's view that the Gospel was written by John Mark in Rome, based on Peter's testimony has been re-examined. James Dunn, for example, notes that it 'makes better sense in the context of oral transmission than most seem to appreciate'. But he concludes that 'the evidence is too sparse for sound hypothesis building.'[15] What might be the response to the points listed above and in favour of the Gospel having been written by John Mark of Jerusalem, in Rome, based on the memories of Peter?

- *Marcus was a very common name in the first century.* But we only know of one who had a significant role in the Church. When this Gospel was named 'according to Mark', which happened before Papias wrote in 130, he was the most likely candidate.
- *Peter is no more prominent in this Gospel than in the others.* While this is true, his role is significantly different. In Mark's Gospel Peter is often an example of failure. This is not so much the case in Matthew's Gospel and still less in Luke's. The most likely person to have taken such a view of Peter was the man himself. In addition, the respected role which Peter later had is reflected in the other Gospels (see Matt.16.17–19; Luke 22.31–2; John 21.15–19), but not in Mark's. As far as the argument that Mark's Gospel is intended as an anti-Peter tract, it is hard to see how, if this were the case, it would so quickly have become identified with Peter. A more plausible explanation is that we have a close portrait of Peter here, which was modified by Matthew, Luke and John to fit more closely with Peter's reputation after his death by martyrdom.
- *Mark does not seem to be at home with the geography of Galilee and Judea.* Once we recognize that Mark's is not necessarily meant to be a sequential, chronological account then the oddity of some of his geographical references becomes much less important. He was writing a Gospel, not a travel guide. However, Bethsaida might be described as being 'on the other side' if what was meant was the move from the territory of Herod Antipas to that of Philip the Tetrarch (Mark 6.45); and

though 'Bethphage and Bethany' are in the wrong order for a traveller coming from Jericho it might well be the way that someone from Jerusalem would speak of them (Mark 11.1).

- *Mark seems confused about the customs of Passover.* The whole issue of the dating of the Passover and the crucifixion of Jesus is fraught with difficulties, which we shall examine in detail in Chapter 9. However, it seems likely that, whatever the explanation for Mark 14.12, it is almost certainly not confusion or ignorance which has led Mark to place the sacrifice of the lambs a day early.
- *The vivid details often used to underpin the claim that this Gospel was based on eyewitness memories are rare exceptions.* This may be the case, but it must be conceded that there are some vivid details, and they are not repeated in the parallel passages in the other Gospels (see Matt. 8.24; 14.19; Luke 8.23; 9.14).

One further point in favour of Papias's view should also be mentioned.

- *Much of the Gospel appears to be told from Peter's point of view.* A frequent feature of Mark's Gospel is what might be called the 'they to he shift': '*they* entered Capernaum and on the Sabbath *he* taught in the synagogue'; '*They* left the synagogue ... Coming close, *he* raised her up, taking her by the hand' (Mark 1.21, 29–31; there are 19 further examples). Who 'they' refers to is not usually specified, but the context makes it clear that the 12 disciples are in view, always including Peter. The 'they to he' shift is a clumsy construction as it stands, as Matthew and Luke seem to have recognized: in their Gospels they often tidy up the awkwardness by changing 'they' to 'he' or missing out the phrase altogether (compare Matt. 4.22–3; 8.14–15; Luke 4.31, 38 with the passages above). But if we substitute 'we' for 'they' the clumsiness vanishes: '*we* entered Capernaum and on the Sabbath *he* taught in the synagogue'; '*we* left the synagogue ... Coming close, *he* raised her up, taking her by the hand.' Richard Bauckham concludes that the shift 'makes the dominant perspective ... within the Gospel's narrative the perspective of Peter and those closest to him. It enables readers to share the *eyewitness* perspective'.[16] But not all of the Gospel is told like this: sometimes Jesus rather than 'they' are the subject (see, for example, Mark 1.39; 2.1; 3.1; there are nine further instances) and the disciples may or may not join in with what he is doing. So Peter's perspective, though dominant, is not the only one in Mark's Gospel, suggesting a weaving together of sources, a mixture of the 'reminiscences' of Peter and material gleaned from others.

So a good case can be made for Peter's as the authenticating voice behind Mark's Gospel. But how strong is the identification of the Gospel with Rome, the place of Peter's death?

Peter had been active for many years in Syria before his likely death at Rome in 65, so it is quite possible that his testimony could have formed the basis of a Gospel written there around the time of the Jewish revolt. But another feature of Mark's Gospel becomes important here: Aramaic phrases and Jewish customs are consistently explained, which would not have been necessary if the Gospel were written in the east (Mark 3.17; 5.41; 7.3–4, 34; 15.22, 34). In the light of this feature, surely it is more plausible that the accurate reflection of first-century political and social pressures in Galilee derive from the original setting of the Gospel's story rather than the circumstances of its writing. If so then, as we saw above, Rome becomes the obvious place for its composition, a city where the church had undergone a brutal and traumatic experience of suffering which chimes with the major theme of Mark's Gospel itself.

The arguments are quite carefully balanced either way. You will be clear by now that I think there's a good case to be made for Mark's Gospel being written in Rome by John Mark in the mid 60s. But of course I'm inclined to that view because it fits with the structure of this book, based around the four pillar apostles, James, Peter, Paul and John. So it's important to ask what you think, once you have weighed up the evidence. Which theory appeals to you more, and why?

Why did Mark write a 'Gospel'?

When Mark wrote the first words of his book, he was quite probably using 'Gospel' (in Greek *eu-angelion*) in a new way. Until this time the word had meant in Christian circles (as it still does) the message of salvation in Jesus Christ. But Mark redefined the word to mean a book-length story about Jesus which went much further than the kind of bare recital of the crucial facts about Jesus which can be found in Peter's sermon at Pentecost, for example (Acts 2.14–36).

Jesus' teachings may have circulated in a written form from very early on and I argued in Chapter 3 that these teachings formed the oldest material in Matthew's Gospel. It is likely that the stories of what Jesus did, including the story of his death, were not written down but related orally. His actions may not have seemed as significant to the earliest church in Jerusalem as they awaited the moment when God would restore Israel. The tradition suggests that the impulse behind Mark's Gospel was the death of Peter, the pre-eminent witness to the stories of what Jesus did. What Mark seems to have done, therefore, is to put Jesus' words and actions, his teachings and his passion, together for the first time into a whole. In doing so he invented a new genre. He had a genuinely blank sheet before him and no clear pattern to follow as he wrote 'the beginning of the gospel of Jesus Christ ...'

Most ordinary readers who picked up a copy of one of the Gospels would probably conclude that it was a biography of Jesus. An unusual biography, certainly, since it includes miraculous stories, but nonetheless, the story of Jesus' life. Many of the form critics disagreed with this reaction, however. Rudolf Bultmann said in 1926 that 'I do indeed think that we can know almost nothing concerning the life and personality of Jesus, since the early Christian sources show no interest in either, [and] are moreover fragmentary and often legendary'.[17] For Bultmann, the Gospels gave access only to the message of Jesus and offered nothing trustworthy about his life at all. Bultmann's views were widely accepted in the middle part of the twentieth century.

More recently there has been a fresh look at this question, and Richard Burridge has clearly demonstrated the link between the Gospels and the kind of biographies which were current in Greek and Roman literature and concluded that 'the Gospels are a form of ancient biography.'[18] However, Burridge also notes that biography was a flexible genre in the ancient world and could be taken in several different directions. Papias complained that, unlike Matthew's, Mark's Gospel was not an 'orderly account',[19] by which he presumably meant that it did not have the carefully worked out patterns and balance of Matthew's. However, ancient biographies were often not clearly ordered, especially if their subjects were philosophers or religious leaders. The aim of an ancient biography was to give a plausible portrait, not a blow-by-blow account of a life. The second-century writer Lucian of Samosata's *Demonax the Philosopher*, for example, has the same 'stringing together' of sayings and events that characterizes Mark's Gospel, as quotations from a random page show: 'Someone else once asked him ... He once ... On one occasion ... He once saw ...'[20] Lucian's intention is to give the flavour of Demonax's personality and sayings.

Mark's Gospel is also more sophisticated than it seems at first. The form critics were diverted by the rough exterior of the Gospel's language from seeing the carefully worked out plot beneath. In contrast to *Demonax* there is a plot at work here, because the words and deeds of Jesus during his ministry are only the prelude for Mark to the climax of the story: the last week in Jerusalem, which culminates in Jesus' death. Burridge characterizes the Gospels as biography, but biography which is 'nothing less than Christology in narrative form'[21] designed to bring out the full significance of who their authors believed Jesus to be. Mark may not have included a statement to say this was what he was doing (as Luke and John do, Luke 1.1–4; John 20.30–1) but he did it all the same. Perhaps he simply found intuitively that the best way to point out the importance of Jesus was to tell his story.

Lucian's *Demonax* may have been a skit on the kind of after-dinner entertainment offered in the ancient world, and Demonax the philosopher may not actually have existed. Most of his sayings are jokes, and Lucian is best known as a satirist who also poked fun at historians in his book *How to Write History*. What *Demonax* does demonstrate, however, is that even a spoof biography would try to give an impression of the subject's character without feeling bound to tell a chronologically ordered story, and in this it reads rather like the early part of Mark's Gospel. A contemporary parallel is with films that tell the story of someone's life. In such a bio-pic, chronology may be rearranged and some real characters removed or sometimes amalgamated with others. The end result is often described in the credits as 'based on a true story' and arguments then rage as to just how true it is. Such films often give a good impression of someone's life, but they have standards of truth and a storytelling grammar of their own which have to be judged differently from a scholarly biography. Like a film director, Mark is concerned to communicate his story in a gripping way and the nature of storytelling has perhaps not changed very much over the centuries. He does this by using a particular 'voice' to narrate the story (as a film-maker today may use a voice-over at key points in the story); could it be that the rough-and-ready Greek of Mark's Gospel is actually an attempt to capture the voice of Peter the Galilean fisherman?

Structuring the drama

In the late 1970s, the actor Alec McCowen performed Mark's Gospel to sell-out audiences in London's West End. He found that it had tremendous vitality as a dramatic story. Ancient biographies were written to be performed, often as after-dinner entertainment. Mark's Gospel lasts only about an hour and ten minutes in performance, and I started using the Gospel this way myself a few years ago. I do a 'performance-reading' where I clearly read from the text, but involve the audience and follow the journey around Galilee and then south to Jerusalem. It's a powerful experience to perform and also, I believe, to watch.

Some features of the Gospel greatly assist in performance. One characteristic of the Gospel is what are sometimes called 'Markan sandwiches'. When the Gospel is read privately these can seem simply to be digressions. A good example is when Jesus sends out his disciples (Mark 6.7–13); the story switches apparently arbitrarily to the death of John the Baptist and its background (Mark 6.14–29) before the disciples report back and Jesus resumes his ministry (Mark 6.30). But in performance this interruption gives the illusion of time passing. This is actually a storytelling technique which is alive and well in contemporary cinema: 'In a film, a scene will change in the middle of the action, leaving the viewer in suspense, while the camera cuts to another scene. The camera will return to resolve the action ... thus creating a frame round the middle story.'[22] Of course there is more to these apparent digressions than simple performance technique. The sandwiches also function as comments on the stories they interrupt, as happens for example in the narrative of Jesus' betrayal which surrounds the story of an unknown woman who anoints Jesus (Mark 14.1–11). The woman's devotion to Jesus is in marked contrast to the chief priests and Judas. (Among other examples are Mark 3.20–35; 5.21–43; 11.12–25; 14:66–72.)

The fact that the other Gospels seem to be primarily literary texts (especially, and self-consciously, Luke's) can distract us from seeing that Mark's Gospel makes sense as a text to be performed, designed to draw the audience in so that they experience the story of Jesus with an immediacy that the other Gospels simply do not have.

New Testament scholars have adopted what has been called a 'literary paradigm' because they generally live in a literate, print-dominated Western culture. But in the Middle East and in Africa, for example, stories are valued and traditions preserved orally. In such cultures, stories are told and retold publicly. In other words, they are performed, rather than read. This process, says J. D. G. Dunn, is surely much closer to what we have in Mark than a text that has been successively edited and pieced together, layer by layer, as the form critics suggested: 'whereas the concept of literary *layers* implies increasing remoteness from an "original", "pure", or "authentic" layer, the concept of *performance* allows a directness, even an immediacy of interaction, with a living theme and core'.[23] Performance is designed to draw the audience in and encourage them to experience the events narrated. It evokes an emotional response rather than a primarily rational one. It re-presents the story in order to make it present, and removes the gulf of time and space between the audience and the past.

Mark's Gospel is often written in the 'historic present' tense which English translations fail to catch, so that 'we miss Mark's vividness and pace'.[24] The effect is to bring an audience straight to the bedside of Peter's mother-in-law, for example, as Mark writes 'they *went* in to the house ... and at once they *tell* him about her ...' (Mark 1.29–30). This is another indication that Mark's Gospel is intended to be a text for performance rather than a historical record. Papias preserved the tradition that Mark had been Peter's 'interpreter' who wrote down the stories which he had heard Peter tell. In other words his testimony was that Mark's Gospel was based on oral performance.

The structure of Mark's Gospel seems to correspond strikingly to the structure of classical drama, as outlined by the Greek philosopher Aristotle in the fourth century BC. Aristotle said that a dramatic tragedy should look like Figure 5.

Of course it is unlikely that Mark knew much about Aristotle, but almost every town of any size in the Greek-speaking world had a theatre; there was even one close to Nazareth, at Sepphoris. So while Mark may not have been consciously following Aristotle's dramatic structure, he could easily have come into contact with it.

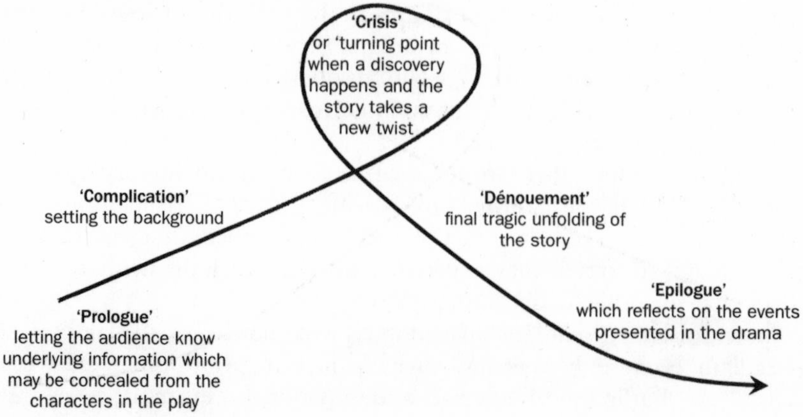

Figure 5 The structure of tragic drama

The structure may have been adopted unconsciously, but it fits Mark's Gospel remarkably well:

- The prologue deftly places the story which is about to unfold in the context of Israel in ancient prophecy (Isaiah) and the reform movement of John the Baptist, before hurrying on to the story of Jesus.
- The complication sets out the story of Jesus' ministry in Galilee, with its whirl of activity.
- The crisis occurs near Caesarea Philippi, where Peter first recognizes Jesus as the Christ. At once Jesus teaches the disciples that this means that he must suffer and die.
- The dénouement is the section which unfolds almost in slow motion compared to the haste of the rest of the Gospel: Jesus enters Jerusalem, and is drawn inexorably towards the cross. This section dominates the Gospel, and seems to present Jesus as a tragic hero, dying a noble and lonely death.
- The epilogue is more problematic. Are the bare eight verses enough or should there be more?

Drawn as a diagram, the Gospel looks like Figure 6.

As a way of combining a wide variety of material about Jesus, this simple structure was a remarkable achievement.[25]

Papias said that Mark's Gospel was 'not in order'. In comparison to Matthew, Mark was not a tidy thinker and he seems to have added things as they occurred to him, rather than ordering them beforehand. Mark frequently uses 'And' (*kai*) to begin a new sentence: he does this 11 times in

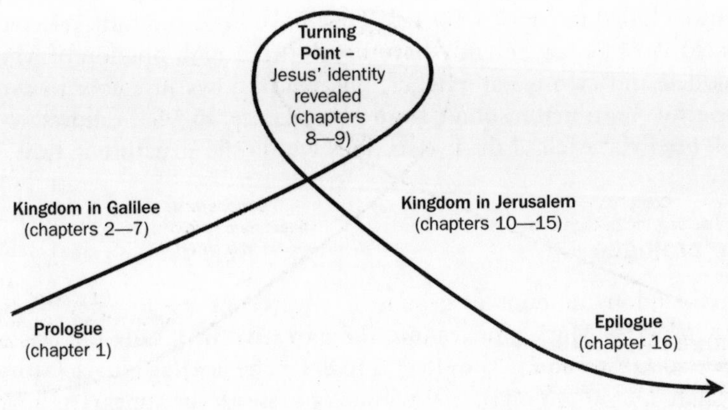

Figure 6 The structure of Mark's Gospel

the first chapter alone. On several occasions, Mark uses the word 'for' (*gar*) out of its normal order: for example, he says that when the women came to the tomb they asked '"Who will roll away the stone from the tomb?" and looking up they saw that the stone had been rolled away – for it was very large' (Mark 16.3–4). The comment about the stone's size has no link with its being rolled away; what Mark meant to say was that they asked the question because the stone was large and they knew they wouldn't be able to shift it. He adds the explanation as an afterthought, exactly as someone would do if telling the story orally rather than writing it.

This aspect of Mark's style tells us something important about him. Writers who write like this 'are not always logical thinkers who develop an argument stage by stage … they mention first the important or striking points … and then fit in the explanatory details afterwards.'[26] As with style, so with structure. Sometimes it seems that a section has ended, only for there to be one last story added on, so the divisions in the diagram are meant to be approximate rather than definitive. Nevertheless there is a genuine flow and development about Mark's story.

The form critics saw Mark's Gospel as essentially a compilation of small units of tradition, strung together 'like pearls on a string'. Yet it is clear that, when we attend to the way in which Mark's Gospel is written, a powerful creative mind has been at work. Morna Hooker comments wryly on the form critics that 'Any woman would have spotted at once the flaw in the analogy: pearls need to be carefully selected and graded.'[27] The narrative may be roughly written, but it is anything but roughly structured. The movement of 'redaction criticism', which followed form criticism, emphasized the role of the 'redactor' or final editor in shaping the material and this seems to be what has happened with the stories of Jesus included in Mark's Gospel. They have been carefully selected and graded. So scholars recently have developed a high opinion of Mark as a skilled and creative storyteller, one who knows just how to evoke a powerful emotional response from his audience. In what follows we shall look briefly at each of the five sections within the structure in turn.

The prologue

A tremendous amount of ground is covered in the first few verses of the Gospel as Mark plunges into the narrative with only the briefest of 'story-so-far' résumés. The effect is to draw the hearers into the story and to catch their attention so that within 15 verses Jesus appears as an adult, embarking on his mission, proclaiming 'The time is fulfilled, the Kingdom of God is here' (Mark 1.15). His first act in bringing the Kingdom is to recruit a band of followers around him (Mark 1.16–20).

Most commentators end the prologue here, as Jesus embarks on his public ministry. However, the analogy of a film script is again helpful. After an arresting opening sequence most films will offer a series of 'establishing shots' before the story really gets going and Mark does a similar thing. There have been snapshot views so far of the Judean desert, the River Jordan and the shore of Lake Galilee. Now the pace slows and the location narrows to the town of Capernaum as Mark uses the device of a single 'day-in-the-life' to establish the pattern of Jesus' ministry (Mark 1.16–34).

A 'day-in-the-life'

Capernaum is the scene of an explosion of the Kingdom of God which looks very like what Jesus will later talk about as the 'mustard seed' effect in one of the parables (Mark 4.30–2). The point of that parable is not just the size of the tree that grows from the seed. Wild mustard grew very quickly and was virtually impossible to remove because its seeds germinated and sprang to life almost at once, suddenly filling a field with a plant which could grow within weeks to a height of 8 to 12 feet. That is the effect of the coming of the Kingdom in Capernaum.

The near frenzy of the situation is neatly captured in a single phrase: 'the whole town was gathered at the door' (1:33). Mark's Greek literally says that the people 'came together around towards' the door, vividly conveying the crush. Archaeological work at Capernaum has given us a picture of several houses facing inwards to a common courtyard, and this seems to be what Mark is describing. It's easy to imagine the crush of people wanting to squeeze in and get a piece of Jesus, the new phenomenon.

But Jesus seems to tire of this mustard-seed impact on Capernaum. He creeps out of Capernaum for some peace and quiet (Mark 1.35–39). Mark shows him moving on. Perhaps the most significant part of this little narrative is Jesus' reply to the disciples when they say, 'Everyone's looking for you'. The need is there in Capernaum. But Jesus responds that they must head out to other places: his call is to bring the good news of the Kingdom to other towns in Galilee as well. It's not enough to stay at home and get people to come to him. So he and the disciples set off on the road.

Meeting a leper

On the road they are ambushed by a leper (Mark 1.40–5). The scene is vivid and focuses on the main characters, and the implied setting is on the road between towns where a leper might be encountered (this is a good example of Mark's economical style). The leper, if he obeys the Law, should call out 'unclean' at the appearance of other people. But he doesn't, instead calling Jesus to him. The atmosphere in the scene is electric. The disciples seem to scatter and hide, leaving Jesus on his own, confronted by a dishevelled bundle of suffering. But the leper throws a challenge to Jesus: 'If you want to, you can make me clean' (Mark 1.40).

Jesus' identity is a key question in Mark's Gospel, and at this point it is posed for the first time. Cleansing the leper meant that Jesus would himself become ritually unclean. The question is put in such a way as to draw out Jesus' choice in the matter. It is a moment of great tension.

What did Mark write next? Some manuscripts say Jesus was filled with compassion, others with anger, and it is not clear which reading is the authentic one. Those who study the manuscripts to determine the best reading tend to opt ultimately for compassion on the grounds that if scribes had felt they needed to change anger to something softer they would have done it on the other occasions in the Gospel when anger appears. Though compassion is the most likely reading, it's worth spending a moment considering why some versions of this story might have said that Jesus was angry. The leper's question puts Jesus between a rock and a hard place. It forces him to make a choice between two courses of action: to side with the explicit instruction of the Law and reject the man; or to act contrary to the Law and heal him, making conflict with the scribes (already implied, Mark 1.22) irrevocable. Being forced to make such a choice might provoke anger as much as compassion. And if the Gospel does derive from Peter's eyewitness testimony then anger is perhaps the more plausible reading.

The choice is made as Jesus reaches out and touches the man. What will happen? Will the infection spread to Jesus? Will he become unclean? 'I do choose,' he says, 'Be clean', and the man is healed (Mark 1.41–2).

Within the world of Mark's story the issue is a simple one of whether

Jesus wants to heal or not. He never raises questions about Jesus' ability to heal as contemporary readers tend to do. It's a good example of how Mark is like a novelist in asking for the 'willing suspension of disbelief' in his readers.

For Mark the decision on the road is a crucial one for Jesus' future direction. Small choices make big differences. Jesus takes the first step on the road to conflict and ultimately the cross. The direction of the rest of the story is set and will inexorably unfold.

Keeping a secret?

Another important theme in Mark's Gospel in the story of Jesus' encounter with the leper is Jesus' command not to tell anyone what has happened (Mark 1.44). This feature of the Gospel was christened the 'Messianic Secret' by Wilhelm Wrede in 1901. Here are some of the other examples:

- Jesus forbids demons to speak about him (Mark 1.25, 34; 3.12).
- He teaches the disciples the meaning of parables in private (Mark 4.10, 34; 7.17; 10.10; 13.3)
- He tells the disciples to keep quiet about his true identity (Mark 8.30; 9.9).
- He conducts some of his healings privately (Mark 5.40; 7.33; 8.23) and asks for people not to talk about them (Mark 5.43; 7.36; 8.26).
- He is inclined to escape the crowds (Mark 1.35; 6.31, 46; 7.24; 8.10; 9.2, 30).

But the reader has known from the very beginning that this is the 'good news of Jesus Christ, the son of God' (Mark 1.1). Jesus' relationship to God is made clear by a heavenly voice at his baptism and his transfiguration (Mark 1.11; 9.7).

So what is going on here? Perhaps the most convincing suggestion is that the secrecy theme keeps Jesus' identity in suspense for the characters in the story, though the audience has already been invited to know the truth. Even when Peter identifies Jesus at the turning point of the Gospel as the messiah, he fails to go further and see that he is the Son of God (Mark 8.29; Matt. 16.16 adds the words 'son of the living God' to Peter's confession). Full disclosure does not come until almost the end of the story. Only on the verge of crucifixion does Jesus cast off the cloak of secrecy and answer the high priest's direct question 'Are you the Christ, the son of God?' with the plain 'I am' (Mark 14.61–2). But the high priest does not understand and accuses him of blasphemy (Mark 14.64). At the cross itself for the first time in the Gospel Jesus' true identity is recognized by a human voice as the centurion says 'Truly this was the son of God' (Mark 15.39). The secret is out at last.

The true identity of Jesus remained in dispute for centuries in the Church until the Council of Chalcedon in 451 brought some measure of agreement. The issue is still alive today and was just as crucial in the early Church. Mark uses the secrecy theme to tease out this question, drawing the audience into his story world and changing the way they see Jesus. It is a very sophisticated and successful technique of persuasion, confirming what he announced at the beginning: that his story is about 'Jesus Christ, the son of God.'

The Kingdom in Galilee

The prologue introduced Jesus and his successful initial work in Capernaum, culminating in his crucial encounter with the leper, which set Jesus on the road to the cross. The next main section of the Gospel is centred on Galilee, mostly around the lake, though there is a single brief foray up to Tyre and Sidon (Mark 7.24–30). (It is highly likely that Mark has hugely simplified the story at this point.)

There is a lot of movement in this part of the Gospel, as Mark draws a picture of the whole region around Lake Galilee alight with the presence of the Kingdom of God. The Kingdom consists of unlikely people (Mark 2.17). The signs of the Kingdom are seen in Jesus' teaching-parables and his miracles. The work is not confined to Jesus himself: he chooses twelve of his followers to be 'apostles', official messengers (Mark 3.14), and sends them out (Mark 6.7, 12–13). People flock to Jesus for healing and great crowds gather to hear his teaching (Mark 6.44, 56). The section is summed up by the comment of the people in the Decapolis area: Jesus 'has made everything right' (Mark 7.37), a good description of what it means for the Kingdom to have come among them.

Feeding miracles

Two similar miracles seem to form the climax to this part of the Gospel: the feedings of the 5,000 and of the 4,000 (Mark 6.30–44; 8.1–9). Mark seems to feel that the meaning of these miracles speaks for itself and does not spell it out (Mark 8.19–21). Unfortunately, commentators ever since have followed the disciples and found that the meaning is not self-evident! Clearly the stories of two similar miracles so close to one another are designed to communicate something important; but what is it?

A traditional interpretation (reaching back to Augustine of Hippo in the fourth century) takes the numbers involved to be symbolic. In the feeding of the 5,000 twelve baskets of leftovers were collected; in the feeding of 4,000 there were seven (Mark 8.19–20). To Augustine five (loaves and thousands) symbolized the five books of Moses; twelve (baskets) the tribes of Israel. Therefore the first miracle is meant to symbolize the salvation Jesus brings to Israel. In the second miracle seven (loaves and baskets) according to Augustine symbolized the rest of the world, since seven was a number representing completeness and 70 in Jewish tradition was the number of gentile nations. It is an interesting way to interpret a text! But it is selective in its choice of numbers. Why is there no significance attached to the 200 *denarii* the disciples have, or the two fish (Mark 6.37–8)? Does seven really represent seventy? What is the significance of the 4,000 in the second story? Interestingly, in his use of these stories Matthew omits the 200 *denarii*, suggesting that he did see symbolic values here (Matt. 14.13–21); as we saw when looking at the patterns in his Gospel, he liked this kind of approach. Mark is much less likely to want to work things out in such a way. Bearing in mind that story is usually the best category to interpret Mark's Gospel, perhaps it is better to stand back from the details and see how these miracles fit into the wider story.

Both miracles take place in the desert. This setting, rather than the numbers involved, is what might suggest that there is an echo intended here of the story of Moses and the people of Israel in the desert. The phrase 'they were like sheep who don't have a shepherd' is also part of the story of the choosing of Joshua to be the leader of Israel after Moses (Mark 6.34; Num. 27.17; Joshua is the Hebrew form of the name Jesus). In the desert the people were miraculously fed by manna, a bread-like substance of which only a daily ration was provided. It had to be eaten up every day and could not be kept. By contrast the bread that Jesus provides is not only real bread, there is so much of it that in both stories a huge amount is left over. And the miracle is not a one-off event, it is repeated. In other words, the point of these miracles lies in the leftovers and their abundance (as Jesus' questions to the disciples imply, Mark 8.19–21). Moses (and also by implication the Law and Jewish faith) can only satisfy so much, Mark suggests. In Jesus the real thing has arrived. There is enough and to spare, an inexhaustible supply (it is striking how much this interpretation echoes the explanation in John's Gospel, John 6.25–40).

There is a link with the gentiles here, though it does not have to be forced from the figures. For between the two miracles Mark tells the story of a gentile woman who meets Jesus (he calls her 'a Greek' to make the point, Mark 7.26). The story again turns on bread. The woman challenges Jesus' reluctance to heal her daughter, which seems to be on the grounds that he has come to feed the people of Israel ('the children') not the gentiles ('the dogs'). She responds to him 'even the dogs under the table eat the children's tiny crumbs' (Mark 7.28). Jesus praises her answer and heals her daughter (Mark 7.24–30). Read together with the two feeding miracles, the implication of this story is that through his disciples, Jesus will satisfy both Jews and gentiles.

Seeing clearly

By the end of this section of the Gospel Mark has shown us Jesus as having power over the created world as master of the wind and waves (Mark 4.35–41); over death as the restorer of life (Mark 5.35–43); and over the needs of the world as the provider of a feast in the desert (Mark 6.30–44; 8.1–10). Jesus has become massively popular on both sides of Lake Galilee, and is the leader of a large and potentially threatening force. Mark says that the 5,000 men sat down in ranks by hundreds and fifties, suggesting a quasi-military organization (Mark 6.40, the other Gospels avoid this language). There can be no doubt: the Kingdom of God has come to Galilee.

But this whole section is framed by opposition from the scribes and Pharisees, from the story of the healing of a paralysed man (Mark 2.1–12) to the demand for a sign of his power after a string of miracles (Mark 8.11), the culmination of their sustained opposition (Mark 2.16, 23–4; 3.22; 7.1–2). What more can they want?

The Pharisees seem to be wilfully blind. They of all people should be able to recognize the work of God. Instead they do the opposite and attribute Jesus' power to 'Beelzebul, the ruler of the demons', an unforgivable blasphemy (Mark 3.22–30). The disciples too are in the dark. Unlike the Pharisees, they want to believe, but it is a gradual process for them. The short story of Jesus healing a blind man in Bethsaida forms a bridge to the next section of the Gospel. In it the man sees very dimly at first; people look to him like trees. As Jesus continues to lay his hands on the man's eyes he begins to see everything clearly (Mark 8.25). The disciples are about to see clearly too.

The turning point

The dramatic plot of Mark's Gospel reaches its 'crisis' halfway through, in the episode which takes place at Caesarea Philippi. This is the turning point of the story. This is where Peter comes to the realization that the audience has known all along. Jesus is the Christ – the messiah (Mark 8.29).

Cross and glory

After Peter's moment of recognition, Mark says that Jesus *began* to teach the disciples, suggesting a decisively new phase of instruction. For the first time Jesus raises the question of what his fate will be. He will suffer and die but after three days will rise again (Mark 8.31). This is defiantly non-violent language, embracing a path of passive resistance to an oppressive regime. Jesus' stress on suffering and the cross means a decisive turn away from a military option. When he later marches on Jerusalem and his army affords him a triumphal entry it is not as other messianic figures like the Maccabees had done in the centuries before, but on an ass, dramatizing his desire for peace and not violence.

Mark portrays these words as a shock for the disciples, and Peter rebukes Jesus. Jesus turns angrily on him and calls him Satan, placing him with the scribes and Pharisees who do not understand (Mark 8.32–3; 3.22–30). Then Jesus speaks directly of the cross and how his followers would also have to take up their crosses (Mark 8.34). At the turning point of the Gospel the end suddenly comes into sight.

To Mark's original audience, whether it was in Rome or Palestine, the cross was not simply an instrument of execution. It also proclaimed that its victims were marginal people: slaves, thieves, rebels, non-citizens. Speaking as Jesus does of the taking up the cross as a mark of following him therefore places his disciples among the poor, the blind, the lame and the unclean. In a nutshell, Jesus leads a ramshackle army of the profoundly unimportant.

Mark has set up a picture of triumph and success in the coming of the Kingdom to Galilee in the first part of the Gospel. Now he lets his audience see that Jesus' vision of the Kingdom is actually radically different from what they might be led to expect. As Martin Hengel comments, 'to assert that God himself accepted death in the form of a crucified Jewish manual worker from Galilee in order to break the power of death and bring salvation to all ... could only seem folly and madness ... [in] ancient times.'[28] Victims even had to carry their crosses: this was execution on the cheap.

The next scene reinforces Jesus' authority. He takes his three closest disciples up a mountain. Jesus is revealed to them as the son of God in the company of Elijah and Moses at the transfiguration. This emphasizes the pre-eminence of Jesus, just as the feeding miracles did. Yet it is a private experience for the disciples and, once again, they are forbidden to speak of it (Mark 9.2–10).

The transfiguration in Mark's story is the moment when the disciples see that in Jesus the Kingdom has come. Peter's confession identifies Jesus as the messiah but he could still be seen as a purely human messenger of God; the transfiguration sets him apart. He is beyond Moses and Elijah and beyond Messiah figures. The voice from the cloud (Mark 9.7) merely emphasizes what has already become plain. But the path to glory will go by way of the cross. And the disciples still don't understand how this can be so (Mark 9.10).

The remaining part of this section fills out the alternative vision of the Kingdom that Jesus has introduced. For the first time the disciples have found the power of God to be limited, as they fail to cast out an evil spirit. Jesus has to come to the rescue (Mark 9.14–29). And Jesus shows the disciples that servanthood, not lordship, is the key role for a leader in the Kingdom of God (Mark 9.33–7).

The Kingdom in Jerusalem

After the excursion to Caesarea Philippi and the transfiguration, Jesus leaves Galilee and heads south (Mark 10.1). The rest of the Gospel's action takes place in Judea and Jerusalem.

At first the story seems familiar. Crowds flock around, Jesus teaches them, the disciples are obtuse and people are healed (Mark 10.2–52). But a note of suffering and service is now present (Mark 10.32–45). Jesus has privately redefined the Kingdom, and the healing of a second blind man suggests that, just as revelation followed the healing of the first, so now Jesus will publicly be revealed as the king (Mark 10.46–52).

The Gospels have been described as 'passion narratives with extended introductions'.[29] This is particularly true of Mark's. Almost a third of the Gospel is devoted to the last week of Jesus' life in Jerusalem. The story of Jesus' triumphant entry into the city (Mark 11.1–11) leads the audience to expect a counterpart to the successful coming of the Kingdom in Galilee. But it doesn't happen that way.

A fig-sandwich and impending judgement

Looking for something to eat, Jesus sees a fig-tree. Fig-trees are unique in producing their fruit before their leaves. It would be reasonable therefore to expect fruit from a fig-tree already in leaf, even if 'it was not the season for figs' (Mark 11.13). But there are none, and Jesus curses the tree. Later, in the sandwich pattern that has by now become familiar, Jesus returns to the tree and it has withered (Mark 11.20).

The filling in this sandwich is the story of Jesus entering the Temple and driving out the merchants and money-changers (Mark 11.15–18). The link is fairly obvious: like the tree, the Temple has the appearance of life from a distance, but on close examination the fruit is simply not there. The busy activity of those who buy and sell and keep the sacrificial system going is like the leaves on the tree, hiding the fact that there is nothing really satisfying in temple worship any longer (echoing once again the theme of being satisfied in the earlier feeding miracles). This is 'the anti-type of a miracle story: instead of life, Jesus brings death, instead of restoration, destruction ... Mark sees what happens as a prophetic sign of coming judgment.'[30] The cursing of the fig-tree is Jesus' last miracle in Mark's story. The fig-tree will return as a warning that judgement is near (Mark 13.28).

This sombre note continues as Jesus takes on the chief priests, scribes and elders in public. The parable of the tenants and the vineyard is clearly about God's judgement on these leaders (Mark 12.1–12). In Galilee Jesus had avoided these confrontations; now he seems to provoke them. Arguments about paying taxes to Caesar, and the absurd nit-picking of the Sadducees about the resurrection, invite ridicule (Mark 12.13–27). Yet there is still genuine faith in Israel, as the story of one of the scribes and then of the poor widow show (Mark 12.28–34, 41–4).

The 'little apocalypse'

Jesus does more talking in this part of Mark's Gospel than in any other. There is an extended passage which goes deeper into the question of judgement and destruction. It is provoked by the disciples' astonishment at the size and solidity of the Temple. Yet Jesus prophesies that the Temple will soon be destroyed (Mark 13.1–2). The whole of Mark 13 is sometimes known as the 'little apocalypse' and it shares some of the characteristics of first-century apocalyptic writings. The Greek word from which 'apocalyptic' is derived means to 'reveal' or 'uncover', and apocalyptic writing therefore claimed to make plain the underlying truth of things. The first century was full of such books, usually offering secrets revealed by a heavenly messenger in a vision, with dramatic pictures of the destruction of the present order of things and a miraculous deliverance and restoration by God for those who had suffered in his cause. They were often linked with precise timetables as to when the predicted events would occur.

Mark 13 has many similarities with this kind of writing. It is full of picture language as Mark relays Jesus' teaching about angels and the Son of Man coming on the clouds (Mark 13.24–7). Yet there appears to be no interest at all on Jesus' part in answering the request of the inner circle of disciples for a timetable and a sign (Mark 13.4). Jesus gives them a series of signs (Mark 13.7–23) but none of them is clear. The disciples seem to want to be given the answer ahead of time, which will let them off the responsibility of watching. But, the 'purpose of [Jesus'] reply is not to impart esoteric information' as contemporary apocalyptic tended to do, 'but to strengthen and sustain faith',[31] by giving them a sense of an alternative reality which leaves timetables for the end of the world behind.

The direct answer to their question is that 'no one knows' (Mark 13.32), not even Jesus himself. Instead Jesus gives them assurance that the present era is balanced by another reality, in which the Son of Man will be vindicated and in which the sufferings of the faithful will count after all. In this reality, the 'stars will fall and the heavenly powers will be shaken' (Mark 13.25). Some contemporary translations choose to render this as if it were literal language – that stars will fall out of the sky and 'heavenly bodies' (presumably meaning planets or comets) will be shaken: It is much more likely that first-century hearers would have taken these things to mean the powers of evil which opposed God. Jesus claims that at that time the stars and the 'powers' (the true translation of *dunameis* here) will be dethroned and broken. This prophecy contrasts with the view of the later first-century Jewish philosopher, Philo of Alexandria, who wrote that 'the powers of the universe are chains that cannot be broken'.[32] Jesus offers a vision of a world no longer enslaved by evil.

The word Mark uses for the (unknown and unknowable) time when this will happen is *kairos*, the right time, the moment of truth (Mark 13.33). That moment is when two realities collide, and the alternative order that is the Kingdom of God is manifest. In a sense Mark has been warming up to this throughout his story. The sense of the heavenly identity of Jesus, the son of God who is unrecognized on earth, has been a major theme, and the audience has been in on the secret from the beginning. Jesus' chosen description as 'the Son of Man', with its echoes of Daniel's apocalyptic prophecy, is also linked (Dan. 7.13–14). The turning-round of expectations about the Kingdom of God from midway through the Gospel also points to the future moment when the two realities will clash. The clash is coming on the cross, but here in Jesus' final teaching to his disciples is a way of understanding what is to happen. The puzzling claim that 'this generation will by no means pass away until all these things happen' (Mark 13.30) makes sense if we read 'these things' as meaning the breaking of the iron cage of predetermination by the heavenly powers. Their grip is broken, as Mark shortly goes on to demonstrate, in the cross.

The grand finale

The pace of the rest of the story is relentless. Mark describes the last days of Jesus in even finer detail. To use a film analogy again, it is as if the rest of the story is told in close-up.

There is little editorial work here. Mark simply tells the story. Jesus and his disciples eat a last supper together. They pray in the garden of Gethsemane. Jesus is arrested. A brief sub-plot shows how Peter first promises loyalty and then fails; this is the last of the 'sandwiches' and the effect is to increase the tension as the story rejoins Jesus at his trial.

The crucifixion is told, uniquely for Mark, with indications of time passing (Mark 15.25, 33). Jesus is hailed ironically as king (Mark 15.18). He came to bring the Kingdom to Galilee, now it looks as if he has failed, as his final words suggest: 'My God, my God, why have you deserted me?' (Mark 15.34). The centurion's words of recognition, important though they are in this Gospel, are muted and equivocal. What does he really mean? Why is it that a Roman sees something that Jesus' own followers and fellow Jews remain blind to (Mark 15.39)? Jesus' body is taken down from the cross and is laid in a tomb. There is no doubt that Jesus is dead (Mark 15.45).

Epilogue – a never-ending story?

The final scene of Mark's Gospel is a funny way to end the story. Mark shows the women coming to the tomb, an encounter with a young man who tells them Jesus is not there, and that they should go to Galilee to see him. Then they run out, filled with fear and amazement, saying nothing to anyone (Mark 16.1–8). And there the text apparently stops. From Eusebius in the early fourth century onwards, it has been recognized that what Mark wrote ends there.

Attempts in the fifth century to 'fix' this inconclusive ending remain printed in most Bibles, but usually with a disclaimer of their authenticity. The 'longer ending' (Mark 16.9–20) was included in the Authorized (King James) Version and certain snake-handling sects in the USA remain attached to it (see Mark 16.18!); but its language and style are not the same as the rest of the Gospel. So the final shot of the story is apparently of the women running in panic through the grey of early dawn, out into the streets of Jerusalem.

Is that where Mark meant to leave the story? After all, the rising of the Son of Man after three days as the climax of Mark's story has been trailed as the natural partner to his suffering and death (Mark 8.31; 9.31; 10.34). The message of the young man at the tomb also affirms a belief that this is indeed what has happened (Mark 16.6), so it is not right to suggest, as some commentators do, that Mark knows nothing of the resurrection. But did he write more?

Tom Wright argues strongly that Mark did write more and that the end of his Gospel has been lost: maybe the manuscript was torn or burned. The overall structure of Mark, he argues, in particular the detailed fulfilment of Jesus' earlier predictions of suffering and death, 'would naturally lead the reader to expect ... a reasonably detailed description of the fulfilment of the other part of the prophecy [his vindication by rising from the dead] as well.' He goes on to claim that the end of the Gospel must have included 'initial meetings with the women and/or Peter; journeying to Galilee and seeing Jesus again there; final teaching and commissioning for worldwide mission.' Wright is open about having a clear apologetic motive for his argument. He wants to show this Gospel 'cannot be used, as [it] has so often been used, as a sign that the earliest Christians knew nothing more than an empty tomb, trembling and panic'.[33] He accuses those who assume that Mark's Gospel ended here as having a hidden agenda to undermine and debunk orthodox Christian faith. Those who think Mark ended his writing so abruptly are living in the uncertain neverland of postmodernism, he says, unable to be sure of their faith, wavering and havering when the incontrovertible truth stares them in the face.

Some of the arguments for Mark having written more lie in the apparently inelegant way that the Gospel ends in mid-sentence with a preposition (*gar* – for, Mark 16.8). But inelegance is one of Mark's hallmarks, and it gives his text an immediacy; his grammar is a bit shaky at the best of times. At times, it is tempting to wonder whether it is deliberate, and the view that this was a text for performance suggests that he is trying to capture the flavour of the spoken rather than the written word.

Ending a book in an inconclusive way had some significant parallels in the ancient world. Homer's *Odyssey*, for example, stops rather than ends. There is no 'rounding off' of Odysseus' ten-year journey home; instead he ends up enmeshed in the local feuds of his native Ithaca as if he'd never been away. In Virgil's *Aeneid,* written only 40 or so years before Mark's Gospel, Aeneas the hero plunges his sword into the traitor Turnus and the book 'ends with an unresolved discord'.[34] In the Bible, the books of Deuteronomy and Jonah also end inconclusively, the latter with a question posed by God to Jonah which he does not answer. In the New Testament, Matthew's Gospel ends literally with a cliff-hanger, as the final scene takes us to the top of a mountain with the disciples ready to be launched on the world and leaves us there, wondering what comes next. Even more notoriously Luke, whose Gospel is neatly wrapped up by Jesus parting from the disciples, ends the whole story he is telling on a downbeat with Paul freely proclaiming the Gospel in Rome but without a resounding conclusion (Acts 28.30–1).

So it may not be so strange that Mark's Gospel ends where it does. To leave this text in some sense unfinished or with a 'suspended ending'[35] may well have been the writer's intention. In doing so, he begs questions of his audience, as in fact he has been doing throughout the Gospel.

Mark was taking material that was already well-known to his audience and casting it in a new way. The resurrection announcement of the young man at the tomb opens a door into the future which the audience in fact occupied. It has the effect of reminding them that out of the anguish and suffering of the cross came the new Christian movement of which they were part, but the structure forces them to recognize their own role by leaving the ending of the story deliberately open. The unfinished nature of the Gospel draws attention to the mysterious quality of the resurrection of Jesus. Mark preserves the first witnesses' sense of surprise at the strange, unexpected nature of what they believed God had done. A tidy conclusion would lose that sense. Perhaps this really is where Mark wished to leave his audience: sensing the shock at a tomb that is untenanted, looking back at a cross that is empty. Morna Hooker suggests that the whole Gospel has shown that 'it is only those who are prepared to believe and who set off on the journey of faith who will see the risen Lord.'[36]

The unfinished fugue

There is another fascinating parallel to Mark's ending. J. S. Bach's *Art of Fugue* ends with Contrapunctus XIV. It is unfinished. His son later said that at the point where he introduced the notes BACH as a counterpoint, he died. But more recently it has been suggested that Bach deliberately left the whole piece this way, especially since the manuscript shows no sign of the deterioration in handwriting through failing eyesight that was characteristic of the last couple of years of his life. Maybe he was trying to express something which he ultimately realized was beyond his capacity to reach. Maybe he was challenging those who came after him to try to complete his work. We shall never know. But if you listen to the piece a strange phenomenon can happen. The intricate, repetitive structure of the fugue echoes in your head, and when the music abruptly stops, it is as if it continues silently and you can still hear it because you know where it is going.

Could Mark have intended something similar? He ends with the abrupt silence of the women, who say 'nothing to anyone' (Mark 16.8). Perhaps they don't need to. The news of Jesus' resurrection will not stay secret for ever. Those who know his story will still hear the music even after it has stopped; they will know intuitively what the next notes must be.

Spotlight on the crucifixion of Jesus

The four Gospel writers come closer to one another in the way they tell the story of Jesus' crucifixion than in any other major section of the Gospels. They seem to be reacting to one another as they retell the story. It is rather like a musical theme and its variations. Mark's account is the theme and the variations are the ways in which Mark's narrative is reworked by the others.

Mark's is easily the shortest account of the crucifixion (Mark 15.22–41), but every detail counts within it, and not a single word is wasted. The features with which we are familiar from the rest of the Gospel are also characteristic of this section: breathless pace, which draws the audience deeper into the story; and Mark's tendency not to draw a conclusion, leaving the meaning open for hearers to puzzle over and maybe even argue with. Whitney Shiner suggests that it is the mockery of Jesus on the cross which shows this technique most clearly (Mark 15.29): 'Mark has focused on the one part of the suffering of Jesus that I can experience. If the performer describes the physical agony of crucifixion, it remains something external to me ... [But if] the performer yells insults at Jesus, I experience that directly.'[37] After the mockery comes darkness. After the darkness comes a cry of desolation in Aramaic. But Jesus no longer speaks to his 'Father' as he has done in the rest of Mark's Gospel; now he addresses 'God'. There is a final loud cry, and Jesus is dead.

How does God respond, according to Mark? The Temple curtain is torn from top to bottom. God has left the building. The world is abandoned, and in Jesus' death, God himself is no more. And here, for the first time in Mark's Gospel, someone recognizes Jesus truly: 'This man *was* the Son of God' says the centurion. But the accent is on the tense here:

as Mark wrote it, it reads 'truly this man Son of God *was*' (Mark 15.39). Mark's message is, in Raymond Brown's words, that 'People can believe and become true disciples only through the suffering symbolized by a cross ... Jesus had been taunted to come down from the cross and save himself, whereas salvation comes only through acceptance of the cross.'[38] This has been the message of the second half of the Gospel, but on the cross it becomes real.

Could Mark's audience bear this image of desolation, degradation and unmitigated suffering? Was Jesus really forsaken by God? The question is left hanging, equivocally answered by the centurion. The other Gospel writers took up the challenge Mark posed.

Matthew followed Mark's telling of the crucifixion and expanded it (Matt. 27.33–56), but where Mark speaks of God vacating the Temple as the curtain is torn Matthew makes a telling addition: 'behold, the curtain of the Temple was torn from top to bottom in two; the earth was shaken and rocks split and tombs opened and the bodies of many holy ones who had fallen asleep were raised and came out of the tombs and after his resurrection entered into the city and appeared to many' (Matt. 27.51–3). Only then does he add the centurion's affirmation: 'truly this was a son of God' (Matt. 27.54). What is the meaning of this interpolation?

Matthew uniquely points ahead to what will follow shortly in the story, using a device which some have called a 'flash forward'. He doesn't want his readers to miss the significance of what has happened in the crucifixion and death of Jesus and fears that they may do so if he leaves the story as he has inherited it from Mark. He uses poetic language to remind his hearers of Ezekiel's great vision of the valley of the dry bones in the past (Ezek. 37), that when all is lost, and the people find themselves in the waste land, the graveyard valley filled with dry bones, then God still has more in store: to bring life out of death. Ezekiel's prophecy will be fulfilled in the resurrection of Jesus.

When Luke came to write his version of the story of Jesus' crucifixion (Luke 23.32–49), he took a different angle from Mark. The early details of crucifixion and mocking are broadly the same, but Luke introduces two new notes: Jesus calls for the forgiveness of those who are crucifying him, and one of the thieves mocking Jesus repents. In Luke's picture Jesus is concerned not for himself but for others. Forgiveness and healing flow from this cross.

Luke records, like Mark, the darkness. But where Mark's crucifixion is overwhelmed by darkness, somehow Luke's is not. It is as if Jesus shines in the midst of it. Luke says that the sun's light failed but Jesus himself seems to illuminate the whole scene. When he dies his last words are not a cry of dereliction but an expression of serene trust: 'Father, into your hands I commit my spirit' (Luke 23.46). This is a child's prayer usually uttered before sleep, in case the child did not wake in the morning. They are uttered to the Father, whose loving care, Luke wants to affirm, still surrounds this scene.

In Mark's Gospel the crowd is vicious; in Luke many of them are moved. The centurion praises God and there is no irony here. He recognizes that Jesus was innocent. There is no torn curtain in the Temple, something which for Mark signifies God leaving the world for a time. Instead, as Walter Moberley notes, 'Luke portrays the crucifixion as a predominantly tranquil scene dominated by the quiet authority and compassion of the suffering Jesus.'[39] Luke affirms that God is still there.

Luke draws a scene that has moved beyond the raw agony of Mark. With the passing of the years the pain dimmed, and the achievement of Jesus became ever clearer as the Church grew and his followers experienced healing and forgiveness. With hindsight the crucifixion became for Luke the quintessential moment of revelation when the light of God shone down on the earth in the triumph of the Son of God on the cross.

Finally, John's Gospel offers such a radical reinterpretation of the crucifixion as virtually to leave Mark's approach behind (John 19.16–37).

John's Jesus is a king. He carries the cross by himself, and is enthroned upon it; he is in control: 'If God is the author of this passion play, Jesus is the protagonist – but also the producer and director!'[40] John tells the story of how Pilate, the Roman governor, recognizes Jesus' kingship only to make the point that Jewish royalty can be executed without a second thought by the imperial authorities. But Jesus responds that Pilate would have no power unless he had been given it 'from above' (John 19.11).

For John, too, the cross is the place where a new community is born. Jesus looks down and sees his mother and the beloved disciple, Mary and John, and gives them to each other. Mary, John says, was from that time taken to the beloved disciple's home (John 19.26–7). This cross is the source of homecoming for Mary.

In John's Gospel Jesus' final words are different again from the previous Gospels. He says 'It is finished' and lays down his life; it is not taken from him as in Mark or Matthew (John 19.30, see also 10.17–18). He bows his head, restricting his breathing and drawing death on himself. Unlike Mark and Matthew, there is no torn Temple curtain or earthquake here; instead there is blood and water, flowing from Jesus' side (see also John 7.38–39). Barnabas Lindars writes that for John 'no sooner is Jesus' sacrifice complete than the flow of life for the world begins.'[41]

What John does in comparison to Mark, Matthew and Luke is to keep two focuses where the others are content with one. Mark's crucifixion story, and its modified form in Matthew, emphasizes pain, loss, dereliction and agony: they show a forsaken Jesus. Luke, seeing the scene from more of a distance, emphasizes Jesus' control and the way in which the cross becomes the source of healing and forgiveness. John somehow manages to combine both: Jesus' care for his mother and his friend points to the essential human relationships that are such a hallmark of this Gospel;

while the cry 'I thirst' draws attention to Jesus' human needs. In these two details is the pain of loss. But in Jesus' cry 'It is finished' is also a sense of accomplishment: the son has completed what the Father sent him to do. He bows his head and gives up his life voluntarily; John affirms that no one takes it from him.

Yet there is also more in John. For his time scheme is different. Where the other three Gospels seem to describe the Last Supper as a Passover meal, John very deliberately says that it was not: it took place before the Passover and therefore the day on which Jesus died was the day of preparation. A hint of what this might mean comes when John specifies that it is hyssop that is used to give Jesus wine when he thirsts (John 19.29). If this is the day of preparation, then hyssop would have been easy to find, for it was specified for use in sprinkling the blood of the Passover lamb on the doorposts of the Israelite houses so that the angel of death would pass over and save the people inside (Ex. 12.22). Noon, the time of Jesus' crucifixion, was also the hour on the day of preparation when the Passover lambs were slaughtered in the precincts of the Temple. It is hard for us to imagine the scene: but in Jerusalem at this same moment as Jesus is crucified, according to John's version, the first of maybe 30,000 lambs were killed. By evening the Temple courtyards would be literally swimming in blood from the sacrifices. Outside the city, on the hill called Golgotha, Jesus' blood would have seemed insignificant in comparison, lost in the crimson sea that washed over Jerusalem at Passover. When Jesus is removed from the cross, in another detail which only John supplies, none of his bones is broken (John 19.33–6): a further reminder of the Passover lambs which were to be without defect or broken limbs.

At Jesus' first entrance in John's Gospel, John the Baptist has said 'Behold the Lamb of God' (John 1.29). This is the theme which John uses to link his twin focuses: human pain and divine accomplishment. Jesus is the sacrificial lamb, who goes meekly to the slaughter. Event and meaning are fused in John's account, and the tension which Mark faced his audience with squarely in his picture of Jesus dying forsaken in agony is resolved.

Draw your own conclusions

- Is a symbolic approach to Mark's Gospel an effective way to study it?
- How likely do you think it is that Peter's testimony lies behind Mark's Gospel?
- What would you say a 'Gospel' is?
- Is Mark's Gospel structured like a drama? How effective is the structure Mark adopted?
- Was Mark 16.8 intended to be the end of the Gospel? What reasons can you find to support or reject this view?

- Why do the Gospel writers draw such different pictures of the crucifixion of Jesus?

Further reading

What are the Gospels?

S. C. Barton (ed.) (2006), *The Cambridge Companion to the Gospels*, Cambridge: Cambridge University Press is a good general introduction to the study of the Gospels.

The last two decades have seen a huge change in our understanding of the genre of the Gospels. Much of this was pioneered by R. A. Burridge (2004), *What are the Gospels? a comparison with Graeco-Roman biography*, 2nd ed., Grand Rapids: Eerdmans, first published in 1992. See R. A. Burridge, 'Who writes, why and for whom?' in M. Bockmuehl and D. Hagner (eds.) (2005), *The Written Gospel*, Cambridge: Cambridge University Press, for a summary and R. A. Burridge (2006), *Four Gospels, One Jesus?*, 2nd ed., London: SPCK, for a more popular introduction. Some of the implications of the change are worked out in R. J. Bauckham (ed.) (1998), *The Gospels for All Christians: rethinking the gospel audiences*, Grand Rapids: Eerdmans.

Commentaries

M. D. Hooker (1991), *The Gospel According to St Mark*, London: Continuum, is a useful and accessible commentary with a number of very helpful 'additional notes' on specific issues. J. R. Donahue and D. J. Harrington (2002), *The Gospel of Mark*, Collegeville: Liturgical Press, is in the Roman Catholic *Sacra Pagina* series. D. E. Nineham (1963), *Saint Mark*, Harmondsworth: Penguin, was ahead of its time when published and is still worth reading as an example of a cogently argued liberal position on the Gospel. From a liberation theology perspective, C. Myers (1988), *Binding the Strong Man: a political reading of Mark's story of Jesus*, Maryknoll: Orbis, is a thought-provoking read, transposed into more popular terms in C. Myers et al. (1996), *'Say to this Mountain': Mark's story of discipleship*, Maryknoll: Orbis.

Other books

W. R. Telford (1995), *Mark*, London: T.&T. Clark, is a brief but comprehensive survey of critical issues with excellent bibliographies. A short but illuminating companion to her commentary on the Gospel is M. D. Hooker (1983), *The Message of Mark*, London: Epworth, which explores several key themes. H. C. Kee (1977), *The Community of the New Age:*

studies in Mark's Gospel, Philadelphia: Fortress, approaches the Gospel text from a sociological perspective and argues that it was written for an apocalyptic Christian community in southern Syria. D. Rhoads, J. Dewey and D. Michie (1999), *Mark as Story: an introduction to the narrative of a gospel*, 2nd ed., Minneapolis: Fortress, is an excellent and accessible example of a literary approach. A more detailed look at how the Gospel might originally have been read, and the parallels with ancient performing arts can be found in W. Shiner (2003), *Proclaiming the Gospel: first-century performance of Mark*, Harrisburg: TPI.

The four Gospels' narratives of the crucifixion of Jesus are monumentally surveyed in the two-volume R. E. Brown (1994), *The Death of the Messiah*, New York: Doubleday; the second part looks at the crucifixion itself. A shorter consideration of the same texts is R. E. Brown (1986), *A Crucified Christ in Holy Week: essays on the four Gospel passion narratives*, Collegeville: Liturgical Press. At 71 pages rather than 1608 it is well worth reading to get a flavour of Brown's approach!

Websites

- Felix Just has compiled an excellent set of links to 'Symbols of the Evangelists' at www.catholic-resources.org/Art/Evangelists_Symbols.htm. The Coventry Tapestry by Graham Sutherland can be viewed from www.coventrycathedraltour.org.uk/#.
- Links to general resources on Mark's Gospel are at www.textweek.com/mkjnacts/mark.htm.
- A good illustration of houses at Capernaum can be found at www.pbs.org/empires/peterandpaul/footsteps/footsteps_2_3.html

Notes

1 R. A. Burridge (1994), *Four Gospels, One Jesus?*, London: SPCK, p. 28.

2 D. Rhoads, J. Dewey and D. Michie (1999), *Mark as Story*, 2nd ed., Minneapolis: Fortress, p. 4.

3 M. Sadgrove (1995), *A Picture of Faith*, Bury St Edmunds: Kevin Mayhew, p. 110.

4 M. Hooker (1991), *The Gospel According to St Mark*, London: A.&C. Black, p. 8.

5 J. G. Crossley (2006), *Why Christianity Happened: a sociohistorical account of Christian origins (26–50CE)*, Louisville: Westminster John Knox Press, pp. 127, 129. See also J. G. Crossley (2004), *The Date of Mark's Gospel: insight from the law in earliest Christianity*, London: T.&T. Clark.

6 Eusebius, *History of the Church* 3.39. See also 2.15.

7 J. L. Houlden (1990), 'Peter' in R. J. Coggins and J. L. Houlden (eds), *A Dictionary of Biblical Interpretation*, London: SCM Press, p. 534.

8 Justin Martyr, *Dialogue with Trypho* 106.3.

9 Augustine, *On the Agreement of the Evangelists* 2.

10 D. E. Nineham (1963), *Saint Mark*, Harmondsworth: Penguin, p. 27.

11 Nineham, *St Mark*, p. 40.

12 Nineham, *St Mark*, p. 203, quoting A. E. J. Rawlinson.

13 G. N. Stanton (1995), *Gospel Truth?*, London: HarperCollins, p. 53.

14 C. Myers (1988), *Binding the Strong Man: a Political Reading of Mark's Story of Jesus*, Maryknoll: New York, Orbis, pp. 39, 417, 431.

15 J. D. G. Dunn (2003), *Jesus Remembered*, Grand Rapids: Eerdmans, p. 146.

16 R. J. Bauckham (2006), *Jesus and the Eyewitnesses: the Gospels as eyewitness testimony*, Grand Rapids: Eerdmans, p. 164 (emphasis removed).

17 R. Bultmann (1934), *Jesus and the Word*, New York: Scribners, p. 8 – originally published in German in 1926.

18 R. A. Burridge (1998), 'About People, by People, for People: Gospel genre and audiences' in R. J. Bauckham (ed.), *The Gospels for All Christians: rethinking the Gospel audiences*, Grand Rapids: Eerdmans, p. 123. See also R. A. Burridge (2004), *What are the Gospels? a comparison with Graeco-Roman Biography*, 2nd ed., Grand Rapids: Eerdmans.

19 Eusebius, *History of the Church* 3.39.

20 Lucian, *Demonax the Philosopher* 33–7.

21 Burridge, 'About People ...', p. 124.

22 Rhoads, *Mark as Story*, p. 51.

23 Dunn, *Jesus Remembered*, p. 249.

24 Burridge, *Four Gospels*, p. 36.

25 See M. D. Hooker (1997), *Beginnings: keys that open the Gospels*, London: SCM Press, pp. 3–6.

26 M. Thrall (1962). *Greek Particles in the New Testament*, Leiden: Brill, p. 47.

27 M. Hooker (1983), *The Message of Mark*, London: Epworth Press, p. 3.

28 M. Hengel (1986), *The Cross of the Son of God*, London: SCM Press, p.181.

29 M. Kähler (1964), *The So-Called Historical Jesus and the Historic, Biblical Christ*, translated by C. E. Braaten, Philadelphia: Fortress, p. 80n.

30 Hooker, *The Message of Mark*, pp. 81–2.

31 C. E. B. Cranfield (1966), *The Gospel According to St Mark*, 3rd ed., Cambridge, Cambridge University Press, p. 394.

32 Quoted in W. Wink (1984), *Naming the Powers*, Philadelphia: Fortress, p. 160.

33 N. T. Wright (2003), *The Resurrection of the Son of God*, London: SPCK, pp. 620, 624, 617.

34 J. Griffin (1986), 'Introduction' in Virgil, *The Aeneid*, Oxford, Oxford University Press, p. xxiii,

35 M. D. Hooker (2003), *Endings: Invitations to Discipleship*, London: SCM Press, p. 11.

36 Hooker, *Endings*, p. 23.

37 W. Shiner (2003), *Proclaiming the Gospel: first-century performance of Mark*, Harrisburg, TPI, pp. 182–3.

38 R. E. Brown (1986), *A Crucified Christ in Holy Week: essays on the four Gospel passion narratives*, Collegeville: Liturgical Press, p. 33.

39 W. Moberley (1988), 'Proclaiming Christ Crucified: some reflections on the use and abuse of the Gospels', *Anvil* 5/1, pp. 38–9.

40 J. Ashton (1991), *Understanding the Fourth Gospel*, Oxford: Oxford University Press, p. 490.

41 B. Lindars (1972), *The Gospel of John*, London: Marshall, Morgan & Scott, p. 586.

6

Paul – Apostle to the Gentiles

Corinth, late 51

Lucius Junius Gallio, proconsul of Greece, was a delicate man. Proconsuls usually served a year governing a province, but Gallio was unable to do so. He left his post early for a sea-cruise, according to his friend Pliny, as a remedy for a lung infection which meant he was coughing up blood. He left, according to his philosopher brother Seneca, because it was the place rather than his body which was diseased.[1] Seneca and others testified to Gallio's charm and the kindness of his disposition. His character and health probably made his appointment as governor of Greece by the Emperor Claudius, prestigious though it was, rather a trial to him.

While Gallio was in Corinth a man named Paul, also known as Saul, was brought before him. Paul's accusers were from the Jewish synagogue, and Paul himself was a Jew. Gallio heard that Paul was encouraging people to worship in ways that were contrary to the Jewish Law. This must have been perplexing to him, and the dispute certainly seemed to be an internal matter of Jewish theology. No wise governor would allow himself to be caught up in such controversies. Accordingly Gallio's judgement was that he could not interfere, and he dismissed the case (Acts 18.12–16).

Gallio returned to Rome eventually, and his path strangely crossed with Paul's once again. In Nero's last frantic years Gallio and Seneca (who had once been tutor to the emperor) were declared public enemies. Both died by their own hands in 65. It was the same year in which Peter and Paul also met their deaths on Nero's orders, in the persecution of Christians following the Great Fire.

If you go to the ruined city of Corinth today you can see the remains of the judgement seat which Gallio occupied. His time in Greece can be dated with remarkable accuracy because of an inscription found at nearby Delphi which includes his name. From it we can pinpoint Gallio's year of office to 51–2. Because he didn't see out the whole term, we can date Paul's appearance before him as being in the latter half of 51, or the spring of 52 when the winter restrictions on sailing ended and Gallio happily left his troublesome province behind.

From the date of this encounter we can reconstruct the chronology of the New Testament.

Paul – man of contradictions

What was Paul really like? Few people seem to like him on first acquaintance through his writings. He can seem angry, pompous, bossy, overbearing – and always right! Yet a deeper knowledge often breeds admiration and the recognition that his was one of the most creative minds in history.

He has been characterized in diametrically opposite ways. To some he has seemed the pioneer of Christian faith, to others the corrupter of Jesus' simple message of love; he has been described both as the arch-suppresser of women and also a feminist before his time.

So what was Paul really like? Something like this question arose when Paul arrived in Jerusalem around the year 37. The disciples of Jesus knew Paul as a Pharisee who, until three years earlier, had been zealously determined to stamp out their heresy about Jesus. Now he wanted to be part of them. Would they believe him and welcome him in or not (Acts 9.26–7)? If you had been in their shoes, how would you have responded? Would you have trusted him or not?

The mixed perceptions of Paul may not be contradictory: he was both passionately concerned to win arguments, and also impatient with those who did not have his intellectual grasp. Of the four apostles around whom this book is constructed, Paul was the only one who had the education and upbringing to develop a fledgling Christian theological system related to, but gradually becoming distinct from, the faith of Israel, and which could also interact with the social and religious currents of the wider Roman Empire.

Paul was constantly thinking through the implications of his faith. Much of his surviving writing is geared to specific situations, and designed to answer particular questions of conduct. An example of Paul's apparently contradictory views lies in the two statements: 'there can be no male nor female, for you are all one in Jesus Christ' (Gal. 3.28), and 'I want you to know that Christ is the head of every man, and the head of a woman is the man' (1 Cor. 11:3). How can these statements, one apparently radically egalitarian (especially when written by a first-century Jew), the other seemingly rigidly hierarchical, be reconciled? The answers, so far as there are any, to these questions, lie in looking carefully at Paul in his context.

Evidence for Paul – How far can we trust the letters and Acts?

Before we begin to follow the story of Paul's life we need to look briefly at the evidence we have. We know more about Paul than anyone else in the New Testament, including Jesus, and more than all but a very few other people in the whole of the first century.

The major sources are the Acts of the Apostles, which is a continuation of Luke's Gospel, and the 13 letters identified as Paul's. But some scholars are highly sceptical both about the value of Acts as a historical source, and also about the authenticity of half of the letters. Drastically reducing the number of trustworthy sources results in a quite different picture of Paul's life from the one which you will find in Acts. Thus you will find that different scholars hold a wide range of views on the pattern and chronology of Paul's life, depending on how trustworthy they think the sources are.

Seven of the letters assigned to Paul in the New Testament are indisputably written by him: Romans, 1 and 2 Corinthians, Galatians, Philippians, 1 Thessalonians and Philemon. But doubt has been cast on Paul's authorship of the other six in varying degrees as follows:

Least likely to be by Paul———			———*Most likely to be by Paul*
The 'Pastoral letters' (1 and 2 Timothy, Titus)	Ephesians	Colossians	2 Thessalonians

Why these letters might not be authentic is a question we shall examine briefly as we meet each of them in the rest of the chapter.

In the context of understanding Paul's life decisions about the authenticity of the letters have varying effects. Ephesians, for example, adds nothing significant to the biographical data about Paul, and nor does 2 Thessalonians. But Colossians and the Pastoral Letters contain a number of clues which, if the letters are authentic, make quite a difference to how we understand Paul's life and his teaching.

It is not only the details of Paul's life which are affected by decisions about the authenticity of his letters. His views on many issues also change if certain letters are discounted. Dominic Crossan and Jonathan Reed's *In Search of Paul*, for example, contrasts the 'authentic, historical' Paul with the 'canonical' Paul. They set Acts and the six disputed letters to one side and this inevitably results in a different portrait of Paul. In Colossians and Ephesians, for example, slaves are firmly admonished to obey their masters (Col. 3.22; Eph. 6.5–8); to Crossan and Reed these statements in letters written after Paul's death are a clear example of the later Church trying to 'sanitize a social subversive, to domesticate a dissident apostle, and to make Christianity and Rome safe for one another'.[2] If we can strip away these later writings, they say, the authentic radical Paul will be revealed. In one sense the Crossan/Reed approach makes the historian's task easier, for there is no longer a mass of apparently contradictory material to reconcile. It leaves a consistent Paul who supports freedom and equality without qualification.

Crossan and Reed's work, compelling though it is, begs the question of how far they have bracketed out source material which is not conducive to liberal Westerners of the twenty-first century. (To be fair to Crossan, this is an issue which he has consistently recognized.) Maybe Paul *was* as awkward and inconsistent as his opponents in Corinth said (2 Cor. 1.17) and as his letter to the Galatians certainly suggests he was.

What of the chronological framework of Paul's life? Acts provides one; but again Crossan and Reed are inclined to discount it. To them, Acts seems to be an apologetic work designed to reassure Roman officials that Christianity was no threat to the political peace of the Empire. Therefore they consider that Paul's encounter with Gallio, with which this chapter began, 'is much more likely ... parable than ... history'.[3] Without Acts as a guide we are in the dark about the details of Paul's life.

Acts is certainly not as straightforward as it seems. There are some marked differences between the Paul presented in Acts and the Paul who presents himself in the letters. Some of the most obvious are:

- *Paul's Roman citizenship*: without it the story in Acts makes no sense, but Paul never mentions it in his letters.
- *Letter-writing*: Paul doesn't write a single letter in Acts, yet it seems to us to be a major facet of his ministry and strategy.
- *Arguments*: Peter's visit to Antioch led to a bitter argument with Paul (Gal. 2.11–16), but in Acts we find no hint of a falling out between the apostles and Peter is consistently presented as supporting the rights of gentiles as full members of the Church. Luke seems to have edited out the disagreement.

These differences lead the respected scholar Jerome Murphy-O'Connor to consider that Luke is a 'tendentious theologian' who has produced a portrait of Paul which is highly unreliable and includes episodes which are 'a tissue of improbabilities'.[4] He concludes that Acts is an unreliable and secondary source, compared to the authentic letters (though Murphy-O'Connor regards only Ephesians, 1 Timothy and Titus as inauthentic, in contrast to Crossan and Reed).

On the other hand there are some 'we' passages in Acts which lay claim to be eyewitness accounts (Acts 16.10–17; 20.5–15; 21.1–18; 27.1—28.16). The writer of Luke's Gospel speaks directly to his audience (Luke 1.1–4; Acts 1.1), and it seems logical that the 'we' passages imply his presence in Paul's story at certain specific points. He does not claim much. Even within the 'we' passages he seems careful to discriminate between events he has seen and those he has not (see the abrupt change in Acts 16.16–24).

Plenty of scholars have argued against Luke being an eyewitness. Perhaps 40 years elapsed between the events described in Acts and its composition – too long for accurate recollection, it is argued. But 40 years is not really too long a time span between an event and its record; it is accepted without question that Josephus, for example, wrote in the early 90s about events that had happened 30 years before.

A more convincing argument against Luke's eyewitness status lies in the genuine differences noted above between Acts and Paul's letters. But Paul's letters and Acts are doing quite different jobs. The letters are not designed (apart from a few autobiographical passages such as Gal. 2.1–10) to reveal much about Paul himself. So Paul's Roman citizenship for most of his life was probably fairly unimportant to him and he had no need to mention it in his letters; even in Acts it only becomes significant in the final chapters. Equally, Acts presents Paul as a man of action and so has no real need to mention his letters. And as far as the arguments between Peter and Paul are concerned, if Luke was writing 40 years later then the original dispute between the apostles was long past and Luke probably saw no point in emphasizing it again. (Anyone who has been part of a heated committee discussion and then seen how the minutes record it even a month or so later may have some idea of what has happened!)

As Martin Hengel, who has strongly defended the accuracy of Acts, states: 'Luke does not always say everything that he knows, and when he does, he can mention facts which are important – to us – only in passing.'[5] Luke's primary aim clearly stated in the introduction to his Gospel is to argue for the faith (Luke 1.1–4); but his method of doing so is by putting the facts accurately. Like any historian, ancient or modern, he has to choose how to arrange the facts he has gathered and which ones to leave out. Luke is hopelessly imprecise by our standards on dates and times. Surprising though it seems to us, who assume that dates are the first things someone studying the history of an event wants to establish, time simply doesn't matter very much to him. But this is consistent with the general rules of history-writing at the time.

Although the arguments are good on either side, in the rest of this chapter I shall take the view that, as David Wenham writes, 'A thoughtful reading of Acts in the light of the historical context ... makes it clear that Acts gets the history right again and again'.[6] But we do need to bear in mind that Luke may have condensed or missed out events for the purpose of telling the story he wants to get across. His framework makes sense and can be read together with the letters. I think that the Pastoral Letters are least likely to be by Paul and that therefore it is not wise to use information from them for Paul's life. Ephesians is problematic, but since it adds nothing to the picture of the events of Paul's life this doesn't matter much in this context. The other letters can, I believe, be used as sources which derive from Paul. But, as with many of the positions taken in this book, my aim is not so much to persuade you as to encourage you to engage with the arguments for yourself. How accurate do you think Acts could be, and why?

Dating Paul's life

Paul was brought to trial in Corinth while Gallio was proconsul of Greece (Acts 18.12–17) in late 51. This is a solid reference point, which forms the basis for working out the rest of the dates of Paul's life.

We can work back from Paul's trial in Corinth to establish when Paul became a Christian. Paul met Gallio in Corinth during his second missionary campaign. This campaign, which was wide-ranging, would have taken perhaps two years to make, so it probably began in late 49 or 50 (Acts 15.41—18.11). This in turn suggests that his first, shorter, missionary campaign during which the churches in southern Galatia were founded began in 48. Between his conversion and this first campaign Paul says he spent three years in Arabia and Damascus, and then 14 years in Syria and Cilicia (Gal. 1.17—2.1). Subtracting the resulting 17 years from 48 places Paul's conversion in 31.

But it is not quite as simple as that because time in the ancient world was counted differently from the way we do it today, using an 'inclusive reckoning' system. A good example of this is the way in which Jesus' burial is recorded in the Gospels as lasting three days; in fact, it is clear that they mean that Jesus was actually in the tomb for about 30 hours or, in our terms, just over a day (Friday night to early Sunday morning). But inclusive reckoning counted all the days involved as complete days. So because Jesus was in the tomb for all of one day and part of two more, the Gospels reckon that up as a total of three.

The same system applied to years. Thus when Acts says that Paul was in Ephesus for two years (Acts 19.10) it might actually mean that he was only there for what we would call two months, that is, one month in one year and one in the next. So the system of inclusive reckoning means that Paul's 3 years in Arabia could have been only 14 months, and his 14 years in Syria and Cilicia just 12 years and 2 months. In other words Paul's conversion could have been 17 years before 48, or it might have been only 13. This means that while 31 is the earliest possible date for Paul's conversion to have taken place, it might have happened in 35, giving a four-year range.

Fortunately there is another clue to the date of this event. Paul says that he had to escape from Damascus because he had offended a representative of King Aretas IV of Nabatea in the city (2 Cor 11.32). This event seems to have happened three years after Paul's conversion (Gal. 1.17–18), which would place it within the years 34–8. Once again some external evidence can help. Although the details are a little hazy, it appears that Aretas took control of Damascus in 37, taking advantage of the power vacuum caused by the death of the Emperor Tiberius that year. This narrows the options for Paul's escape from Damascus to 37–8. If his conversion was three years earlier, it must have taken place in 34 or 35.

After Paul's encounter with Gallio in Corinth in 51, Acts says that he was imprisoned in Judea under the Roman governor Felix and sent to Rome soon after the arrival of the next governor, Festus. The date of the changeover between governors is unclear; it might have happened as early as 55 or as late as 60. But between Paul's encounter with Gallio and his arrest in Jerusalem, Acts places a third missionary campaign which included up to two years in Ephesus (Acts 18.11) and further travels as far west as Illyricum (on the coast of the Adriatic). After his arrest Paul was held for two years in Caesarea (Acts 24.27, the phrase implies this was a full two years). So while 55 is just possible as the year when Paul was sent to stand trial in Rome, a date in 58 or 59 is more likely considering the amount of activity involved. The issue of new coins by Festus dated in the 'fifth year' of Nero (i.e. 58 or 59) probably marks the beginning of his term of office, so we can be fairly sure that Paul was sent to Rome in either late 58 or 59, arriving there the following spring.

Dating Paul's death relies on more circumstantial evidence. The overwhelming consensus in the early Church was that Paul met his death in Rome, and some indirect evidence from Clement (writing around 96) suggests that Paul died in Rome as part of the persecution by the Emperor Nero following the Great Fire in 64. Eusebius, the fourth-century historian of the Church, summed up widespread tradition when he said that Paul 'suffered martyrdom under Nero'.[7] Certainly no other city had a church which boasted the burial place of the apostle and there is no recorded activity of Paul anywhere else after the mid 60s. Therefore in terms of chronology we seem to be on pretty safe ground when we conclude that Paul met his death in Rome while Nero was emperor. Since Nero committed suicide on 9 June 68, Paul must have died before mid 68.

Assuming that Paul had reached the age of 30 when he became a Christian, we can thus reckon with reasonable certainty that he was born between 1 and 5, and that he died between 65 and 68.

Figure 7 is a summary of the main events of Paul's life and the dates of his writings which will be followed in the rest of the chapter.

Cleopatra, Antony and Tarsus

Cleopatra, queen of Egypt, knew how to get a man's attention. Aged 21, she had had herself delivered to Julius Caesar hidden in a linen bedding sack. The surprise gift captivated him. Three years after his death she was summoned to meet Mark Antony, Rome's premier general in the east, who had been hailed as a 'new Dionysus', the god of wine, excess and pleasure. She dressed to match him as Aphrodite, goddess of love, and arrived on a gilded barge surrounded by Cupids and roses. Antony was hooked, and began a wild and tempestuous liaison with Cleopatra whose fame lasts to this day.

The venue for their meeting was Tarsus, 'a not insignificant city' (Acts 21.39) according to Paul, who was born there almost half a century later. Antony's choice of Tarsus as the place in which to meet the Egyptian queen gives an indication of its status in the ancient world. Perhaps Paul's grandparents were among the crowd who remembered Cleopatra's arrival. The story was still being told 1600 years later, when Shakespeare immortalized the scene in his play about the doomed lovers.[8]

Date	Place	Event	Writing
1–5	Tarsus (Cilicia)	Birth	
15	Jerusalem	Education	
34	Damascus Road	Call/conversion	
34–37	Nabatea	Preaching	
37	Jerusalem	Meeting with Peter and James	
37–46	Tarsus and Cilicia	Unknown	
47–48	Antioch	Ministry in the church	
48	Jerusalem	Agreement to go to the gentiles	
48–49	Cyprus, Pamphylia, South Galatia	First missionary campaign with Barnabas	
49	Antioch Jerusalem	Return Conference with Jerusalem apostles	Galatians
50–52	Galatia, Macedonia, Athens, Corinth and Ephesus	Second missionary campaign with Silas	1 and 2 Thessalonians
52	Jerusalem and Antioch	Reporting back	
52–54	Ephesus	Third missionary campaign	1 and 2 Corinthians
55–56	Macedonia, Illyricum, Corinth	Third missionary campaign continued	Romans
56	Jerusalem	Attempted delivery of the collection and arrest in the Temple	
56–59	Caesarea	Imprisonment awaiting trial	
59–60	Mediterranean	Voyage to Rome, including shipwreck on Malta	
60–62	Rome	Imprisonment awaiting trial	Colossians, Philemon, Philippians, *Ephesians (if by Paul)*
62–65	Rome, Macedonia, Ephesus	Final ministry	*1 and 2 Timothy, Titus (if by Paul)*
65	Rome	Death during Nero's persecution	

Figure 7 The life of Paul

Paul's early life

We know little detail about Paul's early life, but from the background we can reconstruct quite a lot about his early years.

Tarsus

Paul was born at Tarsus, the capital city of Cilicia, the region which today roughly corresponds with south-eastern Turkey. In the wars which came before and after Caesar's death Cilicia had been fought over repeatedly. So the defeat of Antony by Octavian in 31 BC and the peace that ensued was the cause of rejoicing in the city, for at long last trade right across the Mediterranean could flourish. Linen was the city's prime export, and was so lucrative that Tarsus was one of the select number of cities which maintained its own office in the forum at Rome to look after the commercial interests of its citizens.

Tarsus was a Greek city-state in origin, but its position made it a crossroads. Westwards it looked to Ephesus and Greece. Eastwards it looked towards the great centre of Antioch in Syria. Northwards, through the Cilician Gates, lay the main route through the Taurus Mountains and the interior of Asia Minor. Throughout Paul's lifetime Tarsus was part of the province of Syria, which included the whole coastal strip as far south as Judea. This position gave the city an almost unique identity straddling West and East. It meant that Paul both had acquaintance with Hellenistic culture and customs, but also kept his eastern roots, as a Jew, firm.

Greek was the first language of Tarsus, and it, rather than Aramaic, seems to have been the language in which Paul thought. When he quotes the Hebrew Scriptures in his letters it is the standard Greek translation (known as the Septuagint) which he uses, suggesting a long familiarity. He could also quote readily from Greek poets when the need arose (Acts 17.28; Tit. 1.12; 1 Cor. 15.33). He shows such a familiarity in his letters with Hellenistic styles of argument and rhetorical practice that Morna Hooker believes that 'Paul had ... been given a Greek education.'[9] This might have happened in Jerusalem, where the high priest Jason had established a Greek school in 175 BC, but it is perhaps more likely that Paul returned to Tarsus and learned rhetoric at the university there, just as many aristocratic Jews sent their sons to the prestigious schools of Alexandria and other Hellenistic cities to complete their studies. Paul himself disclaimed much ability as an orator in his letters (at one point he calls himself an *idiotes*, meaning a lay person who did not speak in a city assembly, 2 Cor. 11.6) but this too may be a rhetorical device. The point is that Paul seems to have been equally at home with Greek rhetoric and rabbinic argument.

Tarsus was a Roman city too. The civil wars which had spilled across Asia Minor in the first century BC seem to have resulted in a good number of Jews becoming Roman citizens. If Paul's family were tent-makers then their products would have been extremely useful to the many Roman generals who needed to shelter their armies as they marched through Cilicia. Citizenship could have been a gesture of thanks for services rendered. Or Paul's grandfather might have become a prisoner of war, become slave to a Roman citizen and subsequently been set free with the gift of citizenship himself. Both of these options are speculative, but would account for Paul being a Roman citizen by birth (Acts 22.28), something which 'sceptics have doubted ... but without justification'.[10] Paul's Roman citizenship would have meant that, from birth, as a Jewish boy in the Greek city of Tarsus, he would have had three identities, reflected in his three names. And this gave him entry to a third cultural identity.

Roman citizens had three (Latin) names:

- *praenomen* (forename)
- *nomen gentile* (clan name)
- *cognomen* (family name)

Gaius Julius Caesar, for example, was of the Julian clan, known personally as Gaius, but identified usually by his last name, Caesar, which his heirs adopted as their family name too. We don't know Paul's praenomen or nomen gentile, but his cognomen would have been Paulus. As a Roman citizen, the cognomen Paulus would have been Paul's for official purposes from birth. It implies a significant social status. That Paul was proud of it can be seen by the way he uses it, rather than Saul, to identify himself in the opening of his letters.

But Paul was also a Jew, the son of a Pharisee (Acts 23.6). His Hebrew name was *Sha'ul* of the tribe of Benjamin, one of the southern tribes whose ancestral land was around Jerusalem. As *Sha'ul* Paul bore the name of the first of the kings of Israel, the most famous of the Benjaminites. It was a name that spoke of a rich and proud heritage. Just as Rome was the home city for a Roman citizen (even if he had never visited it), so Jerusalem was the mother city for Jews. Yet Paul betrays no tension in this dual identity. As a Diaspora Jew he was one of the hundreds of thousands living outside the ancestral homeland who had learned to assimilate to the culture around them while retaining a strong grasp of the faith which they had brought with them. One of Paul's close associates seems to have fitted the same pattern: Silas was also known by the Roman name of Silvanus and seems to have been a Roman citizen too (Acts 16.37–8).

In Greek-speaking Tarsus Paul's Hebrew and Latin names would have been rendered *Saulos* and *Paulos*. Here may possibly lie the clue to why he became known universally as Paul, since *Saulos* was slang for someone who walked like a prostitute. *Paulos* was a much safer name to go by!

Paul claims that, chameleon-like, to the Jews he was a Jew, to the gentiles a gentile: 'to all people I have become all things' (1 Cor. 9.22). His early years in Tarsus would have made him able to handle multiple identities with ease. As Paulus he belonged to the political reality of the Roman Empire; as *Saulos/Paulos* to the Greek-speaking commercial ambience of Tarsus; as *Sha'ul* to the Pharisaic and Jewish world. Three homes remained open to him: Rome, Tarsus and Jerusalem. But to a Jew, as he might have said himself, the greatest of these was Jerusalem.

Jerusalem

Paul said he was brought up in Jerusalem, and the word has the wider meaning of 'formed, educated or nourished' (Acts 22.3), implying that he left Tarsus at quite an early age.

Paul says he was 'brought up in the school of Gamaliel' (Acts 22.3). Gamaliel was the leading rabbi of the early first century, and the phrase may mean that Paul was taught by one of his close disciples rather than the master himself. Paul was a star pupil (Gal. 1.14), and the methods of interpretation which he uses in his letters show how well he had mastered the art of rabbinic argument (see Gal. 3). A Jewish scholar notes that 'Paul's methods for demonstrating religious truth and his treatment of scripture are still distinctly Pharisaic'[11] long after he had become a Christian, and at times Paul seems to have rather enjoyed being able to make common cause with the Pharisees over the resurrection of the dead against the Sadducees who denied it (Acts 23.6–7).

Alongside such academic training, however, came the need to learn a practical skill. Gamaliel's grandfather, the great Rabbi Hillel, had earned his living as a porter and his contemporary Shammai was a stonemason. These rabbis made a virtue of necessity, for 'the major task of the sages ... was to interpret and apply the Torah to everyday life. Thus, if they had one foot in the work-a-day world and the other in the world of the Torah and its Law, it would be easier to make the connection between the two.'[12] Paul's later work as a tent-maker (introduced in Acts 18.3) probably stemmed from an apprenticeship at this stage of his life. Tent-making was a versatile trade, enabling a craftsman to work with linen, leather and canvas, to work almost anywhere and to carry with him a minimum of tools.

Grounded in Greek and in the Hebrew Scriptures, and equipped with practical skills to earn a living, Paul was ready to meet the world.

Paul describes himself at this stage in his life as an 'extreme zealot' (Gal. 1.14). This seems to have put him in line with heroes of the faith such as Phineas (Num. 25.6–13), Elijah (1 Kings 18.40) and Jehu (2 Kings 10.16). Their zeal was expressed in violence, and Paul followed their lead in his desire the stamp out those who, to his Pharisaic mind, were blasphemously following Jesus of Nazareth. Paul's participation in the death of Stephen (Acts 7.58) is entirely believable in this context. (He may also have been one of the Cilicians who met in the 'synagogue of the Freedmen' which led the accusations against Stephen, Acts 6.9.)

Sometime in the year 34, around the age of 30, Paul gained letters to the synagogues of Damascus from the high priest authorizing him to arrest Christians there and bring them back to Jerusalem in chains (Acts 9.2). Damascus lay outside Israel and in territory which swung between Roman and Nabatean rule, which made the trip a risk. It looks as if this was a deliberate attempt on Paul's part to limit the spread of the Christian movement by bringing ringleaders back to the Temple authorities. Like David, he could pray, 'zeal for your house consumes me. Those who insult you insult me' (Psalm 69.9).

Call and early Christian years

On the journey to Damascus Paul received a vision of Jesus. The evidence for this is overwhelming. The story is told three times in Acts (9.3–9; 22.6–11; 26.12–18) as well as by Paul himself (Gal. 1.11–17, also 1 Cor. 9.1; 15.8). Paul seems never to have doubted that he genuinely did meet the risen Jesus as he approached Damascus.

The event which happened on the road to Damascus is often called Paul's 'conversion' and has become a byword for a sudden change of heart. But conversion is probably not the best way to describe it. Paul himself saw a clear continuity between his earlier faith and his later belief in Jesus and certainly never thought that he had ceased to be a Jew by becoming a Christian (see 2 Cor. 11.22). Paul's move from Pharisee to Christian was more of a radical shift within the same overall framework than a 180 degree about-turn.

'Call' is a better description than conversion. Together with the revelation of Jesus as the Son of God, came a specific direction; to 'preach his Gospel among the nations' (Gal. 1.16). As a Pharisee Paul's zeal was devoted to keeping Israel free from gentile influence. That was why he was going to Damascus, where the church was already expanding into gentile territory. The call he received on the way turned him around and sent him to 'the nations', a frequent way of speaking about those who were not Jews. Such a call did not prohibit him from preaching to Jews also; the point is simply that the arena of proclamation was broken wide open to include all the peoples of the world. This was a call similar to those of the prophets of Israel (especially Jer. 1.4–10, the language of which is echoed in Gal. 1.15).

James Dunn suggests that 'Paul's conversion was a conversion for Paul the theologian … a fulcrum point or hinge on which his whole theology turned around.'[13] Instead of keeping people out, defining Israel so tightly that few could meet the demands required, now the doors were open as God welcomed those whom Paul had formerly spurned. Tom Wright is surely correct when he identifies 'that Paul made it his life's work to found and maintain Jew-plus-Gentile churches on Gentile soil within the first Christian generation'.[14] It remained to be seen how this call might be fulfilled, and there were to be several false starts along the way, but the direction and aim of Paul's future life had been settled. The road to Damascus would lead to the world.

Damascus and Nabatea (34–7)

Paul continued on to Damascus. Almost at once he began preaching there (Acts 9.20–2). He now recognized that in Jesus the messiah had come. God had broken into human history, as he had promised through the prophets that he would. In some ways the fledgling traditions of the Church were the least significant of the intellectual influences on Paul. He did not hesitate to argue with those who had been Jesus' disciples about theology (he had a far better training than they did – a point that he may well, somewhat arrogantly, have put to them!); and he never entertained any doubts that he was right (see Gal. 2.11–16 and Acts 15).

Paul's involvement with the Christians had practical rather than intellectual implications for him. The bravery shown in the practical love and ministry of Ananias immediately after Paul's conversion, loving his enemy and literally blessing the one who persecuted him (Acts 9.10–20, cf. 22.12), undoubtedly had a profound effect, reflected in Paul's later attempt to bring a large financial contribution back to Jerusalem to help the poor community there.

Paul did not stay long in Damascus, but as is often the case with Acts it is frustratingly difficult to say how long. For the next three years or so he seems to have operated in the kingdom of Nabatea. Paul himself says he was in 'Arabia' (Gal. 1.17) and this has led some to conclude that he went south to the Sinai peninsula, seeking God in the desert as Moses had done. But it is more likely that he means the area around Damascus, which was well populated and in which he could fulfil the call he had received. How successful this was we don't know. Understandably, the Jews in Damascus whom he had originally been going to support strongly opposed his about-turn. Paul also seems to have annoyed Aretas the king of Nabatea. Paul had to escape the city by night, lowered from the walls in a basket (Acts 9.25; 2 Cor. 11.32–3). It was not the last time he would make an ignominious exit from a city.

First visit to Jerusalem (37)

Paul had not been back to Jerusalem since becoming a Christian, probably wisely. If he was a marked man in Damascus, how much greater was the danger for him in Jerusalem. Yet Jerusalem was also where those who had known Jesus personally lived. Paul visited Peter and also spoke to James the brother of Jesus, but later claimed not to have seen the other apostles there (Gal. 1.18–20). He was introduced to the church by Barnabas, a merchant from Cyprus. After a brief flurry of activity in the city he was sent away, probably for his own good, back to his native Tarsus. This first encounter with the church in Jerusalem set a pattern for later meetings: the leaders there were always ambivalent about Paul. None of them spoke up for him when he was arrested (Acts 21.27–40); he was left virtually on his own by the mother church of the Christian faith.

Tarsus and Cilicia (37–46)

Paul spent almost ten years back in Tarsus and the surrounding province of Cilicia; we know almost nothing about this period. It is quite possible that during this time Paul honed his speaking skills in Greek and supported himself by tent-making. Paul himself says that around the year 42 he had a further vision, and with it received a 'thorn in the flesh' (2 Cor. 12.2–10). These years may also have given Paul the opportunity to think through the implications of his new beliefs for his theology. Yet he may also have been active in planting churches. A later visit to 'strengthen the churches' in Syria and Cilicia, churches of which otherwise we know nothing (Acts 15.41), strongly suggests this. At some point in the year 47, Barnabas who had introduced him to the Jerusalem church knocked on Paul's door and invited him to make the journey with him to Antioch to work with the church there, which Acts tells us he did for a year (11.26).

When Paul went to Antioch he was about 14 years older than the young Pharisee who had received a call to preach among the nations. He had had time to develop a theology, practical skills as a tent-maker and his facility in Greek. He had preached, first in Damascus and Syria, and later in Cilicia and probably founded some churches there. Now in his early forties, he was in the prime of life. The next ten years would see Paul found many churches in the gentile cities of the eastern and Greek provinces of the Roman Empire, cover thousands of miles and write many letters; he would also experience imprisonment and hardship. Though Barnabas was the human agent who invited Paul to Antioch, Paul himself was always clear where his ultimate call came from: 'not from humans or from one man but through Jesus Christ and God the Father who raised him from the dead' (Gal. 1.1). God was calling him to a bigger responsibility.

To the gentiles

Paul's call had been to preach among the nations, and between 47 and 56 he was almost constantly on the move fulfilling that call. He knew that he could not take the Gospel personally to the whole population that surrounded the Mediterranean. He used the new means of transport at his disposal (Roman roads and the sea-trade routes) to establish a network of communications and to create centres of Christian community in particular cities which in turn would send out evangelists into the neighbouring smaller towns and the countryside. The church at Colossae, to which Paul wrote, was one he had never visited: but one of his Ephesian converts, Epaphras, had done the work for him. It is also no accident that his main form of teaching was through letters, often responding to questions which had been sent to him. In the same way much of his evangelism seems to have used local concepts (as at Athens, in Acts 17.22–34) or have been carried out by public debate (as at Ephesus, Acts 19.9). Paul's willingness to suffer for the sake of his beliefs was as powerful as his words, if not more so (see 1 Thess. 2.7–8).

And all the time, Paul was moving westwards. He seems to have had a series of specific goals, which were designed to achieve his grand vision of a series of interdependent Christian communities across the Mediterranean, both Jewish and gentile. His desire to reach Spain (Rom. 15.24) is an example of the way he always seems to have had a future destination ahead of him. The 'missionary journeys' were actually planned with an almost military strategy and for this reason are perhaps best referred to as 'campaigns'.

Antioch – a Door to the Nations (47–8)

If Paul ever had a mentor, it was Barnabas. Barnabas was one of the leaders of the church at Antioch. He seems to have remembered Paul and brought him to work with the expanding group of believers there. Barnabas had a background in business across the Mediterranean (Acts 4.36). This made him different from the ex-fisherman Peter and the carpenter's son James, and may have made him aware of the strategic possibilities for preaching the gospel across the Mediterranean world. It also may have given him some common ground with Paul of Tarsus.

Antioch was the perfect place to begin preaching the gospel to 'the nations' and the church there seems to have included a significant number of gentiles. Paul had not been there long when he and Barnabas went up to Jerusalem with some sort of plan to lay before the leaders of the church there, seeking authorization to plant churches among the gentile nations (Gal. 2.1–10, assuming this is the visit to Jerusalem also in Acts 11.30). Though Paul stresses that this was in response to a revelation he personally had received, the story of the journey as it is found in Acts 13—14 tends to suggest that Barnabas was the leader and Paul the junior partner at this stage.

On the evidence of what Barnabas and Paul did, the plan seems to have been to go to the provinces to the west of their home territory of

Syria and Cilicia, into the centre of what is now Turkey and was then Southern Galatia, moving up into the interior and establishing churches in the main cities there. The new phase in Paul's life is signified by the way in which Acts from this point in the narrative onwards refers to him as Paul, no longer Saul. He was now becoming fully identified as 'apostle to the gentiles'.

Barnabas and Paul were successful. After an initial foray into Cyprus they travelled from the coast of Pamphylia up into the plateau and lake-land of south central Anatolia. There they planted several churches and returned to Antioch with the news that 'God had opened a door of faith to the nations' (Acts 14.27).

'To the Jews first, then to the Greeks'

The first missionary campaign embodied a strategy which Paul was to use throughout his later expeditions. Arriving in a new city, Paul would head first to the synagogue, or, if one had not yet been established, to the place where his fellow Jews gathered for prayer. The primary target of his mission was probably not Jews as such, but the gentile fellow-travellers known as 'God-worshippers' (or 'God-fearers'). Significant archaeological evidence uncovered in the last 40 years has suggested that there were indeed many of them, and that some were wealthy and well-connected (Nero's wife Poppea may have been one).

The God-worshippers were attracted by the Jewish faith, attended synagogue worship and, if they were wealthy, frequently paid for new buildings or decoration (one example from the Gospels is the centurion at Capernaum who had built the synagogue there, Luke 7.5). They worshipped the 'most-high God' of Israel but were not prepared to take the final steps because these would make them unable to bear public office (which required involvement in the pagan cults of city life) and would impose heavy dietary and other requirements which would make social life extremely difficult for them. For men the final step was circumcision, which was not a private matter in the Hellenistic world. Public nakedness in the gymnasium and baths, the primary meeting places, was expected, so Jews could be easily identified. This issue may explain why gentile women seem to have been more likely to become full converts. Most God-worshippers were content to support their local synagogue financially and to watch from the sidelines.

If the God-worshippers were Paul's target, it makes sense of the deal he claimed to have made with the Jerusalem apostles before he and Barnabas set out: 'that we should go to the nations, and they to the circumcision' (Gal. 2.9). Paul seems to have meant that he would concentrate on the God-worshippers among the (gentile) nations, leaving Peter and the others to concentrate on 'the circumcision', that is, those who were full Jews. If the God-worshippers were Paul's target it explains why he was able to use quite technical terms from the Hebrew Scriptures and expect his converts to understand them easily. And if the God-worshippers were Paul's target it also explains why Paul apparently aroused such antagonism from his fellow Jews. A Gospel that attracted wealthy and politically influential God-worshippers could easily jeopardize the future stability of a Jewish synagogue.

The God-worshippers were a crucial group who formed the interface between strict Jews and the wider pagan culture. They had access to both, and would have been hugely valuable in Paul's quest to bring the Gospel of Jesus Christ to the nations. Paul's remarkable success in planting churches may be largely attributed to his strategy of heading first to the synagogues and concentrating on the God-worshippers he found there, offering them a way of becoming full members of the new community of the most-high God they already worshipped. As Crossan and Reed put it: 'The Pauline express thundered along God-worshiper rails, and Paul moved fast because he did not have to lay track.'[15]

Sent to Jerusalem

In the absence of Barnabas and Paul, the leaders of the church in Jerusalem seem to have got cold feet about expansion into the gentile world. Acts suggests that it was a group of Pharisees within the Jerusalem church who instigated this reaction (Acts 15.5).

On returning to Antioch, Paul found Peter had been part of a move supported by James to re-establish rigorous Jewish customs within the Church, in particular enforcing separate eating for Jews and gentiles (Gal. 2.11–14). Barnabas and Paul went to Jerusalem to defend their practice and came back with a decision largely in their favour, but with a few guidelines for how gentiles should behave.

The decision had far-reaching consequences. Paul wrote powerfully that

> Now that faith has come, we are no longer under the guardianship of the Law. You are all children of God through faith in Christ Jesus, for all of you who were baptized into Christ have clothed yourselves with Christ. There is neither Jew nor Greek, slave nor free, male nor female, for you are all one in Christ Jesus. If you belong to Christ, then you are Abraham's seed, and according to the promise, heirs. (Gal. 3.25–9)

For Paul, the Church represented a new community, which transcended barriers of racial and religious origin. This was an extraordinary statement for Paul the ex-Pharisee to make. The decision of the conference to put no real hindrance in the way of gentile believers opened the way to the expansion of the Church right across the Roman Empire. Acts 15, roughly halfway through the Acts of the Apostles, serves as the hinge point on which Luke's narrative of the early Church turns. Luke's instincts as a historian seem to have been right here. Without this decisive shift in emphasis, the Church would have developed very differently.

Paul was not advocating the inclusion of gentiles at any price. The more extreme of his converts sought to promote a 'Law-free' Gospel which claimed that if they were followers of Jesus they could do what they liked (Paul takes them on in Rom. 5—6). The identification of Paul with this group would dog him for the rest of his life, and his attempt, by fulfilling a Temple vow, to prove that he did not agree with them would lead to his arrest and subsequent imprisonment. The accusation that the Church was dedicated to destroying the Law was also crucial in leading to the deaths of Stephen and James in Jerusalem, so it was not to be taken lightly.

Paul was recognized at the Jerusalem conference as the leading spokesman for the gentile churches. He was working in a situation where there were no theological textbooks or guidelines. The early Church was struggling to come to terms with the meaning of what had happened in the events of Jesus' life, death and resurrection. Those who held authority did so because of their companionship with Jesus, and while Jesus himself had taught them, the Gospels are full of comments about how they had either misunderstood or failed to grasp at all what he had told them. Paul had received a far better education than any of the other apostles. The passionate dispute with Peter over circumcision which is described in Galatians is, in part, over Paul the newcomer's stronger grasp of the implications of Jesus' message, against Peter's floundering in waters which the Master had not charted for him.

Paul was in a situation where he saw the implications of the Gospel more clearly than others, yet his authority was always in dispute. Ernst Käsemann puts it well when he says that Paul's letter to the Romans is 'the record of an existence struggling for recognition and of an apostolicity called into question'.[16] In other words, Paul was in an exposed position, improvising his theology at the cutting edge of mission but utterly convinced of the rightness of what he was doing. Implicitly the Jerusalem apostles had recognized Paul's claim, which he had made to them on his earlier visit, to be called to be the 'apostle to the gentiles', just as Peter was apostle to the Jews (Gal. 2.7–8).

Galatians – when, why and how?

It was probably in the midst of the heated debate about the basis on which gentiles could be included in the Church that Paul wrote his letter to the Galatians, though scholars have a variety of opinions on the issue.

A long-running debate has been over whether the letter was written for the 'north Galatians' or 'south Galatians'. The Galatians were a

Celtic tribe which migrated across central Europe from what we now call France and reached central Asia Minor in the mid second century BC. They settled in the northern part of the region and remained distinct from the surrounding Hellenistic culture: 'Inscriptions of the Roman imperial period show that the Galatians preserved their own ethnic identity, not only through the survival of the Celtic language but through their nomenclature, religious cults and forms of social organization.'[17] When the region became a Roman province in the late first century BC it covered pretty well the whole of the Anatolian plateau, fringed by Bithynia in the north and Pamphylia in the south. The whole province was designated Galatia by the Romans, even though the heartland of the Galatian people was in the north (there is some evidence that they had also settled in the south by this stage). Thus, if Paul conceived of the Galatians as an ethnic group he would have been writing only to the Celtic tribes in the north of the province. If, on the other hand, he was simply addressing the inhabitants of the province of Galatia, his letter would have been written to an ethnically mixed group of people across a much larger area. If the first view is taken of Paul's intended recipients, then the letter must have been written after the conference in Jerusalem, since Acts records his activity in the north of the province as part of his second campaign (Acts 16.6).

There is in fact no sign Paul that was writing to the 'ethnic' Galatians; he specifically addresses the 'churches of Galatia', the province, rather than the churches of the 'the Galatians' which would have implied a group of people (Gal. 1.2). Since Paul and Barnabas had planted churches in the cities of Pisidian Antioch, Iconium, Lystra and Derbe within the province of Galatia during their first campaign it seems entirely plausible that Paul intended his letter for the believers in those cities.

Why then would anyone raise the question of the 'ethnic Galatians'? The truth is that the survival of the Galatians' Celtic culture under the Roman Empire was irresistibly attractive to British scholars of the later nineteenth century. If Paul was writing to the 'ethnic' Galatians, then he was writing to people who were distant cousins of those scholars who looked back to their own Celtic forebears in Britain. 'There is every reason ... for believing that the Galatian settlers were genuine Celts ... of which the Welsh are the living representatives'[18] wrote J. B. Lightfoot (1828–89), a Cambridge professor who was later bishop of Durham, and one of the greatest English New Testament scholars. Ironically the words just quoted come from a section of his book which rejects the view put forward by German scholars that the Galatians were in fact a Teutonic tribe. But Lightfoot's counter-argument uses the same kind of unquestioned racial presuppositions as his German opponents. He writes that Paul is speaking to 'a type of character strongly contrasted for instance with the vicious refinements of the dissolute and polished Corinthians ... or again with the dreamy speculative mysticism which disfigured the half-oriental Churches of Ephesus and Colossae'.[19] It was a question of national character, in Lightfoot's view, and the sturdy Galatians were a much more worthy target for Paul's Gospel than the dissolute Greeks.

A slim majority of scholars probably favours a date for Galatians after the Jerusalem conference. This is not on racial grounds, but because they identify the meeting of Paul and Barnabas with the Jerusalem 'pillars' (Gal. 2.1–10) with the conference of Acts 15 itself. Others (and you will have noticed from my reconstruction of Paul's life above that I am with them) see Paul's visit with Barnabas to Jerusalem in Acts 11.30 as Luke's version of Paul's 'private' meeting with the leaders. The main reason for favouring the former view is that 'it is highly unlikely that there were two conferences where the same people debated the same issue with the same outcome.'[20] In addition, the visit to Jerusalem in Acts 11.30 is described as being to bring relief at a time of famine and doesn't mention any discussions regarding Paul and Barnabas's subsequent venture into the gentile world. Therefore, the majority view argues, the letter dates from after the conference and issuing of the decrees which gave guidelines to gentile believers. In response to these points, I believe that Galatians 2.1–10 does record the same visit as Acts 11.30 for three reasons:

- *If the letter were written after the conference it would refer to the decrees*, which though apparently a compromise were actually a pretty clear victory for Paul.
- *Paul is clear that he and Barnabas had a private meeting with the apostles* (Gal. 2.2). The conference described in Acts 15 was not private, and its outcome was very public, resulting in a document intended for widespread distribution.
- *Paul says he went to Jerusalem to see the leaders of the Church about the gospel he preached among the nations* (in other words to get approval for his own calling, Gal. 2). Acts 11.27–30 doesn't speak of this, but says Barnabas and Paul went to bring a gift of money for the poor. But in fact Paul seems to allude to this: 'they asked us to remember the poor, which I wanted to do anyway' (Gal. 2.10).

In terms of the enduring importance of the letter the issue doesn't matter very much. Paul's stirring defence of his Gospel of freedom and grace doesn't depend on its context. But for our understanding of Paul's life it does matter. The conclusion of the view outlined above is that Galatians is Paul's earliest letter to survive and that it was written between his first campaign in southern Galatia with Barnabas and the conference in Jerusalem (i.e. in 49–50). It also implies that Paul's opponents in Galatia held the same views that he found had taken root in Antioch when he returned there, and that they had followed almost on his coat-tails in seeking out the churches which he and Barnabas had just founded. Galatians thus becomes Paul's opening salvo in the struggle which the conference would resolve, perhaps the first written statement of 'my Gospel' (Rom. 2.16; 16.25). The issue would not, however, go away, and seems to have remained a current issue in Antioch for a very long time.

Paul's use of rhetoric

Galatians is perhaps Paul's most heartfelt letter. He pours his heart and soul into it, and centuries later it still leaps off the page for the reader. It provides vital autobiographical clues. But how it is written also provides important insights into Paul.

Paul is angry with his converts and wants to persuade them to return to his teaching. His language is highly emotive and passionate, and for this reason Galatians has been identified as a test-case for rhetorical criticism. In his teaching on rhetoric Aristotle particularly identified three means of persuasion which a speaker might use: *pathos*, the appeal to the emotions of the audience; *ethos*, the appeal to the character of the speaker; and *logos*, the appeal to reason. Can we see Paul using these three means of persuasion in Galatians?

Paul moves between all three forms, but there does seem to be a progression. From the initial attack, which appeals to the Galatians' emotions (Gal. 1.6–9), Paul shifts to a lengthy recital of his credentials, appealing to his own character (Gal. 1.10—2.10); then he proceeds to build his case about the relation of Law and Gospel, appealing to reason and the ancient authority of Abraham (Gal. 2.11—4.31), though this passage also contains a further brief emotional outburst (Gal. 3.1–5). Finally, Paul sums up his argument by telling them how confident he is that they will accept his arguments and agree with him (Gal. 5.1—6.10), specifically raising the issue of 'persuasion' (Gal. 5.8). He is, however, unable to resist a final and personal appeal to his own character (Gal. 6.11–18). This brief rhetorical analysis helps us understand Galatians in two ways: first, it gives us critical tools with which to examine the text, helping us to see the strategy which Paul is employing; second, it enables us to see that Paul does not follow the message slavishly, and the final postscript suggests he is not so sure of his case winning as his magisterial summing up a few verses before had implied. Overall, Paul perhaps echoes Aristotle's own succinct conclusion: *eireka, akekoate, echete, krinate* ('I have said. You have listened. There you have it. Judge.')

The way in which Paul seems to be conforming to Aristotle's overall guidelines is significant for our understanding of him. It implies that he had had some Greek education, and that he was writing to a group of churches which might include some people who would grasp what he was doing: in other words, the 'Greek' cities of the first campaign (Pisidian Antioch, Iconium, Lystra, Derbe).

How much did Paul know about Jesus?

Paul had his vision of Jesus on the road to Damascus at least 15 years before he wrote his letter to the Galatians. He emphasizes early in the letter that he had not received the message he preached from any other human being but 'through a revelation of Jesus Christ' (Gal. 1.12). The fact that Paul then mentions almost nothing of the story of Jesus' life in this letter suggests to some that he actually knew very little about Jesus as a person at all and cared even less (Gal. 4.14 is the only, sketchy, comment). Rudolf Bultmann, for example, argued that 'All that is important for [Paul] in the story of Jesus is the fact that Jesus was born a Jew and lived under the Law ... and that he had been crucified.'[21] Bultmann made a real and significant case. There is very little about the life of Jesus in Paul's letters. In fact, if they were the only source which we had, then, as James Dunn notes, 'it would be impossible to say much about Jesus of Nazareth.'[22]

Paul actually quotes the words of Jesus only in 1 Corinthians (see 1 Cor. 7.10–11; 9.14; 11.23–5). So the fundamental question is, why does Paul not quote Jesus more fully and more directly than he does? The alternative explanations available are that either Paul knew the traditions about Jesus well and could assume that his hearers did too; or that he knew them and didn't think they were important; or that he didn't know them at all.

It is important first of all to remember the patchiness of the sources we have: without 1 Corinthians we might conclude that Paul knew no details of Jesus' teaching on divorce or the story of the Last Supper (see 1 Cor. 7.10–11; 11.23–5). Yet his versions of both are remarkably close to the later formulations of the Gospel writers (on divorce see Mark 10.11; Matt. 19.9–10; on the Last Supper, Mark 14.22–25; Matt. 26.26–29; Luke 22.17–20). This suggests that he was very familiar with at least these segments of the tradition. And although Paul rarely quotes Jesus, there are a good many echoes of Jesus' teaching in Paul's writings which are not word-for-word the same but clearly repeat the same thought or use similar phrasing. Two good examples can be found in Romans 12 and 1 Corinthians 4.

In Romans 12.14–21, Paul turns from his exposition of faith to some practical commands for everyday Christian life. Some of these echo sayings from the Hebrew Scriptures but some are also sayings of Jesus which are not paralleled in the Old Testament (Figure 8).

Paul doesn't note the origin of the sayings which he quotes from the Hebrew Scriptures; neither does he do so with those which the Gospel writers attribute to Jesus. So the fact that Paul doesn't attribute a quotation to Jesus does not mean he doesn't know it's a quotation from Jesus.

In 1 Corinthians 4 language which occurs in the Gospels seems to have been woven into Paul's writing so that it is hard to disentangle:

Romans 12	Saying	OT	NT
v.14	Bless those who persecute you		Matt. 5.44 Luke 6.28
v.15	Rejoice with those who rejoice, weep with those who weep	Sirach 7.34	
v.16	Do not be proud	Prov. 3.7 Isa. 5.21	
v.17	Repay no one evil for evil		Matt. 5.39 Luke 6.29
v.18	Live at peace with all	Ps 34.14	Mark 9.50 1 Thess. 5.13
v.19	Do not seek revenge	Lev. 19.18 Deut. 32.35	
v.20	Feed your enemy if he is hungry	Prov. 25.21–2	
v.21	Conquer evil with good		Luke 6.27

Figure 8 Echoes of Scripture and sayings of Jesus in Romans 12

> Even now we hunger and thirst, are naked, beaten and have no place to settle; we work hard with our own hands; when we're reviled, we bless; when we're persecuted, we endure it (1 Cor. 4.11–12).

Paul's catalogue of sufferings and his actions in response to them evoke the beatitudes (Matt. 5.6, 10–11; Luke 6.1–22) and present him as a model follower of Jesus. Like his master he has no place to call home (Matt. 8.20; Luke 9.58). But there's no direct quotation here. Instead the hearers would probably recognize sayings and phrases which they were already familiar with from the traditions of Jesus' teaching. This is of a pattern with what we found in the letter to James, which only mentions Jesus twice and never quotes him. Instead, it echoes the teaching of Jesus in the same way that the great Jewish sage, ben Sira, alluded to the Hebrew Scriptures. In Richard Bauckham's words, 'James ... has made the wisdom of Jesus his own. He does not repeat it; he is inspired by it.'[23] The evidence suggests that the same could be said of Paul.

There seems enough material to suggest that Paul did know the sayings of Jesus quite well (though of course we don't really know in what form he had them: none of the Gospels had been written down in its present form when Paul was writing his letters). Dunn's conclusion of his examination of what Paul knew about Jesus is that there is a 'fair degree of probability that Paul both knew and cared about the ministry of Jesus prior to his passion and death'. Paul seems to have taken it for granted that the churches he wrote to were already pretty well informed about Jesus' life; but as Dunn says, '"Taken for granted" does not mean "couldn't care less".'[24] There is further evidence in fact that the story of Jesus' life did hold great significance for Paul.

While the words of Jesus were important to the early Christians, his actions were essential to their understanding too. Paul often calls on his audiences to 'Be imitators of me, as I am of Christ' (1 Cor. 11.1), making it clear that they are to emulate the actions of Jesus (see also Phil. 2.5; Rom. 15.3–6). If this appeal was to make any sense Paul had to presuppose a good knowledge of Jesus' life among his hearers: 'Paul uses this knowledge to appeal to his communities to grow as disciples of Christ through imitation of his own way of following Jesus' example, more than by appeal to Jesus' sayings.'[25] The circumstances in which Paul's letters were written mean that we should not really expect to find much information about the life of Jesus within them. Conveying such information was not his concern in the letters, but this doesn't mean that he thought Jesus' life unimportant and his teaching uninteresting. They were the presupposition and heart of Paul's faith.

The second campaign (50–2)

Paul and Barnabas returned to Antioch from Jerusalem with news of the conference. Shortly afterwards they embarked together on a second missionary campaign, with the church's blessing and a strong sense that God was with them (Acts 15.35–36), to revisit the churches they had founded a year or so before. But the relationship between them seems to have been under strain. Paul says that even his mentor was 'led astray' (Gal. 2.13). Perhaps (and this is speculation) Barnabas had been keener for compromise than Paul at the conference, and almost certainly more deferential to the Jerusalem leaders. At any rate they argued violently over the relatively trivial issue of Barnabas's desire to give Mark (his cousin) a second chance. They parted on bad terms and their partnership ended (the Greek word used for the dispute is *paroxysmos*, implying an explosion of fury caused by increasing frustration, Acts 15.39). Barnabas headed back to his native Cyprus, presumably to strengthen the churches which they had founded there. (Luke's willingness to include this painful episode in Acts points towards its overall trustworthiness. If he wished to give his readers a 'whitewashed' account then this part of the story could easily have been suppressed.)

Paul set off without Barnabas but with Silas, a prophet who had been one of the messengers of James's judgement from Jerusalem to Antioch but then returned to Jerusalem (Acts 15.22, 32–3). Silas was a shrewd choice as he was able to confirm the judgement of the conference in person as an 'official spokesman' of the Jerusalem church.

Paul and Silas took a different route from the previous one, going through Paul's home territory of Syria and Cilicia and then probably up through the Cilician Gates and across the mountains until they reached the towns in the central plateau and the churches which Paul and Barnabas had founded a little while before. The aim was to disseminate the decree of the Jerusalem Conference (Acts 16.4). Instead of turning south, however, and heading back to the Pamphylian coast when they reached Antioch in Pisidia, they pressed on westwards, across Anatolia. Luke makes it clear that this was no arbitrary decision, but the result of guidance by 'the Holy Spirit ... of Jesus' (Acts 16.6–8).

This was a new departure. Building on the strategy of the first campaign, they were now heading to virgin territory for the Church. Luke's very specific travel directions perhaps suggest that Paul had planned to go for the heart of the province of Asia – the great city of Ephesus – and perhaps from there across the Aegean to Corinth and the western part of the Empire. But they were 'prevented by the Holy Spirit from speaking the word in Asia' (Acts 16.6). An attempt to head north to Bithynia and the shores of the Black Sea and perhaps then to return eastwards was equally abortive, and they ended up at the port of Troas overlooking the Aegean Sea. Where would Paul go next?

Troas – a symbolic city

Troas took its name from the mythical Troy, the ruins of which could be seen at Ilion, less than 20 miles up the coast. It was the site of the Greek invasion of Asia in the Trojan War, the Persian expedition to Greece under Xerxes in 480 BC, and where Alexander had landed at the outset of his own extraordinary eastern adventure in 334 BC. Julius Caesar arrived three centuries later, claiming descent from Aeneas, the Trojan prince who according to myth had escaped the destruction of the city and eventually founded Rome as 'new Troy'. Romans saw their status as a one-time colony of Troy as legitimizing their rule of the east. Groups of pilgrim-tourists arrived to see the tombs of the heroes and listen for the sound of ghostly armies clashing on the empty beaches. Generations of conquerors had come and gone across this sea, over which Paul looked some time in 50.

Entering Europe

Paul received a vision at Troas. It was of a man of Macedonia who simply called Paul to 'Come over and help us' (Acts 16.9). It was the next stage in Paul's call to the nations, and he took ship at once. It was a decisive and fateful step: 'with Paul, with dusty, tired, much-travelled Paul, came Rome's most dangerous opponent – not legions but ideas, not an alternative force but an alternative faith.'[26] But unlike the conquerors who had come and gone in past generations, he went not in his own name seeking political domination, but as the apostle of Jesus to the nations, bringing good news.

Landing at Neapolis, Paul headed inland to Philippi. It represented a culture change for it was a 'Roman colony' (Acts 16.12) and was legally part of Italy rather than Greece. Latin was the official language and would have been spoken in the streets as well as Greek, a new experience for Paul.

As usual, Paul began the work of evangelizing at once, but he could not head straight to the local synagogue as there does not seem to have been one in the city. Instead the local Jewish population had a 'place of prayer' by the river. There Paul brought a wealthy woman called Lydia to faith, and she and her household were baptized, opening her house as a base for Paul and his companions (Acts 16.14–16). Subsequently Paul and Silas fell foul of the authorities and found themselves in jail, from which they were freed, according to Acts, by a timely earthquake. They played the card of Roman citizenship with the magistrates and were able to leave the city, heading on around the coast to Thessalonica, where there was further trouble, and then to Beroea (Acts 16.16—17.14).

What did Paul really think of women?

From Lydia (Paul's first convert in Philippi) onwards, women take a much more prominent role in the narrative of Acts, and Paul later named two women, Euodia and Syntyche, as his co-workers in Philippi who 'fought alongside' him there (Phil. 4.2–3). Paul would have found that the cities of Macedonia and Greece, which he worked in during this part of the second campaign, were places of much greater freedom and power for women than the cities he was used to. Women seem to have had some role in government in Macedonia, and in Philippi they took a leading part in the conduct of some pagan cults, especially that of Artemis. Women converts are specifically mentioned in the course of the second missionary campaign (Acts 17.4, 12, 34). At Corinth Paul's closest associates were Aquila and his wife Priscilla, who seem to have operated as a team (they are always referred to together, sometimes with Priscilla's name first: Acts 18.2, 18, 19; Rom. 16.3; 1 Cor. 16.19; 2 Tim. 4.19); and his work there may have been funded by Phoebe, a woman deacon from nearby Cenchreae whom Paul commends as a 'benefactor' to himself and to many (Rom. 16.2).

Yet Paul is notoriously prone to being characterized as the original male chauvinist pig. Some of his statements have been (and still are) used to argue that the ministry of women is wrong. On the other hand it has also been said that 'Pauline texts addressing the roles of women in both church and home suggest that Paul be ranked among the most progressive of ancient writers.'[27] Here is one of Paul's apparently greatest contradictions.

Paul lists many women among his 'co-workers': Julia, Junia, Mary, Persis, Priscilla, Tryphaena and Tryphosa, as well as 'Rufus' mother' and 'Nereus' sister'. And these are just in Romans! Four of these women are characterized as 'hard-working', a phrase which Paul never uses of a male colleague. Paul also frequently uses female imagery: he describes himself as a wet-nurse (1 Thess. 2.7) and a woman in labour (Gal. 4.19), and he applies the same metaphor to the creation itself, groaning in labour (Rom. 8.22–5), 'a sound very familiar to Paul from the houses where he stayed and the churches he founded, as indeed it would have been a common experience of household life in the Roman world'.[28] Paul certainly seems to have valued his female colleagues and the experiences of women in a way that was radical (and possibly unwise) in the ancient world.

Yet while Paul speaks of women praying and prophesying aloud (1 Cor. 11.4–5), soon after that he notoriously restricts the role of women when he says 'As in all the congregations of the saints, women should remain silent in the churches. They are not allowed to speak' (1 Cor. 14.33–4). Though there are many and complex explanations for the contradiction between these statements, the simplest is that Paul did not issue a blanket prohibition on women speaking, and that English translations commonly misplace a comma in the second statement (there is, of course, no punctuation in the original Greek text): 'For God is not a God of disorder but of peace, as in all the congregations of the saints. Women should remain silent ...' This means that Paul's comments on women remaining silent can be read as an instruction specifically to the Corinthians, and a response to the chaotic situation during worship there. Despite the virtue of simplicity, however, this explanation does not really carry conviction. After an exhaustive examination of the issue, Anthony Thiselton concludes that Paul is referring here to the activity of 'sifting' prophetic speech (see 1 Cor. 14.29). The prohibition then, understood within the context of Paul's discussion about the right and ordered use of spiritual gifts, is on wives 'sifting or weighing the words of prophets, especially by asking probing questions about the prophet's theology or even the prophet's lifestyle in public'.[29] This is the kind of speaking which they are forbidden to do. Nevertheless we would be foolish to think of Paul as a liberal and politically correct thinker. He has a significant general point in mind here, which is that even in the new community of the Church the old order of the created world remains: so women should remain subject to their husbands and reserve their questions until they can ask them privately (1 Cor. 14.34–5).

Bearing in mind Paul's chameleon-like ability to adapt to the culture around him in order to gain a hearing for the Gospel (1 Cor. 9.22), he may not have had a clear idea of what he thought about the role of women, and tailored what he thought to the audience in front of him. The sociologist Rodney Stark, in his study of the early Church, notes that 'Amidst contemporary denunciations of Christianity as patriarchal and sexist, it is easily forgotten that the early church was … especially attractive to women.'[30] If Paul had been as deeply misogynistic as some commentators have thought, this would not have been the case. Indeed, Stark regards the involvement of women and the fact that within a Christian subculture they could enjoy far higher status than in any other grouping as a significant factor in the Church's growth. And because they married pagan men and produced children who then usually became Christians, women were a very important factor in the rise of Christianity.

A female apostle?

Were the apostles all men, or could at least one have been a woman? The question arises because the name Junia occurs among those to whom Paul sends greetings at the end of his letter to the Romans (Rom. 16.7). The oldest manuscripts of Romans clearly show Junia as a feminine name, twinned with Andronicus, who was presumably her husband.

In the late fourth century John Chrysostom regarded her as a woman apostle. From medieval times onwards, however, scribes and commentators agreed almost unanimously that this must be a misspelling, and that what Paul meant to write was 'Junias', a masculine form of the same name. Then they amended the text to read that way. The only problem with the scribes' solution is that 'Junias' does not exist as a name in any other piece of ancient literature.

So what did Paul mean? Could he possibly have meant that 'Junia' was counted among the apostles in Rome? Earlier in the same passage Phoebe, specifically mentioned as a 'deacon' of the church at Cenchreae near Corinth, seems to be a woman who had a recognized position of ministry (Rom. 16.1). So Junia was probably one of the leaders of the church in Rome, and perhaps even one of its founders, along with her husband Andronicus, Paul's kinsman.

Later scholars believed that male Church leadership was ideologically right and female authority not only wrong but a contradiction in terms. Junia became Junias, and female apostles were written out of the story. On the other hand, however, today's emphasis on gender equality tends to make us ideologically sympathetic to the idea of women apostles and it's important not simply to jump to the opposite conclusion that therefore women and men had equal roles in the early Church. The picture is much more complex than that and Paul seems to have been quite ambivalent on the matter.

Whatever happened to the Kingdom of God? Conflict with the authorities

Although Paul had been in trouble before, at Damascus and during his first missionary campaign, once he crossed into Macedonia he left a trail of conflict with the authorities behind him which ultimately led to imprisonment in Rome. How did Paul end up as such a hardened jailbird?

The accusation against Paul in Thessalonica was that he proclaimed 'another king called Jesus' (Acts 17.7). Jesus himself did not say he was a king, but he spoke a great deal about the Kingdom of God; we find the Kingdom, when we take into account the parallels between the synoptic Gospels, mentioned 89 times by him. But Paul uses the term only 19 times in his letters, and Acts yields just 6 further examples. C. H. Dodd said Luke (in Acts) 'regarded [Paul's] preaching as being just as much a proclamation of the Kingdom of God as was the preaching of the first disciples or of their Master, even though Paul does not himself speak of it in those terms.'[31] In other words, though the message did not change, it seems that the language Paul used about it did.

A clue to what may have happened can be seen in the letter to the Philippians. The conflict Paul met in Philippi landed him in prison. It was partly a matter of economic interest and partly anti-Semitic (Acts 16.19–21). This is one of the 'we' passages in Acts, and Luke may have been representative of Paul's converts in Philippi: Christians from a gentile, not Jewish background. He was like many in Philippi to whom the language of 'Kingdom' (commonplace in Jesus' Judea) would not necessarily have come naturally. They would have understood politics in terms of Greek democracy and Roman imperial citizenship.

Not only that, but Philippi overlooked the plain where Octavian and Antony had defeated the murderers of Julius Caesar in 42 BC. The area had subsequently become the heartland of the cult of the emperor, that quasi-divine being whose word officially held the prosperity of the world in being.

Paul wrote to the Philippians perhaps 10 or 12 years after his visit to found the church there. This was a letter of thanks for a gift they had sent to him in Rome. It also gives us an insight into the situation in Philippi. Paul quotes a hymn which makes it clear that the claim of the God of Israel to be Lord of the world (seen in Isaiah and many other prophets) had been vindicated in Jesus (Phil. 2.5–11). Paul's theology was nothing less than a 'counter-imperial theology' where 'Jesus is Lord and Caesar is not',[32] a challenge to the cult of the emperor, who was routinely referred to in public inscriptions as 'Lord and Saviour', the same titles which Paul used of Jesus.

Thus Paul may use the language of Kingdom sparingly but the concept is clearly embedded in his thought. His phrase 'our citizenship is in heaven' (Phil. 3.20) reinforces the point. The word *politeuma* may mean 'government' as well as citizenship, and Paul was translating Kingdom concepts which Jesus had used in Galilee and Judea into citizenship language, which his Roman colonist audience in Philippi might be able to hear and understand more easily.

Perhaps it is also understandable that the early Church preferred an implicit challenge to the imperial cult rather than an explicit one. Announcing 'King Jesus' in so many words might have raised the spectre of political threat. Indeed, there is some evidence to suggest that this was a real issue. The name 'Christian' (coined apparently in Antioch, Acts 11.26) seems to have been originally a Latin word and would apply to followers of a military or political leader (like 'Herodian' for a supporter of the Jewish royal family). Suetonius' comment that the Emperor Claudius expelled the Jews from Rome because they kept causing disturbances 'at the incitement of *Chrestus*'[33] implies that, though Jesus was dead long before Claudius took power in 41, he was still causing trouble as some sort of political leader much later. This suggests that the early Christian movement did pose a challenge to the authorities.

Christians also used the word *ekklesia* to describe their gathering. To a Jew like Paul this was a sensible carry-over from the Greek translation of the Hebrew Scriptures where the same word was used for the assembly of Israel (e.g. Deut. 31.30; Josh. 8.35; Judges 21.8; 1 Chron. 29.1). But to a gentile convert like Luke it might have had a rather different meaning. For him it would have been a claim, at first sight, to be an assembly of citizens such as any city-state might have. There is a fascinating interplay in Ephesus between the unruly secular and political *ekklesia*, and the Christian *ekklesia* which was able to conduct its meetings without riots and fighting (Acts 19.23–41, this is the only New Testament passage which uses *ekklesia* in its secular meaning).

This was a period when there was much debate about the right form of government and a growing disillusionment with Greek political ideals and the ways the Romans had handled them, combined with a yearning for new and authentic forms of community. Imperial citizens were increasingly becoming subjects of capricious emperors rather than equal members of democratic city states. Adolf von Harnack went as far as to say 'What a sense of stability a creation of this kind [the Church] must have conferred upon the individual! What powers of attraction it must have exercised, as soon as its objects came to be understood! It was this, and not any evangelist, which proved to be the most effective missionary.'[34] The Church's organization and structure was itself a sign of the Kingdom of God.

So the concept of the Kingdom was not so much lost as transformed in Paul's thought, and we see signs of the adaptation of Christian thinking from early in the Church's mission, as it moved away from its Judean base, where Kingdom language was commonplace. The underlying challenge to secular power, perhaps more than anything else, led to the clashes with authority which characterized the latter stages of Paul's life. He was not ashamed of his imprisonments, but boasted of them. He spoke of himself as a 'prisoner of Christ Jesus' (Philemon 1, 9). He also wrote that he was 'in chains' to the mystery of Christ (Col. 4.3), but it is not clear whether he meant to be taken literally or metaphorically. Either way, he certainly saw himself as bound to Jesus not Caesar as his master.

Failure in Athens

Paul's visit to Athens made an irresistible set-piece for Luke as he wrote Acts. Athens was the embodiment of Greek culture. In an extraordinary and unparalleled explosion of creativity covering just the second half of the fifth century BC the city had been host to breakthroughs in tragic and comic drama; in art, architecture and sculpture; and in philosophy and democratic politics. Sophocles, Socrates and Pericles were among the towering figures of the time, their names still remembered today. No wonder Pliny the Elder felt it enough to say that 'Athens is a free city and needs no further publicity, its great fame being more than sufficient.'[35]

But the Golden Age of Athens was short-lived. Ultimately it proved to be a curse, for when a city had such a glorious past, who could resist looking back to it? In the Roman wars of the first century BC Athens had backed the wrong side in the hope of restoring its glory-days; in 87 BC the city was looted by Roman soldiers who shipped many of its treasures back to Rome and ended its independence. Yet the city continued to attract prominent visitors, Antony and Augustus among them, and cultural life was re-established. Wealthy young Romans often visited to complete their education.

By the time Paul arrived in 51 the Athenian market place was dominated by temples, some of which had been relocated from the surrounding countryside. The temples doubled as art galleries and museums; they were the first buildings which a tourist coming from the harbour would encounter. As the contemporary satirist Petronius remarked, 'it was easier to find a god than a man in Athens.'[36] The Parthenon remained on the Acropolis, still towering above the city, and visitors could take home with them replicas of the great statue of Athena within it. If they were wealthy enough they could ask one of the many stonemasons around to knock up a quick copy of any of the other sculptures which took their fancy. But Athens had also been downgraded from the lists of 'wonders of the world'. Sheep wandered in its narrow and crooked streets and rats ran riot. Pliny the Younger, writing 50 years later, urged a friend who was about to become governor of Greece that to take from the Athenians 'the name and shadow of freedom, which is all that now remains ... would be an act of cruelty ... Remember what [the] city was once, but without looking down on it for being so no longer.'[37] It is perhaps an eloquent comment on the nature of the city that one of its major exports seems to have been elaborately carved coffins, available as a memento of Athens, a ghost town in thrall to its remarkable past.

Luke describes how Paul arrived (presumably by sea, since he had come from the coast beyond Beroea, Acts 17.14–15) on his own and was at once struck, like Petronius, by the plethora of gods on offer in the marketplace. Except to Paul these were not gods but idols. He reacted with another 'paroxysm', and began preaching not just in the synagogue, as was his usual custom, but also in the marketplace among the philosophers, apparently a new departure for him (Acts 17.16–34).

Paul's activity among the philosophers seems to have been met largely with incomprehension. Robert M. Grant is probably right to say that 'the more intelligent Gentiles would have found his attack on paganism pointless. They did not worship idols but found in them the symbols of a higher and more spiritual faith.'[38] The picture Luke draws is of a Paul who seems out of his depth.

The philosophers called Paul an 'idle babbler', a *spermalogos,* a word which conjures the image of a bird which picks seeds up indiscriminately and scatters them to grow in strange places (Acts 17.18). Applied to Paul it means someone who foolishly confuses the ideas he has picked up and doesn't really understand them. They accused him of preaching 'strange gods', presumably because his theme was 'Jesus and the resurrection' which in Greek might sound like 'Healing and Restoration'. The crime of inventing new gods was one of the charges which led to the philosopher Socrates' death in 399 BC.

It is unclear whether Paul was taken to the Areopagus (the Athenian ruling council) for a trial on a charge or for a hearing simply out of curiosity. The pattern of Paul's defence suggests that he was facing the same accusation as Socrates. Luke notes that the Athenians were constantly debating new things (Acts 17.21), but they seem to have done so in order to keep fresh ideas out and to safeguard the traditions of the past. In his speech to the Areopagus, Paul stresses that he does not bring innovation, but is disclosing what they had long recognized as unknown (Acts 17.23). The rest of his speech echoes much of the Stoic teaching which was prevalent in the Athenian marketplace: God as creator and Lord who cannot be tied to temples and does not need human attendants (perhaps a sideswipe at the Parthenon, where Athena's giant statue was surrounded by handmaidens who changed the goddess's robes and earrings, styled her hair and held up mirrors to see if she approved!). Paul's God had made humanity to seek and find him, and he backs up his argument with quotations from two poets (Acts 17.28). But then he changes tack and returns to more familiar ground, emphasizing that judgement will come now that the unknown has been made known though the resurrection of Jesus, and calling for repentance.

The response to Paul was muted. Luke says that 'hearing of a resurrection of dead people some sneered, but others said "We will hear you again about this"' (Acts 17.32). A few became Christians, according to Acts, but no church is later recorded in Athens, and Paul himself spoke of the household of Stephanas of Corinth as the first converts in Greece (1 Cor. 16.15). Jesus' instructions to his disciples were to leave a town that gave no welcome by shaking its dust from their feet (Luke 10.11). Paul made no excuses and left Athens (Acts 17.33; 18.1).

Did Paul say what Luke says he said?

Paul's speech to the Areopagus (Acts 17.22–31) is one of the great set-pieces of Acts. But it raises one of the fundamental questions about the book: are the speeches recorded in it genuine, and can we really trust Luke's portrait of Paul?

This speech is one of several that Paul makes in Acts. There are also a number by Peter as well as one each by Gamaliel, Stephen and James. All have a broadly similar style and vocabulary and several seem to have the same structure, even though they are given by different people. Apart from this, a speech such as Paul's to the Areopagus would only take a few minutes to deliver, yet it must have taken considerably longer if it happened in reality. Did Luke therefore make it up?

It is important to remember that Luke is writing after the pattern of Greek historians. This is the thrust of his claim at the beginning of the Gospel to have 'investigated everything from the beginning' (Luke 1.3). Herodotus had been the first to adopt this method in the fifth century BC in his account of the war between the Persians and the Greeks. The name he gave to what he did was *historia*: 'enquiries'. He was followed by Thucydides, who a little later wrote about the war between Athens and Sparta in which he had himself taken part. Where Herodotus was discursive and drew on a wide range of sources, Thucydides was fiercely concerned with accuracy and criticized those who 'simply accept the first story they find'.[39] For this reason he privileged events that had been seen over words that had been said: as the Athenians say early on in his story, 'we do not appeal to the voice of the past but the eyes of those who were present.'[40] Thucydides' approach seems to have been the one broadly followed by Luke in Acts.

But on thirty or forty occasions in his book Thucydides did include speeches. He explained in his preface that, even when he had been present himself, he was not able to remember exactly what had been said: 'So I have given the speakers what, to my mind, they were likely to say given what the situation required, sticking as far as I could to what they actually said.'[41] Ernst Breisach says that for Thucydides the 'speeches set the stage, described situations, and told about motivations without recourse to long enumerations and the use of abstractions ... In other words, the speeches of Thucydides contained what was said, could have been said, or should have been said.'[42] In fact it was only in the nineteenth century that historians stopped using speeches as a device in this way.

In the ancient world, as J. B. Green says, 'speeches are included ... not to provide a transcript of what was spoken on a given occasion but to document the speech event itself'.[43] The evidence of eyes rather than ears took precedence. This convention took a particular twist with Acts, however, since the content of the events Luke was describing was frequently speech. This is why the speeches in Acts loom so large as an issue. With Paul addressing the Areopagus Luke describes the event, but since the event was itself a speech he has to include a report of what Paul said. He seems to have followed Thucydides' pattern: Paul's speech is what the situation demanded, and it seems that Luke has written the script for him. But Thucydides also emphasized that he stuck, as far as possible, to what was actually said; in other words he did not just have a free hand.

Some scholars argue, on the basis of passages like this one, that Luke presents a very different portrait of Paul from the one which his letters give, since here he quotes from Greek poets and argues from his surroundings rather than from the Hebrew Scriptures. There are some parallels in the letters, however. Romans 1—3, for example, attacks idolatry in a way that is in keeping with what Luke says was Paul's initial reaction to the altars of Athens ('paroxysm', Acts 17.16) and the theology of Romans 1—3 also echoes the Areopagus speech in its acceptance that the creation itself reveals the presence of God. A further parallel can be found in 1 Thessalonians, written probably shortly after the visit to Athens. There Paul speaks of turning from idols and surviving the judgement to come through Jesus Christ just as the Areopagus speech does (1 Thess. 1.9–10).

So did Paul say what Luke says he said? Almost certainly not in so many words. But overall Luke does seem to have given a fair picture of what happened. After all, if he were wholly making up the speech, you can't help thinking that he would have made a better job of it than Paul apparently does in Athens! Luke doesn't disguise the fact that the Areopagus was not won over. In this his picture echoes another letter, where Paul emphasizes that he is no philosopher and had no fancy words to spin: 'my message and preaching was not in enticing words of philosophy but in the public demonstration of the Spirit and power' (1 Cor. 2.4). Paul, despite his acquaintance with it, was not really at home in the world of the philosophers, and Luke doesn't hide the fact. The speech he gives to Paul on the Areopagus is appropriate to the occasion. It doesn't hide the fact that Paul left Athens having failed, perhaps for the first time.

Turning point in Corinth

Paul headed to the Isthmus, which divided northern and southern Greece. He made a base in Corinth and stayed there for about 18 months.

Corinth was everything that Athens was not, symbolized by its recent elevation to administrative centre for the province. It was a boom town. It had lain in ruins for 100 years after its destruction in the Second Punic War, but Julius Caesar re-founded it as a Roman colony in 44 BC. By the time Paul arrived it had grown to a population of around 100,000 people, far outstripping nearby Athens.

Like Antioch, Corinth was a melting-pot and a trading centre. The Isthmus was only four miles across at its narrowest point, and there were harbours on either side, 'one leads straight to Asia, the other to Italy'[44] wrote the geographer Strabo. The famous paved *diolkos* ('pull-through') enabled warships and other light vessels to be transported on huge wooden carts from the Ionian Sea to the Aegean without having to travel into the dangerous waters of the Mediterranean off Cape Malea in southern Greece. It also meant that cargoes could be portaged across from one ship to another and at least six days' sailing time saved. This made the city an unchallenged centre for the exchange of news and ensured that it housed a highly mobile population. It was a very open atmosphere and, in contrast to Athens, ready to embrace new ideas.

Where Athens leaned heavily towards the Classical past, Corinth energetically embraced the future. Although it was in Greece, its identity when Paul arrived was strongly Roman. Caesar had repopulated it with freed slaves, ex-soldiers, tradespeople and labourers from Rome itself. The political system was an exact replica of Rome's. Latin inscriptions outnumber Greek ones by almost four to one, according to archaeologists. It was also a city that was hospitable to Jews, many of whom seem to have recently arrived after the Emperor Claudius's edict barring them from Rome.

Corinth was a city that was going places and unashamed about it, with a booming economy and great opportunities for the shrewd or unscrupulous investor to make a fortune. Flaunting one's superior status had become something of an art form in the brash new city, and the absence of aristocratic blood was not the bar to high status that it was in Rome itself. Corinth was also a byword for permissive sexuality, taking its lead from the temple of Aphrodite which was alleged to have owned 1,000 prostitutes: paying for sex with them was also a votive offering to the goddess. In all, Anthony Thiselton considers that

> the self-sufficient, self-congratulatory culture of Corinth coupled with an obsession about peer-group prestige, success in competition, their devaluing of tradition and universals, and near contempt for those without standing in some chosen value system ... provides an embar-

rassingly close model of a postmodern context ... even given the huge historical differences and distances in so many other respects.[45]

If we could travel back in time, Corinth might feel quite like home for a lot of twenty-first-century readers.

The Isthmian Games, celebrated in honour of the sea-god Poseidon, were a huge draw, held every two years and rivalling the better known Olympics. Athletic competitors came from all over Greece and alongside them orators, writers, poets, jugglers, fortune tellers, lawyers and pedlars, all advertising their diverse wares. This would have formed a perfect setting for Paul's preaching, and the length of his stay makes it likely that he encountered at least one of these festivals (and he used the imagery of athletic contest in 1 Cor. 9.24–26). The games had no permanent buildings and so were surrounded by a city of tents. Luke records that Paul quickly found Aquila and Priscilla, recently arrived from Italy and also tent-makers. Paul never claims Aquila and Priscilla as his own converts. They seem to have already been Christians and perhaps had been among the founder members of the church in Rome (though Acts 18.2 says only that they had come from Italy). Whatever their background, they became two of Paul's most enduring colleagues, later moving to Ephesus and working with him there. They took him in to their home and shop and gave him work.

We have to be careful about attributing psychological motives to the people of the first century. They show little interest in such things themselves. Yet there are some indications that Paul arrived on Aquila and Priscilla's doorstep close to despair.

Perhaps it was the magnitude of Corinth which overwhelmed him. Perhaps his experience in Athens had broken his confidence. Perhaps he was lonely. He may have looked back on his ministry since crossing from Troas as a relative failure. It's also quite possible that after being drummed out of Thessalonica and failing to make an impact in Athens he was short of money and needed a job. At any rate he described his arrival in Corinth as being 'in weakness, fear and great trembling' (1 Cor. 2.3). Despite this, Corinth was tailor-made for an itinerant preacher looking to set up a church. Like Antioch, its place at a key intersection of trade routes made it strategically significant. And Paul seems to have taken a deliberate step down in status to manual work in order to challenge the prevailing ethos of Corinth (1 Cor. 9.3–19).

When Silas and Timothy finally arrived from Macedonia (Acts 18.5), Paul had the nucleus of the church in Corinth in place. They followed Paul's usual strategy of arguing in the synagogue, but according to Acts he caused a rift among the Jews and dramatically left to found a rival gathering in the next-door house of Titius Justus, one of the God-worshippers (Acts 18.4–7). Crispus, the ruler of the synagogue, also came over to Paul with his whole household (Acts 18.8). This would have been a major coup, and Luke records escalating conflict with the synagogue. However, unlike his experience in other cities, Paul stood his ground, encouraged by another vision (Acts 18.9–10). More prosaically, despite his step down to manual work, Paul seems to have made some powerful and influential friends.

Crispus would have been one of these, the synagogue ruler of Corinth being a significant figure in the city. Paul also speaks of 'Erastus the city treasurer' (Romans 16.23). A first-century inscription found in 1929 speaks of an Erastus who paved part of the city at his own expense after being elected to office as a magistrate responsible for public revenues. It seems almost certain that these are one and the same man, and the inscription points to at least one of Paul's converts therefore being a very rich and well-respected individual.

The status game

Society in the Roman Empire was highly conscious of status, but status was a shifting and often informal thing with a gap between what was real and what was official.

This went right to the top. The emperor officially ruled only by the invitation of the senate, and his legions marched under the initials 'SPQR' standing for 'the Senate and People of Rome'. But no one was fooled. The emperor was a dictator with absolute power without whose patronage no one, however able, could rise to public office. When a Roman citizen was arrested, as Paul was, his appeal was a personal one to Caesar, not the senate. The emperor was at the top of the patronage pyramid which ran right through the social relations of the empire. It meant that complex networks of friendship and favour gave indirect access to power and prestige. In Rome itself these networks were still regulated to some extent by the aristocracy, who could afford to laugh at the excesses of those with new money who tried to ape their ways.

Trimalchio, the rich ex-slave whose banquet was invented by the satirist Petronius for the amusement of the upper classes, was one of these. He had made his money by speculating on sea-trade, a highly suspect occupation, and designed a huge and tasteless tomb to be decorated with ships, catalogue his fortune and detail the titles he had accepted as well as those he had declined because they were beneath him. The new city of Corinth was full of Trimalchios, indulging in an orgy of self-promotion through tombs and inscriptions to rival Petronius' fictional monstrosity.

One example is a monument in the market-place which proclaims that 'Gnaeus Babbius Philinus, aedile and pontifex, had this monument erected at his own expense and he approved it in his official capacity as duovir.'[46] Babbius gloated over his titles and had his monument set up as soon as he became one of the chief magistrates rather than waiting until his term of office ended, just in case one of his successors vetoed it. In a city like Corinth, gaining status was a huge motivation yet also something of a lottery. It had to be scrabbled and fought for and, once gained, held tight. Modesty was the least of the virtues and boasting of one's own achievements as Babbius did was a huge and all-pervasive social game.

The household was the most important and basic of units, consisting of a wealthy patron (often a merchant), his family, and also his freedmen (ex-slaves known as clients) and slaves. Households centred on blocks, which often contained a villa at their centre and shops and businesses (like that of Aquila and Paul the tent-makers) facing the street, with flats of various sizes on the first floor. In Corinth, rich and poor lived cheek-by-jowl with one another but in a closely defined patron–client relationship.

We know of several such households connected to the church in Corinth: Crispus, Gaius and Chloe are examples, as is Stephanas, with whom are mentioned Fortunatus and Achaicus (1 Cor. 16.17). These two have the kind of nicknames usually assigned to freedmen: 'Lucky' and 'the Greek'; it's hard not to see them as ex-gladiators who had become the enforcers a rich man might find useful on his payroll!

Paul's own description of the church at Corinth was that 'Not many of you were wise by human standards; not many were influential; not many were of noble birth' (1 Cor. 1.26). The implication is that the church was a unique phenomenon in Corinth because it valued those who had no status equally with those who had. Boasting, the chief pastime of Corinth, was irrelevant in God's presence; belonging to the household of Christ was the only status worth having (1 Cor. 1.28–31).

In the meantime the antagonism of the synagogue reached a peak and Paul found himself hustled before the charming and sickly governor Gallio. Gallio's refusal to become involved in the case may have been an important landmark for the Christians in Corinth, for it allowed them scope to continue their preaching without fear of being closed down by the Roman authorities.

Where the encounter with Gallio came during Paul's 18 months in Corinth is unclear (Luke is typically hazy about precise chronology). But at the time it must have seemed that his ministry had turned a corner. Compared to the lone and perhaps despairing figure who had walked in from Athens a year and half before, Paul could set off on his travels again leaving behind a thriving church and some powerful friends, confident that success in Corinth showed that the door was open to the Christian version of Jewish faith in the Western Empire.

At Cenchreae, Corinth's eastern harbour, Paul had his hair cut as part of a Nazirite vow, affirming his Jewish faith (Acts 18.18). His aim would have been to give thanks and to present the hair clippings at the Jerusalem Temple when he had his head shaved there in completion of the vow. After a brief stop at Ephesus, where Paul argued in the synagogue, he left Priscilla and Aquila and continued by sea to Caesarea, arriving in Jerusalem probably in mid 52.

He did not stay long. He headed up to Antioch for a short while and then set off to retrace the steps he and Silas had taken a couple of years before. It was important to get through the Cilician Gates before the winter snows fell and blocked the route to the mountains.

Letters to the Thessalonians

It was during his time in Corinth during the second campaign that Paul wrote two letters to the Thessalonians, building more clearly on the conventional letter forms of the time. These letters were intended to be much more than a private communication; they were 'to be read to all the believers' (1 Thess. 5.27). Although Paul probably wrote Galatians after returning from his first missionary campaign, it was as much a speech in his defence as a letter (he ignores the conventional thanksgiving near the beginning and in effect interrupts himself, such is his anger, Gal. 1.1–9).

The two letters to the Thessalonians are therefore the first time Paul seems deliberately to have used the format of a letter as a pastoral tool. In the process he remoulds the conventions of letter-writing for Christian communication.

First of all Paul replaces the usual opening with a blessing: 'grace and peace' in Greek is *charis*, where the listeners might have expected the similar-sounding *charein*, 'greeting' (1 Thess. 1.1). Paul then moves to thanksgiving but in the name of 'our God and Father ... and the Lord Jesus Christ' (1 Thess. 1.3) rather than of pagan gods. Never one to be constrained by convention, Paul digresses into his memories of the Thessalonians which are interwoven with thanksgiving (1 Thess. 1.4—2.16).

In the body of the letter Paul begins to share the information he wants to impart; he fills them in on what he has been doing since he left them and his desire to return to them again (1 Thess. 2.17—3.13). Then he turns to appeal. Conventionally this is introduced by the word *parakaleo*, meaning 'I call you to ...', which Paul uses (1 Thess. 4.1). Paul appeals to them to continue to follow the instructions he left them (1 Thess. 4.1–8). Then he adds a few extra points about love for one another and the return of Jesus (1 Thess. 4.9—5.11), again employing a stock conventional phrase 'now concerning ...' (1 Thess. 5.1). An indication that Paul wrestled with the conventions of letter-writing is his tendency to put in a 'finally' long before he ends (as in 1 Thess. 4.1). He also reverts to appeals before he really is ready to close the letter (1 Thess. 5.12–22).

The ending is fairly conventional in 1 Thessalonians, but by the time Paul wrote Romans the list of those to be greeted had grown enormously

(Rom. 16). A blessing replaces the customary wish for good health (1 Thess. 5.23–24) and Paul gives them a reminder of his watchword: 'the grace of our Lord Jesus Christ' (1 Thess. 5.28). In 2 Thessalonians Paul adds his own handwritten message (2 Thess. 3.17, see also 1 Cor. 16.21; Gal. 6.11; Col. 4.18).

In this way Paul used and adapted the accepted form of communication and made it into something new. In his hands it was to become a powerful pastoral tool which other apostles were also to use.

Letter-writing

There were plenty of letters circulating in the ancient world. Although there was no public post, merchants needed to communicate with suppliers and travellers far from home wanted to ask their families to send things to them: the copy of one rather touching letter discovered at Vindolanda on Hadrian's Wall is from a young legionary to his mother, asking her to send him some woolly socks!

There was a normal pattern for letters which included the following elements:

- *A. Opening* – the names of the sender (1), the recipient (2), a greeting (3), a wish for good health (4) and sometimes a thanksgiving to the gods (5).
- *B. Body* – reason for writing (6), information and news (7), appeal for help (8), expression of confidence in the recipient's ability and willingness to respond (9), any further minor points sometimes answering queries raised in the letter which is being responded to (10), final comments (11).
- *C. Ending* – farewells and wishes for good health (12), greetings for mutual friends and acquaintances (13). A final personal note was often added by the sender if the letter was written by a secretary or amanuensis.

We can see the pattern at work in this letter found in Egypt. Dionysia, the bridegroom's mother, has asked Apollonius and Sarapias (who seem to be a husband-and-wife team like Aquila and Priscilla) to send flowers for her son Sarapion's wedding. But they can't find the 2,000 roses she wants because it is too early in the season, so they send 1,000 instead and add an extra 2,000 narcissus flowers to the order to make up for the disappointment. The order was sent with the letter through their envoy, Sarapas (names came in rather similar forms in Egypt!).

Apollonius and Sarapias to Dionysia, greeting.

[A] You filled us with joy by telling us the good news of the wedding of the most excellent Sarapion and we would have come at once to serve

him on a day greatly longed for by us and to share in his delight, but because of the assizes and because we are recovering from illness we couldn't come.

[B] There are not yet many roses here, in fact they are scarce, and from all the estates and from all the garland-weavers we only just managed to collect the thousand that we sent you by Sarapas, even by picking the ones that ought to have been picked tomorrow. As to narcissi, we had as much as you wanted, hence instead of the two thousand you wrote for we sent four thousand. We wish you wouldn't condemn us as stingy by writing that you have sent the money, which is an insult when we too regard the kids as our own children and value and love them more than our own and rejoice just as much as you and their father.

[C] Write to us about anything else you want. Give our greetings to the most excellent Alexandros and to his children (may the evil eye not touch them!) Sarapion and Theon and Aristokleia and to Aristokleia's children. Sarapas will confirm to you about the roses – that I did everything to send you as many as you wanted, but we didn't find them.

We pray your health, lady.[47]

I have indicated the sections, but you might like to re-read the letter and see where and how many of the different elements listed above are included.

What did Paul think about the return of Christ?

The letters to the Thessalonians contain much more explicit teaching about the return of Christ than any of Paul's other writings. Paul's stay in Thessalonica had been relatively brief and fraught with danger (1 Thess. 2.1–2, 17; cf. Acts 17.1–9) but it was long enough for the church there to be established. However, Paul had clearly been unable to instruct them very thoroughly in his 'gospel'. In particular, they had heard from him that they should expect the physical return of Jesus to the earth. But when Timothy subsequently visited and reported back the Thessalonians' anxiety that some of the believers had died in the year or 18 months since Paul had been there, Paul set out to address their questions: What would happen to those who had died? Had they lost the chance of salvation by dying before Jesus returned?

In response, Paul attempts to address their lack of knowledge (1 Thess. 4.13) by unfolding the image of the *parousia* of Christ (1 Thess. 2.19; 3.13; 4.15; 5.23). Like many of the words used in the New Testament this is a theological borrowing of a secular word. Paul used it to refer to a visit (his own to Philippi, Phil. 1.26; 2.12 and that of Stephanas, Fortunatus and Achaicus to him in Ephesus, 1 Cor. 16.17) as well as to the coming of Christ, but in the background lay its use for the arrival of a victorious general in a city, accompanied by an entourage of soldiers, servants and administrators. Clearly Paul has something similar in mind here. Christ will not come unaccompanied, but at the head of a retinue of angels and saints, to rally his people to him. For a general approaching a city the first citizens he met would not be the living but the dead: their tombs would line the road. So Paul seeks to reassure the Thessalonians that those who have died will share in the triumphant return of Jesus (1 Thess. 4.14), so they will not be lost.

Then Paul writes 'The Lord himself, with a war-cry, with an archangel's voice, with God's battle-trumpet, will descend from heaven and those who have died in Christ shall rise first' (1 Thess. 4.16). The sound of the war-cry and the battle-trumpet suggest the arrival of a liberating ruler who overthrows the present government. In such a situation the living citizens would then open the gates of the city and go out to meet the conqueror, and Paul says 'Then we, the living who are left, together with them shall be swept up in clouds to meet him in the air' (1 Thess. 4.16–17). The imagery is a fusion of the reality which the Thessalonians might have experienced themselves with Jewish apocalyptic writing, several examples of which have been found among the Dead Sea Scrolls and which is developed in a more thoroughgoing way in the book of Revelation. What Paul is doing is to inspire the Thessalonians with an image of what the coming of Jesus will be like, using pictorial, poetic language which is not meant to be applied literally. His point is that the dead will not be left behind or forgotten.

But *when* this vision of the *parousia* of Christ might be fulfilled is still unknown. Jesus' return will come unexpectedly, as 'a thief in the night' (1 Thess. 5.2). Paul goes on to emphasize this and to draw an ethical implication: they must live as if the 'Day of the Lord' might come at any moment and in the meantime act as 'sons of light and sons of day' (1 Thess. 5.5). However, Paul's sketch of the coming of Christ clearly envisaged that he and most of the Thessalonians would be 'the living who are left' when the Lord came. Thus Paul seems to have expected the return of Jesus to be imminent when he wrote 1 Thessalonians.

Paul may have written 2 Thessalonians, or it could have been written soon after his death by someone close to him. The puzzle here lies in the fact that where previously the Thessalonians had been anxious about the apparent slow arrival of the Day of the Lord, in the second letter they seem to be concerned that it had already come and they had missed it (2 Thess. 2.2)! In these circumstances the hypothesis that Paul did not write the letter seems appealing (especially since 2 Thessalonians 2 includes some of the most impenetrable writing in the New Testament). In fact the Thessalonians' U-turn in belief is not so hard to understand. If the situation in

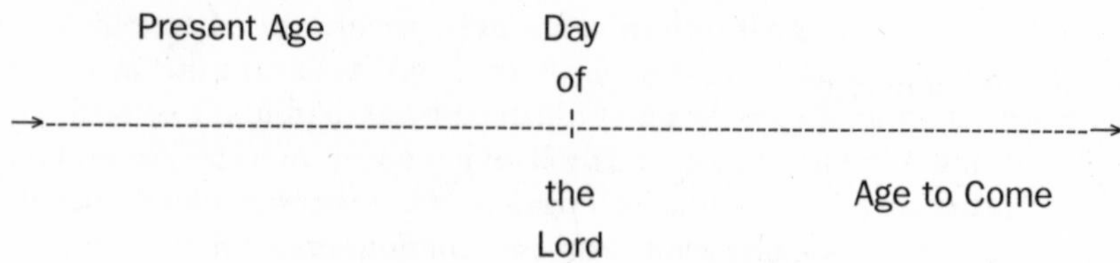

Figure 9 Conventional first-century Jewish eschatology

Thessalonica was one of feverish expectation of Jesus' return it would not be hard for the believers to have swung between contrary views, especially if they thought they had been sanctioned by Paul himself (2 Thess. 2.2).

The confusion is even less hard to understand given what at first seem like elements of double-thinking on Paul's own part. For he can talk of the resurrection of Jesus as the 'first-fruits' of the new age (1 Cor. 15.20), implying that it has already come, yet also encourage the Thessalonians to wait and be ready for Jesus to return. What did this mean?

The early church in Jerusalem shared some contemporary Jewish eschatological beliefs about the coming 'consolation of Israel' (Luke 2.25) and its worship probably focused on that theme. Many contemporary Jews lived in expectation that God would dramatically break into history, ending the 'present age' and bringing in the messianic 'age to come', which would entail judgement for all the enemies of God and his people. This simple scheme is best expressed in a diagram (Figure 9).

The Jerusalem church seems at first to have been essentially passive, waiting for the completion of the Kingdom, which they had seen begun in Jesus. They recognized, and this was where they would part company from many contemporary Jews, that Jesus himself embodied the age to come. The resurrection of Jesus was not just a *sign* of the age to come, it *was* the age to come, the dawn of the day of the Lord. But as the years stretched out, though the hope remained, a more activist approach prevailed. Led by Paul, the Church spread rapidly around the Mediterranean and the gentiles were gathered in. The theological problem Paul encountered was how to reconcile the message that Jesus' life, death and resurrection had been God's definitive act to restore all things, and yet also give full weight to the unchanged reality of everyday life.

The solution was to introduce the idea of an intermediate period *between* the ages, regarding the resurrection of Jesus as the end-point of history, but occurring unexpectedly in the middle of history. Thus it was possible for Paul to say that the Day of the Lord had already come in Jesus and yet to recognize that elements of the Day of the Lord were still awaited. One way Paul explained this was by describing Jesus as the 'first-fruits of the dead' (1 Cor. 15.20); first-fruits being the portion

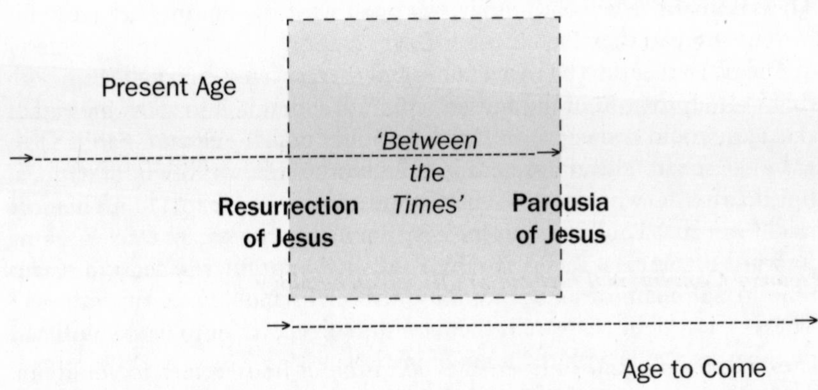

Figure 10 Paul's modified eschatology

of the harvest taken for thanksgiving sacrifice, promising the harvest to come. The period between the resurrection of Jesus and his return was an overlapping period 'between the times' when both ages were in existence. The world still bore many of the characteristics of the old age but Paul believed that Christians should live as citizens of the new, forerunners of the age to come.

Paul's modification of conventional eschatology thus looks like Figure 10.

Paul's view is often described as 'inaugurated eschatology' in which there is a tension between what is 'already and not yet' fulfilled. A classic means of describing it is by drawing a parallel with the end of World War Two in Europe where the Allied landings in Normandy on 6 June 1944 were, it is argued, the decisive act which spelled the end of the conflict (like the cross and resurrection) but the final act of the war waited until VE-Day on 8 May 1945 (like the *parousia* of Jesus). This parallel was first used by Oscar Cullmann soon after the War, who wrote that the early Church believed that 'we already stand in the final phase ... and ... anticipations of the end already exist.'[48] But this view does not do full justice to Paul's belief in the concrete presence of the age to come. In 1944–45 it was still possible for Hitler to have found a way to avert the overwhelming likelihood of an Allied victory by producing an atom bomb, for example; in other words, any judgement that the decisive event happened in 1944 is provisional. Paul's view of the age to come is not like this. The resurrection of Jesus was not, for him, an 'anticipation' of the end: it was the end itself irrupting into history. It was not provisional or partial in any way at all, but decisive, absolute and once-for-all. Paul was utterly convinced that 'the ends of the ages have come' (1 Cor. 10.11) and that he and his churches were living in that time. Yet at the same time he clearly sees the Day of the Lord as lying in the future, as he says to the

Thessalonians. No wonder they were confused by the time he wrote his second letter to them!

The truth seems to be that Paul found no real tension in believing both that in Jesus the end of the age had come, and that in his return the end of the ages would come. James Dunn helpfully points out that 'Paul's Gospel was eschatological not because of what he still hoped would happen, but because of what he believed had already happened.'[49] In a sense we might say that Paul's eschatology is summed up by the phrase, 'looking forward to the past'. This is why Paul shows no interest in, and warns the Thessalonians off, any speculation about eschatological timetables (1 Thess. 5.1). All he really tells them on the subject is not to worry until the final battle begins with the 'man of lawlessness' (2 Thess. 2.3). But this is an unspecific reference too, and implies that they must simply get on with the job of living and serving Christ in the present, not worrying about a future victory that was already secured.

This seems to be how Paul himself lived, and the structure of his thinking about the coming of Christ and living 'between the times' became woven so deeply into his mind that it became an almost unconscious belief, as we shall see when we look at his letter to the Romans.

The third campaign (52–5)

By now Paul was the fully fledged 'apostle to the gentiles' with a strong and independent base far beyond either Jerusalem or Antioch. His apostleship was still disputed, and would continue to be so. Perhaps to the surprise of the leaders in Jerusalem the risks he had taken had paid off, and he, rather than they, was recognized as the leader of a network of churches across Galatia, Macedonia and Greece. But there was a gap in his network: the populous and wealthy province of Asia.

Establishing and consolidating the church in Asia

From Antioch overland through Galatia the journey would have taken at least five weeks, and since Paul was also visiting the churches there it may have been as much as three months before he finally arrived in Ephesus.

For his third campaign, Paul's sights were set on the province of Asia, as perhaps had been his original objective for the second. Paul seems to have become more ambitious as a result of his success in Corinth, where he had left Aquila and Priscilla. When he arrived in Ephesus he found the nucleus of a church already present (Acts 19.1). Rather than seeking to evangelize a single city, or even several of them, he seems to have hit on the strategy of using Ephesus to bring the Gospel to a whole province: as he wrote to the Corinthians from Ephesus, 'a big, wide door opened to me' (1 Corinthians 16.9).

Ephesus

Strange things happened in the seductive air of Ephesus. It was there that Julius Caesar had been first hailed as 'god and saviour of humanity'. Some attributed his lust for dominance to the way such adulation had turned his head. Ephesus and Rome existed in tension with each other, symbolized by the temples of Artemis and Augustus in the city. The Romans attempted to regulate the Artemis cult on the grounds of corruption, but some years later the Ephesians instituted a new ritual commemorating the birth of Artemis and put emperor-worship in its place among the minor cults. Which cult would eventually hold the upper hand?

Ephesus was the strategic centre of a densely populated and fabulously wealthy province. The third-largest city in the world after Rome and Alexandria, it was twice the size of Corinth, to which it was linked by a direct sea-route. But where Corinth was a new Roman city and proud of the fact, Ephesus had retained its ancient identity. In 88 BC the Ephesians had 'ethnically cleansed' their city by slaughtering anyone of Italian blood, even those who sought sanctuary at the great Temple of Artemis. When the Romans regained control of Ephesus four years later they exacted harsh reparations, which crippled the city's economy for 40 years. Once peace came, Augustus raised the city's status to provincial capital at the expense of nearby Pergamum, heralding a period of unprecedented prosperity. Ephesus underwent rapid expansion in population and public buildings. A temple to Augustus dominated one of the two central squares and a splendid residence for the governor made a strong statement about the real location of power by overlooking the 25,000-seat theatre where the city's assembly met.

The city did not lose touch with its past, despite its rapid growth. The ancient assembly of all free citizens remained the city's official government and local culture continued to flourish, especially the worship of Artemis of the Ephesians. Ephesus had a veneer of *Romanitas* but beneath it lay a deep and ancient identity. Many Romans feared the city and its mysterious power.

Asia had become a Roman province in the second century BC. The king of Pergamum had recognized that his realm would eventually be conquered and so he willed it to the city of Rome on his death. The province welcomed the Romans in, and in exchange it had always received lenient treatment. No legions were permanently stationed in the province. But upright Romans considered that it was the acquisition of Asia that had sown the seeds of the destruction of the Republic.

Religion in Ephesus

Paul frequently made idol worship his target. Previously he had worked within cities which either shared his Jewish presuppositions (among synagogues and God-worshippers) or had no strongly felt convictions (Greek and Roman religion being a mixture of cool philosophical speculation and intense superstition). Ephesus offered instead the centre of a visceral and sensual cult, and Paul was ready to take Artemis on.

The cult of Artemis was very ancient, far older than the worship of the Greek deities or Paul's Jewish God. The goddess's original name was Cybele, the earth-mother, and an enormous, many-breasted statue of her stood in the darkness of her temple on a hill behind the city. Artemis was thought to be a goddess of protection who was kindly, listened to prayers and spoke to her followers through oracles. She was the 'great goddess', queen of the heavens and worshipped as lord and saviour. Miniature replicas of the goddess and her temple took her cult far beyond Asia. Runaway slaves could claim sanctuary and freedom at the temple, which was also the central bank for deposits and loans in the province: the awe in which Artemis was held was sufficient protection for slaves and the immense funds stored in the vaults. Six especially powerful spells, known as the 'Ephesian letters', were engraved on the statue of the goddess, making Ephesus a centre for magic and divination. The identities of the goddess and the city were bound so tightly together that few Ephesians could have distinguished between the two. Artemis embodied the city. A threat to her was a threat to the city itself.

Ephesus was host to the temples of a large number of other gods, besides Artemis and Augustus. The city was a religiously tolerant and syncretistic one, similar to Alexandria which lay only five days' sailing away across the Mediterranean. In Alexandria the Jewish philosopher Philo (20 BC–AD 50) produced an impressive synthesis of Greek philosophy and Hebrew theology which united Moses and Plato, and by the early second century the church there had similarly reinterpreted the gospel in Gnostic terms. Ephesus too later became a place where Gnostic Christianity seems to have flourished.

The letters to Timothy are linked closely with Ephesus (1 Tim. 1.3) and they give us an important insight into the situation there in the later first century. A powerful Gnostic presence in the city is suggested by 'falsely named knowledge' (1 Tim. 6.20), which seems to include the characteristic flesh-denying Gnostic practices of extreme celibacy and vegetarianism (1 Tim. 4.3). Women are also prohibited from teaching or having authority over men and are promised that they will be 'saved through childbearing' (1 Tim. 2.12–15).

Some second-century Gnostics held that Eve, not Adam, was the original creation. This would perhaps have seemed natural to those who were used to the worship of the mother-goddess Artemis at Ephesus. It is possible that powerful and charismatic Gnostic women teachers later led the church in Ephesus away from Paul's original teaching, and the prohibition on women teaching was meant to apply only to the peculiar circumstances in Ephesus. The Gnostic emphasis on celibacy may have been a welcome relief to those who had been drawn into some of the fertility rituals associated with the Artemis cult. Therefore what lies behind the mention of childbearing in 1 Timothy may be a judicious attempt to steer between the extremes of celibacy and fertility cult: childbearing women will be saved, and their participation in a normal marriage would not jeopardize their salvation as the Gnostics suggested; but they will be saved only if they behave modestly, in contrast to the festivals of Artemis cult. What matters therefore is 'faith, love and holiness – with propriety' (1 Tim 2.15).

There were many directions in which Christian faith could go. An accommodation or synthesis with Gnostic thought was one of these. But Paul would brook no alternative claims to Jesus as Lord and Saviour. And his proclamation of 'a god who was exclusive, universalist, and intolerant, struck at the very heart of the Ephesians' essentially polytheistic framework of belief.'[50] The stage was set for a pitched battle between belief systems.

Magic, money and merchandise – the silversmiths' riot

Paul's time in Ephesus came to an end, according to Acts, with a riot by the silversmiths who made miniature shrines of Artemis (Acts 19.23–41). Fergus Millar writes that no story 'illustrates better the city life of the Greek East, its passionate local loyalties, its potential violence precariously held in check by the city officials, and the overshadowing presence of the Roman governor'[51] than this one. Most cities were host to regular riots, and Ephesus was no exception. A frequent flashpoint was the relationship between Greeks and Jews over the latter's refusal to join in with the civic worship of Artemis.

Paul had begun his work in Ephesus by attending the synagogue. As usual, he soon fell out with those who worshipped there and moved to the 'Hall of Tyrannus' (Acts 19.9). His association with the synagogue would have inflamed the already simmering unease between Jews and Greeks in the city, but his occupation of the hall daily for two years would have given him a public profile, in contrast to private households where he had set up churches in cities before. Some manuscripts suggest that Paul taught from 'eleven in the morning till four in the afternoon', suggesting a picture of him tent-making in the early morning and evening, and teaching during the hot middle part of the day.

Paul developed a healing ministry, which fits well with what we know of the intense religious atmosphere of Ephesus. A public bonfire which sent 50,000 drachmas-worth of magic spells up in smoke (Acts 19.19 – a drachma was a day's wage) would have certainly drawn attention. Overall, by the end of Paul's time in Ephesus it is quite possible that people all over the city and province had heard of him and his Gospel of Jesus (Acts 19.10). But his good news was not good news to many of them.

The silversmiths had a good deal to lose, but it would be wrong to think that their motives were purely financial. The shrines they made were not, as their equivalents today might be, mere tourist trinkets. They were intended to be a real means of claiming the protection of the goddess in a home. Silver shrines were obviously intended for the rich.

The silversmiths feared the loss of their trade, but perhaps more importantly they feared that the worship of Artemis herself would be undermined by Paul's message. If people turned away from her cult, she herself might withdraw her protection from the city. Ephesus had its problems: the harbour was silting up, and the city relied on the sea for its trade. The fact that Paul came from Tarsus probably didn't help: his home town was an economic rival to Ephesus.

The image of Artemis in her temple was surrounded by small statues of animals given in thanks to the goddess; she was often portrayed accompanied by stags. Homer had called her the 'mistress of the wild beasts'[52] and when Paul wrote to the Corinthians that he had 'fought wild beasts in Ephesus' (1 Cor. 15.32) he was probably talking about his fierce clashes with the silversmiths and other supporters of the goddess.

Paul had achieved what he set out to do: the province of Asia had begun to hear the Gospel, and from his Ephesian base, he had successfully laid the foundations of a new network of churches on the eastern side of the Aegean.

Evangelizing the province

Paul seems to have chosen to base himself at Ephesus and direct operations for this campaign, rather than to travel around as he had done before. To some extent this had been the pattern which he had developed in Corinth, but age or illness may also have contributed to the change in strategy. At any rate, Paul used his base in Ephesus to oversee the growth of the church across the province while simultaneously consolidating the development of the churches he had previously founded in Macedonia and Greece. It is no coincidence that five of the seven letters to churches attributed to Paul relate to this area, and one of the others is to those in the neighbouring province of Galatia. These 'Aegean churches' were the heartland of Paul's mission network.

Although we have direct evidence only for Epaphras's mission to the Lycus valley, where he founded the church in his home town of Colossae as well as Laodicea and Hierapolis (Col. 1.7, 2.1, 4.12–13), we do know that by the late first century there were also churches at Smyrna, Pergamum, Thyatira, Sardis, Philadelphia, Magnesia and Tralles. There is no evidence that Paul personally visited any of these churches himself. How did he keep in touch with them?

Ephesus was the centre for the province's official letter-carriers who delivered official messages using the 'rescript' system, which enabled people throughout the Empire to consult the emperor. They wrote on the upper half of a papyrus sheet and received an answer back on the lower half. This was common business practice too, and it might have been what gave Paul the idea of how to use letters and their carriers as the means to consolidate overall control of the churches.

Paul had probably already written to the Galatians, and he had certainly sent letters to the Thessalonians while he was based in Corinth (1 Thess. 5.27). But it was during this campaign that Paul really hit his stride as a letter-writer and developed the letter form from an expanded private communication into the beginnings of Christian Scripture (though it is highly unlikely that he intended to do this, of course). The two letters to the Corinthians and Romans date from this period; there were at least two further 'lost' letters to the Corinthians; and there may have been a good many others which have not survived.

The letters themselves tell only half the story. An 'epistle' had originally been a verbal communication through a messenger; only later did it include the written instructions they might take with them. (Second Corinthians 3.2–3 suggests that these origins had not been forgotten.) In the absence of a public postal system, finding a trustworthy carrier was an important part of the process of sending a letter, and they were usually entrusted with some supplementary unwritten messages and greetings. The imperial system relied on the messengers to provide interpretation of the correspondence they carried, if asked. Some of Paul's letters include puzzles which have intrigued commentators for centuries, such as the identity of the 'the man of lawlessness' (2 Thess. 2.3), which no doubt caused the Thessalonians to scratch their heads too. Unlike us, they would have had Paul's messenger to tell them what he really meant.

The letter-carriers would have quite quickly gained an important status in the network of churches around the Aegean. Paul mentions about 20 people who may have fulfilled this role, with Timothy, Titus and Tychicus the most prominent. They are often referred to as deacons, which in general usage meant messengers or agents of someone more senior.

Paul and Barnabas had, according to Acts, appointed 'elders' in the churches they had founded in Galatia during the first missionary campaign (Acts 14.23). It has often been suggested that the elders were usually the hosts of the churches, owners of larger houses which could accommodate the gathering of believers (examples are Aquila and Priscilla, and Gaius, Rom. 16.5, 23). These elders were locally based leaders and it was the job of Paul's messengers to bring to them Paul's instructions and teaching as well as having a delegated authority to act for him at times. The terms were fluid, but it is still possible to discern an embryonic system. Luke certainly gives the impression that by the time Paul came to the end of the third campaign there was a network in place, so that Paul could call a conference of elders at Miletus (Acts 20.17).

One of the historical puzzles of the early Church is how it was able to move so quickly from what is often seen as a charismatic grouping without institutional structure in Paul's lifetime to one which within half a century could be described by Ignatius in terms of an accepted and clearly defined threefold order of bishops (overseers), elders and deacons, with the latter group closely associated with the bishop. It seems entirely possible that this structure was based on the system that developed during Paul's time in Ephesus, with Paul himself as the overseer, the elders being locally based leaders and hosts of house churches, and the deacons being Paul's messengers with authority to pioneer ministry in the towns through which they passed. The suggestion is strengthened by the fact that the threefold order runs through Ignatius's correspondence with the churches in Asia in the early second century but seems to vanish when he writes to the church in Rome, suggesting that it was largely distinctive to the church in Asia but had not yet been established further west.

The 'holy internet'

There are some parallels between communication in the first century and the global exchange of information that is such a feature of the twenty-first century. Ships followed well-known routes as they hopped from port to port, and the larger cities tended to become nodal points from which news, goods and ideas could be distributed. The same was true of landlocked cities, linked by Roman roads. In other words, there was a communication network in place which to some bears a resemblance to today's 'information superhighway'.

This network enabled the spread of the Christian Gospel across the Mediterranean within two or three generations, and the dissemination of the books which make up the New Testament. Michael B. Thompson speaks of the 'holy internet' of the first century, in which the 'network "servers" ... were the churches', which 'functioned as the junction or meeting point through which messages passed to and from other individuals and other congregations'.[53] Jerusalem may be seen as the original hub, later joined by cities such as Rome, Antioch, Ephesus and Corinth. What Thompson does with this approach is to use a phenomenon of the twenty-first-century world as a model or framework to illuminate first-century communication networks. It follows, he concludes, that the books of the New Testament were written in an atmosphere of co-operation and communication between churches in different locations. This is in marked contrast to the consensus of previous generations of scholarship, which worked on the presupposition of very limited first-century communication networks and therefore saw the books of the New Testament as having been written within communities isolated from each other.

However, though this is a brilliant analogy, we need to be careful not to import it uncritically into the ancient world. Communication was still difficult and slow most of the time, and our own experience of the almost instantaneous traffic of ideas should not lead us to ignore this fact.

The collection and the saints

Paul's time in Ephesus may also have been the spur to a shift from understanding 'church' as a number of basically singular entities in separate cities (and originally, of course, in some relationship to the local synagogue) to the kind of corporate idea of a universal Church, which approached maturity in the letter to the Ephesians. Paul himself had become the focus of unity in the churches which he had founded and now supervised around the Aegean, and the practical experience of seeing this disparate and unwieldy group of congregations as one may have been what enabled him to see that 'Church' might also refer to God's vehicle to reveal his wisdom (Eph. 3.10), the 'household of God' (Eph. 2.19).

Like any household, this one had an economy. The practical outworking of Paul's time overseeing the Aegean churches was the 'collection for the poor saints'. Paul's motive was that 'if the nations have shared the spiritual things they ought in return to give some material things' to the poor of Jerusalem (Rom. 15.27). From early in his time at Ephesus, Paul seems to have planned to take a collection from the new churches back to Jerusalem. The apostles there had asked him to 'remember the poor' (Gal. 2.10) some years earlier, and he gathered funds from all the churches he had planted: from Galatia, Macedonia, Asia and Greece, devoting a long portion of a letter to the Corinthians to persuading them to part with their cash (2 Cor. 8—9). He also rather craftily let the Roman church know what he was doing while leaving them to decide whether to contribute or not (Rom. 15.25–32).

The model must have been the Temple tax, which Jews throughout the Diaspora sent regularly to Jerusalem. It was an immense practical undertaking; the task of changing the tiny coins, which Paul encouraged all the believers to put aside each week (1 Cor. 16.2), into more easily transportable gold would be remarkable, let alone having to find a way of getting it to Jerusalem safely. But even more importantly it was underpinned by a daring vision of a worldwide Church which he shared in writing to the churches. This vision was one of partnership (*koinonia*) and grace (*charis*). Partnership so that each church helped others, just as individuals were expected to do, and grace because Paul wanted to emphasize that since all good things came from God, Christians had a duty to act generously in imitation: 'God loves a cheerful giver' (2 Cor. 9.7). Paul confessed to the Romans that he feared that the money might not be acceptable in Jerusalem (Rom. 15.31). In fact his attempt to deliver it was to spark the arrest that ultimately meant he arrived in Rome in chains.

After Ephesus – back on the road

After his time in Ephesus, Paul seems to have decided to embark on some further travels. He may have found that the city had become too hot to hold him: he says that 'there is no further room' for him in the area (Rom. 15.23) and he avoided Ephesus when he later passed on his way to Jerusalem (Acts 20.16). (Many scholars advocate a period of imprisonment in Ephesus, and you will often find this mentioned as a fact. But while Acts seems to miss out some important episodes and it is not impossible that an Ephesian imprisonment is one of these – the years pass in just a few verses of Acts after all – there is no real evidence for it.)

Paul had made at least one brief visit to Corinth during his time in Ephesus but now intended to complete the collection for the saints and then head on to Jerusalem. With this in mind he set off to Troas, then to the Macedonian churches, probably launching a further mission to Illyricum on the eastern coast of the Adriatic, which he could easily have visited on his way from Macedonia to Corinth. He stayed at Corinth for three months before beginning the journey to Jerusalem. The letter to the Romans was written from Corinth at this time and in it Paul clearly states that he has completed the work he set out to do during the third campaign, preaching the Gospel 'from Jerusalem round to Illyricum' (Rom. 15.19, Illyricum may be included in 'those regions', Acts 20.2). The next stage in Paul's strategy was to move further west, transferring his base to Rome and then venturing to Spain (Romans 15.24, 28).

Paul gathered around him those appointed by the churches to deliver the collection to Jerusalem (1 Cor. 16.3–4). His life was under threat (Acts 20.3) and he decided not to head directly to Jerusalem after all. Taking a significant amount of money across the eastern Mediterranean was a very hazardous undertaking and Paul was right to be cautious. It was also a violation of imperial restrictions on the transfer of money between provinces (the Temple tax which went to Jerusalem each year was specifically exempted from these rules).

Paul and his companions as a group must have been well-prepared and were probably armed against robbers. Paul's arrest when he got to Jerusalem was because he was mistaken for 'the Egyptian', who had attempted to raise a rebellion in Jerusalem a few years before but escaped with a few supporters (Acts 21.38). Paul and his band must have looked pretty menacing for the comparison to make sense. They headed north via Macedonia and then around the coast until they were able to pick up a direct sailing from Patara on the southern coast to Tyre (Acts 21.1–3).

There are two conspicuous absences from this part of Luke's narrative of Paul's life. First, all we know about the collection comes from Paul's letters: if we only had Acts we would not know why Paul made this journey to Jerusalem. Second, the list Luke provides gives the names of Paul's companions, as well as beginning a 'we' passage that lasts until the end of the book (Acts 20.4). The churches represented were in Asia (Trophimus and Tychicus), Galatia (Gaius from Derbe and Timothy who came originally from Lystra), and Macedonia (Sopater from Berea, Aristarchus and Secundus from Thessalonica, and Luke himself from Philippi). But where were the representatives from Corinth?

We have already noted how conflicts often seem to be smoothed out in Acts. Some scholars have seen this as evidence of a desire by Luke to present an idealized version of the truth, and perhaps it is true that he has omitted some things at this point that might have been embarrassing. As Paul heads to Jerusalem to meet his fate, as Jesus had done, the historian's hindsight shapes the story. In retrospect the quarrels between Paul and the Corinthian church may not have seemed important. But there were real problems between them, as Paul's letters to the Corinthians make abundantly clear. It may be that the Corinthian church declined to contribute to the collection. Whether this is true or not, powerful voices there were raised against Paul. How could this have happened when, only three or four years previously, the Corinthians had been the jewel in the crown of Paul's mission to the nations? What had gone wrong in Corinth?

Corinthian correspondence – the first letters

Paul's strategy of planting churches, moving on and then supervising them from a distance by envoy and letter, was always going to be a risky one. It relied on considerable maturity from the converts and also agreement in matters of belief and behaviour. While churches were small and conformed to a 'household' pattern the first issue was not a problem; nor was the second, so long as the majority of Christians shared Paul's Jewish background. But when the Church began to include a large number of uncircumcised gentiles, trouble brewed quickly and we can see why the Corinthian church went from being the jewel in Paul's crown to the thorn in his flesh. David Wenham estimates that the church in Corinth contained 'several hundred members, even if they did not all gather every Sunday in one place'.[54] And it was composed of people who did not share Paul's frame of moral presuppositions. Without close supervision the Corinthian church was almost bound to overheat.

From his base in Ephesus, Paul re-established contact with the church in Corinth. He wrote a letter to them which is now lost, but in which he asked them to avoid Christians whose behaviour was not up to the standards he had laid down (1 Cor. 5.9–11). Possibly Timothy was Paul's envoy with this letter (1 Cor. 4.17). But the problems did not go away. 'Chloe's people', who may have been involved in trade between Corinth and Ephesus, blew the whistle on major divisions in the church to Paul (1 Cor. 1.11).

This information was confirmed by Stephanas and his henchmen, who visited Paul in Ephesus with a letter from the church in Corinth asking for guidance on a number of questions (1 Cor. 16.17; 7.1). In response Paul wrote what we now know as 1 Corinthians, tackling their divisions in chapters 1—4, returning to the issues of immorality which he had raised in the previous letter in chapters 5—6 and replying to the church's questions in chapters 7—16.

The flashpoint was that a man was having a sexual relationship with his father's wife (1 Cor. 5.1). It was officially illegal under Roman law for a man to marry his father's divorced wife or widow, though it did occasionally happen, usually to keep property in the family. Paul was shocked at this reported relationship, but it was not just because of his Jewish background. This would be abhorrent to anyone, he said, and he was right. Even the brilliant but often crude Roman poet Catullus attacked his friend Gellius for having an affair with his uncle's wife. How much more offensive was the situation Paul faced in Corinth?

Bad though the relationship was it was not the worst aspect of the situation for Paul. His words explode off the page: 'And you're proud of it! You should be mourning instead!' (1 Cor. 5.2).

Why had no one challenged this behaviour? It used to be thought that it was an example of the Corinthians' general sexual openness, their belief that 'everything is permitted' which enabled some of them to continue to use the prostitutes available at the temple of Aphrodite (1 Cor. 6.12–18). But if this is the case, why was Paul so angry with them for not challenging it? More convincing is the suggestion that the man in question was a wealthy patron and host of one of the several house churches that had sprung up in the city, like Erastus the city treasurer. No one challenged him because it would possibly have put the church in jeopardy if it made a powerful enemy. His clients' careers might have been damaged and public honours withheld from them if his patronage was lost. Paul in his 'previous letter' had targeted this man; for him it was crucial that the church, the new society, was not tied to the corrupt practices of the old world around it. The man had to be challenged and Paul did so through his envoy Timothy, pronouncing sentence: 'Cast out the evil man!' (1 Cor. 5.13). Whether the Corinthians obeyed him we do not know.

Similar issues between rich and poor surface in another of the other major questions which Paul faced: the Lord's Supper. Communal meals were a regular feature of first-century life, whether shared by dining clubs or provided for their clients by the wealthy. For dining clubs they underlined who was in and who was out; for the rich they advertised their wealth and generosity and ensured the continued loyalty of those invited. But at the wealthy man's banquet the seating and even the food might be manipulated to reinforce the social positions of those who came. The top table might have the best wine, the lower ones much poorer stuff. Pliny the Younger called this a 'stingy extravagance'[55] where appearance outweighed reality.

The Church had been committed from the first to a pattern of communal eucharistic meals: Paul stresses that he was simply following the pattern of Jesus (1 Cor. 11.23). Paul had fought for an open table at Antioch and again in Galatia. It summed up for him the radical equality of all Christians: here there could be no rich or poor, Jew or gentile, male or female, slave or free. Yet in Corinth the patterns of patronage were so deeply embedded that they had subverted this idealistic vision. When the church was a small gathering it was possible for all to come and share easily. But Corinth seems to have been a fast-growing church, and before long was under pressure of numbers. The floor-plan of a rich man's house consisted of a central courtyard surrounded by smaller rooms, one of which was the dining room. If the Lord's Supper was to be shared there, then it is likely that the ritual actions would have taken place in the dining room, excluding the majority from close contact and perhaps leaving them squeezed in to eat plainer food out in the courtyard. This scenario seems to be what Paul had in mind when he writes that there were divisions between them when they came together to share (1 Cor. 11.17–22). Paul was deeply concerned that appearance and reality should be the same in the church's shared meals, unlike their secular counterparts.

After this Paul embarked on instructions about how the church was a single body, each part contributing to the whole and bound together by love, not competition (1 Cor. 12—14). It was a radical vision of a just world and challenged the status games and patronage pyramids of Corinth. It was underpinned by the final question which Paul addressed, of the resurrection of the dead. There, in the resurrection of Jesus, he argued, was evidence that there truly was a new world coming where old patterns would pass away (1 Cor. 15).

Corinthian correspondence – the second letter

Paul's letter was probably taken to Corinth by Stephanas. Fairly soon afterwards, Paul himself made the week-long sea-trip from Ephesus to Corinth. But he wished he hadn't: it was a 'painful visit' which achieved little and during which Paul seems to have been directly insulted by one of the Corinthian leaders (possibly the 'evil man' himself, 2 Cor. 2.1, 5–6). After returning to Ephesus he wrote a 'severe letter' to the Corinthians, which also does not survive. This was a risk. Had Paul overplayed his hand? Anxiously, he entrusted it to Titus who delivered it to Corinth with instructions to gauge the response and report back to Paul, who now intended to head to Troas and then Macedonia, changing his previous plan to go to Corinth first (2 Cor. 2.12–13; 7.5–7).

Titus was delayed for some reason. Paul suffered agonies waiting for him at Troas and hurried on to Macedonia as quickly as he could (2 Cor. 2.12; 7.5). The disputes with the Corinthians affected Paul deeply. He went so far as to say that 'I was so heavily weighed down that I despaired of life and felt I was under sentence of death' (2 Cor. 1.8–9). Precisely what this means is unclear, but it seems to point to some sort of personal crisis, even breakdown, as well as physical illness. Tom Wright suggests that Paul suffered depression: after three exhausting years in Ephesus the chaos which had broken out in Corinth made him question his whole life's work. 'So had he done it all wrong? ... Was he going to die ... knowing that his work was in ruins, that he'd been called to a unique mission and had just blown it?'[56] Paul claims that the way out of his troubles was finding a deeper trust in 'the God who raises the dead' (2 Cor 1.9). The means by which this happened was his eventual reunion with Titus, the good news of the Corinthians which he brought, and the restoration of his confidence in them (2 Cor. 7.6–16). The risk of the 'severe letter' seemed to have paid off.

The problems in Corinth were not over, however, and so Paul responded with a further letter, 2 Corinthians. This letter has often been considered to be two letters later edited together: chapters 1—9 and 10—13, it is argued, form two distinct blocks with quite different tones, and may have been sent in reverse order. But there are no discrepancies in the manuscripts and it seems always to have circulated as a single entity. It seems more plausible to follow the view that the letter was written as a whole during Paul's work in Macedonia prior to his next visit to Corinth, which lasted three months (Acts 20.3). Its function was to be his 'apology ... a "speech for the defence" ... for Paul's style of mission'.[57] This is why it varies as it does in tone, veering from intense warmth to scathing criticism. It was intended as the warm-up for Paul's arrival, delivered once again by Titus (2 Cor. 8.16–17).

Paul was ambitious and restless. He was not primarily a pastor but a pioneer apostle, always seeking new doors to open for the Gospel of Jesus Christ. Because of this he was vulnerable to criticism. And Corinth had its own specific social dynamics too. Paul was a particularly confusing person in the status game which dominated relationships in Corinth. He was a freeborn Roman citizen (see the byplay in Acts 22.27–9), yet did not mention it in his letters; he had patrons who supported his work, yet chose to work with his hands to earn his own income rather than become the client of a rich Corinthian (2 Cor. 11.8–9); he disputed with philosophers yet called himself an 'idiot' (2 Cor. 11.6). This made him an easy target for opponents in Corinth who were trained orators and better-looking than the rather battered Paul (2 Cor. 10.10; 11.6). In addition they came up with a catalogue of accusations: Paul was not accredited by anyone and he was not a 'real' apostle; he claimed an authority he did not have and 'lorded' over them (2 Cor. 3.1–3; 12.12; 1.24); he was meek when he met them but then bullied them by letter after he left (2 Cor. 10.1, 9–10); he was crafty and shifty, changing his travel plans several times so they didn't know whether he was coming or going, and was not to be trusted in financial matters (2 Cor. 1.12–13; 1.15–17; 12.16–18);

he was a poor speaker, out of his mind, and maybe did not even belong to Christ (2 Cor. 11.6; 5.13; 10.7). It was a devastating critique with a grain of truth in it. Paul was far from perfect. But how could he respond with integrity?

For it was the integrity of Paul's whole ministry that was on the line at Corinth. His refusal to play the status game from the first must have been deliberate; after all, he was serving one who, as he later wrote, 'emptied himself, took the form of a slave and was born as a human being' (Phil. 2.7). Paul was no one's client, but neither had he set himself up as the ruling patron of the Corinthian church himself. He believed passionately that the Church belonged first to God, and then to the believers – whatever their status.

In previous letters, Paul had been at pains to encourage the Corinthians to think things out for themselves, carefully distinguishing between his own words and 'the command of the Lord' (see 1 Cor. 7.10). He recommended that the Corinthians accept Stephanas and others, but he did not impose them as leaders (1 Cor. 16.15–17). When he encountered wrong views about the resurrection, instead of simply condemning them he carefully argued the case for his own views (1 Cor. 15). Thus far he had avoided the temptations of power and leadership for which Corinth above all places was the breeding ground. But now he could play into the hands of his opponents by becoming authoritarian and getting caught in the very traps they accused him of already having fallen into. Yet Jesus had said 'turn the other cheek' and 'love your enemies and pray for those who persecute you' (Matt. 5.39, 44; Rom. 12.14). How should he handle this challenge?

At Hierapolis, far inland in Asia Minor along the Lycus valley can still be seen a first-century tomb celebrating Titus Flavius Zeuxis, a merchant who boasted of having sailed to Italy round Cape Malea 72 times. Two things are striking about this. One is why a seafarer who must have made two voyages a year was based in landlocked Hierapolis; the second is that the route was a highly risky one through 'shipwreck alley', which most merchants avoided by choosing Corinth and its *diolkos* instead. To have made the trip successfully 72 times implies that Zeuxis believed he was an individual highly favoured by the gods. This was his boast, an achievement worth celebrating for posterity. His monument was designed to perpetuate his fame.

Zeuxis's tomb is just one example of the boasting monument-culture which Paul found himself in and which was rife in Corinth. The monuments all around him became the template for his fight-back against his opponents. Rather than out-boast them he brilliantly managed to adopt what can only be called an 'anti-boasting' approach, which is both deadly serious and also very funny. It runs right through 2 Corinthians, as Paul satirizes the status game; but it reaches its climax in a sustained passage which reads like a first-century stand-up comedy routine. Here is Paul's own 'boasting' monumental inscription, an apostle's epitaph:

> I received five 39-lash beatings from the Jews; I was beaten with rods once; I was stoned three times; I was shipwrecked three times and cast adrift for a day and a night.
>
> I have travelled many times: in danger of rivers, in danger of bandits, in danger from my own people, in danger from strangers, in danger in the city, in danger in the desert, in danger from accusing fellow-Christians.
>
> With physical work and effort, nights often without sleep, hungry, thirsty, fasting, cold and naked – all these on top of the everyday responsibility of caring for all the churches; for who suffers and I do not, who is drawn into sin and I am not ashamed? (2 Cor. 11.24–9)

He has made his point. It's a fascinating comparison with Zeuxis. Using his value system, it implies that Paul is far from a favourite with his God. Paul ends by saying, 'If it's good to boast, then I will boast of my weakness'; but he can't resist one final shaft of wit: 'In Damascus King Aretas' governor guarded the city to catch me and I escaped through a window in a big basket' (2 Cor 11.32–3). The image is a deliberately farcical one and to an audience which may have included former soldiers it would have reminded them of the honour given to the legionary who was brave enough to be first over the wall in the attack on a city. Paul presents himself as the opposite: an apostle in a basket making a cowardly escape, first over the wall – backwards.

If we visualize the setting in which this letter might have been delivered, the comparison with stand-up comedy is perhaps not so far-fetched. Titus would have read this, Paul's apology for his ministry, to the church in anticipation of Paul's arrival. Laughter might well have punctured the over-serious spiritual atmosphere, but it was quite a risky strategy. We don't know if it was successful. Chapters 8 and 9 are all about Paul's great project of the collection for the poor of Jerusalem, but how the Corinthians ultimately reacted we can't be sure. Writing to the Romans while he was in Corinth, Paul mentions that the churches in Greece have contributed (Rom. 15.26) but the absence of any Corinthian representatives from Luke's list in Acts 20.4 leaves a question mark hanging over the whole episode.

Paul the mystic and visionary

Paul speaks of 'someone in Christ who was caught up to the third heaven'. In the context – though he disowns any boasting about it – Paul must be making a claim for his own vision of 'paradise', an exalted spiritual experience. If it happened 14 years earlier it would have taken place during the hidden period of his life in Tarsus and Cilicia. It was clearly a mind-blowing event, beyond rational comprehension (2 Cor. 12.2–4).

This was not Paul's only such experience, simply the most dramatic. His call came through a vision of the risen Jesus (Acts 9.3–7; 22.6–10; 26.13–18). At crucial moments in Troas, Corinth and Jerusalem, Acts records Paul receiving specific visions and words from Jesus (Acts 16.9–10; 18.9–10; 23.11). Paul himself says that his visit to Jerusalem with Barnabas was 'in response to a revelation' (Gal. 2.2).

The church in Corinth clearly contained many people who, like Paul, had visions and words from Jesus (this is one reason why Paul mentions his heavenly vision, not to boast but to show that he too has had these experiences). Visions and mystical experiences were a normal (though infrequent) experience, and could account for decisions about travel plans, for example (e.g. Acts 16.7). Larry Hurtado makes a legitimate criticism when he says that 'New Testament scholarship tends to ignore or give little attention to religious experiences in describing and analyzing the features of Jesus and earliest Christianity', tending to give attention to 'social and cultural characteristics ... such as the economic levels of early Christians, the roles exercised by women, and organizational structures or rituals'.[58] Paul stresses again and again that his apostleship is not a matter of human choice, but his response to divine call (e.g. Gal. 1.1). If we want to understand the New Testament world in general and Paul in particular, we have to recognize the power of these experiences, and that those who had them believed in their objective validity.

Yet Paul is diffident about these experiences. He does not seem to value them very highly, though he takes for granted such phenomena as prophecy and tongues-speaking in Corinth. Relating the experience of his heavenly vision to the Corinthians, he goes on to say that the upshot of it was the gift of a 'thorn in the flesh' (2 Cor. 12.7). He doesn't specify what the thorn was, though it seems most likely to have been some form of recurring illness. But the point he wants to make from it is that such mystical experiences do not qualify him to be a 'super-apostle'. He would rather stress his weakness and suffering for the Gospel as credentials, so that the treasure of the message can outshine the 'clay pots' which contain it (2 Cor. 4.7).

The letter to the Romans

Paul's three months in Corinth in early 56 seems to have been the time when he wrote his letter to the Romans. It has proved an incredibly fresh source of theological inspiration through the history of the Church. But why was it originally written? It is unique in being sent to a church which Paul had not founded or visited, and where he had no direct authority.

The church in Rome had probably existed since the late 30s, and initially had a strongly Jewish character. Paul expresses his desire to come to Rome in order to use it as a base for the next missionary campaign he has in mind – to Spain (Rom. 15.28). The letter seems to function as a preliminary to that campaign, which would be new territory in a more ways than one. Paul was getting older, and Spain might have been his final and greatest challenge. The Jewish population of the province was smaller than he was used to from the eastern Mediterranean, being mostly confined to the south-western coast of the Iberian Peninsula, which had once been part of the Carthaginian Empire. Therefore the usual strategy of beginning with the God-worshippers would be less effective. The main language of Spain was Latin rather than Greek, supplemented by local languages similar to the Celtic dialects of Galatia. According to Roman writers, the people of the interior were so barbaric that they brushed their teeth with urine. So Paul's plan would be a hard task, and the need for a sympathetic and supportive community behind him was obvious. Would the Roman church oblige?

With this strategy in mind, Paul seems to aim to summarize his message, perhaps so that they can judge for themselves whether what they might have heard about him as an enemy of the Law is true. But there is also more to Romans. In the absence of Jewish believers after their expulsion by Claudius (probably in 49), the church would have taken on a clearly gentile identity. Some of those who had been expelled (notably Aquila and Priscilla) had returned to Rome, and it seems reasonable to assume that this may have caused tensions in the church there. Paul wants to remove these tensions by giving sustained attention to the relationship of Jew and gentile in the Church, and this is a major theme of the letter. Romans largely explodes the letter-form which is its basis. Although it retains a few of the conventions, it goes far beyond them.

Romans consists of at least five main sections:

- The prologue (Rom. 1.1–17)
- The outline of Paul's Gospel (Rom. 1.18—8.39)
- A sustained reflection on God's choice of Israel (Rom. 9.1—11.36)
- Advice for living (Rom. 12.1—15.13)
- The appeal to join in Paul's vision for future mission (Rom. 15.14—16.24).

It is not really a systematic presentation of Paul's theology, though it is the closest he ever came to producing one. It is an apologetic exposition of his beliefs in the form of a theological *story* full of drama and tension, rather than a theological *system*. What, then, is the story which Paul tells the Romans?

Prologue – introducing the messenger and the message (Romans 1.1–17) The curtain rises on Paul himself, alone in the spotlight in the centre of a bare stage (all Paul's other letters to churches, except for Ephesians, are sent from him and at least one other). He stands before them as the slave of Jesus Christ, his apostle or messenger. In other words he is not here on his own authority but because the Lord has called him, in the long line of prophets. He is here to declare the good news of Jesus, known to be son of God by virtue of his resurrection. Paul is his messenger to the nations, which includes the Romans themselves (Rom. 1.1–6).

These are ambassadorial credentials. In particular they present Paul as *the* intermediary of God and Jesus Christ to the nations. He seeks to rise above any factions that there may be, especially divisions between Jew and gentile: he has the message, and it comes with the authority of God himself. It's a breathtaking claim.

After this magisterial opening Paul rather spoils the effect by breathlessly assuring them that he has longed to come and visit them, perhaps betraying an underlying awkwardness, as if the mantle he has assumed does not quite fit (Rom. 1.8–15). In a way this is appealing and is perhaps meant to seem so to the Romans. For, while Paul comes as the messenger of God, he comes too as a human being with all the frailty which that may imply. But he quickly recovers his balance: his theme is not himself but the good news of God's salvation for all who have faith, both Jew and gentile. He concludes the section with what looks very like a title: 'the righteous will live by faith' (Rom. 1.17). The rest of the letter will unpack this headline statement. Now the story begins.

Outlining the gospel (Romans 1.18—8.39) The first word of the next part of the letter is *apokalyptetai*, the verb form of *apokalypsis* or apocalypse, meaning revelation or unveiling. Paul is announcing something that has been revealed; again like a performer on a stage it is as if he swishes back the curtain to show a scene of teeming life on which the 'wrath of God from heaven' (Rom. 1.18) is coming down. This wrath is not 'a state of chronic ill-temper with humanity, but is something like [God's] constant pressure against evil of every kind'.[59] For this is a world created by God, whose structure bears witness to the goodness of its creator. But humanity has deliberately turned its back on that goodness and over the centuries the world has broken out of control, like a runaway animal (Rom. 1.18–32). As Paul and his audience look down on the scene, with the perspective of God, they see that judgement has been revealed and must fall.

Suddenly Paul turns on his audience as they gaze, perhaps in grim fascination, at the orgy of evil laid out beneath them. He switches from 'they' to 'you': 'do *you* think ... that you will escape the judgement of God?' (Rom. 2.3). Gentiles, by their participation in society, are implicated in this runaway world (Rom. 2.1–16), and while Jews in the audience might think they would escape judgement because they have obedience to the Law to protect them, Paul swiftly makes sure that they know they too are included in it (Rom. 2.17—3.20). Both Jews and gentiles fall under the judgement of God included without distinction in the general indictment of humanity.

And now Paul reveals with a flourish the solution to the problem which he has stated so briefly but effectively. Like a royal proclamation from the messenger who stands before them he announces, 'Now, separate from the Law, God's righteousness has been shown forth' (Rom. 3.21). This is righteousness through Jesus Christ, available for all, since 'all have sinned and come short of the glory of God' (Rom. 3.23, this universal righteousness is the pay-off of the universal condemnation announced earlier). How this righteousness is achieved Paul does not detail at this point, other than to say it comes by grace, a free gift, in the form of an atonement sacrifice in which all believers participate by faith, for God is God of Jews and gentiles (Rom. 3.24–7).

The question with which Paul is wrestling here is about the faithfulness of God (Rom. 3.1–8). It would be easy for him to reject the Law, as his opponents said he did, an accusation that had dogged him for years and was shortly to lead to his downfall in the Jerusalem Temple. But in doing so he would also jettison the story of God's dealings with Israel, in which case the Gospel of Jesus would have no context and lose its power. Even worse, it would suggest that God had taken a wrong turn somewhere and in Jesus had decided to make a new start (effectively the approach which Marcion would take 100 years later, claiming to be Paul's faithful follower). Paul himself could only understand the gospel as the culmination of the story of Israel down the ages, as the prologue to the letter made clear (Rom. 1.2–3). It was the righteousness of God himself that was at stake in Paul's argument, in the sense that it was his justice, fairness and consistency that would be faulted if the Jews and their Law were rejected.

The key was grace. Grace lay at the heart of Jewish faith, the sense that keeping the Law was a grateful response to God's already-made choice of Israel to be his own people. God's righteousness, then, could be shared by him with human beings, received by them by grace and not earned, just as the original covenant had been. This would put both Jew and gentile on an equal footing. But wasn't the Law redundant then? Paul turns to face this accusation, just as if one of the audience has spoken it out loud: 'Not at all! Faith confirms it' (Rom. 3.31).

Now Paul turns from general argument to the introduction, one by one, of three characters who are crucial to his story: Abraham, Jesus and Adam.

First to be introduced is Abraham. His significance lies in being the ancestor of Israel, but pre-dating the Law: he was chosen by God (or 'accounted righteous') before he was circumcised, thus showing that it is possible to be part of God's people without circumcision. Abraham simply had to accept this righteousness with nothing outward to show for it; he accepted it by trust, or faith. Circumcision was the sign following God's choice, not the qualification for it, making Abraham '*our* ancestor' – of gentiles as well as Jews (Rom. 4.1–12).

God's promise to Abraham was always that, through him, the whole world should be blessed. The Law, though it plays a vital part in the story, was therefore a means to an end, that is, to bring to light the grounds for God's judgement (Rom. 4.15). Abraham's faith in this large view of God's mission to save the world, even when it seemed impossible, was the most important thing about him and the aspect of Abraham that Paul wishes his audience to imitate. But they have much more to put their trust in than Abraham had: God's resurrection of Jesus (Rom. 4.13–25).

The focus switches to Jesus, who has been mentioned before but is now brought centre-stage. God's righteousness has been the theme which Paul has been expounding and it is not lost here: English translations tend to switch at this point from 'righteousness' language to 'justification', but it is important to realize that the Greek words which Paul actually used are from the same family, *dikaiosyne*. The problem, as virtually all commentators point out, is that there is no English word such as 'to righteous', which would make better sense of Paul's next statement: 'Having been righteoused therefore by faith, we have peace with God through our Lord Jesus Christ' (Rom. 5.1). Morna Hooker makes the helpful suggestion that an alternative approach would be to use the word '"to right", a verb which normally means "to restore to the proper position" (as with a boat) but can also mean to vindicate or avenge (as in righting wrongs), to rehabilitate or put right'.[60]

Jesus has appeared briefly before in Paul's dramatic presentation as the 'atoning sacrifice' (Rom. 3.25), but again something has been lost in the translation, for there Paul actually refers to Jesus as the 'mercy-seat', within the Holy of Holies in the Jerusalem Temple where sacrifices took place annually on the day of atonement. Does Paul see Jesus as a bit of furniture? Hardly! The symbolism is strange to us, but perhaps not so different from John's transmogrification of Jesus into a lamb in Revelation. Paul's point is that Jesus' body is the place where God and humans are reconciled, which is the function of the Temple's mercy-seat. He is the place to which humans come to be 'righted', and he is God's means of sharing his righteousness with them.

Jesus is the bridge between heaven and earth. At the 'mercy-seat' peace is established between God and humanity and a way to God provided. The picture Paul drew at the beginning of the letter of the unbridgeable gulf between the runaway world and its gracious creator is now miraculously set aside as he shows that Jesus is able to bring both sides together. For, 'while we were still sick, when the time was right' Jesus died 'on behalf of the ungodly' (Rom. 5.6); 'while we were still sinners Christ died on our behalf' (Rom. 5.8); 'being enemies we were reconciled to God' (Rom. 5.10).

Paul has stated the importance of Christ, indeed has hammered the message home; but he has not demonstrated to his audience how it is possible for Jesus to be the one who establishes peace. This is what he now seeks to do, moving forward the third character in his story: Adam.

Adam is, for Paul, a representative human, following the meaning of his name in Hebrew. The entry of death into the world came through Adam, the inevitable accompaniment to humanity's turning away from God which Paul had outlined at the beginning of the letter. All are under condemnation, but the original act of disobedience, according to the Hebrew Scriptures, was Adam's and it brought with it the penalty of death (Gen. 3). However, Paul is at once struck by how inexact the comparison between Adam and Jesus is – he doesn't want the Romans to feel that he is putting the two on the same level. For the 'gift of grace [which must mean righteousness] is not like the sin' (Rom. 5.15): its effect is far greater and more wonderful. In other words, God's righteousness always triumphs over evil. It's an unequal contest: sin cannot win.

Instead through the one man Jesus, grace has broken out. 'Through one man's sin came judgement for all, so through one man's right action came righteousness for all' (Rom. 5.18). There is an echo here of Paul's understanding of the two ages, which we looked at earlier in the discussion of 1 Thessalonians. Adam is the archetypal human of the 'present age', Jesus of the 'age to come'. They are parallel figures and yet the glory of the age to come is so much greater than that of the present that it unbalances the comparison. But, and here Paul might scandalize his Jewish listeners, the Law came in to expose the rampant nature of sin (Rom. 5.20); that is, it functions as a diagnostic tool but is not itself part of the cure. In other words, the role of the Law is limited. By exposing the virulence of sin, the Law provokes God's response leading to 'life eternal through Jesus Christ our Lord' (Rom. 5.21).

Now Paul is caught in a dilemma. For the logic of his position that, by exposing the enormity of sin, the Law has done a good thing suggests that the greater the sin of humanity, the greater the grace-filled response of God will be. Paul does not hesitate to throw out the logic. 'Of course not!' (Rom. 6.1). Again, without spelling them out, the categories of the present age and the age to come are assumed by Paul, creating their own logic. People of the age to come have no business with sin, the characteristic of the old order of creation; instead they identify with Christ, an identification acted out in their baptism where they died to the old order and were raised as Jesus was into a new kind of life. Here Paul employs a favourite and compelling phrase, 'in Christ' which means in some way that the believer participates in Christ, implying an intimate and profound relationship beyond anything merely human (Rom. 6.3–13).

The Law too belongs to the old order, and they are to live in the new by grace (Rom. 6.14). But if they are no longer subject to the Law which defined sin, then comes back the objection, surely sin is a meaningless concept? Paul echoes the title he had proudly employed for himself in the opening greeting of the letter: 'Paul, slave of Christ Jesus' (Rom. 1.1) by responding that where they had been slaves to sin, now they are slaves to righteousness. He has briefly used the concept of redemption – being bought back – earlier (Rom. 3.24); here he uses the same idea to suggest that their experience is like being bought by a good master from a bad one. All they would earn from the old, bad master was death (slaves could usually expect to be paid at least a little pocket money by a reasonable master); from the new, good master the free gift of eternal life would be showered on them (Rom. 6.15–23).

The issue of the Law still bothers Paul, though. So he embarks on a new analogy. The relationship of believers to the Law is just like a marriage, he says. Once one party dies the marriage is over. In the same way their participation in the death of Christ means that they are not bound any longer by the obligations of the Law (Rom. 7.1–6). But does this mean that the old order of sin and the Law are to be identified with each other? No, once again Paul emphasizes the Law's role as a diagnosis, pointing up what's wrong. Diagnosis is neither sickness nor cure, but a necessary (and good) tool between the two. The diagnosis provokes a new awareness of sin, however, and can even make it seem attractive. Caught in the spider's web of temptation and wrong-doing the flesh is weak, though the mind yearns for what is good; but now we are back with the sinful desires of the first part of the letter, and the answer is the same: 'who will rescue me?' Only God through Jesus Christ can do this, according to Paul (Rom. 7.7–25).

The truth Paul proclaims is that there is 'no condemnation for those who are in Christ Jesus' (Rom. 8.1). Slaves of a new master, born through death into a new life, they have a new freedom from the old order of sin and death and by their participation 'in Christ' escape the righteous wrath which God has pronounced upon the runaway world. How do they know this? Paul produces with a flourish the ace in his pack: they are in Christ and so, 'Christ is in you' (Rom. 8.10). They experience the presence of the Spirit, the 'Spirit of the one who raised Jesus from among the dead' (Rom. 8.11), whose life-giving power now extends to them and can bring a halt to the slavish tendencies to sin which Paul has just spoken about. They can break the patterns and habits of the old order and know that they are part of the new (Rom. 8.12–17).

Paul knows it's not quite that simple. This is a time of suffering (as he already knew personally and was to find out even more fully in the months that lay ahead of him). But the suffering which believers encounter is part of the 'birth-pangs' of the new creation, the age to come (Rom. 8.22). Though Paul is talking primarily here of the struggle of the whole of creation as it hangs between the two ages the argument also applies to the individual caught between the tendency to sin and freedom in Christ: the believer's struggle makes their body a battle ground between the present age and the age to come (Rom. 8.26–7). As we saw when looking at Paul's view of the coming of Christ earlier, nothing lies in the balance here. He is unshakably convinced that in the cross and resurrection of Jesus the future is not just assured but has already been made present. So he can conclude that those whom God 'righted [already], these also he glorified' (Rom. 8.30), firmly using past tenses.

How shall Paul sum up this bravura performance? He rehearses highlights of his presentation of the gospel and concludes that nothing at all can ever keep the Romans apart from the love of God (Rom. 8.31–9).

Did God cast off his people? The role of Israel (Romans 9.1—11.36) The knottiest and most tortuous section of the whole New Testament is probably Romans 9—11, where Paul wrestles in anguish with the apparent rejection of his Gospel by the Jews. There is no doubt of his deep feeling on the matter: 'the grief to me is great, the pain in my heart unending, and I would pray myself accursed and cut off from Christ for the sake of my brothers, my family of the flesh who are the people of Israel' (Rom. 9.2–4). Where do the people of Israel, who first received the grace of God and showed the way to salvation, now fit into the plan of God which Paul has outlined in the first eight chapters of the letter to the Romans?

Paul begins by repeating that it is not by sharing blood but by sharing the promise of God that one truly becomes a descendant of Abraham. God's grace is given by him as he wishes (Rom. 9.6–18). Paul's change of language is significant here. Up to this point in Romans he has spoken of Jews and gentiles; but now he begins to speak of Israel rather than the Jews. James Dunn points out that while gentiles and Jews are mutually exclusive terms, since they are primarily ethnic, yet 'it might be possible to include "Gentiles" within "Israel"'[61] if Israel is defined, in the way Paul has done earlier, as the heirs of God's promise. The tragedy which Paul feels so keenly is therefore that, by God's grace, the covenant relationship has been opened to 'the nations', thanks in no small part to Paul's own efforts.

Yet at just this point, when the glory of God can be seen in salvation being proclaimed to the whole world, the Jews who were the original bearers of that salvation seem to be turning their backs on what God has done. But it is not that God has rejected them – whatever they choose to do in reaction – in favour of the gentiles. Paul is convinced that there is still a place for the Jews, for how could God have rejected his people? The idea is unthinkable (Rom. 11.1).

Instead Paul, reflecting on the historical events which he has lived through, sees that it is actually through the 'stumbling' of Israel that salvation has become possible for the gentiles (Rom 11.11–12). He uses the language of 'hardening of the heart' several times (Rom. 9.18; 11.7, 25), evoking the story of Israel's exodus from Egypt, where God hardened Pharaoh's heart in order to bring about deliverance (see Ex. 4.21; 7.3; 14.4, 17). In the same way Paul reflects that if the synagogues had not refused to listen to him, his mission to the nations would not have developed as it did. So he reaches for metaphor again: the Jews are the original 'olive tree' and the gentiles are being 'grafted in' to the original stock (Rom. 11.17–24). And thus Paul finds a solution to his anguish. For the present turning away of Jews is part of the 'mystery' of God's plan (Rom. 11.25), in order to achieve the ultimate aim: the salvation of 'all Israel', which includes both Jews and gentiles (Rom. 11.26). The whole section concludes with a sustained hymn of praise to God, whose wisdom is beyond grasp (Rom. 11.33–6) – except, of course, that Paul has now grasped it!

Paul's strong affirmation in this section of his letter to the Romans is that both Jew and gentile have a place within the Church. If there were tensions between the two groups in the Roman church, as may well have been the case, this was an important affirmation to make. Paul's understanding of 'inaugurated eschatology' with an overlapping period between the present age and the age to come which participates in both forms a crucial background to his thought about the current division between Jews and gentiles; both groups will together be the eschatological Israel in the future. But for now they remained largely apart.

Paul's championing of Israel as one inclusive nation of Jews and gentiles within the plan of God was ultimately unsuccessful: 'Paul carried the day on his first major point: that the grace of God is extended to Gentiles. But on his second major point – that God has not broken covenant with Israel – Paul lost'.[62] It's likely that already within the Roman church the tensions which would pull Jews and Christians in different directions had begun. It is perhaps the first sign that Paul was being left behind by the movement he had helped to create. His practical work in gathering the collection for the relief of the poor in Jerusalem was a means of trying to hold together gentile and Jewish churches and reflect the vision of Romans 9—11.

Advice for living (Romans 12.1—15.13) The next section of the letter to the Romans could have followed directly from the end of chapter 8. For now Paul encourages the Romans to put into practice the implications of what he has been teaching them. There are instructions on how to live as a transformed person, whose whole life bears witness to their faith (Romans 12.1–13). The highly compressed list of sayings which Paul repeats seems to be a summary of Jesus' teaching in the Sermon on the Mount (Rom. 12.14–20, see Matt. 5.38–48; Luke 6.20–36).

Then Paul introduces the difficult question of how to deal with the authorities. Given his brushes with the law (as outlined in 2 Cor. 11.24–5) he wouldn't be the most obvious guide! His practice and theology had clearly put him on a collision course with the 'imperial theology' that was gaining ground across the Mediterranean during the first century. Allegiance to Jesus as Lord and saviour both echoed and strongly questioned the application of the same words to Caesar. In Romans we find a more positive assessment of imperial power, as Paul says 'let everyone be subject to the governing powers, for there is no power except God's and the powers that be have been ordered by God' (Rom 13.1). He goes on to say that therefore those who resist the authorities resist the order God has set up.

This is a passage which has been used to justify appalling abuses on the grounds that rulers have the sanction of God. It is important to read it in context and alongside Paul's implicit challenge to imperial theology. He is writing to the Christians in Rome where disturbances 'at the incitement of *Chrestus*'[63] had, only a few years before, led to the expulsion of the Jewish community. Paul's intention seems to have been not to provoke unnecessary conflict with the authorities. His clashes with them were never direct, but the result of others' accusations. And, as they are portrayed in Acts, Roman officials seem to have been reluctant to act against him.

Paul shows a degree of trust in the fairness of the legal system here. In the course of his letter he has told the Romans to live peaceably and not to seek vengeance, in words that echo Jesus' in the Sermon on the Mount (Matt. 5—7). Understanding the authorities, and the legal system they operated, as at root ordered by God made it possible to leave vengeance to be worked out legally (Rom. 13.3–4). It is important to remember that Paul was writing in the early 50s, before Nero's rule of terror threw legal processes out of the window.

The culmination of Paul's argument is that Christians should pay taxes without question (Rom. 13.6–7). This was a more contentious question in the provinces than in Rome itself, where direct taxation was minimal. Indirect taxes were high in the city, however, and in any economy they hit the poor hardest. Occasionally there were riots over the price of bread, for example, which was inflated by customs fees and sales taxes. It is easy to see how Paul's anti-imperial theology could have been co-opted to refuse payment.

On this point, of course, though Paul does not say so, there was a well-remembered saying of Jesus about paying taxes to Caesar, which probably lies underneath his argument. It is interesting that rather than simply quoting the words of Jesus, he argues his case. The gist of the message seems to be, 'don't pick unnecessary fights'.

Allied to this is the recognition that the present authorities, though ordered by God, are only temporary (Rom. 13.11–12). Paul clearly expected that one day, soon, God would sweep away the present order and bring in the Kingdom. Even the great Caesar was only temporary.

Paul wrote on the verge of heading to Jerusalem. There he would find, ironically, that it was only the Roman imperial authorities that could guarantee his safety and, in the teeth of murderous threats, he would be rescued by a troop of Roman soldiers. He would soon have cause to thank God for the powers that be.

Further instructions for peaceful co-existence in a mixed church, where Jews may already have been a minority, follow, particularly commending patience and understanding for those who still wish to observe the Sabbath and Jewish dietary regulations (Rom. 14.1—15.5). Then Paul returns to the theme of the central section of the letter, the future unity of Jews and gentiles in one people. It is literally by the harmony of their praise that God will be glorified (Rom. 15.6–13).

Paul's appeal (Romans 15.14—16.24) Although Paul was able to greet 26 people by name at the end of the letter (Rom. 16.3–16), he had not visited the church in Rome when he wrote it. The primary function of the letter had been to introduce himself fully and to establish for the Roman believers what 'his gospel' was. Now, finally, he tells them of his plan to use Rome as a base for a further westward expansion of the Church. He has no desire to work in Rome itself, for he wishes to be a pioneer, not someone who builds on 'another's [Peter's?] foundation' (Rom. 15.20). Instead Paul hopes to be 'sent onwards by you' (Rom. 15.24) to Spain. But first he tells them that he must return to Jerusalem, to ensure that he has the backing of the community there in the next stage of his strategy (Rom. 15.25–9).

After a string of personal greetings and a final thanksgiving to God (Rom. 16.1–27) the letter was complete. As it went west with Phoebe the deacon from Cenchreae, Paul prepared to go east to Jerusalem. He wanted to be there for Pentecost (Acts 20.16).

Jerusalem to Rome

At this point in the story the sources about Paul begin to dwindle; there is nothing in his letters (the majority of which he had already written) about this crucial part of his life, so Acts becomes the only source we have. It records Paul's return to the province of Syria, churches where he was welcomed all along the coast, and warnings that he should not go on to Jerusalem. Yet Paul, like Jesus in Luke's Gospel, 'sets his face to Jerusalem' (Luke 9.51) and will not be deterred.

The Jerusalem Paul had known as he grew up and which he had rarely visited since he left nearly 20 years before was no longer there. In its place he found a fragile city increasingly living on its nerves. There had been an escalating series of incidents usually precipitated by the insensitivity of Roman legionaries. In 53 Antonius Felix, an ex-slave whose brother Pallas was Claudius's finance minister, was sent in as governor to sort the province out. Felix had previous experience in Syria and his policy was to act ruthlessly. When the former high priest, Jonathan, who had been his ally, dared to criticize his blatant disregard for normal rules, Felix paid for Jonathan's throat to be cut in broad daylight. No wonder Tacitus loftily declared that 'he had the power of a king – and the manner of a slave'.[64] In 54, Felix put down a rebellion by 'the Egyptian' who had marched on Jerusalem and camped with an army on the Mount of Olives. By the time Paul arrived for Pentecost 56, 'The deployment of troops on the streets – almost unknown in most parts of the Empire – had, in fact, become routine.'[65]

Jerusalem would have been swollen as usual by pilgrims for the festival. The crowded streets and sweaty alleyways were cover for anonymous assassins who threatened anyone vaguely sympathetic to Rome. Soldiers on street corners and around the Temple anxiously awaited this year's inevitable crop of trouble. Into this situation, Paul arrived with a gentile entourage, which was probably armed and carrying a stack of money. It wasn't the best move of his life.

Paul's first task, of course, was to deliver the collection. He met James and the leaders of the church in Jerusalem and gave an account of the 'mission to the nations' (Acts 21.19). Acts doesn't mention the money, though it does feature in a later speech of Paul's (he says he came to Jerusalem to bring alms, Acts 24.17). For this reason, and Paul's own anxiety about whether the collection would be accepted (Rom. 15.31), many scholars have suggested that the Jerusalem leaders rejected the collection outright, painting a dramatic scene in varying degrees of lurid colours, in extreme cases imagining coins being flung down in disdain. There is no evidence of this, however telegenic it might be in reconstruction, but the Jerusalem leaders did attach some conditions to be fulfilled before they would accept the money. Paul was to make a public demonstration, which would confirm that he was indeed an observant Jew and avoid accusations that his money was a bribe to make the leaders accept the 'law-free' gospel, which Paul's opponents believed he preached even to Jews. The background was their perception, probably still true at this time, that the majority of Christians remained faithful to the Law (Acts 21.20).

The deal was this: four men in the Jerusalem church had taken a Nazirite vow, as Paul himself had done some years before when he left Corinth (see Num. 6.1–21); this was the most stringent vow a Jew could take, which conferred the kind of purity on an individual which was normally only expected of priests. Paul was asked to join them (in case of emergency the vow could be completed in a week) and pay for the sacrifices they must make, publicly demonstrating his submission to the Law of Moses. The sacrifices required were three lambs each and a bread-offering. Thus Paul had to pay for 12 lambs in all, a significant sum. The gentiles with him were not asked to submit to the law, in acceptance of the agreement made at the Jerusalem conference seven years before (Acts 21.23–5).

Among the pilgrims were some from the province of Asia, perhaps Ephesus itself. Paul had been recognized in Jerusalem with the gentile Trophimus, the representative of the Asian churches. Seeing Paul in the part of the Temple reserved only for Jews, the pilgrims from Ephesus put two and two together and assumed that he had taken Trophimus where he shouldn't go. A riot broke out, Paul was dragged violently from the inner Temple and into the Court of the gentiles.

Overlooking the outer courts was the Antonia Fortress, where a cohort of about 1,000 Roman soldiers was stationed under the command of a senior officer, the tribune Claudius Lysias. On the lookout for trouble, the legionaries quickly thundered on to the scene, pulling Paul out of the clutches of the mob, chaining him and taking him into the safety of their barracks (Acts 21.27–36).

Claudius leapt to the conclusion that Paul was the Egyptian who had escaped after his defeat two years previously. He calls the Egyptian's followers *sicarii* (Acts 21.38), probably meaning armed men who kept their weapons hidden and mingled with the crowds, perhaps as Paul's entourage had done. Maybe he had been tipped off that the Egyptian was aiming to make an appearance in the Temple at Pentecost, and had already kept Paul under surveillance because he was acting suspiciously. Paul instead announced that he was in fact from Tarsus. He asked for permission to speak to the mob from the safety of the fortress steps, but his attempt to state his case provoked further rioting and the crowd called for his blood. Claudius took Paul into the barracks; clearly Paul's speech about visions of Jesus had cut no ice with him. Paul would have been roughly tied up in preparation for a vicious flogging, during which he would be questioned to find out why he had caused such an outcry.

Twenty-five years earlier, possibly even in the same room, Jesus had been flogged by Pilate's men after the crowd shouted for his death. Here the lives of Jesus and Paul intersected. Then, though innocent, Jesus had been crucified. The same fate probably awaited Paul; the ultimate imitation of Christ lay before him (1 Cor. 11.1). Might his death, by removing the main stumbling block, even accomplish his greatest wish, the end of the conflict between Jew and gentile which threatened to tear the church apart (Rom. 9.3)? No other apostle had been crucified. Might this settle his claim to be part of the elite band, wiping out the fact that he had not shared in Jesus' life by sharing in his death? After all, he had no doubt that God would vindicate such suffering (Rom 8.17).

And yet, was he ready for such an end? Alongside his undoubted bravery there is also an unmistakable and endearing frailty about Paul. This was the man who had first arrived in Corinth in fear and trembling, and who had boasted of his ignominious escape over the walls of Damascus (1 Cor. 2.3; 2 Cor. 11.32–3). There must have been a split-second decision. Acts says that Paul, face down and with the lash about to tear into his flesh, asked an oddly indirect question: 'If a man is Roman and not condemned, is it legal for you to flog him?' (Acts 22.25).

Suddenly the proceedings paused. The centurion in charge of the interrogation hurried off to tell Lysias that Paul was claiming Roman citizenship (Acts 22.26).

Was Paul a Roman citizen?

Whether Paul was a Roman citizen is a contentious issue. Some scholars think it unlikely that he was, since he never refers to it in his letters. Until this point in the story it has had a minor part to play (in Philippi, Acts 16.37–9), but now it assumes major importance. The rest of Paul's story in Acts makes no sense unless it is true, but the puzzle it poses is why Paul revealed it only at the last minute. It is important to recognize the setting. Paul's reason for being in the Temple was to prove he was a true Jew. Claiming to be from Tarsus in public simply marked him out as a Diaspora Jew and would cause no problem. But if he had announced his Roman identity in the Temple courts it would have confirmed the perceptions of many about him and inflamed the situation even further. It was risky but wise to keep quiet. Once inside the fortress, however, it made sense to reveal the truth. The same process had occurred at Philippi, according to Acts, where the citizenship of both Paul and Silas was revealed in a private meeting.

Paul's Roman citizenship may not have been very important to him. It was incidental to his early life; as a Pharisee, he probably wished to distance himself from it, but since he had been born a citizen it was not something he could do much about. Valerie Hope says that 'in the Jewish communities where he lived and worked religious affiliation and religious office were, for the majority of the population, more significant in the assessment of status' and notes that while 'Paul made full use of his Roman citizenship when his activities brought him into contact with other "Romans" ... before this his citizenship may have been of secondary importance.'[66]

Paul in prison

When the tribune hurried down to the torture cell, he found that Paul's citizenship was actually better than his own: born not bought. This put him in a difficult position. Where he could act with impunity in normal circumstances, ill-treatment of a citizen of higher status than himself (and even than the governor, who was still an ex-slave however far he had risen) was potentially a scandal of the highest order. Indeed, given Felix's reputation there was probably already much to hide. Suddenly the brutal crushing of yet another Jewish troublemaker by the Roman military machine shuddered to a halt.

And there it stayed. Claudius had Paul released but wanted to understand the issue that was causing such trouble. Expecting an armed insurgency, he now found himself embroiled in what he probably saw as yet another typically Jewish exercise in theological hair-splitting. Whether he had the authority to call a meeting of the Sanhedrin, the Jewish Council, is irrelevant. Under Felix as governor most of the normal rules were suspended anyway; backed by 1,000 troops, Claudius could get pretty well anything he wanted. Except a resolution to the dispute. The high priest, a corrupt and unscrupulous character whose close links with the Romans both kept him in power and made him hugely unpopular, apparently physically attacked Paul, who in turn denounced him as a 'wall of whitewash', or hypocrite, and disputed his fitness to be high priest (Acts 23.3–4). In his earlier life Paul might have hoped to become a member of the Sanhedrin himself; now he quickly exploited the divisions he knew well between Pharisees and Sadducees over resurrection. The meeting broke down in chaos. Claudius took Paul into custody again for his own safety (Acts 23.10). Paul's status as a prisoner had clearly changed, for now he could receive visitors and give centurions instructions (Acts 23.17).

A further serious plot against Paul's life, revealed by Paul's nephew (Acts 23.16), led Claudius to transfer Paul from the beleaguered garrison at Jerusalem to the Roman provincial headquarters at Caesarea Maritima, handing responsibility over to his boss, the governor. He simply could not afford, in the heightened atmosphere of the festival, for Jerusalem to get out of control. If Acts is to be believed, Paul's guard was perhaps a quarter of the legionaries in the Antonia Fortress as well as some auxiliaries (Acts 23.23). They didn't need to go through the city. Under cover of darkness Paul was bundled out of the fortress on a horse. By morning he was 40 miles away in Antipatris and Claudius could breathe easily once more.

Caesarea

Caesarea was a city of gleaming white walls and cool marble floors built by Herod the Great. Its ruins today are spectacular, as it has been gradually excavated from the sands. As its name suggests, from its grid-pattern streets to its imperial cult temples and four-yearly cycle of Greek games, it was thoroughly Roman.

Any governor could feel at home in the sumptuous palace surrounded on three sides by the sea. This is where Paul was held. Next door was the praetorium complex, the centre of Roman government in Judea. It included administrative offices, which would have housed the registry where official records of legal proceedings were kept. It may have been here that Luke was later able to copy the letter that Claudius Lysias sent to Felix specifying that Paul would be followed shortly by his accusers for a preliminary hearing (it's worth noting how Claudius presents his actions differently to Luke's narrative, implying that he has always been seeking Paul the Roman citizen's safety, Acts 23.26–30). Felix checked with Paul that he came from Cilicia. That meant he could not pass Paul on to another province, because both Tarsus and Jerusalem came under the overall jurisdiction of the legate of Syria.

The high priest and Sanhedrin members duly bustled in five days later, and Tertullus, a professional advocate, outlined the accusations on their behalf: Paul, like an infectious disease, had caused trouble among Jews across the Empire; and he had tried to desecrate the Temple (Acts 24.2–8). Felix invited Paul to respond; his change in status is marked by the way, according to Acts, he speaks with relaxed good humour as one citizen addressing another. Paul admitted to being a Christian, but knew that was not illegal. He had not begun the riot in the Temple, his accusers had. And if the complaints were about his behaviour in other provinces then evidence should be brought from there; perhaps the heart of the matter was that he believed in the resurrection of the dead, as any Pharisee did (Acts 24.10–21). Felix seems to have known about the relationship between Christians and Jews. He adjourned the case until he had received further evidence from Claudius, presumably to ascertain whether Paul had caused the riot in the Temple or whether he had simply been the victim of it.

However, though the legal situation was probably pretty clear and Paul was innocent, it would have been political dynamite to set him free again. The last thing Felix wanted was a Jewish mob besieging his palace as they had done to his predecessor five years before. Tertullus had fawned on Felix in the opening of his speech, but the flattery contained a veiled threat: surely Felix wanted peace to continue? Then he had better listen to how much they hated this man Paul and do something about it. A Roman governor was well aware that legal process sometimes conflicted with *realpolitik*.

Drusilla was one of three princesses who married Felix, the ex-slave. The daughter of Herod Agrippa, king of Judea from 41 to 44, she was well-placed to advise him. Her disregard of Jewish Law in marrying Felix, who was of course uncircumcised, may have made her sympathetic to Paul on precisely the grounds that his accusers in Jerusalem objected to. If there was a way for her husband to join her ancestral faith without actually becoming a Jew, she would probably have liked to know about it. Conversation with Paul appears to have shown Felix that the moral demands of the Christian variation on Jewish faith were just as taxing as the original and he lost interest. However, he also seems to have hoped for money from Paul, a suggestion quite in keeping with his bad reputation (Acts 24.24–6).

Why did Felix think Paul might have money to give him? He was already a rich man and would only have been interested in significant amounts. This brings us back to the collection. The riot in the Temple had prevented Paul from completing his vows, and those who opposed him were clearly not going to believe that completing a seven-day sacrificial vow set aside their objections to him. The Jerusalem church appears not to have spoken up for Paul, although it is hard to know what they could have done in the circumstances. His appeal to Roman citizenship took him into another social world, and given the situation it would not have been sensible for them to have taken his money. This may be a clue to why the collection goes unmentioned in Acts. It was not rejected by the Jerusalem leaders, but neither was it ever received. If this is the case, Luke probably did not want to show how Paul's great vision ended in failure. The money was not, of course, Paul's, but presumably still in the possession of the representatives of the churches. Given the costs of Paul's imprisonment, which he would have been expected to bear himself, it is quite possible that they suggested using some of the money for his upkeep. But we really have no idea what ultimately happened to the money. Maybe Paul did still have it with him, and Felix fancied a cut.

Felix was not an unqualified success in Judea, but he had acted the hard man and restored some form of order, skilfully treading the tightrope between opposing factions. But his days as governor were numbered as soon as his brother, Pallas, who had been Claudius's finance minister, was dismissed by the new emperor, Nero, in 55. Eventually, probably in 58, he was replaced by Porcius Festus.

Like any new official, Festus inherited a backlog of problems from his predecessor. One of them was Paul, who had not been forgotten by his accusers in Jerusalem. Festus decided that the adjourned hearing should be reconvened in Jerusalem, largely it seems in order to make a good impression on the Jewish authorities there. Despite Festus's offer that the hearing should be 'before me' (Acts 25.9) the main charges related to Jewish Law, and Paul was in danger of trial before the Sanhedrin again. He turned down Festus's offer. He had been accused of crimes against the emperor by disturbing the peace of the Empire. If he was not to be tried by Festus on those charges, he decided to exercise his citizen's right to answer them before Nero himself in Rome.

Despite the brief involvement of Agrippa, Felix's brother-in-law, who now ruled the former tetrarchy of Philip and some parts of Galilee and Perea, Festus was left with no real choice but to pass Paul on to Rome. He seems to have been unhappy with this: it would not be a good start to his career as provincial governor to refer a case to Rome which apparently turned on stories about a messiah who had returned from the dead. Paul was clearly mad (Acts 26.24), and Nero would not thank him for the referral. Festus was probably in no hurry to send Paul off, and as much as a year may have passed. Finally Paul was attached to a group of prisoners bound for Rome, though clearly in a different category and treated well (Acts 27.1–3, 43).

By this time it was probably late summer 58 or 59. The sailing season was near to its close and the voyage was a risky one (Acts 27.9). Possibly Festus was hoping Paul would not reach Rome and thus save him embarrassment. Luke takes up the story in close and gripping detail. The overriding question is: will Paul actually make it to Rome or not?

En route to Rome

Festus may not have been very keen for Paul to reach Rome but Paul certainly wanted to get there. He felt that he had a call to 'bear witness' in Rome (Acts 23.11) and had been hoping to visit for a long time (Rom. 15.23). But it was a long and dangerous voyage to make so late in the year and began badly as the winds were against them. In Myra they changed ship and they limped along on an Egyptian grain freighter until they reached southern Crete, less than halfway. With the weather closing in, Paul, perhaps showing his experience as a sea-traveller, advised wintering there. But the harbour was too small for a big freighter to stay in, and they were seeking a safer harbour along the coast when a 'typhoon' (Acts 27.14) hit them and they were forced to run before it for 14 days.

It was a desperate situation, and they had little food with them for they had only expected to be at sea for a couple of days (though at least they were sitting on a cargo of wheat which could be cooked up into a kind of bread, Acts 27.35, 38). In the midst of it, Paul's encouraging vision of an angel was exactly the kind of thing they would have hoped for and trusted (Acts 27.23–6). His later promise to his fellow passengers that 'none of you shall lose a hair from your heads' (Acts 27.34) was probably designed to reassure them, for tossing hair and nail-clippings into the sea was a well-known last resort to appease the gods. At last they were shipwrecked on Malta where they struggled ashore and settled down to wait out the winter. It was probably early November.

Why is the best part of two chapters at the end of Acts taken up with this sea-journey? To us it seems a strange climax to a work of such scope and breadth. Two monuments give an idea of what the significance of the voyage may have been in the first century. The first is a minor one, which we have already seen: Zeuxis the merchant's monument in Hierapolis, which boasted of 72 successful voyages to Italy, implying how much he was blessed by the gods. The second is the massive Trajan's Column, erected in 113 and still standing in the centre of Rome. In over 150 vividly sculpted panels the struggle to conquer barbarian Dacia, beyond Illyricum, is told with an emphasis on travel and transport. Roman legions bridge rivers and hack their way through forests, but this is no simple logistical triumph; they are pushing back spiritual frontiers too. Woods and streams were the homes of local spirits, for each had its own *genius* in Roman eyes. So 'the emperor and his army are victorious not only over the barbarian enemy and his fortresses, but also over the natural forces of rivers, forests and mountains, all with their potentially hostile *genii*.'[67] This was on land; the Mediterranean was much more dangerous, for it was thought to be the realm not of the little wood and water spirits but of Poseidon himself, the 'old man of the sea' who delighted to catch unwary travellers. Voyages would not begin unless sacrifices had been made; ill-omened days had to be avoided; a sailor sneezing or a passenger having a bad dream could put off sailing for days. The winds were also seen as personalized spirits: the north-easterly typhoon which hit Paul and his companions off Crete was called 'Euroclydon'. Travel, especially sea-travel, was as much a spiritual as a physical battle.

Paul's 'anti-boast' epitaph (2 Cor. 11.24–9) was intended to undercut the equation of successful travel and divine favour for a more sophisticated theology of suffering and ultimate victory, which reflected his understanding of Jesus' death and resurrection. In the course of his epitaph, he claimed to have suffered shipwreck three times and once been cast adrift. The point he wanted to put across to the Corinthians was that, despite what would have been seen as very bad luck (and made him something of a Jonah to sailors who took him onto their ship), God had preserved his life: he was still there. The reason, therefore, why the voyage takes up so much space in Acts and was probably equally important in Paul's mind was, in Henry Chadwick's words, because 'the story is there to underline the extreme improbability that the apostle would ever reach Rome ... For the author of Acts the preaching of the apostle of the Gentiles in the capital of the Gentile world is a supernatural fact.'[68] Simply arriving in Rome after such a hazardous journey emphasized that, whatever simplistic explanations might suggest, Paul truly was meant to be there and God had a purpose for him.

On Malta Paul seems to have had a brief period which turned the clock back to his glory days during the missionary campaigns when he had been known as a healer and miracle-worker in Galatia and Ephesus (Acts 28.3–9). But once the weather cleared in the spring they took ship again and finally landed at Puteoli on the Bay of Naples. Paintings from nearby Pompeii show that this was the nearest thing to an industrial port the ancient world could offer. The Egyptian cargo ships docked at massive concrete jetties dominated by huge cranes, which unloaded in the region of 135,000 tons of wheat a year to feed the hungry masses of Rome. Temples in which to give thanks for safe arrival filled the spaces between vast warehouses. Paul and his companions found some local Christians at Puteoli who seem to have let the church in Rome know that, perhaps four years after he had written to them, Paul was finally about to arrive. Within a week Paul was at last in Rome.

Rome

The Appian Way approached Rome from the south-east. Its main traffic consisted of heavy grain carts, creaking and bumping along. Milestones would count down the distance. Seventeen miles out of the city the first of the Roman Christians waited at the 'Three Taverns' to greet Paul and accompany him (Acts 28.15). Seven miles from the city even more welcomed him at the Appian Forum. On the final stretch expensive wayside tombs sprang up with growing frequency until at last the great city itself came in sight.

Even Paul, who was used to Antioch and Ephesus, had never seen anything like it: it was twice the size of these two great cities put together. Here at last was his third home city, after Tarsus and Jerusalem.

Paul was still a prisoner, but a prisoner of a special kind. No charge had yet been proven against him and he was not locked away, but simply left under house arrest at his own expense (Acts 28.16). A single soldier to guard him was very light custody. He seems to have worn his chain as a badge of honour rather than a sign of oppression (Acts 28.20; see Phil. 1.13, Philemon 13). The impression is that he could quite easily have escaped if he had wanted to do so.

Acts presents Paul as speaking to leaders of the Jewish community in Rome and receiving an initially favourable response from them, after they have made it clear that they have heard no bad reports about him (Acts 28.21–2). Later, however, the usual pattern of Paul's dealing with his fellow Jews is reasserted, and the climax of Acts is his condemnation of them and a reaffirmation of his call to 'the nations'. They, he concludes, 'will hear' (Acts 28.28; see also Rom. 11.8). Luke's final image of Paul is of him living in Rome under arrest for two years openly proclaiming the Kingdom of God (Acts 28.30–31).

And there the trail ends. It feels both a cliff-hanger and an anticlimax: quite an achievement! What happened next? Some scholars propose that Paul was executed on Nero's orders when his case came up, but that Luke didn't want to end on a down note or present Paul as the victim of Roman justice. If this had happened, Luke could surely have found a way of presenting it positively: he was at pains to emphasize throughout that Paul's accusers were Jewish and the Romans reluctant jailers. Later Church tradition was very certain that Paul died in around 65 in the widespread culling of Christians in Rome after the Great Fire, and very few scholars would argue with this fact. This leaves perhaps five unknown years between the end of Acts and Paul's death. Was Paul released from his custody and, if so, why doesn't Luke tell us so?

An expert on Roman law, A. N. Sherwin-White, points out that as far as Acts is concerned, 'there is no necessity to construe [it] to mean that he was released at all.'[69] Paul may have remained under arrest till the end of his life.

The implication of Luke's 'two years' (Acts 28.30) may be that no evidence was produced against Paul within that time and that by implication he was innocent. Presumably the documents referring to his case, which must have given Festus quite a headache to prepare, had been lost in the shipwreck and further copies had to be sent for. The Jews in Rome had no information against Paul (Acts 28.21), and no one from Jerusalem or Asia felt it worthwhile making the journey. Failure to pursue charges which had been made would open the accusers up to a fine, but did not mean the defendant could go free. This situation could well have left Paul's case in the courts' ever-growing pending file. After all, Paul had come to Rome at his own request as Agrippa had reflected to Festus (Acts 26.32). Too insignificant to reach Nero, but too enmeshed in the legal system to be resolved, Paul's case probably dragged 'its weary length before the courts' like Dickens's Jarndyce and Jarndyce, 'perennially hopeless'.

A long period of enforced leisure beckoned. Luke suggests Paul was active in Rome as far as he was able, but within the gentile community not the Jewish. Restricted to his house, Paul was able to start writing again. Philippians was almost certainly written during this time, as was the tiny letter to Philemon. Colossians and Ephesians, though their authorship is debatable, may also have been written in prison (all four letters refer to Paul being 'in chains', Eph. 6.20; Phil. 1.17; Col. 4.3; Philemon 13). Colossians also refers to a letter to the church in Laodicea which has not survived (Col. 4.16).

Philippians – 'my joy and my crown'

The last thing the churches around the Aegean had seen of Paul was his departure for Jerusalem in 56. They probably heard news of what had happened there, and of his removal to Rome, but his shipwreck on the way must have led many to assume that he was dead. Then they heard reports that he had finally arrived in Rome and sent Epaphroditus to Paul with a contribution towards his costs (Phil. 4.18).

Something seems to have clicked between the Philippians and Paul from the first. Although Paul appears not to have spent very much time with the Philippians in person, their loyalty and personal support for him was unquestioned. The letter he wrote back to them overflows with his love and concern, a response to their generosity which had clearly touched him deeply.

Philippians has the freshness of a sunny morning after overnight rain. It sparkles with relief and gratitude. Paul tries to make sense of his predicament in prison, and seems to be coming to terms with the end of his active ministry, though he hopes to resume it at some point (Phil. 2.24). Irrepressibly, he finds a silver lining in the dark cloud: 'I want you to know that what has happened to me has helped the advance of the good news'. In fact the Praetorian Guard, the elite group who acted as the emperor's bodyguard and the police force of Rome, have all heard of him, he says. Not only that, but his enforced inactivity means that others have become bolder in preaching the good news (Phil. 1.12–14). The whole letter radiates a sense of submission to God, which strikes a deeper note than in any of Paul's previous letters. The special term which Paul uses to sum up this development is joy (*chara*), a word which sounds very similar to Paul's watchword of grace (*charis*), and which is used 11 times in Philippians.

Paul is able to declare that now he has learned to be content, whatever life throws at him (Phil. 4.11). It seems to have come from the experience of losing everything (Phil. 3.8), and Paul may be talking literally after his shipwreck and imprisonment as well as metaphorically of the lost privileges he once prized highly as a Pharisee (Phil. 3.5). These are statements which it is hard to imagine Paul making during his energetic campaigning years around the Mediterranean. Perhaps with imprisonment came a new maturity and, after years of activity, rest.

Slavery

Just how deeply slavery was embedded in the first-century world is almost impossible for us to grasp. Even quite poor free citizens might own one or two slaves. If you injured someone else's slave, it was the slave-owner, not the slave, to whom you apologized and paid compensation. The slave was simply a 'body', not a human being at all. The slave population of Italy in Augustus's time was probably around 2 million, a figure that would have to be multiplied many times over to find the total in the Empire as a whole. Despite the number of slaves and their constant presence, they were taken for granted and are present in the written records of the first century largely as shadows, unnoticed and unremarked presences in bedchambers, dining rooms and anywhere else which we might regard as private space. Because, in contemporary Western society, we take the absence of slaves for granted, we often fail to detect those shadows. The early Christians did not challenge the institution of slavery, and it would be many centuries before the Church saw the contradiction between its message of freedom and the practice of slavery. This contradiction was a challenge to the imagination as much as anything, and for us it is virtually impossible to imagine a world where it is taken for granted that some people own other people.

Paul used slavery as a metaphor of the incarnation of Jesus Christ, suggesting that Jesus who was 'in the form of God ... emptied himself, took the form of a slave and was born as a human being' (Phil. 2.7), an utterly shocking image in the first century where involuntary enslavement was a nightmare terror, and voluntary enslavement considered a degradation worse than death.

Philemon and the really useful slave

The shortest of Paul's letters is an intriguing glimpse of the many 'occasional' letters which Paul must have written but which have not survived. Its story is a simple one. Onesimus, a slave belonging to Philemon, had escaped from his slavery and run away to Paul. Onesimus was using an acknowledged way of gaining freedom in the Roman Empire. If the relationship between slave and master broke down, slaves could apply to someone who was higher in social status than the master, who might intercede on their behalf. What was Paul going to do about this situation?

Onesimus seems to have become a Christian through his contact with Paul (Philemon 10). Now Paul offers to send Onesimus back to Philemon, but appeals to the master to treat his slave leniently, recognizing him as a Christian brother and perhaps also giving him his freedom (Philemon 16). As a freedman, Onesimus would have remained under obligation to Philemon, who would become his patron. The implication of the letter may be that Paul will happily take on the responsibility of patronage instead, if Philemon grants freedom, for which Paul was prepared to pay (Philemon 18).

The shortness of the letter conceals quite a lot. There is a complex web of social interaction and conflict beneath the apparently simple request from Paul, and a good deal of wordplay too. Paul is treading delicately in a minefield of status issues. He claims higher status than Philemon because he brought him to faith (Philemon 19) and is senior to him in years (Philemon 9). He feels able to command a guest room rather than asking for one (Philemon 22). He puns on Onesimus's name, which means 'useful' (like many slave names this one was probably a nickname, perhaps derived from a comment like 'make yourself useful'). The useful one was useless to Philemon, but is now really useful to Paul (Philemon 11). In Greek the pun introduces another element: Onesimus has gone from being *achrestos* to *euchrestos*, and you can perhaps hear in both those words a deliberate echo of *Chrestus*, the Latin name for Jesus which was indistinguishable to the ear from *Christus*. In other words, Paul is using the nature of the Church, the new society to which all three people belonged, to push accepted boundaries. He plays a double game: claiming higher status than Philemon while at the same time removing the status distinctions between Philemon and Onesimus.

Hidden within the situation is the likely implication that Philemon had ill-treated Onesimus. There is an element of 'naming and shaming' which also operates within the letter. Although private, it is longer than we would expect such a letter to be, and shares characteristics with the public letters by being sent jointly from Timothy and being addressed to a church (Philemon 1–2). Paul nowhere explicitly states that Philemon had treated the useless Onesimus badly, but bringing the issue up in this way put the onus on Philemon to act as a Christian example. Here we see Paul as either a highly gifted pastoral practitioner or the master of social manipulation, depending on your point of view!

Paul had told the Galatians that in Christ the slave/free distinction was abolished (Gal. 3.28). So he has been criticized for not seeing the implications of this and sending Onesimus back, thus implicitly accepting and condoning slavery. While the criticism has some substance, it took the Church in general 18 or 19 centuries to follow Paul's logic. Elsewhere Paul warns slaves not to seek their freedom but to accept their situation in life (1 Cor. 7.21–4). To criticize Paul for this is harsh: changes in Western culture which led to the eventual abolition of slavery were at least partly the result of Paul's radical vision of freedom and equality in Christ, potentially for all of humanity. He did not issue a blanket challenge to the institutions of his day, but in the letter to Philemon we see him playing with the conventions of the age to gain freedom for a useless slave whom he was proud to call a friend and a brother.

Why was this letter preserved? One intriguing suggestion is inspired by the fact that around 110 someone called Onesimus was leader of the church in Ephesus. Some scholars propose that it is the same useless slave, who kept the letter, remembering the apostle who found him his freedom. It is 'doubtful, but chronologically not impossible'[70] comments Geza Vermes, drily.

Colossians – letter and liturgy

The letter to the Colossians is sometimes reckoned to have been written in Ephesus during Paul's stay there. However, this requires an Ephesian imprisonment for which there is no real evidence (pointing to Col. 4.3 is an obviously circular argument). A Roman setting for it is more likely, though some point out that Paul might equally have written 'in chains' from Caesarea. Some of the shifts in theology evident in Ephesians are already under way, and this has led scholars to think that it is a borderline letter, which may be by Paul but could equally well have been written in his name soon after his death to pass on his thoughts to the church in Colossae, which faced some problems (Timothy seems the favourite candidate to have done this, and he is credited as co-author, Col. 1.1). However, the shifts in theology that set Ephesians apart are balanced in Colossians by plenty of parallels with the letters which are undisputed: Galatians, Corinthians and Romans. The jury is out. Whether by Paul or not, the consensus suggests that Colossians was written at some point in the early to mid 60s and that it reflects his mind towards the end of his life.

One of the most notable features of Colossians is the hymn of praise to Christ (Col. 1.15–20). As a poetic section within a letter it is similar to Philippians 2.6–11, and like that passage it focuses on Christ as a cosmic being (it also has similarities with John 1.1–14). Grammar is sacrificed to rhythm and it falls into two full stanzas with a parallel structure and a brief parallel interlude between them, giving it a sort of 'V' shape. You might like to underline the words and phrases that are common to both sides of Figure 11.

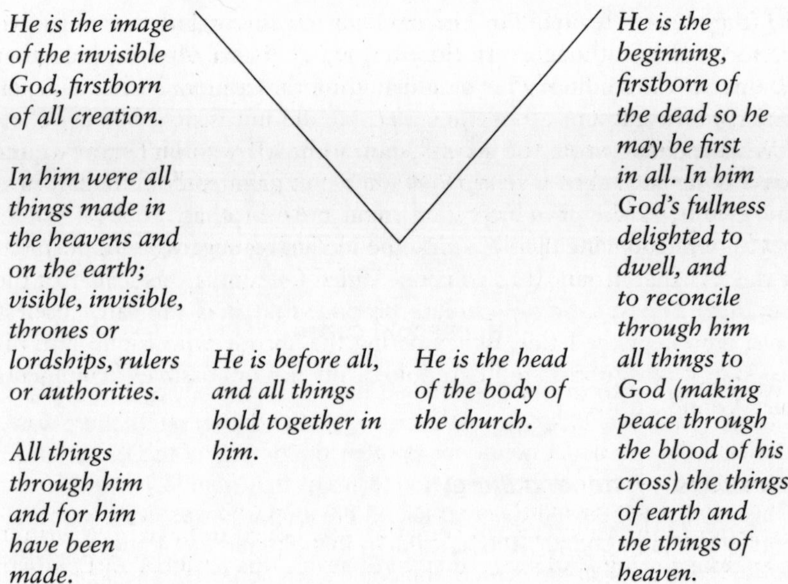

Figure 11 The structure of Colossians 1.15–20

The first stanza is probably a pre-Christian hymn in praise of wisdom. It is very like passages in the Wisdom of Solomon, a Jewish book written at the end of the first century BC, and nothing in these lines need refer to Christ. The coda to the first stanza sums it up. Then begins the prelude to the second stanza, which introduces a Christian response or development: 'he is the head of the body of the Church.' The effect is rather beautifully to place a Christian affirmation about Jesus next to a Jewish wisdom one, emphasizing how the latter grows naturally out of the former. The second stanza then echoes the 'firstborn of creation' with 'firstborn of the dead' and underlines Paul's teaching elsewhere about a new creation in the risen Christ; and as God made all things, so he shall reconcile all things, 'making peace through the blood of the cross'.

What this hymn shows is Paul and the Church coming to a realization of the scope of what had happened in the life and death of Jesus 30 years before. It is significant that this realization seems to have developed out of liturgical material. Their experience of worshipping Jesus the risen Lord led them to see that he was not just the man some of them had known, but ultimately even more than that. So 'Paul was led to conceive of Christ as any theist conceives of God: personal, indeed, but transcending the individual category.'[71] But we must be careful not to overstate this. What is happening in this passage is that Jesus is being interpreted as fitting the attributes of Wisdom. The roots of personified Wisdom can be seen as far back in Jewish tradition as Proverbs (see especially Prov. 8.22–31). But she (the noun is feminine in Hebrew) was clearly regarded as subservient to God, even though very close to him. Not until the fourth century would the Church finally hit on a definition that affirmed Jesus as equal with God the Father.

Whether Paul wrote the second stanza himself we don't know; quite possibly he had taken it over from some unknown early Christian poet and used it, as churches have used songs ever since, as the most potent means of introducing theology into the bloodstream of worshippers.

Household codes

When Paul wrote to the Corinthians, he was giving advice to gentiles about how to live under the new moral regime of Christ, where there was no clear-cut law about behaviour to refer to. The end of the Law's function did not mean that they were free to live as they wanted, however, and this is what led Paul into his attack on the man who was living with his father's wife in Corinth. The scandal in that situation for Paul was that even those outside the church would find such behaviour shocking.

Colossians and Ephesians both feature passages, echoed also in 1 Peter, which are known as 'household codes', general advice on how a Christian household should behave (Col. 3.18—4.1; Eph. 5.22—6.9; 1 Peter 2.13—3.7). The household was the basic unit of society, though it was not until his captivity in Rome that Paul himself became a householder (Acts 28.16). A possible motive for writing down a household code like the one in Colossians, if it is by Paul, was the situation between Philemon and Onesimus and the hints of ill-treatment by the master of his slave. Onesimus is mentioned (Col. 4.9) and the situation of both Colossians and Philemon seems to have been roughly the same.

The codes show a common pattern, giving instructions for wives, husbands, children, fathers, slaves and masters. There is a balance in them, encouraging those who have authority (husbands, fathers, masters) to use it responsibly and wisely (Col. 3.19, 21; 4.1) and those who are subject to authority (wives, children, slaves) to accept it 'in/for the Lord' (Col. 3.18, 20, 23), implying a degree of mutual dependence.

Nevertheless, these codes are deeply patriarchal documents, accepting without question a traditional view of male superiority, and many scholars argue that they are scarcely different from the general moral framework in society at large. The strikingly egalitarian statement that 'there can be no male nor female, for you are all one in Jesus Christ' (Gal. 3.28), for example, seems a long way from 'Wives, be subject to your husbands' (Col. 3.18). Crossan and Reed, who believe that Colossians and Ephesians were not written by Paul but are later attempts to domesticate his radical teaching, conclude that such passages were intended to ensure that 'Christian families were not at all socially subversive' and to move Paul 'into an ultraconservative position of male-over-female superiority'.[72] Others point out, however, that in Colossians and Ephesians the codes are prefaced by a strong encouragement to mutuality: 'bear with one another', 'be subject to one another' (Col. 3.13; Eph. 5.21) and that they do therefore retain a subversive edge. Unlike other contemporary, secular codes, they also assume that wives, children and slaves can choose to 'be subject'; to some degree therefore their submission is voluntary, which assumes that they are fundamentally independent moral beings. For this reason, Elizabeth Schüssler Fiorenza dubs the outlook of the codes 'love patriarchalism'.[73] But it is certainly true that, whatever the original intention of the codes, within a few generations they had been co-opted to require unquestioning humility and silence from women.

Looking back on a life – Ephesians

The debate about Ephesians is complex. There are three major issues. First, the style seems very different from the other major letters, with long rolling pronouncements instead of sharp, combative questions. Second, it is arguable that the vocabulary is different, and though this is not now regarded as decisive it is strange, for example, that the Greek word used for heaven in Ephesians is distinctive to this letter, when the word used in all Paul's other letters would have done just as well. Third and most important are theological questions, for there are some major differences of emphasis in Ephesians:

- The cross and death of Jesus, which are centre-stage in Romans and Corinthians, have been replaced by his resurrection and role as cosmic ruler of the universe (Eph. 1.2–23).
- Where Paul appears to uphold the Law (Rom. 3.31), the writer of Ephesians uncompromisingly declares the law abolished (Eph. 2.15), and the struggle between Jewish and gentile forms of Christianity which dominated Paul's life seems to have ended, perhaps implying a situation after the destruction of the temple in 70.
- Ephesians breathes a sense of a more settled situation and none of the provisionality in the light of the imminent return of Christ that characterized Paul's hard-headed advice on marriage (1 Cor. 7) which is now unequivocally celebrated (Eph. 5.21–32).
- Above all, the Church has now become a universal and cosmic entity (Eph. 1.22–3; 2.11–22) instead of a loose coalition of local congregations.

Aside from these issues, there are also some unusual features.

- The oldest manuscripts do not include a destination for the letter, beginning 'Paul ... to the saints who are faithful in Christ Jesus' (Eph.

1.1), making it a general letter, unlike all the rest of those attributed to Paul.

- There are no personal greetings or references apart from the mention of Tychicus who is the letter carrier (Eph. 6.21).
- Paul speaks in a remarkably uncharacteristic and apologetic way when he says, in effect, 'I'm Paul – you might have heard of me' (Eph. 3.2).

Therefore most scholars agree that Ephesians is the work of a later writer, a close disciple of Paul, who as it were writes on his behalf. The similarities of structure between Ephesians and Colossians suggest a refashioning of Paul's thought to speak to a new situation. Colossians forms a genuinely Pauline substructure (perhaps this is the 'foundation of the apostles', Eph. 2.20), on which a systematic theology is erected.

Ephesians is a general letter which attempts to sum up Paul's work for a generation that had not known him directly (hence the reminder about who he is, Eph. 3.2), and its claim to be by Paul is simply 'a device for passing on authoritative tradition in a creative way'.[74] James Dunn speaks of the disputed letters, especially Ephesians, as being 'an afterwave or tail of the comet or, better, the school or studio of Paul',[75] suggesting both that Paul's intense and concentrated creation of Christian theology caused ripples through the Church, and also that, by analogy with paintings from a great master's studio, not all the brushwork need be the work of the artist himself – his pupils will have filled in spaces and completed the details. Paul's letters are perhaps best thought of as reflecting the views of the apostle and the circle around him, without necessarily claiming to be the precise words which he himself spoke.

And yet ... there remain good *historical* reasons for locating Ephesians in its traditional place: written in Rome during Paul's imprisonment. Ephesians makes sense in that setting. The theological differences between Ephesians and the other major letters cannot be explained away, but they can mostly be accounted for by the passage of time and the fact that they are often anticipated in Colossians. If Colossians was written soon after Paul's arrival in Rome, after a couple of years with little to do except think his theology might well have developed into the form we meet in Ephesians. The sense of the Church as the body of Christ, transcending the local congregations which composed it, was already present in the practical vision for the collection nearly ten years before. It is true that the sense of the imminence of the return of Christ seems to have receded, but the letters to the Corinthians were written at a time of unprecedented success when the spiritual temperature was high. Paul's subsequent experiences must have cooled that temperature down. The death of Christ is not absent from Ephesians (see Eph. 2.13), but the focus on resurrection as a present possession (Eph. 2.6) does dominate; again a change in circumstances and experience might have brought a new emphasis. Perhaps most significantly the issue of gentile and Jew seems to be handled in a markedly different way. Where is the passion of Galatians or the anguish of Romans 9—11? Jews and gentiles are spoken of as equal members of the Church, 'fellow heirs' (Eph. 3.6) whose destiny has been revealed to the 'apostles' (Eph. 3.5). The plural is important: before Paul had fought as the 'apostle to the gentiles' to demand an equal place for them. Ephesians seems to assume the battle has been won and that he is no longer alone: the 'apostles' understand too. This is probably the major theological argument against accepting Ephesians as being written by Paul in Rome in 60. It does seem at first sight to make more sense if the letter was written after 70. However, there is some circumstantial evidence which makes it possible for us to think of a scenario which would make sense of the traditional setting.

One of Paul's associates was Mark, the cousin of Barnabas (Acts 12.12; 15.37–9; Col. 4.10; Philemon 24). Paul had fallen out with him at the start of the second missionary campaign, but mention of him in Colossians and Philemon suggests that he was with Paul in Rome during his imprisonment. Mark was a close associate of Peter, and Peter spent some time towards the end of his life in Rome. Although it may be over-romantic to imagine a meeting between the two ageing apostles, perhaps the first for a dozen years since the Jerusalem conference, it is no more fanciful than most other reconstructions for this part of Paul's life. Their joint link with Mark certainly points to a means of communication between them. And if they did meet, perhaps this holds the key to the change in Paul's perception of the Jew/gentile issue in Ephesians and the agreement of the 'apostles'. In Galatians Paul had claimed that, long before, he and Peter had agreed that there was room for both of them: Paul concentrating on the uncircumcised, Peter on the circumcised (Gal. 2.7). Returning to that agreement in Rome in 60 would have ended the conflict that had dogged the Church for years. Ephesians is specifically written to gentiles and apart from one slightly waspish aside ('the so-called circumcision in the flesh made by human hands', Eph. 2.11) does not engage in old controversies. Perhaps Paul knew their time was past. Ephesians can then be seen as Paul's summing up of his life's work, after a *rapprochement* with his former adversary Peter.

And Paul was growing old (Philemon 9). The journey to Rome as well as his travelling over the years must have taken their toll (he is estimated to have covered 10,000 miles in the travels we know about, and probably many more in those we don't). He did not know how his case would turn out, but it was quite likely that he might die in custody. While it may be said that Ephesians 3.1–13 'reads far more like the estimate of Paul's apostleship on the part of someone looking back than like Paul talking about himself',[76] what would be more natural than for him to write a final, general letter to all the churches of his Aegean network and which had looked to him for leadership? It later came to be associated with Ephesus because that had been where Paul was based. In this sense it bears a resemblance to 1 Peter, sent generally to the Jewish Christian congregations of Pontus, Galatia, Cappadocia, Asia and Bithynia (1 Peter 1.1), which in turn seems to borrow the Pauline public letter-format. Silvanus, the joint author of 1 Peter (1 Peter 5.12), was Silas the Jerusalem prophet who accompanied Paul on his second campaign and was co-sender of the letters to the Thessalonians (1 Thess. 1.1; 2 Thess. 1.1), another link between Paul and Peter. And after six years away, Paul might well have felt he had to tread carefully in reintroducing himself to them. The years had perhaps brought a new humility to him, hence his uncharacteristic 'You might have heard of me' (Eph. 3.2).

A final summing up letter from prison is certainly how Ephesians has been read by most interpreters. In the light of the author's claim to be Paul (Eph. 1.1) and reference to imprisonment and chains (Eph. 4.1; 6.20) we are clearly meant to read it as if it came from this setting whether it was written by Paul or not.

The Dutch painter Rembrandt portrayed this image of Paul brilliantly in his *Self Portrait as the Apostle Paul* of 1661. Paul sits in front of a barred window representing imprisonment. In his hands he holds a scroll at the top of which the word 'EFES' can just be seen. He has half-turned to the viewer, as if surprised out of his contemplation, the top of his head illuminated by a shaft of light. He is, as Simon Schama says,

> the quizzical, confessional Paul, eyebrows arched, as if slightly pained to admit the light of gospel truth, shoulders shrugged, brow crumpled, hapless yet not without hope; the author both of his blind folly and his visionary wisdom; a vessel of sin and a receptacle of salvation; not a Paul of forbidding remoteness, but a Paul of consoling humanity; a Paul for everyday sinners.[77]

And yet ... it remains true that the style of Ephesians is very different from anything else connected with Paul. In some ways this is a subjective judgement, but you can grasp it even in an English translation by comparing Ephesians with Romans. So maybe it was written by a close follower of Paul after all. In this sense it is rather like the speeches in Acts. It is what Paul would probably have said if he had turned to you in the midst of a long reflective afternoon of imprisonment as the sun began to fade, just as Rembrandt painted him many years later. But whether he actually said it in so many words remains for each of us to judge for ourselves.

The vision behind Ephesians seems to be darker than the other letters, especially Philippians. Its conclusion sets its audience in the midst of an apocalyptic scenario where enemies of flesh and blood pale into insignificance compared to cosmic powers and spiritual forces (Eph. 6.10–17). The 'armour of light', as has been noted for centuries, closely parallels the equipment of a Roman soldier, though it may apply equally well to descriptions of God as a warrior in the Old Testament or echo the speeches of generals rallying their troops before a decisive battle in Greek and Roman literature. Perhaps it was meant to evoke all three. It certainly seems to reflect an awareness of the trials which broke upon the church in Rome, whether prophetically before the event or consolingly after it. Either way, the last words read as Paul's farewell message, praying for 'Grace on all those who love our Lord Jesus Christ, and immortality' (Eph. 6.24). Grace will be enough – in this life and the life to come.

Sources for the rest of Paul's life – the case of the Pastoral Letters

Philippians, Colossians and Ephesians are the last of the major letters attributed to Paul in the New Testament. None of them add very much to our understanding of Paul's life. But the Pastoral Letters (1 and 2 Timothy and Titus) positively overflow with personal information.

They offer a picture of Paul active again in Macedonia and Asia (1 Tim. 1.3; 2 Tim. 4.13, 20; Tit. 1.5; 3.12) but also expecting an imminent end to his life (2 Tim. 4.6–7). Because there is no obvious way in which this information can be fitted into the framework of Paul's missionary career in Acts, and the premonitions of death suggest a setting in the mid 60s, the only point in Paul's life when it seems that these letters could plausibly have been written is after being released from prison in Rome.

Most scholars think that these letters were written some considerable time after Paul's death, intended to pass on his teaching about church leadership. They were not included in lists of Paul's letters until after 150, though from that point on they became an undisputed fixture. They just don't read like Paul, the style is flat and they use different vocabulary from Paul's other letters. A. T. Hanson sums it up neatly: 'it is as if ... W. B. Yeats ... ended by writing the poetry of John Betjeman.'[78]

The letters present Timothy and Titus as young men, just starting out in the task of church leadership; but we know from Acts and the other letters that they had both been working with Paul for quite some time by the mid 60s (at least ten years in Timothy's case). They also assume a strongly developed structure of authority in the Church, with bishops, elders and deacons having clearly designated roles (e.g. 1 Tim 3.1–7, 8–13; 5.17–22). While it is quite possible that the roots of this structure were planted by Paul during his time in Ephesus, its developed form in the Pastorals has much more in common with the letters of Ignatius in the first decade of the second century. This leads most scholars to think that the letters were written in the late first century by someone who was trying to summarize the kind of advice Paul had given to his co-workers and envoys, such as Timothy and Titus. Since the period in which Paul seems consciously to have adopted a delegated pattern of ministry was the third missionary campaign, then the references to Macedonia and

Asia may be introduced to make the setting clear and also quite possibly fill out the curiously abbreviated account of that time in Acts 19. In this sense it is quite reasonable to accept the *thought* as a genuine reflection of Paul's views even if the words are a long way from his and the structure of the Church has developed hugely since his time. Several writers have remarked on the similarity between the Paul of the Pastorals and the Paul of Acts and therefore suggested that this is a church-leaders' handbook written by Luke (if you compare Acts 20.25–35 and 2 Tim. 4.1–8 you will see why they think this).

If it is legitimate to read these letters in this way, then some scholars see significant implications. The process of the writing of the Pastoral Letters was a creative reinterpretation in the name of the apostle for a new situation. Paul himself was forward-looking, always seeing new perspectives in the application of the Gospel. Perhaps he would have welcomed a reinterpretation. J. C. Beker suggests therefore that

> the adaptation of Paul's gospel by the church today should perhaps more closely resemble the imaginative and creative process undertaken by a composer who takes a theme from a previous era and allows it to speak in the musical idiom of his or her own day ... a creative and skilful composer or musician maintains the integrity of the original motif yet allows its emotive and communicative power to come through in the hearer's own musical language. The challenge and mandate to the church today is to engage in a similar creative act. May it so reenact the powerful word of Paul's Gospel that it transforms our lives today in the same way it transformed those who heard it in the past.[79]

That is to say, since the early Church accepted these letters, which were *adaptations* of Paul's teaching, as canonical and therefore authoritative, then the means of holding to Paul's apostolic faith is not necessarily by following his teaching as such, but the method behind it, guided by the example of the post-Pauline church community, but without being tied wholly to its conclusions.

It seems unlikely that the writer of the Pastoral Letters would have agreed with this view, however. The concluding instruction of the first letter is for Timothy to keep safe the faith that has been entrusted to him: 'Guard the deposit' (1 Tim. 6.20, the phrase has become a watchword for those anxious to maintain the faith; so much so that Cuddesdon Theological College near Oxford adopted it as a motto and had it written on the chamber pots without any apparent awareness of the double-entendre).

A case can be made for the authenticity of all of the Pastoral Letters, largely on the grounds that the personal information contained in them is superfluous unless they are genuine, but the cumulative nature of the arguments about the Pastoral Letters means that they cannot be relied upon as sources for the later period of Paul's life.

We left Paul under house-arrest in Rome, having waited two years for his accusers to appear. They seem not to have turned up. It's quite possible that Paul was released without the case ever coming to trial. Preliminary hearings would have been inconclusive, and emperors periodically released prisoners in a show of clemency in order to clear the legal backlog. Given the Romans' love of bureaucracy, however, the charges may have remained on file deep in the state archives.

So what did happen next to Paul?

Finishing the race

There is little evidence for the end of Paul's life. Clement of Rome at the end of the first century is unclear: he records that Paul reached 'the furthest limits of the west',[80] and many have taken this to mean that Paul fulfilled his dream of going to Spain on the grounds that, from Rome, the furthest west was Cadiz. This major city was also known in the first century as the 'ends of the earth', which can be correlated with the instruction of the risen Jesus for the disciples to 'be my witnesses ... to the ends of the earth' (Acts 1.8). However, if Luke knew that Paul had been to Spain and would have associated such a visit with reaching 'the ends of the earth', why on earth would he not say so? Answers to this conundrum range from the view that Acts must have been written around 62, which is highly unlikely, or that Paul's work in Spain was such a failure that it didn't last long and Luke was embarrassed to talk about it.

A strong tradition persisted in the early Church that Paul went on his travels once more, revisiting Ephesus and the Aegean churches, but this may be the later Church putting the clues together from the Pastoral Letters. However likely the scenario seems, since we have ruled out the Pastoral Letters as reliable sources we are left with silence. The only real evidence of such a journey from Rome to Asia is Paul's hope that he will visit the Philippians (Phil. 2.24) and his request that Philemon keep a bed ready for him (Philemon 22); but these may be courtesies rather than firm plans and cannot be taken as evidence of anything more than Paul's desire to visit.

It is far more likely that Paul, whose plan to go to Spain had been communicated to the Romans at least six years earlier, remained in Rome. Rome itself seems to have been interpreted in Acts as the goal of Paul's travels, and the Greek word Clement uses for 'limits' is *terma*, which literally means a target which is aimed at; Rome had become Paul's aim. Apart from that, if Clement did mean Spain he could simply have been using Paul's plans in Romans 15 as his guide, which leaves him no better informed than we are.

In fact Rome would have been an excellent base for Paul. It 'provided a potted experience of empire'. Here were found 'exotic beasts in the arena, defeated prisoners on display, varied tongues and modes of dress in the street, inscriptions and maps listing distant places and peoples, and monuments and sculptures which ... recalled the wealth and extent of the empire'.[81] The poet Ovid said that 'the world and Rome are the same place'.[82] There was much for Paul to do there.

The tradition of the early Church and some circumstantial evidence points to the likelihood that Paul died in the chaotic aftermath of the Great Fire at Rome. As a Roman citizen, if convicted, Paul was entitled to death by the sword, but in Nero's later years of madness such niceties were not likely to be observed. Perhaps Paul had been released on some kind of bail, the charges against him unproven but still on file; perhaps the law took its due course if he was arrested in the crackdown on Christians in 65. But it is more likely that Paul was rounded up as a Christian with many others and herded to his death without being identified as a ringleader in the mayhem. It was a squalid and anonymous death at the hands of the state whose power Paul had first opposed and later sheltered beneath.

Paul's reputation and legacy

The Second Letter of Peter, probably written towards the end of the first century, speaks about how 'our beloved brother Paul, according to the wisdom he received, wrote to you, speaking in all his letters concerning some things which are hard to understand, which the unlearned and unstable twist, as they do with the other Scriptures, to their own destruction' (2 Peter 3.15–16). The significant points in this statement are, first, that the early Church recognized that Paul's letters were not always easy to interpret (a conclusion echoed by those who have studied them down the ages!); and second, that some of Paul's letters were being referred to as 'Scriptures' and had been collected together within 50 years of his death. It is also clear from Acts that Paul had become a hero to many in the early Church by the end of the first century.

Paul was certainly a hero to Marcion, who arrived in Rome around 135 with a bundle of Paul's letters under his arm. But, despite the Church's rejection of Marcion and his teaching, Paul's reputation was strong enough to survive. This suggests that the arguments about Paul's status as an apostle, and the bitter controversy which he aroused, soon faded after his death. He was recognized as what he was: the leading intellect of the early Church.

As we have seen, however, his influence may have been more profound after his death than it was in his lifetime. His letters disseminated his teaching more widely than that of other apostles, and hindsight perhaps elevates him to a higher position than he actually occupied. Heroic man of action and profound thinker he may have been, but he worked almost without exception with teams of associates from his early partnership with Barnabas to his later connection with the strings of messengers who took his letters out and read them to the congregations they were addressed to on his behalf.

Above all Paul was faithful to the call he had received on the road to Damascus: to go to the nations. The place which later came to be revered as his tomb (a modest affair compared with Peter's) lies on the outskirts of ancient Rome, in what was then a poor and crowded area. It is quite possible that this was the area which Paul had come to call home, the arena of his ministry shrunk from the eastern Mediterranean to a couple of poor districts in the suburbs of Rome. Beneath the church later built around his tomb lies a burial ground which dates from the first century. It is not a Jewish or Christian cemetery, but a pagan one. If Paul was buried there he remained faithful to the call to go to the nations, even in death.

Draw your own conclusions

- How sympathetic a person do you find Paul? Did he have an inner consistency or was he a man of contradictions?
- Do you think we can trust Acts to provide a framework for Paul's life? What kind of history does it offer?
- Call or conversion? Which word best describes Paul's experience on the Damascus Road?
- Why is Paul so angry in Galatians? What was really at stake?
- How much did Paul know about Jesus' life? How strong is the evidence?
- Did Paul recognize the implications of his statement about equality in Galatians 3.28 as far as the role of women was concerned? How might Priscilla have discussed the issue with him?
- Are the speeches in Acts imaginative recreations of what happened, or has Luke just put words in the speakers' mouths?
- What effect do you think Paul's critique of the status game in Corinth had?
- Do you think Paul changed his mind about how soon the end of the world would come?
- How would you summarize Paul's Gospel as he presents it in Romans 1—8?
- What was Paul's view about the future of the Law and of Israel?
- Do you think Paul wanted Philemon to release Onesimus? What was his view of slavery?
- How would you describe Paul's view of Jesus in Colossians?
- Do the Pastoral Letters genuinely reflect Paul's views or are they evidence of a conservative backlash after his death?
- How do you think Paul passed his final years, and how did he look back on his life?

Further reading

The most useful starting point is D. Horrell (2006), *An Introduction to the Study of Paul*, 2nd ed., London: T.&T. Clark, which gives succinct summaries of the main issues in the study of Paul's life and theology. More detailed is J. D. G. Dunn (ed.) (2003), *The Cambridge Companion to St Paul*, Cambridge: Cambridge University Press. B. Witherington (1998), *The Paul Quest: the renewed quest for the Jew of Tarsus*, Downers Grove: IVP, surveys the range of views on Paul while coming to generally conservative conclusions. G. F. Hawthorne, R. P. Martin and D. G. Reid (eds) (1993), *Dictionary of Paul and His Letters*, Downers Grove: IVP, is an exhaustive compendium of information on Paul.

On Paul's life, see D. Wenham (2002), *Paul and Jesus: The True Story*, London: SPCK, a helpful account of Paul's life based on Acts. J. Murphy-O'Connor (2004), *Paul: his story*, Oxford: Oxford University Press, shortens the same author's (1996), *Paul: a critical life*, Oxford: Oxford University Press. Both contain valuable insights and a deep understanding of the social background but are sceptical about the historical value of Acts, substituting instead some highly speculative views. C. Roetzel (1999), *Paul: the man and the myth*, Edinburgh: T.&T. Clark, is an impressive reconstruction of Paul's life and teaching based on the seven letters generally agreed to be genuine. J. D. Crossan and J. L. Reed (2005), *In Search of Paul: how jesus' apostle opposed Rome's empire with God's kingdom*, London: SPCK, makes fascinating use of archaeological evidence.

Paul's theology is examined in M. D. Hooker (2003), *Paul: a short introduction* Oxford: Oneworld. This is a gem of a book. C. K. Barrett (1994), *Paul: an introduction to his thought*, London: Geoffrey Chapman, is a valuable extended essay on the concepts in Paul's theology. N. T. Wright (2005), *Paul: fresh perspectives*, London: SPCK, considers several themes in Paul's thought. It largely replaces Wright's earlier (1997), *What St Paul Really Said*, Oxford: Lion, which nevertheless remains useful. Other short summaries of Paul's thought include E. P. Sanders (1991), *Paul: a very short introduction*, Oxford: Oxford University Press, and J. Ziesler (1990), *Pauline Christianity*, revised ed., Oxford: Oxford University Press.

Larger treatments of Paul's theology are led by J. D. G. Dunn (1998), *The Theology of Paul the Apostle*, Edinburgh: T.&T. Clark, a huge, magisterial and endlessly stimulating attempt to explore the details of Paul's thought. D. Wenham (1995), *Paul: follower of Jesus or founder of Christianity?*, Grand Rapids: Eerdmans, carefully explores the links between the teaching of Paul and Jesus and concludes that the former is much more strongly indebted to the latter than has often been thought. E. P. Sanders (1977), *Paul and Palestinian Judaism*, London: SCM Press, is a landmark study which changed our understanding of Paul and gave birth to what is often called the 'New Perspective'. A good, very short, introduction is provided by M. B. Thompson (2002), *The New Perspective on Paul*, Cambridge: Grove Books. R. Bultmann (1952), *Theology of the New Testament* I, London: SCM Press, Part II remains a compelling presentation of an older view.

More specialized studies of important aspects of Paul's churches can be found in G. D. Fee (1997), *Paul, the Spirit and the People of God*, London: Hodder, and R. Banks (1994), *Paul's Idea of Community: the early house churches in their cultural setting*, revised ed., Peabody: Hendrickson. W. Meeks (1983), *The First Urban Christians: the Social World of the Apostle Paul*, New Haven, Yale University Press, is a fascinating study of the social setting. The hidden role of women in Paul's churches was examined in E. S. Fiorenza (1992) *In Memory of Her* 2nd ed., London: SCM Press, and has been brought to light in C. Osiek, M. Y. MacDonald and J. H. Tulloch (2006), *A Woman's Place: house churches in earliest christianity*, Minneapolis: Fortress. Slaves were an invisible presence in the ancient world: they are revealed in J. A. Glancey (2006), *Slavery in Earliest Christianity*, Minneapolis: Fortress.

Websites

- Details of the Gallio Inscription can be found at www.kchanson.com/ANCDOCS/greek/gallio.html.
- Six alternative views on 'The Chronology and Writings of Paul' (including Jerome Murphy-O'Connor's) can be compared in a chart at www.anchist.mq.edu.au/251/PaulChron.htm
- 'Peter and Paul and the Christian Revolution', linked to a PBS series, has very good material on Paul at www.pbs.org/empires/peterandpaul/footsteps/index.html
- Two good websites offer pictures and maps covering the travels of the apostle: 'The Journeys of Paul' at www.luthersem.edu/ckoester/Paul/Main.htm and 'The Footsteps of Paul' at www.abrock.com/Greece-Turkey/FootstepsIntro.html.
- 'The Text this Week' offers links to background articles on Paul at www.textweek.com/pauline/paul.htm.
- 'Conflict and Community in the Corinthian Church' are explored at www.gbgm-umc.org/umw/corinthians/, particularly taking into account how the issues looked to women.
- The Paul page at www.thepaulpage.com/ is an excellent resource for exploring the 'New Perspective' on Paul.

Notes

1 Pliny, *Natural History* 31.33; Seneca *Moral Epistles* 104.

2 J. D. Crossan and J. L. Reed (2005), *In Search of Paul*, London: SPCK, p. 106.

3 Crossan and Reed, *In Search of Paul*, p. 34.

4 J. Murphy-O'Connor (1996), *Paul: A Critical Life*, Oxford: Oxford University Press, pp. vi, 6.

5 M. Hengel (1986), *Earliest Christianity*, London: SCM Press, p. 119.

6 D. Wenham (2002), *Paul and Jesus: the true story*, London: SPCK, p. 179.

7 Eusebius, *History of the Church* 2.22.

8 William Shakespeare, *Antony and Cleopatra*, Act II, Scene 2.

9 M. Hooker (2003), *Paul: a short introduction*, Oxford, Oneworld, p. 36.

10 M. Goodman (2007), *Rome and Jerusalem*, London: Penguin, p. 163.

11 A. F. Segal (2003), 'Paul's Jewish Presuppositions' in J. D. G. Dunn (ed.) *The Cambridge Companion to St Paul*, Cambridge: Cambridge University Press, p. 163.

12 K. E. Bailey (2003), *Jacob and the Prodigal; how Jesus retold Israel's story*, Oxford: BRF, p. 20.

13 J. D. G. Dunn (1997), *The Theology of Paul the Apostle*, Edinburgh, T.&T. Clark, p. 179.

14 N. T. Wright (2005), *Paul: fresh perspectives*, London: SPCK, p. 169.

15 Crossan and Reed, *In Search of Paul*, p. xii.

16 E. Käsemann (1980), *Commentary on Romans*, Grand Rapids: Eerdmans, p. 20.

17 S. Mitchell (2003), 'The Galatians: Representation and Reality' in A. Erskine (ed.), *A Companion to the Hellenistic World*, Oxford: Blackwell, p. 290.

18 J. B. Lightfoot (1865), *St Paul's Epistle to the Galatians*, London: Macmillan, p. 251.

19 Lightfoot, *Galatians*, p. 1.

20 G. W. Hansen (1993), 'Letter to the Galatians' in G. F. Hawthorne, R. P. Martin and D. G. Reid (eds), *Dictionary of Paul and his Letters*, Downers Grove: IVP, p. 328.

21 R. Bultmann (1952), *Theology of the New Testament* I, London: SCM Press, p. 188.

22 Dunn, *Theology of Paul the Apostle*, p. 184.

23 R. J. Bauckham (2001), 'James and Jesus' in B. Chilton and J. Neusner (eds), *The Brother of Jesus*, Louisville: Westminster John Knox Press, pp. 115–6.

24 Dunn, *Theology of Paul the Apostle*, pp. 206, 185.

25 R. A. Burridge (2007), *Imitating Jesus: an inclusive approach to New Testament ethics*, Grand Rapids: Eerdmans, p. 148.

26 Crossan and Reed, *In Search of Paul*, p. 8.

27 C. S. Keener (1993), 'Man and Woman' in Hawthorne et al., *Dictionary of Paul*, pp. 591–2.

28 C. Osiek, M. MacDonald and J. H. Tulloch (2006), *A Woman's Place: house churches in earliest christianity*, Fortress: Minneapolis, p. 63.

29 A. C. Thiselton (2000), *The First Epistle to the Corinthians*, Grand Rapids: Eerdmans, p. 1158.

30 R. Stark (1997), *The Rise of Christianity*, San Francisco: HarperCollins, p. 95.

31 C. H. Dodd (1936), *The Apostolic Preaching and Its Developments*, London: Hodder & Stoughton, pp. 8–9.

32 Wright, *Paul: fresh perspectives*, p. 69.

33 Suetonius, *Life of Claudius* 25.4.

34 A. von Harnack (1908), *The Expansion of the Church in the First Three Centuries* II, London: Williams & Norgate, p. 50.

35 Pliny, *Natural History* 4.23.

36 Petronius, *Satyricon* 17.

37 Pliny the Younger, *Letters* 8.24 (tr. Radice).

38 R. M. Grant (2001), *Paul in the Roman World*, Louisville: Westminster John Knox Press, p. 4.

39 Thucydides, *The Peloponnesian War* 1.20.

40 Thucydides, *The Peloponnesian War* 1.73.

41 Thucydides, *The Peloponnesian War* 1.22.

42 E. Breisach (1983), *Historiography: ancient, medieval, and modern*, Chicago: University of Chicago Press, p. 17 (emphasis added).

43 J. B. Green (1997), 'Acts of the Apostles' in R. P. Martin and P. H. Davids, *Dictionary of the Later New Testament and its Developments*, Downers Grove, IVP, p. 11.

44 Strabo, *Geography* 8.6.

45 Thiselton, *The First Epistle to the Corinthians*, p. 17.

46 Thiselton, *The First Epistle to the Corinthians*, p. 8.

47 P. Oxy 46.3313 translation from P. Parsons (2007), *City of the Sharp-Nosed Fish: everyday life in the Nile valley 400BC–350AD*, London: Weidenfeld & Nicholson, pp. 135–6.

48 O. Cullmann (1967), *Salvation in History*, London: SCM Press, p. 240. See also pp. 44–5.

49 Dunn, *Theology of Paul the Apostle*, p. 465.

50 G. M. Rogers (1991), *The Sacred Identity of Ephesos*, London: Routledge, p. 146.

51 F. Millar (1981), *The Roman Empire and its Neighbours*, 2nd ed., London: Duckworth, p.199.

52 Homer, *Iliad* 21.470

53 M. B. Thompson (1998), 'The Holy Internet' in R. Bauckham (ed.), *The Gospels for All Christians*, Edinburgh: T.&T. Clark, p. 53.

54 Wenham, *Paul and Jesus*, p. 142.

55 Pliny the Younger, *Letters* 2.6 (tr. Radice).

56 N. T. Wright (1994), *Following Jesus*, London: SPCK, p. 59.

57 F. Young and D. Ford (1987), *Meaning and Truth in 2 Corinthians*, London: SPCK, p. 27.

58 L. Hurtado (2005), *How On Earth Did Jesus Become A God?*, Grand Rapids: Eerdmans, p. 183.

59 J. Ziesler (1989), *Paul's Letter to the Romans*, London: SCM Press, p. 74.

60 Hooker, *Paul: a short introduction*, pp. 74–5.

61 Dunn, *Theology of Paul the Apostle*, p. 506.

62 R. Hays (1996), *The Moral Vision of the New Testament*, Edinburgh, T.&T. Clark, p. 417.

63 Suetonius, *Life of Claudius* 25.4.

64 Tacitus, *Histories* 5.9.

65 N. Faulkner (2002), *Apocalypse: the great Jewish Revolt against Rome*, Stroud: Tempus, p. 121.

66 V. Hope (2000), 'Status and Identity in the Roman World' in J. Huskinson (ed.) *Experiencing Rome: culture, identity and power in the Roman Empire*, London: Routledge, pp. 148, 134.

67 J. Coulston (2001), 'Transport and Travel on the Column of Trajan' in C. Adams and R. Laurence (eds.), *Travel and Geography in the Roman Empire*, London: Routledge, p. 129.

68 H. Chadwick (1959), *The Circle and the Ellipse*, London: SPCK, p. 16.

69 A. N. Sherwin-White (1963), *Roman Society and Roman Law in the New Testament*, Oxford: Oxford University Press, p. 57.

70 G. Vermes (2005), *Who's Who in the Age of Jesus*, Harmondsworth: Penguin, p. 206.

71 C. F. D. Moule (1977), *The Origin of Christology*, Cambridge: Cambridge University Press, p. 95.

72 Crossan and Reed, *In Search of Paul*, pp. 118, 122.

73 E. Schüssler Fiorenza (1992), *In Memory of Her: a feminist theological reconstruction of Christian origins*, 2nd ed., New York: Crossroads, p. 218.

74 A. T. Lincoln (1990), *Ephesians*, Dallas: Word, p. lxix.

75 Dunn, *Theology of Paul*, p. 13.

76 Lincoln, *Ephesians*, p. lxiii

77 S. Schama (1999), *Rembrandt's Eyes*, London: Penguin, p. 658.

78 A. T. Hanson (1982), *The Pastoral Epistles*, Grand Rapids: Eerdmans, p. 7.

79 J. C. Beker (1992), *Heirs of Paul*, Edinburgh: T.&T. Clark, p. 128.

80 *1 Clement* 5.

81 V. Hope, 'The City of Rome: capital and symbol' in Huskinson (ed.) *Experiencing Rome*, p. 87.

82 Ovid, *Fasti* 2.684.

7

The Gospel of Luke and the Acts of the Apostles

Bithynia, 110

When Pliny the elder saw the eruption of Mount Vesuvius from the terrace of his villa in August 79 his 17-year-old nephew was with him. The boy declined the offer to sail across the bay with his uncle in his fateful expedition. When news came that Pliny had died, his nephew found himself heir to his uncle's wealth and name. He is usually known as Pliny the Younger.

A year after the disaster at Pompeii, aged 18, Pliny the Younger embarked on the glittering career available to a young Roman aristocrat. He began to practise as a lawyer, and attachment to the staff of the governor of Syria during military service revealed a formidable gift for understanding finance. He entered the Roman Senate around the age of 30 and reached the highest office of consul in 100, three years after his friend, the historian Tacitus.

Pliny subsequently became known for his prosecution and defence of various provincial governors, deftly untangling the financial confusion which dogged many of them. In 109, the Emperor Trajan sent him to the province of Bithynia in northern Asia Minor to sort out the financial and administrative chaos there.

Pliny had ambitions as a writer, and he became known for his speech of gratitude to the Emperor Trajan, which developed into a meditation on the perfect ruler. Pliny delivered it to his friends as an after-dinner entertainment in three parts, each two hours long. When the friends observed that it was not very diverting for them, Pliny replied that just because they were friends it didn't mean that they shouldn't suffer. But it was letters to those friends which Pliny chose as the medium for his literary art. He wrote nine books, designed to be read publicly, containing his thoughts on life, love, friendship and the virtues, especially moderation and modesty (the latter especially being a quality Pliny seemed to think he had in abundance!). Together they form 'the nearest [thing] we have to a Roman autobiography'.[1] The tenth book is different. It consists of the record of Pliny's administration in Bithynia.

Bithynia had problems, and Pliny wrote to the emperor about them all. He also wrote about a baffling group he found in the province: Christians. Pliny asked Trajan what he should do about them: 'I have never taken part in the trials of Christians, and thus do not know what crimes it is usual to punish or to pursue, or to what lengths' he wrote.

Pliny went on to explain what he had done so far. Some he had tortured, others who were Roman citizens had been shipped off to Rome. But, whatever he did, he could get only this from them:

> that they used to meet on the same day at sunrise and sing by turns a hymn to Christ as to a god; they would then pledge themselves not to commit a crime but instead not to commit fraud, theft or adultery and not to break trust with others. After doing this they would go away and gather later to share food – but ordinary and innocent food. And they swore that they had stopped doing even this after my decree, in accordance with your instructions, outlawing political gatherings.

Pliny thought this too good to be true and tortured two 'female slaves, called deaconesses' to get at the truth. They refused to change their story. Somewhat rattled, Pliny decided to ask for guidance because this 'excessive and depraved superstition'[2] had wide support and he feared it would turn people away from traditional pagan rituals.

The Christians in Bithynia emerge from Pliny's letter as a puzzle to him. They were a peaceful group who pledged themselves not to do harm but good, and who were obedient to the decrees of the emperor. Yet they were enticing people away from traditional worship and this scared Pliny: what would happen if such behaviour angered the gods? What was Pliny to do? Who could tell him more about this faith?

The correct form of address for Pliny as proconsular legate of a Greek-speaking imperial province was *kratiste*, 'most excellent'. This is how Luke addresses the mysterious Theophilus, for whom the Gospel and Acts were written (Luke 1.3, see Acts 1.1), and also how, later in Acts, Paul addresses both Felix and Festus the governors of Judea (Acts 24.2; 26.25). Luke's Gospel and Acts were not written for Pliny, but they would have been ideal for briefing him about the Christians. Remembering too Pliny's eulogy about Trajan delivered in three two-hour sittings, the Gospel and Acts might have been designed for reading in a similar setting (Pliny's friends might have found them more interesting than his thoughts on the perfect ruler).

The name Theophilus might be code, for it means 'lover of God' and could point to a 'God-worshipper', that group which was so crucial for the growth of the churches Paul founded. On the other hand he might have been a real aristocratic Roman who, like Pliny, needed to know more about the Christian faith.

Who was Luke?

Luke's Gospel stands out from the other three gospels because it has a sequel, Acts, which tells the story of what happened after Jesus. The two books were clearly conceived as a unity, but were split up by the arrangement of the canon of the New Testament. Only quite recently have they been seen once again as a single story. In terms of breadth and ambition Luke's work outstrips all the other Gospel writers.

Luke's Gospel was linked with Paul in the early Church: he was the apostle whose authority guaranteed it. Irenaeus in the late second century claimed that the third Gospel was written by 'Luke the companion of Paul, [who] wrote down the gospel preached by him in a book.'[3] No alternative author ever seems to have been proposed, and Luke was a slightly odd choice. Paul mentions Luke in the letters to the Colossians and Philemon, as 'the beloved physician' (Col. 4.14; Philemon 24). Some have tried to underpin the case for Luke's authorship of the Gospel on the grounds that it contains a good deal of medical vocabulary, but Henry J. Cadbury successfully demonstrated in 1933 that the Greek of the Gospel was consistent with that used by any educated person of the time (and so Cadbury was said to have gained his doctorate by taking Luke's away!).

It is chronologically possible that a companion of Paul in his twenties could have lived long enough to write the story down in the last decade of the first century, and there is a claim to eyewitness status by the author of Acts (Acts 16.10–17; 20.5–15; 21.1–18; 27.1—28.16), though these passages could be the accounts of someone else which have simply been included verbatim. But we cannot be sure who Luke was, or if he had any connection with Paul's 'beloved physician'.

We gain a strong impression of the author, however. He showed compassion and human warmth as well as intelligence and the ability to organize a mass of complex material. He was clearly very familiar with the Hebrew Scriptures, but his great theme is the way in which the Church grew beyond its Jewish roots. For this reason many believe him to have been a gentile 'God-worshipper'. Paul's letters suggest that Luke was active in the Lycus valley churches, and later traditions linked him with Antioch. Most likely he travelled and lived in different places at different times. Perhaps above all he was a masterly writer whose Greek prose flows elegantly. Cadbury called him 'a gentleman of ability and breadth of interest',[4] a quaint but accurate description.

When was Luke–Acts written?

Luke, like Matthew, used Mark's Gospel as his main source for the life of Jesus. If Mark's Gospel was written in the mid to late-60s, then Luke–Acts must have been written later than that. However, the enigmatic ending of Acts, which fails to mention the deaths of James, Peter or Paul raises many questions. Why, if Acts was written after these crucial events are they not even alluded to?

The obvious answer is that these events had not happened when the work was completed. But this is hard to accept, because it calls into question the common dating of Mark's Gospel, which rests on reasonably secure grounds. Some argue that perhaps Acts was written *before* the Gospel, possibly based on Paul's defence, prepared for a trial before the emperor), but the careful structure of the two books together as well as the opening of Acts (Acts 1.1) make this view seem like special pleading.

The alternative view is that the books were written much later and the author felt no need to include material which was common knowledge. This seems rather strange to us: why miss out the end of the story? We shall return to this question at the end of the chapter. For now it is enough to recognize that Luke–Acts has been carefully structured to fit within the usual limits of two scrolls. Therefore the decision to end the story before the deaths of some of the key characters seems to have been deliberate.

Luke–Acts must have been written later than Mark's Gospel, but how much later? On the grounds that in Luke's Gospel Jesus' predictions of the destruction of the temple are widened to include the whole of the city of Jerusalem, it seems likely that Luke was writing after the events of 70 (Luke 19.41–4; 21.20–4, see also Mark 13.14–20). There are no other indications of date, however, and as a result scholars generally propose a date of between 75 and 95.

Luke says that he is writing after 'many' have attempted to do the same thing (Luke 1.1). He had Mark's Gospel available to him, as well as a lost common source (Q) with Matthew's Gospel. Luke had a good deal of his own distinctive material too, most clearly seen in his narrative of the passion: only an eighth of this part of his Gospel is shared with Mark's version and it would stand on its own, suggesting that Luke already had a complete account of the crucifixion to hand. Clearly, the more material there was available to Luke, the later his Gospel was likely to have been composed. In addition, despite the presence of some shared material with Paul's letters in the Gospel, there seems to be a sense of distance from the events narrated in the writing. The description of the early years of the church in Jerusalem has a kind of 'golden age of innocence' quality about it. The differences between the Paul of Acts and the Paul of the letters (though these are often exaggerated) make more sense if a longer time had passed between Paul's lifetime and the writing of the book. For these reasons, I feel safest dating the composition of Luke–Acts to the 90s.

What kind of book is Luke–Acts?

Luke–Acts is a wide-ranging and structurally ambitious work. But how can we describe its genre? Luke's Gospel fits the biographical pattern and explicitly takes its cue from those who had gone before (Luke 1.1), but the continuation took the genre in a new direction, borrowing from history. For this reason many scholars suggest that the example of Luke–Acts undermines the category of biography as a controlling genre for the Gospels. For some, the similarity of Luke's Gospel to the other three wins out over its unity with Acts (a view which led the early Church to place John's Gospel between Luke's and Acts in the New Testament). They argue that it is actually two books of different types: biography in the Gospel, history in Acts.

A counter-argument suggests that ancient biography was a flexible enough category even to embrace a book like Acts, and at least one example of a collective biography exists. The title of 'Acts of the Apostles', though we cannot be sure that the book was known by this name until the late second century, certainly suggests that the early Church recognized it as being concerned with a group of people. Seeing Acts within the overall category of biography (while struggling to be contained within it) explains, for example, why the focus changes after Acts 13 to be exclusively concerned with Paul, who then effectively becomes the subject of a biography. As a result other figures, notably Peter, vanish; but this may be simply due to the constraints of the genre.

Richard Burridge's proposal that the Gospels be seen within the category of ancient biography has been widely accepted. Burridge found that the 'hero' of a biography was characteristically the subject of around a quarter to third of the verbs in a book. The four Gospels clearly conform to this statistical pattern. A similar analysis of verb-subjects in Acts throws up an intriguing suggestion: God is the subject of a high proportion of the verbs. On this basis perhaps he, rather than the apostles or Paul, should be seen as the 'hero' of the story. It might have been better entitled 'The Acts of the Holy Spirit'.

Luke–Acts is probably best described as 'biographical history'. It shares traits with both genres and the blurring of boundaries may be deliberate. Perhaps the story was too revolutionary to fit the constraints of either genre, and was designed to provoke questions. If Luke's Gospel and Acts were read, like Pliny's eulogy to Trajan, as after-dinner entertainment for Theophilus and his friends, you can imagine the kind of questions that might follow: 'Who is the real hero?'; 'Was that biography or history?' and so on. The questions would be the same as those which dominate the study of Luke–Acts today. All of them would be seeking to provoke further discussion and argument. In this sense Luke–Acts seems to function with an apologetic purpose, encouraging its hearers to learn more.

The Aims of Luke–Acts

At the opening of his Gospel Luke writes

> Since many have undertaken to draw up a narrative of the things which have come to fruition among us, as handed on to us by those who were eyewitnesses from the beginning and those who became servants of the message, it seemed good to me also, having carefully investigated all things from long ago, to write to you a well-ordered account, most excellent Theophilus, so that you should know that the things which you have heard are a sound basis. (Luke 1.1–4).

This opening is quite different from the other three Gospels, written in a 'deliberately secular style [which] invites comparison of his work with that of the historians of his day'.[5] History was a popular branch of literature in the first century: short fragments from works by almost a thousand historians have survived, but tantalizingly none are long enough to bear comparison with Luke–Acts. The boundaries between history and other prose genres were blurred, and the creation of hybrid forms was probably quite common.

As a Christian writer Luke was continuing the work which Mark had done in creating the Gospel genre. But at the same time he outlined his method and implicitly set standards by which a historian might provide an account in which the reader could have confidence (Luke 1.4). Such faith in the relation of past events as a means of discovering truth was rare in the ancient world, but it was a hallmark of the thinking of the early Church. Martin Hengel writes that the four Gospel writers had a common aim: 'to report a real past event which is the foundation for present (and future) salvation ... by relating "stories" which together refer to a unique "history"'.[6] While Mark had created the Gospel genre intuitively, Luke seems to have figured out why he had done so, and therefore he could claim to be the first Christian historian.

Luke's preface consciously reaches out to a wide audience and has a wide horizon. Luke–Acts is recognizably a 'universal history', aimed at edification rather than entertainment, of the kind pioneered by Polybius in the second century BC. Polybius wrote a history of the rise of Rome, with many asides on method. For him history, according to Robin Lane Fox, 'is the history of events and actions as they affect cities, peoples and individuals, and it must be written by a "pragmatic" individual, someone who travels to the sites in question, interviews participants and personally studies documents.'[7] Polybius's geographically wide-ranging history seems to have been a model for Luke both in its aims and its execution.

Historians are only as good as their sources. Luke notes that 'many' have previously recorded the traditions, but says that he has returned to the sources and gathered information from both eyewitnesses and also those who were 'servants of the word'. Most historians of the time considered that traditions were sufficient and that history was written simply by quoting past authorities, concluding that 'historical narrative could be created without primary research ... New interpretations of past events were generally derived from rationalizing or from new perspectives, rarely from new research.'[8] But Polybius had stressed the importance of eyewitnesses, regarding evidence from any other source as 'hearsay at one remove'. Luke seems to have followed both courses. Like Polybius he claimed to have spoken to eyewitnesses, but also to have received information from 'servants of the word'. Who formed this latter group?

The term 'servants of the word' (*hyperetai*) was applied by Jews to the synagogue official who looked after the scrolls of Scripture (Luke 4.20). Luke uses it of John Mark (Acts 13.5) who was also, of course, widely identified as the author of Mark's Gospel. Paul himself is described as a 'servant of the word' (Acts 26.16), someone who 'though not an "eyewitness from the beginning", is portrayed as an authoritative "servant" of the traditions "from the beginning"'.[9] Paul said that he had 'passed on what I received' (1 Cor. 11.23; 15.3), emphasizing the continuity of tradition and his own responsibility in handing it on. It follows that there may have been a group of people in the early Church who were recognized to have responsibilities in guarding and transmitting the traditions of the Church. Luke's aim was to provide Theophilus with a 'sound basis'. To do this, following Polybius's strictures on eyewitness testimony, Luke emphasizes his use of primary sources; but he also uses controlled tradition. These two kinds of sources imply a check on the kind of unfettered imagination which characterized much contemporary history-writing. Where it is possible to assess Luke's sources his handling of them seems careful and accurate. What he also does, again following the example of Polybius, is to 'order' them.

An 'orderly account'

The key to writing history in the way that Polybius had done was to find an ordering principle. Luke's 'well-ordered account' takes the traditions and reminiscences he had received and carefully frames and arranges them.

In 1957, Hans Conzelmann wrote a book whose central thesis was brilliantly expressed in its title, *Die Mitte der Zeit,* 'the middle of time'. What Conzelmann spotted was that Luke's Gospel is more than a simple narrative of the life of Jesus. Its canvas spreads across nothing less than the entire history of the world. Jesus' life is the heart of history, the 'middle of time' itself, the hinge on which the world's destiny turns. This theological framework sets Luke's Gospel apart from both his sources and the other Gospels because it means that Luke rejected their view that the end of time was imminent; hence his unique desire to write a continuation. Luke saw Jesus' resurrection as the beginning of a new instalment of the story rather than a moment which brought history to a close. Luke extended the concept of a 'between the times' period which seems to have become part of Paul's later thinking, where the present age and the age to come overlapped. He recognized that this period might last a long time and that it could be defined as the age of the Church.

Rather than being the beginning of the story, in an important sense Luke's Gospel is the second part of a trilogy, of which the first is what Christians (following Luke's thinking) have come to call the Old Testament. Luke's scheme of salvation looks like Figure 12.

With this framework in the background, Luke was able to shape the material he had received and gathered. So the story he tells is set out like Figure 13.

The pattern is made explicit in Jesus' final words to the disciples: 'you shall be my witnesses in all Judea and Samaria and to the ends of the earth' (Acts 1:8). Rome seems to be the end of the earth in view. The ordering principle which Luke used was thus to tell 'how we brought the good news from Jerusalem to Rome'.

The structure outlined in Figure 13 shows that the Gospel and Acts mirror each other. The sense of continuation is underlined by the opening of Acts: 'The first book I wrote, Theophilus, concerned all the things which Jesus *began* to do and teach' (Acts 1.1); so the Gospel is only the beginning of what Jesus did, and by implication Acts will complete the story.

The ordered and schematic structure shows why Luke's narrative differs at certain points from those of his fellow Gospel writers. Unlike Matthew, he has reordered the skeleton which Mark provided and also introduced material which the others seem not to have known, especially in the birth and passion narratives (though, intriguingly, his passion material has some significant echoes in John's Gospel). Luke's Gospel begins at Jerusalem with Zechariah, includes material from Nazareth and Bethlehem and also tells of Jesus in Jerusalem at the age of 12. Luke includes a good deal of Nazareth material. He often introduces things 'once, when Jesus was ...', giving him freedom to cut loose from Mark's geographical pattern, and to group his material thematically. Luke describes a kind of triumphal procession by Jesus from Galilee to Jerusalem. He has simplified the account so that his audience doesn't need to worry about the geography, and he also tidies up Mark's rather rough Greek.

The Age of Israel → The Age of Jesus → The Age of the Church

(Old Testament)	(Gospel)	(Acts)

Figure 12 Luke's scheme of salvation

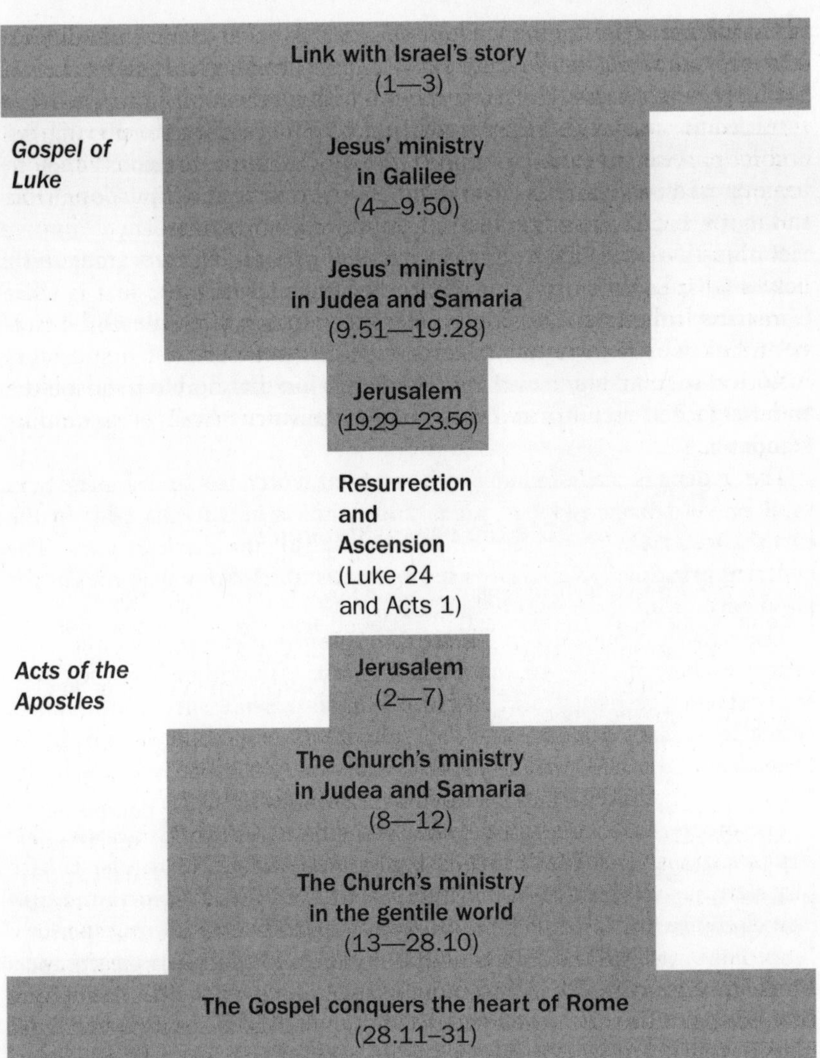

Figure 13 The structure of Luke's Gospel

One effect of Luke's order is that Jerusalem assumes a greater significance in Luke–Acts than in the other Gospels, notably in the central section, which embraces the end of the Gospel and the beginning of Acts. Jesus' journey to, his passion and resurrection in, and the growth of the Church within and then beyond Jerusalem sets the city at the heart of the whole work. Luke's 'spiritual geography' is different from that of the other Gospel writers.

At an even more detailed level, Luke's order means that he has also 'tidied up' the resurrection stories; where the other Gospels speak of

Jesus appearing in Galilee (in Mark's case, by implication solely there, Mark 16.7), Luke doesn't include Galilee in this part of the story at all. He firmly situates all Jesus' appearances in, or close to, Jerusalem. As a result some suggest that here we have an example of Luke playing fast and loose with the historical facts, fitting them into a scheme which he has imposed on them, ignoring those that do not serve his purpose. Does this mean that he has eliminated stories which do not conform to his own views, just as he seems to have downplayed the undoubted antagonism between Paul and Peter?

Paradoxically this leads to the conclusion that, while Luke is the Gospel writer who most clearly conforms to the standards of first-century historical scholarship, he is for the same reason therefore the most likely to be regarded as untrustworthy by the equivalent twenty-first-century standards.

Did the census happen?

Luke wanted to offer Theophilus a 'sound basis' for what he had already heard (Luke 1.4). But since D. F. Strauss first raised the question in 1835 this claim has seemed to be suspect because of the Bethlehem census, which conveniently places Mary in Bethlehem in time for Jesus to be born in the 'city of David'.

Both Matthew's and Luke's Gospels clearly place the birth of Jesus 'during the time of Herod' (Matt. 2.1; Luke 1.5). Herod the Great died in 4 BC, but Luke also says that 'It happened in those days a decree went out from Caesar Augustus that the whole world should be registered. This first registration came about when Quirinius was governing Syria' (Luke 2.1–2). Strauss spotted a discrepancy here. There was no record of Quirinius being governor of Syria during Herod's lifetime; he did not become governor of Syria until around ten years after Herod's death, and ordered a census of the Roman province in 6/7 according to Josephus. Since Luke uses the registration as a means of explaining the presence of Joseph and Mary in Bethlehem when Jesus was born the implication is that, if such a major early point is untrue and Luke has manipulated the facts, why should we trust him on anything else?

Objections to Luke's accuracy here usually make four additional points:

- No Roman historian mentions a decree of Augustus to assess the world.
- If such a decree existed, Herod's states would have been exempt from it since they were not yet Roman provinces.
- If a Roman decree were enacted within Herod's states it would surely have followed Roman rules, which taxed people where they lived, not (on the Jewish pattern) where they came from originally.

- Such an assessment would not have involved Mary, since the Romans did not include women in the registration.

These objections are not really decisive, however.

- Augustus's interest in the world was what led to the making of Agrippa's map of the world. Luke speaks of a 'registration', which may not imply a formal census: all it really means is a systematic attempt to describe an area. So although it is technically true that no other historian mentions a worldwide census that is not necessarily what Luke means here. His general statement that Augustus wanted a listing of the world is in fact hard to argue with.
- Herod, as a client king of the Roman Empire, would not have been required to carry out a survey, but knowing Herod's prudent desire to please Augustus it is quite likely that he could have done so. Client kingdoms were usually set up to prepare the local population for eventual Roman rule, bringing in Roman customs and manners. Their rulers also paid tributes to the emperor and efficient taxation depended on accurate record-keeping. Herod would have had to develop some form of tax-collection system.
- Since Herod was semi-independent he would not be bound by Roman rules for collecting tax; indeed he was likely to have adapted existing Jewish practices and expected people to return to their native towns.
- Mary's presence in Bethlehem is to accompany her husband: the Gospel does not say she went to be counted too.

Thus far Luke's picture is coherent with the historical circumstances, though there is a great deal of supposition on either side of the argument. What does seem decisive is the fact that the dates of Herod and Quirinius simply don't match.

For this reason, Dominic Crossan, in typically trenchant style, comments that the story 'seems a brilliant explanation of why Jesus of Nazareth was born at Bethlehem, unless, of course, one knows anything of Roman history and Roman, or indeed any, bureaucracy'.[10] But the problem with such a comment is that it assumes Luke and his audience, including Theophilus, must have been ignorant of Roman history and bureaucracy to accept this account. This seems a highly patronizing judgement to make, and only serves to deepen the puzzle. It seems reasonable to assume that Luke understood Roman and pre-Roman administration better than we do.

Some scholars have pointed out that the Greek phrase in question bears at least two alternative translations. Instead of the more obvious 'this first registration came about when Quirinius was governing Syria,' it could be translated 'this registration came about before Quirinius was governing Syria,' since the word *prote*, while it usually means 'first', can also mean 'before', and may refer not to the registration but to Quirinius.

This is a slightly forced reading, but in the circumstances not an impossible one. Therefore Luke would be pointing out that this census or survey was before the Roman ones began, hence explaining why Joseph needed to return to Bethlehem.

The second alternative is that the phrase could read 'this registration came to be most important when Quirinius was governing Syria', and again *prote* is the key word, since it can also mean 'most important'. On this reading, Luke would be emphasizing that the registration in which Joseph was involved was a preliminary to the later, famous, census under Quirinius.

On the other hand, how important a matter is this? If Luke was wrong in suggesting that a census under Herod was also under Quirinius, which does seem to be the most obvious reading of the text, does this really invalidate the accuracy of everything else he wrote? It's another matter on which you will need to make up your own mind. How trustworthy do you think Luke is, and why?

Writing Luke's Gospel

Luke's Gospel is the most complex in terms of the sources which it draws from. Almost half of its material is not found in the other Gospels; a further third is taken over from Mark's. Roughly a tenth is shared with Matthew (and so probably comes from Q, the hypothetical document which scholars have reconstructed from the passages common to both Matthew's and Luke's Gospels). The remaining tenth is Luke's own blending of two or three other sources.

Luke took over the structure of Mark's telling of the story of Jesus. The story is told in two parts: early success in Galilee, a turning point at Caesarea Philippi and the final act in Jerusalem. But the balance has shifted: the turning point occurs about a third of the way through the Gospel instead of half-way, because Jerusalem has a deeper significance for Luke.

The whole story begins in the Temple at Jerusalem, with the appearance of an angel to Zechariah (Luke 1.5–25); Jesus is dedicated in the Temple as a baby (Luke 2.21–40); his own visit to Jerusalem at the age of 12 is included and once again the story centres on the Temple (Luke 2.41–52). The second part of the Gospel is framed as a more deliberate approach to Jerusalem than either Mark or Matthew had suggested. In Luke's Gospel Jesus is always aware of the fate that awaits him in Jerusalem, and is purposefully drawn to it; so he 'set his face towards Jerusalem' (Luke 9.51). In the Gospels of Mark and Matthew it is the recognition of Jesus as the messiah (Mark 8.29) and Son of God (Matt. 16.16) for the first time, followed by the transfiguration (Mark 9.2–9; Matt. 17.1–9), which is the turning point in Jesus' life. For Luke these events are the prelude to Jesus' increasingly triumphal procession into Jerusalem. Subsequent events unfold inexorably and there is nothing contingent or accidental about them for Luke. The confrontation in the Temple, which looms so large in Mark's dramatic account of the last week of Jesus' life, tends to surprise the reader of his Gospel because until that point the Temple has been unmentioned in the story. Luke's early scenes centring on the Temple have the effect of making the reader of his Gospel see that the final confrontation there is what Jesus had been born for.

The way Luke handles the recurring theme of Jerusalem is a good example of how he took over material from others, but made it his own. The clearest examples of this can be seen by comparing the parables and miracles of Jesus in the first three Gospels (in Figure 14 the miracles are shaded).

Luke's Gospel contains 18 miracle stories and 30 parables, Mark's 17 and 10, and Matthew's 15 and 25. The space Luke devotes in his Gospel to the birth and childhood stories at the beginning and the resurrection appearances of Jesus at the end means that he actually has less room in his book for the story of Jesus' ministry, yet he still manages to fit in significantly more parables than his fellow writers, and also slightly more miracles than Matthew. Clearly he wants to show Jesus as a miracle-worker and prophetic teacher.

Looking at Figure 14 we can see that the decisive shift, which happens as Jesus sets his face to Jerusalem (Luke 9.51), is reflected in the distribution of miracles and parables. Only a fifth of the parables occur before this point in the Gospel, and only a third of the miracles after it. Thus Luke seems to be locating Jesus' wonder-working activity largely in Galilee, and his teaching ministry mostly in Judea. In Mark's Gospel it is striking how little room there is for either teaching or miracle-working after the turning point at Caesarea Philippi (8.29); there are only three miracles after that point and a mere three parables, all set in Jerusalem. Luke observes the order of Mark's Gospel in the miracle stories which he uses, but he feels free to scatter the parables (of which he uses all but one) across his Gospel without regard for their original setting in the overall story. No fewer than 13 parables are unique to Luke's Gospel, and some of those which are shared with Matthew's Gospel seem to have come by separate routes (so the great feast in Luke's Gospel is a wedding feast in Matthew's). Luke also seems not to know a good many of the parables which Matthew includes in his Gospel, especially those which occur in the teaching block about the Kingdom (Matt. 13). Many people see this as evidence that Luke could not have had access to Matthew's Gospel as a source.

Luke thus seems to show a good deal of flexibility with regard to where he placed the sayings of Jesus but very little when it comes to the miracles. He reduces the contrast which Mark had drawn between Galilee

Miracle/parable	Luke	Mark	Matthew (Q)
Man with unclean spirit	4.33–5	1.23–6	
Peter's mother-in-law	4.38–9	1.30–1	
Leper	5.12–13	1.40–2	8.2–4
Paralyzed man	5.18–25	2.3–12	9.2–7
Man with withered hand	6.6–10	3.1–5	12.10–13
Wise and foolish builders	6.47–9		7.24–7
Centurion's servant	7.1–10		8.5–13
Widow's son at Nain	7.11–5		
Two men in debt	7.41–3		
Sower	8.4–15	4.1–20	13.1–23
Lamp under a jar	8.16–18	4.21–5	
Calming a storm	8.22–5	4.37–41	8.23–7
Legion	8.27–35	5.1–15	8.28–34
Jairus' daughter and the bleeding woman	8.41–56	5.22–42	9.18–25
Feeding 5,000	9.12–17	6.35–44	14.15–21
Boy with unclean spirit	9.38–43	9.17–19	17.17–19
Samaritan	10.25–37		
Friend at midnight	11.5–8		
Children and father	11.11–13		7.9–11
Exorcising a mute demon	11.14		12.22
Strong man	11.21–3	3.22–7	12.29–30
Rich fool	12.13–21		
Returning master	12.35–40	13.34–6	24.42–4
Faithful and unfaithful slaves	12.42–6		24.45–51
Empty fig tree	13.6–9		
Crippled woman	13.11–13		
Mustard seed	13.18–19	4.30–2	13.31–2
Woman baking	13.20–1		13.33
Narrow door	13.23–7		7.13–14
Man with dropsy	14.1–4		
Great feast	14.15–24		22.1–14
Preparing to build and fight	14.28–33		
Salt and saltiness	14.34	9.50	
Lost sheep	15.1–7		18.12–14
Lost coin	15.8–10		
Lost son	15.11–32		
Dishonest steward	16.1–8		
Rich man and Lazarus	16.19–31		

Miracle/parable	Luke	Mark	Matthew (Q)
Humble slave	17.1–10		
Ten men with leprosy	17.11–19		
Widow and the bad judge	18.1–8		
Pharisee and tax-collector	18.9–14		
Blind man near Jericho	18.35–43	10.46–52	20.29–34
Pounds/talents	19.11–27		25.14–30
Evil tenants	20.9–19	12.1–12	21.33–46
Fig tree	21.29–33	13.28–32	24.32–6
High priest's servant	22.50–1		
Parables and miracles in Mark or Matthew but not in Luke			
Secret seed		4.26–9	
Good and bad trees			7.16–20
Wheat and tares			13.24–43
Hidden treasure			13.44
Great pearl			13.45–6
Fish net			13.47–50
Walking on water		6.48–51	14.25
Syro-Phoenician woman's daughter		7.2–30	15.21–8
Deaf man		7.31–7	
Feeding 4,000		8.1–9	15.32–8
Blind man at Bethsaida		8.22–6	
Unkind slave			18.23–35
Vineyard workers			20.1–16
Withered fig tree		11.12–14, 20–5	21.18–22
Two sons			21.28–32
Wise and foolish bridesmaids			25.1–13
Sheep and goats			25.31–46

Figure 14 Parables and miracles in the synoptic Gospels

and Judea and portrays Jesus as a prophet more familiar with Judea than we might have expected him to be (as John's Gospel also does).

But perhaps most striking is how many of the best remembered parables belong to Luke's Gospel alone, especially the Good Samaritan, the rich fool, and the lost sheep, coin and son.

We can tentatively suggest that Luke had a wider range of independent sources for Jesus' sayings than he had for the miracles. In Acts he quotes an otherwise unknown saying of Jesus: 'It is more blessed to give than to receive' (Acts 20.35). The nature of Luke's account of the passion also suggests that he had an independent narrative of Jesus' last days available to him, into which he added a few of Mark's details, though he generally let it stand for itself.

Overall, Luke seems to have done an extraordinary job in blending his sources together. But what does the process tell us about why he did it? Mark Goodacre speculates that Luke may have acquired a copy of Matthew's Gospel and thought that, just as Matthew had added to Mark's Gospel and tried to 'fix' it, he could 'do the same kind of thing, but do it better'.[11] Goodacre is perhaps the leading contemporary antagonist of the Q theory; but it is not necessary to accept that Luke actually used Matthew's Gospel as a source to think that Goodacre is right in suggesting that Luke was trying to do the same thing that Matthew had done: to expand Mark's Gospel into a fuller and less enigmatic document. Not only that, but if his aim was to speak to a Hellenistic-Roman audience (rather than an eastern, Semitic, one as Matthew sought to do), then Mark's Gospel and the other sources became the raw material which he could sift and reorder. It is striking how much of Mark's Gospel Luke could use while also decisively shifting and developing Mark's portrayal of Jesus to convey a subtly different understanding of him.

In writing history, the earliest interpretation is not always the best. Mark's Gospel takes its audience vividly close to Jesus. Luke takes a different approach, one which is more distant and measured, and adds perspective and depth. Luke also, crucially, always has an eye to the future development of the Church.

Luke, Matthew and Q

For many years scholars have held to a consensus that the material which appears both in Matthew's Gospel and Luke's came from a common source, labelled Q. But it doesn't take long to spot the logical possibility that Luke might have used Matthew's Gospel as a source, or that Matthew could have used Luke's. The dilemma here is that, while both Mathew and Luke seem to have been scrupulous in preserving what they took from Mark's Gospel, each would have been positively cavalier in their treatment of the other's work if it is true that they took material from it. In particular, if Luke used Matthew's Gospel, why would he have scattered the carefully crafted material in the Sermon on the Mount (Matt. 5 – 7) so randomly across his Gospel?

Figure 15 gives a flavour of how marked a feature this is by setting the first part of the Sermon on the Mount in parallel with Luke's Sermon on the Plain (Luke 6.17–49). You can see at a glance that the bones of the same Sermon are present in both Gospels: the beatitudes and 'turn

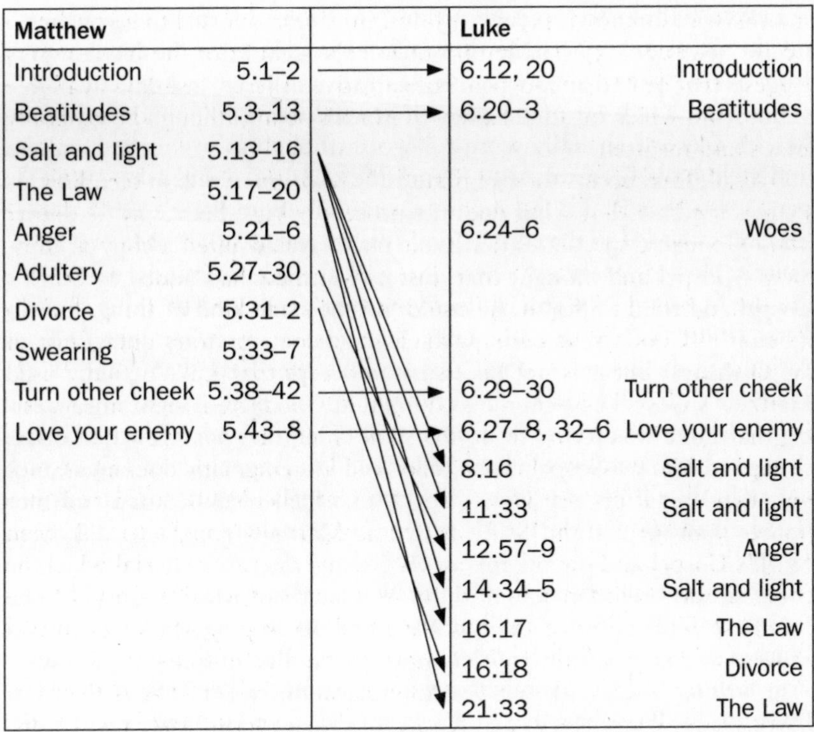

Figure 15 The Sermon on the Mount and the Sermon on the Plain

the other cheek/love your enemy' sayings. But a closer look at the texts reveals that the flesh on the bones is slightly different: the Beatitudes according to Matthew are much longer, and Luke's version really only focuses on the literally poor and hungry (not those who are 'poor in spirit' and 'hungry for righteousness' as Matthew has); the 'woes' which denounce the rich have no direct parallel in Matthew's Gospel. The rest of the material which Luke's Gospel and Matthew 5 have in common is scattered across the former; the 'salt and light' saying is split, with the light part being repeated. Overall it is clear that Luke tends to place the bulk of Jesus' sayings within the framework of Jesus' journey to Jerusalem (after the turning point of Luke 9.51).

This scattering is what makes most scholars convinced that Luke could not have had a copy of Matthew's Gospel available to him. Graham Stanton says, 'If Luke has used Matthew, then he has used this major source extremely freely indeed: he has "dismantled" Matthew in order to write his own very different Gospel.'[12] And this would be in marked contrast to the scrupulous way in which Luke seems to have used Mark's Gospel as a source.

Luke usually seems to prefer Mark's version of a story to Matthew's on the occasions when Matthew has expanded what he has received from Mark. The clearest example of this is in the key episode of Peter's confession that Jesus is the messiah at Caesarea Philippi. Luke follows Mark's account virtually word-for-word (though as usual the grammar and style have been tidied up) from the question Jesus asks: 'Who do people say that I am?' All he adds materially is in Peter's reply, where 'of God' is added to the confession 'You are the Messiah' (Mark 8.27–9; Luke 9.18–20). Matthew's reworking of this passage adds, after 'You are the Messiah', 'the son of the living God', followed by Jesus blessing Peter (Matt. 16.16–19). But Luke, like Mark, jumps straight to Jesus forbidding the disciples to tell anyone what they have seen (Mark 8.30; Luke 9.21). If Luke knew Matthew's additions to this story, why would he not have used them? The same is true of stories which Mark's Gospel does not have, notably the birth stories and the genealogy of Jesus which are radically different between the two Gospels. Again, scholars argue, if Luke had known Matthew's version, why is there no hint of it in his Gospel?

Surely it is conceivable that Matthew might have used a copy of Luke's Gospel and expanded it, pulling the disparate sayings into his teaching blocks? At first sight the shorter forms of the Beatitudes and the Lord's Prayer in Luke's Gospel might suggest this, on the principle that briefer texts are likely to be earlier ones (see Luke 6.20–3; Matt. 5.3–12 and Luke 11.2–4; Matt. 6.9–15). Here is some evidence that Luke's Gospel came first.

But the arrangement of the 'turn the other cheek/love your enemy' sayings are good evidence for the opposite conclusion. In Matthew's Gospel these are separate; in Luke's they have been woven together to make a pithier saying altogether (see Matthew 5.38–48; Luke 6.27–36). Surely Matthew would not have split up these sayings once they had been put together? So here is possible evidence that Matthew's Gospel came first.

The existence of the lost source, Q, to which both Matthew and Luke had independent access, was proposed as the way through of resolving the question of whether Luke borrowed from Matthew or vice versa. Since in some cases the shared material between the Gospels of Matthew and Luke has identical Greek vocabulary it makes sense to regard Q as a written document. Jesus' sayings were originally in Aramaic and had to be translated into Greek. The chances of Matthew and Luke both translating Jesus' sayings into identical Greek are non-existent. Therefore both must be working with the same Greek translation of his words. But is the Q hypothesis really the best way to deal with the relationship between the Gospels of Matthew and Luke?

The 'Case Against Q'

The Q theory has certainly been an effective and useful strategy, but there is only circumstantial evidence for it and in recent years it has come under some sustained criticism, though it continues to be widely accepted. What then is the 'case against Q'?

For a start there seem to be several examples of Luke preferring Matthew's longer version of some episodes. The temptations of Jesus are a good example: Mark simply notes that Jesus was tempted, Matthew adds the detailed threefold story of Jesus' testing, which Luke shares but characteristically reorders (see Mark 1.13; Matt. 4.1–11; Luke 4.1–13). In general, where Matthew has added to Mark's account, Luke prefers Mark's version. But Luke's aims were wider and more ambitious and this led him to simplify and précis his sources. So it is not surprising that Luke often prefers Mark's terser approach, nor that occasionally he uses Matthew's material when it suits his purposes.

The last point is a crucial one. The usual arguments for Q tend to see the source relationship between the Gospels of Matthew and Luke in a fairly mechanical way, overlooking the slant or 'spin' which each has introduced. If we take the different perspectives of Matthew and Luke into account we can see that the differences between the two versions of the Beatitudes, for example, make sense. Luke's focus on the poor and hungry in the Beatitudes fits perfectly with his concern for them throughout his Gospel. Matthew's emphasis on piety, a major theme of his Gospel, is also reflected in this passage. The birth stories are another example; though the accounts differ substantially, they have a surprising number of details in common: the placing of the birth in Bethlehem, Joseph's name, the idea that Mary was a virgin when Jesus was conceived. There is no direct contradiction between the two accounts, rather a striking difference of focus.

What about the argument that, if Luke used both the Gospels of Mark and Matthew, he seems to have treated the former with great care and the latter much more freely? This is overstated; we saw earlier that, while Luke observed Mark's order for the miracles, he redistributed his parables significantly. Since most of the material which Luke's Gospel shares with Matthew's also consists of sayings and parables, Luke in fact seems to be treating both Gospels in the same way. Why he does not feel free to redistribute the miracles in the same way is unclear to us; but it should not obscure the fact that he reorders Jesus' words with more freedom than his deeds.

Mark Goodacre sums up the 'case against Q' by appealing to 'Occam's Razor', the principle that, in cases of difficulty, the simplest explanation is to be preferred. The simplest explanation on offer here, says Goodacre, is that 'the theory of Luke's use of Matthew enables us to dispense with Q.'[13] Goodacre's arguments are compelling, and I would expect them to enter the scholarly mainstream gradually in the future. The question of Q will remain an open one for a long time to come, and many scholars will be reluctant to give up a theory which underpins much of their work. More research needs to be done to examine the deeply unfashionable but logically possible use of Luke's Gospel by Matthew.

Examining the 'case against Q' helps to make the distinctive character of Luke's Gospel clearer. Goodacre considers that 'Luke avoids his predecessor's more rigid, thematic approach in order to develop a plausible, sequential narrative of the events he sees as having been fulfilled in the midst of his readers.'[14] Whether they had a common source or not, and whatever the precise relationship between them is, this is a fairly good summary of the differences between these two Gospels.

Turning the world upside-down

According to Luke, when Paul and Silas arrived in Thessalonica they were greeted as 'those who have turned the whole world upside down' (Acts 17.6). Luke's Gospel differs from the others by making clear the radical and indeed potentially revolutionary implications of the story of Jesus and his followers. It is full of inexplicable reversals of fortune – inexplicable, Luke implies, unless God is behind them – that turn the world upside down.

For an audience hearing Luke's Gospel in the last quarter of the first century the notes of irony would have been deafening. The atmosphere of ancient piety which suffuses the opening scenes could only draw attention to the 'heap of ashes' that Pliny the Elder said the great city had become. How could salvation come from such unpromising ground? Yet the barren Elizabeth becomes pregnant, and the unmarried Mary who is still a virgin conceives (Luke 1.24–38). Jesus' birth is revealed not to the rich and powerful but to poor shepherds (Luke 2.8–18), while in the Temple the teachers of Israel are astonished at the wisdom of their 12-year-old pupil (Luke 2.47). Jesus announces his mission in the synagogue at Nazareth as being 'to bring good news to the poor, to proclaim release to the captives and give sight to the blind, to send out the broken to freedom, and to proclaim a year of the Lord's favour' (Luke 4.18–19); the unstated bad news must be for the wealthy and powerful.

This is a topsy-turvy world, and the parables which fill Luke's Gospel emphasize this. They challenge the conventions of the audience, throwing surprises at the listeners which often hinge on generosity or extravagance and upset the accepted pattern of normality. In the story announced as a single parable which is then told in three parts (Luke 15.3) of the lost sheep, coin and son, a sensible shepherd would cut his losses and certainly not go and search for the 1% of his flock which has got lost (Luke 15.4–7); a woman who is foolish enough to lose a valuable coin probably wouldn't boast about it (Luke 15.8–10); and neither of them would be wise to gather their friends and neighbours together to have a party to rejoice because they would surely end up out of pocket. As for the story of the father whose younger son takes his inheritance and runs off, the voice of sanity is represented by his other son who is diligent and hard-working (Luke 15.11–32). Yet in all three cases Jesus seems to praise extravagant and foolish behaviour, commending what the audience would naturally see as the 'wrong' response as the way of the Kingdom of God.

These reversals reach their climax in the death and resurrection of Jesus. The reversal of death itself is the ultimate act of God. But the theme then continues through Acts; Paul the arch-persecutor becomes the pillar of the Church; his apparent failure in Athens is followed by success in Corinth (Acts 17.16—18.11); the last chapters of the book contain his epic struggle against the odds to reach Rome (Acts 27.1—28.16).

There are echoes of the Hebrew Scriptures in such reversals: barren women who give birth and a shepherd boy who defeated a giant warrior are variations of the same theme (see the stories of Sarah and Hannah in Gen. 18.1–15; 21.1–7 and 1 Sam. 1, and the story of David and Goliath in 1 Sam. 17). But would such a story appeal to Theophilus and his friends, an educated gentile audience?

The reversal theme was also a feature of the Hellenistic-Roman world. The fall of the wise and the mighty underpins Homer's *Odyssey*, for example, as well as Sophocles' dramatic trilogy about Oedipus. The Romans also pondered the fleeting nature of worldly success. As Scipio Africanus watched the smoking ruins of once-mighty Carthage after its savage defeat at the hands of his troops, he wept and explained that his tears were for Rome's own future fate. Theophilus would have recognized a common theme.

There was a further reason why the idea of reversal might have appealed in the later first century. Augustus's consolidation of the Empire in the early first century had been intertwined with the promise of a new golden age, which would last forever. Skilful use of visual propaganda proclaimed the eternal rule of Rome, and after Augustus the cult of the emperors and their families grew and developed rapidly. As Steven J. Friesen observes, the Empire 'constituted a utopian vision that had the misfortune of succeeding. The transcendent claims for the emperor and his rule clashed with obvious contradictions in the experiences of real lives.'[15] Nero's later years of madness and terror shocked many into questioning the Empire's future. Many of the Roman upper classes had participated in his orgiastic excesses, and after his death a new seriousness spread across Roman society. Robin Lane Fox suggests that the last three decades of the first century 'are in part the history of a moral reaction, in part the story of an older generation who were trying to put an inhibited past behind them'.[16] Judaism, an appealing alternative, was itself undermined by the destruction of the Temple in 70. In such a setting, Luke's story of the reversals in fortune and unexpected triumphs of Jesus and his followers would at least have been worth a hearing.

The place of women

Women are more visible in Luke's Gospel than in any of the others, another reversal of the accepted social order of the first century.

Luke's distinctive material brings in the stories of Elizabeth and Anna and the birth of Jesus is told from Mary's perspective, in contrast to Matthew's concentration on the role of Joseph (Luke 1—2). Later in the story Luke introduces the woman who anointed Jesus and was commended by him (Luke 7.37–50), and portrays Jesus as the guest of Martha and Mary, the latter incurring her sister's anger by sitting at Jesus' feet to listen to him, a role normally reserved for men (Luke 10.38–42).

Mary Magdalene, Joanna and Susanna are named among a group of women who supported Jesus (Luke 8.1–3). Compared to the Gospels of Mark and Matthew 'where it comes as something of a surprise to the reader to learn, during the passion narrative, that many women had accompanied Jesus from Galilee ... Luke makes clear that these women disciples were constant companions of Jesus from an early stage'.[17] Not only this, but there is no real distinction between them and the male disciples for Luke: all are following Jesus on the way. This feature is shared by the description of the early Church in Jerusalem which specifically includes Mary (Acts 1.14), and women play an important part in the growth of the Church. Dorcas in Joppa is described as a 'disciple' (Acts 9.36); Lydia from Thyatira is Paul's first convert in Philippi (Acts 16.14–15); leading Greek women in Athens show interest in Paul's preaching, in contrast to most of the men there (Acts 17.4, 12, 34); in Corinth Paul's hosts are the married couple Priscilla and Aquila (Acts 18.2, 18); and at Caesarea, Paul meets Philip's four unmarried prophetic daughters (Acts 21.9).

Two of Luke's unique parables feature women: the lost coin and the bad judge; in the first of these God is compared to the woman (Luke 15.8–10; 18.1–8). It is Luke who introduces the poor widow in the Temple who is commended by Jesus, and also the weeping women of Jerusalem on the way to the cross (Luke 21.2–3; 23.27).

Statements like Peter's sermon at Pentecost (Acts 2.17–18) and Paul's letter to the Galatians (Gal. 3.28) implied a radical equality between men and women, but the early Church was embedded in a society which was deeply unequal and patriarchal in its assumptions. Indeed, the Church seems to have reverted to a more traditional understanding of the role of women by the end of the first century and had certainly done so by the first decades of the second. Yet Luke's Gospel makes women more visible than the other Gospels, and this cannot be accidental. Women feature within an overall social framework which Theophilus would have recognized, but they are in many cases noticed and named by Luke. This too would be a destabilizing and disorientating manifestation of the Kingdom of God for the audience.

There is one curious feature of Luke's Gospel, with regard to women, compared to the others: women are not the primary witnesses of any of Jesus' resurrection appearances. In fact Luke points out that the disciples considered the women's report of the empty tomb as 'silly words' (Luke 24.11). It is Peter who is presented as the first witness (Luke 24.34). This seems to be at odds with the rest of the Gospel.

Interestingly, it is Paul's list of witnesses to the resurrection which most closely parallels Luke's account by failing to mention any women (1 Cor. 15.5–8). Tom Wright suggests that the motive behind their omission is that 'women were simply not acceptable as legal witnesses.'[18] Luke may in fact imply their presence, since the picture he draws of the band of disciples includes women, and he specifies that those gathered in the upper room were 'the eleven and those with them' (Luke 24.33). At this crucial stage in his narrative Luke may not wish to draw attention to the women in case it undermines the credibility of the resurrection, but it is still a strange feature.

Overall, then, Luke portrays women more positively than the other Gospels do, but this is not saying a great deal! Feminist interpreters rightly point out that, even in this Gospel, assumptions of male superiority remain intact, as the example of the resurrection witnesses clearly shows. Nevertheless, Luke brings many women to the surface of his story and enables some different interpretative strategies as a result. Nicola Slee suggests three: 'recovery of neglected texts'; 'reading texts "in memoriam"'; and 'the "golden thread" approach.'[19]

In the first, the interpreter works to articulate the actions and feelings of the women who feature in (or behind) the texts but whose experience is overlooked. An example would be to imagine the story of the prodigal son as told by his mother, who is strangely absent (Luke 15.11–32); or to do the same thing from the point of view of Mary, who scandalously sits like a man at Jesus' feet to listen to his teaching (Luke 10.38–42). This is not an attempt to reconstruct the historical past, but an imaginative attempt to engage with the feelings the interpreter brings to the text.

The second strategy, 'reading texts "in memoriam"', concentrates on women who have been victims of men and seeks to honour them. An example here would be of the prostitute who weeps over and kisses Jesus' feet, wipes them with her hair and anoints them with costly ointment (Luke 7.36–50). This was scandalous and inappropriate behaviour of a highly sexualized kind. Yet it is accepted by Jesus. In interpreting such a passage inevitable questions about sexual abuse arise: what do the words of Jesus about forgiveness mean in that context?

The third, 'golden thread' approach, sees the theme of liberation in the whole of the Bible as an interpretative key and recognizes that it lies behind statements such as 'in Christ there is neither male nor female' (Gal. 3.28). The parable of the widow and the bad judge (Luke 18.1–8), for example, which portrays a strong woman opposing a corrupt male authority figure, can be seen as a significant part of an overall narrative which proclaims liberation to all those who are oppressed, including women.

This last approach may remind us that Luke was attempting to articulate how to live in a new world while remaining firmly embedded in an old one. Like Paul, he did not grasp fully the implications of the Kingdom of Jesus where gender was transcended. But in Luke–Acts he gave some hints of how the radically inclusive Church of Jesus Christ might one day help to bring about huge changes in society.

The place of empire

Luke lays great stress on the importance of the humble and poor in both his Gospel and Acts. To someone like the younger Pliny this would have raised serious questions. We saw that Pliny was baffled by the Christians he arrested in Bithynia in 110. They pledged themselves to do good, kept the peace and were loyal to the emperor. Yet their beliefs were dangerous and subversive, for they were attracting people away from pagan temples. To Pliny it would have been dangerous and subversive to suggest that the poor had a special place in the world.

Romans still shivered at the memory of Spartacus, the former soldier who had led an army of 70,000 slaves in a bid for freedom in southern Italy in 72 BC. The revolt had eventually been crushed, and a 100-mile stretch of the Appian Way into Rome was decorated with crucified slaves at 40-yard intervals to discourage anyone who might have ideas above their station in future.

In this context two issues arise very clearly from the story which Luke told. The first key figure is Jesus, who was executed on a cross; the second is Paul, who had died under Nero. How could a group which celebrated the lives of these notorious troublemakers possibly be tolerated within the Roman Empire?

Alongside the story of how a small group of the poor and humble were used by God to bring good news of salvation to the heart of the Roman Empire, Luke also tends to show the Roman authorities in a good light. Pontius Pilate tells the Sanhedrin and the chief priests no less than three times that he can find no grounds for the death penalty for Jesus, according to Luke (Luke 23.4, 14, 22). This response is also characteristic of Roman officials dealing with Paul in Acts: Gallio in Corinth, Claudius Lysias in Jerusalem, and Festus in Caesarea all see the accusations against Paul as groundless (Acts 18.14–15; 23.29; 25.25). Sergius Paulus, the proconsul of Cyprus, actively believes (Acts 13.12). Lower down the social scale, centurions in Capernaum, Jerusalem and Caesarea, are presented positively (Luke 7.1–10; 23.47; Acts 10.1–33); the centurion at the cross recognizes Jesus as a 'righteous' man, by contrast with the chief priests, the official representatives of righteousness.

Yet the picture of the Roman Empire in Luke–Acts is ambivalent. Though Jesus was declared innocent by Pilate, it was a Roman execution that he suffered, and Pilate is himself declared one of the guilty men by Peter (Acts 4.27). The governor Felix is portrayed as corrupt and inefficient, delaying the process of Paul's case for his own ends (Acts 24.25–6); his successor Festus tries to do a deal with the Jews which will keep the peace at Paul's expense (Acts 25.9–10). Paul's last-minute assertion of his Roman citizenship prevents him from suffering the same fate as Jesus but also pushes him into the slowly grinding machinery that was the Roman legal system, from which he may never have escaped (Acts 22.25; 26.32).

Luke–Acts is not, then, quite the demonstration that Christians have nothing to fear from the Empire or the Empire from Christians that some have argued it to be. The position is more complex than that. Once again, looking at the political situation of the later first century may illuminate what is going on. After the chaotic final years of Nero, and the power struggle that led to the 'year of four emperors' in 69, questions about responsible conduct and government came to the fore in Rome, and across the Empire. During the reign of Domitian (emperor 81–96) some of Nero's excesses were reproduced. Tacitus explored these issues through his history-writing, concluding pessimistically that the imperial regime was fundamentally corrupt. Pliny the Younger was part of the move to 'clean-up' corrupt governing practices in the provinces, which was why Trajan sent him to Bithynia in 109. Many Romans across the Empire were conscious of the dangers of power and wondered how it could be used responsibly. Acts, written while such questions were open for debate, draws attention to corrupt Roman officials such as Felix, whose name was a byword for bad practice, as well as responsible ones. Like Paul's citizenship, the Empire seems to be viewed ambivalently. It is a force for good, through which God may work when honest and moral officials are involved. It can also be evil when administered by the corrupt and immoral.

The spectrum of New Testament views on the Roman Empire is sometimes represented by the two extremes of Romans 13 and Revelation 13. In the former Paul exhorts the Romans to 'be subject to the governing powers, for there is no authority except from God, and the powers there are have been established by him' (Rom. 13.1). In the latter, John sees the power of the Empire as the great beast which makes war on the Church (Rev. 13.7). Steve Walton proposes that Luke–Acts 'falls at *both* ends of the spectrum',[20] affirming responsible use of power but also challenging its misuse. The implication for 'most excellent' Roman officials such as Theophilus or Pliny was that they had nothing to fear from the subversive power of Jesus' followers, so long as they acted justly and honourably.

Such a reading also gives rise to a further, intriguing possibility. The abrupt ending of Acts is one of the book's most noticeable features. Readers over the centuries have been puzzled as to why Luke gives no indication of the outcome of Paul's case at all. Within the context of debate about the appropriate use of power, however, might the open ending not be a way in which Luke challenges Theophilus'? If he were the presiding judge, how would he rule? The technique is familiar on a much smaller scale in parables like the prodigal son, where the audience is left pondering, like the elder son, whether they would join the party or not (Luke 15.25–32).

Knowing the fact which Luke doesn't narrate, that Paul was executed by Nero, then adds a new dimension. Nero was the archetypal corrupt wielder of power and so the verdict Theophilus seems to be invited to give would be more than a legal one. For accepting Paul's innocence would mean also accepting the truth of the whole story: it would be a strong argument for Theophilus to become a believer himself.

Spotlight on the resurrection of Jesus

The first two Gospels are quite reticent about the resurrection of Jesus. Mark, famously, ends his story with the empty tomb and the women fleeing panic-stricken and dumb-struck, with only the promise that Jesus will appear in Galilee (Mark 16.1–8). Matthew adds a little, but not much, more: a brief appearance of Jesus to the women at the tomb, a slightly laborious dismissal of the possibility that Jesus' body might have been stolen from the tomb, and then a farewell appearance on a mountain-top in Galilee (Matt. 28.1–20).

Luke's Gospel is quite different. It goes far beyond its predecessors. After the discovery of the empty tomb it includes the story of Jesus' appearance on the road to Emmaus, his appearance to the 11 disciples and his departure from them near Bethany, caught up into heaven. Luke reprises the story in his second volume, beginning Acts by expanding the ascension story (Luke 24.1–53; Acts 1.1–12).

John's Gospel has even more material about the resurrection than Luke's. There, as with the other three Gospels, we hear of the empty tomb. But John adds a story of Mary Magdalene meeting Jesus outside the tomb, and two meetings of Jesus with the 11, the second of which is for the benefit of Thomas. John's Gospel originally ended there, but the later epilogue relates one further resurrection appearance of Jesus, primarily to Peter, in Galilee (John 20.1—21.25).

There's something a bit strange about the way these later Gospels have so much more material about the resurrection of Jesus than the earlier ones, but also tell quite different stories. Yet Paul, writing a good ten years before any of the Gospels were written, could assume that the Corinthians knew all about the resurrection of Jesus. The words he uses are widely recognized to be a summary of belief which he himself received within a few years of Jesus' crucifixion and which 'was formulated as tradition within months of Jesus' death'[21] (1 Cor. 15.3–8). So the traditions about Jesus' resurrection were known as part of the story of Jesus. But they only appear in the Gospels in any detail with Luke and John. Why is this?

James Dunn suggests that these stories were essentially private traditions rather than public property. The common traditions of Jesus' teaching and his passion, which form the earlier parts of the Gospels, were kept corporately in the memory of the early churches. But the stories of risen appearances belonged to those who had experienced them, not to the Church as a whole. 'The appearances could be confessed by the churches and their teachers. But they were not (could not be) elaborated as stories by elders and teachers, because as stories they belonged first and foremost to the one(s) who witnessed the appearance.'[22] Therefore we would expect them to appear in the later Gospels, simply because the supply of eyewitnesses would have been dying out as the years passed. Thus the reason why the accounts of Luke and John diverge is because they were choosing representative examples of resurrection stories, not attempting any systematic collection of them.

If the question behind the opening paragraphs of each Gospel was 'who was Jesus and where did he come from?', then the obvious question we might expect behind the closing paragraphs might be 'What happened to Jesus and where did he go?' But, perhaps to our surprise, there is fairly limited interest in 'what actually happened' on the third day to Jesus. Historical questions about the events of the resurrection are not asked or answered by these accounts. Instead the emphasis falls much more strongly on 'Where is Jesus *now*?'[23] The only Gospel which takes a slightly different view, indeed seeks to answer the question about what happened to Jesus after the resurrection, is Luke's.

Mark's Gospel is almost off-hand about the resurrection of Jesus. Assuming that the Gospel was intended to end at 16.8, it leaves the story incomplete and without a clear ending. The women arrive at the tomb, find that the stone has been rolled away and meet a young man – clearly meant to be an angel – who points out the emptiness of the tomb to them and gives them a message for the disciples and Peter: 'He goes before you into Galilee. There you will see him, just as he told you' (Mark 16.7). But, as so often with those who follow Jesus in this Gospel, they flunk the test. 'They fled from the tomb for they were gripped by trembling and amazement; and they said nothing to anyone because they were frightened' (Mark 16.8).

What Mark brilliantly draws attention to is the mysterious quality of the event, which the stories of Luke and John inevitably disperse as the risen Jesus interacts with the disciples. The atmospheric setting ('early on the first day of the week, just after sunrise'); the anxiety of the women; their determination to offer a final service to Jesus; the shock and awe of going into the tomb and meeting a mysterious young man there; all these details are brilliantly drawn, so that we experience the scene through the eyes of the women. They flee, struck dumb at what has happened.

Mark preserves the sense of the surprise, the strangeness, the awe at what God has done in their midst. A tidy conclusion would lose that sense. Perhaps this really *is* where he wants to leave his audience.

Indeed, the interesting thing about this ending is that dramatically it works when the whole Gospel is read as a performance piece. An audience's imaginative response is to follow the women as they run, helter-skelter, away from the tomb, heading to Galilee. It points to the future and its simplicity avoids the anticlimax of attempting to describe the risen Jesus. I remember being part of a theatre group which attempted to dramatize the resurrection. In the end we simply turned a spotlight onto the audience. Mark faced the same dramatic challenge and met it brilliantly. If Dunn is right, then in its original setting Mark's scene at the empty tomb might have been followed by the testimony of one of those who had a personal story to tell of a meeting with the risen Jesus. And, although there is no evidence that it was ever used this way, it has often struck me that a perfect response to this unresolved end would be the liturgical dialogue at the opening of the eucharistic prayer: 'The Lord is here ...'

So if Mark is off-hand about the events of the resurrection it is probably not because he thinks they are unimportant, but because he does not want his audience to be stuck there, looking back. Instead he wants them to look forward to the day when they will themselves meet Jesus Christ, when he comes in power and glory (Mark 13.26).

Matthew presumably found Mark's approach to telling the story of the resurrection too risky. Uniquely among the Gospel writers he gives a preview of the resurrection in the story of the crucifixion. The sequence of events there is paralleled by what happens three days later: there is an earthquake, tombs open, the dead are raised, the guards fear and the witnesses are women (Matt. 27.51–5; 28.2–8). Matthew is keen that his hearers do not miss the significance of Jesus' return from the dead. Earthquakes and angels were widely recognized eschatological symbols: 'Jesus' resurrection is an end-time event ... the end of the world in miniature'[24] (see Matt. 24.7, 31; Mark 13.8, 27; Luke 21.11). The angel at the tomb is not Mark's understated young man in a white robe but a full-dress member of the heavenly host: 'His appearance was like lightning and his garment was white as snow' (Matt. 28.3).

There are signs that Matthew is answering the most obvious questions about the resurrection. How do you know that the empty tomb was the right one, or that the body was not stolen? There were guards there. How then was the stone moved? An angel did it. Why were the women so frightened? The angel was terrifying and they must have thought the end of the world had come. Why did the guards not tell what had happened? They were bribed to keep quiet.

The angel's message to the women is the same as it was in Mark's Gospel. They must go to Galilee and there they shall meet Jesus. They leave the tomb, but their fear in Mark's version is replaced by joy, and they do not keep silent but rush to tell the disciples what they have seen and heard.

On the way, however, they meet Jesus himself. Their appropriate response is one of worship – an interesting echo of the story of Thomas which John will later tell. They hold on to Jesus' feet, which may be another answer to an obvious question – was the risen Jesus a spirit or still a physical presence? Ghosts don't have feet you can touch (Matt. 28.9–10). But this is only a brief appearance, for Galilee is where the grand climax of Matthew's Gospel will happen.

Although Matthew seems to have felt able to develop Mark's brief resurrection scene he does not seem to have done so with a completely free hand. Tom Wright is probably correct to say that 'Precisely because we can see his hand at work in so much editing, we can also see where he was bound to restrain editorial licence. This was the story all the early Christians knew.'[25] Matthew feels obliged to tell more than Mark, but not as much as Luke and John will do.

And so to Galilee. The scene is strongly reminiscent of Moses' farewell to the people of Israel, on a mountain looking into the promised land (Deut. 34). Though it is very short, a mere five verses, within it are packed connections with the rest of Matthew's Gospel, making it 'almost a compendium of Matthean theology'.[26] Jesus gives instructions to those who will continue his work, on a mountain, as Moses did. Matthew's answer to the question 'Where is Jesus now?' seems to be 'Within the Church', in the activity of 'making disciples of all the nations [that is, significantly, gentiles as well as Jews], baptizing them in the name of the Father, and the Son and the Holy Spirit, and teaching them to keep all my commandments' (Matt. 28.20). The disciples worship Jesus, as the women coming from the tomb did, though reality creeps in for 'some doubted' (Matt. 28.17). Matthew's risen Jesus is a figure worthy of worship, to whom 'all authority in heaven and on earth' has been given, a clear echo of the prophecy in Daniel 7. He towers over Moses, and unlike Moses he will be with them, 'every day till the age comes to an end', a fulfilment of the prophecy made right at the beginning of the Gospel (Matt. 1.23).

Yet Jesus' primary command to the disciples is to go out and continue his work. There is no ascension here, but like Mark, Matthew directs the attention of his hearers into the future – a future which they already occupy. And now they understand why Matthew has laid such stress on Jesus' teaching in his Gospel. For the content of their message is the commandments of Jesus, as well as the story of his life. How they live matters as much as what they say.

This ending, though not as abrupt as Mark's, is also a suspended one. It, too, points to the future, and is full of the conviction that Jesus is alive in the world, and that that is where his followers will meet him. Matthew has embroidered Mark's story but not added much about the resurrection itself. Speculation about it just doesn't seem that important to him.

John's Gospel tells the by now familiar story of the empty tomb. But according to John it was found by only one woman, Mary Magdalene, who then also meets the risen Jesus on her own. Some men, Peter and John, become witnesses of the empty tomb. Then Jesus appears to the disciples, but in Jerusalem not Galilee, and he commissions them and sends them out to continue his work (John 20.1–23). Setting aside the development of details, this seems to be a variation on the basic pattern that Mark and Matthew used: tomb – individual appearances – appearance to the disciples and commissioning. Even some of the details seem, as has happened earlier in John's Gospel, to say similar things to the other Gospels but in a different and more personalized way. So Jesus' warning to Mary Magdalene, 'do not cling to me for I have not yet ascended to the Father, but go to my brothers and tell them ...' (John 20.17) conveys the same thought that Mark and Matthew offer when they direct their audiences away from the tomb and towards the future.

The surprises begin with what was originally the conclusion to the Gospel, a kind of coda which centres on Thomas (John 20.24–9). Thomas is an intriguing character, known ever after for his scepticism, though as David Runcorn says, 'he might equally be remembered for his unfortunate lack of timing. This is the man who managed to miss the resurrection!'[27] The figure of Thomas dramatizes the doubt that Matthew noted among the disciples (Matt. 28.17), and also the failure to believe, which Mark credits to the women at the tomb (Mark 16.8).

John's treatment of Thomas suggests a time when significant questions about the resurrection of Jesus had begun to arise. If John's was the last of the Gospels to reach its final form, perhaps at the end of the first century, we can understand why these questions might have acquired a new force. Those who could say 'I was there' would be virtually all gone. Thomas's failure lay in not trusting the word of his fellow disciples when they said that Jesus had risen. So, by analogy, those who were sceptical many decades later also needed to trust the word of the witnesses, now passed on by the traditions of the Church.

In fact, doubt is also a hidden theme in John's retelling of the resurrection appearances earlier in the chapter, as he subtly anticipates possible questions. Thus, Peter and John become witnesses to the empty tomb, perhaps in case the testimony of the women was not thought to be enough (John 20.3–9); and the physicality which Matthew merely hints at is now emphasized, along with the continuity between the crucified and risen Jesus (John 20.20). But such questions are not really important, suggests John. For these are the kinds of questions which Thomas asks, but when faced with the opportunity to touch the wounds of Jesus he does not need to do so. Like the women and the disciples in Matthew's Gospel, Thomas is compelled to worship and makes the climactic confession of John's Gospel: 'My Lord, and my God!' Jesus responds with words that echo across the decades to the doubters: 'Is it because you have seen me that you have believed? Blessed are the ones who have not seen but have believed' (John 20.28–9). Like Mark and Matthew, John is not really interested in offering information about the resurrection of Jesus. He is much more concerned to encourage others to believe (John 20.31) and to continue Jesus' work, as the disciples were commissioned to do (John 20.22–3).

The encounter between Jesus and Thomas forms a perfect end to John's Gospel, as it was evidently intended to do (see John 20.30–1). But at some point a further resurrection story was added, an appearance to the disciples in Galilee. There is no sign that John's Gospel ever circulated without this epilogue.

The scene takes the audience back to Galilee and the early parts of the Gospel, and to fishing once again. There are some unusual features of this story. Peter is clearly the leader here, as he appears in the synoptic Gospels, but is not in John's (John 21.3). And the carefully worked out structure of John's Gospel, which has offered the perfect number of seven signs of Jesus' power, seems to be supplemented by another sign here.

The story falls into two parts: the appearance of Jesus and a shared meal, and the rehabilitation of Peter. The appearance of Jesus and the meal includes a huge catch of fish, 153 of them. So precise a figure is obviously meant to carry significance, but it's not clear what it is. (Many commentators have noted that it is a triangular number, the sum of the first 17 numbers, and represents completeness in some way, though not explicitly so.)

Jesus' encounter with Peter is a charming story of forgiveness, but also includes a note of commissioning. Peter's story had been left unresolved in the main body of John's Gospel. He had denied Jesus (John 18.15–18, 25–7, see also John 13.37–8); and though a witness of the empty tomb, he had not understood its significance (John 20.8–9). This epilogue therefore tidies up any possible misunderstanding that Peter was a faithless and failed disciple. Jesus puts the question to Peter three times, 'do you love me?' in parallel with his three denials (though John's Gospel only contains two of them). In return for Peter's pledge of love he is given the commission to take care of the flock Jesus leaves behind (John 21.15–17). But then a darker note intrudes, and Peter's death is predicted by Jesus and remembered by the writer. This is what obedience to the command 'Follow me' will mean for him (John 21.18–19). It does not mean martyrdom for all, however, and the peaceful (and probably recent) death of the 'beloved disciple' whose testimony lies behind the Gospel is explained (John 21.21–4). Andrew Lincoln sums up that 'Disciples are to be faithful followers in whatever role the risen Lord assigns them.'[28]

John's Gospel does leave a few loose ends, however. Most significantly the text alludes to Jesus' ascension but does not narrate it (John 20.17). So John doesn't clearly answer the question 'Where is Jesus now?' He is close to Matthew in seeing the continuing life of Jesus in the work of his disciples, but the presence of Jesus is also mediated through the Holy Spirit, breathed into them (John 20.22, see also John 16.7).

This epilogue to the Gospel answers some questions but leaves others open. The writer explains that all the books in the world would not be enough to hold the tales he could tell about Jesus (John 21.25). The end of this Gospel, like those of Mark and Matthew, is in a sense ragged and unfinished. For the story continues.

Luke's Gospel is different. Mark, Matthew and John give an impression of an indeterminate period during which the risen Jesus appeared to his disciples. They do not attempt to give a definitive account of this time, nor do they say how it ends. They just seem to expect their fellow Christians to know, or not to be bothered by the question. Luke has committed himself to write for Theophilus in 'an orderly way' (Luke 1.3), and the raggedness of the accounts of the resurrection seems to have been a challenge to him. How could he order them and make them tidy?

The traditions about the resurrection of Jesus included appearances in both Jerusalem and Galilee. Mark sees Galilee as the place where Jesus will be revealed. Matthew tells the story of what happened in Galilee, but adds a brief preliminary appearance in Jerusalem. John too ends the story in Galilee, but with a significant role now for earlier appearances in Jerusalem.

Luke's Gospel locates all the appearances of Jesus in Jerusalem, and concentrates them into a single day (Luke 24), reminiscent of Mark's similar 'day-in-the-life' approach at the beginning of his Gospel (Mark 1.21–45). He creates a beautifully balanced and choreographed narrative, 'a small masterpiece'.[29] The centrepiece is the appearance of Jesus on the road to Emmaus, which none of the other Gospels even mention. Luke's writing invests the story of Cleopas and his companion with a rich emotional intensity, so that the audience travels the road with the disheartened disciples, and feels their shock, surprise and joy when Jesus' familiar bread-breaking action makes his presence plain to their eyes. Then we are on more familiar ground, as Jesus appears to his disciples, shows them his wounds, and eats with them. Finally he leads them out to the Mount of Olives and 'moved away from them and was carried up into heaven' (Luke 24.51). The disciples worship Jesus, just as they do in the climaxes of the Gospels of Matthew and John, before returning to Jerusalem.

This is the only account in the Gospels of Jesus' ascension, although John's alludes to it (John 20.17). Luke thus gives a clear and unambiguous answer to the question 'Where is Jesus (physically) now?' He is in heaven.

It was a widespread early Christian belief that 'God lifted [Jesus] up and gave to him the name above every name' (Phil. 2.9, see also 1 Tim. 3.16). If Jesus was 'the son of God from the heavens, whom he raised from the dead', who 'will come down from heaven' (1 Thess. 1.10; 4.16), then Luke logically enough, wants to tell his audience how he ascended to the heavens.

The story invokes the departure of two of the heroes of the Hebrew Scriptures who had played a pivotal role in Jesus' transfiguration: Elijah and Moses (Luke 9.29–31; 2 Kings 2.11; Deut. 34.6; in the first century Moses, whose tomb was unknown, was believed to have been taken up to heaven in a cloud[30]). But, as is often the case with Luke, the story would also have had a double resonance. Subjects of the Empire were accustomed to accounts of emperors becoming gods after they died, as their souls ascended heavenwards, usually witnessed by a couple of companions. Yet there are also crucial differences between Luke's story of the ascension of Jesus and similar Jewish or Roman stories. For Jesus had, of course, gone through the experience of death and come out on the other side. Therefore Jesus is a more significant figure even than the holiest prophets or the most powerful rulers.

Luke only gives his audience two resurrection appearances by Jesus (another, to Peter, takes place 'off-stage', Luke 24.34). In each of them Jesus emphasizes how his suffering and death connect not just with his overall mission, but with the plan of God for salvation. The travellers heading to Emmaus occupy the time with an extensive Bible study, 'beginning from Moses and all the prophets he opened up to them what was said about him in all the Scriptures' (Luke 24.27). And when Jesus meets his disciples he reminds them that he had predicted his passion (Luke 24.45–6). The repetition underlines the significance of what Jesus says to the disciples. What has just happened in Jerusalem is the point on which the salvation of the world turns, the fulfilment of the prophecies of old.

Because Luke has a sequel in mind, we can almost sense the caption 'To be continued ...' at the end of his book. He uses an 'overlapping' device, which Morna Hooker points out is characteristic of 'some of the historical books of the Jewish Scriptures',[31] and will reprise the story at the beginning of Acts (Acts 1.1–11). This second bite at the ascension story changes the time frame of Jesus' post-resurrection presence with the disciples from a single day to 40 (Acts 1.3). Luke's total lack of embarrassment about the contradiction suggests that neither figure is meant to be taken literally. Instead, more in line this time with the other Gospels, Luke sees the life of Jesus continuing in the life of the Church (this is the force of 'began' in Acts 1.1). Like John, Luke wants to emphasize the role of the Holy Spirit as the continuing power and presence of Jesus (Luke 24.49; Acts 1.5, 8; 2.1–4). The specific story of Jesus is ended. With his departure to heaven the transition to the third act of God's history of salvation can begin.

Draw your own conclusions

- What advice do you think Luke would have given to Pliny about what to do with the Christians in Bithynia?
- When do you think Luke–Acts was written?
- What makes Luke–Acts different from the other Gospels?
- Does Luke's emphasis on order and structure make his work more or less historically useful?
- Do you think the census happened as described in Luke 2? Does it matter whether it did or not?
- How would you say Luke portrays Jesus in his Gospel?
- What is your evaluation of the 'case against Q'?
- Did Luke break new ground in his portrayal of women as disciples of Jesus?
- What, in Luke's eyes, should be a Christian attitude to the state?
- Why does Luke lay such a strong emphasis on the resurrection of Jesus?

Further reading

Commentaries

L. T. Johnson (1991), *The Gospel of Luke* and (1992), *The Acts of the Apostles*, Collegeville: Liturgical Press, is the best commentary on both Luke and Acts. Though now dated, G. B. Caird (1963), *St Luke*, Harmondsworth: Penguin, is still clear and full of good sense. C. F. Evans (2009), *Saint Luke*, 2nd ed., London: SCM Press, is a heavyweight in all senses of the word. D. J. Williams (1990), *Acts*, Peabody: Hendrickson, covers Acts well.

Other books

J. B. Green (1995), *The Theology of the Gospel of Luke*, Cambridge: Cambridge University Press, surveys the widespread appreciation of

Luke's role as a theologian, something first raised by H. Conzelmann (1960), *The Theology of St Luke*, London: Faber, the original German title of which (*Die Mitte der Zeit*, 'the centre of time') more aptly summarizes the author's argument. Luke's special awareness of the role of women is examined in A. J. Levine and M. Blickenstaff (eds) (2001), *A Feminist Companion to Luke*, Sheffield: Sheffield Academic Press.

For discussion about the historical value of Acts (and by implication of Luke) see the previous chapter on Paul.

On the narratives of the resurrection of Jesus in the four Gospels, see the comprehensive treatment in N. T. Wright (2003), *The Resurrection of the Son of God*, London: SPCK, Part IV. Far shorter but packed with insight is M. D. Hooker (2003), *Endings: invitations to discipleship*, London: SCM Press.

Websites

- Links to general resources on Luke can be found at www.textweek.com/mtlk/luke.htm.
- Luke's arrangement of his sources can be seen at a glance at 'Color-coded Luke' developed by James Tabor at www.religiousstudies.uncc.edu/jdtabor/luke.html.
- There is 'A Synoptic Gospels Primer' at www.virtualreligion.net/primer/; and the Gospels arranged in parallel can be found at www.utoronto.ca/religion/synopsis.
- Mark Goodacre offers common passages viewed synoptically at www.markgoodacre.org/maze/synopses.htm and also provides a good introduction to 'The Case Against Q' at www.markgoodacre.org/Q/.
- Stephen Carlson hosts a 'Synoptic Problem Web Site' at www.hypotyposeis.org/synoptic-problem/ and offers some interesting thoughts on the Census in Luke 2 on 'Hypotyposeis' at www.Hypotyposeis.org/weblog/2004/12/putting-luke-22-in-context.html

Notes

1 R. Lane Fox (2006), *The Classical World*, 2nd ed., London: Penguin, p. 569.

2 Pliny the Younger, *Letters* 10.96.

3 Irenaeus, *Against Heresies* 3.1.

4 H. J. Cadbury (1957), *The Making of Luke–Acts*, London: SPCK, p. 220.

5 J. Nolland (1989), *Luke 1–9:20* Dallas: Word, p. 11.

6 M. Hengel (2000) *The Four Gospels and the One Gospel of Jesus Christ*, London: SCM Press, p. 111.

7 Fox, *The Classical World*, p. 339.

8 Kenneth S. Sacks (1998), 'Hellenistic Historiography' in S. Hornblower and A. Spawforth (eds), *The Oxford Companion to Classical Civilization*, Oxford, Oxford University Press, p. 345.

9 D. P. Moessner (2005), 'How Luke Writes' in M. Bockmuehl and D. A. Hagner, *The Written Gospel*, Cambridge: Cambridge University Press, p. 166.

10 J. D. Crossan (1991), *The Historical Jesus: the life of a Mediterranean peasant*, San Francisco: HarperCollins, p. 372

11 M. Goodacre (2001), *The Synoptic Problem*, London: Sheffield Academic Press, p. 127 (emphasis removed).

12 G. N. Stanton (1989), *The Gospels and Jesus*, Oxford: Oxford University Press, pp. 87–8.

13 Goodacre, *The Synoptic Problem*, p. 160.

14 Goodacre, *The Synoptic Problem*, p. 161.

15 S. J. Friesen (2001), *Imperial Cults and the Apocalypse of John*, New York: Oxford University Press, p. 131.

16 Fox, *The Classical World*, p. 507.

17 R. J. Bauckham (2002), *Gospel Women*, Grand Rapids: Eerdmans, pp. 112–13.

18 N. T. Wright (2003), *The Resurrection of the Son of God*, London: SPCK, p. 607.

19 N. Slee (2003), *Faith and Feminism*, London: DLT, pp. 19–21.

20 S. Walton (2002), 'Luke's View of the Roman Empire' in P. Oakes (ed.), *Rome in the Bible and the Early Church*, Carlisle: Paternoster, p. 35.

21 J. D. G. Dunn (2003), *Jesus Remembered*, Grand Rapids, Eerdmans, p. 855 (emphasis removed).

22 Dunn, *Jesus Remembered*, p. 863.

23 J. Fenton (1993), 'The Four Gospels: Four Perspectives on the Resurrection' in P. Avis (ed.), *The Resurrection of Jesus Christ*, London: DLT, p. 49 (emphasis added).

24 W. D. Davies and D. C. Allison (2004), *Matthew: a shorter commentary*, London: T.&T. Clark, pp. 541, 544.

25 Wright, *Resurrection*, pp. 641–2.

26 Davies and Allison, *Matthew*, p. 548.

27 D. Runcorn (2006), *Rumours of Life*, 2nd ed., London: SPCK, p. 95.

28 A. T. Lincoln (2005), *The Gospel According to St John*, London: Continuum, p. 522.

29 Wright, *Resurrection*, p. 647.

30 Josephus, *Antiquities* 4.8.

31 M. D. Hooker (2003), *Endings: invitations to discipleship*, London: SCM Press, p. 51.

8

John – Apostle and Prophet

Smyrna, 155

Polycarp walked into the amphitheatre at Smyrna in Asia Minor on 23 February 155. He was met by a wall of noise, the cheers and boos of a crowd hungry for spectacle, excitement, danger and bloodshed. Spanish bullfights are the last remnant of the Roman games today, still staged in an intense and intimate arena, the original theatre of cruelty. But Polycarp had not come to fill the role of *toreador*: he was there to play the bull. It was his blood which the crowd had come to see.

Polycarp stood before the Roman governor. He was a very old, very proud and very stubborn man. The governor spoke kindly, out of respect for Polycarp's age, and asked him to swear an oath to the emperor. It would be enough to get Polycarp off the hook. But Polycarp did not respond. The governor invited him to condemn his own faith by saying 'down with the infidels.' Polycarp looked around at the yelling crowd before glancing up to the sky. He gestured to them: 'Down with these infidels' he said gruffly to the governor.

Polycarp had been bishop of Smyrna, 30 miles north of his native Ephesus, for more than half a century. As a young man, it was said, he had known John the apostle and others who had been eyewitnesses of Jesus. He was one of the last to have known those who had known Jesus. Irenaeus, who also came originally from Ephesus, remembered Polycarp well. For Irenaeus, this link with Polycarp, and through him to the teaching of the apostles, guaranteed the authenticity of the traditions about Jesus which he had received. By the mid second century, conflict between those like Polycarp who insisted they were in touch with the apostles' interpretation of Jesus and those (usually called Gnostics) who took different views had become vicious. Polycarp was outspoken in his refusal to have anything to do with the Gnostics. He would refuse to argue with those he disagreed with, putting his fingers in his ears and crying out 'O good God, why have you brought me to this, that I should suffer such things?'[1] before running out of the room. When he met Marcion, who tried to reduce the four Gospels to one, in Rome once, Marcion asked if Polycarp knew who he was. Polycarp growled in reply, 'I know the first-born of Satan.'[2]

So Polycarp had never been ready to compromise, as the governor found. He asked Polycarp for a final time to recant his faith in Jesus. But Polycarp would not: 'Eighty and six years have I served him, and he has done me no wrong. How then can I blaspheme my king and my saviour?'[3] Polycarp was burned to death and his bones preserved by the local church as a reminder of his sacrifice. His martyrdom was powerful propaganda for his beliefs.

The Gnostic groups which Polycarp and Irenaeus opposed rarely produced martyrs. Gnostic teachers saw the physical realm as a distraction from the spiritual realities which they believed Jesus had come to illuminate. To them Polycarp's death was a tragic mistake. For most Gnostics, Jesus' suffering and death had been an appearance only: how could they be real, the Gnostics argued, if Jesus' nature was divine, for surely a god cannot suffer and die? It was better, they argued, if faced with martyrdom, to deny Christ and make reparations later.

On the other hand, Polycarp and Irenaeus emphasized the human suffering and physical death of Jesus; for them a martyr's death was a literal imitation of Christ, and beyond it lay the promise of a bodily and physical resurrection: they really did not believe they had anything to lose. As Elaine Pagels remarks, 'the attitude towards martyrdom corresponds to the interpretation of Christ's suffering and death.'[4] The passion and commitment of the martyrs who followed Polycarp's example reinforced their message. Tertullian, late in the second century, said 'the more we are cut down by you, the more we grow: the seed is the blood of Christians.'[5] The Jesus followed by the martyrs was real flesh and blood. As he had experienced suffering and death so he had also, in their eyes, wholly shared their human experience.

The conflict between rival understandings of Christianity dominated the story of the Church in the second and third centuries and was only really resolved at the insistence of Christian emperors after Constantine, who wanted an 'approved' version. The roots of the conflict can be seen in the New Testament most clearly in the writings associated with John. These writings signify a shift in emphasis. They have more in common with Polycarp than Paul. For Paul, the major conflicts were to establish the Church's differences from Judaism (while still retaining a common theological background) and paganism (while still appealing to many gentiles from a pagan background). For the Gospel, the letters and Revelation of John the questions are internal ones about a Christianity which has grown beyond its Jewish roots and become a predominantly gentile movement. It is under attack from without, but perhaps more importantly also from within. Though there are differences between the letters, Gospel and Revelation of John, they are united in responding to a situation of conflict, where the truth is under attack.

John, disciple and apostle

What relationship the writings ascribed to John, and the situations which gave rise to them, have to the disciple and apostle of the same name is extremely hard to say. Our knowledge of John is very limited and what information there is in the New Testament relates to the first few years of the church in Jerusalem. Irenaeus said that John's death occurred 'in the reign of Trajan' (98–117); he seems also to say that John had been seen 'not long ago, almost in our own time, towards the end of the reign of Domitian'[6] (81–96), but it is unclear from the context whether Irenaeus had John himself or the book of Revelation in view. There is a faint suggestion that he might have been martyred like his brother James, but the view that John lived to an old age in Ephesus was almost unanimous in the early Church, and there are references to his tomb in the city from the late second century. Yet it is a big jump to move from Jerusalem in the 40s to Ephesus in the 90s: the situations were very different. What can we say with any certainty about John in the New Testament?

In the first three Gospels John is called to discipleship by Jesus; he and his brother James are described as sons of Zebedee and fishing partners with Simon and Andrew (Mark 1.19; Matt. 4.21; Luke 5.10). John is always listed in the first four among the disciples, with Peter, Andrew and James (Mark 3.16–19; Matt. 10.2–4; Luke 6.13–16). He and James, with Peter, seem to have been closest to Jesus and accompanied him, for example, as he went to heal Jairus's daughter, up the mountain of transfiguration, and into the garden of Gethsemane (Mark 5.37; 9.2; 14.33; Matt. 17.1; 26.37; Luke 8.51; 9.28). These three with Andrew are the ones who listen to Jesus' predictions of the doom of Jerusalem (Mark 13.3), while it is Peter and John who are entrusted with the important task of preparing for the Passover (Luke 22.8).

According to Mark's Gospel the two sons of Zebedee were given a nickname by Jesus: '*boanerges*', which means 'sons of thunder' (Mark 3.17). What this signified is hard to say, but the brothers are the cause of an argument among the Twelve because they ask for the top seats in the Kingdom (Mark 10.35–41; Matt. 20.20–4) and they also call for Jesus to blast an unsympathetic Samaritan village with fire (Luke 9.52–6). In both cases their requests are not granted. On the basis of these stories the nickname has been thought by many to refer to the impetuous character of the two brothers.

After Pentecost, John came much more to the fore according to Acts. He was involved in the healing of a man in the Temple, brought before the Sanhedrin and was sent to the Samaritans to see what had happened among them as a result of Philip's ministry (Acts 3.1–10; 4.1–22; 8.14–25). Bearing in mind the close connection of Luke's Gospel and Acts it is likely that Luke intended his audience to pick up the irony in the last of these episodes. The disciple who had once called for fire to fall on the

Samaritans now recognizes the coming of the fire of the Holy Spirit upon them. Yet in Acts John is hardly ever mentioned in his own right, being portrayed as 'simply the "sidekick" of Peter, having no voice or function of his own'.[7] He fades from the picture as Peter does, mentioned finally as the brother of James the first of the apostles to be martyred (Acts 12.2). Paul includes him as one of the 'pillars' in Jerusalem around 48 (Gal. 2.9). After that all trace of him vanishes, except for the connection of John, the author of Revelation, with Patmos (Rev. 1.9).

In this chapter we shall explore Revelation, the book which explicitly claims to be written by John (Rev. 1.1). In the following one we shall look at the letters and the Gospel which are attributed to him.

John the author of Revelation

The author of Revelation introduces himself simply as John, the slave of Jesus Christ (Rev. 1.1–2). He clearly commands authority within the seven churches of Asia (Rev. 4.1); this seems to be the authority of a prophet rather than anything else (his call is recorded in Rev. 10.8–11). But he is also their brother and one who has shared with them in 'the troubles, the Kingdom and the endurance in Jesus' (Rev. 1.9). He writes from the island of Patmos (Rev. 1.9), one of the Sporadic Islands, which was maintained by the citizens of Miletus as a defensive outpost for their city in the Aegean. John may have been held prisoner on Patmos, though this is not clear from the text: he simply says he was there 'through the word of God and the witness of Jesus' (Rev. 1.9), which may mean that he had been called there to receive the vision. His comments about the Jews suggest that he also is Jewish (Rev. 2.9; 3.9), while the Greek style of his writing (described as early as the third century by Dionysius of Alexandria as 'barbarous', and recently as 'pidgin Greek'[8]) seems to reflect the thought of someone whose first language is Aramaic.

Though this is sparse evidence on which to base a conclusion, these few indications do seem to fit John the apostle. He does not claim the title of apostle, and mentions the 'twelve apostles' (Rev. 21.14) without apparently connecting himself with them; but since he is describing the content of a vision which he is communicating perhaps this is not so strange. The author seems to expect his name to speak for itself, and to carry its own authority.

Is it plausible that John the Galilean fisherman of the 20s was active as a prophet in Asia Minor in the 70s, 80s or 90s? Although many scholars struggle with this idea it is no stranger than the widely accepted tradition that Peter met his death in Rome in the 60s and wrote to the churches of northern Asia Minor (1 Peter 1.1). There is also good evidence that Philip, one of the seven deacons in Jerusalem, later relocated to Hierapolis in Asia Minor.[9]

Objections to John the apostle's authorship of Revelation began in the third century with Dionysius, but his reasoning stemmed from certainty that the Gospel of John came from the apostle and that therefore the differences in style and content between the two books meant that Revelation must have had a different author. We shall look at the complex question of the authorship of John's Gospel in the next chapter, but if the authorship of Revelation is looked at purely on its own merits there is really only one outstanding candidate: John the apostle.

Yet the discussion reveals a long-standing and early ambivalence about Revelation. It is not comfortable reading, or easily understood. Of all the books in the New Testament, Revelation is the weirdest and the most prone to lead its readers into serious confusion and obsession. To some that has seemed sufficient reason to query whether it could really have come from an apostle. In fact it reveals something of the variety of belief that flourished in the early Church.

Number games

When my wife used to catch the bus home from school, she played a game with her friends by adding up the numbers on the tickets. Any number between 1 and 26 was then converted into a letter of the alphabet by counting A as 1, B as 2 and so on. The object of the game was to find out the initial of the name of the man she was to marry. It is an ancient pastime. Among the excavated ruins of Pompeii are the words, scratched on a wall, 'I love her whose name is 545.' But the knowledge of whose name translated into 545 remains known only to the young man who carved it there just before the city met its fate.

The opening of Matthew's Gospel plays with numbers, but in an amateur way compared to how Revelation makes use of them. The most famous of Revelation's symbolic numbers is the 'number of the beast'. The audience ('if you have understanding') is invited to 'count the number of the beast, for it is the number of a man. And the number is 666' (Rev. 13.18). This game (though it was of course deadly serious in the first century) is sometimes called *isopsephism* in Greek or *gematria* in Hebrew. As with the bus-ticket game, each letter has a numerical value but on a rather more complex basis. So the first nine letters (A–I in English) are numbered 1 to 9, the tenth letter (J) corresponds to 10, the eleventh (K) to 20, and so on up to 100 (S), then 200 (T), 300 (U) and beyond to the end of the alphabet (24 letters in Greek, 22 in Hebrew).

The point of number games was both to conceal and reveal meaning; so the historian Suetonius records the political gossip that surrounded the recognition that both the name Nero and the phrase 'killed his own mother' added up to 1005 in Greek letters.[10] But unless Nero had already been under suspicion no one would have thought to make the calculation. These are codes that only work one way: if you have the answer then hearing the number will confirm it, but if you don't then the possibilities are endless. This simple game is therefore a good way of hiding subversive messages which will not arouse suspicion among those who don't know their meaning.

The word beast in Greek letters does not add up to 666, but if it is transliterated into Hebrew it does:

T R Y V N
400 + 200 + 10 + 6 + 50 = 666

By the same process the Hebrew letters for the Greek name 'Emperor Nero' (*Neron Kaisar*) also add up to 666:

N R V N Q S R
50 + 200 + 6 + 50 + 100 + 60 + 200 = 666.

Proof that the number was widely understood to point to Nero lies in the text of the New Testament itself: many early manuscripts have 616 as the number of the beast, a figure which can be arrived at by the same process, but using Latin rather than Greek as the starting point.

The identity of the beast points to two things which are significant in the study of Revelation. First, the one-way number code and the ease with which it can be cracked if you already know the answer shows that John's aim is to reveal not to conceal meaning from his audience. Second, it locates the book in the second half of the first century and suggests that Nero himself is a significant figure in the background. This is an important clue to when it was written.

The number of the beast

The identity behind the number of the beast has been calculated using number codes in many different ways. One of my favourite recent candidates was Bill Clinton. Since Clinton was the third American president to be called William and the Hebrew letter W (or V) has the value of 6, then the answer of 666 was obvious (wasn't it?)! If you're not convinced you should note that Clinton was the forty-second holder of the office, and that 4 + 2 rather spookily also add up to 6.

Dating Revelation

Several dates have been canvassed over the centuries for Revelation. Irenaeus seemed to date it to the end of Domitian's reign (96) and commentators have suggested evidence of persecution around this time as a setting for the book, as well as Domitian's reputation as the 'bald Nero' (that is, Nero but without the hair or good looks). Others, however, propose a date in 69, during either the short-lived reign of Galba (June 68–January 69) or the beginning of Vespasian's decade in power (69–79).

The dating usually turns on attempts to identify the 'seven kings', of whom 'five fell, one lives and one is not yet come. When he comes he shall stay a short time. And the beast which was and is not, he is an eighth, but also one of the seven, and goes to destruction' (Rev. 17.10–11). The seven kings are associated with a place of seven mountains, which must be Rome, the famous city of the seven hills. As with the number of the beast, the audience is invited to identify the person referred to (Rev. 17.9): we are looking for rulers of Rome, five dead and one still alive when Revelation was written.

The obvious place to start is with Augustus, the first emperor; he and his successors, Tiberius, Caligula, Claudius and Nero, make up the five dead and Galba the one who is living. Galba was soon murdered by his own guards and he was succeeded by three further emperors before the year was out. The next 'king' was Otho, whose disputed three-month reign was short-lived as predicted. This would make Vitellius, the next emperor, the eighth in the sequence, 'who was and is not ... but also one of the seven'.

Accepting this scheme makes Galba the living emperor; but this also makes the time frame for the writing of Revelation incredibly tight: a book written in late 68 could not have come quickly into widespread circulation. And by the time it did the audience would know that Vitellius had been defeated and killed by Vespasian's armies in December 69, invalidating the prediction. In such a situation why would anyone have listened to any more of John's prophecies?

An alternative view omits Galba, Otho and Vitellius from the list on the grounds that they reigned only briefly and did not command widespread allegiance across the Empire. Therefore Vespasian is really to be seen as Nero's successor, which not only gives a much wider time frame but also fits well with the prophecies of what is to come: Titus succeeded his father as emperor but only reigned for a short time (79–81); he was followed by Domitian, who would be eighth in the sequence and was also seen by many as a reincarnation of Nero, who had been one of the original seven. This seems the most likely possibility, except for the fact that no other ancient source discounts Galba, Otho and Vitellius from a list of emperors.

Irenaeus apparently claimed that Domitian was the emperor living at the time Revelation was written. This leads some scholars to count backwards through Titus, Vespasian and the three emperors of 69 to identify the five dead. But the sequence then stops short of Nero who must surely feature in it somewhere if he is 'the beast'. Once again skilful historical gymnastics enable some scholars to find ways of making the list include

Nero, usually by discounting those emperors with short reigns, but the attempts are not very convincing. On the other hand, if the sequence started with Nero then Titus would have been the reigning emperor. On the face of it this seems appealing. Domitian then becomes the emperor who is to come and the eighth emperor is interpreted as Nero returned from the dead, an event expected on a fairly widespread basis across the Empire (a pretender claiming to be Nero raised an army in the east in 80, though his campaign against Titus seems to have come to nothing; another claimant did the same thing in Domitian's reign).

It is ironic that, in the midst of a book so heavy with symbolism, commentators have tended to demand such a literal interpretation of this particular passage of Revelation. John may have intended to identify the individual rulers, but perhaps it is more likely that the number seven was symbolic, as it frequently is in the rest of the book. Seven usually stands in Revelation for completeness and 'the one point John wishes to emphasize is that the imperial line has only a short time to run before the emergence of a monstrous new Nero'.[11] This interpretation seems to make most sense in terms of the wider themes of Revelation, which predict the ultimate ruin of Rome and Roman power. The only time reference that can be derived is that Nero is one of the dead five emperors (and most commentators identify him as the charismatic beast healed of a mortal wound, Rev. 13.3).

The price of accepting a symbolic interpretation of this passage is to let go of any prospect of dating Revelation from its text. Some see details such as the description of the earthquake which happens at the opening of the sixth scroll as reflecting the eruption of Vesuvius in 79 (Rev. 6.12–17); others read the command for John to measure the temple as proving that the book must have been written before the destruction of Jerusalem in 70 (Rev. 11.1–3). In fact the only lower limit on a date for Revelation comes from recognizing that Nero is among the dead emperors: therefore it cannot have been written before 68. There is no upper limit. All we can say is that it is likely to have been written before the end of the first century.

The situation of Revelation

The first word of Revelation in Greek is *Apokalypsis*, meaning an unveiling. This allies it with a particular style of writing which had been popular in Jewish circles for a couple of centuries. It was a relatively late development out of the well-established genre of prophecy. The book of Daniel, probably written in the mid second century BC, is usually reckoned to be the first apocalypse, though elements of apocalyptic can be found in earlier Hebrew prophets. Other Jewish apocalypses, like Daniel itself, were written in the names of such long-dead people as Ezra, Enoch and Abraham.

Some examples of apocalypses in circulation in the first century have been found among the Dead Sea Scrolls. The remaining fragments of the War Scroll depict the final conflict between the powers of light and darkness in a seven-year war, at the end of which the Roman Empire (known by a pseudonym) is defeated by the armies of God. The War Scroll includes detailed instructions as to how the army of God is to be dressed, and even how deep their camp toilets should be dug! After the final battle, Israel will rule over the defeated nations and the poor, by the power of God, will be vindicated. The Temple Scroll includes a description of a new Temple which would have extended from the centre of Jerusalem right across the Kidron valley and up to the Mount of Olives (an architectural and engineering impossibility, but that is the glory of visions). It was to be built in three concentric squares. The first two squares would have three gates in each wall, making a total of twelve gates, each carrying the names of one of the tribes of Israel. In the central square an angel measures the dimensions of the buildings, which the writer then reports as what he had seen in a vision. The parallels between these two scrolls and Revelation's description of a war led by the Lamb and the coming of the new Jerusalem are not hard to see. It is important to notice too that Revelation is the story of the opening of a scroll (Rev. 5.1).

Yet Revelation is also different from these apocalyptic writings from Qumran. It begins as a series of letters, which seem to be prophetic rather than apocalyptic (Rev. 1—3). It also narrates essentially a single vision, rather than several. Perhaps most importantly it is not written in the name of an ancient faith-hero but by someone well-known to contemporaries. The significance of these differences is to ground the vision much more clearly in a historical situation. This book is a vision of 'what is soon to take place' that invites the audience to share the writer's perspective, which he says has been given to him by God himself (Rev. 1.1).

The destination cities of the opening sequence of letters follow exactly the route of the messenger who would carry them. This clearly shows that John was writing to real churches and with a real grasp of the challenges which faced them. There are strong connections between the prophetic messages contained in the letters and the local circumstances of the churches to which they are addressed:

- Those 'who overcome' in Ephesus are promised the right to eat from the tree of life in paradise (Rev. 2.7); the great temple of Artemis included a tree-shrine where slaves who sought asylum could gain their freedom.
- Thyatira supported a well-known metal industry and the image of Christ for them is one 'whose feet are like burnished bronze' and those who overcome will be rewarded with an 'iron sceptre' (Rev. 2.18, 27).
- The Laodiceans receive the sharpest rebukes and are castigated for being 'lukewarm – neither hot or cold' and urged to buy white clothes

and eye ointment (Rev. 3.16, 18); their city was famous for producing medicines and clothes made of local black wool, and it lay close to the hot springs of Hierapolis, which flowed in a river across the plateau and over a cliff opposite Laodicea where the waterfall left a gleaming white encrustation of lime which could be seen for miles. Drinking this lukewarm, lime-flavoured water would make you feel sick (Rev. 3.16).

As for the challenges the churches faced, John was concerned that the Ephesians had lost their original passion and zeal (Rev. 2.4); that the Smyrneans and Philadelphians were under attack from the local synagogues (Rev. 2.9; 3.9); that the Pergamenes and Thyatirans listened to other prophets and compromised with idol-worshippers (Rev. 2.14–15, 20); that the Sardisian church was in danger of dying out (Rev. 3.2); and that the Laodiceans' wealth had blinded them to true discipleship (Rev. 3.17–18). A group called the 'Nicolaitans' were clearly causing problems across the province (Rev. 2.6, 15). Summarized like this, we can see that the church in Asia was not in the best of health. The vision John had received and wanted to share with them was designed to help them overcome these problems and, perhaps above all, to encourage them to keep going in the face of increasing difficulties. What were those difficulties?

Encountering difficulties

A new religion is a hard plant to grow, especially in such a competitive religious environment as the province of Asia in the first century. Statistics of any meaningful kind are impossible to come by for the growth of Christianity in the first two or three centuries. But it does seem clear that in the early decades the numbers were, compared to the size of the population of a city like Ephesus, tiny; even 1,000 believers (which is probably many more than there actually were) would represent less than 0.5% of the inhabitants. Beginning from such a low base, sociologist Rodney Stark says that 'Progress must have seemed terribly slow during the first century.' In addition the early Christian groups, with their emphasis on caring for the poor and sick and sharing goods, were vulnerable to what Stark terms the 'free-rider' problem, where less committed members join a group for their own benefit without offering anything in return. The solution lies in making 'costly demands',[12] which is exactly what we see in Revelation.

Revelation emphasizes suffering and persecution, but it is significant that this is usually seen as a future possibility rather than a present reality (e.g. Rev. 2.10; 16.6; 17.6). Although armies of martyrs march through its later chapters, the only actual death recorded is that of Antipas of Pergamum (Rev. 2.13). Commentators often read Revelation against a background of persecution of the Church by Domitian and the allegedly aggressive late first-century growth of the emperor-cult. But there is no clear evidence for either of these things. There may have been a short-lived campaign against aristocratic Christians in Rome in 95, but it does not seem to have spread across the Empire. In fact when Polycarp met his end in the arena in 155 he was only the twelfth martyr in the history of the church at Smyrna. Pliny the Younger in Bithynia at the turn of the century was baffled that he could find no crime for which he could justify punishing the Christians he had arrested.

The script from which the Church worked was the story of Jesus of Nazareth, the original martyr. His followers expected to share his sufferings, but it is a striking fact that none of them were executed in the aftermath of his arrest and crucifixion. Indeed, though Peter and John suffered imprisonment in the early days according to Acts, it is the freedom to preach which the church in Jerusalem had that is striking. Stephen, James the brother of John, and James the brother of Jesus were all martyred in Jerusalem, but their deaths were spread over a period of 30 years. Paul and some of his associates were often imprisoned, but rarely for long; Paul escaped execution in Jerusalem by appealing to his Roman citizenship. The only major persecution of the Church in which a large number of Christians died was Nero's in 65. While this event undoubtedly sent a shock wave through the Church and may have caused some to abandon their faith, it seems to have been a one-off event. Probably many more Christians died in the Jewish War of 66–70 than in any first-century campaign of persecution.

If there are no signs that Christians were persecuted into conformity by the authorities, perhaps a more insidious threat was social pressure. Paul's battle in Ephesus had been to establish a distinctive and uncompromising faith in the city, whose followers would not be seduced into a bit of emperor-worship to maintain their social status. Christian Jews could claim existing privileges to exempt them from sacrificing to the emperor. Gentiles who became Christians could not. They faced a dilemma. In some ways the issue is not so different from the way in which, in England between the mid sixteenth and early nineteenth centuries, it was necessary to be a member of the Church of England and swear allegiance to the crown in order to be awarded a degree at Oxford or Cambridge or to become an MP. Refusal to do so meant automatic disqualification from political power and social advancement. As the temples of the emperor-cult spread across Asia in the later first century, and grew grander in style, participation in the cult became an unavoidable part of municipal and social life. These temples, set in the heart of the cities, proclaimed Roman rule and were 'a permanent architectural stage set, against which people played out their lives ... a constant reminder of the emperor ... a unique means of honouring the world ruler on a scale never seen before'.[13] They were an ancient means of mass communication, reinforcing the visual message of Roman cultural, economic and above all political domination. Becoming the *neokoros*, or guardian of the emperor's shrine, was the highest honour available in Asian society by the late first century.

The oldest and most prestigious of the imperial temples in Asia, dedicated to Augustus and Rome, was at Pergamum, the city where 'Satan's throne' is located, according to John (Rev. 2.13). In Revelation the 'Imperial cults are portrayed as deception, a blasphemous lie, one crucial aspect in the Roman practice of dominating and exploiting the world',[14] and the book was written to enable the audience to see what was wrong with the Empire of Rome, as the chilling end to the enumeration of its merchandise shows:

> gold, silver, precious stones and pearls;
> fine linen, purple, silk and scarlet;
> scented woods and ivory goods, precious carvings and bronze, iron and marble;
> cinnamon, spices, perfumes, ointments and frankincense;
> wine, oil and the finest flour, wheat and cattle and sheep and carriages
> – and the bodies and souls of men. (Rev. 18.12–13)

After all, it was the power of Rome that had killed the son of God. How then could people in the churches even think of compromising with it?

This leads Steven J. Friesen to conclude that 'John's critique was not aimed at particular cults or institutions; it was directed at an imperial way of life.'[15] Luke's perspective in Acts was different and ultimately more successful: he saw that the Empire could be an instrument of God for good, though it was not always so. Paul's perspective seems to have been more mixed: the logic of his theology was anti-imperial and caused him problems with the authorities, but his later life under the protection of Roman citizenship had been foreshadowed by his call to the Roman church to 'be subject to the governing powers'. The latter perspective was balanced by a recognition that the present order would not last long (Rom. 13.1, 11–12).

Revelation predicts persecution and martyrdom because the logic of the book sees Roman power as inextricably linked with the power of Satan. This is why Nero, the beast, is such an important figure in Revelation. Romans like Theophilus and Pliny the younger, as well as Christians like Luke, saw Nero as an anomaly and an aberration. Vespasian, and later Nerva and Trajan, were the acceptable faces of Roman imperialism, moderate men who upheld classical values and avoided excess. But John saw Nero as the real face of Rome, the snarling beast revealed behind the actor's comic mask which the emperor had loved to wear. Nero was no aberration for John. The proof lay in his persecution of the people of God.

The cities to which John wrote at the beginning of Revelation were probably good places to live in the second half of the first century, prosperous and peaceful. But the vision which John had seen while on the island of Patmos showed him a different reality. After concluding the seven letters which are addressed as the words of Christ to the churches the scene shifts and the book properly begins, as John's gaze is lifted up and a door into heaven opens upon a new reality (Rev. 4.1).

John's vision

Everyone agrees that Revelation is a carefully structured book; less widespread is agreement on what the structure actually is. Almost as many theories have been proposed as there are commentators, and opinion is divided on whether the book should be read as a linear sequence of visions, a cycle which keeps repeating, or simply the gradual building-up of images into a glorious poem which intuitively conveys John's vision without any logical sequence to it at all.

Alan Garrow divides the book into six fairly equal sections of between 1600 and 2,000 words each. These sections may have been intended to make the text suitable for reading in instalments 20- to 30-minutes long. The instalment-based structure of the book, according to this view, makes it like a television series. Serials often use a 'cliffhanger' technique between episodes, and Garrow neatly illustrates this by a comparison with the TV series *Doctor Who*. He notes that the 'link between the generic characteristics of ancient apocalyptic and contemporary science fiction ... makes an analysis of a science fiction serial particularly appropriate here.'[16] Each section begins as something is opened: heaven (Rev. 4.1), the seventh seal (Rev. 8.1), the temple in heaven (Rev. 11.19), the tabernacle (Rev. 15.5) and finally heaven again (Rev. 19.1). The prelude and introductory sections function as 'foreshadows', which announce 'a future occurrence in the story-line which leaves the audience partially uncertain as to the exact nature or timing of that event',[17] thus creating suspense.

According to Garrow's interpretation, the book falls clearly into a prelude (the letters to the churches) and two introductory sections (the seals and the trumpets) before the opening of the scroll which reveals 'what must soon take place' in the final three sections. The function of each part of the text, once it is analysed this way, becomes much clearer; this is especially true of the apparently anomalous sections, such as the triumph of the Lamb, which seems to be out of sequence and has often puzzled commentators as a result (Rev. 14).

In the reading of Revelation which follows I shall use this interpretation of the text's structure, though it is important to recognize that there are many other ways of looking at it. Figure 16 outlines the structure of the book according to this interpretation.

Prelude: this is the revelation of 'what must soon take place' (1)

Letters to the angels of the churches at

Ephesus	Smyrna	Pergamum	Thyatira	Sardis	Philadelphia	Laodicea
(2.1–7)	(2.8–11)	(2.12–17)	(2.18–29)	(3.1–6)	(3.7–13)	(3.14–22)

A vision of heaven (4)

Introduction of the scroll and the lamb who is worthy to open it (5)

Opening of the seven seals of the scroll

Seal 1	Seal 2	Seal 3	Seal 4	Seal 5	Seal 6
War	Civil strife	Famine	Plagues and death	an army of martyrs	destruction of the earth
(6.1–2)	(6.3–4)	(6.5–6)	(6.7–8)	(6.9–11)	(6.12–17)

Interlude – the sealing of the faithful from twelve tribes and the triumph of the lamb (7)

Seal 7 – whose contents are not revealed. There is silence in heaven for half an hour (8.1–5)

Blowing of seven trumpets
to announce the imminent opening of the scroll

Trumpet 1	Trumpet 2	Trumpet 3	Trumpet 4	Trumpet 5	Trumpet 6
Disasters in the natural world				A plague of locusts	An army from hell
(8.7)	(8.8–9)	(8.10–11)	(8.12)	(8.13—9.12)	(9.13–21)

Interlude – the 'little scroll' and the two witnesses (10.1—11.14)

Trumpet 7 – God's Kingdom announced (11.15–18)

The contents of the scroll part 1 – the cosmic conflict begins

The birth and death of the messiah	War in heaven	The dragon makes war on earth	Two beasts arise
(11.19—12.6)	(12.7–12)	(12.13–17)	(13.1–18)

Interlude – a future vision of the triumph of the lamb (14)

The contents of the scroll part 2 – God's wrath poured out on the earth

Seven angels receive seven bowls of wrath (plagues) (15.1—16.1)

Bowl 1	Bowl 2	Bowl 3	Bowl 4	Bowl 5	Bowl 6	Bowl 7
(16.2)	(16.3)	(16.4–7)	(16.8–9)	(16.10)	(16.12–16)	(16.17–21)

Interlude – a vision of the evil of Babylon (Rome) and its fall (17.1—19.10)

The contents of the scroll part 3 – the final defeat of the beast and the triumph of God						
The beast captured and thrown into a lake of fire	Satan captured and cast into an abyss for a thousand years	Faithful martyrs reign with Christ for a thousand years	Satan released and makes war again. He is cast into the lake of fire with the beast	The final judgement of the dead. Death and hell are consigned to the lake of fire	The new heaven and new earth where God will dwell with his people	The new Jerusalem described
(19.11–21)	(20.1–3)	(20.4–6)	(20.7–10)	(20.11–15)	(21.1–8)	(21.8–22.7)
Epilogue (22.8–21)						

Figure 16 The structure of the Book of Revelation

The throne of heaven and the opening of the seals

The story begins in the heavenly throne-room (Rev. 4.2). The time is the present not the future. Like much of Revelation, this passage is a densely packed tapestry of allusions to the Hebrew Scriptures, though John has used the materials to describe what he saw in a fresh way (compare Rev. 4 with 1 Kings 22.19; Job 1.6; Isa. 6; Ezek. 1.4–28). John finds himself in the operations centre of the high command of heaven, before the throne of God. In the hand of God there is a scroll, but it is closed by seven seals and the writing inside it which will reveal 'what must happen soon' is not yet known.

Who can open the scroll? Only 'the lion of Judah, the root of David' (Rev. 5.5) is able to do so. This title is obvious Christian code for Jesus, and understanding him as the revealer of the mystery of God's plan 'which has for long been hidden' is echoed by Paul (Rom. 16.25).

When John looks for the lion he sees instead a 'lamb that has been slain' (Rev. 5.6). The lamb takes the scroll and is met by an avalanche of heavenly praise: 'Worthy is the lamb' (Rev. 5.12).

One by one the seals are broken by the lamb. The visions connected with the seven seals are not themselves the revealing of 'what must soon take place'. That information is contained inside the scroll itself, and the seals are only the outer packaging. But the seals show what signs will accompany the opening of the scroll. The first four seals reveal messengers, lone horsemen who suggest that, when the scroll is finally opened, it will unleash armies from the east (signified by the bow, Rev. 6.2); civil war (destroying the peace of the Empire, Rev. 6.4); famine (as the Empire's economy collapses, Rev. 6.6); and death itself will stalk the earth as plagues and wild animals are let loose (Rev. 6.8). The fifth seal reveals the cost to the people of God: the righteous victims of what has already been described (Rev. 6.9–11). The sixth seal reveals the destruction of the earth as its people flee from the wrath of the lamb against his enemies in images reminiscent of Pliny the Younger's description of the horrific demise of Pompeii (Rev. 6.12–17).

The first six seals parallel Jesus' words in the apocalyptic passages in the Gospels (Mark 13.7–31; Matt. 24.6–31; Luke 21.9–27). Wars, civil strife, earthquakes and famines, persecutions and natural disasters are listed there, suggesting that John's vision does not stand on its own, but is a development of earlier tradition. There is one significant difference, however, which is that Jesus' apparent prophecies of the destruction of Jerusalem (see especially Luke 21.20) have disappeared. This may suggest that part of John's aim is to reinterpret these images of the coming of Christ in the light of the destruction of the Temple, which might have been expected to be the prelude to the final judgement and wrath of the lamb.

Before the seventh seal is opened there is a pause. As we read through Revelation, we begin to recognize this as a characteristic storytelling device, which heightens the tension and suspense for the audience. Picking up the vision revealed by the fifth seal, John sees the faithful from the tribes of Israel, who are identical with the Church, being sealed with the mark of God (Rev. 7.3). This crowd of 144,000 is 'a multitude no one could count' (Rev. 7.9) and their song of praise proclaims the triumph of the lamb. In the midst of the chaos foreshadowed by the visions of the seals, John's picture of the faithful also foreshadows the final revelation of the new Jerusalem (there are clear parallels between Rev. 7 and Rev. 21).

Finally, at the end of this instalment, the seventh seal which the audience has been anticipating is opened. Now, surely, the contents of the scroll will be revealed. The audience waits with bated breath. But there is silence (Rev. 8.1). Nothing happens.

Revelation and imagination

Revelation calls for an imaginative response. The audience is invited to visualize the amazing images, to hear the sweet music of the heavenly choirs and the harsh dissonances of disasters, to taste and smell the acrid smoke of destruction, and the perfume of incense before the throne. Ian Boxall notes that an hour or so looking at how artists have interpreted Revelation may be more helpful than wrestling with the intricacies of a scholarly commentary. Such exploration is 'to set the exegetical task within a wider framework. For artists, like poets and prophets, have not lost that capacity to see … that which is so often hidden from our eyes'.[18] Revelation engages the senses as no other book in the New

Testament does, and dares its readers to look beyond the world they know and see, to the profound reality that underlies it.

The Victorian poet and Jesuit priest, Gerard Manley Hopkins, wrote that 'design, pattern or what I am in the habit of calling "inscape" is what I above all I aim at in poetry.'[19] 'Inscape' was, for Hopkins, an insight into the ultimate spiritual reality of an object, something he tried to capture in poems like 'The Windhover', which describes the flight of a falcon. His sonnet 'God's Grandeur' is close in vision to Revelation. Though 'The world is charged with the grandeur of God' the footsteps of generations have almost worn its traces away, 'And all is seared with trade; bleared, smeared with toil;/And wears man's smudge'. The inscape of the world, in other words, is hidden and easily missed. Yet, 'for all this, nature is never spent;/There lives the dearest freshness deep down things', and Hopkins closes the poem with the recognition that the cause of this freshness is 'Because the Holy Ghost over the bent/World broods with warm breast and with ah! bright wings.'[20]

Revelation can be read as John's attempt to describe the inscape of the first-century world. Like Hopkins, he can only do so by using images and symbols, metaphors and poetic figures. In particular, he assumes that, besides the world which his audience knows, there is a heaven and an underworld. Much of John's story moves between these different realities and to follow him the inner eye of imagination must be opened.

The seven trumpets

The scene is silent; the audience is reminded by the vivid gold of the altar of the kaleidoscope of colours described earlier (Rev. 4.3). Incense curls upwards and you can imagine the smell as well as perhaps the gentle hiss of the grains as they meet the fire in the censer. Then an angel casts fire on to the earth. Thunder, lightning and an earthquake erupt.

The audience anticipates that, once the seals have been opened, the message of the scroll can be read. But the angels around the heavenly throne receive trumpets to announce the ceremonial opening of the scroll. The next section once again increases the suspense as each trumpet heralds another foreshadowing of the judgement that will fall when the scroll is finally opened. The judgements that fall as the trumpets are blown seem to echo the plagues of Egypt described in Exodus, perhaps pointing to the fact that a new deliverance is at hand.

Before the fifth trumpet sounds the screech of an eagle is heard, announcing that the remaining three trumpets will be accompanied by three woes. This signals that the remaining judgements, like the Exodus plagues, are aimed at those 'who do not wear the seal of God' (Rev. 9.4). The sixth trumpet is accompanied by the coming of a ghastly army from the east mounted on horses breathing fire, smoke and sulphur (not, as some have said, a prediction of gunpowder, but symbols of the underworld showing this to be an army 'straight from the jaws of hell'[21]). Yet, despite this army's awesome destructive power, the people of the world who survive it do not turn to God, just like Pharaoh in the Exodus story (Rev. 9.20–1).

Then, as we might expect from the sequence of seven seals, as the anticipation is heightened, the seventh trumpet about to blow and the contents of the scroll are at last about to be revealed, there is another interlude. Down from heaven comes another angel, holding a 'little scroll' (Rev. 10.1–2). This little scroll has caused immense confusion among commentators, but it seems to function primarily as a confirmation of John's prophetic vocation. Like the scroll given to Ezekiel in Babylon this scroll is not to be read but to be eaten (Ezekiel 3.1–3; Rev. 10.9). Unlike Ezekiel's scroll, which remained sweet, the taste of this one quickly becomes bitter to John's stomach (Rev. 10.9–10), perhaps symbolizing the bitter-sweet balance of joy and sorrow of the story that is about to be revealed.

The strange episode of the two witnesses follows (Rev. 11.1–13). At first sight the city where these events take place is Jerusalem, home of the Temple and the place where Jesus was crucified (Rev. 11.1–2, 8). If this is the case then the two witnesses (or martyrs, the word means the same thing in Greek) might be the two Jameses, brothers respectively of John and Jesus. But the most famous two witnesses, twinned in tradition from early on, were Peter and Paul. It is 'the beast', who has not yet been mentioned or identified but who will later be seen to be Nero, who is the cause of the witnesses' deaths (Rev. 11.7). Rome is always called 'the great city' elsewhere in Revelation (see Rev. 16.19; 17.18; 18.10) and it was also much more likely to be a place where all the nations could see the deaths of two prophets who had 'said terrible things to the people of the world' (Rev. 11.10). As for the city being the location of Jesus' death, his death was brought about by the power of Rome even if it did not take place in the city itself. The important point is that, whoever the witnesses may be, John stresses that after three and a half days they would be vindicated and raised to heaven. Their ultimate fate foreshadows that of all God's people at the end of the book, just as the interlude before the opening of the sixth seal did.

Now, at last, the seventh trumpet sounds. The coming of the Kingdom is proclaimed. This is the end of the instalment and the contents of the scroll can be revealed.

The first part of the scroll – cosmic conflict

The scroll will tell the secret of 'what must soon take place', but first the story backs up a little to reveal that some of what is to take place has already been accomplished. The audience, in other words, suddenly find themselves in the midst of the events which they have come to hear about.

The opening scene narrates the birth and death of the messiah who is raised to heaven, but the woman (the Church) who gave him birth remains on earth (Rev. 12.1–6). There is war in heaven between the angels and the dragon (Satan) who is cast down to earth (Rev. 12.7–12). The dragon on earth makes war on the woman (Church) that gave birth to the messiah (Rev. 12.13–17) and two beasts arise, which worship the dragon (Satan) and also make war on the Church. The beast is identified by the number 666 (signifying Nero) (Rev. 13.1–18).

In the midst of this depressing scenario there is once again an interlude which shows the future triumph of the saints and the lamb and foreshadowing the fall of Babylon (Rome) and the final judgement (Rev. 14). The Church's suffering and struggle will not be in vain. This concludes the first instalment of the scroll.

The second part of the scroll – God's wrath and the destruction of Babylon

In response to the excesses of the beast, the wrath of God is poured out for the last time (Rev. 15.1—16.1). Seven angels receive seven bowls of wrath, which contain plagues. Like the foreshadowing plagues that accompanied the trumpets, these plagues are similar to the plagues of Exodus. First, sores come upon those who worship the beast, then the sea is depopulated (Rev. 16.2–3). The third bowl causes rivers and water to turn to blood, and the fourth to make the sun scorch the people of earth, who continue to curse God (Rev. 16.4–9). At the fifth bowl, the kingdom of the beast is turned to darkness but people still curse God; the sixth bowl dries up the great river the Euphrates. The kings of the earth gather at Armageddon for battle (Rev. 16.10–16).

The seventh bowl follows, which is a surprise, for by now the audience is accustomed to the pattern of an interlude before the final element in a sequence of seven. Instead a voice calls 'It is done' and the 'great city' of Babylon is punished for its sins (Rev. 16.17–21).

Then follows the interlude, closing this instalment. It is a vision of the evil of Babylon and its fall, completed by the rejoicing of heaven over it (Rev. 17.1—19.10).

The final part of the scroll – the defeat of the beast and the triumph of God

A rider on a white horse, the Word of God, leads the armies of heaven to war against the beast, which is captured and thrown into a lake of fire (Rev. 19.11–21). Satan is also captured and cast into the abyss for 1,000 years (Rev. 20.1–3). The faithful martyrs are raised to life and reign with

Christ for 1,000 years (Rev. 20.4–6). After 1,000 years Satan is released from the abyss and makes war again, besieging the faithful, but he is defeated and his army consumed by fire from heaven. He is cast down into the lake of fire with the beast (Rev. 20.7–10). The final judgement of the dead follows. Death and hell are consigned to the lake of fire (Rev. 20.11–15). The new heaven and new earth where God will dwell with his people is described (Rev. 21.1—22.7). The book ends with a brief epilogue.

Reactions to Revelation

John's vision was written with a clear audience in view. In the prosperous cities of Asia where Christianity was becoming a comfortable option, John gave his hearers a glimpse of the hidden reality of the world, setting their existence in a new context. As Richard Bauckham says, the 'power, the profusion and the consistency of the symbols ... create a symbolic world which readers can enter so fully that it affects them and changes their perception of the world'.[22] The very weirdness of the book, which leads many readers today to recoil from Revelation, is what made it appealing in the first century.

By his construction of a way of seeing the universe that offered a radical alternative to the Roman world-view, John was trying to radicalize the Christians of the seven churches. He wanted them to see themselves as a dissident, even deviant, group, at odds with the Empire in which they lived. It is perhaps no accident that language of 'the Kingdom', so rare a feature of Paul's writings, occurs 19 times in Revelation. For John there could be only one king and one kingdom.

John was right to see Nero's attack on the church in Rome and the deaths of Peter and Paul as straws in the wind. The day would come when Empire and Church would clash, and clash violently. Sporadic incidents such as the death of Polycarp finally gave way to deliberate systematic persecution of Christians by the Emperor Decius in 249–51. It reached a horrific crescendo under Diocletian and Galerius in 303–11, when ordinary criminals had to be released from prisons in order to accommodate the thousands of Christians who had been arrested. The Church survived the onslaught, but only just. Shortly after, under Constantine, the tables were turned. In 390, Ambrose, the bishop of Milan, demanded that before receiving communion the Emperor Theodosius should do public penance for ordering the massacre of thousands at Thessalonica. This was the kind of activity that had been the stock-in-trade of many emperors. Remarkably, Ambrose got what he wanted and it seemed that the imperial beast had at last been tamed, as John had believed it would eventually be.

Although there was little persecution in the first century, the rhetoric of martyrdom was well established from very early in the Church's history, partly through the influence of Revelation itself. Deaths that did occur were widely publicized: we have seen how Nero's persecution in Rome brought Christians to Tacitus's attention. We know from our own time the counter-intuitive truth that those who are willing to die for a cause strengthen it, especially through the publicity their actions bring. Perceived martyrdom can be a rational choice and those who suffer it become heroes. Tertullian, who later said that the blood of the martyrs was the seed of the Church, was attracted to Christian faith in the late second century by the martyrdoms he had witnessed. He said that such people, who took their faith so seriously, intrigued and humbled him.

Not many Christians died through persecution, but the few who did were an example of sacrifice to be followed. It was much easier to encourage believers to make the smaller sacrifices required in everyday living in the light of the example offered by the martyrs. By setting their present existence in the context of a cosmic battle, John's vision made it possible to ask much more of the Christians in Asia. What was social prestige and status when weighed against the eternal destiny of the world? In this sense Revelation gave guidance for everyday ethical decisions: was it acceptable to make a sacrifice in the imperial temple in order to further a political career? John's answer is clear: no, because to do so is to ally one's self with the beast, and alliance with the beast is alliance with Satan.

Some might see such reasoning as oppressive and manipulative, and it can become so. But in the early Church, as Rodney Stark points out, such high demands actually led to 'a very potent religion ... while membership was expensive, it was, in fact, a bargain. That is, because the church asked much of its members, it was thereby possessed of the resources to *give* much.'[23] The benefits were not just other-worldly, through participation in the 1,000-year reign of the saints promised in Revelation (Rev. 20.4–6). They were this-worldly too: when Christians were sick, they received care; when they fell on hard times, they received money and food; when they loved others, they received love in return; when they made the sexual sacrifices asked of them, they stepped off the first-century merry-go-round of relationships, and women especially gained far greater security in marriage. The emphasis on costly discipleship in Revelation was thus the way in which the 'free-rider' problem could be counteracted. Revelation explained why Christian faith might be worth struggling for.

Yet many have remarked that violent imagery pervades Revelation. Does the book therefore encourage a violent response by Christians? Certainly it has been used to justify violence over the centuries. Some commentators see a lurid fascination in the book with the destruction of the wicked, verging on sadism. Others argue that the violence portrayed is of a 'cartoon' kind, deliberately stylized: the hellish army of the east is a fantastic creation, for example, which lays waste a third of the world (Rev. 9.13–21).

Perhaps more significant than the violence is the fact that the underlying emphasis of the book is on the 'lamb that was slain' (Rev. 5.6). When the lamb is revealed the audience is expecting a lion will appear; but, as G. B. Caird comments, instead the lamb is used as the controlling image throughout the book, as if John were to say, 'Wherever the Old Testament says "Lion", read "Lamb",' and 'Wherever the Old Testament speaks of the victory of the Messiah or the overthrow of the enemies of God, we are to remember that the Gospel recognizes no other way of achieving these ends than the way of the Cross',[24] by suffering, not militant action.

The violent destruction of the wicked in Revelation echoes Old Testament images of the ultimate fate of those who turn away from God. But, as in those prophecies, the emphasis lies on the fact that the violence is deferred to the future, for 'vengeance is mine, says the Lord, I will repay' (Deut. 32.35; Rom. 12.19). In other words, though the final judgement will be awful and violent, it is not for God's people to anticipate it by their own violent actions, just as it had been Jesus' choice not to raise armed revolution in Jerusalem. Instead, 'Martyrdom, like the cross, is the cost of divine patience.'[25]

Some third-world commentators have also pointed out that the queasiness of Western scholars over the scenes of violence in Revelation may come from a cultural inability to read the book from the 'underside of history'. Allan Boesak, for example, a black South African liberation theologian who was heavily involved in the struggle against the Apartheid system, takes Caird to task. Caird suggests that John laments over the destruction of the great city of Babylon (Rev. 18.18) 'with infinite pathos'.[26] Boesak protests that this is 'typically the viewpoint of those who do not know what it means to stand at the bottom of the list'.[27] To those who do know what it means to be at the bottom of the list the violent destruction of Babylon is a matter for rejoicing not sadness (Rev. 18.20; 19.1).

Read from this perspective, Revelation becomes a profoundly liberating book which exposes the inner workings of world power. Most non-Western commentators identify the 'beast' today as America and its allies, an empire whose economic needs shape the world through overt and covert military operations in a way that is eerily reminiscent of ancient Rome. Revelation gives a voice, rarely heard, to those whose story was told in counterpoint to the imperial ideology that dominated the first-century world. In doing so it continues to give hope to those who 'stand at the bottom of the list' and to persuade them that the dream of divine justice is worth waiting and suffering for. Revelation's deferred violence is perhaps what gives John's vision its power. After all, the Empire was littered with the bodies of those who had challenged the power of Rome directly. The Christian strategy was a different one. Rome could not deal with the kind of passive resistance that Christians offered. Ultimately Christians overcame the Empire not through hate but love.

Gnostic reactions

Resisting the Empire by being prepared to suffer without fighting back (as Jesus had commanded, Matt. 5.39) was part of the reaction to Revelation. Another response was to give up the struggle altogether. This was the attraction of the strands of Christian belief labelled as Gnostic, the opponents of Polycarp and Irenaeus. Like 'New Age' beliefs today, Gnosticism covers a diverse and bewildering variety of beliefs. It was not an organized movement, but rather 'a cast of mind neither wholly separable from Christianity nor dominant within it'.[28] Gnostics tended to believe that salvation could only come through access to secret knowledge (*gnosis*), which gave one a 'cosmic password' to use when the spirit was liberated from the material body by death and freed to soar through the heavens, eluding the obstacles placed in the way by the use of the password. (Yes, it does sound rather like a computer game!) The password need not be a literal word – it could be acquired by sharing in a special food (which is why the early Christians' ritual meals seemed Gnostic to some).

Implicit in Gnostic beliefs were three main strands: a dualistic contrast between the material world (bad) and the spiritual world (good); an emphasis on secret knowledge only available to the select few who were initiates; and a profoundly unethical approach to life: it didn't matter what you did, so long as you had 'the knowledge'. In its later form it was this emphasis on knowledge, which Christian Gnostics claimed was passed on in a secret tradition from the apostles themselves, which forced the Church to define more clearly which books were to be regarded as scripture and to establish a commonly held tradition of interpretation.

Revelation's overall thrust was opposed to such thinking. John's desire was to provide an open 'revelation' where the only hidden elements, such as the number of the beast, were not difficult to work out. (Revelation was sometimes later seen as a Gnostic text because this identification, which would have been obvious in the first century, was forgotten.) Perhaps above all John's vision was of a heaven and earth which were inextricably intertwined.

The ultimate image of Revelation is not the ascent of the faithful to be with God in heaven, but the radical and shocking descent of heaven to earth, as the New Jerusalem comes down and God dwells with his people (Rev. 21.2–4). In other words, the battleground for humans is earth, and the triumph of God will be a physical as much as a spiritual one. The earth is not to be thrown away as a mistake, as the Gnostics believed; it will become a new paradise. This is a city which needs no temple, for God is always present (Rev. 21.22), where the gates are never closed for defence but remain open in peace for ever (Rev. 21.25–6). It is a city in some ways like the seven cities of the prelude to the book, but utterly transformed by the presence of God.

All shall be well

Revelation begins with the statement that it is a vision from God designed 'to show his servants what must soon take place' (Rev. 1.1). Did it come true? There have been many complex and intricate attempts to locate Revelation in a specific historical context. Alan Garrow, for example, sees the rise of someone claiming to be Nero who allied himself with a pretender to the Parthian throne in 80 as the background situation to the book. Therefore he identifies the fifth and sixth bowls of wrath specifically with the reincarnated Nero and the Parthian army (Rev. 16.10–12). Revelation then effectively becomes a prediction of the success of Nero and the Parthians and their dominance of the Roman Empire until their defeat in the final battle with the Word of God (Rev. 19.11–21). The Romans were certainly anxious at this time about the Parthian threat, but the upshot was not the overthrow of the Empire by the eastern hordes. Instead the usual Roman strategy of road and town building literally paved the way for the annexation of the two provinces of Armenia and Mesopotamia under Trajan in the early second century.

If Revelation had been so tied to historical circumstances it is hard to see why people would have continued to read it, especially when it became clear that its predictions had not been fulfilled. This makes it likely that Revelation was never intended to be a blueprint or timetable for the future. It is visionary in the sense that it places its readers in a new context and enables them to see what they had been blind to before. It affirms the triumph of God over the powers of evil, identified in general terms as the Roman Empire, and the ultimate vindication of the suffering servants of the messiah.

The emphasis that the vision will be fulfilled soon produces an urgency which would otherwise be lacking. There is little in the way of specific signs of the end time that can be clearly identified, as countless interpreters since have seen. This is something entirely coherent with the words of Jesus which the Church preserved: 'it is not for you to know the times or the moments which the Father has set in place on his own authority' (Acts 1.7).

The power of Revelation lies in its extraordinary re-imagination of the world, its depiction of 'inscape'. Its poetic grasp and depth are unparalleled in the New Testament and it is amazing how rich a harvest of creativity has sprung from its seeds in Western art: Dante's *Inferno*; Dürer's *Four Horsemen of the Apocalypse*; El Greco's *Opening of the Fifth Seal*; Milton's *Paradise Lost;* the 'Hallelujah Chorus' and 'Worthy is the Lamb' from Handel's *Messiah*; J. M. W. Turner's blazing *Angel Standing in the Sun,* to name just a few. Such art speaks at a depth beyond words, as Revelation itself does. Perhaps above all this is because it articulates the deep Christian conviction that 'All shall be well, and all manner of thing shall be well,'[29] that God will 'wipe every tear from their eyes and death shall be no more, nor shall sorrow or lament or pain' (Rev. 21.4).

Draw your own conclusions

- How likely is it that John the apostle wrote Revelation? Why do you think the early Church was reluctant to accept this identification?
- Is it important when Revelation was written? What do you think is the most likely date?
- Could martyrdom have attracted converts to the Church?
- How important is imagination in interpreting Revelation?
- What was John's view of the Roman Empire? Was it justified?
- Is Revelation too violent a text?
- What is the value of Revelation for those who are 'bottom of the list'?

Further reading

For a useful introduction to Revelation, see I. Boxall (2002), *Revelation: vision and insight*, London: SPCK. Also helpful is S. Woodman (2008), *The Book of Revelation*, London: SCM Press. On the background and setting, L. L. Thompson (1990), *The Book of Revelation: apocalypse and empire*, New York: Oxford University Press, gives a good overview of life in the province of Asia, while S. J. Friesen (2001), *Imperial Cults and the Apocalypse of John*, New York: Oxford University Press, draws together archaeology and text. A. J. P. Garrow (1997), *Revelation*, London: Routledge, makes sense of the structure of the text; G. B. Caird (1984), *The Revelation of St John*, 2nd ed., London: A.&C. Black, remains useful despite its age. I. Paul (2003), *How to Read the Book of Revelation*, Cambridge: Grove Books, and (2005), *The Ethics of the Book of Revelation*, Cambridge: Grove Books, are very useful, very short introductions.

The 'thousand year rule of the saints' has given rise to hundreds of millenarian movements. N. Cohn (1957), *The Pursuit of the Millennium*, London: Secker & Warburg, deals with the medieval period, while D. Thompson (1996), *The End of Time*, London: Sinclair-Stevenson, brings the story to the end of the twentieth century.

On martyrdom, R. Stark (1997), 'The Martyrs: Sacrifice as Rational Choice' in *The Rise of Christianity* San Francisco: HarperCollins, is a superb essay showing the value of social-scientific analysis in the hands of an expert.

Websites

- The 'Cities of Revelation' are explored at *www.luthersem.edu/ckoester/Revelation/main.htm*
- The website of the PBS series 'Apocalypse!' offers background on first-century apocalyptic writing as well as Revelation and the story of its subsequent interpretation at www.pbs.org/wgbh/pages/frontline/shows/apocalypse/

- 'The Text this Week' provides links to articles on Revelation at www.textweek.com/epistlesrevelation/revelati.htm.
- Felix Just has compiled an excellent site linking with artistic interpretations of John's apocalyptic vision at www.catholic-resources.org/Art/Revelation-Art.htm and more general resources at www.catholic-resources.org/Bible/Apocalyptic_Links.htm

Notes

1 Irenaeus to Florinus, in Eusebius, *History of the Church* 5.20.
2 Eusebius, *History of the Church* 4.14.
3 *The Martyrdom of Polycarp* 9 (tr. Staniforth).
4 E. Pagels (1979), *The Gnostic Gospels*, Harmondsworth, Penguin, p. 105.
5 Tertullian, *Apology* 50.13.
6 Eusebius, *History of the Church* 3.23, 7.8.
7 J. P. Meier (2001), *A Marginal Jew* III, New York: Doubleday, p. 220.
8 Eusebius, *History of the Church* 7.25; J. Ashton (1991), *Understanding the Fourth Gospel*, Oxford: Oxford University Press, p. 197.
9 Eusebius, *History of the Church* 3.31, 39.
10 Suetonius, *Nero* 39.
11 G. B. Caird (1966), *The Revelation of St John the Divine,* London: A.&C. Black, p. 219.
12 R. Stark (1997), *The Rise of Christianity*, San Francisco: HarperCollins, pp. 7, 175–6.
13 P. Zanker (1988), *The Power of Images in the Age of Augustus*, Ann Arbor: University of Michigan Press, p. 299.
14 S. J. Friesen (2001), *Imperial Cults and the Apocalypse of John*, New York: Oxford University Press, p. 147.
15 Friesen, *Imperial Cults*, p. 151.
16 A. J. P. Garrow (1997), *Revelation*, London: Routledge, p. 15.
17 Garrow, *Revelation*, p. 37.
18 I. Boxall (2002), *Revelation: vision and insight*, London: SPCK, p. 7.
19 Letter to Robert Bridges, 15 February 1879 in C. Phillips (ed.) (1986), *Gerard Manley Hopkins*, Oxford: Oxford University Press, p. 235.
20 'God's Grandeur' in Phillips (ed.), *Gerard Manley Hopkins*, p. 128.
21 Caird, *The Revelation of St John*, p. 122.
22 R. J. Bauckham (1993), *The Theology of the Book of Revelation*, Cambridge: Cambridge University Press, p. 10.
23 Stark, *Rise of Christianity*, p. 188.
24 Caird, *The Revelation of St John*, p. 75.
25 Caird, *The Revelation of St John*, p. 295.
26 Caird, *The Revelation of St John*, p. 227.
27 A. Boesak (1987), *Comfort and Protest*, Edinburgh: St Andrew Press, pp. 121–2.
28 P. Rousseau (2002), *The Early Christian Centuries*, London, Longman, p. 12.
29 Julian of Norwich, *Revelations of Divine Love* 27.

9

The Gospel of John

P52

One afternoon in 1934, Colin Roberts was sifting through a box of papyrus scraps. They looked unpromising: fragments of bills, letters and receipts for taxes which had been lying uncatalogued in the depths of the John Rylands Library in Manchester for a decade.

Roberts scanned a little piece of papyrus no bigger than the palm of his hand. He recognized the writing, scratched in black ink on the dull brown surface, as Greek. There were fragments of words on both front and back. As he turned the fragment over he realized that he recognized these words. This was no bill, letter or tax receipt, but something quite unexpected instead.

The words formed part of John 18.31–4 and 18.37–8, the story of Jesus' trial before Pilate. Roberts blinked and looked more closely: as an expert palaeographer, trained to distinguish the date of a document by the style of the handwriting, he knew that this manuscript almost certainly dated from the reign of the Emperor Hadrian in the early first century.

The scraps of rubbish had been picked up from the rubbish dumps of the ancient Egyptian cities of Fayum and Oxyrhynchus, where the dry climate and the shifting sands had preserved the waste which, anywhere else in the world, would have decayed and disappeared. Excavations had begun in 1897 and revealed that, in the first few centuries AD, the cities had had a large Christian population. On only the second day of excavation at Oxyrhynchus a fragment of 'Sayings' of Jesus had come to light, which were later recognized to be part of the lost *Gospel of Thomas*. Priceless papyrus treasures could be found, reported Bernard Grenfell (one of the directors of the dig), by 'merely turning up the soil with one's boot'.[1]

The box Roberts was sifting had taken a long time to catalogue because it wasn't part of the main finds from Oxyrhynchus. The excavations had been interrupted by World War One, and Grenfell had bought the material which later went to Manchester from an Egyptian dealer when he returned to the site in 1920. Since Grenfell was not sure exactly where his purchases had come from, they had not seemed to be very important.

Roberts's palaeographer's instinct told him that the scrap of paper he held could be dated to between 80 and 130. He concluded that 125 was a reasonable date to assign to it, and in 1935 published his results, designating the John Rylands' papyrus 'P52' (the fifty-second manuscript of the New Testament to be discovered).

Later scholars would err on the side of caution and put the date of P52 back to around 150–75. But on that Manchester afternoon Roberts realized that the Egyptian rubbish in his hands was the oldest surviving manuscript of any part of the New Testament, as it is still recognized to be today.

When, where and who?

Clement of Alexandria, writing about the year 200, said that 'last of all, John, seeing that the physical facts had been made clear in the Gospel [of Mark], urged by his friends and inspired by the Spirit, put together a spiritual gospel.'[2] Any reader of the other three Gospels who comes upon John's story of Jesus is bound to agree with the distinction: this Gospel has a haunting and poetic quality which goes far beyond the achievement, great though it is, of its three New Testament counterparts.

On the face of it, Clement's is a pretty good distinction. For one thing, this Gospel invokes the role of the heavenly realm in a way that the other Gospels do not, and it is easy to think that the emphasis on worshipping 'in spirit and in truth' (John 4.20), for example, means that it is the heavenly plane of existence that really matters, not the earthly one. Another example of the difference between John's and the other Gospels is the picture of Jesus. In the synoptic Gospels Jesus is remarkably cagey about his identity, using only the ambiguous phrase 'son of man' about himself, and constantly deflecting attention to God instead. In John's Gospel, by contrast, Jesus repeatedly draws attention to himself and speaks at length about his identity as the son of the Father, the stranger from heaven who is sent to do the Father's will on earth. John's Gospel is also perhaps the most difficult of the four to understand fully, a book, as Augustine said in the fourth century, in which a child might paddle and in which an elephant also might swim!

John's Gospel is at first sight another version of the story of Jesus, but the more you read it, the more complex it becomes. Wayne Meeks has commented that 'The reader cannot understand any part of the Fourth Gospel until he understands the whole'.[3] It appears to be the fruit of longer reflection than the other Gospels, especially reflection on the identity of Jesus. For this reason it has long been accepted that John's Gospel was the last of the four New Testament Gospels to be written.

The date and nature of John's Gospel

The view of the early nineteenth-century scholar, F. C. Baur, that John's Gospel was written around 170 has cast a long shadow over New Testament scholarship. Baur settled on 170 because Irenaeus, writing in 180, mentions John's Gospel, making it impossible for it to have been written any later. Baur would have set the date in the third century if he could have done so, reasoning that the process of reflection which underlies John's Gospel must have taken many decades, and that John's Gospel represented the highest form of thought in the New Testament, the synthesis which had resulted from the clash of Jewish and Greek forms of Christianity.

Colin Roberts's publication of P52 in 1935 pulled the rug from under any scholars who remained convinced by Baur, but the view that the Gospel was the fruit of long reflection has continued to be influential, and most scholars date John's Gospel, in its present form, to between 90 and 100. This also follows the view of Clement of Alexandria that John's Gospel was written 'last of all'.[4]

One of the features of John's Gospel which supports Baur's view is the long discourses which punctuate the narrative and which are quite at odds with how Jesus speaks in the other Gospels. A good example is the speech about the 'bread of life' (John 6.26–65), which has strong overtones of the eucharistic worship of the early Church.

Yet if you read the section of John's Gospel which immediately precedes the 'bread of life' discourse you will find yourself on much more familiar ground. The story of the feeding of the 5,000 is one of the few episodes common to all four Gospels (John 6.1–15; Matthew 14.15–23; Mark 6.34–46; Luke 9.10–17), and if you read the four accounts side by side it becomes clear that John's version has a strong eyewitness flavour to it compared to the others. The structure of the story is the same, but John includes details that the others do not have, particularly identifying the disciples who speak in the conversation with Jesus (John 6.5–8), and mentioning the boy who offers his loaves and fishes to feed the crowd (John 6.9). John's Gospel also includes the significant detail that the crowd wished to make Jesus king (John 6.15).

As well as apparent examples of eyewitness reportage, John's Gospel is also more precise about the geography of Judea and Galilee than the other Gospels, which specify only 12 locations between them. John's Gospel mentions all of these, and another 13 besides. Not only this, but where Luke speaks about 'a certain village' (Luke 10.38) as the home of Martha and Mary, it is John's Gospel which gives distances: 'Bethany ... the village of Mary and Martha ... near Jerusalem, about fifteen *stadia* [i.e. a mile and three-quarters] away' (John 11.1, 18). John's measurement is remarkably accurate, and from it you can see why Luke might not want to locate Jesus so close to Jerusalem at that point in his telling of the story: it would upset Luke's scheme of the journey to Jerusalem (and imply that Jesus was going round Jerusalem in circles!).

John's Gospel is more sure-footed on Aramaic terminology than the other Gospels: Peter is called '*Cephas*' (John 1.42, see also Gal. 1.18); Pilate's judgement seat is identified as being at '*Gabbatha*' (John 19.13); Mary's response to the risen Jesus is preserved as '*Rabboni*' (John 20.16). In each case the phrase is carefully translated for a Greek-speaking audience.

In addition, Jewish feasts have a higher profile in John's Gospel: three Passovers (John 2.13; 6.4; 11.55), Tabernacles (John 7.2), Dedication (*Hanukkah*, John 10.22), and a further unnamed one (John 5.1) feature. There are also frequent indications of time (for example John 2.1; 12.1).

As John Robinson remarked, 'It is hard to believe that such detail is put in purely for symbolic purposes or that it does not rest upon genuine memory';[5] suggesting therefore that John's Gospel is grounded in eyewitness testimony to the ministry of Jesus. Robinson argued that the Gospel reached its present form around 65 (the point he wished to make was that John's Gospel is therefore as close as, or closer than, Mark's was to Jesus himself). John's is also the only Gospel to include the claim that it reflects the witness of one who was actually there (John 19.35; 21.24).

Yet alongside the deep grasp of the background to Jesus' life stand equally deep insights into the theological significance of that life. Surely these must have taken far longer than a couple of decades to develop?

Awareness of the significance of Jesus was not slow to develop. It's worth remembering that Paul's letters which deal with this same issue (Philippians and Colossians, in particular) probably date from around 58, before any of the Gospels were written. This was already about 25 years after Jesus' crucifixion, so in theory it need not have taken a further 30 or 40 years for John's understanding of the importance and significance of Jesus to develop. But what is distinctive about John's Gospel is the way the theology and the background details of Jesus' life are so closely woven together that they cannot be divided from one another. It is this fusion which suggests, though it cannot be definitely proved, that what we have in John's Gospel is a comparatively late development.

So there is a dichotomy: on the one hand the precision of the background in the Gospel suggests that we have first-generation, possibly eyewitness, material here; on the other hand there are also signs of long gestation which point to this Gospel being a late composition. Can this dichotomy be resolved?

The answer may lie in some oddities in the text. First of all, the Gospel seems to end twice. There is a concluding summary statement at the end of chapter 20, which seems to round off the Gospel (John 20.30–1) – only for chapter 21 to follow with a further story of an appearance of Jesus in Galilee, ending in much the same way (John 21.24–5). Second, Jesus' farewell discourse to the disciples at the Last Supper seems to end with the decisive command 'Rise, let us go' (John 14.31) – only for Jesus to embark on a further long speech and a prayer (John 15 – 17) before he and the disciples finally set off for the garden of Gethsemane (John 18.1). This looks very much like a text that has been added to, and rather awkwardly so at that. These are the most obvious examples, but once you start looking others begin to appear. So chapter 6 (the feeding of the 5,000) and chapter 11 (the raising of Lazarus) have been suggested as additions to the original flow of the Gospel (try skipping from John 5.47 to 7.1, or 10.42 to 11.45 and you will see the point), while the prologue (John 1.1–18) seems to be a wholly different kind of writing to what immediately follows it.

We don't have to accept all these suggestions to see that there is some evidence here for at least two stages in the development of this Gospel. Some commentators have really gone to town on the reconstruction of the Gospel, and imagined a process where separate sections became dislocated and were put back together in the wrong order by a rather clumsy editor. Others suggest a series of editions – as many as seven – but there's no strong evidence for either of these theories, appealing and well-argued though they may be. They also seem to rely too strongly on what James Dunn calls the 'literary paradigm', which assumes that books were composed in successive written stages and were then widely 'published' in definitive forms. This is not what happened in the first century, when every copy of a book had to be made by hand and would contain variations in the text, usually tiny but sometimes much greater.

The later addition of the story of the woman taken in adultery (John 7.53—8.11), a passage clearly not part of the original Gospel of John (the style of writing is quite different from the rest and it does not appear in the earliest manuscripts of the whole of John's Gospel that have survived), particularly suggests that, as Leslie Houlden concludes, John's Gospel is, 'despite its profundity, not tidy in its structure or "finished" in its presentation'.[6] John's Gospel seems to have been more fluid in terms of its composition than the other three Gospels and slower to reach a definitive version.

So a number of scholars suggest that John's Gospel was originally composed in Judea out of eyewitness material, but later thoroughly reworked in the light of long reflection and hindsight. This theory neatly explains the dual personality of the Gospel. It may mean that there were two 'editions' of John's Gospel, but it's probably more likely that the text represents the final coalescence of a series of floating traditions which were blended together into the Gospel as we have it.

This conclusion actually leaves us with a process, rather than a tidy date, for the composition of the Gospel. The process began orally in the aftermath of Jesus' death and resurrection and continued until the Gospel was written down in the form that has reached us, perhaps as late as 100. It looks as if the traditions about Jesus were developing but did not reach a completed form so much as being 'frozen' at some point and passed on as the Gospel of John without the loose ends being tied up and tidied away. (You have probably noticed that P52 is only a scrap of John 18 and this is not evidence for the completion of the whole Gospel. P66 is the earliest manuscript of the whole of John 1–21 that we have, and it dates from 175–200. This might mean that F. C. Baur was right after all!)

If the text of John's Gospel suggests that it has a Judean origin, where was it completed? Since the P52 manuscript was found in Egypt, it might indicate Alexandria. A rare Egyptian form of the word for palm branches is used in the story of Jesus entering Jerusalem (John 12.13), and Alexandria was the home of the Jewish philosopher Philo who developed the idea of the 'Word' (*logos*), which may have echoes in the prologue to John's Gospel. But there is not much more to the case for Alexandria than this, and since all the early manuscripts of the New Testament have an Egyptian provenance it could logically be argued that they were all written there.

Clement of Alexandria would almost certainly have claimed the Gospel for his own city if he could have done so, but he is one of the strongest witnesses to a connection between John the apostle and Ephesus, the traditional place for the Gospel's final composition. Ephesus was only a five-day voyage away from Alexandria and if John's Gospel was completed there in the late first century it could have been in circulation in Egypt soon afterwards. There is no internal evidence in the Gospel itself for a connection with Ephesus. Instead we have to rely on the testimony of Christian writers of the second century and later, and they are unanimous: 'when John and his Gospel are referred to in the ancient world it is always in association with Ephesus.'[7] We can't definitively say that John's Gospel was completed in Ephesus; northern Syria and Antioch could be strong candidates too; but the claim makes sense. It is not all that Clement said about the composition of John's Gospel, however. He also noted that 'John [was] ... urged by his friends and inspired by the Spirit',[8] emphasizing that the composition of John's Gospel took place within a community of 'friends'. Given the extended process which probably lay behind the Gospel reaching its final form, it is important to give some attention to what the implications of Clement's statement might be.

'What we have seen'

John's Gospel ends with the statement that 'we know that his witness is true' (John 21.24). This implies that the book is guaranteed by a community of people. The same idea can be found in the first letter of John (1 John 1.1–3). The writer is so gripped by what he has to say that the words tumble forth and he interrupts his own careful announcement of the subject, 'the word of life', with the claim that the eternal word was heard, seen, gazed at and touched on earth and within living memory. Words about visual recognition are used no less than six times in the short passage. There can be no doubt in the writer's mind that what he's speaking about really happened. But the voice is plural: so who are the 'we' who speak here?

The first thing to notice is that this letter, like the Gospel of John itself, is anonymous. The other two letters attributed to John are sent from 'the elder' (2 John 1; 3 John 1), but do not make his identity any more specific than that. Neither the letters nor the Gospel makes a direct claim to authorship by John the apostle. The early Church linked all four with him, though not without some argument. Revelation does name John as its author (Rev. 1.1, 4, 9; 22.8), and dispute arose about its authorship largely because of discomfort with its eschatological themes. Dionysius of Alexandria, later followed by Eusebius, suggested that its author was 'John the elder', whom Papias appears to mention as distinct from John the apostle. Dionysius arrived at this view on the somewhat counter-intuitive grounds that, since John preferred to remain anonymous in the Gospel and letters, the emphasis on his name in Revelation showed that it could not be the self-effacing apostle who had written it!

Approaching Revelation on its own merits, there are good grounds for accepting that John the apostle was its author. But Dionysius was right to point to the differences of style and theology between Revelation on the one hand and John's Gospel and letters on the other. Though he overstated his case when he concluded that there was 'scarcely, so to say, a syllable in common between them',[9] he was surely correct to spot that it seems highly unlikely that one author would write in two such different styles.

There are strong thematic echoes between the Gospel and the letters: for example Jesus' command to 'love one another' (John 13.34–5; 15.12; 1 John 3.11, 23; 4.7, 11–12; 2 John 5) and the symbolism of light (John 1.4–9; 3.19–21; 8.12; 9.5; 12.35–6, 46; 1 John 1.5–7; 2.8–10), as well as striking similarities of vocabulary. But there are differences on minor (but significant) points of style which suggest that the actual writer of the Gospel was not the same person who wrote down the letters, and the understanding of eschatology seems to vary between them (though the same problems occur between different letters written by Paul, too). Overall it seems that, while different hands may have put the finishing touches to these books, they were written within a community which shared a common outlook. To put things another way, there is a strong 'family likeness' between the Gospel and the letters, which suggests that they come from a shared mindset rather than from a single mind.

Revelation is clearly the odd writing out here, and if its writer had not identified himself as John probably no one would have thought to link it and the Gospel of John. But Revelation also shares a few thematic similarities with the Gospel: both use the image of Jesus as the Lamb of

God (though the Greek words employed for 'lamb' are different), and the concept of testimony and witness features in both. These features give Revelation more common ground with the Gospel and letters of John than with any other New Testament writings. So we may characterize Revelation as a distant cousin of the Gospel and letters, though the relationship doesn't seem to be very close.

If the author of Revelation was the apostle John, it therefore seems that he could not also have been the direct author of the Gospel and letters. Who did write the Gospel and letters of John, then? We have seen that the first letter emphasizes that it is written from 'us'. So who are 'we'?

The chain of memory

Irenaeus seems to have been the first to link John the apostle with the Gospel, around 180: 'John, the disciple of the Lord, who leaned on his breast, published his Gospel while staying at Ephesus.'[10] Three important connections are made here: John is identified (1) with the 'beloved disciple', (2) with the author of the Gospel and (3) with the city of Ephesus. None of these statements is self-evident: the 'beloved disciple' is not identified as John in the Gospel itself; the Gospel is anonymous; there is nothing to link it or the letters directly with Ephesus. So why did Irenaeus make this threefold link?

Most commentators assume that since Irenaeus apparently knew Polycarp (the bishop of Smyrna, near Ephesus, who died in 155) and Polycarp may have known John the apostle, then Irenaeus was claiming the authority of Polycarp for this statement.

Scholars have questioned this claim with the following argument. Irenaeus says that he had heard Polycarp's reminiscences of 'John and others who had seen the Lord'[11] when he was young, but elsewhere he says that Papias was a friend of Polycarp's and also heard John. However, Papias himself seems not to have claimed to have heard John directly, and mentions 'the elder John', from whom he also received information about the composition of the Gospels of Mark and Matthew.[12] Maybe Irenaeus was mistaken and the John about whom Polycarp spoke was the otherwise unknown John 'the elder'. In addition, Polycarp (born in 70) may have been too young to have known the apostle John anyway. Although the elder John was introduced into the debate about John as an alternative (non-apostolic) author for Revelation, the argument runs that in fact he was much more likely to have been the author of the Gospel. Since the second and third letters of John say they come from the 'elder', and the same person may have written the Gospel, the mysterious John the elder is revealed as the creative genius behind the Gospel and letters. QED! This whole argument is incredibly complicated, requiring the Gospel's author to have been both 'after Paul, the greatest theologian in all the history of the church' but also someone who was almost immediately

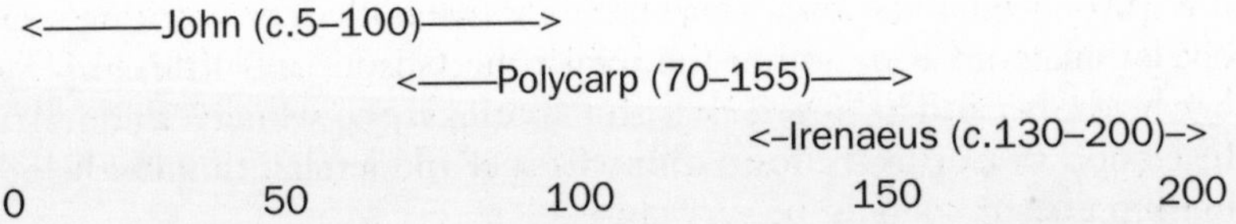

<———John (c.5–100)———>

<——Polycarp (70–155)——>

<–Irenaeus (c.130–200)–>

0 50 100 150 200

Figure 17 A chain of memory?

'forgotten'.[13] As John A. T. Robinson noted, appealing to the principle of 'Occam's Razor': 'Geniuses, like entities, are not to be multiplied beyond necessity.'[14] The elder John as the author of the Gospel is a convenient figment of the imagination for whom there is no real evidence.

If we look again at the evidence we see, first, that if the dates of birth and death of the three people concerned are compared it does seem possible that a reliable chain of memory could connect them (Figure 17).

But we must be wary. First, only Polycarp's dates are certain and he is the key link in the chain. Second, Irenaeus does not actually say that the information in his statement about John's Gospel came from Polycarp: the link between John and Ephesus is strong both in early tradition and in Revelation, but Irenaeus was here repeating what everyone believed to be true and he didn't need Polycarp to have given him special information. More significant is the link Irenaeus makes between John and the beloved disciple. That these two individuals are the same person is an obvious reading of the Gospel if it comes to you with the title 'according to John', whether or not the identification is true. Again, Irenaeus didn't need Polycarp for this piece of information since he could easily have arrived at the conclusion himself by reading the Gospel.

Yet the fact remains that Revelation on the one hand and the Gospel and letters of John on the other seem to be only distant relatives. They surely cannot all have come directly from John the apostle, so who did write the Gospel and letters? Irenaeus's statement about the 'publishing' of the Gospel is part of his wider survey of the origins of all four Gospels. His comments about the composition of Matthew's Gospel can be interpreted to mean that the roots of that Gospel go back to the apostle Matthew, rather than Matthew the apostle himself directly being the author. It seems possible that something similar may be meant here.

The text of the Gospel itself suggests this. The last chapter seems to have been added to the body of the Gospel, and it concludes, 'This is the disciple who bore witness concerning these things and caused them to be written. We know that his witness is true.' (John 21.24, see also 19.35) Some translations have 'who bore witness concerning these things and wrote them down', but the same word used for 'writing' is used about the placard placed on Jesus' cross (John 19.19). There it means that Pilate ordered, or caused, the placard to be written. No one would expect the governor of a Roman province to get out the pen himself; in the ancient world authoring a book was very different from physically writing it oneself. It makes sense to assume the same process is meant in this appendix to John's Gospel. The impression given is of a group who have completed the Gospel in its present form, but whose work is reliant on the beloved disciple as their source.

How likely is this? In Matthew's Gospel, Matthew himself is not a major player and the link with him lies only in his possibly being the vehicle by which some extra teaching material about Jesus was introduced into the bulk of the Gospel which the final writer had borrowed from Mark. Mark's Gospel itself was widely believed to be composed of the stories which Peter had told about Jesus, and Peter has within it a role which is similar to that of the beloved disciple in John's Gospel. But Peter was never credited as the author of Mark's Gospel, probably because Mark himself was well-known enough in the early Church as the companion of both Paul and Peter to command his own authority. Luke to some extent was the same, though he was an eyewitness to Paul rather than to Jesus. The writer of Matthew's Gospel is a more shadowy figure than Mark or Luke. In this he was just like the writer of John's Gospel. The onus was on these two writers to show how their writings linked with the earliest stories about Jesus.

The writer of Matthew's Gospel solved the problem by relying on Mark's Gospel and therefore Peter as his main source. The material which might possibly have come from Matthew the apostle is significant but subsidiary. John's Gospel is different. It includes a great deal of extra material and, unlike Matthew's, does not share the structure of Mark's Gospel. Where did this extra material come from? The comment at the end of the book suggests that the source was the 'beloved disciple'. It is time to consider who he might have been.

The beloved disciple

Who was the beloved disciple? Serious candidates include Lazarus, Nathanael, Thomas, Mark (whose first name was John) and even Paul, as well as John himself. Mary Magdalene also has some followers. Of these Lazarus is probably the most likely, on the grounds that Jesus 'loved him' (John 11.3, 5, 36). Of his presence at the Last Supper, Mark Stibbe suggests that his recent 'resurrection would have marked him out as something of a celebrity guest'![15] But there is no strong evidence here.

John the disciple was identified by Irenaeus as the beloved disciple. Three important points support Irenaeus's identification:

- John the disciple is never named in this Gospel – alone among the four, the only John in its pages is the Baptist – and this has been taken to imply that, if John the disciple was the author, he omitted his name out

of modesty (the 'sons of Zebedee' appear in John 21.2, but this is in the appendix not the main body of the Gospel).
- The beloved disciple is paired with Peter at crucial moments (the Last Supper and the visit to the empty tomb, John 13.23–4; 20.2–8), just as John is in the early chapters of Acts.
- The Last Supper seems to have been a gathering of the Twelve, therefore John would have been present.

But these grounds are not strong enough to support Irenaeus's view. They can all be countered:

- Half of the twelve disciples whom we know from the other Gospels are not present in John's: Bartholomew, Matthew, James the son of Alphaeus, Thaddeus and Simon the Zealot; John's omission may not therefore be as significant a detail as it at first appears (and hiding behind the rather exclusive title of 'the beloved disciple' hardly seems to suggest modesty, anyway!).
- Since Peter and John became such a celebrated 'double act' it seems strange that, if John were the beloved disciple, his identity should remain hidden.
- The gathering of the Twelve at the Last Supper is not a feature of John's Gospel (the information derives from Mark 14.17); however the absence of several of the names of the Twelve implies logically that any of the other absentees have as good a claim to be the beloved disciple as John.

In addition, and perhaps most significantly, the beloved disciple actually only appears in the second half of the Gospel, and not until the Last Supper, the night before Jesus died. If he is to be identified with John, where had he been until then? (Claims are sometimes made that he appears at the beginning of the Gospel, John 1.35 but this identification is far from obvious.)

The identity of the beloved disciple is 'a riddle wrapped in a mystery inside an enigma'. The more we look at the evidence, the more it begins to seem deliberately opaque: the writer of the Gospel 'deliberately chooses not to identify [the beloved disciple] ... If later readers were meant to discover his identity, [he] would have provided far clearer clues.'[16] This conclusion suggests that the beloved disciple is not to be identified with a historical person at all. He seems to be a representative figure, whose function is a literary one, who draws attention to key episodes: the betrayal of Jesus (John 13.23–4); the dying words and death of Jesus (John 19.26, 35); the empty tomb (John 20.2–8); and the risen Jesus (John 21.7).

Some pursue this conclusion and argue that, therefore, John's Gospel is an imaginative reconstruction, and that this was what Clement meant when he called it a 'spiritual Gospel'. But this is to go further than is necessary: imaginative interpretation and historical testimony are not polar opposites, as if you can only do one and not the other at any one time. R. G. Collingwood noted that the historian and the novelist share in composing 'works of imagination' but that their ways part because the historian's picture 'must be localized in space and time', that is to say, it must be recognizably consistent with the other events of history for 'there is only one historical world'. Collingwood also noted that 'the historian's picture stands in a peculiar relation to something called evidence.'[17] Thus, while imagination plays an indispensable role in any writing about the past, such writing is also anchored in a way that prevents it from straying too far away from reality.

The imaginative freedom of John's Gospel does not therefore necessarily make it historically worthless; it simply means that it is often hard to tell where fact ends and elaboration begins, just as it is often difficult within it to see where Jesus' words end and the writer's begin. It would surely be ironic if the Gospel were unchecked imaginative fiction since its primary claim is that the events it describes did happen, that 'the Word became flesh' in real time and in a real place.

So perhaps we should rethink what it means for the beloved disciple to 'bear witness' (John 21.24). It actually seems to be about far more than simple eyewitness experience. The claim for the beloved disciple is not so much (just) that 'he was there' as that (also) 'he understood'. The poet T. S. Eliot once wrote that 'We had the experience, but missed the meaning'.[18] This Gospel claims that the beloved disciple knew both experience and meaning.

Raymond Brown suggests that the reason why this enigmatic figure appears only towards the end of the Gospel is that he 'was not *yet* the Beloved Disciple because at the beginning of the Gospel story he had not yet come to understand Jesus fully'.[19] He grows into discipleship as the story unfolds, as perhaps the readers of the Gospel are intended to do. In this Gospel discipleship is far more important than apostleship: 'remaining' (John 15.4) matters more than being sent out, though mission has its place (John 20.21). Being a disciple of Jesus is the highest honour anyone can aspire to.

The beloved disciple has a deeper sense of the meaning of the events of Jesus' life than his fellow disciples do, as at the empty tomb, where the beloved disciple believes and Peter does not (John 20.8). Therefore the search for the elusive beloved disciple has been refined: we are looking now for the creative mind behind the Gospel, the visionary who saw not just the surface of the events in front of his eyes, but the deeper 'inscape'.

Once again, there are many candidates for this creative mind, but one does seem to stand above the others. Who, in the early Church, saw Jesus not just as a human being but as the key figure in a cosmic struggle, with a relationship so close to God as to be virtually indistinguishable from him? Paul is one possibility, but as Tom Wright puts it, 'With Paul we are in the seminar room: we are arguing the thing out, looking up references, taking notes, and then being pushed out into the world to preach the Gospel to the nations.' In John's Gospel, by contrast, the writer 'takes us up the mountain, and says quietly: "Look – from here, on a clear day, you can see for ever."'[20] The other book in the New Testament which offers a similar perspective is Revelation. There are good grounds for identifying John the apostle as the author of Revelation. Though the visions of Revelation and John's Gospel are different, we also noted earlier that there is a kinship between them. The John who wrote Revelation was primarily a prophet. His gift was to see things others did not see, to reimagine the world around him. The same qualities seem to lie behind John's Gospel, which presents Jesus in a cosmic context and is aware of the significance of Jesus in a way that the other three Gospels are not.

The early Church probably followed a similar process of reasoning in identifying this Gospel with the apostle John. There is no conclusive evidence, it is all circumstantial, and there are good arguments against it, particularly the question of why John was not clearly identified as author of the Gospel. But it does seem to be the best reading of the evidence to suggest that the basis of this Gospel's theological interpretation of Jesus comes from John the apostle, and that his role was remembered in the figure of the beloved disciple in the Gospel, even though it is probably not meant to be a direct portrait of him. If this is so we can return to the question with which we began this section: who formed the community which seems to have turned this theological interpretation into the Gospel and letters of John?

The 'school' of John?

To sum up where we have reached so far, while there is a close family likeness between the letters and Gospel of John they are unlikely to have been written by the same person. They probably came from a community which shared the same basic theology and thought forms. Their relationship to Revelation is more distant, but John's Gospel shares a breadth of theological imagination with the Apocalypse. Both the appendix to the Gospel and the first letter strongly suggest that a group of people rather than one individual is behind the writings.

That the apostles had a circle of people around them is fairly self-evident. Paul had a group of helpers whom James Dunn describes as 'the school or studio of Paul',[21] which collected his letters. Peter had Mark as his 'interpreter', and possibly others also. John too is unlikely to have been a hermit.

The description which Irenaeus passed on about Polycarp paints a scene of discussion within a group at Ephesus, presumably around 90 (when Polycarp would have been 20 years old). 'John and the others who had seen the Lord' spoke 'concerning his miracles and his teaching'. This was the context in which Polycarp listened to 'eyewitnesses of the Word of Life'[22] (Irenaeus's quotation from the first letter of John implies a connection between it and the discussion he describes).

This group has been described as a 'school' by analogy with the kinds of schools which philosophers gathered around them and has been described in great detail by some scholars, who also reconstruct the times and circumstances of the community's move from Judea to Ephesus. But it is not necessary to seek philosophical parallels. Just as Jesus gathered disciples, so those disciples more than likely replicated his pattern. The limited evidence we have suggests simply this:

- that John was active in Jerusalem until at least 50;
- that Revelation was written some time before the Gospel but after 70;
- that John had visited Ephesus and the other six churches of Revelation by then;
- that John was still active in Ephesus during the 90s.

This scenario allows for John to have been active in Ephesus in the 80s and 90s, and gives ample time for a group of interpreters to have gathered around him. These were the people behind the Gospel and the letters of John.

This doesn't mean that the letters or the Gospel were written by a committee. Barnabas Lindars says that 'full recognition must be accorded to the evangelist as a creative writer, who should not be dissolved into a mass of hands in a "school"'.[23] The apostle John may have been the man with the vision behind the Gospel, but its actual writer – whose work was affirmed by his colleagues in the circle around John – was, like Matthew, Mark and Luke, a creative artist of genius. Indeed, in this aspect of the Gospel writers' art, he was the perhaps the greatest of them all.

The structure of John's Gospel

John's Gospel is split between a first half which focuses on Jesus' ministry and miracles and a second half which tells the story of Jesus' passion and death. These two sections were called by C. H. Dodd the 'Book of Signs' and the 'Book of the Passion',[24] though most scholars now prefer to describe the latter as the 'Book of Glory'. The prologue (John 1.1–18) and the epilogue (John 21), which form a kind of 'frame' around the whole Gospel, and an interlude between the Books of Signs and Glory, which tells the story of Lazarus's return to life and Jesus' preparation for death (John 11.1—12.50), contribute to form a basic fivefold structure. Richard Burridge describes the structure of the whole Gospel (using the traditional animal symbol for John) as 'like an eagle, with the two main sections being the "wings" on which it flies, separated by a thin body of material in between with the prologue and appendix forming extensions on the wingtips'.[25] The image draws attention to the sophisticated balance of the Gospel as a whole.

Opposing forces

Matthew and Luke followed Mark in their arrangement of the story of Jesus. John takes a different approach. Mark organizes his story around Jesus 'going up to Jerusalem' (Mark 10.33), implying that Jesus did not visit the city until his triumphal entry, but John's Gospel shows Jesus as a frequent attender at the Temple festivals. John's story, for all Jesus' movement to-and-fro between Jerusalem and Galilee, is more static than Mark's. The only sense of progression and development comes in the growing opposition of the Jewish authorities to Jesus.

It is the motif of opposition rather than movement which gives John's Gospel its shape. It rises to a climax midway through the Gospel as the plot to kill Jesus becomes explicit (John 11.45–53), and the second part of the Gospel provides the unfolding of the plan of the authorities. But this is also a darkly ironic Gospel, and the plot to kill Jesus is articulated by Caiaphas the high priest with the words, 'it is better that one man should die for the people than that all the nation should die' (John 11.50). Caiaphas's words are true, as the text points out, but not in the way the high priest intended (John 11.51). So the balance between the two main sections of the Gospel does not represent the same kind of dramatic tension that Mark pioneered in the writing of his Gospel.

Sign–discourse–saying

John's Gospel is almost seamless in its structure and, for all the balance it displays, it is an immensely complex book. A good example of this complexity lies in the mutual relationship between the three distinctive features of miracles, usually called signs, discourses, and the sayings which employ the formula 'I am', an important pointer to Jesus' identity, since this was the designation God chose for himself (Ex. 3.14).

Stephen Smalley devised the table in Figure 18 to show how they might relate to each other.

While the relationship is comparatively straightforward between the sign of the feeding of the 5,000, followed by the 'bread of life' discourse, which also includes the saying 'I am the bread of life' (John 6.35), in the other cases it is less obvious, and really only begins to become clear after sustained reflection and thought.

Smalley uses his scheme to argue that the 'centre' of John's Gospel 'is to be found in seven signs, bound together with discourses and ... sayings which expound various aspects of the theme of eternal life as that is to be found in and through Jesus the Christ'.[26] This is a helpful analysis, but, just as Jesus cannot be pinned down by the authorities (John 10.39), so the text itself resists such organization: there is a further miracle in the story of Jesus walking on the water (John 6.19–21) that lies outside this scheme. This makes eight signs and not seven, and it does not seem to relate to any discourse or 'I am' saying. It's also not immediately obvious that Jesus' brief words with the Samaritan woman can be counted as a 'discourse'.

There certainly seem to be some strong links between the signs, discourses and sayings, but John's Gospel is not neat and tidy, nor does it seem to have been written to a particular pattern. It shows signs of being a work still in progress. Though there does seem to be an underlying structure we should be wary of trying to make any pattern fit too tightly. The nature of John's Gospel itself resists such tidiness.

	Sign	Discourse	Saying – 'I AM'
1.	Water into wine (2)	New Life (3)	True Vine (15.1)
2.	The official's son (4)	Water of life (4)	Way, the truth, the life (14.6)
3.	The sick man (5)	Son, life-giver (5)	Door of the sheep (10.7)
4.	Feeding of the 5,000 (6)	Bread of life (6)	Bread of life (6.35)
5.	The blind man (9)	Light of life (8)	Light of the world (8.12)
6.	Lazarus (11)	Shepherd, life-giver (10)	Resurrection and life (11.25)
7.	The catch of fish (21)	Discipleship (14—16)	Good shepherd (10.11)

Figure 18 Signs, discourses and sayings in John's Gospel

The prologue (John 1.1–18)

Where to start? The roots of a human life go back much further than birth or the moment of conception. Family and ancestry matter, but so does the society into which someone is born, its history and currents of thought. So where can we make a beginning?

'In the beginning was the Word' (John 1.1) is one of the most economical yet breathtaking openings to any book. 'In the beginning (*arche*)' means both when the world began and also the principle beneath the world, its inner being. The next phrase, 'was the word (*logos*)', points not just to a spoken word but also its inner reason, the key which unlocks all mysteries. In other words, where the first three Gospel writers locate Jesus within what may be an ancient context but is still a strongly human one, John raises the stakes incredibly high. The roots of Jesus' life go right back to the dawn of time, indeed before there was time at all. Here is where we must start the story of Jesus, according to the evangelist. 'Read this book,' he is saying, 'and I shall unfold the mysteries of the universe for you.'

The climax of this opening is the phrase 'the word became flesh' (John 1.14). The Nicene Creed expressed the same idea three centuries later in the words 'he became man', an obvious turn of phrase. But John's Gospel avoids the obvious choice. The reason for this is probably to emphasize the novelty of what is being expressed here. Gods in human form were a staple part of Greek and Roman mythology, and the emperor was routinely worshipped as a human god who thus formed a bridge between earth and heaven. Angels in human form crop up in the Hebrew Scriptures in a visit to Abraham and Sarah (Gen. 18), and in the book of Tobit. Moses meets God face to face (Deut 34.10) and Isaiah, Ezekiel and Daniel all have visions of the glory of God. Yet none of these encounters, pagan or Jewish, come close to 'the word became flesh'. Even Paul's phrase, probably quoted from an early Christian hymn, that Jesus was 'born in human likeness' (Phil. 2.7) remained open to misinterpretation: was Jesus only 'like' humans, but not actually one of them?

The word 'flesh' (*sarx*) is shocking in its directness and hits the reader like a sudden splash of cold water. The Greek text juxtaposes *logos* and *sarx,* abstract concept and tangible physicality. *Sarx* means meat or the human body, and in Paul's writings it applies, usually negatively, to natural human desires. But flesh, says John, is the vehicle of the word coming into the world and there can be no question that it is a wholesale adoption of humanity that is meant, not simply a guest appearance.

The word 'dwelt among us': from the abstract and cosmic, even the slightly distant description of John the Baptist, there is a sudden urgent claim that the word, the life, the light, is known to the writer and his community. The 'word dwelt among *us*' localizes all that has gone before. Like the visions of Isaiah, Ezekiel and Daniel, John's Gospel speaks of the glory of God; but, unlike theirs, this is not a majestic vision but a simple one focused in a single human being who is 'full of grace and truth'. The phrase may echo the Hebrew idea of 'loving kindness' or 'faithfulness', a shorthand description of the character and nature of God. Here is the majestic and holy God of Israel among humans in a way no one could have thought to imagine or even conceive – and yet, he is here.

The structure of the prologue is remarkably visual. Starting with the swirling mystery of the universe, it gradually closes in on the green banks of the river Jordan among the brown of the wilderness, and the Baptist surrounded by crowds. But where is the word, the life, among the hundreds of faces gathered there (John 1.10–13)? The question is answered as the face of Jesus, full of the grace and truth of God, is revealed (John 1.14). In a masterpiece of build-up, however, he is not actually named until the climax of the passage (John 1.17).

The Book of Signs (John 1.19—10.42)

Once the proper context of Jesus has been set in the prologue, John embarks on a narrative of his life. After reading the accounts of Matthew, Mark and Luke it is strange to find in John's Gospel almost none of the familiar stories which they tell, nor their strongly Galilean setting. Even the calling of the disciples is different: there is no first meeting here by the Sea of Galilee but instead an encounter between Jesus and his future followers in the orbit of John the Baptist near Jerusalem (John 1.19–51).

Gathering the nucleus of a small band, Jesus heads north to Cana in Galilee, where a first miraculous sign is quickly followed by a return to Jerusalem (John 2.1–12). There Jesus cleanses the Temple around Passover time and meets Nicodemus, a senior figure among the Jewish authorities (John 2.13—3.21). After further time near Jerusalem, linked still with John the Baptist (John 3.27–36), Jesus and his followers return north to Galilee via Samaria. His encounter with a woman there leads many Samaritans to believe (John 4.1–42). Back in Galilee, Jesus returns to Cana and works another 'sign' there, healing the son of a royal official (John 4.43–54). Once again, after a brief stay in Galilee, Jesus returns to Jerusalem. There, on a Sabbath, he heals a man by a pool where the sick cluster. This provokes Jesus' first clash with the authorities and also the first hint that he claims to be 'equal with God' (John 5.1–47).

With a large crowd following, Jesus heads back to Galilee. There he feeds 5,000 people, a sign of power that the people take to show that he is a prophet and which encourages some of them to try to make him king. Jesus manages to withdraw and explains to his disciples that he is the bread of life (John 6.1–71). From Capernaum, Jesus travels through Galilee, but once again returns to Jerusalem for the Festival of Tabernacles where he teaches in the Temple, again leading to confrontation with the authorities (John 7.1—8.59). In Jerusalem, Jesus heals a man born blind, an incident which increases the tension between Jesus and the Pharisees. He then heightens the tension by taunting them with the contrast between himself as the Good Shepherd and themselves as the hired hands who neglect their duty (see Ezek. 34) to the point where he is threatened with stoning at the Festival of Dedication. Jesus escapes arrest and flees across the Jordan (John 9.1—10.42).

Interlude – returning to life, preparing for death (John 11.1—12.10)

Shortly afterwards, Jesus is summoned back to the close vicinity of Jerusalem, to Bethany and the graveside of his friend Lazarus. He raises him from the dead, the greatest of his miracles. It is also the turning point in the Gospel, for by now orders have gone out for Jesus' arrest and execution. Such a powerful and public sign performed so close to Jerusalem is like Jesus putting his head into a lion's mouth. The tone of the Gospel darkens, and when Jesus returns to Bethany on the eve of the Passover festival week, Mary, Lazarus's sister, anoints Jesus for burial as a sign of what lies ahead (John 12.1–11).

The Book of Glory (John 12.11—20.31)

Jesus enters Jerusalem in triumph, hailed as the conqueror of death because of the raising of Lazarus. Jesus reaffirms his claim to have come from the Father (John 12.12–50).

The story shifts quickly forward to the eve of the Passover. Jesus washes his disciples' feet, they eat together and Judas goes out to betray his whereabouts to the chief priests (John 13.1–30). Jesus explains that the hour of glory has come. He embarks on a long discourse, which makes clear his relationship to the Father, the disciples' relationship to him and to one another, and the gift of the Holy Spirit who will take his place as the Father's messenger to them (John 13.31—16.33). Then Jesus prays for the disciples, turning from addressing them to addressing his Father, before he sets out to meet his fate (John 17.1—18.1). Judas is ready for them and guides a detachment of soldiers to the garden where he knows Jesus will be. Jesus is arrested and questioned by the chief priest and then Pilate. At the crowd's request Jesus is condemned to death, despite Pilate's anxious attempts to uncover Jesus' real identity (John 18.2—19.16).

A small cluster of Jesus' faithful followers gather around the cross, which has a placard on it proclaiming that Jesus is 'King of the Jews'. They hear his last words and witness his death. Joseph of Arimathea and Nicodemus, by now secret disciples of Jesus, arrange for the burial of the body (John 19.17–42).

Two days later, Mary Magdalene goes to the tomb and finds Jesus' body is gone. Peter and another disciple also see that it is so, but it is Mary who meets the risen Jesus first, before he appears to all the disciples except Thomas. He breathes on them, as God breathed into Adam (Gen. 2.7), bestowing the promised Holy Spirit. Jesus' meeting with Thomas forms a final encounter, a week later, where Thomas's scepticism evaporates and he declares that Jesus is 'My Lord and my God!' (John 20.1–29). A brief summary statement ends the Gospel (John 20.30–1).

Appendix – return to Galilee (John 21.1–25)

The Gospel is supplemented by an appendix, which seems to have been added later and which tells of another appearance this time in Galilee and a further miracle (a tremendous catch of fish), the prelude to the restoration and commissioning of Peter after his denial of Jesus (John 21.1–23). The final ending of the Gospel affirms that the disciple who 'bears witness' has been the one who is behind the Gospel (John 21.24–25).

The eschatology of John's Gospel

Paul's characteristic way of talking about eschatology was as a linear sequence. He shared with most contemporary Jews a view that he lived in the 'present age', but claimed that in Jesus the Kingdom of God had broken in, the sign of the 'age to come'. The same overall sequential understanding is also there in Revelation. But we don't find the same thinking in John's Gospel. Instead of a horizontal sequence of ages there is a vertical one, and the important categories here are not 'before and after' but 'up and down' or 'below and above' (see John 3.31; 8.23). For Paul the two ages run side-by-side for a while, but in John's Gospel the new descends and replaces the old. The paradoxical 'already–not yet' tension which characterizes Paul's inaugurated eschatology is not possible in this scheme. In its place is a thoroughgoing dualism which insists on clarity. It cannot be both night and day in John's Gospel: it must be one or the other.

What's the time?

Time has a special quality in John's Gospel. There are several reminders that 'the time/hour had not yet come' early in the Gospel (John 2.4; 7.6, 8, 30; 8:20; 12:27–8), leading to the point when the fateful moment strikes. Then the final act of the Gospel begins (John 12.23; 13:1).

When the moment strikes, people have to make a choice, and in doing so they bring judgement on themselves. Rudolf Bultmann perhaps catches this best when he writes that, when Jesus is encountered, then a split 'between faith and unfaith, between the sighted and the blind, is accomplished ... He who believes is not judged (i.e. not condemned), but he who does not believe remains in darkness ... and is thereby judged (i.e. condemned)'[27] (see John 3.19; 9.39). Judgement begins now, not in the future, as the other New Testament writers tend to think, and it is based squarely on reaction to Jesus. Turning from Jesus means condemnation, but turning to Jesus leads to salvation, which is why he says that he comes not to condemn but to save (John 3.17). The offer is like deciding whether to join a lifeboat that is leaving a sinking ship: if you don't make the choice and go at once you condemn yourself to drowning. There is no time to get ready for judgement to happen: it's already there.

Judgement is worked out through characteristically dualistic language, which poses opposites such as light and dark (John 1.4–5; 3.19–21), God and the devil (John 8.44–7), blindness and sight (John 9.39). Eternal life is not something for the age to come, but a present possession (John 5.24; 11.24–5) in contrast to the spiritual death which accompanies turning away from the light of Jesus. The life Jesus offers – now – is 'life in all its abundance' (John 10.10). The eschatological perspective of John's Gospel has therefore often been described as 'realized eschatology', in the sense that the future age is seen as present already in all its fullness, even if 'the world' cannot perceive it.

Yet the perspective of uncompromising judgement cannot be maintained all the time. A future perspective is still present in the occasional mention of the 'last day' (John 6.39, 40, 44, 54; 11.24; 12.48), suggesting that this Gospel is not so far away from the thinking of the rest of the New Testament as it seems at first glance. Perhaps most significantly the dualities are frequently overcome: 'The gap between heaven and earth is constantly being bridged'[28] by Jesus himself. Therefore, Barnabas Lindars observes that the eschatology of John's Gospel 'is not strictly realised ... because it does not imply that the future is wholly swallowed up in the present. It is much more an anticipated eschatology, and its crucial feature is the dynamic concept of salvation now, but not yet.'[29] The emphasis falls more strongly on now and less strongly on not-yet than it does in Paul's writings, but the difference is like the opposite ends of a pendulum swing. Both writers seem to be expressing the same thing, but John's Gospel is 'further along the eschatological time line'.[30]

The difference in emphasis seems to be for rhetorical effect. The writer of John's Gospel is like a salesman who wants to close the deal now: today is the day to decide, the offer can't last much longer! So the present dimension of salvation is exaggerated. Casting alternatives into such extremes was not unusual in the first century, especially in some of the documents found at Qumran. The 'Community Rule' speaks in strikingly similar dualistic language of the way those 'born of injustice spring from a source of darkness', while 'the children of righteousness are ruled by the Prince of Light and walk in the ways of light'.[31] The implication is that John's Gospel is written in a similar rhetorical style in order to make a point.

The emphasis on present experience of the eschatological future had a very important effect. It raised the stakes for community life within the Church, for if (and when) disputes and splits occurred they posed grave questions about the reality of fellowship and love which were to be the hallmarks of the new life Jesus' followers were to live (John 13.34–5). This became an even more pressing and serious issue in the letters of John, which emphasize the need for a practical demonstration of unity and love (1 John 3.11–24). In 1 John, love is the acid test of discipleship, for, 'someone who does not love his brother, whom he has seen, cannot love God whom he has not seen' (1 John 4.20).

Present glory and the cross

Glory (*doxa*) is a word that recurs through the first 17 chapters of John's Gospel. When it does it almost always points forward to the last chapters which deal with the crucifixion of Jesus. Reading the prologue to the Gospel, which culminates in the statement that 'we saw his glory' (John 1.14), you might expect to find a story in which Jesus is transfigured to shine with the light of heaven (Mark 9.2–7). But glory is a much more subtle thing in John's Gospel. It is hidden, open only to those with eyes to see through the outward appearance of things.

Jesus reveals his glory to the disciples (John 2.11). They are the ones who see it. The aim of their apprenticeship in the first three-quarters of the Gospel is to help them to perceive glory in the cross. Jesus announces that now, at last, the hour has come for him to be glorified (John 12.23), but the readers are left to work out for themselves how that glorification takes place. At the moment of betrayal, when the machinery of crucifixion begins to move to its unstoppable conclusion, Jesus declares that his glorification has begun (John 13.31–2).

The revelation of glory in the cross is a function of the eschatological understanding of John's Gospel. Where the other Gospels are content to think of glory as a future element (see Mark 13.26), John's Gospel, with its emphasis on the present, must find a way of representing the cross not as the vindication of Jesus now.

This requirement is perhaps what lies behind the radically different approach to telling the story of Jesus in John's Gospel. The crucifixion does not dominate this Gospel as it does the others, where the journey of Jesus moves inevitably towards the cross. In John's Gospel Jesus moves back and forth from Jerusalem, circling closer and closer to his destiny. Only at the appointed hour, however, will that destiny happen, so it is clear that the cross must be the will of God and cannot be an accident. When the crucifixion happens, Jesus is still in control. He dies with the words 'It is finished' (John 19.30) on his lips, and returns to his Father (John 14.12; 16.28). John Ashton points out that 'what the world sees as defeat is really a triumph ... the end of Jesus' hopes and aspirations is really the beginning of his ascent into glory', and goes on to say that readers of the Gospel are expected 'to *see past* the physical reality of Jesus' death to its true significance: the reascent of the Son of Man to his true home in heaven'.[32] In a strange way, therefore, John's Gospel hardly needs the resurrection stories, and its first version concluded with Jesus blessing those who, unlike Thomas, 'have not seen but have believed' (John 20.29) the glorified and risen Jesus.

Signs and sayings – miracles and discourses

All four Gospels agree strongly that Jesus was a miracle worker and a teacher whose words had great impact on those who heard them. But Jesus performs only a few miracles in John's Gospel, while his teaching is not in the form of pithy parables but long, often repetitive, discourses.

Signs

The relatively small number of miracles in John's Gospel suggests that they have been carefully selected both for their symbolic value (as the endings of the Gospel say, John 20.30; 21.25), and also because they are the most impressive. The use of the term 'sign' for them literally suggests that they are pointers to a greater reality. This greater reality is described as 'glory' (John 2.11), evoking the splendour of the divine.

(Some scholars have suggested that a 'signs source' was the basic layer of John's Gospel. But, though plausible, this is a theory for which there is no real evidence. The miracle stories in John's Gospel show no sign of having been written by someone else: the vocabulary and style is the same as the rest of the Gospel. If these stories did form the first layer of the Gospel there is no longer any independent sign of it.)

Though fewer, the miracles in John's Gospel are similar to the miracles in the other Gospels: the sick are healed, the blind see, the hungry are fed and the dead are raised. In the case of the official's son from Capernaum there is a good argument for this miracle being John's version of the same event described by Matthew and Luke, even though there are many differences between them (John 4.46–53; Matt. 8.5–13; Luke 7.1–10). In other cases, for example healing the paralysed on a Sabbath (Mark 2.1–12; John 5.2–9), the details of the story and the location is different (Capernaum in Mark, Jerusalem in John) but the crucial saying attached to the event ('take up your mat and walk') is the same.

The real differences lie not in the details of these miracles but in their significance in John's Gospel. Raymond Brown concludes that 'The different final form ... does not stem from the miracle but from the Johannine expansion of the miracle through interpretative theological dialogue.'[32] These stories may have been reworked in a sermon-like way, until they have ended up in their present form.

Each of the miracles described by John offers a wealth of interpretative possibilities, and one intriguing feature is the way in which almost all of them can appeal to two audiences: to those of a Greek background, steeped in the traditions of Hellenistic mythology and worship, they would have one message; to those of a Jewish background they could have another, though the meanings were complementary.

The story of turning water into wine would spark immediate connections with Dionysus or Bacchus, the pagan god of wine (John 2.1–11).

Stories of Dionysus turning things into wine were a regular part of his cult, but the scale of this miracle suggests that Jesus was 'out-Dionysusing Dionysus' (the capacity of the jars suggests around 180 gallons!). But in Jewish terms this miracle would point to the joy of the last days, when God would set the world right and it would flow with an abundance of wine (Amos 9.13–14, Hosea 14.7, Jeremiah 31.12).

The other miracles offer similar double meanings. Healings took place in the stories about the Greek god Asclepius, as well as in the Hebrew Scriptures, giving a dual application to the signs of the healing of the official's son who is on the point of death (John 4.46–53) and the lame man at the pool of Bethesda (John 5.2–9); archaeological excavations show there was a Roman temple to Asclepius next to this pool. The miracles of feeding 5,000 and walking on water (John 6.1–14, 19–21) point to Jesus' mastery over the natural world. The recovery of sight by a man born blind (John 9.1–41) points to the coming of light into the world (see John 1.5), echoing the creation story for Jews (see Gen. 1.3), and Apollo the Sun-god for pagans. The raising of Lazarus forcibly points to the significance of death, an enduring theme in all religious reflection, but also to Jesus' power to overcome it (John 11.38–44). The final miracle in the Gospel, the catch of fish (John 21.2–11), is another nature miracle pointing to the generosity of God.

The miracles in John's Gospel function as signs pointing to greater truths, but they are also pegs to hang discourses on. So the feeding of the 5,000 leads naturally into Jesus' teaching about the bread of life (John 6.25–59) and the teaching about the light of the world (John 8.12–20) links well with the story of the healing of the man born blind (John 9). Signs and speech have a symbiotic relationship in John's Gospel, designed to point to the greatest question of all: what is the meaning and identity of Jesus?

The raising of Lazarus – did it happen?

The raising of Lazarus is a pivotal moment in John's Gospel. It is the point at which the plot of the authorities becomes fatal for Jesus (John 11.45–57), and also the basis of his fame as he enters Jerusalem (John 12.17–18). The story is told in great detail, with the characters of Lazarus's sisters, Mary and Martha, vividly drawn (John 11.1–44). It is a superbly told tale, 'unique in that everything is subordinate to the overriding aim of making the maximum emotional impact'.[34] The episode clearly has a major function in the Gospel, but its absence from the other Gospels forcibly raises the question, how far we can trust John's Gospel to relate what really happened?

The other three Gospels offer miracle stories about people raised from the dead, but since all of these occur soon after the death has taken place they do not strain credulity so much (see Mark 5.35–43, Luke 7.11–17). Lazarus, John is at pains to emphasize, has been dead four days and his body is already decaying badly (John 11.39). Scholars are divided over whether the raising of Lazarus was a historical event or not. A primary reason for scepticism is, naturally, that some dismiss the possibility of miracles at all. This is an important issue, but it is not the main focus here. The question is, rather, did John think Jesus raised Lazarus from the dead, or is this story meant to be 'a kind of parable of what Jesus does not only for Lazarus, but for all who believe in him'?[35]

The strongest argument to explain why the first three Gospels fail to mention the event, if it happened, is that Peter does not seem to be among those who are around Jesus at the raising of Lazarus, and Mark's and Matthew's Gospels are essentially based on the witness of Peter. The absence of the story from Luke's Gospel is more problematic since Luke includes a good deal of his own independent material in his Gospel, which sometimes echoes John's Gospel. A good and possibly relevant example is the way that Luke describes the crowd welcoming Jesus into Jerusalem as praising God for the miracles they have seen (Luke 19.37), an echo of Jesus' entry into Jerusalem according to John (John 12.18). But though Luke mentions the sisters Martha and Mary, their brother Lazarus is notable by his absence (Luke 10.38–42). Surely if Luke knew of the story of Lazarus's raising from the dead, he would have included it?

It can be argued that the narrative scheme of the other Gospel writers does not allow them to include the story, since they place Jesus in Galilee until the final confrontation in Jerusalem, but this seems like special pleading. Placed where John puts the episode, on the brink of Jesus' entry to Jerusalem, it could fit quite happily into the storyline which Mark, Matthew and Luke follow. Alternatively, Richard Bauckham has suggested that Lazarus might, if he was under threat as John's Gospel says he was (John 12.9–11), have needed 'protective anonymity',[36] but while this might (just) apply to the situation in which Mark's and Matthew's Gospels were written, it is hard to see its relevance to Luke's. Nor does it explain why the whole episode was ignored: it would have been perfectly possible to tell the story without mentioning names, as is frequently the case in other miracle stories.

In all, then, it looks unlikely that the event actually happened as John described it: the crowning miracle of Jesus' career shortly before his final Passover festival. Dominic Crossan argues therefore that, paradoxically, 'while I do not think this event ever did or ever could happen, I think it is absolutely true.'[37] He means that John has invented a story which expresses symbolically what Jesus did. Crossan uses the analogy of a high school named after Abraham Lincoln which might have a statue showing the president using an axe to break the chains of a slave. This was not a literal event in Lincoln's life, but an accurate symbolic representation of what he did; in other words it would depict an event that never happened but is nevertheless true. John's story of Lazarus is the same, argues Crossan, in depicting Jesus as one who brings life out of death. However, though Crossan's argument is characteristically ingenious and worth considering carefully, a surprising number of scholars are convinced that there is a bedrock of fact in this story. John P. Meier, whose analysis is perhaps the most exhaustive, concludes that

> I think it likely that John 11.1–45 goes back ultimately to some event involving Lazarus, a disciple of Jesus, and that this event was believed by Jesus' disciples even during his lifetime to be a miracle of raising the dead. In other words, the basic idea that Jesus raised Lazarus from the dead does not seem to have been simply created out of thin air by the early church.[38]

To arrive at this conclusion Meier has reconstructed an early version of the story which excludes much of the detail. He argues that there was a simple tradition of a sick man called Lazarus whose sisters, Mary and Martha, knew Jesus. Jesus raised Lazarus from the dead, calling him out from his tomb. As such this story was similar to those of Jairus's daughter (Mark 5.35–43) and the widow of Nain's son (Luke 7.11–17) and it was either not known about or not selected for use by the other Gospel writers. John exaggerates the miraculous element (only in this account 'has the corpse been buried for four days and begun to stink'[39]), creates dialogue and tells the story as dramatically as possible. In doing so it becomes the means by which he gathers up the strands of the story so far and anticipates what will happen to Jesus in the rest of the Gospel.

As it stands, the Lazarus story is a powerful and unforgettable encapsulation of the main theme of John's Gospel: that Jesus has come to bring life. Most significantly the life of Lazarus can be restored only by Jesus submitting himself to death, as Thomas notes (John 11.16), and as Jesus' own deep agitation may show too (John 11.33, see also 12.27; 13.21). Meier paraphrases C. H. Dodd to say that 'the raising of Lazarus is Jesus' victory *over* death ... which symbolizes and points forward to Jesus' victory *through* death.'[40] In typically ironic fashion, Jesus' words to the crowd, 'loose him; let him go' (John 11.44), spell freedom for Lazarus but foreshadow captivity for Jesus himself. In particular Jesus' conversation with Martha on the way to the tomb sets the whole episode in context. Martha's hope is the conventional one of the time for a future resurrection 'on the last day' (John 11.24). Jesus responds to her that, in him, the 'last day' has already come: 'I am the resurrection and the life' (John 11.25).

John's Gospel poses the raising of Lazarus as the basis for the ultimate and implacable opposition of the Jerusalem authorities to Jesus (John 11.45–53). The other Gospels make the cleansing of the Temple incident the reason for Jesus' arrest, but John makes it clear that Jesus' threat is far greater and deeper than a matter of politics and religious observance. The implications of Jesus' actions, in other words, stretch much further than the Temple and Israel. Jesus the life-giver does not so much challenge as completely overshadow the Temple and render it irrelevant, and for this reason the authorities cannot tolerate him any longer. So they seek to do the impossible, and put to death the man who is actually the cause of life.

In this examination of the Lazarus story we have seen how John took a basis of fact and embroidered and developed it for his own theological purpose. John Ashton comments, 'Suppose ... that the ... answer to the question whether Lazarus actually rose from the dead ... is "No". Does this mean that the Gospel narrative has no truth and no validity? Only if there is no truth in narrative other than historical truth'.[41] In effect John creates a free meditation on events which enables him to draw out the deeper meaning and implications of them in a way which straight narration would not do: we have here, according to Andrew Lincoln, 'a narrative which contains a substratum of core events from the tradition with substantial claims to reliability, but one which is now shaped by an interpretive superstructure which contains a considerable amount of embellishment, including some legendary or fictive elements.'[42] How much is the 'considerable amount' here? John seems clear that the authority for embellishment is the guidance of the Holy Spirit (John 15.26; 16.13), which forms the guarantee that, whatever embellishments have been made, they do not stray too far from the true meaning of the events described.

This exploration of John 11 tells us a good deal about the nature of this Gospel. Though the events themselves matter, it is their meaning that is the most important thing. Meaning matters to Luke and the other Gospel writers but it has an overriding importance for John. Oscar Cullmann suggested that 'the Gospel writer presents his theology in the form of a *life* of Jesus'[43], which is to say that where the theology is drawn *from* the events of Jesus' life for Matthew, Mark and Luke, in John's Gospel the theology comes first and the events then illustrate it. The process seems to be a recursive one: the events gave rise to the theology, which was then read back into the events.

Which is more real? The plain narrative of what took place before their eyes? Or the secondary version which John offers, confronting the audience with the true meaning that the bare event itself could not disclose, which could only be seen in retrospect?

The discourses

In John's Gospel Jesus often teaches by means of long speeches. In the first three Gospels Jesus teaches in short stories and sayings. Both forms are representations of what Jesus said rather than verbatim reports, of course, and a moment's thought reveals that this is the case: in Mark's Gospel a 'huge crowd' gathers to hear Jesus (Mark 4.1), but they would have felt short-changed if they heard only the three stories which are recorded (though there is a vague mention of 'many similar parables', Mark 4.33). Jesus must have taught at greater length and it may be that the discourses in John's Gospel are an alternative way of trying to capture this. But the speeches which are placed in his mouth are probably like Paul's in Acts: appropriate to the occasion but unlikely to be the actual words that were said, normal procedure for a work of history or biography in the ancient world.

The first major discourse comes as part of the encounter with Nicodemus. It is unusual in not being public; it takes place 'by night'. Like many of the discourses, it begins as a conversation (John 3.1–13) and becomes a monologue (John 3.14–21). Its subject is Jesus as the revealer of a fresh beginning, the salvation of the world which is a new departure in the story of Israel. The emphasis is on Jesus being the one sent from heaven for the sake of the world.

Where Jesus' words are meant to end is unclear: does he or the writer say 'For God loved the world like this: he gave the son, the only one, so that everyone who believes in him may not be destroyed but have everlasting life' (John 3.16)? Unlike Paul, who is scrupulous in distinguishing between his own words and those of Jesus (see 1 Cor. 7.12), the author of John's Gospel seems so confident of his ability to interpret Jesus' words that he takes for granted his licence to do so. Some scholars suggest that passages like the second part of this discourse had their origin in the preaching of the early Church, introduced by preserved sayings of Jesus which are signalled by the phrase 'Amen, amen, I say to you ...' (John 3.3; unfortunately the formula is not always clear in contemporary English translations). Such sayings may have functioned as the 'text' from which the preacher then developed his interpretation.

The second discourse follows the healing of the lame man by the pool of Bethesda on a festival Sabbath (John 5.1, 9). God works on the Sabbath, and Jesus does too (John 5.17), the first example of how Jesus replaces or sets aside the traditional pattern of observances. The authorities accuse Jesus of breaking the Law by healing on the Sabbath, part of the escalating theme of the opposition of the authorities which provides much of the tension in the storyline of the Gospel and leads Andrew Lincoln, for example, to see this discourse as part of a 'defence in an interrogation or trial'.[44] But the discourse quickly moves from the specific issue to become a vindication of the very thing of which the authorities accuse Jesus, making himself equal to God (John 5.18). In other words, the accusation is right: Jesus *is* deliberately breaking the old covenant boundaries. The discourse goes on to emphasize the fundamental unity between the Father and the Son (John 5.19–47).

The third discourse concerns the bread of life, following the feeding of the 5,000. Bread was a potent symbol, connected in Jewish thought with the Law, the true bread by which one might live. Jesus in this discourse sets himself in the place of the Law (John 6.35), but there is also a glimpse forward to the symbolic sharing of Jesus' body and blood in the Eucharist (John 6.53–6).

The Feast of Tabernacles (John 7.2) forms the background to the next major discourse (which straddles the intruded section of John 7.53—8.11). Tabernacles was a time to pray for rain, but Jesus' announcement of himself as the source of living water (John 7.37–8) once again suggests that he supersedes the festival. The same note is sounded in Jesus' proclamation that 'I am the light of the world' (John 8.12); Tabernacles was an autumn festival, its rituals, as the evenings drew in, illuminated by the lighting of huge lamp stands in the Temple. Once again, dispute with the Jewish authorities leads Jesus to turn defence into attack, accusing them of no longer being the descendants of Abraham. The discourse concludes with outright confrontation between Jesus and his opponents as he is threatened with being stoned (John 8.31–59).

The discourse about the Good Shepherd forms the last of this sequence in the first half of the Gospel. In a way that is now familiar, Jesus both points to the shortcomings of his opponents, described as 'hired hands' or time-servers, and claims to be the true shepherd who will lead the flock to safety even at the expense of his own life (John 10.1–18, see Ezek. 34). The setting in the Festival of Dedication (*Hanukkah*) once again forms a perfect background to this discourse. Dedication was a time to remember the triumphs of the Maccabees in freeing the Temple but also a time when discussion about the coming of the messiah took place. It would pointedly raise questions about the fitness of the rulers to rule, and thus forms the ideal climax to the first half of the Gospel in terms of Jesus' teaching.

At this halfway point in the Gospel there has been a great deal of public teaching by Jesus. But it is significant that it has almost all taken place in the context of conflict, and it has rarely picked up the theme of the Kingdom of God which is the basis of Jesus' teaching in the first three Gospels (John 3.3, 5 are the exceptions). In fact, as Rudolf Bultmann observed, 'it turns out in the end that Jesus as the Revealer of God reveals nothing but that he is the Revealer ... John ... in his Gospel presents only the fact ... of the Revelation without describing its content'.[45] In other words, looking at the discourses shows that the teaching in John's Gospel is solely geared towards understanding Jesus. Even more than the other Gospels, John's focuses on Jesus himself and his significance.

Famous last words – the farewell discourse

Jesus' public teaching comes to an end after his entry into Jerusalem. A rather terse summary draws together the main themes of identity between Jesus and God, and his role in bringing judgement and salvation to the world (John 12.44–50). This may be intended as a refresher for the audience of the Gospel rather than being an integral part of the story itself (Jesus is still apparently in hiding, John 12.36). The story itself moves quickly forward to the end of Jesus' life and the supper which he has with his disciples. But the supper is hardly narrated at all. Instead the next five chapters (a quarter of the Gospel) are occupied by Jesus' farewell discourse, more than twice as much space as the crucifixion itself will occupy. This teaching is private, intended for the disciples not the often uncomprehending or hostile crowds.

The farewell speech was a regular feature of much ancient biographical writing: the best example is Plato's *Phaedo*, a sustained narrative of Socrates' teaching to his close followers on the night before he was put to death by the Athenian authorities. On a much smaller scale Paul's address to the Ephesian elders fulfils a similar function (Acts 20.17–35).

Jesus' farewell discourse, in its dramatic context in John's Gospel, is Jesus' last chance to get through to his disciples. His later comments suggest that he has done so and that now they have heard all they need to know (John 17.7–8). The disciples therefore take a rather more central place in this discourse than they have done in the others. This is Jesus' last will and testament to them.

Mark's Gospel has private teaching for the disciples in a similar setting in Jerusalem, though not on the eve of the crucifixion. This is the so-called 'little apocalypse' which looks for future cosmic signs of the end of the world (Mark 13). Jesus' farewell discourse in John's Gospel faces some similar questions, but they are in a very different key, and are relocated to the present. The disciples are anxious (John 14.1). But Jesus' departure will not leave them alone, for his place will be taken by 'another advocate', the Spirit of truth who will dwell with them for ever (John 14.16–17). The idea of a future return of Jesus, evident in Paul's thinking, seems to have been collapsed into his return to the disciples after the resurrection, followed by the gift of the Spirit who will replace Jesus and become the animating force of their community (John 14.26). The glorification of Jesus will not be obvious, it will come about through the obedience of his followers and the fruit that they bear (John 15.8). In other words, the business of manifesting the Father in the world which has been the role of Jesus, the messenger from heaven (and which has formed the basis of the earlier discourses) now becomes the role of his disciples under the leadership and guidance of the Spirit. Therefore their own unity and close fellowship is a vital part of their future mission (John 15.1–17). The final part of the discourse is Jesus' prayer for the disciples in their new responsibility (John 17).

Recognizing this transference from Jesus to the community of disciples is crucial for understanding John's Gospel. The high claims of the first half of the Gospel that Jesus is the revealer of the Father now become the basis for the claim of the community behind the Gospel to possess the 'authorized version' of the meaning of Jesus. Their role is also to take on the function of Jesus in bringing the truth to the world (John 17.15–18). After the resurrection, Jesus authorizes and commissions the disciples with words that make their link with him explicit: 'as the Father has sent me, so also I send you'. Then he breathes his Spirit on them, just as God breathed into Adam in the creation story (Gen. 2.7), and gives them the authority he himself has had to forgive and retain sins (John 20.21–3). The identification is complete. As Jesus and the Father are one, so also are Jesus and his disciples.

John's Gospel and the others: spiritual versus physical?

Clement of Alexandria's comment that John's was a 'spiritual Gospel' shows that the question of why John's Gospel was different from the others was a live issue almost as soon as it was written. For centuries John's Gospel had been prized for supplementing and filling out the picture of Jesus offered by the other Gospels. But as the critical study of the New Testament gathered pace in the nineteenth century scholars increasingly began to point out that the differences seem in fact to be discrepancies or contradictions.

How different is John's Gospel?

At first sight it looks as if a conflict between John's and the other Gospels can be resolved by simple arithmetic: it's three against one, so John's version is likely to be suspect. But since the Gospels of Matthew and Luke are based on Mark's it's really a head-to-head contest, Mark versus John.

Four major issues strike anyone who tries to harmonize these two traditions:

- The cleansing of the Temple happens at the beginning of Jesus' ministry in John, not at its end (John 2.13–16; Mark 11.15–17).
- Jesus moves back and forth between Galilee and Judea in John, frequently attending festivals; in Mark, Jesus' triumphal entry to Jerusalem a few days before his crucifixion is his first visit.
- The raising of Lazarus is the reason for the plot against Jesus in John (John 11.53), but Lazarus is unmentioned in Mark and it is the Temple-cleansing that antagonizes the Jewish authorities (Mark 11.18).
- Jesus eats a meal with his disciples on the eve of Passover in John (John

13.1), so his crucifixion is on the eve of Passover too; in Mark the meal is the Passover itself (Mark 14.16), so Jesus dies one day later.

Consequently it became obvious that both could not be right.

On the basis that John's Gospel laid claim to an eyewitness source (John 19.35; 21.24) it was generally preferred when there was a conflict. F. C. Baur overturned this view, writing in 1847 that John's Gospel 'does not intend to be a strictly historical Gospel. It subordinates its historical content to an overriding idea.' In the conflict between the Synoptics and John's Gospel, he judged that

> when two different reports concerned with the same subject are so related to one another in their difference that only one of the two – not both at the same time and in the same way – can be historically true, it is to be assumed that the overwhelming historical probability lies on the side of that report which least of all betrays any interest, beyond the purpose of purely historical narration, that could have an influence on the historical record.[46]

John's Gospel was, therefore, so ideologically skewed that it had, in Baur's view, very little historical value (though he was genuinely at pains to say that it had immense theological value). Instead, Baur favoured Matthew's Gospel as providing the best access to historical information about Jesus on the grounds that he believed it to be the oldest of the four and least affected by any 'overriding idea'. Just after Baur's death in 1860, H. J. Holtzmann proved to the satisfaction of almost everyone that Mark's was in fact the earliest Gospel, but Baur's basic conclusion that the synoptic version of Jesus' life was to be preferred has remained virtually uncontested ever since, a remarkable tribute to him. John's Gospel is often regarded as theological, the Synoptics as historical. And thus Clement's spiritual/physical distinction was vindicated.

Yet a close look at John's Gospel doesn't really bear out the spiritual/physical distinction in this way. As D. Moody Smith comments, 'Clement's assessment ... works much better ... on the macro-level than the micro-level. That is ... it breaks down repeatedly when specific aspects of John are compared with the other Gospels.'[47] John's Gospel appears to give more precise historical details than the other Gospels do. This is not what you might expect if it were designed to be concerned solely with theological matters.

To some extent we are back to questions about what kind of books the Gospels are. If we understand them as first-century biographies, then while what we would regard as historical facts are clearly not irrelevant, neither are they the primary concern. Luke seems to be the New Testament author most concerned to present his work as historically responsible but he is also probably the most creative of the synoptic Gospel writers in terms of recasting his narrative according to a literary pattern and giving the least attention to detailed questions of chronology. Richard Bauckham has argued that, in this setting, there is a good case for regarding John's Gospel as at least as firmly situated within the genre of biography/history as the other Gospels, while its presentation of geography and chronology 'would have made it look, to competent contemporary readers, more like historiography than the Synoptics.'[48] Of course, as Bauckham points out, this is different from saying that the information which John's Gospel provides is reliable according to the standards of modern historical writing. It is simply a claim that, according to the standards of the time, the intention of the writer of John's Gospel was to provide some historical information. In this sense, Clement's contrast between 'physical' and 'spiritual' should not be read as an opposition between mutually exclusive categories. The message of John's Gospel is, above all, that in Jesus heaven and earth touch, the spiritual and physical are interwoven and no longer opposed: 'the Word [spiritual] became flesh [physical]' (John 1.14). John's Gospel is designed to tell the story of Jesus again but in such a way that the spiritual meaning beneath the surface of events is revealed.

Did the writer of John's Gospel know Mark's?

For those who compare only the four Gospels of the New Testament, the differences between John's and the others are very marked. However, looked at from a wider perspective they seem to have a strong 'family resemblance':[49] they are all trying to do the same kind of biographical task in a similar way. Comparisons with other Gospels, such as *Thomas* or *Philip* or the *Gospel of Truth*, which have very little regard for what actually happened, reveal much greater differences. The overall structures of the two Gospels of Mark and John actually have strong similarities:

- Both begin with John the Baptist (Mark 1.4–8; John 1.19–36).
- Both show a ministry based in Galilee 'after John was arrested' (Mark 1.14; see John 3.24; 4.43).
- The feeding of the 5,000 and Jesus' walking on water occupy a central place in the story of Jesus' ministry (Mark 6.34–52; John 6.1–20).
- Peter makes an important confession about Jesus' identity (Mark 8.29; John 6.69).
- Jesus goes to Jerusalem for a final confrontation with the temple authorities (Mark 11.1–10; John 12.12–15).
- Jesus is anointed in advance of his death (Mark 14.3–9; John 12.1–8);
- Jesus is betrayed by Judas and arrested (Mark 14.43–6; John 18.1–12).
- Peter denies knowing Jesus (Mark 14.66–72; John 18.15–27).
- Jesus is reluctantly condemned to death by Pontius Pilate (Mark 15.15; John 19.16).

The order of events is often slightly different (the anointing, for example, occurs before the entry into Jerusalem for John, but after it for Mark). But the broad outline is the same.

So did the writer of John's Gospel know the Gospels of Mark, Matthew or Luke? For the last few decades the scholarly consensus has been that John's Gospel came from an independent source and was not connected with the synoptic Gospels except through the sharing of very early traditions about Jesus. Yet a close look at the issue suggests otherwise. Careful comparison of John's Gospel with the other three suggests some sort of dependence between them, though it is hard to be specific about exactly what it is. Andrew Lincoln notes in his commentary on the Gospel that, though he was initially disposed to think that John's Gospel was not directly connected with the others, constant contact with the text has led him to conclude that 'the Fourth Gospel provides evidence that its writer and editor not only knew Mark, to which it is most substantially indebted, but also knew and used Matthew and Luke.' *How* the writer of John's Gospel used Mark's (and Matthew's and Luke's) is unclear. It was obviously not in the same way that Matthew and Luke had used Mark's Gospel for it shows far more 'creative and imaginative freedom'.[50] But the overall storyline and many of Jesus' sayings are the same.

There are some clear indications within the text that a Gospel like Mark's is presupposed. For example, there is no narrative of either the actual baptism of Jesus, or of Jesus' symbolic actions at the Last Supper in John's Gospel. The most obvious explanation of this is that the writer of John's Gospel felt the stories were known well enough not to need repeating. Some characters in the story simply appear, without explanation or identification (notably Pilate, John 18.29). There is a clear presupposition that they don't need to be introduced because the audience will already know who they are.

John's Gospel, then, may plausibly be another attempt to 'fix' Mark's, just as Matthew's and Luke's seem to have been. But where Matthew and Luke rewrote the text and added to it, John's Gospel seems to be more of a supplement, which endeavours to bring out the implications of Jesus' life more fully. So Lincoln concludes that the 'evangelist supplements the other Gospels ... by enhancing [the Synoptics'] portrait of [Jesus] through a further narrative that makes more explicit the significance of his oneness with God'.[51] The writer of John's Gospel seems content to leave some episodes of Jesus' life untold because they are narrated by Mark, but there are three areas in particular where there seem to be definite conflicts between the two traditions. These are Jesus' ministry in Judea, the cleansing of the Temple and the trial and crucifixion of Jesus.

Jesus' ministry in Judea

The Gospels of Mark and Matthew have a simple geographical pattern. After his baptism in the wilderness of Judea, Jesus heads north to Galilee and doesn't come south again until the Passover at which he dies. John's Gospel by contrast shows Jesus as a regular visitor to Jerusalem, and this picture is partly echoed by Luke's Gospel (see Luke 4.44; 5.17; 6.17; 7.17).

In fact Mark's narrative has a strong implied Judean background to the story. Jesus has followers from Judea (Mark 3.8); he has contacts near Bethany that he can call on (Mark 11.3); he knows someone in Jerusalem at festival time who is able to provide a room at very short notice (Mark 14.13–15); and his followers include a member of the Jewish council (Mark 15.43). In addition, Matthew and Luke include a lament over Jerusalem: 'How often have I longed to gather you as a hen gathers her chicks under her wing' (Matt. 23.37; Luke 13.34); the force of 'how often' would be lost if this were Jesus' first adult visit.

Since the triumphal entry into Jerusalem is the first time Jesus has entered the city, according to Mark, it looks as if he has streamlined his narrative which is built around the final 'assault' on Jerusalem, and that John's Gospel (backed up by Luke's) is the more realistic. Interestingly, Fergus Millar, perhaps the leading contemporary historian of the ancient Near East, takes the view that 'John presents ... an incomparably more detailed and circumstantial picture of Jewish life in Palestine, punctuated by the annual rhythm of the festivals, than do the Synoptics.' He argues that therefore a choice must be made: 'Either Jesus went only once to Jerusalem, for the fatal Passover, or he went several times ... I suggest that the narrative of Jesus' ministry which brings us closest to the real world of first-century Palestine is that of John.'[52] But if we take the Gospels seriously as biographies it is surely not necessary for us to choose: it is just that Mark has simplified the story and told it more economically. What is significant is that in Millar's judgement it is John's Gospel which seems to reflect the Palestinian background more authentically. (As we said earlier, this is in itself no guarantee of accuracy. Millar's argument is simply that John's Gospel appears to be the more plausible account.)

The cleansing of the Temple

John's Gospel begins the ministry of Jesus with an incident in the Temple (John 2.13–21); Mark's Gospel, on the other hand places this event on the day after Jesus' entry into Jerusalem (Mark 11.15–18). Matthew and Luke broadly follow Mark, but place the event on the same day as the entry into Jerusalem (Matt. 21.10–17; Luke 19.45–8).

Because most scholars assume that the concern of John's Gospel is with theology rather than history, it is generally reckoned that the writer has taken this story from the place it has in Mark's Gospel as the prelude to Jesus' passion and used it for another purpose, that is 'as a headline under which or window through which to read the whole Gospel'.[53] In particular, locating this episode early in the story explains the continuing opposition of the Temple authorities to Jesus in John's Gospel. Their antagonism would make no sense otherwise, but the plot of the Gospel turns on it. The story of Lazarus replaces the Synoptics' cleansing, both physically and in terms of the plot of the Gospel. The cleansing of the Temple is what leads to Jesus' death according to Mark; for John it is Lazarus' return from the dead which is the last straw for the authorities (Mark 11.18; John 11.53).

There are more differences between the two accounts than simply the timing. Placed side by side, it becomes clear that, while they share close similarities, the common elements are not honestly much more than you would expect of two narratives set in the same place. There are two major differences between the accounts. John's Gospel speaks of Jesus driving out cattle and sheep (John 2.14–15), while Mark's states quite clearly that Jesus 'would not allow anyone to carry a vessel through the Temple' (Mark 11.16); and the words of Jesus in each version are completely different.

John's version suggests that sheep and cattle available to be purchased for sacrifice had been introduced into the Temple area, and that the initial force of Jesus' anger is against this practice: he takes a whip of cords and uses it to drive out the animals and those who were selling them. After this he turns on the money changers and the dove-sellers. In other words, this event seems to be a one-man protest which becomes a stampede.

Mark's Gospel omits any mention of the cattle but includes a comment about Jesus not allowing anyone to carry vessels (or merchandise) through the Temple, implying a far more significant intervention in the regular process of ritual than John's Gospel does. To enforce such a prohibition would require barring the entrances and symbolically halting the sacrificial system. If nothing could be brought into the precincts the sacrifices would stop. This would be a large-scale protest (requiring a significant number of supporters) and would have caused major disruption. It fits more logically as the aftermath of the entry into Jerusalem than a demonstration with just a small, not yet fully formed, band of disciples, which is the situation in John's Gospel.

As far as the words of Jesus recorded in these passages are concerned, John includes material about the destruction of the Temple, while Mark adds a saying about the Temple becoming a 'den of robbers (or bandits)' which is usually taken to be an attack on the nationalist aspirations attached to the Temple at this time and possibly on the Herod family's abuse of power. The strangest aspect of this difference lies in the fact that Mark uses the saying which John records here as the accusation against Jesus at his trial (Mark 14.58), but refers to it nowhere else.

The differences can be explained (and usually are) by seeing the account in John's Gospel as having been rewritten to fit the theological context. But it is actually Mark's account which seems better attuned to this purpose: the symbolism of the destruction of the Temple system fits neatly with the tearing of the sanctuary curtain at Jesus' death which points to the end of the Temple as the dwelling-place of God (Mark 15.38). The symbolic value of John's version, by contrast, is not clear at all, though it helps to explain the consistent opposition of the Temple authorities to Jesus throughout his ministry.

There are three alternative ways of explaining the differences:

- Mark's Gospel is right both in its timing and description of the event.
- John's Gospel is right both in its timing and description of the event.
- The two Gospels are talking about different events.

It is worth pausing to consider that the reason why the vast majority of scholars opt for the first or second options (but almost always the first) is that it seems unlikely that such an event could have happened twice. But this is a presupposition rather than evidence.

If we look for evidence, then we find an intriguing story in Josephus's *Jewish War* about Jesus Ben Ananias who prophesied about the Temple at the Feast of Tabernacles in 62, just before the Jewish revolt of 66. Jesus Ben Ananias's protests led to his arrest by the Temple authorities. He was savagely beaten and then taken before the Roman governor, Albinus. Under questioning from Albinus he refused to answer and continued his prophecies of destruction. Albinus concluded that the man was mad and released him to resume his dismal ministry for 'seven years and five months'. Until the Temple was indeed destroyed, Josephus notes that 'his voice was heard most of all at the feasts.'[54] The importance of this story lies in the similarity of a prophetic announcement within the Temple precincts at a festival and implies that an isolated prophetic announcement in itself did not lead to arrest. It was only Jesus Ben Ananias's persistence that finally led the authorities to deal with him.

Could something similar have happened with Jesus of Nazareth? Certainly if Jesus had caused two incidents in the Temple it would make it more likely that they should be the basis for accusations against him, as Mark's Gospel suggests. As it is, John's Gospel skips straight from five days before the Passover (John 12.1, 12) to the day before (John 13.1), missing out the period which covers both the cleansing of the Temple and Jesus' teaching there which forms the basis of Mark's narrative of the same period (Mark 11.7—12.44).

It's not possible to come to a definitive answer on the question, but the point of the analysis is to show that it is at least possible for both Gospels to be right: there is not an inevitable contradiction here, and of the two accounts it actually seems in this case that Mark's is more likely to be governed by symbolic considerations than John's. This throws further into question the consensus that Mark's Gospel is generally more historically reliable than John's. This is not to deny that the material in John's Gospel has been heavily reworked and embroidered (see the analysis of the Lazarus story above). Instead it is to suggest that a similar process may have been at work in the other Gospels too, even Mark's, making all four Gospels more alike than is often thought to be the case.

Can you have your unleavened bread and eat it? When was the crucifixion of Jesus?

The third and most obvious disagreement between John's Gospel and the Synoptics is over the day on which the crucifixion of Jesus took place. Jewish festivals began at sunset, so the chronology of John's Gospel shows Jesus eating a meal on the eve of Passover, being arrested that night and executed the following day. Thus he is dead and buried before the Passover feast itself begins. The Synoptics on the other hand unanimously agree that Jesus ate the Passover with his disciples before being arrested, making the day of execution the feast day itself. Either one or the other is correct.

There are a huge number of explanations offered on this subject, including the ingenious one that there were two calendars in operation in Jerusalem at the time. None of these explanations can command a consensus. But the initial presupposition that Mark's Gospel must be chronologically accurate and that the story in John's Gospel has been altered to fit theological concerns cannot be demonstrated.

The Passover feast was celebrated on the fifteenth day of Nisan, the first month in the Jewish calendar, followed the next day by the feast of unleavened bread which lasted for a week (Lev. 23.5–6). By the first century it seems that both feasts were rolled into one, and the week-long feast of unleavened bread was often seen as beginning on the Passover day (see Mark 14.12). The lambs which were needed for the Passover meal were killed in the Temple at twilight on Nisan 14, before the beginning of the feast day at sunset with its night-time meal. In view of the numbers of lambs required by the first century, this slaughter had been pushed back to begin in the early afternoon of Nisan 14.

The different accounts all agree that Jesus died on a Friday, that is, the day before the Sabbath (Mark 15.42; Matt. 27.62; Luke 23.54; John 19.31). They also agree that Jesus was arrested during the previous night, the only chronological marker for the event in the oldest source (1 Cor. 11.23). The Synoptics suggest pretty clearly that Jesus had just eaten a Passover meal with his disciples (Mark 14.12–16; Matt. 26.17–19; Luke 22.1–14, though Luke 22.15 may imply that this is the eve of Passover). John's Gospel does not describe the meal as such, but since it is clear that

	Mark 14.43—15.47	Luke 22.47—23.56	John 18.1—19.42
Night	• Arrest of Jesus by Jewish police • Jesus taken to the high priest • Chief priests, elders and scribes gather in council (Sanhedrin)	• Arrest of Jesus by Jewish police • Jesus taken to the high priest	• Arrest of Jesus by Roman soldiers and Jewish police • Jesus taken to the former high priest, Annas • Jesus taken to the high priest, Caiaphas
Morning	• Council takes Jesus to Pilate • Pilate condemns Jesus • Jesus crucified (9 a.m.)	• Chief priests, elders and scribes gather in council (Sanhedrin) • Council takes Jesus to Pilate • Pilate sends Jesus to Herod Antipas • Pilate condemns Jesus • Jesus crucified	• Jesus taken to Pilate • Pilate condemns Jesus (noon)
Afternoon	• Jesus dies (3 p.m.) • Jesus buried (before sunset)	• Jesus dies (3 p.m.) • Jesus buried (before sunset)	• Jesus crucified • Jesus dies • Jesus buried (before sunset)

Figure 19 Three accounts of Jesus' last hours

the chief priests have not yet eaten their Passover meal the next morning then that day must be the day of preparation (John 18.28; 19.14).

The events of the following day have three variations, summarized in Figure 19 (Matthew follows Mark in structure, though he adds a few details, such as Caiaphas's name, Matt. 26.57).

The broad outlines are similar, though the details are very different. Luke's Gospel and Mark's differ over the timing of the meeting of the Sanhedrin to condemn Jesus, and most strikingly Luke's version includes

Jesus being sent to Herod Antipas. The differences in John's account are much more marked. According to him, the Sanhedrin had met some weeks before to decide on Jesus' death (John 11.47–53), so he has no need to relate a midnight meeting as Mark does. John's Gospel also suggests that Roman soldiers came to arrest Jesus alongside the Temple police (the technical words for 'cohort' and 'officer' are used, John 18.3, 12). Most obviously the time of the crucifixion is different (after midday, John 19.14; 9 a.m., Mark 15.25). And woven into the story in John's Gospel is the importance of these events taking place on the day *before* the Passover. This is why the Jewish authorities will not enter Pilate's headquarters, lest they become impure for the feast itself (John 18.28). Yet Mark's Gospel seems to say that Jesus ate a Passover meal with his disciples before his arrest.

All the writers have been selective in what they have chosen to say and how they say it. John's Gospel often provides a more 'close-up' view of the events. The major discrepancy is over the day on which Jesus' death occurred. The key question is whether the Synoptics really think that Jesus had eaten a genuine Passover the night before.

Although it looks as if this is their view, the crucial ingredient in a Passover meal was a lamb, and it is absent from the narrative. Whole lakes of ink have been used to discuss this question by scholars, with the argument going back and forth without any clear resolution. While it seems clear that this meal was '*some kind of* Passover meal', it was not celebrated by Jesus with his family as the Law commanded and, given Jesus' reinterpretation of many of the most important elements of Jewish faith 'there is no reason to suppose that Jesus might not have celebrated what we might call a *quasi*-Passover meal a day ahead of the real thing.'[55] The discussion cannot reach a definite conclusion since the information available is not comprehensive ('When arguments are so finely balanced it is wise not to press for one alternative as against another'[56]), but it seems that the account in John's Gospel is just as likely to be accurate as the one largely shared by the Synoptics.

To my mind John's chronology fits the situation better, and the main reason for this conclusion is that it does not seem likely that Jesus' arrest, trial and crucifixion took place on the Passover day itself, as the Synoptics have it. Such activity would have meant a widespread flouting of the regulations for a holy day, and 'there are really too many anomalies to make this convincing.'[57] Raymond Brown considers that, contrary to the argument that the date of the crucifixion has been altered in John's Gospel to allow a clearer identification of Jesus with the Passover lamb, 'the odds do not favor John's having created the chronology to fit that theological insight'[58] (a view echoed by Fergus Millar: 'we should give our preference to John'[59]). Aside from all other considerations, we should acknowledge that the early Christians kept a Friday as the day of the week when the crucifixion took place from very early on, another point in favour of the chronology in John's Gospel.

If the chronology of John's Gospel is accepted, then it allows for some precision in dating Jesus' death. During Pilate's governorship (26–36), Passover fell on a Friday only twice, in 30 and 33. Brown concludes that, therefore, the crucifixion of Jesus took place on 'April 7, 30 or April 3, 33', and observes that 'the political situation in 33 (after the fall of Sejanus in Rome in Oct. 31) would explain better Pilate's vulnerability to the pressures of the populace.'[60] The most likely date for Paul's experience on the Damascus Road is 34, which probably makes 30 a more likely date for the crucifixion, though we shall never know exactly.

Overall this exercise shows that the traditions in John's Gospel are as capable of yielding historical facts as Mark's. Or, conversely, that Mark's Gospel is as theologically motivated in its selection of events and the editing of Jesus' story as John's is. In this case Mark has (mis)identified the Last Supper with the Passover meal 'after the event' but in such a way that his 'account reflects the significance given to the tradition by the Christian community in the light of Jesus' subsequent death'.[61] Both John's and Mark's traditions need to be handled carefully and understood as forms of ancient biography which include the kind of historical information we want to find, but do not see their primary responsibility as being to provide it for us.

James Dunn puts the point well when he says that 'if John's Gospel was not intended to serve as a source of *historical* information about Jesus in his ministry on earth ... [then] an inquiry which sought to *vindicate* John by demonstrating the historical roots of his tradition would in fact be missing the point, *John's* point.'[62] I think this point can be extended to all four Gospels. None of them offers 'history' in the form that we have come to expect it in the twenty-first century.

All of the Gospels sought to vindicate Jesus, but John's perhaps more consciously so than the others. This is the fundamental aim of the Gospel, as its first epilogue shows: 'these things have been written so that you might believe that Jesus is the Christ, the Son of God; and believing this, that you may have life in his name' (John 20.31). It's the same idea that dominates the opening of John's first letter. While the claim is that Jesus, the life, appeared in history, it is also a more than historical claim: who Jesus really was cannot be answered by history alone.

Synagogues and mystagogues: opposition without and within

The Gospel of John is a story of how people loved darkness rather than light (John 3.19); of how they put to death the one God had sent them. The opposition to Jesus reaches its climax with the high priest's unwittingly prophetic saying that it may be necessary for 'one man to die for the people' (John 11.50).

The hatred Jesus attracts is also the birthright of the new community he leaves behind (John 15.18). There is evidence in the text that opposition to the Christian community at the time the Gospel was written came externally, from Jewish synagogues who did not accept Jesus as the son of the Father, and internally, from mystagogues who too readily accepted Jesus as a heavenly being and claimed to have fresh revelations from him. Both kinds of opposition meant that the Gospel was formed against a background of controversy and argument. As Raymond Brown has commented, 'If the Johannine eagle soared above the earth, it did so with talons bared for the fight.'[63] The Jesus portrayed in John's Gospel is far from meek and mild. He is a master of polemic and controversy.

The 'Jews'

Throughout John's Gospel Jesus' opponents are labelled as 'the Jews' (see John 2.18–20; 6.41–52; 7.1–15; 8.31–59; 9.18–22; 10.31–33). In the arrest and trial it is clear that Jesus' accusers, who manipulate Pilate into executing him, are also 'the Jews' (John 18.28–40; 19.4–15). In one passage Jesus denounces those who claim Abraham as their father as in fact the children of the devil (John 8.44).

Richard Hays summarizes John's teaching on the subject as 'Jews who do not believe must be children of the devil. The reason that they do not believe is that they *cannot* ... One shudders to contemplate the ethical outworking of such a theological perspective on the Jews.' Some scholars see the outworking in second-century writings such as the *Epistle of Barnabas*, which argued that Judaism was a false faith. The outworking continued through the persecution of Jews in Europe throughout the Middle Ages and Martin Luther's calls for synagogues to be torched at the Reformation. It culminated in a Nazi picture book of the 1930s which began with the words 'The father of the Jews is the devil'[64] (see John 8.44). Hays concludes that the outspoken statements of John's Gospel against the Jews are a 'theologically misconceived development',[65] where the long anti-Semitic tradition in Europe began.

When John's Gospel was written, as opposed to later centuries, Christians were not in a position of power to persecute Jews. In fact the reverse was the case, and it seems that the portrayal of the Jews in John's Gospel may reflect a particular period in Jewish–Christian relations. A strange feature of the Gospel is the claim that, during Jesus' lifetime, his followers feared being 'put out of the synagogues' by the Pharisees if they identified with him (John 9.22; 12.42). In the farewell discourse, Jesus predicts that his disciples will not simply be cast out of the synagogues but that they will also face death (John 16.2, see Mark 13.12).

Many commentators follow the lead of J. L. Martyn who notes that around 85, as part of the Pharisaic attempt to give coherence to Judaism in the aftermath of the destruction of the Temple, the *Birkat ha-Minim* was produced to be used in synagogues, proclaiming a curse on

'Nazarenes' and 'heretics'. Clearly Christians would have been unable to pronounce such a curse and therefore, Martyn argues, the effect was to exclude them from synagogues after that date. Martyn's influential interpretation of John's Gospel takes its starting point from the 'highly probable correspondence' between 'the expressions "to be put out of the synagogue" [in the *Birkat ha-Minim*] and "to put someone out of the synagogue" [in John's Gospel]'. He says that 'In this trauma the members suffered not only social dislocation but also great alienation, for the synagogue/world which had been their social and theological womb, affording nurture and security, was not only removed, but even became the enemy who persecutes.'[66] The year 85 fits very neatly into the probable period for the composition of John's Gospel, and so Martyn argues that John's Gospel is a 'two-level drama', using the events of Jesus' life as a means of reflecting on the contemporary experience of a community grappling with the traumatic effects of expulsion from the synagogue.

The story in John's Gospel which lends itself to Martyn's two-level approach is the healing of the man born blind (John 9). This is one of the set pieces of John's Gospel and, like the Lazarus story, is told in graphic and gripping detail. Jesus heals the man, but unusually Jesus himself is not the focus of the story (he is 'off-stage' for more than half of the episode, John 9.8–34). Instead the once-blind man is interrogated by the 'Pharisees' and the 'Jews' about Jesus and the healing (John 9.13, 18), and he becomes a witness for Jesus. The niceties of theological dispute are beyond him, and he simply says to them 'one thing I know: I'm a blind man but now I can see ... It's never been known for someone to open the eyes of a man born blind. If this man wasn't from God, he couldn't have done it' (John 9.25, 32–3). In contrast to the robust response of the man, his parents are afraid that if they become involved in the discussion they will be 'put out of the synagogue' (John 9.22).

The story lends itself, especially because of Jesus' absence from most of it, to being seen as the means by which a later community came to terms with opposition in the synagogue. The blind man testifies, simply but openly, to what Jesus has done for him. In the process of confrontation with the Pharisees his understanding of Jesus becomes clearer, as does the stark choice he must make: will he be the disciple of Jesus or of Moses (John 9.28)? There seems to be no halfway house between the two, and, according to John's Gospel, the choice is being enforced by the Pharisees rather than the followers of Jesus. As David Rensberger says, Jesus' disciples 'must either suppress their own experience or stand by it in defiance of those who, in their society, are in charge of communal norms and their interpretation'.[67] The onus of this interpretation is that the community of Christians from which John's Gospel came were victims of Jewish persecution, and that the antagonism towards the Jews in the Gospel itself is a howl of pain against the spiritual homelessness which that community experienced at the end of the first century.

Unfortunately, neat as this interpretation is, there are at least two grounds on which it must be questioned. The first is that the *Birkat ha-Minim* cannot bear the weight that is put on it. It's unclear how widely it was used, and it seems unlikely that it included Christians before the mid second century. Also, it appears to have been an attempt to bar Christians from leading synagogue worship rather than a blanket ban on Christian attendance. The latter would, anyway, have been almost impossible to enforce. There is not enough evidence to assume that it was the cause of a dramatic rupture between Christians and the synagogue in 85. The second ground is the nature of Jewish–Christian antagonism in the first century. There is evidence of animosity between some Christians and some Jews, but we must be careful to define which parties of Jews we are talking about, rather than talking in blanket terms. Some Pharisees (especially Paul in his early years, of course) and some Sadducees (including those who, according to Josephus, were behind the death of James in Jerusalem in 62) opposed the followers of Jesus. More widely Paul, according to Acts, met antagonism in some of the synagogues of the Diaspora because of his 'Law-free' Gospel. Revelation predicts persecution and martyrdom, but it is seen as a future test rather than something that already existed to any marked extent. There is therefore evidence of occasional clashes, which could be violent, between Jews of certain theological persuasions and Christians, but they were neither widespread nor co-ordinated. Martin Goodman points out that, while clashes probably did happen, they were not seen as very significant by most Jews: 'the rabbis in fact had very little to say about Christians of any kind, treating Christians born as Jews within the general category of heresy and those born as gentiles simply as idolaters.'[68] Three references in John's Gospel seem too slight a foundation on which to build the case for a campaign to cast Christians out of the synagogues.

At some point there was a 'parting of the ways' between Jews and Christians. The process was a long one and has been both under- and overstated. It is understated because there is evidence of some antagonism between Jews and Christians right from the beginning of the movement: it was not a new development after 85. Alongside Jewish attacks on Christians, Paul in the early 50s wrote that 'the Jews, who killed the Lord Jesus and the prophets, threw us out, displeasing God and opposing everyone' (1 Thess. 2.14–15). This must be a reference to his own experiences in being drummed out of various synagogues. He also claimed to have received the '39-lash beating', a punishment which signified being removed from the synagogue, five times (2 Cor. 11.24). Juxtaposed with this, Paul agonized about the salvation of Israel in Romans, which certainly shows that he did not consider all Jews implacable enemies of the Church (Rom. 9—11). Matthew's Gospel contains probably the most anti-Semitic text in the New Testament: at the trial of Jesus the crowd cry out: 'may his blood be upon us and our children!' (Matt. 27.25). Yet

Matthew's Gospel is also deeply concerned to present Jesus in his Jewish context as a second Moses, which tends to make commentators think that this statement has been misappropriated by anti-Semites. Nevertheless, these examples show that some conflict between Jews and Christians was present right from the beginning of the movement.

The process of separation has been overstated when it is assumed that there was a definite point at which Church and synagogue divided. Other than the *Birkat ha-Minim* there is simply no evidence that there was ever any widespread expulsion of Christians from synagogues. Who would have had the authority to orchestrate such a campaign in the confused decades after the destruction of the Temple? Rather, both Christianity and Judaism drew away from each other as they defined themselves in the light of the destruction of the Temple in 70. Neither Christians nor Jews knew at the time that they were at the beginning of movements which would ultimately follow diverging paths. Although Christian leaders became increasingly outspoken against the synagogues as the second century progressed, many ordinary believers may have been happily oblivious to the differences between what were developing into separate faith-systems but which still had a great deal in common. Jews who became Christians may have attended both church and synagogue at times, just as gentiles who became Christians occasionally frequented pagan temples (whether Church leaders forbade them to or not). In fact it seems that as late as the end of the fourth century enough Christians were still attending synagogues in Antioch for John Chrysostom to preach a series of vitriolic sermons against the practice.

These considerations make it unlikely that John's Gospel was composed, as Martyn argues, in reaction to traumatic expulsion from a synagogue. It might be so if it were tied very tightly to a particular localized historical moment, but John's is the Gospel which is most obviously the result of a long process, making it more likely to reflect a wider setting.

What are we to make of the threats of persecution and violence which are so clear in John's Gospel? Jesus actually says similar things in the 'little apocalypse' of Mark's Gospel and the parallel passages in the Gospels of Matthew and Luke (Mark 13.5–13). Revelation also anticipated violent opposition. A solution to the puzzle may lie, not in supposed traumatic expulsions from the synagogues, but in traditional Jewish expectations that the age of the messiah would include a 'great tribulation', an idea given a new twist by Jesus. Therefore his followers confidently expected that the 'road to the new world passes through the land of suffering and death'[69] and led to what can seem to us an almost pathological willingness to embrace suffering and martyrdom by the second-century Church. This anticipation of suffering and persecution may well go back to Jesus himself.

Nevertheless, John's Gospel clearly has a problem with 'the Jews'. But, as has often been pointed out, when the term is used negatively it is usually aimed at the Jewish authorities rather than a whole race. In the context it is clear that Jesus is making a polemical point against his opponents and not taking aim at every Jew. The thinking behind the Gospel is not as systematic as that, and Jews themselves are described as being 'afraid of the Jews' (John 9.22). Yet Jews are much more clearly the focus of opposition to Jesus in John's Gospel than elsewhere in the New Testament, and Martyn is right to point out that the situation reflected here is a step beyond the situation portrayed by Paul and Matthew's Gospel. Whatever the precise status of the *Birkat ha-Minim*, it shows that by the later first century, or the very early second century, there was a movement within Judaism to draw the boundaries of what was acceptable teaching in the synagogues more tightly than had been done before. Such a setting would require Christians to define themselves more clearly. So, Goodman concludes,

> The impetus to the parting of the ways between Judaism and Christianity had come less from the Jewish side than the Christian ... When the Christians claimed that Jesus was the expected Messiah, in the eyes of non-Christian Jews they were simply mistaken. They could be pitied or mocked for their folly, but there was no need to expel them from the Jewish fold.[70]

In other words, Christians needed to mark out their territory clearly. By the later first century one way to define who Christians were (and it was still only one way among several) was to say that they were no longer Jews. John's Gospel does this by stressing the opposition of 'the Jews' to Jesus during his lifetime.

The teaching of the Gospel goes further than that. The careful structure of the discourses is designed to show Jesus as the replacement for Jewish festivals. Who needs prayer for rain at the festival of booths when you have Jesus, the living water (John 7.37–8)? Or a Passover lamb, when Jesus' death is the ultimate sacrifice? This replacement theology is deeply grounded in John's Gospel.

The dualistic language which is such a marked feature of John's Gospel is a rhetorical device designed to heighten tension. It forces the issue and encourages people to choose. Though the anti-Jewish language in the Gospel is unfortunate (especially in John 8.44), it was part of standard literary technique in the first century. Opponents, especially those who were bound closely by ties of family and blood, were denounced in words which seem crude and inflammatory today. Yet the Community Rule at Qumran had no scruples about denouncing (Jewish) opponents as children of darkness, led by the angel of darkness (Satan). The Gospels of Mark and Matthew show no qualms over Jesus calling Peter 'Satan' (Mark 8.33; Matt. 16.23), an accusation which had no lasting effect on Peter's reputation in the Church. In fact in the first century 'Satan' seems to have been seen often as the poser of choices for human beings, as he is portrayed in the stories of the temptations of Jesus (Matt. 4.1–11; Luke 4.1–13). He is seen as 'a strange servant of the living God'[71] who had yet to morph into his medieval caricature with horns and a tail. The aim of the anti-Jewish passages in John's Gospel was to put sharply the question of identity. The choice was put in sometimes lurid terms, but it was not intended to be a source of racial hatred.

The community which gave rise to John's Gospel was small in comparison to the network of synagogues around it, and it would have taken immense imagination and faith to see a time when the boot might be on the other foot and Christians would become the majority. Sadly when that did happen in the fourth century, much of Jesus' teaching was ignored by his followers, especially in the way they treated their Jewish neighbours. The replacement theology of John's Gospel would win out in the Church of later centuries against Paul's more reconciliatory understanding of one Israel, the ancient olive tree into which the gentiles were being grafted (Rom. 9—11). It led ultimately to Christians being seen as the 'new People',[72] a 'third race' which was neither Jewish nor gentile (the phrase was first mentioned by Tertullian, *c.*200, but it was rejected by him since he was keen to retain the Jewish roots of Christian faith). In this sense it is the development of the theology behind John's Gospel rather than the text itself that has caused problems.

This issue remains a salutary reminder of the need to understand the New Testament in its appropriate historical setting before trying to interpret it. Reading Jesus' attacks on the Jews without some knowledge of the way in which the language of conflict and polemic were used in the first century is hugely problematic. But ultimately, the basic stumbling block between Jews and Christians was Jesus himself. John's Gospel recognizes this fact more clearly than the other Gospels. As a result later conflicts between Jews and Christians are foreshadowed in it. Whether the anti-Semitic tradition and its excesses can be laid at the door of this Gospel, however, is another matter.

Mystagogues – the 'spiritual Gospel'

It used to be very popular to see John's Gospel as having been heavily influenced by Gnosticism. However, since no texts which survive from earlier than the second century can really be labelled Gnostic, the consensus that the Gospel must have been completed by the end of the first century has largely brought this approach to an end. Gnosticism offered a 'thought-world of metaphor, poetry and paradox',[73] in Keith Hopkins's words. John's Gospel was inevitably appealing to those who lived in such a thought-world, and so certain aspects of it have come to be seen as 'a step on the way to what happened in the second century, when Gnostic teachers used the device of secret teaching by the risen Jesus as a vehicle for their own views'.[74]

John's Gospel clearly posed the distinction between good and evil. Jesus was 'from above', his opponents were 'from below'. The Gospel did not attempt to explain how this state of affairs came about. The Hebrew creation stories were no real help, simply assuming that the power of evil already existed before Adam and Eve. Even Paul's appropriation of these stories (Rom. 5) did not raise the question of how the power of evil had got there in the first place. This gap has created perhaps the most enduring debate in Christian theology in the ensuing centuries: how do we account for evil?

John's Gospel opens out the question of a higher, deeper or greater reality more than any other of the writings of the New Testament do, with the marked exception of Revelation. Jesus is the messenger who brings heaven to earth. This may be what lies behind Clement of Alexandria's view that this is a 'spiritual Gospel', for John's Gospel at least approaches the question of where Jesus came from in cosmic terms, as the other three Gospels do not. Later Gnostic Gospels (such as the *Gospel of Thomas*, the *Gospel of Philip* and the *Gospel of Truth*, all found at Nag Hammadi in Egypt) increasingly divorced Jesus from earthly reality. They used the same kind of thought seen in the prologue and discourses of John's Gospel to offer, according to Philip Rousseau, a 'poetic and symbolic vision and a shift from the horizontal of scriptural narrative to the vertical of spiritual ascent'. This transformed 'the history of Jesus, as Mark and others had presented it, into a series of tableaux, windows onto the cosmic realm within which the "real" Jesus operated.' The Gnostics were convinced that that they were 'like the disciples talking with the risen Jesus, hearing from his lips fresh wisdom as yet unrecognized'.[75] In the course of these conversations they believed that they came to understand the truths of universe which lay behind and beyond anything the Gospels of Matthew, Mark, Luke or John revealed.

The Gnostics received such truths through visions and prophecies inspired by the Spirit of Jesus. Charismatic activity of this sort had clearly been a major strand in the worship of the early churches. The book of Acts in particular gives the sense that direct instructions from the Spirit were a regular experience (as in Acts 13.2, for example). Paul warned the Thessalonians, 'do not quench the Spirit, and do not look down on prophecies' (1 Thess. 5.19–20), and expected worshippers at Corinth all to bring 'a psalm, a teaching, a revelation, a tongue, an interpretation' (1 Cor. 14.26), inspired by the Spirit. But, just as Gnostics later caused problems by producing new revelations which went beyond accepted traditions about Jesus, so Paul put in checks to balance the weirder words produced in his churches: he told the Thessalonians to 'test everything' (1 Thess. 5.21), and urged the Corinthians to make sure that what they offered the assembly was 'for building up [the church]' (1 Cor. 14.26).

The passages of John's Gospel which deal with the 'Paraclete' (the distinctive term used for the Holy Spirit in this Gospel, John 14.16, 26;

15.26; 16.7) seem to fit the same setting and to show the same mixture of sanction and reserve about charismatic utterances.

The identification of the Spirit with Jesus is very clear in John's Gospel. The Spirit is often referred to as the Paraclete, a word which can be translated in many different ways – comforter, counsellor, advocate – none of which quite catch the full meaning of the Greek word which refers to 'a person of influence, a patron or sponsor, [who] could be called into a court to speak in favour of a person or their cause'.[76] Jesus introduces the Spirit as '*another* paraclete' (John 14.16), and in fact in 1 John it is Jesus, not the Spirit, who is referred to as an advocate (1 John 2.1). The clear implication is that, within the community, the Spirit replaces the presence of Jesus after his departure and that, just as Jesus has shown the Father to the disciples, so the Paraclete will continue to reveal Jesus to them. The role of the Paraclete is to help the disciples, both by developing fresh understanding (teaching) and helping them to recall what Jesus had said (reminding them). As such the role is one which functions both in the present and in the past: remembering Jesus' words, but also helping the disciples to see the full implications of what he had said, which might open up fresh insights and new possibilities. Richard Hays points out that while this might suggest to us 'some sort of intuitive knowledge in the hearts of individual believers', a much more likely first-century scenario is one where 'we should think of the Paraclete as guiding the community through Spirit-inspired prophecy uttered in the worshiping assembly.'[77] There is thus a strong community aspect to the activity of the Spirit.

Equally significantly, on closer examination it turns out that the Paraclete will offer no new revelations. The function is purely to elucidate what Jesus has said and to remind the disciples of his sayings. The Paraclete, in other words, is Jesus' authorized interpreter within the community of disciples. It follows, therefore, that any apparently charismatically inspired new revelation about Jesus would be discounted unless it echoed what was already believed by the community. It also follows that the Paraclete is the guarantor of the interpretation of Jesus that John's Gospel offers.

The tradition of the community was vulnerable to alternative interpretations of Jesus which claimed to be Spirit-inspired. This seems to be precisely the situation addressed in 1 John, where some teachers ('the antichrists' 1 John 2.18) are claiming that Jesus was not the Christ (1 John 2.22) and that he had not been human (1 John 4.2). The recipients of the letter are instructed to 'test the spirits to see whether they come from God' (1 John 4.1). The fundamental issue in the letters is that some members of the community have left (1 John 2.19), apparently led by someone called Diotrephes (3 John 9).

If we read John's Gospel against this same background of division within the community, then its conservative emphasis in terms of the Paraclete makes a good deal of sense. Tom Thatcher notes that 'The

Spirit ... can only point back to and affirm what Christians have already been taught ... "from the beginning," making the Paraclete's work parallel to that of human beings like the Beloved Disciple in the preservation of the true witness.' It is tempting to speculate that, if the split in the community came at around the time the last eyewitnesses of Jesus' ministry died out, the Gospel of John was a means to 'fix and freeze [the] community's memory once and for all'.[78] It is important to note, however, that the Gospel is not against Spirit-inspired activity as such. The target is what the community regarded as false teaching about Jesus. Prophetic warnings about future events (such as Agabus's about the famine, Acts 11.28), or personal words for individuals (such as Paul's 'thorn in the flesh' and the saying that went with it, 2 Cor. 12.7–9) are not ruled out. But the kind of speculations about the origin of the evil powers, which were later to be the Gnostics' stock-in-trade, and correspondingly mythical retellings of Jesus' story, are resolutely resisted.

John's Gospel has a kind of unfinished quality to it: it is not neat and tidy and it constantly bursts out of the interpretative systems which scholars try to impose. In the same way the Gospel opens the door to further metaphysical speculation, but then refuses to pass through it. Wayne Meeks comments that the 'picture is never rationalized by a comprehensive myth, as in Gnosticism, or by a theory of predestination, as later in the Western Catholic tradition'.[79] This suggests that the community was conscious of what it did not know as much as it was conscious of what it did. Above all the aim of the Gospel was not to reproduce simple memories of Jesus, but a specific way of remembering him, an authorized interpretation of who Jesus was. The statement at the end of the Gospel suggests as much: 'but these things have been written down in order that you should believe that Jesus is the Christ, the Son of God' (John 20.31). The claim of the Gospel is that this view goes back to Jesus himself.

Spotlight on 'Who is Jesus?'

The heart of the difference between John's Gospel and the other three lies in how they understand and present Jesus himself.

John's Gospel does not present a fully fledged picture of Jesus as the second person of the Trinity but it was the single most important source of that description of him, arrived at by the Council of Nicea in 325. The question, 'how divine was Jesus?' provoked intense debate from the late first through to the mid fifth centuries. And, while an answer was agreed at that point, precisely what the formula 'fully God and fully man' means has never been wholly explained. The great theologians argue that it can never be wholly explained because it is beyond human comprehension anyway. For them theology grinds to a halt at this point, and prayer begins.

The first three Gospels had a high view of Jesus and his significance. The very first words of Mark's Gospel, for example, are 'The beginning of the good news about Jesus Christ, the Son of God' (Mark 1.1). The last phrase may possibly have been added later, but, as Morna Hooker says, it is 'certainly in keeping with Mark's own beliefs, and forms an appropriate heading to his book'.[80] Mark's use of the secrecy motif seems to tease the reader into following the clues until the climactic announcement by the gentile centurion at the crucifixion: 'Truly this was the son of God' (Mark 15.39). The phrase 'son of God' could have many meanings, as the Church for the next four centuries explored. Did it mean that Jesus was God incarnate or simply a child of God, one among many? A unique agent from heaven, or someone who spoke with the voice of God, as the prophets did, but who was otherwise wholly human? In Mark's Gospel the identity of Jesus as God's son is gradually revealed, but precisely what it might mean is unclear.

Matthew and Luke also grapple with this question. Matthew tends to present Jesus as the rightful teacher and king of Israel, in succession to Moses and David. Luke emphasizes Jesus as a person filled with the Spirit. In both cases they introduce material about Jesus' origins which may point in the direction of a unique relationship between Jesus and God, and in subsequent centuries was seen as showing just that. Yet neither draws that conclusion, and while they go a step further than Mark they stop short of finally attributing identity with God to Jesus.

Paul, of course, wrote before any of the Gospel writers, but he does not really approach the question of the identity of Jesus in the same way. Partly this is because he was writing letters, not a Gospel, and so his focus on Jesus is different. Paul definitely treats Jesus as something more than simply a man who was highly aware of God. He offered prayers through Jesus (see Rom. 1.8 and 1 Thess. 3.11–13), and he describes Jesus as the one to whom 'every knee shall bow, in heaven and on earth and beneath the earth, and every tongue confess' (Phil. 2.10–11), a plain echo of the prophecy that all the nations would turn to God himself (Isaiah 45.23). Though Paul comes tantalizingly close to the kind of understanding of Jesus as God that would later develop, James Dunn considers that he 'points the way forward to the subsequent agonizing of Christian theologians over how Jesus could be seen as both God and human being'[81] but doesn't quite seem to get there himself. Nevertheless Paul does come to the point, as C. F. D. Moule puts it, where he 'was led to conceive of Christ as any theist conceives of God.'[82] His strong Jewish attachment to the idea of one God only, however, kept him from seeing the implications of this. (Some scholars think that Paul may have explicitly identified Jesus with God in Romans 9.5, but the case is not proven. Titus 2.13 may be an example, if it was written by Paul himself.)

John's Gospel stands out from the rest of the New Testament on this matter, for there is no longer any secret about the identity of Jesus. From the beginning of the Gospel the declaration is made loud and clear: Jesus was the Word, he was in the beginning with God himself, he is the one who makes God known (John 1.14, 18).

Matthew and Luke seem to have written their Gospels as a means of 'fixing' what they felt was lacking in Mark's, adding teaching material in Matthew's case, tidying up the structure and much of the language and style in Luke's as well as adding in many parables. While both were drawing out the significance of Jesus himself as well, their primary focus was on his life-story and his teaching. John's aim seems to be different. Tom Thatcher says that 'John did not ... write a Gospel to help people remember information about Jesus, but rather to ensure that they remembered Jesus in a specific way'.[83] Understanding Jesus rightly is a primary concern in John's Gospel, and this is what lies behind the emphasis on Jesus' true identity. For this reason, Thatcher goes on to suggest that the aim of the Gospel is to portray Jesus 'as a figure from the past and to keep him locked in that past ... to suppress the living memory of Jesus and replace that memory with a fixed image of a person who lived and died decades earlier'.[84] In other words, John's Gospel deliberately offers Jesus 'as he really was', or perhaps 'as he really should have been'. In this way it 'freezes' the changing interpretation of Jesus, and says to its audience: this is who Jesus was in the beginning, and he is the same now. It was a means of protecting the memory of Jesus from the pressure of new revelations received by Gnostics, claiming to be the living voice of Jesus speaking in the present. The value of its eyewitness testimony lay in being able to say, 'I was there; so my interpretation of Jesus is the right one.'

It has often, and rightly, been observed that where Jesus in the first three Gospels proclaims the Kingdom of God, in John's Gospel its place is taken by Jesus himself. The clearest expression of this can be seen in the set of 'I am' sayings. 'I am' was identified in the Old Testament with the name of God. When Moses asked to know who he was speaking with in the burning bush, the reply was 'I am who I am' (Ex. 3.14). Jesus proclaims that he is:

- the bread of life (6.35);
- the light of the world (8.12);
- the door of the sheep (10.7);
- the good shepherd (10.11);
- the resurrection and life (11.25);
- the way, the truth, the life (14.6);
- the true Vine (15.1).

Jesus also uses the phrase elsewhere. The first time he does so is when he meets the disciples while he is walking on the water, just after the feeding of the 5,000. He says, 'I am; don't be frightened' (John 6.20). Andrew Lincoln comments that Jesus 'is being presented as the embodiment of the God who walks on the water [in Job 9.8] and whose self-proclamation [in Isaiah 40—66] is "I Am; do not be afraid".'[85] Mark's parallel account includes exactly these words but he probably does not invest them with the same significance (Mark 6.50). Maybe the community which lies behind John's Gospel picked them up and developed their meaning.

The Jesus of John's Gospel is concerned to make clear his subordinate position to the Father. When he is accused of making himself equal to God, he responds that he only does what he sees the Father doing (John 5.19). He is, in the final analysis, the servant of God and not God himself. The imagery used is that of the trusted servant who is given licence to act on the master's behalf. He both is, and is not, the master himself. So Jesus can do nothing on his own authority (John 5.30). There is a way to go here before the Nicene doctrine of 'fully human, fully God' can flower. But the path is set, and though the journey was a long one, the creed can fairly be said to be based on the theological insights of John's Gospel.

John's Gospel begins with the revelation of Jesus' identity and it is not in doubt as the story unfolds. People must decide for or against Jesus, but they do not have the luxury of ignorance about him. His identity is plain for all to see; unless, of course, they are blind. So where Jesus frequently hides his identity in Mark's Gospel, in John's he proclaims it fearlessly. And he is recognized. So Thomas's statement forms the climax of the Gospel, when he says to the risen Jesus, 'My Lord, and my God!' (John 20.28). Bringing others to the same realization is the aim of the Gospel: 'These things have been written so that you might believe Jesus is the Christ, the son of God. And, believing this, that you may have life in his name' (John 20.31).

Draw your own conclusions

- What do you think Clement had in mind when he said John's was a 'spiritual' Gospel?
- What is the function of the beloved disciple? Is it important to discover his identity or not?
- Why is the structure of John's Gospel so different from that of the other Gospels?
- What would you say are the main differences between the eschatologies of Paul and John's Gospel?
- What role do the discourses play in John's Gospel?
- Do you think the Last Supper was a Passover meal or not? Why do John's Gospel and the Synoptics disagree over this?
- Can John's Gospel be held responsible for anti-Semitism?
- How would you summarize John's view of Jesus?

Further reading

Commentaries

Two recent commentaries can be recommended: A. T. Lincoln (2005), *The Gospel According to St John*, Black's New Testament Commentaries, London: Continuum, is an excellent, comprehensive and up-to-date guide to the Gospel, organized around the idea that Jesus is on trial throughout his public ministry; J. Neyrey (2007), *The Gospel of John*, Cambridge: Cambridge University Press, is more experimental in its use of social scientific approaches as well as the insights of rhetorical and narrative criticism. Of older commentaries, B. Lindars (1972), *The Gospel of John*, London: Marshall, Morgan & Scott, is both profound and simple; C. K. Barrett (1978), *The Gospel According to St John*, 2nd ed., London: SPCK, is masterly, but requires some familiarity with Greek from the reader. The significantly older E. C. Hoskyns (ed. F. N. Davey) (1947), *The Fourth Gospel*, London: Faber, remains useful. R. A. Burridge (1998), *John: the People's Bible Commentary*, Oxford: BRF, is a simply written commentary which contains helpful insights.

Other books

There are many introductions to John's Gospel. R. Edwards (2003), *Discovering John*, London: SPCK, is a good first step, covering most critical issues fairly and well. D. Moody Smith (1995), *The Theology of the Gospel of John*, Cambridge: Cambridge University Press, surveys the setting, themes and theology of the Gospel. B. Lindars (1990), *John*, Sheffield: Sheffield Academic Press, is the distillation of a lifetime's study designed to be easily accessible to students. J. Ashton (1991), *Understanding the Fourth Gospel*, Oxford: Oxford University Press, is a complex book, reflecting its subject matter, but will amply repay those who invest time in it. Older but still helpful is C. H. Dodd (1953), *The Interpretation of the Fourth Gospel*, Cambridge: Cambridge University Press, which includes summaries of the leading motifs and ideas in the Gospel; so also are the early chapters of R. Bultmann (1955), *Theology of the New Testament* II, tr. K. Grobel, London: SCM Press. D. Moody Smith (2001), *John among the Gospels*, 2nd ed., Columbia, South Carolina: South Carolina University Press, is a comprehensive survey of the interpretation of John's Gospel since the nineteenth century. J. Ashton (ed.) (1986), *The Interpretation of John*, London: SPCK, collects eight of the most significant essays on the Gospel written between 1923 and 1972.

More specialized studies include J. A. T. Robinson (1985), *The Priority of John*, London: SCM Press, a book which has waited two decades to be taken seriously; characteristically of Robinson it is simultaneously well-argued and argumentative! It develops some of the insights of C. H. Dodd (1963), *Historical Tradition in the Fourth Gospel*, Cambridge:

Cambridge University Press. Recently the view that eyewitness testimony lies behind John's Gospel has been developed in R. J. Bauckham (2006), *Jesus and the Eyewitnesses*, Grand Rapids: Wm. B. Eerdmans. M. Hengel (1989), *The Johannine Question*, tr. J. Bowden, London: SCM Press; R. E. Brown (1979), *The Community of the Beloved Disciple*, London: Geoffrey Chapman; and J. L .Martyn (1979), *The Gospel of John in Christian History*, New York: Paulist Press, all take different views of the original setting and authorship of the Gospel. D. Rensberger (1989), *Overcoming the World: politics and community in the Gospel of John*, London: SPCK, broke new ground when it was published by drawing attention to the radical, practical, political implications of what had been assumed to be a 'spiritual' Gospel. M. W. Stibbe (1992), *John as Storyteller*, Cambridge: Cambridge University Press, uses narrative criticism to analyse John 18—19, while T. Thatcher (2006), *Why John Wrote a Gospel*, Louisville: Westminster John Knox Press, helpfully uses social memory theory to consider why there was a need to write down the Gospel at all. J. D. G. Dunn, 'Let John be John; A Gospel for its time' in Dunn (1998), *Christ and the Spirit; Collected Essays of James D. G. Dunn* Vol. 1, Edinburgh: T.&T. Clark, is a penetrating insight into the character of the Gospel.

Websites

- P52, the oldest manuscript of the New Testament, can be seen at www.kchanson.com/ANCDOCS/greek/johnpap.html. There is a 'Virtual Exhibition' on Oxyrhynchus at www.papyrology.ox.ac.uk/POxy/VExhibition/exhib_welcome.html, which includes texts, background to the city and some fascinating photographs of Grenfell and Hunt's excavations.
- The 'Text this Week' offers links to articles on the Gospel of John at www.textweek.com/mkjnacts/john.htm and the letters at www.textweek.com/epistlesrevelation/1john.htm.
- Felix Just provides helpful resources on both the Gospel and the letters of John at www.catholic-resources.org/John/.

Notes

1 Quoted in W. Dalrymple (1997), *Towards the Holy Mountain*, London: HarperCollins, p. 398.

2 Eusebius, *History of the Church* 6.14.

3 W. Meeks (1972), 'The Man from Heaven in Johannine Sectarianism' in J. Ashton (ed.) (1986), *The Interpretation of John*, London: SPCK, p. 161.

4 Eusebius, *History of the Church* 6.14.

5 J. A. T. Robinson (1985), *The Priority of John*, London: SCM Press, p. 53.

6 J. L. Houlden (1990), 'Gospel of John' in R. J. Coggins & J. L. Houlden (eds), *A Dictionary of Biblical Interpretation*, London: SCM Press, p. 363.

7 Robinson, *Priority of John*, p. 45.

8 Eusebius, *History of the Church* 6.14.

9 Eusebius, *History of the Church* 7.25; see also 3.39.

10 Eusebius, *History of the Church* 5.8.

11 Eusebius, *History of the Church* 5.20.

12 Eusebius, *History of the Church* 3.39.

13 C. K. Barrett (1978), *The Gospel According to St John*, London: SPCK, p. 134.

14 Robinson, *The Priority of John*, p.118.

15 M. W. Stibbe (1992), *John as Storyteller*, Cambridge: Cambridge University Press, p. 79.

16 A. T. Lincoln (2005), *The Gospel According to St John*, London: Continuum, p. 22.

17 R. G. Collingwood (1946), *The Idea of History*, Oxford: Oxford University Press, p. 246.

18 T. S. Eliot, 'Dry Salvages'.

19 R. E. Brown (1979), *The Community of the Beloved Disciple*, London: Geoffrey Chapman, p. 33.

20 N. T. Wright (1994), *Following Jesus*, London: SPCK, pp. 27–8.

21 J. D. G. Dunn (1998), *The Theology of Paul the Apostle*, London: T.&T. Clark, p. 13.

22 Eusebius, *History of the Church* 5.20.

23 B. Lindars (1990), *John*, Sheffield: Sheffield Academic Press, pp. 31–2.

24 C. H. Dodd (1953), *The Interpretation of the Fourth Gospel*, Cambridge: Cambridge University Press, p.289.

25 R. A. Burridge (1994), *Four Gospels, One Jesus?*, London: SPCK, p. 137.

26 S. S. Smalley (1978), *John: Evangelist and Interpreter*, Exeter: Paternoster, p. 91.

27 R. Bultmann (1955), *Theology of the New Testament* II, London: SCM Press, p. 38.

28 J. Ashton (1991), *Understanding the Fourth Gospel*, Oxford: Oxford University Press, p.207.

29 Lindars, *John*, p.70.

30 D. C. Allison (1985), *The End of the Ages Has Come*, Edinburgh: T.&T. Clark, p. 60.

31 *1QS* III.18–19 (tr. Vermes).

32 Ashton, *Understanding the Fourth Gospel*, p. 496.

33 Brown, *The Community of the Beloved Disciple*, pp. 27–8.

34 B. Lindars (1972), *The Gospel of John*, London: Marshall, Morgan & Scott, p. 382.

35 D. Moody Smith (1995), *The Theology of the Gospel of John*, Cambridge: Cambridge University Press, pp. 35–6.

36 R. J. Bauckham (2006), *Jesus and the Eyewitnesses*, Grand Rapids: Wm. B. Eerdmans, p. 196.

37 J. D. Crossan (1994), *Jesus: a Revolutionary Biography*, San Francisco: Harper, p. 94.

38 J. P. Meier (1994), *A Marginal Jew II – Mentor, Message and Miracles*, New York: Doubleday, p. 831.

39 Lincoln, *The Gospel According to St John*, p. 334.

40 Meier, *Marginal Jew II*, p. 800.

41 Ashton, *Understanding the Fourth Gospel*, p. 427.

42 Lincoln, *Gospel According to St John*, pp. 46–7.

43 O. Cullmann (1967), *Salvation in History*, London: SCM Press, p. 270.

44 Lincoln, *Gospel According to St John*, p. 202.

45 Bultmann, *Theology of the New Testament* II, p. 66.

46 Quoted in W. G. Kümmel (1973), *The New Testament: the history of the investigation of its problems*, London: SCM Press, p. 138.

47 Moody Smith, *The Theology of the Gospel of John*, p. 62.

48 R. J. Bauckham (2007), 'Historiographical Characteristics of the Gospel of John', *New Testament Studies* 53, p. 25.

49 R. A. Burridge (2004), *What are the Gospels?*, 2nd ed., Grand Rapids: Eerdmans, p. 237.

50 Lincoln, *Gospel According to St John*, pp. 32, 38.

51 Lincoln, *Gospel According to St John*, p. 38.

52 F. Millar (2006), 'Reflections on the Trials of Jesus' in F. Millar (ed. H. M. Cotton and G. M. Rogers), *The Greek World, the Jews and the East*, Chapel Hill: University of North Carolina Press, p. 147.

53 J. D. G. Dunn (2003), *Jesus Remembered*, Grand Rapids: Eerdmans, p. 323.

54 Josephus, *The Jewish War*, 6.5.3.

55 N. T. Wright (1996), *Jesus and the Victory of God*, London: SPCK, pp. 555–6.

56 Dunn, *Jesus Remembered*, p. 773.

57 M. D. Hooker (1991), *The Gospel According to St Mark*, London: A.&C. Black, p. 333.

58 R. E. Brown (1994), *The Death of the Messiah* II,, New York: Doubleday, p. 1372.

59 Millar, 'Reflections on the Trials of Jesus', p. 160.

60 Brown, *The Death of the Messiah* II, p. 1376.

61 Hooker, *Mark*, p. 334.

62 J. D. G. Dunn (1998), 'Let John be John; A Gospel for its time' in *Christ and the Spirit: collected essays of James D. G. Dunn* Vol. 1, Edinburgh: T.&T. Clark, pp. 352–3.

63 Brown, *Community of the Beloved Disciple*, p. 24.

64 Quoted in R. Edwards (2003), *Discovering John*, London: SPCK, p. 112.

65 R. Hays (1996), *The Moral Vision of the New Testament*, Edinburgh: T.&T. Clark, pp. 427, 434.

66 J. L. Martyn (1979), *The Gospel of John in Christian History*, New York: Paulist Press, pp. 92, 104.

67 D. Rensberger (1989), *Overcoming the World: politics and community in the Gospel of John*, London: SPCK, p. 45.

68 M. Goodman (2007), *Rome and Jerusalem: the clash of ancient civilizations*, London: Penguin, p. 526.

69 Allison, *The End of the Ages Has Come*, p. 141.

70 Goodman, *Rome and Jerusalem*, p. 582

71 W. Wink (1986), *Unmasking the Powers* , Philadelphia: Fortress, p. 23.

72 *Epistle of Barnabas* 5.7; 7.5.

73 K. Hopkins (1999), *A World Full of Gods*, London: Weidenfeld & Nicolson, p. 260.

74 Lindars, *John*, p. 37.

75 P. Rousseau (2002), *The Early Christian Centuries*, London: Longman, pp. 71–2.

76 Lincoln, *Gospel According to St John*, p. 393.

77 Hays, *The Moral Vision of the New Testament*, p. 151.

78 T. Thatcher (2006), *Why John Wrote a Gospel*, Louisville: Westminster John Knox Press, pp. 90, 112.

79 Meeks, 'The Man from Heaven in Johannine Sectarianism', p. 161.

80 Hooker, *Mark*, p. 34.

81 J. D. G. Dunn (1997), *The Theology of Paul the Apostle*, Edinburgh: T.&T. Clark, p. 293.

82 C. F. D. Moule (1977), *The Origin of Christology*, Cambridge: Cambridge University Press, p. 95.

83 Thatcher, *Why John Wrote a Gospel*, pp. 157.

84 Thatcher, *Why John Wrote a Gospel*, p. 165.

85 Lincoln, *Gospel according to St John*, p. 219.

10

Jesus of Nazareth

The crucified man

This nail gave them a lot of trouble. First it had to be driven through a piece of olive wood which would act like a washer to stop the victim tearing his legs free. Then it was hammered through his heel, as several soldiers tried to hold him still. Finally, it was attached to the side of the cross's upright beam, but a knot in the wood bent the nail's head, making it hard to hammer home. His arms were tied, not nailed, to the cross-piece. Maybe the soldiers had had enough of nails for that day. After the man was dead it would prove impossible to remove the nail from the bone. He was buried with the nail still there.

In 1968, the troublesome nail came to light in an ossuary in Jerusalem. The heel-bone to which it was attached belonged to a young man named Yehohanan, who was in his mid-twenties and about five feet, five inches tall. His family must have recovered Yehohanan's body from the cross and eventually buried his bones in the family tomb, together with his four-year-old son.

Most crucifixion victims were poorer than Yehohanan, and their families were powerless to rescue their corpses. Their bodies were thrown out as rubbish, to be picked over by crows and scavenged by dogs. It was the final humiliation to have no burial place, cast out from the dead as well as from the living. But Yehohanan's family was wealthy and had a tomb in which his bones could lie undisturbed for centuries. We don't know why he was crucified or when in the first century he died. All we have is the bent nail, still fixed to his heel-bone, a dumb witness to the terror that was crucifixion.

This was the fate that Jesus of Nazareth too would suffer. Yet, strangely, this instrument of torture would be the symbol of salvation for subsequent generations of Christians. The cross would itself be redeemed.

Jesus of Nazareth

In this final chapter we shall focus on Jesus of Nazareth, the man behind the New Testament: his life, death and what happened afterwards. What was it about that life and death which had such a profound effect that, two millennia later, he is still remembered and worshipped right across the globe?

Critical historical study of the life of Jesus really began in the eighteenth century and was a growth industry in the nineteenth. In 1910, Albert Schweitzer published a book called *The Quest of the Historical Jesus* (the original German edition of 1906 was the less romantically titled *From Reimarus to Wrede: a History of the Life-of-Jesus Research*). The imagery was perfect for the time, with its undertone of chivalry and noble ideals echoing the Arthurian 'Quest for the Holy Grail'. The quest for the Grail was a never-ending one, and so, Schweitzer implied, was the quest to find the real Jesus. He posed a sharp dichotomy to his readers. Either they could accept that the Gospels point to a Jesus who was an apocalyptic prophet who forecast the end of the world and died in an attempt to bring it about; or they could accept the argument of Wilhelm Wrede that all the Gospels were theologically motivated reworkings of Jesus' life in the light of the Church's later belief in the resurrection and so provided no useful historical information at all. The choice lay between an incomprehensible or inaccessible Jesus.

The theologian Martin Kähler had already in effect called a plague on both Schweitzer's and Wrede's houses in his 1892 book *The So-Called Historical Jesus and the Historic, Biblical Christ*. In this, Kähler argued that the historical study of Jesus was a false turn anyway. What mattered about Jesus was the message his followers preached about him. A scholar could spend years seeking out the details of Jesus' life and yet still not understand who he really was. By contrast the poorest peasant with the Gospels in her hands could see the true, historic Jesus for herself and be in touch with him. The historic Jesus was mediated by faith, not historical knowledge.

Study of Jesus largely followed these three routes through the twentieth century. Schweitzer believed that it was possible to recover the real Jesus, but only by intensive historical study of the contemporary Jewish background, and that the result was at odds with the portrait the Church later drew of Jesus. Wrede believed that it was only the later portrait that could be recovered from the texts of the New Testament, and that therefore intensive literary study of the texts was the way forward. Kähler rejected both approaches in favour of present-day religious experience.

Schweitzer himself came to a similar conclusion to Kähler, and gave up his academic career to become a doctor in Africa. This has tended to suggest that his approach was a dead-end and to obscure the fact that many scholars did follow his lead and continue the 'Quest', especially in Britain and North America. This movement has borne fruit especially in the last two decades, and is sometimes called the 'Third Quest', though, as Dominic Crossan mischievously points out, 'the third quest is always the successful one ... in all good fairy-stories'![1] Though not all contemporary scholars would agree, there is a measure of agreement that the Gospels can be trusted as sources for the life of Jesus because, in James Charlesworth's words, 'of the intentionality of the texts ... Jesus' sayings ... were transmitted within a decade of his death, and within a somewhat controlled environment'. For Charlesworth, this is because we can now see the Gospels more clearly within the context in which they were written. Charlesworth is not naively trusting, however, and he also recognizes that 'the Evangelists certainly did take incredible liberties in shaping the Jesus tradition',[2] that is to say their idea of historical fact and ours may be different and require some careful sifting. Scholars vary in how critically they assess the sources for the life of Jesus.

Overall I believe that we can have a lot of confidence that it is possible to reconstruct the life of Jesus, though it is important to recognize that all historical work can only be reconstruction and carries no guarantee that it is correct. We have to be critical interpreters of the first-century documents because, as David Catchpole says, a 'sensible and constructive scepticism' is required 'which recognizes that the first-century world of the documents is not identical with the twenty-first-century world of those who study the documents'.[3] The reason for the reconstruction is because we want to understand what it was about Jesus' life that led to such an extraordinary effect.

Some facts about Jesus

There is a general consensus about many of the facts about Jesus. Below is a list of 15 facts with which few scholars would take issue (though some are more widely agreed than others).

- Jesus was born during the reign of Herod the Great, probably in 4 BC.
- He grew up in Nazareth, a small town in Galilee.
- He spoke Aramaic and Hebrew and probably also, as a skilled worker, some 'functional' Greek.
- Jesus was initially associated with the Jewish apocalyptic renewal movement of John the Baptist in Judea, and may have been one of his close disciples though he later became more distant from him.
- Jesus gathered his followers in Galilee and worked there for between eighteen months and three years, based in the fishing village of Capernaum. While there may have been visits during this time to Jerusalem, only in the last week of his life did he have a major impact on the capital.
- The major theme of his preaching was the Kingdom of God. He taught in parables.
- Jesus had a reputation as a healer and worker of miracles, prophetic signs of the Kingdom.

- He had many followers, but the closest ones were called 'the Twelve'. Since there seem to have been more than 12 of them, the number is probably symbolic of the 12 tribes of Israel; that is to say, Jesus was proclaiming a new version of Israel (only two tribes had returned from exile centuries before).
- Jesus was criticized for not keeping the ceremonial laws, and he associated with people good Jews would not want to be seen with, such as tax-collectors and prostitutes.
- He made comments and took actions attacking the Jerusalem Temple, which formed the basis of the charges that led to his arrest.
- On the night before he was arrested, he celebrated some form of Passover meal with his disciples, implying his own status as a kind of sacrifice on behalf of the people of Israel.
- The Temple authorities arrested him, but the Roman governor Pontius Pilate ordered his execution.
- He died on a cross in Jerusalem at Passover sometime between 29 and 35.
- After his execution his followers claimed that he had unexpectedly appeared to them alive.
- They told others that Jesus was alive; many of them were persecuted and some were executed rather than deny the truth of their experience.

This is a pretty standard list, but of course scholars would disagree on how much weight to put on each element in it.[4] As a result their interpretations vary significantly. But the facts themselves are not substantially in dispute. On the basis of these 15 facts we shall try in the rest of this chapter to reconstruct the life of Jesus.

Dates and times

The date of Paul's conversion in 34/35 is a key factor in dating Jesus' death. There are two main candidates for the actual day of the crucifixion: 7 April 30, or 3 April 33. The later date is probably too close to Paul's conversion in 34/35 to be likely. Therefore the crucifixion of Jesus probably took place at Passover 30.

When did Jesus' ministry begin? The Gospels all say that it was connected with the work of John the Baptist. In fact Luke places the opening of John's work in the 'fifteenth year of Tiberius Caesar's rule' (Luke 3.1). This sounds pretty precise but in fact Tiberius had been co-ruler for a couple of years with the ailing Emperor Augustus before he became sole ruler when Augustus died in 14, so the 'fifteenth year' of Tiberius's reign could therefore be any time between 25 and 29. However, since Pontius Pilate did not arrive as governor until 26 (Luke 3.1) we can narrow the field by one year. If we turn to John's Gospel we find a two-year framework for Jesus' ministry, based around three Passover festivals, the first of which took place while Jesus was still effectively working with John the Baptist and before he began his proclamation of the Kingdom (John 2.13; 6.4; 11.55). Working back from Passover 30, this would suggest that John the Baptist probably began his ministry in 27, comfortably within the range for Tiberius's fifteenth year. Since Jesus was 'around thirty' (Luke 3.23) when he began his ministry, this would convincingly place his birth in the last years of Herod the Great's reign (he died in 4 BC) – say 5 BC.

Bethlehem and boyhood

Missing from the list of facts above is any mention of Jesus' birth at Bethlehem. Many scholars claim that the miraculous elements in the birth stories rule out their use as any kind of trustworthy historical sources. These are passages which derive from the 'symbolical imagination of the storyteller';[5] and Luke's possible mistake over the census under Quirinius does not foster confidence in this section of his narrative. The story of Jesus' birth in Bethlehem, then, is generally taken to be a means of bolstering the claim that Jesus was of the line of David, born in his ancestor's city. Nazareth is often held to be the more likely place of his birth.

Bethlehem doesn't contribute much to the story of Jesus' life. Jesus' connection with the line of David is a relatively minor strand in the New Testament, and nothing really hangs on it. There was no real need for Matthew and Luke to introduce the idea, but Paul independently refers to it (Rom. 1.3) and these may be reasons for trusting the report. Bethlehem is a possible and plausible location for Jesus' birth, but it should not obscure the fact that both Matthew and Luke emphasize later that Jesus was, to all intents and purposes, a Galilean. He was always known as Jesus of Nazareth.

The question of who Jesus' father was is, of course, beyond historical investigation. The Gospels of Matthew and Luke both affirm that Jesus' mother was a virgin when she conceived him, but go into no details about the matter. James Dunn is prepared to leave the issue open, simply pointing out that these passages do not tell us much more historically than 'the core conviction that Jesus was born of God's Spirit in a special way'.[6] If he was born in Bethlehem, then his designation 'of Nazareth', his mother's home town, suggests something irregular about his parentage. In a later story of Jesus' return to Nazareth he is referred to as 'the son of Mary' (Mark 6.3, see also Matt. 13.55, though in Luke 4.22 he is called 'the son of Joseph'). Beyond this we cannot go in historical terms.

Clearly Jesus did not suddenly burst upon the scene in Galilee after his baptism, as Mark suggests (Mark 1.14). Matthew and Luke offer a little more by way of Jesus' context, which we explored when looking at the upbringing of Jesus' brother James in an earlier chapter. Boys ended their schooling around the age of 12 and it was usually followed by a period of apprenticeship to learn a trade. Jesus became a carpenter like Joseph (Mark 6.3; Matt. 13.55 form the thin but generally accepted basis for this).

Jesus seems to have had more than just a basic education. The Jewish scholar David Flusser concludes that 'When Jesus' sayings are examined ... it is easy to observe that Jesus was far from uneducated. He was perfectly at home both in holy scripture and in oral tradition, and he knew how to apply this scholarly heritage.'[7] Flusser also notes that Jesus was addressed as Rabbi, a term which had not yet been formalized but implies a learned or wise man. Luke suggests that Jesus benefited from occasional contact with the Temple in Jerusalem, on one occasion joining in the discussions of the Law, asking questions, showing a deep knowledge of the Scriptures, and giving answers that amazed those who listened (Luke 2.41–51).

For some young men who sought to grow in wisdom there was a further stage of education, after they had mastered the basics of a trade. They followed a teacher and we have two examples of this in Paul and Josephus. Both of these were more privileged than Jesus and grew up in Jerusalem. Nevertheless it is quite possible that Jesus followed the same pattern. Paul, perhaps ten years younger than Jesus, became a follower of the Pharisaic teacher Gamaliel. Josephus was born a generation later, around 37, into a wealthy and respected priestly family. At the age of 16 he spent three years with a hermit, Bannus, in the desert.

There are some signs that Jesus may have done something similar. Around the age of 20 he would have been expected to get married. There is no sign at all that he did, and this strongly suggests that he left Nazareth at that time in search of something else, very much as Josephus did at an earlier age. Paul found Gamaliel as his teacher, Josephus found Bannus as his mentor. Jesus seems to have found John the Baptist. This is where the story really begins.

John the Baptist

On a clear day you can see the Mount of Olives from the terrace of Herod Antipas's mountain fortress of Machaerus. Here, according to Josephus, John the Baptist was brought after he had been arrested.[8] Perhaps he gazed across the desert and the Dead Sea towards Jerusalem, 30 miles away, wondering what had gone wrong.

John was probably a much better known figure in the first century than Jesus was, certainly he figures much more strongly in Josephus' writings. If Jerusalem had had gossip columns, he would have figured in them;

both for his unusual dress-sense and diet, designed to draw attention to his prophetic vocation (Mark 1.6) but also for his outspoken criticism of the marital shenanigans of the Herod family which, according to Mark's Gospel, led to his imprisonment (Mark 6.17–18).

Josephus says that John had been arrested because he was politically dangerous and Herod feared that he might incite the crowds to rebellion. These two reasons are probably both true: John told it like it was and had announced the judgement of God upon the corruption of Israel, symbolized most clearly in the chaotic morals of the royal family. The specific target of John's criticism was Antipas's marriage to his brother's former wife, something illegal under Jewish Law but perfectly acceptable to the Romans. It was an eloquent example of what was wrong with the Herod family, whose power was based solely on Roman support. Denouncing the marriage could easily have been seen as inciting rebellion.

John may have been Antipas's tame prophet rather than his oppressed prisoner. Mark says that Antipas both feared and protected John, for he knew him to be a 'righteous and holy man' (Mark 6.20). John may have had quite a lot of freedom within the fortress. Being bound (Mark 6.17), even in chains as Josephus says, was not perhaps as onerous as it sounds. John's imprisonment may have been like Paul's later captivity in Caesarea, with light shackles on hands or feet. Machaerus was so remote that there was no chance of escape from it.

In the clear light of early morning perhaps John walked on the terrace facing towards Jerusalem, glimpsed the Mount of Olives and wondered what had happened. The Mount of Olives was the place where, according to the prophecy of Zechariah, God would stand in judgement (Zech. 14.4). Imminent judgement had been the theme of John's preaching, and the baptism which he introduced was a preparation for it. John had predicted the coming of a 'powerful one' who would bring the Holy Spirit (that is, the presence of God) and fire (that is, purification) (Mark 1.7–8; Matt. 3.7–11; Luke 3.16). Vast crowds had flocked to him, as both the Gospels and Josephus show. The atmosphere must have been intense, the air thick with excitement. But with John's arrest, which many expected to be the trigger for the Day of the Lord, came – nothing.

John sent two of his disciples north to Galilee, where Jesus was declaring the coming of the Kingdom of God. The question he posed to Jesus was a simple one: 'Are you the coming one, or should we expect someone different?' (Matt. 11.3; Luke 7.19). Was Jesus' ministry in Galilee a continuation of John's work or something else altogether, perhaps unrelated to the judgement which John had foretold?

Jesus' reply was positive: 'Tell John what you hear and see: blind people receive sight, lame people walk, lepers are made clean, deaf people hear, dead people are raised and the poor hear good news' (Matt. 11.4–5). In other words the presence of God had already come in Galilee.

But this would have been a puzzle for John. He seems to have taught the people to be ready for the judgement, after which the Kingdom of Heaven would come as God's presence filled Jerusalem. It was surely not yet time for the Kingdom, and Galilee was the wrong place for it be manifest.

According to Mark's rather lurid tale, John later met his death as an act of revenge by Antipas's wife who resented his criticism. His head was dramatically served on a dish at a banquet, and his disciples buried him (Mark 6.17–29).

A disciple with a difference?

The relationship between John and Jesus is a good example of the 'criterion of embarrassment' in action. John was more famous than Jesus in the first century. He also had followers in Ephesus at least 20 years after his death (Acts 19.1–5). It is clear that Jesus had received John's baptism, a story which was deeply embedded in the traditions about Jesus. The potential embarrassment was that it looked as if John was Jesus' teacher, and therefore the greater figure. So the texts suggest that the Baptist's role in the story of Jesus' life was downplayed. John's Gospel, for example, begins with a strong denial that John was 'the light', even before Jesus himself has been mentioned by name (John 1.6–8, 20).

Strong traces of John's importance survive. The most obvious and yet the most easily overlooked is the opening to Mark's Gospel: 'The beginning of the good news about Jesus Christ, the Son of God ... John came, baptizing in the desert ...' (Mark 1.1, 4). As Morna Hooker comments, 'We are so used to the story that we do not realize the oddity of its opening lines. The beginning of the good news about Jesus is not a story about Jesus himself but about John.'[9] In the Gospel of Matthew John is not introduced until the story of Jesus is well under way. The other two Gospels follow Mark's example, if not his narrative. Luke begins his Gospel with the annunciation and birth of John in close parallel with Jesus. John introduces the Baptist by name before Jesus. Both these two Gospel writers are concerned to define John's place as clearly subordinate to Jesus, but neither can conceive of a story of Jesus that does not in some way begin with John.

In Acts we find some further evidence that an important element has been downplayed. When the disciples of Jesus look for a replacement for Judas they set these criteria: 'someone who was with us in all the time the Lord Jesus went about among us, beginning with the baptism of John until the day he was taken up from us' (Acts 1.21–2). Peter's outline of the good news later in Acts also begins with the 'baptism that John preached' (Acts 10.37), as does Paul in the synagogue at Antioch in Pisidia (Acts 13.24), showing that for the first Christians the story of Jesus began with the mission of John and the baptism he proclaimed.

How then should we understand the relationship between Jesus and John? John seems to fit the role of mentor or teacher for Jesus well.

There are some strong similarities between Jesus' teaching and John's. Jesus' disciples, according to Luke, ask him to 'teach us to pray as John taught his disciples' (Luke 11.1), which might suggest that the prayer which follows was one which John used. Certainly its themes fit well with what we know of John's message with its blend of apocalyptic expectation and practical piety. Even if this was not so, it is still illuminating that the disciples apparently looked to John as the role model for a teacher and wanted Jesus to emulate him. John's message of judgement focused on the idea of separation, expressed by him in the image of wheat and chaff (Matt. 3.12; Luke 3.17) and by Jesus in several alternative images in the parables of judgement (e.g. Matt. 13.24–30, 36–43, 47–50; 22.11–14; 25.1–13, 31–46). John's audience included tax-collectors and sinners (Luke 3.12–14), as Jesus' also was later to do (Luke 5.27; 15.1; 19.1–10; see also 18.10–14).

A further strong similarity is that both John and Jesus were celibate. This was highly unusual in the first century. Strict Essenes were celibate, but marriage was highly valued in Jewish society, a sign of God's favour and part of one's obedience to the Law. However, the prophet Jeremiah had never married and had children because of impending judgement on Judah (Jer. 16.2). One of Jesus' sayings speaks about those who 'become eunuchs for the sake of the Kingdom of Heaven' (Matt. 19.12), suggesting that the state of celibacy was linked with waiting for the Kingdom to come. That Jesus was still unmarried by the age of 30 (when Jesus was baptized, Luke 3.23) implies that he had made a decision early in his adult life to dedicate himself to God in this way. Perhaps he had been preparing for God's call under John's guidance for a long time.

The hallmark of John's work was baptism. Although there were some parallels to what he did in ceremonial washing, especially as it was practised at Qumran, John's baptism was unprecedented. Proselyte baptism, for gentiles who became Jews, was similar; but there is no evidence that it was being administered before John began to baptize and is more likely to have been an imitation of John's ritual than the other way round. John P. Meier comments of John that 'Certain great religious figures stand out in history precisely because they take the raw material of traditional religious vocabulary and symbol and forge something new out of the old.'[10] Both Josephus and the Gospels identify John as 'the Baptist'. It was this unique action rather than his teaching which drew attention to John and marked him out from any other contemporary figure.

Jewish ceremonial washing was a repeated ritual, but John's baptism was administered only once. John's practice seems to have been to gather groups of people together in mass baptisms in the River Jordan as an initiation rite (see Luke 3.21). The pattern seems to have been gathering, followed by teaching, culminating in immersion as a sign of renewed commitment to the covenant through repentance and a new life. Josephus says that John urged the people to 'come together in baptism'.[11] David

Catchpole deduces from this phrase, which is a reminder of rituals such as the dedication of the Temple, the gathering of pilgrims for a festival, or the meeting at which a new king was chosen and anointed, that John was gathering a 'community of salvation' which was 'no shapeless or randomly spontaneous gathering of Jewish people, but a somewhat formal gathering on a set basis and for a set purpose'.[12] The implication of John's teaching was that those baptized would return to their former lives, but would act righteously in preparation for, and eager expectation of, the coming of God (see Luke 3.10–14).

There is some evidence that Jesus himself baptized. John's Gospel says that he did so while John was still active and that Jesus became more successful than John (John 3.22–4; 4.1). But there is then a rather perplexing comment that while 'Jesus himself did not baptize, his disciples did' (John 4.2). The other Gospels do not mention baptism as part of Jesus' ministry in Galilee. But the importance of John's baptism as the beginning of the story of Jesus, the practice of the Church immediately after Jesus (the mass baptism at Pentecost in Jerusalem for example, Acts 2.41), and the way in which Matthew's Gospel ends with an instruction by Jesus to baptize (Matthew 28.19), all suggest strong continuity between John's baptism and the rituals of the early Church. The comment that Jesus did not baptize is widely regarded as an addition made at some point during the composition of John's Gospel. It seems to reflect Jesus' later practice of not baptizing, but the other evidence in John's Gospel outweighs it, largely because it was an embarrassment (as John 4.2 shows). So, although the evidence is slender, it seems reasonable to conclude that Jesus did, for a time, baptize and that this suggests that he had been a close associate of John and his mission.

The most embarrassing issue for the Gospel writers, as far as Jesus' relationship with John was concerned, is the strong tradition that John baptized Jesus. John's Gospel sidesteps the issue by not narrating the episode at all. The other three Gospels go into varying degrees of detail, in the case of Matthew suggesting that John was reluctant to baptize Jesus (Matt. 3.14–15). All three emphasize the event as a moment when the Holy Spirit was given to him and when he heard words that marked him out: 'You are my Son, the beloved one, in whom I delight' (Mark 1.11). John's Gospel places the same affirmation of the coming of the Spirit upon Jesus in the Baptist's mouth (John 1.32).

Whether or not we are prepared to take the voice from heaven as a direct communication from God, it seems that this was a decisive moment for Jesus. If it were not so, the Gospel writers would surely have written it out of the account. The words are a mixture of quotations from Psalm 2.7 and Isaiah 42.1; as David Flusser says, 'Heavenly voices were not an uncommon phenomenon among Jews of those days, and frequently these voices were heard to utter words from scripture.'[13] Following this visionary experience, the synoptic Gospels say that Jesus spent a period of time fasting in the desert (Mark 1.12–13; Matt. 4.1–2; Luke 4.1–2), though the episode is often ignored because of the subjective narrative of temptations connected with it. While there are clear echoes of the story of the people of Israel wandering in the wilderness for 40 years, it is still entirely plausible that Jesus spent some time alone in the desert. The first three Gospels take this period as the immediate prelude to Jesus' ministry in Galilee, but John's Gospel suggests a different picture, with a passage of time between Jesus' baptism and his ministry in Galilee.

John's Gospel portrays Jesus baptizing around this point in the story. The most likely interpretation is that he was initially a kind of assistant to the Baptist, leading a detached group of John's disciples who later formed the basis of Jesus' own band of twelve (John 1.35–49). John's Gospel introduces here a visit to Cana (John 2.1–12), a return to Jerusalem (and a demonstration in the Temple, John 2.13–17) followed by baptism ministry back in Judea, and a mission to Samaria (John 4.39–41) before Jesus fully begins his ministry in Galilee. That this, or something like it, is an accurate reflection of Jesus' activity between his baptism and his announcement of the Kingdom of God in Galilee is borne out by a stray reference in Luke's Gospel, which says that Jesus 'carried on preaching in the synagogues of Judea' (Luke 4.44), after a period of activity in Galilee which included a visit to Nazareth where Jesus said 'a prophet is not without honour except in his own country' (Luke 4.24), a saying which John's Gospel also places at this point in the story for no apparent reason (John 4.44).

We need not expect that all the pieces will fit perfectly, and that is not the point of the exercise. Rather, if we try to make sense of the information provided by the Gospels, we can see that a preliminary phase of Jesus' ministry closely connected to John's seems likely. We can also see that the early Church may not have wanted to draw attention to it, and that Mark and Matthew skipped over the episode altogether in their Gospels. For them the watershed moment is 'after John was arrested' (Mark 1.14; Matt. 4.12).

To sum up, we have a picture of a preliminary phase of Jesus' ministry as an assistant to John, eventually leading a detached group of the Baptist's disciples. Some of the things Jesus would later do were part of John's ministry, such as preaching to large crowds. The content of Jesus' preaching at this stage would have come from John's message too. During this phase, bearing in mind the possibility that there may have been two demonstrations in the Temple, Jesus may also have foretold the destruction of the Temple itself (John 2.19). Jesus penetrated areas untouched by John's own ministry, and a move into Samaria perhaps represented a new step in the campaign of baptism.

Once John was arrested, Jesus would have been forced to reappraise what he was doing. Should the campaign of repentance continue, or should it take another turn? But one more aspect of the relationship between John and Jesus remains to be explored: did John identify Jesus as the 'powerful one', the one who was to come?

Who did John think Jesus was?

According to John's Gospel John specifically identified Jesus as 'the one of whom I said, after me comes someone who ranks before me, because he was the first' (John 1.30). The phrase plays on the concepts of before and after, but it is concerned largely with rank and not with timing. C. H. Dodd suggests that the whole phrase might be better put, 'There is a man in my following [i.e. among my disciples] who has taken precedence of me, because he is and always has been essentially my superior.'[14] John expected the coming one to begin as part of his own group, but ultimately to surpass his master.

John seems to have envisaged himself as the prophet of a new age, heralding the moment of judgement, when God would act. In Matthew's Gospel John is credited with originating Jesus' slogan 'Repent: the Kingdom of heaven is near' (Matt. 3.2). Baptism with water was the first of a two-part act, the second of which was baptism with fire (Matt. 3.11; Luke 3.16; see also Mark 1.8), a prediction easily associated with passages such as Ezekiel 36.25–7, which speaks of cleansing by water, the removal of idols and the gift of a new heart and a new spirit. Thus, after cleansing came judgement followed by renewal and the new regime called the Kingdom of God.

Whether John actually identified Jesus as the person who was the coming one we cannot tell. John's Gospel says that this person is the one on whom 'I have seen the Spirit falling as a dove' (John 1.32) but only the synoptic Gospels mention a dove being present at Jesus' baptism (Mark 1.10; Matt. 3.16; Luke 3.22). There seems no obvious connection between the Holy Spirit and a dove in pre-Christian symbolism. Luke emphasizes that 'the Holy Spirit fell upon him *in bodily form* like a dove' (Luke 3.22), an addition to Mark's bald version. Joan E.Taylor concludes that 'This is not a symbolic story, constructed so that everyone hearing it would immediately recognize the motifs. Luke tries to explain that the Spirit was in bodily form like a dove, clearly trying to make something of a simile that has no meaning for him.'[15] Behind the introduction of the dove into the story of Jesus' baptism, well-enough known for John's Gospel to allude to it, may therefore lie a historical incident associated with Jesus' baptism, a visionary experience which was interpreted as marking him out in some special way. John's Gospel records a later, surer, identification by the Baptist of Jesus with the one who was to come (John 3.27–30, though as so often with this Gospel it is unclear where the character in the story stops speaking and the narrator's comments begin), but at this stage still, as John Robinson shrewdly points out, 'Jesus is to be understood as *John's* coming one.'[16] John, as the warm-up man, continues to hold centre stage at this point.

The arrest of John ended this phase, as the first three Gospels point out explicitly and John's does implicitly (John 3.24; see also 5.35: 'John *was* a light ...'). If John had a clear picture of how the one to come would fulfil the prophecy it makes sense of his puzzlement at what Jesus in fact did, and where he did it. The Kingdom coming *before* judgement? And in *Galilee* not Jerusalem? For Jesus' Galilean ministry took the good news in a new and unexpected direction.

Galilee

Why did Jesus return to Galilee? Obviously it was the place where he had grown up and where his family lived, but if he had had an extended period of ministry with John the Baptist he had probably become much more accustomed to Judea. It's not clear why Jesus headed back north, but it was to prove a successful choice.

Settling in Capernaum

Jesus' return to Galilee seems to have been connected with John's arrest (Mark 1.14; Matt. 4.12). John's seizure by Antipas's men must have been alarming for those closely associated with him: would they be next on the list? This in itself could have been a motive for leaving Judea.

According to Luke's Gospel, Antipas was very disturbed by reports of Jesus' activity. He feared that Jesus was John the Baptist come back to haunt him. He tried to see Jesus. Later Jesus received reports that Antipas was out to kill him. Finally, Pilate sent Jesus to Antipas during his trial in Jerusalem, something for which Antipas was grateful because he had wished to meet him for a long time (Luke 9.7–9; 13.31–3; 23.7–11).

Jesus' response to the report that Antipas was after him was to call him a fox (Luke 13.32). It's a good summary of Antipas's sly and tricky character, and one of several sharp remarks about him. Jesus' saying that 'Foxes have lairs and birds have nests but the Son of Man has nowhere to lay his head' (Luke 9.58) is probably a coded criticism of Antipas. Sepphoris, a city which Antipas built, meant 'little bird' in Hebrew, and Antipas was famous for the fine buildings he created, but which were largely built on the taxes he had taken from the people of Galilee, rendering some of them homeless. Jesus' question to the crowds about John the Baptist contrasts Antipas with the true messenger of God; the reed which bends to whatever wind is blowing, the man who dresses in silk and lives in a fine palace (Luke 7.24–8), must be Antipas. Perhaps Antipas feared that Jesus was a ghostly version of John because Jesus continued the campaign of criticism against him. Yet if there was antagonism between Jesus and Antipas it seems strange that Jesus returned to Galilee, the heartland of Antipas's power.

In fact Jesus' choices were limited. Staying in Judea was probably more dangerous. It was easier to police than Galilee and also under the more efficient jurisdiction of the Romans. The Decapolis, across the Jordan, was also under Roman control and it was Greek rather than Jewish in character: an unlikely place for a Jewish prophet to flourish. Perea, also east of the Jordan and further south, was ruled by Antipas. It was where John had been arrested and was being held captive; it was also bare and mountainous: a hard place to hide. So Galilee was the best option available, a place where it was far easier to give the authorities the slip and hide in the hill country (as bandits had done for centuries). Two pieces of evidence suggest that this might be why Jesus returned to Galilee.

The first is the motif of secrecy which features in Mark's Gospel. Mark uses this theme for his own purposes to introduce the question of Jesus' true identity. But there may well be a historical core to this tradition: Jesus' repeated (and ineffective) injunctions to secrecy, his apparent reluctance to associate with crowds, and the absence of any mention in the Gospels of Sepphoris and Tiberias, the two major cities of the region, all make sense if he had chosen to return to Galilee in order to avoid detection.

Second, Jesus chose Capernaum rather than his home town of Nazareth as his base. Capernaum was on the edge of Antipas's territory: it would be easy to slip across the Jordan into the Tetrarchy of Antipas's brother Philip from there. It would also have been easy to hide among the steep mountains and valleys of Upper Galilee to the north, or to sail across the lake to a different location altogether. Nazareth, among the more populated villages of Lower Galilee and only five miles from Antipas's administrative capital of Sepphoris, would have been much more dangerous. Capernaum had the advantages of good communications links but was also easy to disappear from, should the need arise. It was not rich, though it did have 'a thin layer of provincial bureaucracy'[17] represented by the presence of a tax-collector and a royal official. In short, Capernaum was a pretty good place 'to win the cat-and-mouse game with Antipas'[18] and also from which to announce the coming of the Kingdom of God.

Galilee and Judea

It would be a mistake to think that, by basing himself in Capernaum, Jesus vanished into isolation and obscurity. Though there were divisions of political authority, Galilee and Judea were pretty closely linked and shared the same culture. In the nineteenth century it was commonplace to emphasize the 'purity' of Galilee by contrast with Judea, and their isolation from each other. The ancient nickname of 'Galilee of the gentiles' (Isa. 9.1) even led some scholars to suggest that Galilee had been imperfectly colonized in the second century BC, leaving its inhabitants religiously Jewish but ethnically gentile.

The view that Galilee was ethnically gentile was useful for those who wished to argue that Jesus was not racially a Jew, a position which reached its extreme in Hitler's Germany in what has been described as 'the Nazi Quest for an Aryan Jesus'.[19] Though few scholars ever followed this Nazi path, the stereotype of division between Galilee and Judea has been remarkably persistent, so that Jesus emerges as a northerner who 'invades' the foreign city of Jerusalem at the end of his life. However, recent archaeological evidence shows the Galileans in the first century to have been indistinguishable from their Judean cousins: 'in terms of ethnicity, the Galileans should be considered Jewish' summarizes Jonathan Reed, and 'many Galileans at the time of Jesus likely had great-grandparents or grandparents, or perhaps even parents, who were born in Judea, so that contacts still existed between families and clans.'[20] The practice of pilgrimage several times a year to Jerusalem would have regularly reinforced these connections, so that 'spiritually, and religiously ... , the chief city of ... Galilee was Jerusalem.'[21] The Gospels of Mark and Matthew, which concentrate the early part of their narrative about Jesus on Galilee, may have unwittingly caused scholars to miss the close links between Galilee and Judea. John's Gospel redresses the balance in a much more plausible and realistic way, while Luke's Gospel follows the pattern of Mark but gives a stronger sense of Jesus' occasional activity in Judea (for example, Luke 4.44; 6.17; 7.17; 23.5).

The game's afoot

Another reason for Jesus to settle in Capernaum was that he had met a group from the village while he was with John the Baptist. When John was arrested it made sense for him to go home with them.

Mark's Gospel begins the story of Jesus' ministry with the call of the disciples to follow Jesus (Mark 1.16–20). John's Gospel makes it clear that Andrew and Peter were initially followers of the Baptist and that they met Jesus while they were with him (John 1.40–2). Like them, Philip came from Bethsaida (John 1.44), just three miles or so round the lake shore from Capernaum. These three and Nathanael made up an initial group of disciples of Jesus. Luke's Gospel also suggests that Peter knew Jesus well before he embarked fully on his mission to Galilee, since Jesus seems to have been living in Peter's home before Jesus called him to be his follower (Luke 4.38).

The Gospels of Luke and John depict a period of ministry by Jesus before he embarks on a more purposeful campaign in Galilee, while Mark and Matthew say that Jesus came into Galilee proclaiming the good news before they tell the story of how he called his disciples (Mark 1.14–15; Matt. 4.12–17). Luke uses this gap in the record to include Jesus' visit to Nazareth, and his announcement of a programmatic statement in the synagogue there, a visit which Mark and Matthew place in the midst of Jesus' Galilee mission (Luke 4.16–30; Mark 6.1–6; Matt. 13.54–8). This 'Nazareth Manifesto' is almost certainly an example of Luke's characteristic approach as a historian in 'ordering' his material and providing a speech which outlines what Jesus should have said. This sermon in the synagogue helps Luke's audience to grasp what Jesus' mission is about.

Whatever the detailed sequence of events, the synoptic Gospels agree that John the Baptist's arrest precipitated a new departure in Jesus' mission, marked by a definite step by the disciples: 'they left their nets and followed him' (Mark 1.18; Luke 5.11). Jesus' call to them was to become 'fishers for people' (Mark 1.17, see also Luke 5.10). A new era had begun.

Galilee or Israel?

John the Baptist had foreseen the coming of the 'powerful one', and may have identified Jesus in some way with this figure. But the 'Day of the Lord' was due to come first. Something seems to have spurred Jesus on to announce the coming of the Kingdom in Galilee as not just near but as a present fact.

The identification of the first phase of Jesus' ministry purely with Galilee may be misleading. There are signs that Jesus was active in Judea even while he was based in Capernaum. And though Mark's Gospel definitely locates the first part of Jesus' ministry in Galilee and nowhere else, it does say that 'a great crowd from Galilee, Judea, Jerusalem, Idumea, the far side of the Jordan and around Tyre and Sidon, followed him because they had heard what he was doing' (Mark 3.8). Clearly the news had spread far beyond Galilee.

All the Gospels show Jesus and his disciples travelling extensively. Mark's Gospel especially offers a glimpse of activity to the north and east of Galilee, up to Tyre and Sidon (Mark 7.24), then across to the Decapolis (Mark 7.31). Later Jesus goes to the villages around Caesarea Philippi (Mark 8.27), and into Judea itself (Mark 10.1), though this may be the prelude to the journey to Jerusalem (Mark 10.32).

These travels look like Jesus spreading his message right across the 'ideal Israel' of old, which had been promised to Abraham. Jesus' sayings about being sent to the 'Lost Sheep of Israel' (Matt. 10.6; 15.24) point to a special concern, as Sean Freyne says, for 'People living in border areas [who] might well have felt themselves marginalized, even excluded ... they were invited to participate in ... the banquet with Abraham,

Isaac and Jacob.'[22] Jesus seems to have been consciously 'gathering-in' those who lived on the fringes of Israel and calling them home. He was also extending the boundaries of Israel and effectively recolonizing lands which had once been thought part of Israel, but were so no longer. In this he was continuing the pattern he would have learned in Nazareth as a boy, a settlement village designed to reclaim Galilee as part of Israel and whose name probably derives from the Hebrew *Nezer* (branch) echoing the prophecy of the future rule of the branch of David. This perspective may also make sense of Jesus' call to the first disciples to come and fish for people, gathering up in the net all those who belong to the Kingdom of God (see Ezek. 47.10). The promise of salvation given to Abraham had been worldwide in scope, not restricted to Israel; through him 'all the families of the earth' would be blessed (Gen. 12.3). It was a big vision, and Jesus began to put it into action.

The difference was that, where John told people to wait, to prepare and to be ready, Jesus told them that God was already at work among them. Unexpectedly, like the thief in the night (Matt. 24.43; Luke 12.39), the Kingdom was suddenly among them. The future had broken in.

Jesus and the gentiles

Was Jesus' message only for Jews? It's pretty clear that John the Baptist's was, but Jesus seems to have shown an openness to gentiles that is surprising. Though many scholars have discounted this evidence on the reasonable grounds that it was convenient for the later Church to discover that Jesus had welcomed gentiles among his followers, it nevertheless seems plausible.

Northern Galilee and especially the Decapolis were areas where there were large gentile populations. Jesus seems to have been unconcerned by the niceties of purity rituals (though if his contact with gentiles had been frequent we would expect it to figure in the Pharisees' accusations against him), and the record of his encounter with a Syro-Phoenician woman is just anti-gentile enough to suggest that it is a genuine incident which led to a reappraisal of his thinking (Mark 7.25–30). The coming of the nations to worship at Jerusalem was a staple part of prophecy about the last days (see, for example, Isa. 56.6–8; Zech. 2.11–13; 8.20–3), and E. P. Sanders points out that, when Barnabas and Paul began the mission to the gentiles, no one objected to the principle: 'they disagreed only as to its terms and conditions'. Sanders concludes that, though Jesus' activity among gentiles was limited, the gathering of the nations into God's Kingdom was part of his plan: 'Jesus started a movement which came to see the Gentile mission as a logical extension of itself.'[23] All of this points to Jesus taking a step which was to lead far beyond where John the Baptist had gone.

The Kingdom of God

Jesus began a new pattern of ministry in Galilee. He seems to have abandoned the practice of baptism, turned his back on the fasting and austerity of John the Baptist and begun to heal the sick, something completely absent from John's ministry. John had proclaimed that the Kingdom of God was imminent. Jesus said that, in his own presence, the first signs had already come.

Jesus and the Kingdom

What did it mean for Jesus to come into Galilee, proclaiming that 'The time has been fulfilled!' (Mark 1.15)? The Kingdom of God is seen here as a time as much as a place: it is where and when God's presence comes in a fuller way than is normally experienced. It is where and when God rules. It is when God's peace and wholeness (*shalom*) is experienced in right relationships between God and his people; within people and between them, and between them and the rest of creation. The Kingdom is also where strange things happen, and where, as it were, the rules of normality are suspended and reality undergoes a 'phase change'.

The ingredients announced in Jesus' message ('The time is fulfilled, the Kingdom of God has come close. Repent and believe in the good news!') are fourfold:

- *The time is fulfilled*, so the message is urgent; it is no longer future, as John the Baptist had announced it. God's time is fulfilled and the moment is now.
- *The Kingdom of God has come close*; the presence and the power of God touching and changing the world are the Kingdom of God. Describing it as close suggests that the Kingdom has not come finally and definitively, it is more tantalizing than that. In Jesus the power and presence of God is manifest; it can be reached out to and touched, but also, sometimes, the power is absent (see Mark 6.1–6). Therefore the full manifestation of the power of God is still something future.
- *Repent*; Jesus continued the ministry of John the Baptist. His hearers are to turn away from their former ways of life and embrace the Kingdom, the power and presence of God.
- *Believe in the good news*; how do the hearers show their belief in the good news announced to them? By acting on it, and recognizing the signs which authenticate it. They participate in the arrival of the Kingdom by their active belief, which will include doing the kinds of things that Jesus himself did (Mark 6.7–13).

Declaring the Kingdom or rule of God in this way made a very deliberate statement and clearly invited a comparison in Galilee with the rule of

Antipas. It was a message, as Dominic Crossan has put it, that was 'one hundred percent political and one hundred percent religious'.[24]

But a Kingdom needs a king. This is the Kingdom of God, of course, so God is the king, but such a close identification between the Kingdom of God and the man who announced it, and whose actions were bringing it into being, implied a special status for that man: it identified him so closely with God as to be almost the same as God. Sanders offers the term 'viceroy' as a means of capturing the nuances of this view: 'God was king, but Jesus represented him and would represent him in the coming kingdom.'[25] This was an immense claim to make, even if it was implicit rather than explicit.

The Kingdom was present – and yet it was also still to come. This has been a perennial problem for scholars to make sense of. Perhaps the best way to do so is to recognize that Jesus, while being clear that the Kingdom had indeed come, did not necessarily expect it to remain. The Kingdom over which he presided was a foretaste, a 'first instalment' as Paul would later describe the gift of the Spirit (2 Cor. 1.22; 5.5). But it is probably a mistake to think that the question of logical consistency mattered very much to Jesus anyway. Paradox is, after all, the stock-in-trade of the poet and the prophet, and Jesus seems to have been content to let the Kingdom remain a riddle as much as a reality. John P. Meier comments that 'the kingdom of God ... is a ... multifaceted reality, a whole mythic story in miniature that cannot be adequately grasped in a single formula or definition.'[26] The Kingdom was real, and it manifested God's future rule in the present, but it was also elusive. Yet even in its elusive presence, it was clear that it had arrived in some way. And this meant that it had appeared *before* the judgement which John the Baptist had warned about. Therefore it was out of the expected sequence.

To understand or grasp the Kingdom meant a challenge to the imagination. It was not the kingdom of the Herods, nor was it the future expectation of John the Baptist. What was it, then? Crossan again succinctly offers a summary: 'The Kingdom of God is what the world would be if God were directly and immediately in charge.'[27] Through his actions and through his teachings, Jesus demonstrated what this reality might look like.

In what follows we shall look first at Jesus' actions – his *praxis* of the Kingdom – and only then at his teachings. The order is deliberate and is partly influenced by the approach of E. P. Sanders, who argues that, if Jesus is primarily viewed as a teacher then it 'is difficult to make his teaching offensive enough to lead to execution or sectarian enough to lead to the formation of a group which eventually separated from the main body of Judaism.'[28] A parallel with Paul may be drawn: if we had only his letters, then we would be unlikely to give credibility to the strong tradition that he was executed under Nero. Acts, as an account of what Paul did, makes his fate plausible. If the task is to draw a picture of Jesus in which he is, in Tom Wright's phrase 'a comprehensible and ... crucifiable first-century Jew'[29] then actions really do speak louder than words. Jesus Ben Ananias, who prophesied the destruction of the Temple from 62, was allowed to continue his denunciations for seven years. Subversive words alone meant little, but when added to subversive actions they became dynamite.

Followers of Jesus

Kingdoms in the ancient world were more a matter of 'who' than 'where'. A kingdom was not primarily a geographical concept but was defined by who owed allegiance to a particular king. So when Jesus announced the Kingdom of God the natural question to ask was, 'so who are the subjects of this Kingdom?' Jesus had a close, inner group of 12 followers, and then a wider circle around him. Beyond them came the tax-collectors and sinners, a group that Jesus' opponents claimed he should not have been associating with.

The 'Twelve'

It is not very easy to identify the 12 disciples. There are four lists (Mark 3.14–19; Matt. 10.1–4; Luke 6.12–16; Acts 1.13) and there is a slight discrepancy between the names in them. There are some ingenious ways of making them correspond to 12 individuals, but at least 14 names have good claim to be part of 'the Twelve'.

This suggests that, in E. P. Sanders's words, 'the conception of the twelve was more clearly anchored than the remembrance of who precisely they were.'[30] Certainly we know nothing, beside their names, of the majority of the disciples, but for this reason the number 12 becomes more important, not less. Twelve pointed unequivocally to the 12 tribes of Israel. The connection between the role of the Twelve and the 12 tribes is made explicit in one saying: 'you shall sit on twelve thrones, judging the twelve tribes of Israel' (Matt. 19.28; Luke 22.30 is the same thought in tidier Greek). The disciples were to be associated with Jesus in his role as judge of Israel. Therefore the symbolic choice of 12 disciples also suggests that Jesus considered his mission to be directed to the whole of the people of Israel.

Ten of the 12 tribes had become the 'lost tribes' after the destruction of the northern kingdom of Israel and the exile of its people to Assyria in 722 BC (see 2 Kings 17.1–6). This left only the two southern tribes in the kingdom of Judah as the remnant of the whole. Thus Jesus' choice of 12 was a symbolic action which claimed that he was reconstituting the long-lost and God-given identity of Israel as a whole.

There was more for the Twelve to do than sit and wait for the judgement. Their group may have originated in a detached group of John's followers, but Jesus had a different job description in mind for them.

A disciple (*mathetes*) is someone who learns from a master, and rabbis and philosophers alike attracted them in the ancient world. Jesus' disciples were different from the norm: the Gospels do not use the verb related to the noun disciple for what they do. They don't learn (*matheteo*) from Jesus, they follow (*akoloutheo*) him. John P. Meier points out that 'They were called ... to share and be formed by Jesus' own prophetic ministry of proclaiming the Kingdom, with all its consequent dangers, and not simply to learn or memorize certain doctrinal, legal or ethical statements'.[31] They were not simply to watch him at work, they had an important role in the Kingdom. They were to be, like Jesus, part of its coming.

They were also called by Jesus. Normally disciples chose to follow a master, not the other way round. A greater imperative was at work here, perhaps reflecting Jesus' own call from God at his baptism. So, as well as assisting Jesus and being taught by him (sometimes in private), the Twelve were also his messengers and were sent out to do the same kinds of things that he did, including preaching the good news, healing the sick and casting out demons (Mark 3.13–19; 6.7, 12–13; Matt. 10.1, 7–8; Luke 9.1–6).

The instructions for the 12 Jesus sent out are clear, but they differ a little between the synoptic Gospels (Mark 6.8–9; Matt. 10.9–10; Luke 9.3). The bulk of the saying is clear: take nothing on the road, no food, money pack, or spare clothes. But there are also some differences: Mark says take sandals, Matthew says don't and Luke doesn't include an opinion on the matter; and what about taking a stick? Mark thinks it's a good idea, Matthew and Luke don't. This is the kind of passage which confirms the need for some careful sifting, a good example of how we should handle such sayings. The gist has been preserved, but did Jesus say the disciples should take a stick and wear sandals or not?

A stick was obviously a means of defence: no sensible traveller went without one to ward off wild animals and robbers. Bare feet were a sign of penitence, but not practical for long journeys. Mark's version of the saying probably reflects the form of words used when commissioning Christian messengers. It took its lead from Jesus' saying but had been altered for a new situation. Matthew and Luke preserve an older version, which is likely to be closer to the actual words of Jesus because of the 'criterion of embarrassment'. To travel so nakedly was probably a utopian statement of faith in the Kingdom and a new regime of harmony between animals and people (see Isa. 11.6–9).

Why did Jesus send out his disciples like this? If they were fishermen or farmers, or even in one case a tax-collector, then they would have had to abandon their work to travel (a craftsman like Jesus would not have had to do so, of course). So lacking money and food, wearing clothes worn to rags, walking on bare feet and carrying no means of defence, their appearance would speak of poverty and radical dependence on God (see Matt. 6.25–34; Luke 12.22–31). They would become living symbols of the Kingdom they proclaimed.

In the synoptic Gospels the Twelve are also designated apostles (Mark 3.14; Matt. 10.2; Luke 6.13). Although this term may be a later addition, it catches their function well, as those who are sent out as messengers or ambassadors. It was certainly the description which the early Church felt fitted their role.

Jesus recognized the risks involved in sending the Twelve out so ill-equipped ('I send you out like sheep among wolves', Matt. 10.16), but the instructions also assume that they will quickly set up a network of support (Matt 10.11–13; Luke 9.4–6). This may have been part of the plan. Criss-crossing Israel, they were laying the foundations of a movement much wider and bigger than a little group in Capernaum.

The wider circle, women and crowds

The Twelve formed the core of Jesus' followers, with a special role to fulfil. But there were many others who followed Jesus. Luke says that, as well as sending out the Twelve, Jesus also later sent out 70 others, with similar instructions (Luke 10.1–12). Seventy, like twelve, is a symbolic number which stands for all the nations of the world according to the list in Genesis 10. Therefore, Luke is suggesting that Jesus was anticipating the worldwide mission that would follow Pentecost.

Even though 70 is a symbolic number we should not therefore discount Luke's evidence that there was a wider circle around Jesus. The replacement of Judas by one who 'was with us in all the time the Lord Jesus went about among us, beginning with the baptism of John until the day he was taken up from us' (Acts 1.21–2) suggests a wider pool of disciples who were part of the travelling group. There is also evidence of supporters who were not on the road all the time, but who provided food and shelter when it was needed: the provider of the donkey for Jesus to enter Jerusalem and the host of the Last Supper in Jerusalem are the most obvious (Mark 11.2–6; 14.13–15). Some of these closet disciples may have been quite influential, such as Joseph of Arimathea and Nicodemus (Mark 15.43; John 19.38–9).

Some of the disciples were women, the most natural reading of Luke's phrase 'the Twelve were with him and some women' (Luke 8.1–3). This was unique (suggestions that women sometimes took on important roles, for example as synagogue rulers, seem to be based on a misunderstanding of titles used by the wives of such officials). It is remarkable that so many of the women who were followers of Jesus had their names recorded: Mary Magdalene, Joanna (whose husband was Antipas's steward and who may have been the Junia of Romans 16.7, as we saw in chapter 6), Susanna, Mary the mother of James, Salome, Mary and Martha (Mark

16.1; Luke 8.2–3; 10.38–9; John 11.1). The presence of this group is startling, given that 'early Christianity was on the whole not a hotbed of anti-discriminatory gender-blind liberalism.'[32] There are other indications that some of Jesus' disciples were female. The saying about the 'lilies of the field which do not toil or spin' (Matt. 6.28; Luke 12.27) only really makes sense if some of the audience were women, for men would not be found weaving; and a number of parables feature women and domestic tasks (for example, Luke 15.8–10; 18.1–8).

The inclusion of women in Jesus' close circle was a cause for scandal, but it is worth noting in passing that no whiff of it seems to have been attached to Jesus. Their presence was also probably a sign of the presence of the Kingdom of God where there was no distinction between genders (see Joel 2.28, used in Acts 2.17). Normal distinctions were suspended.

Beyond the committed supporters lay the crowds. Mark's Gospel portrays Jesus in his early ministry as being constantly hemmed in by crowds, scarcely able to breathe (Mark 2.4, 13; 3.9, 20, 32; 4.1; 5.21, etc.). The other three Gospels do not emphasize the point as strongly as Mark's, but the crowds are still frequently present.

How many people make a crowd? Mark's Gospel offers two examples of the size of crowds: 4,000 and 5,000, in the miracles of feeding (Mark 6.44; 8.9). These figures do not appear to be symbolic ones: it is the number of baskets of leftovers which symbolize Jesus' mission to both Israel and the world as a whole: 12 and 7 (standing for 70), as the Gospel itself makes clear (Mark 8.19–21). The numbers are not impossible, though we should treat them with care. At any rate, it was a large following.

Though we should not place too much trust in Mark's geography, unusually he gives a location to both stories: close to Bethsaida (Mark 6.45) and in the Decapolis (Mark 7.31; 8.10). John's Gospel, as usual more geographically precise, locates the feeding of the 5,000 in the same place (John 6.1, 17). This is strong evidence for Jesus having had, at one stage, a large group following him in the hills of Upper Galilee around the Jordan Valley, and rather weaker evidence for another crowd around him across Lake Galilee in the Decapolis.

It was John the Baptist's large crowd of followers, according to Josephus, which got him into trouble and made Antipas anxious, lest they should turn rebellious. Anyone with a crowd around him was a potential danger, and one little detail in Mark's version of the feeding of the 5,000 raises questions about this. The men sat down, he says, 'in companies of hundreds and fifties' (Mark 6.40). The word used is one which often relates to the ranks of a military parade and may 'hint that the crowd could easily become an army prepared to march behind Jesus'.[33] John's Gospel adds more substance to this possibility by saying that Jesus had to escape into the hills because he knew that 'they were about to come and take him so that they might make a king of him' (John 6.15). Alongside Jesus' network of supporters across Israel, we can also imagine a network of informers channelling information about Jesus' activities to Antipas, and also to Pilate, the Roman governor at his headquarters in Caesarea.

But Jesus did not seem to envisage recruiting an army. His instructions for those who followed him predicted hardship and suffering (see Mark 8.34–5; 10.38–9; 13.9–13). Jesus rejected the violence which was endemic in his society and demanded that those who followed him should love their enemies, 'a hitherto unheard-of application'[34] of the command to love one's neighbour (Matt 5.44; Luke 6.27).

For these reasons it is unlikely that Antipas or Pilate would have been very worried by Jesus' following. He seems to have made less immediate impact than John the Baptist, but he was worth keeping an eye on. Rulers of Galilee and Judea had to maintain a delicate balance, holding back from action lest they provoke trouble but also keeping close watch on potentially dangerous people. This may be why Jesus was later able to advance on Jerusalem with the Passover pilgrims and to cause an incident in the Temple without opposition, only to be arrested a few days later under cover of darkness and hastily condemned to death. The crowds would have had no time to react in Jesus' defence and Pilate probably congratulated himself on a clinical and characteristically efficient piece of Roman policing which had averted a crisis.

Jesus and the sinners

A major accusation against Jesus was that he routinely ate with 'tax-collectors and sinners' (Mark 2.15–16; Matt. 11.19; Luke 15.1). This points up his relationship with the Law, for he and his disciples were also accused of not keeping the Sabbath as they should (Mark 2.27; 3.2; Luke 13.14; 14.3) and not observing the rituals of hand-washing (Mark 7.2). Jesus also objected to the misuse of the laws of Corban, which dedicated money to the Temple (Mark 7.11). The significance of these controversies about the Law and how it should be obeyed lies in the way some Pharisees used relatively minor strictures of the Law as touchstones to define the boundaries of who was in and who was out of Israel.

Incidental episodes in the Gospels take the continued existence of the Law and its traditional functions for granted, such as the leper whom Jesus heals and then sends on his way to the Temple to make a sacrifice of thanksgiving (Mark 1.44, see also Lev. 14). Jesus seems not to have been opposed to the Law as such, only to the way in which some people in his day interpreted it.

Matthew's Gospel records Jesus as saying, 'Don't think I came to set aside the Law or the Prophets' (Matt. 5.17), and the dispute about his observance of the Sabbath was over what it is permissible to do, not whether the day should be observed or not. That particular dispute provides an insight into the thinking that lay behind what Jesus' critics believed to be his lax approach to the Law. Jesus explains the actions of his disciples in picking grain on the Sabbath with the saying, 'the Sabbath came into existence for the benefit of humanity, not humanity for the benefit of the Sabbath' (Mark 2.27); the function of the Law (and the customs which had grown up around it) was to help the people be the children of God. Too tight an interpretation would stifle that relationship. Jesus' actions with regard to the Law and customs were designed to emphasize the love and generosity of God. His criticism was reserved for those who sought to become gatekeepers and use the Law to exclude those who did not share their understanding (see Matt. 15.15–20).

This was of a piece with Jesus' mission to the whole of Israel. His vision of the Kingdom included those who lived in border areas who had been marginalized by progressively tighter boundary-drawing. In the same way Jesus seems to have deliberately associated with those who were reckoned by the Pharisees to have excluded themselves from Israel and her covenant relationship with God. The 'tax-collectors and sinners' were the most obvious of these, though extending healing to lepers and associating with Samaritans was probably equally controversial. Who were the tax-collectors and sinners, and what had they done to put themselves outside the pale?

Tax-collectors were a deeply unpopular group of people throughout the ancient world. In Judea their profession made them agents of Roman authority; in Galilee they were the chief providers of Antipas's growing fortune. The heavy tax burden on ordinary people was experienced in the shape of a tax-collector's demand: they were at the front line of the tensions between the rulers and the ruled.

Tax collection was not a job for shrinking violets. As Thomas Schmidt delicately points out, 'an occupation which depends for success on suspicion, intrusion, harassment and force tends not to attract the most pleasant personalities.'[35] Yet this group had been prominent among those who came to John for repentance and baptism. According to Luke they had received the advice from John, 'don't collect more than you are ordered to do' (Luke 3.12–13), implying that tax collection in itself was not wrong, only the exploitation of it for personal profit. Some commentators, reasonably enough given Luke's generally pro-Roman stance, are sceptical about such a saying as this. However, the other Gospels clearly suggest that Jesus, like John, included tax-collectors among the covenant people of Israel and did not suggest that they look for another job (see, for example, Mark 2.15–16; Matt. 21.32). Zacchaeus, the 'chief tax collector' of Jericho was a case in point. Although the story of his encounter with Jesus is often told as a paradigm of repentance and restitution, in fact close attention to the text suggests that Zacchaeus was, probably unusually for a tax-collector, not corrupt. He says to Jesus, 'I give half my possessions to the poor and if I defraud someone I pay it back fourfold' (Luke 19.8), and the tense is a present not a future one, most obviously suggesting that he 'describes repeated, customary practice, rather than a single spontaneous act of generosity.'[36] If this reading is correct, then Zacchaeus was a pious man. Paying back fourfold was what the Law required for the stealing of a sheep, for example (Ex. 22.1), and far beyond the compensation the rabbinic writings demanded. As chief tax-collector, Zacchaeus would have been responsible for the mistakes of his subordinates. He seems to have paid back and compensated those who had suffered from 'administrative oversights', deliberate or otherwise. Giving half of his possessions was a very generous act, though he could probably afford it. To Jesus, Zacchaeus's actions showed him to be a true 'son of Abraham' (Luke 19.9). Even tax-collectors could belong to the Kingdom of God.

Tax-collectors were often bracketed with 'sinners'. Originally sinners were simply those who did not keep the Law; the word was routinely used to describe gentiles, for example, so it was not necessarily pejorative (see Matt 5.46–7; 18.17, also Gal. 2.15). But by the first century it had become an insult, what Dunn calls 'a dismissive "boo-word" to warn off members of the in-group against conduct outside the boundaries which defined the group'. As an example of how this worked, we can return for a moment to the dispute about the action of Jesus' disciples on the Sabbath. The point at issue was not the Law itself, for this did not prohibit plucking ears of corn on the Sabbath. The issue was a strict Pharisaic interpretation, which took any such effort as work and a violation of the spirit if not the actual letter of the Law. This strict interpretation would therefore define even Jesus' disciples as 'sinners'. Dunn concludes that 'They were "sinners" ... *only from a sectarian viewpoint* and only as judged by the sectarians' interpretation of the law.'[37] Tax-collectors fitted neatly into this category, and seem to have been something of a test case. Their general unpopularity undoubtedly made labelling them as sinners a shrewd move, and equally undoubtedly many of them lived up to the label and used their position to extort and cheat. They were extreme sinners. An honest tax-collector was like a 'good' Samaritan – a contradiction in terms.

But taxes were not bad in themselves, and someone had to collect them. The Temple, for instance, could only run because of the tax to support it, which Jesus himself paid (Matt. 17.24). The Law did not prohibit the collection of taxes. It's likely that few tax-collectors were glowing examples of integrity and righteousness, but it was possible for them to live by the Law if they tried. Jesus' association with them, to the extent of including one within the Twelve (Mark 2.14), showed very clearly that they should not be automatically written off as sinners. They too could have a place in God's Kingdom.

To those who said Jesus should not associate with such people he retorted that 'the healthy don't need a doctor, but the sick do. I did not come to call the righteous but sinners' (Mark 2.17). But what did he require from the sinners whom he called into the Kingdom? E. P. Sanders has argued that Jesus offended the Pharisees particularly because he asked for no change in behaviour from the tax-collectors, no concrete act of repentance. Examples of Jesus doing so, he contends, are only to be found in Luke's Gospel, which adds 'to repentance' to Mark and Matthew's 'I came to call sinners' (Luke 5.32). In Sanders's view, it was John who was the preacher of repentance, not Jesus, whose mission was simply to proclaim the acceptance of God to those who had been constantly told that they were outside God's love. Sanders concludes that 'Luke's Jesus, who got tax-collectors to repent and repay, would not have irritated anyone'[38] and would therefore not have ended up on a cross. However, the interpretation of Zacchaeus outlined above suggests that Jesus offered places in the Kingdom of God to those whose behaviour marked them out as righteous, but who were usually excluded from Israel by the attitudes and prejudices of others.

The parable which Matthew records of the two sons, the elder of whom refuses to work in the vineyard but then does so while the younger readily agrees but then doesn't turn up for work, makes the point: it is in actions rather than words that the truth is revealed (Matt. 21.28–30, see also 25.31–46). Sanders is right that Jesus does not seem to have preached repentance in the same way that John had done. The reason why Sanders wishes to emphasize this fact is because he rightly believes that Jesus stressed God's unconditional covenant love as primary, to be followed by repentance: Jesus did not require repentance and a change of life as a condition of entry into the Kingdom. But Sanders is perhaps wrong to assume that Jesus then made no significant demands on those who had entered. It is perhaps more likely that Jesus looked for evidence of God's Kingdom in unlikely and unexpected places, such as among tax-collectors where no one else imagined that God could be at work.

For most people it was impossible to imagine that these worst of 'sinners' could be part of the Kingdom. But the barrier was one of imagination, not reality, and had to be challenged primarily by actions, not words. So Jesus, taunting his righteous, strictly law-observing opponents, said 'Truly I tell you, the tax-collectors and prostitutes are ahead of you on the way into the Kingdom of God' (Matt. 21.31). The point of the saying is a rhetorical one. There is no evidence that prostitutes formed part of Jesus' entourage but if the grace of God might be at work among such as them, who could be beyond the pale of God's Kingdom?

Food, glorious food!

Jesus was well-known as a party-goer. 'The son of man has come eating and drinking and you say "Look, someone who's a glutton and a drunkard, a friend of tax-collectors and sinners"' (Luke 7.34, Matt. 11.19).

The opposite of the glutton and the drunkard would be an extreme ascetic – John the Baptist for instance. It was hard to imagine John as the perfect party guest.

Jesus was thoroughly at ease in such surroundings and his convivial behaviour contrasted sharply with the practice of his former mentor. The contrast was another demonstration that Jesus believed the Kingdom of God had come.

Those who seriously sought the coming of God's Kingdom fasted voluntarily. Jews were bound by the Law to fast only on the Day of Atonement, the most solemn festival of the year (Lev. 23.26–32). John's disciples and the Pharisees fasted two days a week (Mark 2.18; see Luke 18.12) and on occasion for longer periods. The post-exilic prophet Zechariah mentions four fasts to be kept in commemoration of the exile to Babylon, which would one day become days of feasting (Zech. 8.19).

Jesus did not fast regularly. Only in the account of the temptations, following the baptism by John, is he said to have done so at all (Matt. 4.2; Luke 4.2). Fasting defined John, but feasting defined Jesus. Again and again the Gospels show him eating in company, across a social spectrum from tax-collectors to Pharisees (for example, Luke 5.29; 7.36; 10.38; 11.37; 13.26; 14.1; 19.7).

When questioned about why he and his followers did not fast, Jesus replied 'do the attendants of the bridegroom fast while he is with them? While the groom is with them they cannot fast. But once he's gone, then they can fast' (Mark 2.19). In the Hebrew Scriptures the imagery of a wedding had become a regular one to express the future unity of God and his people (for example, Isa. 54.1–8; Hos. 2.19–20). Jesus' practice of feasting seems deliberately to have invoked this imagery and a more pithy paraphrase of the saying would be 'Who weeps at a wedding? It's not a time for mourning, but rejoicing.' The implication is clear: the Kingdom has come and it's time to celebrate.

Jesus often ate with tax-collectors and sinners, but he also ate with Pharisees (see Luke 7.36; 11.37; 14.1). The use of the word 'reclined' in these contexts suggests that these were feasts or banquets. The Pharisees criticized Jesus for his laxness about hand-washing (Mark 7.1–23), but were perhaps most concerned by his indiscriminate choice of dining-companions (see Luke 14.7–24). He appeared to make no distinction between tax-collectors and Pharisees, and careful social grading at meals was very important not only among Jews but right across ancient society. In the stories of the feeding miracles too, there is no sign of regular etiquette being observed: all were fed equally and everyone had enough (Mark 6.41–2).

The theme of Jesus' feasting was clear. It was an acting-out of the great banquet prophesied by Isaiah, when God would be with his people (Isa. 25.6–9; 65.13–14). As Tom Wright neatly puts it, 'Jesus was ... celebrating the messianic banquet, and doing so with all the wrong people.'[39] Jesus vividly showed a Kingdom without boundaries by eating with tax-collectors and 'sinners' on the one hand, and Pharisees on the other. He seems to have looked forward (as Isaiah had also done) to the drawing of the gentile nations to the same banquet (see Matt. 8.11; Luke 13.29).

Was there a ritual pattern to these feasts? Although the evidence is slight, Luke's suggestion that the way in which Jesus blessed bread and broke it was a characteristic action (Luke 24.30–5) may point in this direction (see also Mark 6.41; 14.22). Eating a symbolic eucharistic meal together would become the distinguishing mark of Jesus' followers after the crucifixion, a means of reaffirming their master's practice of the Kingdom of God.

Good news for the poor?

Jesus lived in an economically divided society, which had extremes of wealth and poverty. Luke's Gospel emphasizes Jesus' mission to 'the poor' (see Luke 4.18; 6.20; 7.22; 14.13; 16.20, also 1.52) and records Jesus' beatitude, 'Blessed are the poor, for yours is the Kingdom of God' (Luke 6.20). Yet the Gospels do not record Jesus denouncing the rich in the way that some of the Hebrew prophets, such as Amos, had done, or even in the terms his own brother James was later to use (James 5.1–6). The closest he came was apparently in saying that it would be hard for the rich to belong to the Kingdom; but it was still not impossible for them to do so (Mark 10.23–7). Nor does Luke's Gospel exclusively show Jesus with the poor: Zacchaeus, a 'chief tax-collector', was probably one of the richest men in Judea at the time.

Matthew's Gospel records Jesus' beatitude about the poor slightly differently from Luke's: 'Blessed are the poor in spirit, for theirs is the Kingdom of Heaven' (Matt. 5.3). Guessing which version of a saying is closer to the original is always hazardous, and it is of course likely that sayings were repeated and they may have existed in different, equally authentic forms, varying slightly according to the audience. Tax-collectors, while unlikely to be poor, might nevertheless have been regarded as 'poor in spirit'. The materially poor and the tax-collectors shared something important: the judgement by others that they were outside the Kingdom of God. The poor, because riches were usually seen as a sign of God's blessing, the reward of righteousness. The tax-collectors, because they were immersed in a dirty trade. Maybe this judgement by outward appearance was what Jesus was challenging.

The other Gospels do not stress Jesus' concern for the poor in the way that Luke's does, but they do show Jesus healing lepers and beggars (Mark 1.40–5; 10.46–52). These people were not just poor but destitute, removed from ordinary society and living off the scraps it left them. They were the homeless and the hopeless. And in fact the lepers and beggars, to whom Jesus physically reached out, rather than 'the poor' in general, seem to be those in view in Luke's Gospel. The clue lies in the Greek word *ptochos*, usually translated as 'poor' but which carries with it the more precise meaning of a beggar, someone who has absolutely nothing at all. So the Lukan beatitude might be better translated, 'Blessed are the destitute, for yours is the Kingdom of God.' Jesus himself seems to have chosen deliberately to live a lifestyle which might classify him as a *ptochos*, dependent on the charity of others and intentionally homeless (Matt. 8.20; Luke 9.58). Yet he was also the leader of the movement.

Why did Jesus embrace this lifestyle, and why might the destitute especially be blessed? Jewish tradition certainly did not see poverty as a virtue. But in a complex web of social relations where everyone had someone else to protect them, the destitute stood out because they had dropped off the social scale and were uniquely vulnerable. In the absence of anyone else to look out for them, the destitute had to rely on God and became his special concern – not because of any intrinsic righteousness they possessed or any virtue in poverty itself, but because they were helpless (see, for example, Ps. 35.10; 113.7; 140.12; Prov. 17.5; 19.17; 22.22–3; Isa. 11.4). In the Psalms especially, being poor became a metaphor for helpless dependence on God (see, for example, Ps. 34.6; 40.17; 70.5). It may have been Jesus' desire to characterize himself as wholly dependent on the Father which led him to identify practically with the destitute.

Jesus' actions seem to be less a radical new departure than a reminder of the obligation to provide for the utterly helpless which was laid upon Israel in the Law. Seen this way, his concern and care for the beggars and lepers is part of his general mission to include all Israel in the Kingdom of God.

Jesus also singled out another group of vulnerable people: children. Like the destitute, fatherless children had no one to protect them and were seen as God's special concern (see, for example, Deut. 24; Ps. 10.18; 68.5; Prov. 23.10–11). Like the destitute, Jesus suggested that there was a special place for them in the Kingdom of God and used them as examples of discipleship (see Mark 9.33–7; 10.13–16). In the ancient world in general, children were expendable, prone to be exposed on hillsides as babies if they were unwanted. Jews valued and protected their children in a way that many Greeks and Romans found surprising, but still generally treated them as insignificant and unimportant. Yet Jesus said that the Kingdom even belonged to 'such as these' (Mark 10.14).

Jesus' actions graphically set forth an acted-out vision of a Kingdom where Pharisee and prostitute, beggar and tax-collector, child and wise elder were all included. This was the restoration of Israel that the people had longed and prayed for. But now it was here, would they join in or not?

Signs of the Kingdom

Jesus' initial impact was through signs or healing miracles. Mark's Gospel paints a picture of Capernaum swollen with people seeking help: the whole town tried to get into the doorway, and a man has to be let down through the roof to get to Jesus because of the crowd; the sick eventually flock to him from all parts (Mark 1.33; 2.4; 6.54–6). When John the Baptist's disciples enquire whether Jesus is the one John had predicted, it is the signs to which Jesus points in reply (Matt. 11.5; Luke 7.22). They are a counterpart to Jesus' teaching, so much so that John Painter describes their role in Mark's Gospel as 'active parables'[40] which form an indispensable part of his ministry.

Jesus' miracles fell into three categories: physical healings, exorcisms and 'nature miracles'. Of these it was perhaps the healings which were the most significant as 'signs of the Kingdom': Gerd Theissen sums the matter up well when he writes that 'The miracles of Jesus were initially meant to bring concrete, material, healing help. They contain a protest against human distress.'[41] Many of Jesus' healings violated the Pharisees' strict purity code.

Reports of miracles are a non-negotiable element within the sources which we have about Jesus, and although it is quite likely that some of the stories were embroidered in the retelling there seems to be a bedrock of fact here; so much so that John P. Meier is led to conclude that 'the tradition of Jesus' miracles is more firmly supported by the criteria of historicity than are a number of other well-known and often readily accepted traditions about his life and ministry'.[42] Although the text of Josephus' comments about Jesus has almost certainly been tampered with since the first century, the undisputed part of what he says is that Jesus was 'a wise man ... who did amazing deeds'.[43] Jesus' reputation as a miracle-worker is one of the most secure facts about him. It is also one of the most disputed.

Miracles or myths?

There were several miracle-workers in Galilee and Judea around Jesus' time, known as *hasidim* or wise men. One was Honi the circle-drawer, who lived about a century before Jesus and got his name from the time when he drew a circle on the ground during a time of drought and told God that he would not leave it until rain had fallen. The rain fell and his prayer was answered. The rabbis excused Honi's disrespect on the grounds of his evident intimacy with God. Another, Hanina Ben Dosa, was a few years younger than Jesus and also a Galilean. He was once asked to heal the son of the Rabbi Gamaliel in Jerusalem. Hanina refused to go to Jerusalem, but prayed on the roof of his house for the boy who was healed from that moment. Asked how he knew that the healing had happened, Hanina replied 'If my prayer is fluent in my mouth, I know that he [the sick man] is favoured; if not, I know that it [the disease] is fatal.'[44] The story is very similar to Jesus' healing of the centurion's servant (Matt. 8.5–13; Luke 7.1–9).

Beyond Israel there were also reports of miracles. When Vespasian became emperor in 70 he benefited from well-known prophecies that a 'world-ruler' would come from Judea where he had just suppressed the Jewish revolt of 66–70. En route from Judea to Rome Vespasian passed through Alexandria, and while there he apparently healed a blind man and a lame man who both claimed they had been promised healing by the god Serapis.

There are other stories of miracles in first-century literature but they are by no means widespread. In the cases of Honi and Hanina it is clear that God performed miracles at their request and that sometimes he did not answer their prayers. Vespasian was pretty cynical about religion (on his death-bed he commented, 'I think I am becoming a god', knowing that previous emperors had been deified by order of the Roman Senate), and the Roman historians Tacitus and Suetonius imply that his healings were a publicity stunt to boost his shaky claim to the imperial purple. In all, then, while there are some parallels with Jesus' miracles, the number he was credited with and their context, as part of the Kingdom which was to come, sets him apart from his contemporaries.

It's often argued that modern science leaves no room for the miracles reported in the Gospels to have happened. Since the Enlightenment, philosophy and science have been dominated by the assumption that only those things which can be rationally proved to have happened can be real. This made contemporary personal experience the standard by which all events had to be judged, something often known as the 'principle of analogy'. Its weakness lies in the possibility of events which lie outside our own personal experience. Logic textbooks of the 1750s, for example, derived from consistent observation the law that 'all swans are white'. The arrival of Europeans in Australia uncovered the fact that this was not an immutable law: black swans existed too! Nevertheless, the rationalist approach dominated through the nineteenth and twentieth centuries, culminating in Rudolf Bultmann's programme of 'demythologizing' which ruled out any supernatural claims. In 1941, he famously wrote that 'We cannot use electric lights and radios and, in the event of illness, avail ourselves of modern medical and clinical means and at the same time believe in the spirit and wonder world of the New Testament.'[45] More recently the academic world seems to have become more open to the possibility of miracle, so that Gerd Theissen, for example, who is far from a credulous fundamentalist, is able to sum up the issue like this:

> Miracle only becomes a problem when one's own experience knows no analogy to miracles. We all judge historical reports on the principle

> of analogy: we tend to regard the elements in them that contradict our own experience as unhistorical. We cannot imagine anyone walking on the water or multiplying loaves in a miraculous way and are therefore rightly sceptical about these reports. But the same principle of analogy which is the basis of our scepticism obliges us to recognize the possibility of healings and exorcisms. For in many cultures there is an abundance of well-documented analogies to them – and even in the 'underground' of our culture, although that may officially be denied.[46]

Imagination is the key element in this discussion. Theissen says we 'cannot imagine anyone walking on the water', because imagination is constrained by what experience tells us of reality. But there are many examples of human inability to accept real events because they are beyond the limit of experience. When the Wright brothers first flew at Kittyhawk in 1903, for example, reports took many weeks to be included in the local newspapers because the experience of the editors was that heavier-than-air flight was impossible. The event had happened, but the imagination of the pressmen could not accept that it was true.

Developments in scientific thinking, especially the 'quantum revolution' and 'chaos theory' in physics suggest a world which is no longer so confidently explained as Bultmann believed it could be. It is far more random and unpredictable. The scientist and theologian, John Polkinghorne, points out that if you had never seen water boil, its behaviour in a kettle at 100°C would appear wholly freakish and bizarre. For, at that point, the gradual and predictable rise in temperature of the water, which is directly related to the heat source applied to it, suddenly stops. Some of the liquid assumes a quite different state, and becomes steam. When you make a cup of tea you expect this change and accept it as normal and wholly predictable. Yet what happens is that, while the laws of physics remain the same, their consequences radically alter in the changed state. Within the new regime, different events occur, which, if you didn't boil a kettle every day, you would not predict. 'Miracles' may therefore simply be manifestations of what scientists term a 'phase change', suggests Polkinghorne: they are a manifestation of a 'new regime'. He goes on to suggest that it is not at all strange, in the light of this scientific thinking, to consider that 'If it is true ... that God was present in Christ in a way that he has not been present in any other person, then Jesus represented the presence of a new regime in the world. It is at least a coherent possibility that that new regime was accompanied by a new phenomenon.'[47] This 'new regime' may be what Jesus knew as the Kingdom of God.

Jesus seems to have had what the sociologist Max Weber termed 'charisma': that is, an extraordinary personal power and authority. Theissen connects this idea with Jesus' possession of '"paranormal" gifts to an extraordinary degree'. These gifts, he argues, can be seen in other people, cultures and times right across the world and lie behind the miracle-stories of the Gospels. It is notable that the miracles usually take place through a combination of Jesus' power and the faith of others, either of those who come for healing (see Mark 5.34; 10.52), or those who have brought them (Mark 2.5). When little faith is present, miracles are hard to come by (Mark 6.5–6). The power to work miracles seems, at least partly, to be derived from the context of the community in which the miracles take place. But Jesus also 'knew how to combine them with the centre of his message and give them a fascinating religious interpretation: he saw them as the dawn of the new world'.[48] His deeds were not incidental to the message of the Kingdom, they formed the heart of the experience of the Kingdom itself.

Nevertheless, as John P. Meier points out, any decision about the possibility of miracles 'is always a philosophical or theological judgment'.[49] Yet this does not mean that a historical investigation can ignore the question. Philosophical and theological presuppositions must be recognized and cannot be bracketed out. Ignoring the miracles impoverishes a historical investigation of Jesus. Sanders shrewdly remarks that it was reports of healing which attracted the crowds: 'if ... large crowds surrounded him in Galilee, it was probably more because of his ability to heal and exorcize than anything else.' Simply saying that the Kingdom had come was not enough in the first century, as it would not be today. The audience would be entitled to ask for evidence, and the Gospels suggest that it was primarily the miracles which provided it. In characteristically cautious fashion Sanders observes that the miracles in themselves 'do not require us to think that [Jesus] was an eschatological prophet, but they are compatible with that view.'[50] As signs they are significant in their wider context, and they are closely connected with Jesus' teaching.

Polkinghorne's suggestion provides a scientific possibility for the understanding of Jesus' miracles, but only if they are recognized as eschatological signs. That, however, is what the Gospels claim about them. A decision on whether the Gospels were correct in this identification will depend on the theological and philosophical beliefs which you bring with you to the texts. But the overwhelming evidence is that miracles, however we understand them, played an important part in Jesus' impact on the people of Galilee and Judea.

Magic

The atmosphere in which Jesus worked was very different to the rational, scientific world-view of the contemporary West. While our imaginations can stretch (just) to entertain the notion of a healing miracle, the Gospels' language about Jesus casting out demons is foreign to Western contemporary thought. But if we are to grasp the historical reality of Jesus the issue will not go away.

Magic was endemic throughout the Roman world, including Israel. Magicians offered a means of controlling the caprices of fate by manipulating the unseen forces to which humans were prey through the use of incantations, curses and charms, alongside appeal to pagan gods. But even very simple matters could be dealt with by magical means. The papyrus finds at Oxyrynchus in Egypt include tips against infestation, 'To keep fleas out of the house, wet rosebay with salt water, grind it and spread it', as well as advice on the question of 'How to eat garlic and not stink? Roast beetroots and eat them'[51] which might seem to us to be common sense rather than magic. Jesus was therefore part of a world in which magic was a means of understanding and controlling reality. (The same psychological process is at work today in the widespread reading of horoscopes in the West and the continued appeal of animism in many parts of Africa.)

With the magical world-view went, in Jewish eyes, an understanding of the world as divided between the powers of light and the powers of darkness as the Dead Sea Scrolls clearly reveal. The world was in the grip of Satan, the prince of darkness, and occupied by him. It was not hard to extend the idea to Roman or Herodian rule, for these too were rulers who had usurped authority. But while it is tempting to think that the rule of Satan was a metaphor for political reality, in fact it was probably the reverse that was the case: concrete political reality was probably seen as an earthly reflection of the true spiritual reality of Satan's dominance.

Today we might diagnose the symptoms of a child 'possessed with a spirit' (Mark 9.18) as epilepsy, but Marcus Borg observes that, however we explain the child's condition, 'Jesus and his contemporaries (along with people in most cultures) ... did not simply *think* of these as cases of possession and exorcism; rather, all of the participants – possessed, exorcist, onlookers – *experienced* the event as an exorcism of a spiritual force'.[52] The accepted way of interpreting such an affliction was not through a medical model, as it is today, but by seeing the child as a hostage to malign spiritual powers.

In this sense a magical view of the world is really just another form of discourse, with its own concepts, values and vocabulary. Within this discourse, Jesus did not act in the characteristic way of magicians. He did not use the mechanics of magic such as charms, amulets or incantations. In healing he seems to have used touch and occasionally applied spittle, but these were hardly magical practices (saliva was recommended by Pliny the Elder as a treatment) and they are absent from the stories of exorcism. The only technique that Jesus used in exorcism, according to the Gospels, was a simple word of command.

Exorcisms and nature miracles

Exorcisms loom large in the synoptic Gospels, especially those of Mark and Luke. There are four major examples: the man in the Capernaum synagogue; the man among the tombs of the Gerasenes; the Syro-Phoenician woman's daughter; and the child at the foot of the mountain of transfiguration (Mark 1.21–8; 5.1–20; 7.24–30; 9.14–29). Besides these there are several summary statements of Jesus' activity which emphasize his exorcisms (see Mark 1.32–4, 39); and when the disciples are sent out by Jesus, casting out demons is very much part of their job description (Mark 6.7, 13). Luke's Gospel does not distinguish as clearly as the other two synoptic Gospels between healing and exorcism. This seems to be because, for Luke, sickness is simply another manifestation of Satan's dominion (see, for example, Luke 13.11, 16). There is sufficient evidence here to show that a ministry of exorcism was, perhaps to an even greater extent than his ministry of healing, a major strand in the traditions about Jesus.

Jesus did not pray for spirits to be expelled, or invoke a name, as was common practice. Instead he addressed the spirits directly on his own authority (see Mark 1.25; 9.25, for example). By doing so Jesus made the claim that he was in conflict with evil powers on his own behalf. This is the heart of the stories about exorcisms. But because 'magic' was a form of social discourse, it could mean different things to different people and might be a false and hugely dangerous claim to make. Jesus' exorcisms represent, in John P. Meier's words, 'not individual acts of kindness, or even individual acts of power [but] ... part of the eschatological drama that is already underway and that God is about to bring to its conclusion.'[53] Such a claim perhaps inevitably led opponents to characterize Jesus as in league with Satan himself, to which his response was to tell a parable about someone who breaks into a strong man's house and 'plunders' the goods (Mark 3.22–7). This parable suggests that Jesus saw himself as raiding the realm of Satan in his ministry of exorcism. Jesus appears as a kind of guerrilla leader, attacking those in possession of power and strength on behalf of the rightful but presently dispossessed ruler, God himself.

Some of the signs of the Kingdom are nature miracles. This group includes the stilling of the storm; the feeding miracles; and Jesus walking on water (Mark 4.35–41; 6.32–44 and 8.1–9; 6.45–52). They have often been dismissed as theological elaborations added much later to the Gospels, and the theological pay-offs are not hard to find: the story of the stilling of the storm easily and elegantly illustrates the point that in Jesus harmony between humanity and creation has been restored, for example. Yet they seem too full of incidental detail to fit this explanation entirely comfortably: why invent the detail that Jesus was 'asleep on the cushion' (Mark 4.38)? James Dunn suggests that 'despite the theological overlay ... some reminiscences do still seem to poke through.'[54] But what those reminiscences were it is not possible to say. What the stories demonstrate is the perception that Jesus was master not only of sickness and evil spirits, but also of the natural world, though we cannot definitely say whether this perception existed during Jesus' own ministry or developed later.

Stories of the Kingdom

Jesus offered a vision of the Kingdom of God in action, but he accompanied it with teaching. The Kingdom was a hard concept to grasp, and his teaching about it was likewise elusive, mostly given in the form of parables (see Mark 4.10, 33). In Greek the word *parabole* literally means something thrown against something else. It implies a creative juxtaposition of unrelated things, and the English word 'parabola', describing a curve, reminds us that the function of a parable is to 'tell all the truth, but tell it slant' in the words of the poet Emily Dickinson. Jesus' parables are a means of expressing important truths in a form which is not dry and detached and is often shocking in its originality. Tom Wright trenchantly proposes that they show Jesus as 'a thinking, reflecting, creative and original theologian',[55] and C. H. Dodd describes the parables as having 'the ring of originality. They betray a mind whose processes were swift and direct, hitting the nail on the head without waste of words',[56] Kenneth Bailey notes that 'Jesus does not say "God's love is boundless." Instead he tells the story of the prodigal son.'[57] In parables the abstract was made concrete and popular. This was teaching with which ordinary people could engage without years of study and dedication to the finer points of the Law.

The stories are vivid ones, often with an edge of humour to them. Jesus had a sharp eye for the reality of the world around him: a beaten-up traveller, a harsh landowner leaving money with his servants, workers in a vineyard; all of these were real-life situations which Jesus must have watched or heard about. Beneath the stories there is a framework which assumes with confidence the loving goodness of the Father. 'No circumstance of daily life is too trivial or commonplace to serve as a window into the realm of ultimate values, and no truth too profound to find its analogue in common experience.'[58] God is central to these stories, even though he is rarely mentioned directly.

The point of parables

What were the parables designed to do? From very early on in the Church's history, the parables were seen as allegories, that is to say a story which could be translated, point by point, to give a message about something completely different. Tertullian, in the second century, for example, used the story of the Prodigal Son in this way. He interpreted the elder son as the Jews who are envious of the younger son, the Christians, who are welcomed by the Father, who stands for God, with a ring, which stands for baptism, and a feast, which represents the Eucharist.

In later hands this approach tended to become virtually interpretation by numbers, where the interpreter used inconsequential details 'like a set of pegs on which favourite doctrines are hung'.[59] So, for example, the two coins which the innkeeper receives to pay for the recovery to health of the victim in the parable of the Good Samaritan were often held to represent the Old and New Testaments, given for the healing and salvation of humanity (Luke 10.35). Though questioned by reformers such as William Tyndale and John Calvin in the sixteenth century, this allegorical approach to interpreting the parables of Jesus continued into the late nineteenth century and is still occasionally used today.

Allegorical interpretation was stopped in its tracks by Adolf Jülicher in 1888–9. In a landmark two-volume study of the parables, he argued strongly that they were not intended by Jesus as allegories with a complex range of references, but were instead simple teaching illustrations intended to establish a single point.

Jülicher was heavily influenced by Greek rhetorical theory as expounded by Aristotle, who commended the use of parables for speechmakers who want to convince their audiences.[60] Aristotle's advice is strikingly similar to the technique employed by the prophet Nathan when confronting King David over his behaviour with Bathsheba (2 Sam. 12). In Jülicher's view, Jesus' parables were both striking and simple illustrations of general moral principles, such as the need to make sacrifices for the greater good (the parables of the field and the pearl, Matt. 13.44–6) or to use one's gifts to the full (the parable of the talents, Matt. 25.14–30; Luke 19.12–27).

Yet allegory is present in some of the parables. The parable of the vineyard for example, is based on Isaiah's Song of the Vineyard – which is an allegory where the vineyard transparently stands for Israel, as it must also surely do in Jesus' teaching (Mark 12.1–9; Isa. 5.1–2). The parable of the sower was seen as an allegory from a very early stage, as the explanation of it shows (Mark 4.1–20). Jülicher dealt with these parables by claiming that any allegorical teaching must have been added by the later Church; but here his argument became circular: because Jesus must have taught simple one-point parables, therefore anything more elaborate could not have come from him. The case was far from proved.

While Jülicher was right to deliver the parables from the hands of the allegorists, he restricted them too tightly by his use of Aristotle's category of the one-point illustration. Behind the New Testament's Greek word *parabole* lies a Hebrew word, *mashal*. This primarily means 'proverb' or wise saying, but it was also used more popularly for any saying that was deliberately puzzling, such as a riddle, and even for allegorical stories and prophetic oracles.

Jülicher seems to have missed this wider background partly because of a desire, shared by many who followed him, to see Jesus as wholly original. So Joachim Jeremias, for example, claimed that 'Jesus' parables are something entirely new' and speculated that they may therefore have been 'an important influence on the rabbis adopting parables as a narrative form'.[61] It is true that scarcely any Jewish rabbinic parables are recorded earlier than Jesus' own. But the fact that the first three Gospels can take it for granted that Jesus' audience understood and accepted his means of teaching 'in parables' (Mark 3.23; 12.1) suggests that the form was not new in Jesus' day. The term parable seems to have been well enough known that the majority of Jesus' teaching could be characterized in this way, whether it was a brief saying (such as the log and the speck, Matt. 7.3), a much longer narrative (such as the Prodigal Son, Luke 15.11–32), or even an allegory (such as the Sower and the Vineyard, Mark 4.1–20; 12.1–9).

Riddles and surprises

One of the greatest puzzles about Jesus is that, according to Mark, he told his disciples that he intended his sayings to be incomprehensible: 'to you the secret of the Kingdom of God has been given, but to those on the outside everything is in parables, so that they may look but not see and may listen but not hear, in case they should turn and be forgiven' (Mark 4.11–12). The distinction between insiders and outsiders is not maintained neatly, however. Mark characteristically shows that even the disciples were frequently baffled by what Jesus said (see Mark 8.21; 9.32). He spoke to them in riddles.

Riddles are not meant to be easily understood. They are a kind of code which is generally impossible to crack unless someone has already given you the answer. Perhaps this is what Jesus meant by emphasizing to the disciples that they, the insiders, had been given the secret of the Kingdom. Tom Thatcher notes that 'The ability to answer a riddle, especially riddles that seem vague, is a mark of membership ... [of] a community of knowledge.'[62] The question begged by many of Jesus' parables, is what the right answer might be.

The parable of the Good Samaritan is a riddle in the sense that several answers ought to be possible to Jesus' concluding question: 'which of these three do you think became the neighbour of the one who fell among the robbers?' (Luke 10.36). It plays on accepted ideas of who the 'neighbour' and therefore 'good' person might be in such a situation. Clearly the Samaritan is more neighbourly than either the priest or Levite. But can a Samaritan be good and if so does this imply that the priest and the Levite are not? Thatcher suggests that it 'utterly defies the way that Jews in Roman Palestine thought about reality'[63] to suggest this. Yet that is what Jesus did, with all the implications about who might therefore be included in, and perhaps also excluded from, the Kingdom. The answer might have been plain to the disciples, on the inside of Jesus' novel and radical way of understanding the Kingdom, but to those on the outside the story would have been a baffling one – even when Jesus trapped them into the answer he wanted (Luke 10.37).

What marks the parable of the Good Samaritan as part of a 'riddling session' is the context of conflict in which it was told, according to Luke. The lawyer who asks Jesus 'who is my neighbour?' is intent on trapping Jesus (Luke 10.25, 29). Jesus turns the question on him (Luke 10.36), and a sophisticated game of wit takes place, marked by move and counter-move. In twenty-first-century Western society, riddles are generally restricted to primary schoolchildren or Christmas crackers, but in many other societies they are deadly serious and highly prized examples of wisdom which often occur in semi-formal contests of wit. Riddles in such a setting contain easily memorable arresting images or short stories, cast in a pithy form. Once you start looking for them in the Gospels, it becomes evident that they are widespread, and that Jesus was a master at playing this game.

A further example is the parable of the mustard seed (Mark 4.30–2; Matt. 13.31–2; Luke 13.18–19). Because it was tiny, the mustard seed easily infiltrated carefully cultivated wheat fields. Once set, it produced an effect out of all proportion to its size, growing within weeks to a height of 8 to 12 feet, so that 'the birds of the sky may nest beneath its shade' (Mark 4.32). Dominic Crossan comments that 'it tends to take over where it is not wanted ... it tends to get out of control, and ... it tends to attract birds within cultivated areas where they are not particularly desired.'[64] Farmers hated it.

How can the Kingdom of God be like that? The most obvious response is that the Kingdom's arrival is unexpected and that it comes in ways which look humble and inconsequential at first sight. Yet it also implies that the Kingdom might be unwelcome. Each question would cause the hearer to check his or her own reactions. Surely the Kingdom would be welcome? But if so a more appropriate image would be one used by the prophet Ezekiel, of a cedar tree in whose shade the birds might nest (Ezek. 17.23). Jesus might have been alluding to this, but his choice of mustard seed instead of the regal cedar undercuts the grandeur of the image. How can this despised mustard seed be a metaphor for the Kingdom? The image is absurd.

There may be a political comment here, too. For in Galilee and Judea the owners of the 'garden' (Luke 13.19) might have been seen as Herod Antipas and the Roman governor. How much of a threat might the weed-like growth of the Kingdom of God be to those for whom the well-ordered garden represented wealth? Seen in this light the parable of the mustard seed has a distinctly subversive angle to it. Yet the subversive angle is cleverly hidden. Questioned by Herod's police, Jesus and his disciples could take refuge in playing dumb. It is, after all, only a story about a weed ...

Many of the parables have a deliberately absurd, almost cartoon-like, quality to them. They contain a high level of ambiguity, which seems to be designed to cause the listeners to question and wonder. To say the Kingdom of God is like a mustard seed is no clear manifesto for action, whatever the political connotations of the saying might be. The parable is a riddle which leaves the audience scratching their heads, seeing things in a new light, perhaps asking why Jesus is talking about mustard not cedar and what it is about the difference that illuminates the Kingdom of God. Turid Karlsen Seim suggests that a 'parable proper implies a discrepancy between two stories: the story as already known to the hearers, that is, as their experience predicts it, and the unpredictable story being told'. Interpreters have often tried to iron out discrepancy, Seim argues, but it is integral to the way parables work: 'It is ... a hermeneutical device whereby we gain access to the meaning of the story' which does not make the 'inner logic of the story collapse', but renders it 'unstable'.[65] Thus, when seeking out the meaning of Jesus' parables, it's important to do two things: understand the 'inner logic' of the story; and search for the surprise or twist involved. Seeing how the story shifts is usually a clue to the questions the audience would have been left with. But this can be hard to do because we read the parables after 20 centuries of Christian interpretation, which tends to rob them of the surprises they contain.

The original shock impact of the parable of the Pharisee and the tax-collector (Luke 18.9–14), for example, is hard to hear today, especially since we are accustomed to Pharisees getting a worse press in the Gospels than tax-collectors. Amy-Jill Levine points out that, originally, 'the Pharisee would be the equivalent of Mother Teresa or Billy Graham. The idea that either would not be in a right relationship with God is preposterous.' Thus the function of the parable is to leave the listener thinking 'Thank heaven, I am not like Mother Teresa; thank heaven, I am not like Billy Graham'[66] – an absurd reaction. The effect is to destabilize the categories in which the audience thinks, and to force them to see and accept the tax-collector as righteous too. Therefore he too has a place within the Kingdom.

Teaching in this form would have marked Jesus out as a wise man or sage, a distinctive category set apart from those primarily devoted to the Law, as the Scribes and Pharisees were. Jesus' teaching often echoed the

Book of Proverbs, such as the sayings about doing good to your enemies (Matt. 5.44; Prov. 25.21–2, cf. Rom. 12.20); the treasure in the field (Matt. 13.44; Prov. 2.4–5); taking the lowest seat at a banquet (Luke 14.10; Prov. 25.6–7). Many other sayings have the 'feel' of the wisdom literature of the Hebrew Scriptures (of which the Book of Proverbs is just one part), perhaps especially those collected in the Sermon on the Mount in Matthew's Gospel.

If Jesus was seen as a sage he was a sage with a difference. In the hands of sages like Ben Sira in the second century BC, the wisdom tradition had come to be seen as primarily a source of common-sense advice for rulers. By contrast Jesus was a 'sage from below'[67] who used the wisdom forms subversively, to puncture pomposity and to make mischief, questioning values which were taken for granted. His parables were designed to liberate imagination and encourage people to see how his actions demonstrated the new order of the Kingdom of God. But so far we have really only considered one group of parables, those concerned with the growth of the Kingdom. There is also another important group of parables: those which speak of future judgement.

Crisis and judgement

Some of Jesus' parables focus on being ready for an expected event of which the timing is uncertain: slaves who are waiting for their master to return (Mark 13.34–6; Luke 12.35–8); a thief in the night (Matt. 24.43–4; Luke 12.39–40) or wise and foolish bridesmaids (Matt. 25.1–13). Others emphasize judgement: notably the wheat and the tares (Matt. 13.24–30), the talents (Matt. 25.14–30; Luke 19.11–27), and the sheep and the goats (Matt. 25.31–46), all of which speak of a moment of division, when good will be separated from bad.

Impending judgement had been the keynote of John the Baptist's message. While its importance for Jesus was secondary to the announcement that the Kingdom was present, judgement was clearly still a major theme for him. What do these parables suggest about Jesus' understanding of judgement?

They seem to imply that when the Kingdom comes more fully than it already has done humanity will be divided into two: those who are in relationship with God and those who are not. The language is apocalyptic, a toned-down version of what is found in the Dead Sea Scrolls, though there are stock images of eternal torment and weeping and gnashing of teeth for those who do not share the presence of God (Mark 9.43–8; Matt. 5.22; 13.42, 50; Luke 12.5; 13.28). The descriptions of division tend to emphasize that those outside the Kingdom are excluded because they have chosen to be (see Matt. 25.34–45).

Some of the judgement-sayings include the figure of the 'Son of Man' (see Mark 8.38; 13.26; 14.62; Matt. 16.27; 24.30; 25.31; Luke 9.26;

21.27). If these occurred on their own, we would almost certainly conclude that Jesus was speaking about someone else, based on the Son of Man in the apocalyptic vision of Daniel who receives the authority of God (Dan. 7.13–14). But the name 'son of man' is one which is used routinely by Jesus in the Gospels to describe himself and is strikingly never used by anyone else about him. It is ambiguous: it might mean something close to God's viceroy, or it might simply mean an ordinary person – 'someone like me'.

Did Jesus see himself as the 'Son of Man', the agent of God's future judgement? This seems likely, largely on the grounds that such an idea seems to have been a new one, unparalleled among Jesus' contemporaries. The ambiguity around it is similar to the kind of ambiguity which we find in the parables, and such ambiguity offered a measure of protection.

How Jesus saw himself and what the claims he made for the coming of God's Kingdom meant are still contested issues. Perhaps this is not surprising, because these same issues would ultimately lead to his death.

Heading to Jerusalem

The arrest of John the Baptist had marked a new stage in Jesus' life. He had emerged in Galilee proclaiming that the Kingdom of God had arrived and based himself in Capernaum in the far north. In the following 18 months he had gathered around him both close disciples and much greater crowds. News about him had spread across the whole of Israel. Now John was dead. As the signs of spring began to be seen and lambs were gathered across the country ready for sacrifice at the Passover, what would Jesus do next?

During this time Jesus had been elusive. The authorities found him hard to track down, and his actions and his words seemed calculated to shroud his intentions in mystery. His visits to Jerusalem had been, in effect, under cover and not part of his public ministry. He had shown what the Kingdom of God was like in Galilee, but sooner or later he would have to face the challenge of bringing that Kingdom to Jerusalem. That, after all, was where the prophets had said that God would appear. Jesus' work in Galilee had been remarkable, but had it really changed anything?

All four Gospels identify a decisive turn by Jesus towards Jerusalem (Mark 10.1, 32; Matt. 19.1; 20.17; Luke 9.51; John 11.7). The accounts are pregnant with the knowledge that this would be Jesus' last journey. But did Jesus think this too? To understand what he was doing we have to look at the question, who did Jesus believe he was?

'Who do you say I am?'

The first three Gospels place Jesus' change of direction in the immediate aftermath of the disciples' recognition of Jesus' real identity and of his transfiguration (Mark 8.27—9.13; Matt. 16.13—17.13; Luke 9.28–36). While these episodes are crucial to the movement of the plot of the synoptic Gospels, and are therefore probably told in stylized form, they raise an important question: what did the disciples believe Jesus' role to be?

Jesus asked the question, 'Who do people say that I am?' The disciples offered various answers: John the Baptist, Elijah, a prophet. None of these options caught the novelty and range of Jesus' role in the Kingdom of God, hence the next question: 'You, who do *you* say that I am?' Peter's response is to say, 'You are the Christ'.

The setting of this story is important. It takes place on the road to the villages around Caesarea Philippi. The area was under the rule of Herod Antipas's brother Philip and well-known as a place of sanctuary. It was a safe hiding-place, at the furthest extent of ancient Israel, tucked into the foothills of the Mount Hermon range from whose snows, it was believed, the waters of the Jordan were born. It was also dominated by the worship of the pagan god Pan, whose shrine Herod the Great had augmented with temples dedicated to Rome and Augustus. So to most Jews it would have seemed to be holy ground which needed to be reclaimed.

Jesus' recognition by Peter as the Christ, the anointed one, the messiah, placed him in the role of being the one to revive the nation and to reclaim its ancient borders. Accepting such a role would carry implications with it which would take the bearer south along the road to Jerusalem. It would also mean that Jesus was 'the one who was to come' about whom John the Baptist had prophesied.

Although the whole episode of Peter's confession is often rejected by scholars as being a post-Easter invention, it fits very plausibly into the historical setting of Jesus' ministry. After the initial phase of the Kingdom in Galilee a journey north in secret with his closest followers to plan the next move makes sense. Integral to that move must have been some reflection on what the right steps should be. The Gospels record both Jesus' warning about weighing up the consequences of an action before taking it (Luke 14.28–30) and also later struggles with what he felt called to do (see Mark 14.36).

Yet, according to the story, Jesus was ambivalent about Peter's response. He pledged the disciples to secrecy and offered them an interpretation of his role that required suffering and death as the way to ultimate vindication. Again the uncertainty of many scholars over the authenticity of this passage is outweighed by its preservation of the sharp antagonism between Jesus and Peter (Mark 8.33) which the later Church was unlikely to have introduced, given Peter's subsequent authoritative role.

What might Peter have meant by recognizing Jesus as the messiah?

There was no clear blueprint or job description for a messiah, nor probably any widespread popular expectation of someone who would fill the role. In the circumstances of royal rule by the Herod family, whose claim would not have stood a chance without Roman patronage, there had been a revival of interest among some in the return of a king (who would be an 'anointed one' or messiah) in the line of David, possibly through a sub-branch of the family.

This figure was unequivocally a military one (it was hard to see royalty in any other way in the first century), who was to restore David's kingdom. But there were many ways of interpreting what this actually meant: in practice 'the idea of Israel's coming king was one that different movements and different claimants could quite easily reshape around themselves ... Messiahship, it seems, was whatever people made of it'.[68] In the circumstances of heightened eschatological expectation aroused by John the Baptist and Jesus himself, however, it would have been very odd if the disciples had not speculated over whether Jesus' Davidic family connections fitted him for the role.

One interpretation current in the first century connects the expectation of a Davidic messiah with the promise made by the prophet Nathan to David – a son of David who would build a temple and be accepted as God's son (2 Sam. 7.12–14). Significantly, the same three elements emerge in the high priest Caiaphas's interrogation of Jesus about whether he intended to destroy and rebuild the Temple: does this mean, Caiaphas asks, that Jesus is 'the messiah, the son of the Blessed One [i.e. God]?' (Mark 14.61). James Dunn notes that 'if a messianic reading of Nathan's prophecy was "in the air" at the time of Jesus, that would provide all the explanation necessary for Caiaphas's question'[69] which has otherwise largely baffled commentators. This, or something like it, may be what lies in the background of the brief conversation at Caesarea Philippi that has come down to us. This kind of messiah would have to head to Jerusalem, because that was where the Temple was; and he would be seen to be a special figure; worthy to be called God's son, as was the king in the Psalms (see Ps. 2.7).

Jesus' response suggests that he had a rather different understanding of being the messiah, which completely undermined the triumphalist Davidic image. In the scene at Caesarea Philippi, and twice later in Mark's Gospel, Jesus tells the disciples that 'it is required that the son of man suffer many things and be rejected by the elders, the high priests and the scribes, and be put to death – and after three days to rise' (Mark 8.31, also 9.31; 10.33–4). Wilhelm Wrede rejected any possibility that these passages could reflect the actual thought of Jesus, arguing that the only way to get prophecy so exactly right is to compose it after the event. Certainly it does look as if later events have affected the prophecies, to the extent that, by the third time the prediction is made, the fit with what Mark is about to narrate of Jesus' passion is almost perfect: 'the son of man will be betrayed to the high priests and the scribes and they will sentence him to death and will hand him over to the gentiles and they will mock him and spit on him and whip him and put him to death – and after three days he will rise' (Mark 10.33–4); this is the passion story in a nutshell. Matthew and Luke in their revisions make a telling alteration: rising 'after three days' becomes 'on the third day' (Matt. 16.21; 17.23; 20.19; Luke 9.22; 18.33), a neater match with the story of Jesus' resurrection as it was later told.

Though Wrede's view has put a large question mark against these predictions, once we move away from the precise words to the thought behind them a surprising degree of unanimity among scholars breaks out. The key phrase is 'after three days', preserved by Mark. With hindsight this became a prediction of Jesus' resurrection 'on the third day', but its more obvious meaning would probably have been the general 'after a little while', as it is sometimes used in the Hebrew Scriptures (see Hos. 6.2). This makes it likely that Jesus said something which both set his mission within a framework of suffering and death, and also looked for future vindication from God, but that he was not specific about the timing.

Some of Jesus' contemporaries seem to have expected that the messiah would begin a period of 'tribulation', which would be followed by a vindication at the time when God would raise the faithful dead to life once again. In essence, this seems to have been Jesus' own expectation, but with a distinctive twist. Sanders suggests that Jesus was expecting an event like the Exodus, where God would act to 'create an ideal world ... would restore the twelve tribes of Israel, and peace and justice would prevail. Life would be like a banquet.'[70] The word exodus is in fact used by Luke in his account of the transfiguration, where Jesus 'spoke of his exodus which he was soon to bring about in Jerusalem' (Luke 9.31). Unlike the general expectation, however, this action of God would decisively include Jesus himself and perhaps his followers too in its accomplishment. Dale Allison writes that 'The picture originally painted was of Jesus and the community around him facing the great tribulation, yet confident in the hope that glory lies on the other side of suffering.'[71] Victory therefore had to be won, and 'unless a seed falls into the ground and dies it remains a single seed. But if it dies it produces many seeds' (John 12.24). Allison summarizes Jesus' teaching as 'The road to the new world passes through the land of suffering and death.'[72] John the Baptist had predicted judgement; Jesus sought to bring it upon himself. His role therefore would be like that of the Passover lamb in the original Exodus, deflecting the judgement which should fall on Israel but at the cost of his own life.

This view of messiahship implies that Jesus set out for Jerusalem in a deliberate attempt to bring about the tribulation. This would require enormous and unshakeable faith. Jesus took the road to Jerusalem knowing that he faced a likely death, but believing that through his martyrdom God would achieve a new Exodus, or something even greater.

The first three Gospels record the story of the transfiguration of Jesus as a confirmation of what had been established at Caesarea Philippi, a heavenly endorsement of Jesus' understanding of his role, a week or so later (Mark 9.2–8; Luke 9.28–36). Once again, debate rages over what this event might have been and whether the episode is a symbolic one, invented to bolster the story as a whole. But it is at least possible that it was a visionary experience, reaffirming the call he had received at his baptism and confirming to him that he was on the right path.

The period of six days (Luke says 'about eight') between Peter's confession and the transfiguration experience suggests a period of retreat and reflection accompanied by the inner circle of his disciples among the Hermon mountains, paralleled by Jesus' withdrawal to the desert before his baptism. It seems likely that, after this period of reflection, Jesus was ready for the challenge that lay ahead. Passover was a few weeks away. From the Hermon mountains in the far north of ancient Israel, Jesus and his disciples made the fateful turn south towards the destiny which he knew awaited him in Jerusalem.

Jesus and the cities

Jesus seems to have avoided towns and cities for most of his ministry. The Gospels do not mention Sepphoris, and only John's speaks coincidentally of Tiberias (John 6.23), yet these were the major cities of Galilee.

Some scholars suggest that Jesus had a deep and perhaps romantic preference for the simplicities of rural life over urban luxury. But his avoidance of them may have been more to do with safety than ideology. These towns were much more tightly controlled by Antipas's troops than the surrounding villages. On the other hand, with their theatres and bathhouses, they were also centres of Hellenistic culture and as such perhaps suspect to many Jews.

Jerusalem too had become in many respects a Hellenistic city under Herod the Great's architectural patronage. Yet it was dominated by the Temple, centre of Jewish religious life and faith. Jews could not avoid Jerusalem if they wished to be devout, however compromised they might feel it had become through foreign influences. (Strict Essenes had come to the conclusion that they must boycott the Temple, as the Dead Sea Scrolls show, but this was an extreme minority reaction.)

John's Gospel portrays Jesus as a regular visitor to Jerusalem, but he is often reluctant to go and attends the festivals almost covertly (see John 7.1–53). John's Gospel sees Jesus as being at loggerheads with the Temple authorities from the outset of his public ministry, and while this theme may be exaggerated in order to develop the plot of the Gospel, it is plausible that Jesus was seen as a threat. While he was in Galilee the threat was probably not a very serious one; but once he entered the city itself the authorities would have been justified in keeping a close eye on him.

There is evidence that Jesus foretold the destruction of the Temple, and that he had done so throughout his ministry. It was a major accusation against him that he had done this (Mark 14.58; 15.29; Matt. 26.61; 27.40; see also Mark 13.2; John 2.19; Acts 6.13). Yet, on the other hand, he cannot have been dramatically opposed to the Temple as such, or else why did his followers subsequently continue to worship there after the crucifixion?

Jesus does not seem to have rejected the Temple as such; he paid the Temple tax (Matt. 17.24–7), and in his last week in Jerusalem he taught in the outside courts and apparently commended a poor widow who contributed to its upkeep (Mark 12.41–4) which might have seemed strange if he was violently opposed to the Temple. Yet he also seems to have predicted destruction and caused an incident which at least temporarily disrupted normal business (Mark 11.15–19).

The prophets of the Hebrew Scriptures offered a vision of a new Temple, to which all the nations of the world would come (for example, Isa. 60.3–7, 10–14; 66.18–24; Micah 4.1–7). This vision had not been fulfilled by Herod's rebuilding, and a number of sources (notably in the Dead Sea Scrolls) suggest that there was widespread, though not uniform, hope that in the age to come God would provide a new temple and fulfil these prophecies.

Setting Jesus' sayings about the destruction of the Temple in such an eschatological context helps us to see why Jesus could apparently simultaneously attack and support the Temple. Sanders concludes 'that Jesus publicly predicted or threatened the destruction of the temple, that the statement was shaped by his expectation of the arrival of the eschaton, [and] that he probably also expected a new temple to be given by God from heaven'.[73] Proclaiming this message in Galilee would not be especially dangerous; but proclaiming it within the Temple itself would be likely to lead Jesus into trouble.

The long and winding road

The road from Galilee to Jerusalem was thronged with crowds. Spring flowers bloomed and daytime temperatures rose. The pilgrims camped close to the Jordan River each night, huddling round campfires and exchanging news and gossip as new people joined the crowd. Scattered families were reunited on the road, and the pilgrims chanted psalms as they prepared to celebrate their Passover feast of national liberation. Alongside them clustered flocks of sheep being driven towards the Temple for the Passover sacrifice. Sometimes it must have seemed that the whole of Israel was on the move.

Most pilgrims arrived a week early, in order to observe a period of purification from corpse impurity. In small communities contact with a dead body would have been almost impossible to avoid during the preceding year; just being in the same room as a dead person or walking over a grave would lead to it. So though the Passover was celebrated on 15 Nisan, it was in the days before 8 Nisan that the crowds, perhaps as many as half a million people, converged on Jerusalem and its surrounding villages.

Such a large number of people waiting for the festival to begin also made it easy for the carnival mood to turn ugly. A moment's reflection on what God had done to set his people free from Egypt prompted the thought that he might do it again and liberate them from the contemporary 'pharaohs' of Rome and the Herod family. After Herod the Great's death in 4 BC, and again under the governor Cumanus around 50, Passover became the flashpoint for protest and violence. So in parallel with the gathering of people from Galilee and Judea, detachments of soldiers would be marching east from Caesarea Maritima to reinforce the garrison in Jerusalem. Passover was always a tense time for those in authority.

Jesus' journey south to Jerusalem assumes the aspect of a royal progress in Luke's Gospel, but it looks as if Luke has arranged his material to create this impression. The Gospels of Mark and John make the journey south seem more understated, though still full of incident. At any rate, Jesus, his disciples and his other followers probably blended with the other pilgrims on their way to Jerusalem. There was safety in numbers: it would be hard for Antipas or Pilate to arrest Jesus quietly when he was surrounded by so many people, and finding him among the crowds would be next to impossible.

They passed from the lush landscape of Galilee down the Jordan valley, probably skirting the grand buildings of Scythopolis, one of the ten towns of the Decapolis, before following the steep road out of Jericho through the dry and suddenly bare hills on the last lap towards Jerusalem itself.

Climbing this road the pilgrims would chant the 'Psalms of Ascent' (Ps. 120—34) until at last they crested the hill, and found the city spread out before them, the white stones and gold finishings of Herod's breathtaking Temple gleaming in the sunlight.

For Jesus it was the beginning of the last act.

Jesus' last week

Jesus' last week dominates the Gospels. Six of Mark's 16 chapters, seven of Matthew's 28, five of Luke's 24, and an astonishing nine out of John's 21 focus on Jesus' last days. This was not unusual in ancient biographies, where there was a 'tendency to describe the subject's death at some length to reveal the true character'.[74] Even so there is a discrepancy here. Sebastian Moore notes that Jesus is often remembered as a great teacher, someone of whom 'Harnack can say … that he refers to the deepest and most searching spiritual truths as though they grew on trees for anyone to pluck.' Yet the Gospel writers' attention is only partly on this extraordinary teaching. Moore goes on, 'It is as though an admirer of Shakespeare the man, having gone on and on about the special circumstances attendant on his death, added "by the way, he also wrote plays" – and handed us for the first time the Shakespeare corpus.'[75] Why this relative downplaying of Jesus' teaching in favour of the story of his death?

The answer lies in that last week. It clearly had a huge impact on those who experienced it, and for those who came afterwards it threw up many questions. What kind of messiah was this, that he suffered and died with a cry of dereliction on his lips? 'The cross was the part of their experience of Jesus that demanded immediate and detailed interpretation', writes Luke T. Johnson, and 'Precisely the need for interpretation – indeed the problematic nature of that event – argues for its basic historicity. This community would not have invented a crucified messiah, since it showed itself so eager to escape the implications of that proposition.'[76] Jesus' last week was a conundrum. How could the man who died on a cross in an efficient piece of Roman counter-terrorist strategy end up a few years later worshipped as God? The cross needed both context and explanation.

'Prophecy historicized' or 'history scripturized'?

The four Gospels offer four different accounts of Jesus' last week. The variations are as basic as whether Jesus' demonstration in the Temple happened on the same day as his triumphal entry into Jerusalem (Matt. 21.1–17; Luke 19.28–45), or a day later (Mark 11.1–19) – or did not occur then at all (John 2.13–22).

These discrepancies offer good reasons to dismiss the accounts altogether. Dominic Crossan, for example, argues that little can be known of the last week of Jesus' life other than the bare fact that he died on a cross. Crossan disputes even the burial story, claiming that Jesus' body was never found because it was eaten by scavenging dogs beneath the cross. The details of Jesus' final days are an example, according to him, of '*prophecy historicized* and not *history memorized*'.[77] That is to say, they have been created by the Gospel writers out of a tapestry of biblical texts and echoes of ritual actions. One example he offers is of the humiliation of Jesus in the palace of the Roman governor. Jesus is clothed in purple robes, crowned with thorns, beaten with a reed and spat upon (Mark 15.16–20). This shows a striking resemblance to the punishment suffered by the scapegoat, which was also beaten, abused and spat upon (Lev. 16.7–10, 21–2). Crossan suggests that, once the early Christians had decided that Jesus' death should be understood as a sacrifice for sin, the scapegoat naturally came to mind as a means of explaining it. So Mark's narrative used the details of the punishment which the scapegoat underwent to imagine what had happened to Jesus. Thus prophecy became history. Matthew and Luke simply continued the process, according to Crossan, while John did basically the same thing but took a slightly different route.

Others have not been so sceptical. Crossan clearly makes an important point when he emphasizes the vital, complex and subtle role which biblical allusion plays in the last chapters of the Gospels. But the match is not as close as he asserts between the Gospels and their supposed sources. Between the poles of 'prophecy historicized' and 'history memorized' may lie a third alternative; what Mark Goodacre has christened 'history scripturized'.[78]

The accounts of Jesus' death contain a number of details which are unnecessary if the texts really are prophecy historicized, as Crossan contends. The role of Simon of Cyrene, the mention of the 'place of the skull' and the hour of the crucifixion, for example, have no obvious scriptural or symbolic value at all. This implies that these details are in the accounts for the simple reason that they were part of the memories of those who were there. Therefore, suggests Goodacre, while the bones of the accounts reflect actual events, the Gospel writers have used biblical texts at certain points to add interpretative flesh. So the history has been 'scripturized'.

A similar process seems to apply to the whole story of Jesus' last week. The overall sequence of events is a common one: Jesus entered Jerusalem on a donkey to acclaim, created a disturbance in the Temple, taught in the Temple, ate a meal with his disciples, was arrested in the Garden of Gethsemane, condemned to death by Pilate and then was crucified and buried. But there are gaps between these events which have been filled in differently by the different Gospel writers, even to the extent of placing the crucifixion on alternative days.

The differences between the Gospel accounts of Jesus' last week, therefore, reflect the different emphases of their writers, something that can be seen very clearly when their narratives of the crucifixion are compared. But this does not mean that they have imagined almost everything. The basic events seem to have solid evidence behind them, but were interpreted in the light of the Scriptures.

Arrival in Jerusalem

The Gospels suggest that this Passover was to be a special one. John's Gospel has a running theme of 'the hour', which at last strikes as Jesus enters Jerusalem (John 12.23); it had not come when earlier festivals occurred and was the source of antagonism between Jesus and his brothers (John 7.6–8). While this theme serves the eschatological scheme of John's Gospel, there may be some historical root to it. Luke also notes that Jesus' final journey to Jerusalem was surrounded by eschatological speculation which he says Jesus sought to damp down (Luke 19.11). Paula Fredriksen proposes that this particular Passover may have been fraught with even greater than normal expectation, and that during the journey to Jerusalem perhaps 'Jesus announced that this Passover would be the last before the Kingdom arrived'[79] (see Luke 19.11, Mark 10.37). Three actions make up the story of Jesus' arrival in Jerusalem: his appearance on a donkey at the Mount of Olives, his triumphal entry into the city and the incident in the Temple. When read together against a background of heightened eschatological expectation, these three actions seem deliberately provocative.

Entering the city

It is easy to overlook the significance of Jesus' arrival on the Mount of Olives (Mark 11.1), since the road from Jericho made the Mount the obvious way to approach Jerusalem from the east. Until this point Jesus had been one among the pilgrim crowd, but his demand for a donkey marks a new development. Riding down the Mount of Olives was significant because it was here that God would stand to bring judgement, according to the prophets (Zech. 14.4). Appearing on the Mount of Olives might be a claim to be the 'strong one' whose coming John the Baptist had prophesied.

All four Gospels record Jesus' entry into Jerusalem in an atmosphere of jubilation and to the kind of welcome which went far beyond what a prophet and holy man from Galilee might be expected to arouse. Casting down clothing in front of him was the mark of homage to royalty.

Jesus arrived in the city mounted. The Gospels never record him riding anywhere else, so this was an important departure from normality. Matthew's Gospel, followed by John's, catches an allusion to the prophet Zechariah about the arrival of a king riding on an ass (Matt. 21.5; John 12.15, see Zech. 9.9) and the choice of an ass rather than a horse is often interpreted as a sign of Jesus' peaceful intentions. It probably was, but only in the sense that riding a horse was reserved for times of war, and asses made perfectly good royal mounts the rest of the time.

The crowd waved branches, though only John's Gospel specifies that they were palms (John 12.13). Palms were a national symbol: Roman coins issued after the destruction of the Temple in 70 showed an enslaved figure beneath a palm tree with the words *Captive Judea* on them, and palms were a reminder of Simon Maccabeus, the last leader of Israel to ride victoriously into Jerusalem (1 Macc. 13.51). Waving palms in front of Jesus was a political and nationalistic act. As Tom Wright notes, 'riding on a donkey over the Mount of Olives, across Kidron, and up to the

Temple mount spoke more powerfully than words could have done of a royal claim.'[80] Riding into Jerusalem was a royal act.

From the Mount of Olives, the pilgrims descended towards the city. But the approach is not a simple one, as anyone who has walked it will know. The steep Kidron valley must be traversed, and from this direction in the early first century the options for entering the city were limited. The Temple dominated the eastern side of the city and its wall formed the wall of the city on this side. It was possible to enter the city by the Golden Gate of the Temple into its outer courts, but this gate was primarily used for ceremonial duties. North of the Temple lay the Bethesda pools, but these lay outside the city walls, and were directly beneath the walls of the Antonia fortress with its Roman garrison. Most likely the pilgrims went down the Kidron valley and then climbed up to enter Jerusalem through the ancient city of David. This was also the most obvious way to approach the Temple, since most visitors to the precincts entered through its southern gates, beneath the Royal Portico.

If Jesus entered Jerusalem through the city of David the crowd's acclamation of him as 'Son of David' (Mark 11.10) was particularly appropriate. It was also probably the safest route, at some distance from the barracks of Roman soldiers and Temple guards and through a densely populated area into which it would be easy to vanish if trouble occurred. James Dunn suggests that for some Jesus' entry into Jerusalem 'was nothing beyond the boisterous procession of a bunch of pilgrims ... But for those who looked for the coming of God's reign the event carried clear overtones of import.'[81] Jesus' third action on arrival in the city, the demonstration in the Temple, would amplify those eschatological overtones.

Turning the tables on the Temple

According to Mark, Jesus took a brief look at the Temple after arriving in Jerusalem and then left the city for the night (Mark 11.11). Matthew and Luke streamline the story and have him entering the Temple straightaway to turn out those buying and selling (Matt. 21.10–17; Luke 19.45–8), but Mark's version is probably more likely. John's Gospel virtually jumps straight from the entry into Jerusalem to the eve of the crucifixion (John 12.1, 12; 13.1).

It is possible to make a case that there were two similar but distinct demonstrations in the Temple, one at the beginning of the ministry of Jesus and one at the end. This is not popular with scholars in general, who assume that there can have been only one such event. Perhaps a slim majority favours John's chronology over Mark's and thus would bracket a demonstration in the Temple out of Jesus' final week. In John's Gospel, tension between Jesus and the Temple authorities is the basis of the plot, so it makes sense to narrate a story of conflict with them early on. In Mark's Gospel Jesus enters Jerusalem for the first time at the beginning of his final Passover week, so his attitude to the Temple can logically only be explored at that point in the narrative.

Scarcely anyone considers that a significant incident in the Temple did not happen at all, and even the normally cautious Sanders judges that 'it is overwhelmingly probable that Jesus did something in the temple and said something about its destruction'.[82] Whether it happened early or late in Jesus' career (or both), it suggests some important things about Jesus' attitude to the Temple.

There are several possibilities for what Jesus intended his demonstration in the Temple to mean (though we should heed James Dunn's warning to 'beware of the easy assumption that [Jesus] was following out a clearly-thought through strategy'[83] – this may have been a spur-of-the-moment action). The traditional title of 'cleansing' for this episode implies that Jesus' action was fundamentally religious in its motives, concerned to restore true worship and cast out money-making abuses, an understanding which leans heavily on the saying 'my house shall be called a house of prayer' (Mark 11.17). Some groups did see the Temple establishment as 'wealthy, corrupt, often greedy, and sometimes violent',[84] and no doubt some pilgrims complained about the price of pigeons. The requirement to pay the Temple tax in Tyrian shekels might well have induced money changers to charge a little more than they need have done in commission. Yet overall there are few signs that the Temple was seen as corrupt in the first century, though there was occasionally some anti-priestly feeling. Jesus' action would not really have changed any such corruption anyway. It was a short-lived protest which, if it was an attempt to reform Temple practices, must be judged a failure. In which case it is unlikely that the Gospel writers would have given it such importance.

An alternative explanation is that Jesus attempted an armed coup, designed to take over the most powerful symbol of Jewish nationalism. Though rightly dismissed, this view may have more substance than it is usually credited with, in the sense that Jesus' actions might have looked like a possible coup to the authorities, both Jewish and Roman. John the Baptist had been seen by Antipas as a possible focus for armed rebellion, and the Temple was potentially a very effective military stronghold, as was shown in the siege and final battle of the Jewish revolt in 70, as well as a religious centre. But however it looked to Pilate and Caiaphas, this was surely not Jesus' intention and it does not fit with the picture the Gospels offer of his preliminary ministry in Galilee. Armed conquest does not seem to have been any part of Jesus' vision of the Kingdom of God, though the authorities may have rightly feared what could happen if his followers decided to make it so.

More convincing is a third option, which sees Jesus' demonstration as a symbolic, prophetic act with messianic overtones. Seeing Jesus' action in this way locates it very clearly within an understandable first-century context. Jesus Ben Ananias prophesied against the Temple at all the feasts from

62 until it was actually destroyed in 70, and he provides an example of a prophet whose actions were in some ways similar to Jesus of Nazareth's. If it was a symbolic action then its short-lived character is explained.

Yet symbols are, by their nature, susceptible to many meanings. To take just three recent interpretations, Tom Wright considers that Jesus' action was one of judgement, aimed at those who turned the Temple into a 'talisman of nationalist violence', but also proposing that Jesus 'saw himself, and perhaps his followers with him, as the new Temple'.[85] Therefore his action symbolized the end of the system of sacrifice. E. P. Sanders understands the symbol to be of imminent destruction and rebuilding: Jesus meant 'to indicate that the end was at hand and that the temple would be destroyed, so that the new and perfect temple might arise.'[86] This action is symbolic of God's future restorative action. Dominic Crossan considers that Jesus simply 'exploded in indignation at the Temple as the seat and symbol of all that was non-egalitarian, patronal and even oppressive on both the religious and political level. His symbolic destruction simply actualized what he had already said in his teachings'.[87] So Jesus' action was essentially a protest against privilege and the misuse of power. How do we find a way through these differing interpretations?

According to Mark, Jesus 'threw out those selling and those buying in the Temple, and overturned the tables of the moneychangers and the chairs of the dove-sellers, and did not allow anyone to carry anything through the Temple' (Mark 11.15–6). Three separate actions are detailed here: throwing out sellers and buyers; overturning the tables of the money changers; banning any movement within the Temple. Paula Fredriksen questions whether, in the vast area of the Temple courts ('twelve soccer fields could fit neatly into the space'), overturning some tables would actually have made any impact: 'If Jesus had made such a gesture, who would have seen it?'[88] But as described by Mark this action amounts to clearing the courts of everyone within them. Fredriksen's point may be reversed: if this event did occur as described, who would have missed it, since it would have caused hundreds of people to leave the precincts and, at least temporarily, closed the Temple?

Matthew and Luke, coming later to Mark's account, seem to be a little uneasy about it. Matthew omits the ban on movement within the Temple and Luke merely says that Jesus threw out the sellers (Matt. 21.12; Luke 19.45). Does this perhaps suggest that they felt Mark's account overstated the impact of Jesus' action? Maybe so, in which case Fredriksen's question about who would have seen the event arises again. But how many people would have needed to see it? The three actions detailed by Mark, and even the reduced versions of Matthew and Luke, point in the direction of the end of the Temple's sacrificial system as it was practised. The most obvious meaning of throwing out the buyers, sellers and money changers was that they would not be needed any longer, and that could only be the case if the sacrificial system came to an end. Only a small demonstration would be needed to begin the report that Jesus had prophetically foretold the destruction of the Temple, as Jeremiah had done centuries before (see Jer. 19).

According to the synoptic Gospels, Jesus spent the next few days teaching in the Temple precincts; and his followers continued to worship in the Temple in the years that followed. Neither of these actions suggests an implacable opposition to the Temple itself and the system of sacrifice which was its *raison d'être*. There is a world of difference between a picture of Jesus himself seeking to bring judgement on the Temple as the agent of God by causing chaos in the courts, and a prophecy that in the future rule of God the Temple will no longer be needed.

That Jesus was looking to the future, perhaps long-term, is also suggested by the saying which is connected with the event. 'He said to them: "Has it not been written that my house will be called a house of prayer for all the nations? But you have made it a cave for robbers"' (Mark 11.17). Only Mark includes the emphasis on the inclusion of gentiles (see Isa. 56.7), but this detail points to the future when all people may be drawn into the worship of the Temple and envisages the eschatological future when all the nations would be gathered to Jerusalem. The most obvious contemporary application of the second part of the quotation (drawn from Jer. 7.11) was to the priests, who ran the Temple, and the Herod family, who had rebuilt it. The 'cave of robbers' means a bandits' hideout, where they store their spoils after raids. The Temple, like all ancient temples, was also a bank, a safe place to store money and valuables. (This was one of the reasons why its destruction was welcome to Vespasian and his son Titus in 70, since its looted wealth formed the basis for their family fortune.)

Herod the Great and his sons had spent a great deal on the rebuilding of the Temple, but in doing so they had also made a secure treasury for themselves. The Galilean taxes, which yielded such a good financial harvest for Herod Antipas, fetched up in the Temple vaults with the acquiescence of its authorities. So Jesus' criticism would have pointed not at the priests in general, but specifically at those who were at the top; and also to the Herod family itself. The sharpness of the cave image is striking. The caves of Arbela loom over the western shore of Lake Galilee, easily visible from Capernaum and from the lake itself. Here Herod the Great had famously destroyed brigands who had made Galilee and Judea a dangerous place, and brought peace. But perhaps the result of this peace was simply that the biggest robbers of all were now in charge, storing their loot under cover of God's protection in the Temple. The coming of God's Kingdom would spell an end to all that.

Jesus had been content to leave a good deal of his teaching in Galilee enigmatic, for the hearers to work out his meaning. Possibly his action in the Temple was the same. Did he foresee an end to the sacrificial system, or did he envisage a new Temple given by God which would replace the present one? The combined intelligence of hundreds of scholars has yielded no clear-cut answer to these questions, and contemporaries too may have been puzzled as to what he actually meant. Perhaps this was the aim, to keep everyone guessing and raising questions which did not have simple answers. James Dunn says that 'among the reverberations set off by Jesus' action in the Temple would be the question, "Could this be the expected Davidic messiah?"'[89] What seems certain is that the Temple authorities were behind Jesus' arrest, and 'if one has to explain what disturbed that group about Jesus, something that could be interpreted as presenting a danger to the Temple/sanctuary would be the most plausible factor.'[90] Prophetic action and utterance in the heart of the Temple itself, on however large or small a scale, and whatever they might mean, drew a line in the sand. Mark cites this as the moment when the authorities finally determined to eradicate the Galilean preacher (Mark 11.18).

Teaching in the Temple

Mark portrays Jesus teaching in the Temple courts for the intervening few days between his arrival in Jerusalem and the Passover itself (Mark 12—13). Matthew and Luke follow his lead and suggest that Jesus delivered a substantial body of teaching in the Temple (Matt. 21.23—25.46; Luke 19.47—21.38). All these Gospels relate this period as the only time in his adult life when Jesus was in Jerusalem. Therefore if there was a strong tradition of Jesus teaching in the Temple the writers had no alternative but to locate it at this point in their narratives. John's Gospel shows Jesus teaching in the Temple on several earlier occasions (notably John 7.14—10.39), and omits any record of public teaching in the Temple at this point in the story, moving directly from Jesus' entry into Jerusalem to his private teaching of the disciples (John 13.1).

It seems likely that Jesus had been to Jerusalem in previous years and that a good deal of his teaching, which focused on the destiny and fate of Israel, had been delivered before. Jesus may have appeared then no more dangerous or significant than his namesake Jesus Ben Ananias did three decades later. But if Passover 30 was heralded with heightened eschatological expectation, Jesus' presence in the Temple courts telling parables which could be interpreted as attacking those currently holding power (see Mark 12.1–12) might have suddenly raised the stakes and made the authorities very anxious indeed.

Jesus' predictions of his fate had outlined the need for sacrifice, for suffering and death in Jerusalem (Mark 8.31; 9.31; 10.33–4). The same teaching formed the basis of his vision for those who followed him (Mark 13.1–23). His role was to be the new Passover lamb, deflecting judgement from those who followed him, and inviting ultimate vindication (Mark 13.24–7). On those who did not follow him, judgement would fall heavily. Tension mounted through the week.

Apocalypse in the Temple?

Eschatological expectation was a hallmark of Jesus' ministry. Within Jesus' message of the Kingdom, the motif of reversal, the overturning of the accepted order, had an important place. Dale Allison points out that several of Jesus' judgement sayings have an 'Honor now/Shame then' pattern, which looks forward to a time when 'Wrongs will be righted once and for all at the consummation'[91] (see Matt 10.39; 23.12; Mark 8.35; 10.31; Luke 14.11; 17.33; 18.14). Luke's Gospel foreshadows the theme in Mary's song of joy: 'He has frustrated the plans of the proud, tumbled the rulers from their thrones, lifted up the humble and filled the hungry with good things; the rich he has sent away with nothing' (Luke 1.51–3). It was one thing to proclaim this as a generality. But to announce that the time was imminent when it would be fulfilled was extremely dangerous. To do so would set Jesus very clearly at odds with those in authority.

This is what seems to have happened. One of Mark's 'sandwiches' provides the frame for his explanation of Jesus' threat to Jerusalem. He tells how a fig tree at Bethany, cursed by Jesus, withered in a day (Mark 11.12–14, 20–5, see Matt. 21.18–22). The story alludes to the Hebrew prophets who saw the fig tree as a symbol of Israel, its barrenness a sign of the nation's failure. In response God will bring judgement, and in this acted parable that is Jesus' role. And if judgement were to fall on Israel, then the Temple authorities would bear the brunt of the reversal it would bring.

The synoptic Gospels place Jesus' teaching on judgement and the future in the Temple. What all three preserve, despite their differences, is Mark's theme of conflict between Jesus and the Temple authorities (Mark 11.27; 12.13, 18, 35, 38–40), which is immediately intelligible, and his apocalyptic predictions of the future (Mark 13), which are much harder to understand.

The 'Little Apocalypse' sounds strange to twenty-first-century ears. Albert Schweitzer argued that Jesus expected an imminent act of God, quite possibly the end of the world itself, and was simply misguided and mistaken. George Caird later responded that Schweitzer misunderstood how language was being used: biblical writers 'regularly used end-of-the-world language metaphorically to refer to that which they well knew was not the end of the world'. Therefore the message of Jesus was actually 'directed to Israel as a nation with a summons to abandon the road of aggressive nationalism and return to a true understanding of her historic role as the people of God'.[92] Jesus was not literally predicting the end of the world in judgement, according to Caird, but rather the crisis with Rome which came to a head with the destruction of the Temple in 70.

Yet Schweitzer seems to have been on to something important about Jesus' apocalyptic message. Caird's influential attempt to sidestep the obvious implications of Jesus' words helpfully points out their political resonance but fails to catch the cosmic dimension of them. If Jesus made predictions of God's imminent judgement at Passover 30 itself, what did he expect would happen next?

Fundamentally Jesus hoped for a world set right, where God was in control, where the poor and powerless were lifted up and the rich and powerful toppled from their places. If a significant element of his message during this last week in Jerusalem was an apocalyptic one, it may not have offered those who heard him a blueprint for the future, but rather 'as it were a film full of flash-forwards' which poses a 'problem for the viewer. If we're not confused, then something is wrong: we are imposing our order on an intrinsically unordered narrative', writes James Dunn: 'The shattered mirror of prophecy gives a Picasso-esque image, and how the often jagged fragments fit into a whole is by no means clear.'[93] Pressing the apocalyptic imagery of Mark 13 for precise details of Jesus' plan of salvation is the wrong thing to do and, as the history of interpretation shows, doomed to fail. It is more realistic to see Jesus in his last week offering to the Temple crowds the kind of imprecise, enigmatic, but enticing vision which had already drawn many followers in Galilee. As Mark puts it, 'the whole crowd was spellbound by his teaching' (Mark 11.18, NRSV).

Cat and mouse in Jerusalem

One of the oddities of the story of Jesus' last week is why someone who made such an entrance into Jerusalem, prophesied against the Temple and criticized its leaders from within its precincts was not immediately arrested. Pilate was not slow to react to provocation, as we know from other episodes in his career, and Jesus would die on his orders within a few days under the caption 'king of the Jews'. If, as Paula Fredriksen says, 'A straight line connects the Triumphal Entry and the Crucifixion', why do the 'Gospels depict [Pilate] as doing nothing?'[94] Jesus seems somehow to have entered the city without arousing the opposition which he himself had predicted (Mark 8.31; 9.31; 10.33–4).

Some scholars explain this by suggesting that the story of Jesus' entry has been exaggerated and that it had more impact on Jesus' disciples than on the city as a whole. 'Perhaps' says E. P. Sanders, 'the event took place but was a small occurrence ... only a few disciples unostentatiously dropped their garments in front of the ass ... [and] quietly murmured "Hosanna".'[95] Fredriksen rightly dismisses this argument as lacking conviction, and in its place suggests that Pilate would have had sufficient information about Jesus to believe that his teaching was harmless and therefore that he was no threat to Rome. She concludes that it was only later in the week, under pressure from Caiaphas, that Pilate reluctantly recognized Jesus' threat to public order and then acted swiftly.

The Gospels themselves offer a simpler explanation: the authorities 'sought to arrest him but they were afraid of the crowd' (Mark 12.12). If this is true, then rather than Jesus' entry into Jerusalem being a low-key affair that did not attract much attention, the opposite may have been the case. If it was a major event which aroused excitement and anticipation in the crowd, Jesus' role at the centre of it may paradoxically have protected him. As John P. Meier says, 'Jesus' crucifixion is much easier to understand if he attracted large, enthusiastic crowds and much more difficult to understand if he was largely ignored by the populace and failed to gain any wide following.' He concludes that 'the more probable scenario is that Jesus not only attracted large crowds for a good part of his ministry but also continued to do so up until his arrest.'[96] Large crowds would have raised the stakes for Pilate and Caiaphas, forcing them into a waiting game, wary of putting a match to the combustible Passover crowds.

Pilate and Caiaphas

Pontius Pilate emerges from other ancient sources as a harsh governor, unafraid of cruelty and lacking subtlety. This is a contrast both with the portrait of him in the Gospels, and also with the view that he played Passover 30 with the skill necessary to avoid a bloodbath in Jerusalem. Yet, Pilate held office as governor of Judea for 11 years, a remarkably long time. He was a survivor, and despite his sometimes heavy-handed and provocative actions, he seems to have navigated the confusing currents of Judean politics very adeptly before they finally led to his downfall in 36. In these circumstances the Gospels' account that Pilate waited cautiously for the right moment to strike at Jesus because he had entered the city on a popular tide of nationalist fervour is not implausible.

Caiaphas was also a survivor. He served as high priest for 18 years, longer than anyone else in the first century. As high priest, Caiaphas was both the leader of the Jews (far more respected because of his religious authority than any member of the Herod family), yet also the chief agent of Roman government in Judea. Caiaphas formed a highly effective team with Pilate, which ensured a period of relative quiet in Judea and Jerusalem, and remained high priest, remarkably, for the whole of Pilate's governorship. But at festivals like the Passover, Caiaphas wore the magnificent ceremonial robes of the high priest, which were normally kept under Roman guard. Caiaphas only wore them when Pilate let him. It was quite clear who was in charge.

Caiaphas was, in Geza Vermes's words, 'just an efficient quisling'.[97] He played no significant part in any of Pilate's various altercations with Jews, according to Josephus, and Raymond Brown concudes that 'history would remember Caiaphas as little more than a name in the list of high priests were it not for his being "high priest that (fateful) year"' (John 11.49; 18.13).[98] He made no other mark and his survival in office for a record period was probably a sign of his weakness, pliability and inoffensiveness to the Roman governor. Caiaphas seems to have been Pilate's poodle.

The knowledge that Caiaphas was under Pilate's thumb has caused many scholars to question the Gospels' portrayal of the high priest backing the governor into a corner over the execution of Jesus. Would Caiaphas have been able to procure the death of Jesus even though Pilate considered him innocent? Perhaps the answer to this question lies in the shadowy figure of Annas, Caiaphas's father-in-law. Annas is mentioned only in John's Gospel in connection with Jesus' last week, but he is coupled with Caiaphas by Luke at other points (John 18.13, 24; Luke 3.2; Acts 4.6). Josephus considered him 'a most fortunate man'[99] because five of his sons, as well as his son-in-law, became high priest, as he had been himself for nine years. Annas emerges from the various sources about him as 'a powerful manipulator of the political scene even after he was dismissed from office'.[100] Since former high priests retained their status and title after leaving office (as US presidents do today) it is possible that when the Gospels speak of the 'high priest' they may mean Annas rather than Caiaphas. Annas may also have been the one behind the scenes who was pushing for the execution of Jesus, putting steel into his pliable son-in-law.

The Betrayer

In a city without a civil police force, identity documents or any means of recording images of those under suspicion, it was comparatively easy for potential troublemakers to evade arrest. Paul's experience in 56 of being mistaken for 'the Egyptian' after his arrest in the Temple (Acts 21.38) shows how hard it was for the authorities to identify suspects. Among the Passover crowds it would have been fairly simple for Jesus to come and go as he wished. What Caiaphas and Pilate needed was an informer to lead them to him. They found one in Judas Iscariot.

Judas plays a relatively minor role in the Gospels, albeit a crucial one. The historical basis of his betrayal passes the test of embarrassment: early opponents of Christianity were quick to point out the fallibility of Jesus' judgement if one of his closest associates betrayed him. The motive for Judas's approach to the Temple authorities was, apparently, financial, but only Matthew states the price of 30 pieces of silver for handing Jesus over. If this was paid in Tyrian shekels, the usual currency of the Temple, it represented about a third of a year's wages, a good but not extraordinary reward (Mark 14.10–11; Matt. 26.14–16, see Zech. 11.12).

Some have speculated that Jesus knew all along what was happening. The Gospels themselves suggest this (Luke 22.21–3; John 13.26–7). Given the predictions Jesus had made about his own fate in Jerusalem there may have been an element of staging about his arrest. If he was convinced that his death was necessary, then some means of being handed over to the authorities had to be found. But Jesus may simply have let the events unfold and not intervened to stop them; after the time he had spent with all the disciples he presumably had a pretty shrewd view of their capabilities and potential actions. Perhaps it was not so hard to predict that Judas was the most likely to turn informer.

Jesus' practice seems to have been to travel into Jerusalem from Bethany each day and to pause on returning at the foot of the Mount of Olives, beneath the imposing silhouette of the Temple (Mark 11.11; 13.3; 14.3; Luke 21.37; 22.39; John 18.2). Judas knew this pattern and could take the authorities to Jesus, who was otherwise anonymous amidst the tide of pilgrims which swept in and out of Jerusalem each day.

The deal was agreed, and a code set: Judas would lead them to Jesus and greet him with a kiss, perhaps then, as later, a sign of membership of Jesus' movement (Mark 14.44; see also Rom. 16.16; 1 Peter 5.14). As Geza Vermes points out, 'the surprise treachery of Judas [must have] struck the chief priests as a godsend ... they grasped the opportunity without hesitation'.[101] The opportunity for a 'surgical strike' to remove Jesus was too good to miss.

As the detachment of guards gathered their weapons and strapped on their armour, ready to ambush and kidnap Jesus, he and his disciples were eating together in another part of the city in a meal fraught with symbolism.

The Last Supper

That Jesus shared a meal with his closest disciples on 'the night he was betrayed' is one of the most solid pieces of information we have about him. Paul is the earliest witness, writing about it only 20 years or so after the event (1 Cor. 11.23). Precisely when the Last Supper happened, and whether it was a Passover meal or not, is unclear. Dispute over these matters forms the greatest discrepancy between the stories of Jesus' last days which Mark and John tell. There are good reasons to follow John's chronology and to place the Last Supper on the eve of the Passover (13 Nisan), a Thursday. This means that the meal was not a conventional Passover celebration, but something which Jesus adapted to his own purpose. It was, specifically, a meal eaten in the shadow of the eschatological expectations of Passover 30, when Jesus looked for God to act (Mark 14.25; Luke 22.16).

Meals had had an important role in Jesus' practice of the Kingdom and may even have had some kind of ritual nature. This lies in the background of the Last Supper just as much as the Passover does. But there was something different about this meal. Jesus had regularly feasted with tax-collectors and 'sinners', a sign of the open and all-embracing nature of his vision of God's Kingdom. Now, on the eve of the crucial Passover, it was just his closest followers, the symbolic twelve, that he drew together. To them he tried to explain what he believed was about to happen.

Those who argue most strongly for the Last Supper being a genuine Passover concede that it 'would still be surrounded by the atmosphere of the Passover even if it ... occurred on the evening before the feast'.[102] It is clear that Jesus' meal with his disciples was both like and unlike the conventional Passover. Was there a lamb? None of the accounts mentions one and it was the centrepiece of the Passover meal, making it less likely that this meal was a normal Passover. But it was, in Tom Wright's words, '*some kind of* Passover meal'.[103] Indeed, if the Last Supper was celebrated on the night before the Passover, that would have allowed Jesus more freedom to reinterpret the fundamental message of the feast.

A key part of the Passover meal was the explanation of its different elements by the head of the household. The youngest member of the family asked 'Why is this night different from all other nights?' and the story of the people of Israel and their deliverance from Egypt was recounted in reply (Deut. 26.5–11; Ex. 12.26–7). The electrifying moment in Jesus' meal must have come when, using the same explanatory pattern, he said, 'this is my body ... this is my blood of the covenant', referring to the bread and wine which the disciples shared (1 Cor. 11.24–5; Matt. 26.26, 28; Mark 14.22, 24; Luke 22.19, 20). Joachim Jeremias notes that Jesus was 'applying to himself *terms from the language of sacrifice* ... each of the two nouns presupposes a slaying that has separated flesh and blood. In other words: *Jesus speaks of himself as a sacrifice.*'[104] The role of the lamb at the original Passover had been to die in place of the first-born of Israel, and thus make the exodus of the people from slavery possible. This is what the sacrificial lambs of the Passover feast symbolized. Now Jesus seemed to be taking upon himself that same sacrificial role.

Did Jesus mean by this to replace the Passover sacrifices in particular and the Temple system itself in general? A significant number of scholars believe that to be the case. Theissen and Merz say Jesus 'wanted to replace provisionally the temple cult which had become obselete'.[105] Yet this proposal seems inherently unlikely, given that not long afterwards the disciples apparently continued to participate in Temple worship and 'break bread' together in their homes without seeing any contradiction between the two things (see Acts 2.46). Instead James Dunn proposes that 'Jesus spoke of his anticipated death in terms of a *covenant sacrifice* rather than a sin offering' such as was offered in the Temple. This was not so much to replace the Temple as to stand alongside and go beyond it, in a new stage of God's action among his people that would establish a new covenant where the Law would be written in their minds and in their hearts (Jer. 31.33). Dunn concludes that 'If God was indeed to make a fresh covenant with his people, then presumably a covenant sacrifice was also required; Jesus' death would serve as that sacrifice.'[106]

Judas' role was vital. The Gospels describe Jesus' reaction to Judas as remarkably acquiescent. According to John's Gospel, Jesus himself gives Judas the cue to begin the events which will soon lead to his arrest (John 13.27). Judas' departure may have been the trigger for what followed, but there was still time to escape the net. Jesus chose not to do this. Instead he and the disciples set off through the city to the Garden of Gethsemane, at the foot of the Mount of Olives. Judas and the guards would know where to find him.

Was Jesus 'weird'?

A significant question is raised by E. P. Sanders; is it really plausible that 'Jesus determined in his own mind to be killed and to have his death understood as sacrificial for others, and ... he pulled this off by provoking the authorities'? Sanders continues that, 'It is not historically impossible that Jesus was weird ... [but] other things we know about him make him a *reasonable* first-century visionary.'[107] In other words, martyrdom is irrational and not easily delivered to a timetable.

Yet there are many examples of others behaving in just such a 'weird' fashion if they believe their deaths will make a difference in the long run. The chilling footage of suicide bombers preparing for their final missions has made it clear that a strong belief in a cause can make people rationally undertake actions which, under other circumstances, they would reject.

Under the circumstances of Passover 30 Jesus' actions were not 'weird', though they may seem so to us. Within the framework of eschatological expectation and the promise of a new covenant his self-sacrifice would have made perfect sense, additionally so if he had travelled from Galilee to Jerusalem under the conviction that God had called him to make this sacrifice.

It is one thing to court martyrdom, but another to make sure that it happens to you. Jesus could not be certain that Caiaphas and Pilate would play along: 'a historian must be uncomfortable with an explanation which leaves other actors out of the drama'[108] says Sanders. As Carlos Eire puts it, in an entertaining and thought-provoking essay, 'what might have happened if Pilate had listened to his wife?'[109] (see Matt. 27.19). History is the arena of the contingent and unforeseen event, so it is right to question what Jesus expected his fate to be. Perhaps he envisaged something akin to John the Baptist's last months: imprisonment before execution. He may not have expected death to follow as quickly as it did. Nothing implies, in his words to the disciples, that he would be dead before the following day began at sunset. Rather they imply that he saw before him a time of suffering and, ultimately, sacrifice.

In Eire's essay, Pilate does listen to his wife and Jesus goes free. The erstwhile messiah returns to Galilee and visits Jerusalem each Passover under protection of the Romans, who favour the 'docile submission' he preaches 'especially if he also encouraged people to pay their taxes.'[110] This counterfactual scenario, transferring Jesus Ben Ananias's later experience on to Jesus of Nazareth, could only really convince if it were true that Jesus' threat to Jerusalem was limited and that he genuinely preached 'docile submission'. We have seen that this was far from the truth. Jesus' teaching was dangerous and he had, at least potentially, a large force at his command. He must have known, as Sanders says, that he was 'a marked man',[111] but this does not imply that he foresaw the precise sequence of events to follow. He may not have predicted the cross.

Understanding the passion narrative

Up to this point in the story we have been drawing together scraps of information in order to build up a picture of roughly what happened to Jesus. From here on, however, there is a huge array of detailed information available to us; the only problem is that the Gospel writers do not agree on the details, and the reports of Jesus' trial (if that is what it was) 'teem with difficulties'.[112] It is important briefly to consider how to find a way through the minefield.

The outline of the events at the end of Jesus' life was already agreed before the Gospels were written. The clearest example of this lies in Paul's narrative of the Last Supper. This was clearly so well-known by the time Paul wrote to the Corinthians, at least ten years before Mark completed his Gospel, that he could refer to it quite casually (1 Cor. 11.23–5). Paul also reminds the Corinthians of a simple summary of this pre-Gospel tradition: 'that Christ died for our sins, according to the Scriptures, and that he was buried and that he was raised on the third day according to the Scriptures' (1 Cor. 15.3–4). This part of Jesus' story, the passion narrative, was therefore part of the pre-Gospel tradition.

But that pre-Gospel tradition about the final hours of Jesus' life was not standardized, and since we may assume that it was largely handed down by word of mouth, it was an organic and developing story during at least the 30s and 40s. Probably the passion was the part of Jesus' story most prone to 'performance elaborations'[113] around a centrally agreed core. Inevitably, therefore, the attempt to disentangle what happened becomes extremely difficult. The tendency for the early Church to imagine the story in the images and words of the Hebrew Scriptures can also, to our minds, distort the picture.

For the Gospel writers the aim was to take the bare facts that they had received and tell them in such a way that the hearers experienced the drama of the story for themselves. They were remarkably successful in doing this, as centuries of yearly recitals in Holy Week have shown. History and story are not mutually exclusive categories, but what I am suggesting here is that in the passion narrative the Gospel writers took the freedom granted to ancient historians to its extreme. This has the paradoxical effect of making Luke, the best historian among the Gospel writers by ancient standards, the most suspect by contemporary ones, since he tells the story with his trademark clarity and efficiency, ruthlessly reordering the sources. Because Luke has reworked the raw material more thoroughly than his fellow evangelists, his account may be less useful than theirs in providing the kind of information which historians today want to find.

There is a venerable tradition of attempting to harmonize the details of the passion story, most marked in the 'seven words from the cross'. This approach ignores the fact that none of the Gospels includes all seven words, and that each narrative of the crucifixion is complete in its own right. The same is true of the passion narrative as a whole. Raymond Brown notes that there are three stories here, not one, with distinctive retellings by Mark (followed, with slight embellishments, by Matthew), Luke and John; 'No matter how it arose, each arrangement would give the impression of being the full picture of what happened, not part of a considerably larger whole.'[114] Mark, Luke and John share the same basic outline of events, but they develop it in different ways.

According to Mark, Jesus was condemned by the Jewish council, the Sanhedrin, immediately after Jesus' arrest, by night, as he was brought before the high priest Caiaphas as a prisoner. Luke places a similar examination after daybreak on the following morning. John has the Sanhedrin judge Jesus in his absence some weeks before Passover (Mark 14.53–65; Matt. 26.57–68; Luke 22.63–71; John 11.47–53). The core fact is agreed: Jesus was condemned by the high priest. But how that actually occurred is filled in by the imagination of each writer.

Similarly, Luke introduces a hearing before Herod Antipas (Luke 23.6–16), which the other writers apparently know nothing about. Is there a historical core here? It is possible that Luke had access to information which the others did not possess, but this scene also fits with a theme of Luke's Gospel, which is Antipas's fear of Jesus. It underlines Jesus' status as innocent victim: even Antipas, who has been out to get Jesus for a while, finds no fault in him (Luke 23.15). It also neatly parallels the later experience of Paul's questioning by Antipas's great-nephew Herod Agrippa when he too was in Roman custody (Acts 26). Therefore many scholars conclude that the hearing before Antipas is an addition to the story by Luke, perhaps based on Psalm 2.1–2, which mentions the 'kings of the earth and the rulers' standing against the Lord's anointed one (see also Acts 4.26–7). The argument is evenly balanced: there may be a historical core here or there may not. At the very least the episode 'serves to underline the freedom of Luke's use of whatever material he had before him',[115] but the price of that freedom is that we cannot be sure, with Luke's distinctive material, whether it actually happened or not. It *could* have happened: but that does not mean that it did.

As a final example, Mark and Luke have Jesus enigmatically keeping virtual silence in the face of Pilate, while in John's Gospel there is a dialogue about the nature of kingship and truth (Mark 15.2–5; Luke 23.2–5; John 18.29–38). The differences between the accounts can be understood if we recognize that they are not meant to be reportage, but elaborations from a basic core designed to explain that core. So, in the case of the exchange between Pilate and Jesus, that core is the charge of being 'King of the Jews' against Jesus, which was displayed on the cross. The Gospel writers use Jesus' encounter with Pilate as a 'dramatically effective ... vehicle of proclaiming who Jesus is', rather than being interested in 'telling readers how Pilate got his information, why he phrased it as he did, or with what legal formalities he conducted the trial'.[116] In doing so they prompt reflection on the reality of true power and in what sense Jesus really was a king. But in terms of historical information all we can draw from this part of the passion story is the likelihood that Jesus was brought before Pilate, not what was said when they met.

The same process goes on today in retellings of the passion narrative. Some years ago I developed a way of telling the story of the crucifixion and resurrection for primary schoolchildren through the experience of Barabbas, who was released by Pilate instead of Jesus (Mark 15.6–15). The story has plenty of drama in it: Barabbas first hears the crowd cry out his name from his cell and assumes they are calling for his death; then comes the fateful approach of a soldier's footsteps down the corridor, the turning of the key in the door and Barabbas assumes he is about to be led out to die. But instead he is given freedom, and later meets Peter who tells him about Jesus, who took his place. The idea was not original but developed from someone else, who in turn had taken it on from someone before him. It is a way of developing the story so that it makes a fresh impact and also imaginatively conveys the theological association between the death of Jesus and life for others. Like the Gospel writers' retelling of the passion story, it could have happened but imagination and storytelling have filled in the gaps left in the account. Mark, Matthew, Luke and John were probably engaged in the same kind of activity.

A final word needs to be said on the accuracy of John's passion narrative. In contrast with previous generations of scholarship, today there is a growing sense that John may preserve a more accurate account of Jesus' arrest, trial and execution than the other Gospel writers do. In part this is because it is recognized that Mark's Gospel is just as affected by theological considerations as John's is. But it is also because, alongside the elaboration for theological effect, there are some small details in

John's passion narrative which ring true but are not included in the other accounts. An example of this is the way that John alone suggests that the arresting party included Roman soldiers (he uses the technical terms *speira* and *chiliarchos* for a detachment of Roman troops and their commander, John 18.3, 12). It is also John alone who has Caiaphas and Annas say to Pilate 'it is not lawful for us to execute anyone' (John 18.31), reflecting the reservation of this power to the governor in Roman provinces. And it is John who gives details of the precise location of Pilate's place of judgement at the 'Stone Pavement' (John 19.13).

The differences between John and the Synoptics are often exaggerated. Some of them are insuperable, the most obvious being whether Jesus died on Nisan 15, as Mark says, or 14, as John does. Others show underlying agreement, but the accounts have so reordered the events that we can't tell which (if either) may be chronologically accurate. Jesus was condemned by the Sanhedrin, but we can't tell whether it was immediately before he was sent to Pilate, or some weeks earlier. John may have placed this incident early in order to bring out the irony that the result of Jesus' gift of life to Lazarus is death for himself. On the other hand, since Mark waits till the end of his story to move the location to Jerusalem, he cannot afford to narrate such a clearly Jerusalem-based event until then. These are plausible reasons why either writer might have reordered the story. Brown concludes that 'A serious possibility is that John's arrangement is more original ... Historically, having a Sanhedrin session weeks before Passover would be more plausible than one gathered hastily in the middle of the night.'[117] Either version works imaginatively, but John's is the more plausible historically. This doesn't automatically mean that John's version is chronologically accurate, but it does explain why a number of historians now think that, where a choice has to be made, 'we should give our preference to John.'[118]

In what follows, therefore, I shall not embark on an exhaustive attempt to judge the historical truth of each detail of the passion narrative. It is best to read those narratives for themselves, on their own terms, recognizing that they are at least in part imaginative retellings. It is also important to recognize that the three narratives of Mark/Matthew, Luke and John have material to offer, but that John's may provide more raw data for the contemporary historian than the others. The overall outline adopted follows the work of Geza Vermes, and though at certain points I think Vermes may be a little too sceptical (he does not credit John's mention of Roman troops, for example), his work is a short, accessible but thorough examination of 'What really did happen on the day of the Crucifixion of Jesus'.[119] The underlying facts of Jesus' last hours are not substantially in dispute. So let us follow them through.

Arrest and trial

After the Last Supper, Jesus and the disciples went to pray in the garden of Gethsemane. According to Mark, Jesus was desperately conscious of the enormity of the fate that awaited him (Mark 14.36). As the pagan Celsus pointed out in the third century, this is not what might be expected of someone portrayed as the Son of God, or even of a martyr.[120] It is another instance of embarrassment in the account, and therefore almost certain to be a genuine historical memory. Jesus feared what might happen on the great adventure – or would it be nightmare? – of faith which was about to begin.

Judas entered the garden of Gethsemane, looking for Jesus. Behind him came armed servants of the high priest and a detachment of Roman soldiers (Mark 14.43; John 18.3). Millar considers that the presence of Roman troops 'places [Jesus] closer to the category of the long succession of popular religious leaders, all viewed as instigators of popular disorder, who are known from the pages of Josephus, and all of whom ... were repressed by Roman forces.'[121] The presence of swords among Jesus' disciples, and a sudden flare of violence (Mark 14.47; Luke 22.49–51; John 18.10–11), may explain the Roman presence as a means of making sure that the arrest did not get out of hand and escalate into a fight between Jesus' supporters and the authorities. Jesus had not been arrested earlier in the week because Caiaphas feared the popular reaction. Roman troops would have made anyone wishing to defend Jesus think twice.

Judas's kiss may be dramatic licence, but he identified his master by some means and Jesus was soon taken back to the city itself and put under interrogation by the former high priest, Annas. Annas was then able to report the following morning to the Sanhedrin, which Martin Goodman notes 'played a judicial role in first-century Jerusalem, but only as an adjunct to the High Priest'.[122] It was effectively the high priest's advisory council.

Constraints on the enforcement of Jewish Law were set by the rule of Rome. The Roman imperial system allowed local legal systems autonomy at the lower end of the scale, but provincial governors reserved to themselves the highest powers of life and death, except perhaps for clearly religious offences. Thus the high priest and his council might decide that Jesus should die, and even pronounce sentence (Mark 14.64), but they could not carry it out. The worst punishment they could authorize was scourging. (This is what happened with Jesus Ben Ananias in 62, whom the governor released. A few months earlier the Sanhedrin had executed Jesus' brother James during a period between governors, but the high priest, Annas's son, was dismissed as a result.)

Why might Caiaphas have pronounced the death sentence on Jesus? Sanders considers that the simplest explanation is that 'Caiaphas had Jesus arrested because of his responsibility to put down trouble-makers ...

Caiaphas was primarily or exclusively concerned with the possibility that Jesus would incite a riot.'[123] While this view is satisfactory at the most basic historical level, it fails to do justice to some of the theological issues which were undoubtedly at stake.

Mark's version of Caiaphas's questioning of Jesus may link three issues which occur together in the prophet Nathan's messianic prophecy to David: the expectation of a son of David who would rebuild the Temple and be recognized as God's own son (2 Sam. 7.12–14). Caiaphas's question to Jesus, 'Are you the Messiah, the son of the blessed one?' (Mark 14.61) is glossed by James Dunn as 'You are charged with promising to build the Temple. Do you then claim to fulfil Nathan's prophecy? Are you the royal Messiah, God's son?' Although Mark's setting for this accusation is suspect (a Sanhedrin meeting in the middle of the night seems unlikely), the accusation itself commands credibility. Dunn goes on to note, 'since royal Messiah translated readily enough as "king of the Jews" ... one who claimed to be a king was likely to receive short shrift' from the governor.[124] Jesus' triumphal entry into Jerusalem, evoking memories of David; his demonstration in the Temple precincts with its implication of judgement on its present form; and his frequent pronouncements and actions which seemed to carry with them a claim to possess the authority of God; all these were enough to convince Caiaphas and his advisers that Jesus was highly dangerous and had the capacity, unchecked, to cause a religious frenzy. If there was heightened expectation around Passover 30, perhaps they were justified in their fears of what might happen next.

Pilate appears to have been less easily convinced. There are strong signs that he was, ironically for someone stationed in Judea for so long, tone-deaf to the nuances of Jewish faith. He had coins adorned with pagan symbols, brought military standards bearing images of the emperor into the Temple, and he took money dedicated for religious purposes to finance a new water supply for Jerusalem. All of these events caused great offence to observant Jews and suggest that Pilate made no effort to understand their views. The otherwise unknown scandal of the 'Galileans whose blood Pilate mixed with their sacrifices' (Luke 13.1) suggests that the major incidents were accompanied by many minor ones. In the light of this, it's perhaps not so surprising that Pilate might have refused to rubber-stamp Caiaphas's decision.

Instead Pilate decided to question Jesus himself. According to all the Gospels, he could not get a straight answer. Asked, 'Are you the King of the Jews?' Jesus replied 'You have said so' (Mark 15.2; Matt. 27.11; Luke 23.3; John 18.37), which essentially means 'What do you think?' Pilate was presumably satisfied that Jesus was not the threat to public order that Caiaphas and the council believed him to be. Perhaps he would have preferred that Jesus should simply be imprisoned, surely an adequate rebuttal of his more grandiose claims. After all, if the crowds were on Jesus' side an execution might inflame the situation rather than pacify it.

Pilate may have sent Jesus to Herod Antipas, who was in Jerusalem for the feast, for a second opinion (Luke 23.6–11). Perhaps he also thought that Antipas might like to take Jesus off his hands: had Jesus not caused trouble in Antipas's Galilee? Only Luke's Gospel mentions this episode, so we cannot assume its authenticity. But it does convey graphically the dilemma in which Pilate found himself, charged with keeping the peace at Passover, caught between the rock of the Temple authorities calling for Jesus' blood and demanding firm leadership from the governor, and the hard place of allegedly widespread popular support for Jesus which might easily spill over into an uprising.

It was not the first or last time Pilate would find himself in such a situation, nor was he unique as a Roman governor in being caught up in local squabbles that escalated into major incidents. What then could he do?

Rescue appeared, apparently, in the form of a custom of releasing a prisoner at the festival (Mark 15.6; John 18.39). Vermes calls it 'a surprise, the unforeseen legal custom (or fiction) of the ... Passover amnesty'.[125] It certainly has a 'too good to be true' ring to it and it is not a custom that has any evidence to support it outside the Gospels. Yet it could have happened, and in the circumstances it might just have been Pilate's only route out of trouble. Barabbas, apparently an insurgent (Luke 23.19; John 18.40), 'was not the kind of person a Roman administrator would have felt at liberty in ordinary circumstances to let loose in a turbulent country. But maybe the circumstances were not normal on that particular Passover?'[126] By offering the crowd a choice between Jesus and Barabbas, Pilate made a smart move, though it was a risky one. Essentially he asked whether the crowd would back the Temple authorities in their desire for Jesus' death. It was a means of finding out whether the spectre of popular support for Jesus was real. The crowd gave its verdict, which was not so much in favour of Barabbas as a vote of confidence in Caiaphas's judgement (Mark 15.6–15; Luke 23.18–25; John 18.39—19.15). Pilate theatrically washed his hands of the decision, according to Matthew's Gospel (Matt. 27.24). Again this is one of those details that may have been added by the Gospel writer's imagination, but which perfectly expresses the truth of the situation. Pilate had abdicated judgement on Jesus, and in the process a crisis had been averted.

Pilate may have abdicated judgement, but he could not abdicate giving the order for execution. The scene in front of Pilate's judgement seat where the crowd claimed responsibility for Jesus' death (Matt. 27.25) became the basis for much anti-Semitic propaganda and inexcusable action in later centuries. At most it implicates a group of first-century Jews in the condemnation of Jesus. But sadly the accusation that 'the Jews were those who had killed him ... is too familiar to appreciate readily how bizarre it is.' Pilate's hand-washing could not absolve him from responsibility: Jesus' 'death was engineered by the High Priestly authorities in the Temple [but] ... the order to execute Jesus was given ultimately by Pontius Pilate as Roman governor'.[127] Indeed, Pilate's insistence on his exclusive right to the power of life and death is what the whole story hinges on. So he completed his duties by passing sentence of crucifixion (Mark 15.15; Luke 23.25; John 19.16). The charge, which a prisoner had to carry on a placard to his own cross, read 'Jesus of Nazareth, King of the Jews' (Mark 15.26; Luke 23.38; John 19.19). John's Gospel catches the irony by having the chief priests complain that it should read 'the *alleged* king of the Jews' and Pilate responding that 'I have written what I have written' (John 19.21–2). A broken figure of fun, mocked and abused by Roman soldiers (Mark 15.16–20; John 19.1–5) – that was the only kind of king of the Jews which Roman power would tolerate.

It is unlikely that Pilate gave much thought to the death sentence passed on Jesus as he changed his clothes for dinner that evening. As far as he was concerned he had done his job and preserved the peace. He had kept Caiaphas and the Temple authorities on his side, and he had neatly side-stepped the possibility of an uprising in defence of Jesus. However much sleep the incident cost Pilate's wife (Matt. 27.19), her husband almost certainly lost none.

Crucifixion

It is easy to lose sight of Jesus as he is shuttled between Annas, Caiaphas, Pilate and Antipas in the passion narratives. The rulers are powerful; Jesus is powerless. The impression is heightened by the way the story is told. In Mark's Gospel, once Jesus has been arrested, he is 'in a grammatical sense, the subject of just nine verbs, [but] … the object, direct or indirect, of fifty-six'.[128] What was true of a man under arrest was even more strikingly true of a man being crucified: he became merely an object.

To Romans crucifixion was the worst of punishments and the cruellest of deaths. To Jews an ancient curse was invoked on anyone who was executed and 'hung upon a tree' (Deut. 21.22–3, see Gal. 3.13). Crucifixion was public deterrent, torture and means of execution all rolled into one. Roman citizens, unless the circumstances were exceptional, were exempt from it; it was known as the 'slaves' punishment'[129] and brought shame to the families of those who suffered it. This was what Jesus now faced.

He was flogged and mocked, part of the kind of vicious games which were the regular pastime of troops in such a situation. Then, as was customary, Jesus carried the beam on which he was to be hung out to the execution ground, 'the place of the skull' (Mark 15.22; Luke 23.33; John 19.17). It was probably not a long journey, but after the flogging Jesus seems to have been weak and a passer-by was compelled to help him with his burden. This man, Simon of Cyrene, is identified in Mark's Gospel as 'the father of Alexander and Rufus' (Mark 15.21). Many scholars see this as an acknowledgement of an eyewitness source for this part of Mark's narrative.

One of the clearest disagreements between the Gospels in the passion story is over the time of the crucifixion. Mark states 'the third hour', 9 a.m. (Mark 15.25, 33; Luke 23.44; John 19.17). John, on the other hand, does not have Pilate even give sentence until 'the sixth hour', noon (John 19.14). Mark's careful dividing of the day into three-hour blocks (6 a.m. to 9 a.m.; 9 a.m. to noon; noon to 3 p.m., Mark 15.1, 25, 33) suggests that there is a stylized scheme behind his presentation, which some have speculated has a liturgical basis. On the other hand, John's afternoon crucifixion on the day of preparation for Passover identifies Jesus' death as happening at the exact time that thousands of lambs were sacrificed in the Temple and the drains in the eastern wall ran with blood; many consider this too neat a theological juxtaposition to be true.

Given the amount of activity involved in the condemnation of Jesus during the morning, John's timing perhaps carries greater plausibility, but it is unlikely to have been as important an issue in the ancient world as it is today. Precision in timing was far less significant. More important was the fact that Jesus was crucified during the daytime, publicly, and for all to see. If John's placing of the events on Nisan 14 is correct, then the crucifixion of Jesus would indeed have been accompanied by the noise of the bloody slaughter of the Passover lambs in the Temple.

Jesus was crucified in company with at least two others (Mark 15.27; Luke 23.33; John 19.18). Crucifixion was often a mass event, and the eve of Passover might have appealed to Pilate as a good time for it, when a significant percentage of the population of Judea were gathered in Jerusalem. It was also the one time of the year when the governor was resident in the city for a while, so it is possible that a number of executions were reserved until then. Jesus was not singled out for any special or unique treatment. His cross took its place among a number of others outside the city wall.

Looking out from the cross, Jesus did not see his disciples gathered around him to share his final torment. As the hours passed, no doubt those who did watch came and went. There was little they could do. The Synoptics specify a number of women, and John's Gospel also Jesus' mother and the 'beloved disciple' (Mark 15.40–1; Luke 23.49; John 19.25–6). Also present were crowds who jeered, and some who mourned Jesus' death (Mark 15.31–2; Luke 23.48). And perhaps a centurion who disagreed with Pilate's sentence. He considered Jesus either 'a son of God' or 'innocent' (Mark 15.39; Luke 23.47). For Mark this is 'an unconscious acknowledgement of Jesus' identity ... the climax of Mark's Gospel'.[130] But it would take the later eyes of faith to see divine revelation in this squalid scene.

Crucifixion was meant to last a long time. Agonized bodies, struggling for air, parched by the sun, calling out for mercy or death; these made up the deterrent Pilate and other governors across the Empire wanted. But the approaching Passover created a problem. Jesus may have been added to the list of the crucified at the last minute, and where the others around him were approaching death he was probably expected to last into the night and perhaps even the next day, which might require others to work on the feast day that counted as a Sabbath. According to John's Gospel, therefore, the soldiers attempted to hasten the death of all the crucified. They found Jesus already dead. Any doubt is dispelled by the *coup de grâce* dealt by another soldier, and the note of eyewitness testimony to the events (John 19.31–5).

Why had Jesus died so quickly (in six hours according to Mark's Gospel, and no more than five according to John's)? All four Gospels specify that the moment of death was accompanied by some significant last words, a common feature of ancient biographies. However, as James Dunn points out, from the briefest survey of the seven 'last words from the cross', a 'stunning feature immediately becomes apparent: that only one of the "last words" is attested by more than one author'. Dunn sums up: 'The uncomfortable conclusion probably has to be that most of the words from the cross are part of the elaboration in the diverse retellings of Jesus' final hours.'[131]

One of the words does have a strong claim, if only because of its unlikely content. This is Jesus' cry, recorded in Aramaic, *Eloi, Eloi, lema sabachtani*, which in translation means 'My God, My God, why did you forsake me?' (Mark 15.34). It is a quotation from Psalm 22.1, but the fact that it is quoted in Aramaic rather than the Hebrew of synagogue and Temple worship suggests that it had a strong memory behind it. The psalm itself ends confidently (as many commentators since have noted, seeking to soften the rawness of its opening verse). Yet it seems highly unlikely to have been added as a 'performance elaboration' in later retellings of the story. Mark also notes that some of the crowd misunderstood what Jesus said and thought he was calling for the prophet Elijah, an incidental detail which adds nothing to the scene in terms of either theology or plot (Mark 15.36). Vermes suggests that 'the phrase had become in the vernacular of the time of Jesus a kind of proverbial saying, expressing religious incomprehension and bewilderment.'[132] The cry perhaps expresses Jesus' confusion. How had the great adventure of the Kingdom of God come to this? Maybe he had expected some vindication at this Passover, some intervention by God, some sign that his death was not in vain. In this cry of pain we may speculate on the cause of Jesus' relatively quick death on the cross. Feeling for the first time abandoned by the heavenly father whose presence he apparently had never doubted, weighed down by bitter disappointment, perhaps he died of a broken heart.

Burial

Victims of crucifixion were usually not buried. Their bodies were left for the dogs to eat, and the birds to dissect. Yet we know that the crucified Yehohanan was buried conventionally and so, despite attempts to suggest otherwise, it seems certain that Jesus 'was buried', as Paul could assume the Corinthians took for granted less than two decades later (1 Cor. 15.4).

The Church of the Holy Sepulchre in Jerusalem has a very good claim to be the site of the stone tomb in a garden in which Jesus' body was buried (Mark 15.46; Luke 23.53; John 19.41). It lay just outside the city walls in the early first century, adjacent to the place of crucifixion. All the Gospels say that the tomb belonged to Joseph of Arimathea who was, according to Mark, 'awaiting the Kingdom of God' (Mark 15.43; Matt. 27.57; Luke 23.50–1; John 19.38). Joseph was a member of the high priest's council, which suggests that, just as the centurion at the crucifixion apparently disagreed with Pilate's death sentence, so some members of the Sanhedrin may have dissented from Caiaphas's condemnation of Jesus.

Speed seems to have been of the essence with this burial, as the sun began to set and the day of Passover was about to commence. The body of Jesus was hastily washed and prepared for burial before the city closed down for the festival. The tomb was sealed with a stone (Mark 15.46).

The empty tomb

About 36 hours later some of Jesus' female disciples walked through the dark streets in order to be at the tomb as soon as it was light. They would complete the work of anointing which had been so rushed two days before. It would have been a matter of some urgency since the process of decay and its accompanying smell would by then have been well advanced (see John 11.39).

The women, led by Mary Magdalene, saw the tomb open and the body gone. They experienced a vision there, accompanied by the words 'He is not here, he is risen'. The tomb's emptiness was confirmed shortly afterwards by Peter (Mark 16.1–8; Luke 24.1–10; John 20.1–9).

Various options have been suggested for why the tomb might have been empty: grave-robbers might have broken in; the women could have gone to the wrong tomb; Jesus, like other crucifixion victims, was never buried anyway; he did not really die and was revived by the therapeutic coolness of the tomb. But these objections to the emptiness of the tomb do not convince. It seems as solid a conclusion as any about the life of Jesus that when the women got to the tomb it was empty.

If it had simply been the case that the tomb was empty and the body gone, there the matter would almost certainly have ended, whatever the visionary experience of the women. But then began a series of appearances of the man who had been crucified two days earlier. The rumour spread quickly that Jesus had been seen alive again, returned from the dead.

Rumours of resurrection

There are two problems with examining the basis for the rumour of resurrection. It is absolutely clear, first, that the early Church believed that Jesus had risen from the dead. Yet it is, second, almost impossible to find any evidence for what happened because the accounts are either very sketchy or incredibly diverse.

The belief that Jesus had risen from the dead is widespread across the New Testament. Setting aside the Gospels and Acts, we can see that the writings of Paul are shot through with this conviction and studded with references to the resurrection of Jesus from the dead (see Rom. 1.4; 4.24, 25; 6.4, 5, 9; 7.4; 8.11, 34; 10.9 1 Cor. 6.14; 15.4, 12–17, 20; 2 Cor. 4.14; 5.15; Gal. 1.1; Eph. 1.20; Col. 1.18; 2.12; Phil. 3.10; 1 Thess. 1.10; 4.14; 2 Tim. 2.8). Non-Pauline writings are the same (see Heb. 13.20; 1 Peter 1.3, 21; 3.18, 21; Rev. 1.5, 18). On into the second century it continued to be the case, as Tom Wright says, that 'belief in the resurrection ... was foundational to early Christianity' in a remarkably uniform way. Apart from a few Gnostic groups, 'Christianity ... never seems to have developed even the beginnings of a spectrum of belief'[133] about the resurrection. The resurrection of Jesus lay at the heart of the early Church's understanding of its own origins.

The many New Testament references do not specify what happened at all, with a single brief exception. Thus, assuming that the Gospels of Mark and Matthew and virtually all the writings listed above were written before about 90, there was next to no written source offering detailed evidence for the resurrection appearances of Jesus until the Gospels of Luke and John came along, as much as 60 years after the crucifixion. These later Gospels offer more detailed accounts (Luke 24.13–53; John 20.11—21.23), but do not agree on the details and have little in common.

Small wonder then that many have questioned whether there is any historical basis at all to the after-death appearances of Jesus. Dominic Crossan suggests that the appearances of Jesus were the kind of hallucinations frequently experienced by people who have been traumatically bereaved. For him the story of Jesus' resurrection appearances was a means of rescuing hope from amidst the ruins of his death: 'What happened historically is that those who believed in Jesus before his execution *continued* to do so afterward ... It is a terrible trivialization to imagine that all Jesus' followers lost their faith on Good Friday and had it restored by apparitions on Easter Sunday.'[134] Jesus' impact in Galilee and his message of the Kingdom were so powerful and had such an influence on his followers that they continued to do his work. According to Crossan, the stories of the empty tomb and his risen appearances were metaphorical ways of describing their sense of his continuing presence which were later (wrongly) taken literally.

All of this makes the only early indication of what happened a supremely significant piece of evidence. One of Paul's references to the resurrection of Jesus does offer some details. Writing to the Corinthians, Paul says that

> I handed on to you the most important things that had been handed on to me. *That Christ died for our sins according to the Scriptures; and that he was buried; and that he was raised on the third day according to the Scriptures; and that he was seen by Cephas, then by the Twelve.* Afterwards by over five hundred brothers at one time, of whom most are still alive though some have died. Afterwards he was seen by James, then by all the apostles and last of all, as if to one born at the wrong time, he was seen by me too. (1 Cor. 15.3–8)

The part of the quotation in italics is widely recognized to be what Paul claimed had been 'handed on' to him. Its vocabulary and structure suggest that it originated as a primitive statement of belief, a shorthand summary of the key points of early Christian belief.

When had this been handed on to Paul? His own first visit to Jerusalem as a Christian took place around 37, at most seven years after the crucifixion, when he met Peter and James (Gal.1.18–19). Perhaps significantly they are the two named individuals among Paul's list of witnesses of the resurrection. C. H. Dodd claims that what Paul 'handed on' to the Corinthians had been 'derived from the main stream [of tradition] at a point very near its source'.[135] This evidence of Paul's reaches right back to a popular summary of belief in the first decade after the crucifixion.

The empty tomb is not specifically mentioned by Paul, a fact that some have found disturbing. The mention of 'was buried' is unexpected and in such a compressed statement is surely intended to imply that the tomb was later found empty. Without it, the appearances could have been dismissed as hallucinations and the resurrection of Jesus as non-physical.

Paul's argument in this part of 1 Corinthians rests on the physicality of Jesus' risen existence. He is seeking to demonstrate that Jesus' resurrection was in bodily form, but quickly moves on to a more complex and philosophical discussion of the nature of the resurrection body (1 Cor. 15.12–58). He does not develop the story of the appearances in any detail at all. But he leaves us in no doubt that they formed a very early part of Christian belief.

Thus we are forced back to the double problem outlined above. On the one hand the resurrection of Jesus as a phenomenon of belief is very well attested. But on the other we know very little about it beyond the comparatively late information supplied by the Gospels of Luke and John.

Why is this so? The reports of the appearances in the Gospels of Luke and John are fragmentary and complex. Yet they are also, in some ways, remarkably sober and matter-of-fact accounts, lacking much of what we might expect to have been added in the way of elaboration. An example of this lies in Luke's angels. The choir which had heralded Jesus' entry into the world (Luke 2.13–15) might be expected to make a reappearance. After all, Matthew introduces an angel and an earthquake into the story and Luke himself expands Mark's 'young man in a white robe' who meets the women in the tomb into 'two men in dazzling clothes' (Matt. 28.2–3; Mark 16.5; Luke 24.4). But there is no choir and no more individual angels, even though they will be frequent figures in the early chapters of Acts. Clearly there has been some control on the development of legendary and colourful elements in these stories.

The resurrection stories in the Gospels fall into a unique category. James Dunn observes that 'there is nothing quite like them in the Jesus tradition and an effective synoptic analysis is almost impossible'.[136] Yet even within the variety there are some shared elements. Perhaps most striking is the way in which the underlying structure of the resurrection accounts in all the four Gospels follows the primitive outline of which Paul reminded the Corinthians. That is, they tell of the death of Jesus, his burial, his resurrection on the third day and his appearance first to individuals and then to the group of disciples (Mark's Gospel ends before the appearances begin, and John 21 adds some extra appearances to the original Gospel which ends at John 20.31). Of course there are many differences of detail, especially among the identities of the individuals to whom Jesus appeared. But 'Amid all the diversity, we seem to have variations upon a common pattern.'[137] So, although it looks as if the detailed written narratives about the resurrection appearances of Jesus were a comparatively late development, there are signs that they were controlled and conformed to a particular structure. Luke and John did not have a free hand to invent these stories.

The fact that the stories of Jesus' resurrection include the personal names of the earliest eyewitnesses lends weight to this view. Mary Magdalene, Mary the mother of James, Salome and Cleopas are specified in different Gospels (Mark 16.1; Matt. 28.1; Luke 24.10, 18; John 20.1). Strikingly, all but Cleopas were women, and a good case can be made for his unnamed companion being his wife, 'Mary of Clopas' (John 19.25). Since women were not accepted as legal witnesses in Jewish circles, such reliance on their testimony for the resurrection of Jesus is quite unexpected. This would be bound to prejudice any Jew who listened to the story against it, which is a strong reason for accepting the women as the earliest witnesses; this is not something which anyone would have fabricated. Richard Bauckham speculates that 'these women were well known not just for having once told their stories but as people who remained accessible and authoritative sources of these traditions as long as they lived.' The differing accounts of the visit of the women to the tomb 'may well reflect rather directly the different ways in which the story was told by the different women.'[138] Paul addresses the issue of eyewitnesses directly when he speaks of 'more than five hundred brothers ... most of whom are still alive, though some have died' (1 Cor. 15.6). The implication of his words is that members of this group are available to confirm what Paul has said. The absence of the women from his summary may suggest an element of embarrassment about their being the first people to whom the risen Jesus appeared.

Overall it seems that belief in the resurrection of Jesus was widespread in the early Church, but that paradoxically the evidence for what actually happened is scarce. Sanders sums up the situation well when he writes 'That Jesus' followers (and later Paul) had resurrection experiences is, in my judgement, a fact. What the reality was that gave rise to the experiences I do not know.'[139] Something happened. What exactly it was is very hard to say.

Expecting resurrection

The resurrection of Jesus did not occur like lightning from a blue sky. There was a background of expectation in first-century Galilee and Judea that God would raise the faithful dead to life again at the end of time, though such expectation was not universal. (It was, of course, not shared by the powerful elite of the Sadducees.)

Such beliefs in resurrection had their roots in the Hebrew Scriptures (see Ezekiel 37; Daniel 12.2–3; Hosea 6.2), but those roots were not deep. The Sadducees, as guardians of Israel's traditions, could point to any number of scriptural passages which emphasized that 'dust you are, and to dust you shall return' (Gen. 3.19) and held out little hope of future existence.

It seems to have been the experience of martyrdom under various invaders during the two centuries before Jesus was born which forced the growth of ideas of resurrection. One example is the seven brothers in the time of the Maccabees who embraced death in the hope that God would honour their sacrifice with a future reward (2 Macc. 7.9, 11, 14). How could such heroism for the sake of God not call forth a response from him in terms of the restoration of life?

Belief in new life as a reward for martyrdom gradually widened to include all those who were righteous, that is those who observed the Law. E. P. Sanders considers that by the first century 'most Jews expected death not to be the end, though they may have conceived the future quite vaguely.'[140] That vagueness led to a wide variety of views, traces of which are scattered through the Gospels in the form of popular beliefs about the reincarnation of prophets, or the Sadducees' ridicule of the hope that husbands and wives would ultimately be reunited (Mark 6.14; 8.28; 12.23). Burial customs changed too, to reflect the growing belief that God would physically raise the dead. So bones were carefully preserved in ossuaries because they would be needed at the resurrection, and though it was claimed that God could resurrect the dead even if only the smallest bone survived (the tip of the coccyx would do, apparently), no one wanted to take any chances.

At the heart of such beliefs was the conviction that it was only on the 'last day' that the dead would be raised. It was, as Tom Wright points out, not a hope for individual survival, 'never simply a way of speaking about "life after death" ... but [rather] the *reversal* or *undoing* or *defeat* of death'.[141] Resurrection came as an eschatological package, bundled with hope for the restoration of the Kingdom to Israel in a new age.

Jesus seems to have shared the widespread belief in the future resurrection of the righteous at the last day, and applied it to himself and the suffering and martyrdom he believed he was called to undergo. He predicted that 'after three days' he would rise again (Mark 8.31; 9.31; 10.34). What did he mean by this? Almost certainly not what his disciples later said happened: the Jewish writer Pinchas Lapide notes that '"On the third day" has nothing to do with the date or with the counting of time but contains ... a clear reference to God's mercy and grace which is revealed after two days of affliction and death by way of redemption.'[142] It was not a prediction of imminent resurrection, therefore, but rather an expression of faith that God would ultimately vindicate the righteous person who suffered. Jesus thus placed himself in the context of the Jewish tradition of martyrdom and shared the hope of future vindication, which had spurred on many young men since the days of the Maccabees, when God raised all the righteous dead to life again.

Seen in this way the cross need not have been a cause for despair, argues Dale Allison: 'when [Jesus] met his end, the disciples would have been down but not out – that is, emotionally down but not theologically out.' They would have had an interpretative framework within which to place Jesus' death, for 'There was nothing in the crucifixion itself to undo the basic structure of anybody's eschatological expectations.'[143] This is true up to a point. What it fails to take account of is the strong possibility that Passover 30 was surrounded by the expectation that God would act, and quite likely bring about judgement on Jerusalem along with the new eschatological age of his Kingdom. This expectation is a plausible interpretation of Jesus' actions during his last week, the reactions of the authorities and the crowds, and also makes sense of his final cry of despair and sense of abandonment. The sense of dashed hope, and fear for the future, is reflected in the resurrection accounts themselves: the travellers on the road to Emmaus say 'we were hoping that he was the one who would redeem Israel'; the disciples meet behind locked doors in case they are the next to be arrested (Luke 24.21; John 20.19).

What no one seems to have bargained for, including Jesus himself, was that Jesus might return from the dead alone.

Resurrection was understood as a wholly corporate idea. A legitimate question, on hearing the report that Jesus had been seen alive again, might have been to ask where the other signs of God's new age were, and why there were no other resurrected bodies. Allison notes a Jewish story which tells how a rabbi, hearing reports of the 'Messiah's arrival, opens his window, sniffs the air, and then declares "The Messiah has not come." This anecdote vividly depicts the conviction that, when the redeemer comes, everything will be different.'[144] Tom Wright puts it graphically when he says that 'Jesus interpreted his coming death, and the vindication he expected after that death, as the defeat of evil; but on the first Easter Monday evil still stalked the earth from Jerusalem to Gibraltar and beyond, and stalks it still.'[145] One of the reasons why the disciples were apparently slow to accept the possibility of Jesus' resurrection appearances, and why some continued to doubt (Matt. 28.17; Luke 24.25, 38; John 20.24–5), was that everything was not different.

To put it another way, there are no signs that, if the disciples had wanted to rescue something from the wreckage of their hopes, they would have invented an individual resurrection. It simply did not make sense. And this in turn is an argument in favour of the truth of their assertion that Jesus had risen from the dead. Later they would integrate Jesus' resurrection with their other beliefs, and come to understand it as the 'first-fruits' of the great resurrection to come, though there are also traces of other ideas left in the New Testament (1 Cor. 15.20; see also Matt. 27.51–3; 1 Peter 3.19). Jesus' unexpected return from the dead 'split into two the one eschatological act of redemption that Jesus' words had held together'.[146] Jesus' resurrection was a problem for the disciples because it overturned their expectations. Their previous beliefs would have disposed them to expect that God would vindicate Jesus, and would raise him from the dead, but not in the way that they later claimed had happened.

Can we tell what happened?

Beyond the bare fact that the disciples believed that Jesus had appeared to them, can we say any more about his resurrection? Rudolf Bultmann influentially held that historical investigation of what happened is inappropriate because 'This would mean that one was trying to justify faith in God's word ... in relation to which we cannot raise the question of legitimation, but which rather asks us whether we are willing to believe it.'[147] Yet there is no reason in principle why the resurrection of Jesus should not be investigated historically, since the empty tomb and his post-crucifixion appearances were events within time and history. Indeed Tom Wright regards the 'secure historical conclusion' that 'the tomb was empty, and various meetings took place ... between Jesus and his followers' as 'coming in the same sort of category, of historical probability so high as to be virtually certain, as the death of Augustus in AD 14 or the fall of Jerusalem in AD 70.'[148] Wright seems to confuse what can be established in principle with what can be established in practice. For there is simply not enough detailed evidence available about the resurrection of Jesus for a firm historical conclusion to be drawn. As Dale Allison puts it, the accounts we have are 'emaciated historically' and 'come to us as phantoms. Most of the reality is gone.'[149] We are still left with the gap between the early Church's manifestly central belief in the resurrection of Jesus and almost no information about the events themselves.

In some ways perhaps this is not surprising. The claim of the disciples was that Jesus' return from the dead inaugurated a new age. Therefore he was an eschatological figure, a visitor from God's future. It is striking how, in the stories of the resurrection appearances, Jesus is almost always either at first unrecognized, or inspires fear (Matt. 28.10; Luke 24.16, 37; John 20.14–15; 21.4, 12); he is a physical being who eats with his disciples (Luke 24.39–43; John 21.12–15); yet he is also able to come and go at will through locked doors (John 20.19, 26). Tom Wright has coined the word 'transphysical' in an attempt to express the sense that 'the early Christians envisaged a body which was still robustly physical but also significantly different from the present one ... not ... *less* physical, as though it were some kind of ghost or apparition, but more.'[150] If the risen Jesus truly was an eschatological figure, the fact that he seemed both to some extent the same yet different is perhaps to be expected.

But the evidence is scant. And it is evidence on which historians rely. They are not trained or paid to make metaphysical judgements, which is what speculations about the nature of the risen, eschatological body of Jesus are. If we want to go further into what really happened we must therefore leave historical methods behind, for they have no more to yield on the question. In the epilogue, therefore, we shall consider briefly some of these deeper questions.

Where history comes to an end

The first Christians not only affirmed that Jesus had risen from the dead. They also claimed that, by this act, 'God made him both Lord and Christ' and that he was 'appointed son of God in power' (Acts 2.36; Rom. 1.4). The resurrection appearances of Jesus were 'the historical ignition points for the Christological convictions linked to them'.[151] Within a very short time the risen Jesus was being worshipped in terms that were reserved by any Jew for God himself. The primary evidence for this is the set of documents which we call the New Testament.

What adequate explanation can there be for this development, and the spread of Jesus-worship across the Mediterranean inside a few decades? Tom Wright affirms that 'no other explanation could or would do' to account for the rise of the Church except 'the bodily resurrection of Jesus'.[152] If this were really true then all argument would be at an end and the truth of the Christian faith would not be in dispute. Yet it has been contested for 2,000 years. The evidence is simply not strong enough for a judgement to be made on solely historical grounds.

The answer you make will depend on the beliefs you bring with you to the question. The philosopher Anthony Flew once asked some Christian apologists with whom he was debating the reality of the resurrection to supplement their arguments with 'a rich and relevant antecedent revelation or by a rich and relevant natural theology'.[153] He was making an important point. In the early centuries of the Church's history, writes Gerard O'Collins, 'the factuality of Jesus' own resurrection slipped somewhat into the background' of beliefs about resurrection in general. But 'a change which began with the Renaissance' led to 'a certain erosion of Easter faith'.[154] This was determined more by a shift in presuppositions than any change in the facts about the resurrection of Jesus, as people began to challenge the dogmas of the Church, and questioned whether ancient beliefs could be trusted any longer.

Flew's plea for a world-view which might make the resurrection of Jesus intelligible is a vital one. It was particularly anticipated by the German theologian, Wolfhart Pannenberg. In the 1960s, Pannenberg offered an unfashionable but vigorous defence of the resurrection of Jesus as a public event, open to historical scrutiny. This approach he labelled as 'from below'.[155] However, he has gradually realized that the resurrection of Jesus makes no sense unless it is seen in its wider context, and that wider context includes the recognition of his own presuppositions about the existence of God. In his later work he concludes that 'the human and historical reality of Jesus of Nazareth can be appropriately understood only in the light of his coming from God.'[156] That, of course, begs the question of whether God exists, and if he does whether a Judeo-Christian understanding is a reasonable one. Pannenberg has thus ended up back with 'an updated version of case for the resurrection in general',[157] which the theologians of the early and medieval Church used. Once again, it seems, history does not provide all the answers. But where else can we look?

The present-day experience of Christian believers should not be ignored. Many people across the globe report the sense that Jesus is somehow alive and present to them, even if not in the 'transphysical' sense in which the disciples apparently saw him. Christians across the world continue to pray, and sometimes feel that they have heard Christ speak back to them. Whatever the basis for these phenomena (which I have experienced myself) they raise questions about the continued existence of Jesus of Nazareth.

There are many different answers to whether the life, death and reported resurrection of Jesus are enough to explain the sudden and extraordinary rise and growth of the Church and its continued existence. Those answers will depend on the background beliefs you bring with you, but studying the historical evidence may question some of those beliefs, and world-views can shift. Religious experiences, whether positive or negative, will also play their part in determining how sympathetic you are to the idea that Jesus rose from the dead.

The enigma of Jesus

In his life and work Jesus was characteristically enigmatic. His parables puzzled; his actions upset expectation. In his death too he remained an enigma. Rumours of his risen presence could not and cannot be proved. Can a man rise to new life after death? Could rumour alone have sustained the faith of his followers, often leading them to their own deaths? Was the story of a carpenter from Galilee enough ultimately even to overcome the might of the Empire which had executed him?

Perhaps it is best to return to the resurrection stories themselves, and specifically to the empty tomb. Rowan Williams points out that, in the scene depicted in John's Gospel, two angels sit at either end of the stone on which the body of Jesus had lain (John 20.12). This may be a reminder of the two cherubim who sat at either end of the Ark of the Covenant, which occupied the Holy of Holies in the Temple (see Ex. 25.18–20). They face each other and 'define a space where God would be if God were anywhere ... but there is no image between the cherubim. If you want to see the God of Judah, this is where he is and is not'.[158] Was Israel's God present in the absence at the heart of the Temple? Was the risen Jesus present in the absence at the heart of the empty tomb?

There was a gap in the Temple which had to be filled by faith. The same kind of gap existed in the empty tomb, and we cannot definitely say what it represents, because the historical evidence is too slight. It is a gap that must be filled with faith, either for or against Jesus. Here each one of us is left with more questions than answers. I can't help thinking that Jesus would be happy with that. Is he a presence or an absence?

Stooping down into a Jerusalem tomb one spring morning in the year 30, a group of women saw the absence of Jesus. In the centuries ahead extraordinary things would be done in his name, as a sign of his continuing presence. But he resists the attempt to tie him down and contain him, just as he always did.

Catch him if you can.

Draw your own conclusions

- What do you think made people begin the 'Quest of the Historical Jesus' in the eighteenth century?
- What was Jesus' relationship with John the Baptist and his movement? Why do you think John was the more famous in their own day?
- What might Jesus' motives have been for settling in Capernaum?
- How would you describe the meaning of the Kingdom of God?
- What made Jesus choose the followers he did? What made them follow him?
- Why did food play such an important part in Jesus' ministry?
- Could Jesus have performed the healing miracles described in the Gospels?
- What was Jesus aiming to do in the parables he told?
- Why did Jesus avoid the cities of Galilee?
- Why do you think Jesus turned south to Jerusalem for Passover 30?
- Do you think that the authorities in Jerusalem were worried about Jesus? How might a report to Pilate from Caiaphas on Jesus' activities in the early part of Passover week have looked?
- What did Jesus anticipate would happen at Passover 30? Was he mistaken if he expected the end of the world?
- If much of the Passion narrative is an imaginative retelling of the story does that affect how you read it?
- Do you think the tomb was empty? If it was, what reasons could there be for this?

Further reading

The story of the 'Quest'

Histories of the 'Quest' really begin with Schweitzer's own *The Quest of the Historical Jesus*, which is still in print and also available online. It surveys (in a rather partisan way) the nineteenth-century 'Old Quest'. A readable, though not comprehensive, survey of the same material which continues into the twentieth century is C. Allen (1998), *The Search for the Historical Jesus*, Oxford: Lion.

Many of the large books on Jesus survey the history of the Quest. J. D. G. Dunn (2003), *Jesus Remembered*, Grand Rapids: Eerdmans, chapters 3–5, is, to my mind, the best of these. David B. Gowler (2007), *What Are They Saying About The Historical Jesus?*, New York: Paulist, is a useful and up to date guide to the more recent debate. Jaroslav Pelikan (1999), *Jesus Through the Centuries – His Place in the History of Culture*, 2nd ed., New Haven: Yale University Press, looks at 2,000 years' interpretation of Jesus.

The Historical Jesus

The note at the end of John's Gospel about how 'all the books in the world' could not do justice to Jesus is strikingly true. A helpful survey of both the 'Jesus of History' and the 'History of Jesus' is provided by M. Bockmuehl (ed.) (2001), *The Cambridge Companion to Jesus*, Cambridge: Cambridge University Press. This is a good place to start. To get to grips with different contemporary approaches to the historical Jesus it's best to tackle the leading scholars directly and I have picked out below a selection of those which are of most interest.

- J. P. Meier (1991, 1994, 2001), *A Marginal Jew: Rethinking the Historical Jesus*, New York: Doubleday, is an almost inexhaustible mine of information in three volumes (so far). Meier's approach is rich and painstaking, but his concern to satisfy an imaginary panel of a Roman Catholic, Protestant, Jew and agnostic in a search for objectivity often leads to extremely cautious and meagre results. As a quarry for research his books are second to none, however.
- G. Theissen and A. Merz (1998), *The Historical Jesus: a comprehensive guide*, London: SCM Press, is an excellent survey, with exercises at the end of each chapter and it makes good use of insights from the social sciences. Complementary but quite different is G. Theissen (2001), *The Shadow of the Galilean: the quest of the historical Jesus in narrative form*, SCM Classic edition, London: SCM Press, a fictional account of Jesus' life and mission which remains one of the best introductions available.
- E. P. Sanders (1985), *Jesus and Judaism*, London: SCM Press, is a learned, dispassionate, sane and complex book committed to rigorous historical method. Sanders's more popular (1993), *The Historical Figure of Jesus*, London: Penguin, is probably the best available single volume on the subject.
- J. D. Crossan (1991), *The Historical Jesus: the life of a Mediterranean peasant*, San Francisco: HarperCollins is equally full of insight and idiosyncrasy. Crossan is always worth reading for a fresh perspective, incorporates much fascinating detail from the archaeology and literature of the wider Roman Empire, but his views are not widely shared. Crossan continued the story in (1998), *The Birth of Christianity*, San Francisco: HarperCollins, attempting to disentangle the processes by which the disciples came to believe that Jesus had risen from the dead. The popular (1995), *Jesus – a revolutionary biography*, San Francisco: HarperCollins, covers the same ground and gives a flavour of the bigger books. Crossan represents a liberal approach to the historical Jesus.
- N. T. Wright (1996), *Jesus and the Victory of God* and (2003), *The Resurrection of the Son of God*, both London: SPCK, offer a robust alternative to Crossan. Fascinating and compelling as these books are,

Wright often seems impatient of those who do not share his broadly conservative views. He has written many popular books, of which perhaps the most interesting is (1999), *The Meaning of Jesus: two visions* London: SPCK, co-authored with Marcus Borg, who writes alternate chapters from a different perspective.

- Paula Fredriksen (1999), *Jesus of Nazareth, King of the Jews*, London: Macmillan, approaches Jesus as an apocalyptic prophet from the perspective of a Jewish historian.
- Dale C. Allison (1998), *Jesus of Nazareth: millenarian prophet*, Minneapolis: Fortress, builds on (1985), *The End of the Ages has Come*, Edinburgh: T.&T. Clark, to offer a compelling interpretation of the apocalyptic and eschatological views of Jesus. The final chapter of (2005) *Resurrecting Jesus*, London: T.&T. Clark, is a wide-ranging and nuanced examination of the evidence for the resurrection of Jesus.
- James D. G. Dunn (2003), *Jesus Remembered*, Grand Rapids: Eerdmans, breaks genuinely new ground in its treatment of how the memories of Jesus were preserved and the trustworthiness of the tradition. Dunn's work opens up the prospect of many more books about Jesus in the future.

Websites

- The nail through the heel-bone of Yehohanan can be seen at the Israel Museum website: www2.imj.org.il/eng/exhibitions/2000/christianity/jesusdays/crucifixion/index.html. Archaeologist Joe Zias's article 'Crucifixion in Antiquity', which explains the details of Yehohanan's death, is available at www.joezias.com/CrucifixionAntiquity.html.
- The 'Quest of the Historical Jesus' is outlined at www.historicaljesusquest.com/christianity.htm, and theories are summarized at www.earlychristianwritings.com/theories.html. Albert Schweitzer's book is available online also at www.earlychristianwritings.com.
- K. C. Hanson's 'Palestine in the time of Jesus' at www.kchanson.com/PTJ/ptj.html explores the social background to Jesus' life, linked to the book of the same name.
- 'Into his Own – perspective on the world of Jesus' also provides useful background at http://virtualreligion.net/iho/.
- James Tabor offers a good introduction to 'The Jewish Roman World of Jesus' at www.religiousstudies.uncc.edu/JDTABOR/indexb.html.
- 'The Many Faces of Jesus' at www.pbs.org/wgbh/pages/frontline/shows/religion/jesus/ is part of the generally excellent 'From Jesus to Christ' website.

Notes

1 Quoted in D. Allison (2005), *Resurrecting Jesus*, London: T.&T. Clark, p. 14.

2 J. H. Charlesworth (2000), 'The Historical Jesus: sources and a sketch' in J. H. Charlesworth and W. P. Weaver (eds.), *Jesus Two Thousand Years Later*, Harrisburg: TPI, pp. 101–2.

3 D. Catchpole (2006), *Jesus People: the historical Jesus and the beginnings of community*, London: DLT, p. 57.

4 Similar outlines can be found in N. T. Wright (1996), *Jesus and the Victory of God*, London: SPCK, pp. 147–8; E. P. Sanders (1993), *The Historical Figure of Jesus*, London: Penguin, pp. 10–11; J. D. Crossan (1991), *The Historical Jesus: the life of a Mediterranean peasant*, San Francisco: HarperCollins, pp. xi–xiii; Charlesworth 'The Historical Jesus ...' pp. 107–13; J. D. G. Dunn (2003), *Jesus Remembered*, Grand Rapids: Eerdmans, pp. 312–24.

5 Dunn, *Jesus Remembered*, p. 344.

6 Dunn, *Jesus Remembered*, p. 348.

7 D. Flusser (2007), *The Sage from Galilee*, Grand Rapids: Eerdmans, p. 12.

8 Josephus, *Antiquities* 18.5 (119).

9 M. D. Hooker (1983), *The Message of Mark*, London: Epworth Press, p. 4.

10 J. P. Meier (1994), *A Marginal Jew II – Mentor, Message and Miracle*, New York: Doubleday, p. 52.

11 Josephus, *Antiquities* 18.5.

12 Catchpole, *Jesus People*, p. 16.

13 Flusser, *The Sage from Galilee*, p. 21.

14 C. H. Dodd (1963), *Historical Tradition in the Fourth Gospel*, Cambridge: Cambridge University Press, pp. 274–5.

15 J. E. Taylor (1997), *The Immerser: John the Baptist within Second Temple Judaism*, Grand Rapids: Eerdmans, p. 274.

16 J. A. T. Robinson (1985), *The Priority of John*, London: SCM Press, p. 186.

17 Dunn, *Jesus Remembered*, p. 319.

18 J. Reed (2000), *Archaeology and the Galilean Jesus: a re-examination of the evidence*, Harrisburg: TPI, p. 166.

19 P. M. Head (2004), 'The Nazi Quest for an Aryan Jesus' in *Journal for the Study of the Historical Jesus* 2.1, p. 55.

20 Reed, *Archaeology and the Galilean Jesus*, pp. 53, 58.

21 P. Fredriksen (2000), *Jesus of Nazareth, King of the Jews*, London: Macmillan, p. 183.

22 S. Freyne (2004), *Jesus, a Jewish Galilean*, London: T.&T. Clark, p. 77.

23 E. P. Sanders (1985), *Jesus and Judaism*, London: SCM Press, p. 220.

24 J. D. Crossan interview in 'From Jesus to Christ – the world of the first Christians' at www.pbs.org/wgbh/pages/frontline/shows/religion/

25 Sanders, *The Historical Figure of Jesus*, p. 248.

26 Meier, *A Marginal Jew II: Mentor, Message and Miracles*, p. 452.

27 J. D. Crossan (1994), *Jesus: a revolutionary biography*, San Francisco: HarperCollins, p. 55.

28 Sanders, *Jesus and Judaism*, p. 4.

29 Wright, *Jesus and the Victory of God*, p. 86.

30 Sanders, *Jesus and Judaism*, p. 101.

31 J. P. Meier (2001), *A Marginal Jew III: Companions and Competitors*, New York: Doubleday, p. 71.

32 Catchpole, *Jesus People*, p. 76.

33 M. D. Hooker (1991), *The Gospel According to St Mark*, London, A.&C. Black, p. 167.

34 Dunn, *Jesus Remembered*, p. 587.

35 T. E. Schmidt (1992), 'Taxes' in J. B. Green. S. McKnight and I. H. Marshall (eds), *Dictionary of Jesus and the Gospels*, Downers Grove: IVP, p. 806.

36 L. T. Johnson (1991), *The Gospel of Luke*, Collegeville: The Liturgical Press, p. 286.

37 Dunn, *Jesus Remembered*, p. 530.

38 Sanders, *The Historical Figure of Jesus*, p. 233.

39 Wright, *Jesus and the Victory of God*, p. 431.

40 J. Painter (1997), *Mark's Gospel*, London: Routledge, p. 35.

41 G. Theissen and A. Merz (1998), *The Historical Jesus: a comprehensive guide*, London: SCM Press, p. 313.

42 Meier, *A Marginal Jew II: Mentor, Message and Miracles*, p. 630.

43 Josephus *Antiquities* 18.3 (63), see J.P. Meier (1991) *A Marginal Jew I: The Roots of the Problem and the Person*, New York: Doubleday, p. 61.

44 Sanders, *The Historical Figure of Jesus*, p. 138.

45 R. Bultmann (1985), *New Testament and Mythology, and other basic writings* (ed. S. M.Ogden), London: SCM Press, p. 4.

46 Theissen and Merz, *The Historical Jesus*, p. 310.

47 J. Polkinghorne (1990), 'God's Action in the World', (J. K. Russell Fellowship Lecture), CTNS Bulletin 10:2. Available at www.starcourse.org/jcp/action.html

48 Theissen and Merz, *The Historical Jesus*, p. 312.

49 Meier, *A Marginal Jew II: Mentor, Message and Miracles*, p. 514.

50 Sanders, *Jesus and Judaism*, pp. 164, 173.

51 P. Parsons (2007), *City of the Sharp-Nosed Fish*, London: Weidenfeld & Nicolson, p. 192.

52 M. J. Borg (1993), *Jesus: a new vision*, London: SPCK, p.64.

53 Meier, *A Marginal Jew II: Mentor, Message and Miracles*, p. 453.

54 Dunn, *Jesus Remembered*, p. 688.

55 Wright, *Jesus and the Victory of God*, p. 479.

56 C. H. Dodd (1971), *The Founder of Christianity*, London: Collins, p. 49.

57 K. E. Bailey (2003), *Jacob and the Prodigal*, Oxford: BRF, p. 18.

58 Dodd, *The Founder of Christianity*, p. 53.

59 G. N. Stanton (1989), *The Gospels and Jesus*, Oxford: Oxford University Press, p. 211.

60 Aristotle, *Rhetoric* 2.20.

61 J. Jeremias (1972), *The Parables of Jesus*, 3rd ed., London: SCM Press, p. 12.

62 T. Thatcher (2006), *Jesus the Riddler: the power of ambiguity in the Gospels*, Louisville: Westminster John Knox Press, p. 24.

63 Thatcher, *Jesus the Riddler*, p.71.

64 J. D. Crossan, *The Historical Jesus*, pp. 278–9.

65 T. K. Seim (2000), 'Parable' in A.Hastings et. al. (eds.), *The Oxford Companion to Christian Thought*, Oxford: Oxford University Press, p. 514.

66 A.-J. Levine (2006), *The Misunderstood Jew*, San Francisco: HarperCollins, pp. 38, 40.

67 B.Witherington (1994), *Jesus the Sage: the pilgrimage of wisdom*, Minneapolis: Fortress Press, p. 165

68 Wright, *Jesus and the Victory of God*, p. 482.

69 Dunn, *Jesus Remembered*, p. 634, see also 4Q174.1.10–13 among the Dead Sea Scrolls.

70 Sanders, *Jesus and Judaism*, pp. 183–4.

71 D. Allison (1987), *The End of the Ages Has Come*, Edinburgh: T.&T. Clark, p. 139.

72 Allison, *The End of the Ages*, p. 141.

73 Sanders, *Jesus and Judaism*, p. 75.

74 R. A. Burridge (2004), *What Are the Gospels?*, 2nd ed., Grand Rapids: Eerdmans, p. 337.

75 S. Moore (1972), 'The Search for the Beginning' in S. W. Sykes and J. P. Clayton (eds.), *Christ, Faith and History: Cambridge Studies in Christology*, Cambridge: Cambridge University Press, p. 94.

76 L. T. Johnson (1999), *The Writings of the New Testament*, London: SCM Press, pp. 146, 149.

77 J. D. Crossan (1994), *Jesus: a revolutionary biography*, San Francisco: Harper, p. 152.

78 Quoted in Dunn, *Jesus Remembered*, p. 779 n.83.

79 Fredriksen, *Jesus of Nazareth*, p. 251.

80 Wright, *Jesus and the Victory of God*, p. 490.

81 Dunn, *Jesus Remembered*, p. 649.

82 Sanders, *Jesus and Judaism*, p. 61.

83 Dunn, *Jesus Remembered*, p. 638.

84 C. A. Evans (1995), *Jesus and His Contemporaries*, Brill: Leiden, p. 342.

85 Wright, *Jesus and the Victory of God*, pp. 420, 426.

86 Sanders, *Jesus and Judaism*, p. 75.

87 Crossan, *The Historical Jesus*, p. 360.

88 Fredriksen, *Jesus of Nazareth*, p. 232.

89 Dunn, *Jesus Remembered*, p. 640.

90 R. E. Brown (1994), *The Death of the Messiah* I, New York: Doubleday, p. 458.

91 D. Allison (1998), *Jesus of Nazareth – Millenarian Prophet*, Minneapolis: Fortress, pp. 132, 133.

92 G. B. Caird (1980), *The Language and Imagery of the Bible*, London: Duckworth, pp. 256, 265.

93 Dunn, *Jesus Remembered*, p. 485.

94 Fredriksen, *Jesus of Nazareth*, p. 242.

95 Sanders, *Jesus and Judaism*, p. 306.

96 Meier, *A Marginal Jew* III, pp. 24, 26.

97 G. Vermes (2005), *The Passion*, London: Penguin, p. 119.

98 Brown, *Death of the Messiah*, p. 411.

99 Josephus, *Antiquities of the Jews* (tr. Whiston) 20.9 (198).

100 Meier, *A Marginal Jew* II, p. 397.

101 Vermes, *The Passion*, p. 33.

102 J. Jeremias (1966), *The Eucharistic Words of Jesus*, London: SCM Press, p. 88.

103 Wright, *Jesus and the Victory of God*, p. 555 (emphasis original).

104 Jeremias, *Eucharistic Words*, p. 222 (emphasis original).

105 Theissen and Merz, *The Historical Jesus*, p. 434.

106 Dunn, *Jesus Remembered*, p. 816 (emphasis original).

107 Sanders, *Jesus and Judaism*, p. 333.

108 Sanders, *Jesus and Judaism*, pp. 332–3.

109 C. M. N. Eire (2002), 'Pontius Pilate Spares Jesus: Christianity without the Crucifixion' in R. Cowley (ed.), *More What If? Eminent historians imagine what might have been*, London: Macmillan, p. 55.

110 Eire, 'Pontius Pilate Spares Jesus', p. 57.

111 Sanders, *Historical Figure of Jesus*, p. 264.

112 Vermes, *The Passion*, p. 45.

113 Dunn, *Jesus Remembered*, p. 773.

114 Brown, *Death of the Messiah* I, p. 417.

115 F. Millar (2006), 'Reflections on the Trials of Jesus' in F. Millar, *The Greek World, the Jews and the East*, Chapel Hill: University of North Carolina Press, p. 152.

116 Brown, *Death of the Messiah* I, p. 725.

117 Brown, *Death of the Messiah* I, pp. 425–6.

118 Millar, 'Reflections on the Trial of Jesus', p. 160.

119 Vermes, *The Passion*, p. 115.

120 Origen, *Contra Celsum* 2.9, 17, 24.

121 Millar, 'Reflections on the Trial of Jesus', p. 160.

122 M. Goodman (2007), *Rome and Jerusalem*, London: Penguin, p. 327.

123 Sanders, *Historical Figure of Jesus*, p. 269.

124 Dunn, *Jesus Remembered*, pp. 633–4.

125 Vermes, *The Passion*, p. 57.

126 Vermes, *The Passion*, pp. 61–2.

127 Goodman, *Rome and Jerusalem*, pp. 583–4.

128 W. H. Vanstone (1982), *The Stature of Waiting*, London: DLT, p. 20.

129 Tacitus, *Histories* 4.11.

130 Hooker, *Mark*, p. 379.

131 Dunn, *Jesus Remembered*, pp. 779–80.

132 Vermes, *The Passion*, p. 75.

133 Wright, *The Resurrection of the Son of God*, p. 552.

134 Crossan, *Jesus: a revolutionary biography*, p. 190.

135 Dodd, *The Apostolic Preaching*, p. 16.

136 Dunn, *Jesus Remembered*, p. 841.

137 D. C. Allison (2005), *Resurrecting Jesus*, London, T.&T. Clark, p. 239.

138 R. J. Bauckham (2006), *Jesus and the Eyewitnesses*, Grand Rapids: Eerdmans, p. 51.

139 Sanders, *The Historical Figure of Jesus*, p. 280.

140 E. P. Sanders (1992), *Judaism: practice and belief 63* BCE*–66*CE, London: SCM Press, p. 298.

141 Wright, *The Resurrection of the Son of God*, p. 203.

142 P. Lapide (1984), *The Resurrection of Jesus*, London: SPCK, p. 92.

143 Allison, *Resurrecting Jesus*, p. 323.

144 Allison, *Jesus of Nazareth*, pp. 156–7.

145 Wright, *Jesus and the Victory of God*, p. 659.

146 Allison, *Resurrecting Jesus*, p. 324.

147 R. Bultmann (1984), 'New Testament and Mythology' in *New Testament Mythology and Other Writings* (ed. & trans. S. M. Ogden), London: SCM Press, p.39. This essay was written in 1941.

148 Wright, *Resurrection*, p.710.

149 Allison, *Resurrecting Jesus*, p.338.

150 Wright, *The Resurrection of the Son of God*, pp. 477–8.

151 L. Hurtado (2005) *How on Earth did Jesus become a God?* Grand Rapids: Eerdmans, p. 194.

152 Wright, *Resurrection*, p. 717.

153 G. Habermas and A. G. N. Flew (1987), *Did Jesus Rise from the Dead? The resurrection debate*, San Francisco: Harper & Row, p. 7.

154 G. O'Collins (1987), *Jesus Risen*, London: DLT, pp. 8, 32.

155 W. Pannenberg (1968), *Jesus: God and Man*, London: SCM Press, p. 33.

156 W. Pannenberg (1994), *Systematic Theology* II, Edinburgh, T.&T. Clark, p. 288.

157 O'Collins, *Jesus Risen*, p. 60.

158 R. Williams (1996), 'Between the Cherubim: The Empty Tomb and the Empty Throne' in G. D'Costa (ed.), *Resurrection Reconsidered*, Oxford: Oneworld, p. 90.

Appendix

Maps

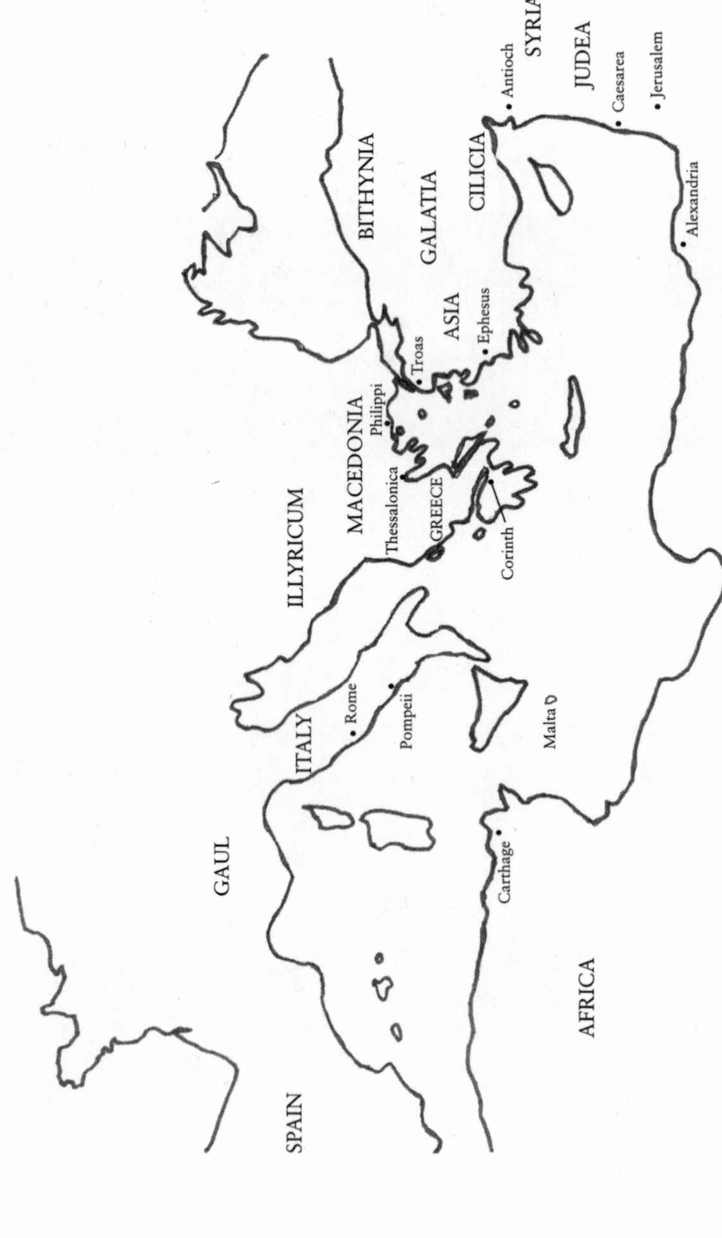

Map 1 The Mediterranean in the first century

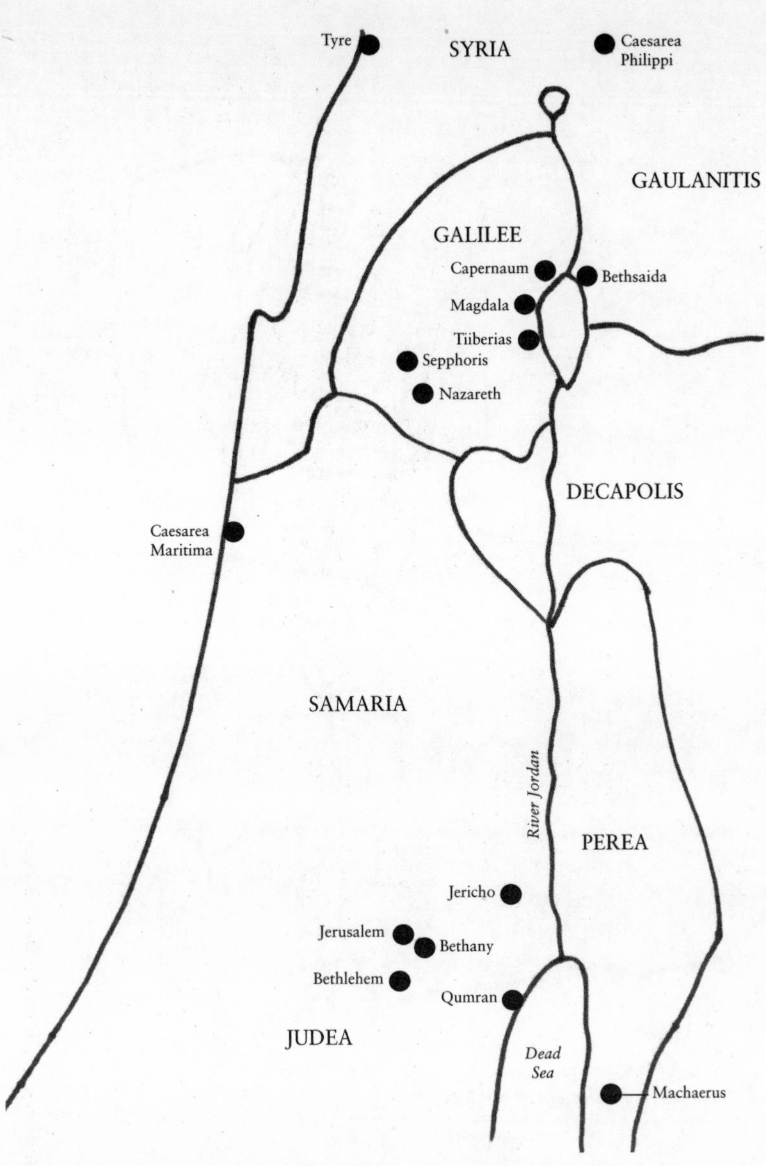

Map 2 Galilee and Judea in the early first century

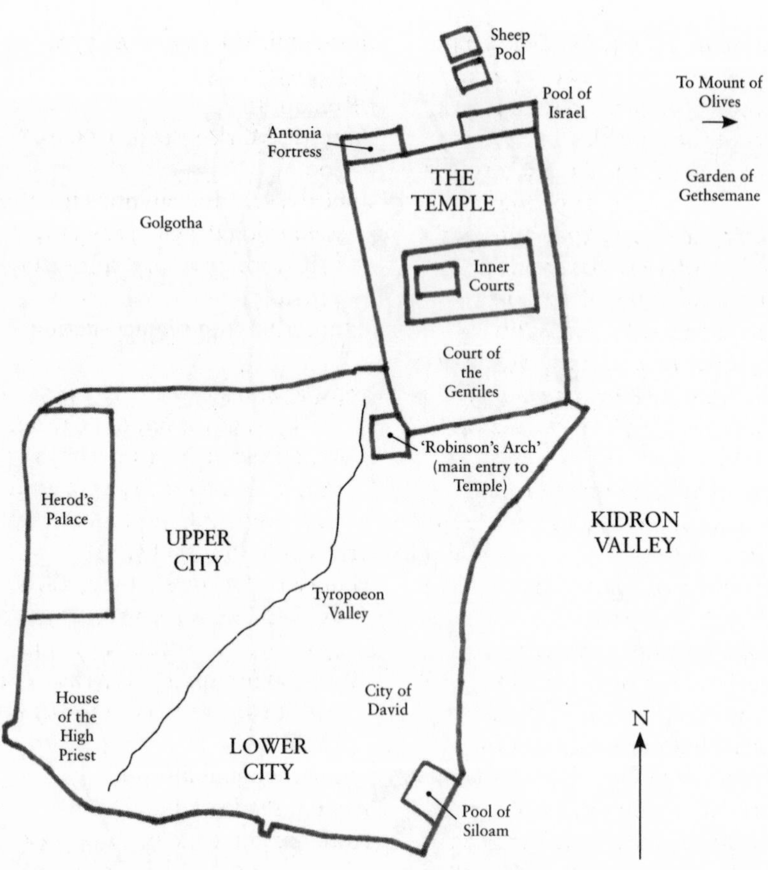

Map 3 Jerusalem in the early first century

Index